BEING IN CHRIST

BEING IN CHRIST

A Biblical and Systematic Investigation in a Reformed Perspective

Hans Burger

WIPF & STOCK · Eugene, Oregon

BEING IN CHRIST
A Biblical and Systematic Investigation in a Reformed Perspective

Copyright © 2009 Hans Burger. All rights reserved. Except for brief quotations in critical publications or reviews, no part of this book may be reproduced in any manner without prior written permission from the publisher. Write: Permissions, Wipf and Stock Publishers, 199 W. 8th Ave., Suite 3, Eugene, OR 97401.

Wipf & Stock
A Division of Wipf and Stock Publishers
199 W. 8th Ave., Suite 3
Eugene, OR 97401

www.wipfandstock.com

ISBN: 978-1-4982-5207-2

All scripture quotations, unless otherwise indicated, are taken from the HOLY BIBLE, NEW INTERNATIONAL VERSION®. NIV®. Copyright © 1973, 1978, 1984 by International Bible Society. Used by permission of Zondervan. All rights reserved.

Manufactured in the U.S.A.

Contents

Contents

Contents

Foreword

AT THE MOMENT that the work on my doctoral dissertation is coming to an end, I feel very grateful. I owe much to many people, but especially I want to express my gratitude towards God, Father, Son, and Spirit. Working on this study has enriched my life and my understanding of the gospel of Jesus Christ—at least in my own perspective. It is up to others now to judge whether my understanding of the gospel is right. Nevertheless, it is my prayer that this book may contribute to a deepening of the Christian life of others—a life in Christ.

Further, I want to thank prof. dr. Barend Kamphuis in the first place. I am very grateful for his willingness to be my supervisor. If he had seen nothing in my plans, I would have not been given a place as PhD student (AIO) at the Theological University in Kampen (Broederweg), the Netherlands. I appreciated the room he offered me to do theology in freedom. At the same time, he was present if needed, as a conversation partner or to ask critical questions. His knowledge of the Reformed tradition as well as his willingness to read my texts carefully were very helpful.

Secondly, prof. dr. I. U. Dalferth (Zürich) has to be mentioned. I wish to thank him for his time during our conversations in Zürich and in phone calls. He criticised the first version of my research plan, wanted to be my co-supervisor at a distance, and continued to encourage me with valuable suggestions. His methodological sharpness and his reactions on my texts improved the result significantly. Moreover, a word of thanks to prof. dr. Rob van Houwelingen. He supervised the New Testament-part of the project. I was often surprised by the quickness of his reactions on my texts, which were not hasty yet but always to the point.

Thanks are also due to the other members of the examining committee: prof. dr. Gerard den Hertog (TU Apeldoorn), prof. dr. Kees van der Kooi (VU Amsterdam), prof. dr. Kees de Ruijter (TU Kampen).

I could not have done this work in solitude. It has meant a lot to me that I could work in community with others. These were in the first place the other systematic theologians of Broederweg 19: dr. Ad de Bruijne downstairs, and my neighbours on the 'attic,' dr. Hans Schaeffer and drs. Dolf te Velde. Together with the systematic theologians of the Theological University Apeldoorn—prof. dr. Gerard den Hertog, prof. dr. Hans Maris, and drs. Arnold Huijgen—we met monthly as a research group. It was always a joy to see each other and discuss a text of one of the members.

More PhD students populated the 'attic' of Broederweg 19. I have good memories to our discussions and lunches. But the library of the Theological University should not be forgotten. Almost every book I needed was present in their collection, and their service was excellent.

Happily the theological world is bigger than Kampen. It was good to join other company regularly. I was accepted as a member of NOSTER, the Dutch Research School of Theology and Religious Studies; I could visit the annual XART-conferences; and have been part of the 'promovendi beraad' of the Gereformeerde Bond. I have enjoyed all different meetings as well as the conversations with various theologians in the lobby. What also encouraged me were the meetings of the study group 'Christocentric Community.' They remembered me always of the church I was working for.

That I could do my research, visit Zürich and work as a PhD student was made possible financially by different foundations and persons. I could study a semester in Zürich thanks to support of, among others, the Dr. Hendrik Mullers Vaderlandsch Fonds. And from the sponsors who enabled me to finish my project I want to mention the Jagtspoel-foundation and the Reformed Church of Hilversum (the Netherlands). The publication of my doctoral dissertation was made possible by a donation of the foundation Afbouw in Kampen.

In the final phase of the completion of my manuscript also different people played a role. I am delighted with the theological friendship of three of them, friends from the beginning of my theological study in 1992 up to this day: drs. Pieter Both, drs. Wim van der Schee and drs. Thijs Tromp. They read the entire manuscript and gave their comments.

I could not have missed Ed Pieffers (Kampen) as well as Andy Draycott (Edinburgh). They both checked over all of my English. If my style still needs improvement, it is not they who are to be blamed for it. I am very glad that they both took the time to read my texts and correct my English. Ria Kuijper-Versteeg (Franeker) helped me in the latest phase of making the manuscript ready for the publisher.

Some material in this book has been published before in Dutch. Sections 3.3.2. and 3.4.1 appeared in a slightly different version as 'Een eeuwigdurende verbondenheid. Bavincks concept van de *unio mystica*.' In *Ontmoetingen met Herman Bavinck*, Barneveld: De Vuurbaak 2006, 265–86. A small part of section 10.3.2 appeared in 'Theologia crucis, theologia gloriae, of geen van beide?' In: *Levend water. Gereformeerd debat over charismatische vernieuwing*. Barneveld: De Vuurbaak 2006, 135–50. I would like to thank the publishers, De Vuurbaak Barneveld, for their permission to use this material.

I have finished this book in Franeker, where I have been working for two years as a minister in the Reformed Church 'De Voorhof.' I feel privileged that I have worked in their midst. I hope that they may enjoy some fruits of the work that has gone into this book.

Life is more than theology and work. I am grateful to God for the parents He gave me and who were the first to teach me a Christian life; the first stones on which this study builds. Comparably, I am grateful to God for my sharpest critic, my colleague, the one who continues to remind me of the questions of daily (Christian) life, the mother of our children Christi and Boaz, my friend: my wife Janneke. It is great to share my life with you.

Franeker, August 2008
Hans Burger

1

INTRODUCTION

1.1 Necessity of Renewed Reflection on 'Being in Christ'

1.1.1 THEOLOGICAL CLIMATE

TO BE OR NOT to be—in Christ—that is the question. To quote Christof Gestrich: 'Christian faith and 'being in Christ' are one.'[1] However, whereas one would expect 'being in Christ' to be a central theme in the message of the church and in theology, often this is not the case. Instead, according to Gestrich the weakness of Christianity is the absence of Christ in the faith of Christians; many Christians believe in God yet bypass Christ.[2] More empirical research would be necessary to determine the extent to which Gestrich is right. Nevertheless, a tendency to neglect Christ is one that I recognise.

This neglect of Christ has its place in the post-Barthian context. The disappearance of the dominance of Karl Barth's christocentric theology

1. Gestrich, *Christentum und Stellvertretung*, 415.

2. Gestrich, *Christentum und Stellvertretung*, 415.

created space for new theological ideas and orientations. Different themes like immanence, pneumatology (or pneumatheology), reality, liberation, spirituality, mysticism, narrative, and biography received an important place on the theological agenda.[3] In reaction to Karl Barth, this new theological agenda often implied a move away from Christology. This move is reinforced by the problem of religious pluralism. As a result, theological concepts can lose Christological weight, and a neglect of Jesus as Christ, the Son of God, easily arises. In this way, Jesus Christ becomes an inspiring 'shape' of love and emancipation,[4] a symbol of God's mercy,[5] a human being inhabited by the healing Spirit of God and giving voice to the call of God's love,[6] or 'a thin place' transparent for the Holy to be followed in his own Spirit.[7] Salvation in Christ is presented in a pluralistic theory of religious ends as salvation among salvations.[8] If interest in religion is growing, the place of Jesus Christ has become an open question for many.[9] At the same time, the language of 'being in Christ' has only rarely been made the central subject of discussion and conceptualisation, although it is central to Pauline soteriology.[10] Consequently, the significance of Jesus Christ is in danger of being reduced to a moral or spiritual example. In him we see how we should live with God and with each other. But Jesus Christ does not himself determine the relationship between God and the believer.

However, this neglect of Christ can take a different, more conservative form. Accordingly, Jesus Christ is reduced to the one who died for our sins but who, in the present, does not really play any role. He made it possible to live with God again by his satisfaction for our guilt. But he determines only the *past* of the relationship between God and believer,

3. See e.g. Grenz, Olson, *20th Century Theology*, 113–285.

4. The concept of 'shape' for Christology is used in Hodgson, *Winds of the Sprit*. See for his Christology *Winds of the Sprit*, 231–75.

5. In the theology of H.M. Kuitert, Jesus becomes a symbol for God's mercy; see Kuitert, *Zeker weten*, 149. Cf. his Christology, Kuitert, *Jezus*.

6. See the Christological chapters of the pneumatheology of G.D.J. Dingemans, Dingemans, *De stem van de Roepende*, 425–545.

7. De Lange, 'Semper Reformanda,' 4, 47–48.

8. Heim, *Salvations*.

9. See e.g. for the Dutch discussion on 'Ietsisme'—believing that there must be Something—Biezeveld, De Boer et al., *In iets geloven*.

10. Nüssel, "Ich lebe, doch nun nicht ich, sondern Christus lebt in mir," 480.

and not the present. Within the smaller orthodox-Reformed churches in the Netherlands, I notice an inclination towards this second form, at least within my own church.[11] In a reaction to liberal theology, the doctrine of satisfaction by penal substitution has been stressed. The danger looms that the significance of Jesus Christ is reduced to the doctrine of satisfaction by penal substitution. Jesus Christ himself remains someone of the past. Where the law is preached as a rule for the Christian life, it is done too often in isolation from the new life given in Christ, resulting in a legalistic way of life. These reductions make it increasingly difficult to live a Christian life today.[12] Again, modernity's question to Christology rears its head: how can a historical person who lived 2000 years ago be relevant for my salvation? Is it true as Kuitert writes, 'Jesus remains where he was, in the past'?[13]

Within this climate of a neglect of Christ, it is important to reflect anew on the question of what it is to be in Christ. Reflection on this theme may show that it is a theme with a great integrating power. If it can be shown that 'being in Christ' embraces Christology, pneumatology, spirituality, biography, and ethics, a concept of 'being in Christ' can be used to do justice to a post-Barthian agenda without losing Christology.[14] Further it might be used to bridge the gap between the past and the present. In the light of the conservative form of the neglect of Christ, it is significant that 'being in Christ,' communion with Christ or 'unio mystica cum Christo' used to be a central theme within the tradition of the Reformation.[15] It is a central theme in the theology of e.g. John Calvin,[16] and one of the

11. As a signal of this second form within the Reformed Churches ('Vrijgemaakt') of which I am a member, see Van Benthem, De Vries, 'Meer dan genoeg,' 159–60; De Bruijne, 'Romeinen: pionierswerk nodig?,' 91–92; De Bruijne, 'Christelijke ethiek tussen wet, schepping en gemeenschap,' 132–34; Douma, 'Preken is Christus preken,' 723–25, 741–43; 761–63; 775–78; 797–800; Harmannij, *Jezus leed wat wij nu lijden*, 7–9, 29–46, 111–14; Kamsteeg et al., 'Antwoord op vragen,' 72–74; Meijer, 'De preek,' 163–66; Meijer, 'Christus preken,' 179–82; De Ruiter, *De hartkwaal van de kerken*, 85–104. See further for the broader Reformed Dutch context the issue *Kontekstueel* 20 (2005) 1.

12. Cf. Van der Kooi, 'Enkele perspectieven en uitdagingen voor de dogmatiek,' 12–13.

13. Kuitert, *Zeker weten*, 149.

14. For an attempt in the same direction, using concepts like intercession and a 'Christomorph community,' see Van der Kooi, *De ziel van het christelijk geloof*.

15. Van 't Spijker, *Gemeenschap met Christus*. Cf. Hoekema, *Saved by Grace*, 54; Smedes, *Union with Christ*, xii.

16. See on this theme in John Calvin's theology e.g. Baars, *Om Gods verhevenheid en*

treasures of the Reformed tradition that needs to be rediscovered. At the same time, the critical question must be asked: is the Reformed tradition itself to be blamed for this present neglect of Christ?

Another problem concerns the question of the presence of salvation in the present. Within the Dutch Reformed context, two poles to this discussion can be discerned. On the one hand A. van de Beek reacts to the idealism of the '60s and '70s. He claims in his theology of the cross that the Son of God came to share our problems, not to solve them or to improve us in this world. Salvation will bring another world, but does not result in progress in the present reality.[17] On the other hand, under the influence of the Pentecostal and Charismatic movement notions such as victory, liberation from demonic possession and healing are emphasised. Reflection on 'being in Christ' will not settle these questions, but can be helpful to create a conceptual context in which it will be easier to deal with them.

To conclude, the present-day theological climate can be understood as an invitation for renewed theological reflection on the theme of 'being in Christ.'[18]

1.1.2 CULTURAL-PHILOSOPHICAL CONTEXT

Apart from the theological climate, grounds for the choice of this theme can be given in relation to the cultural-philosophical context. Our time has been characterized as 'time of uneasiness.'[19] It is a time of cultural crisis, in which Islam becomes more important while at the same time a new 'post-enlightenment modernity' emerges in Western Europe.[20] It may be debatable whether our context still can be characterized as post-modern, but still the problems of (post)modernity and nihilism need to

zijn nabijheid, 405–7, 436–37; Garcia,'Imputation and the Christology of Union with Christ,' 222, 231–35; Hartvelt,*Verum Corpus*; Kolfhaus,*Christusgemeinschaft bei Calvin*; Tamburello, *Union with Christ*; Wallace, *Calvin's Doctrine of the Christian Life*,; Won, *Communion with Christ*, 12–75. See further Schaede, *Stellvertretung*, 347–93.

17. Van de Beek, *Jezus Kurios*, 80, 229–31, 246–54.

18. The book of Gestrich, *Christentum und Stellvertretung*, and the inaugural address of Nüssel, "'Ich lebe, doch nun nicht ich, sondern Christus lebt in mir'" support this conclusion.

19. Verbrugge, *Tijd van onbehagen*.

20. 'Post-enlightment modernity' is a term of Irshad Manji's, used by Mak, *Nagekomen flessenpost*, 30.

be solved. In the postmodern context, we can trace a tension between a disengaged, nihilistic self on the one hand, and on the other hand a self that desires to express himself.[21] In the former case, the self-confident modern subject, who has his own sources for orientation and morality within himself, has become more and more problematic. The voluntarist and liberal orientation of early modernity has resulted in nihilism.[22] The confidence in the capacity of the self to control its own destiny has been shattered; a development from active agency to passive situatedness.[23] At the same time modernity has failed to conceive and practise relationality.[24] Disengagement and loss of contact are characteristic outcomes of modernity.[25] In the latter case, the subject wants to express himself.[26] Individual identity has become a project, narrating a unique story, and the surface of a person's life, and even skin, has to be designed in a fashionable way. Although a firm rooting of the self in moral sources has become problematic, nevertheless the postmodern subject builds himself a beautiful house on the sand. Disengagement and expressivism go hand in hand.[27]

In theological perspective, the first aspect can be interpreted as the life of a sinner who has lost contact with God and his surrounding world, the second as a sinner who nevertheless justifies himself and tries to make the best of it, living without God. Here theological reflection on the theme of 'being in Christ' may offer a message of hope. Can Christ be offered to the sinner who has lost contact with God, with his neighbour, his world and his moral sources, as the one in whom God comes to meet us and restore contact and relatedness?[28] Is the theme of 'being in Christ' a saving message to the self-righteous sinner, because it offers release from the impossible task of pulling oneself out of the marsh by one's hair, a la Baron

21. Taylor, *Sources of the Self*, 495–519.

22. Cf. the analysis of John Milbank in Milbank, *Theology and social theory*. On the problem of voluntarism see further Frigato, *Leven in Christus en moreel handelen*, 52–56; Gunton, *The One, the Three and the Many*, 119–23.

23. Thiselton, *Interpreting God and the Postmodern Self*, 11, 121–26.

24. Gunton, *The One, the Three and the Many*, 37.

25. Glas, 'Geloofszekerheid,' 19–34, esp. 21; Gunton, *The One, the Three and the Many*, 13–15; Taylor, *Sources of the Self*, 41, 44, 88, 97.

26. Cf. Taylor, *Sources of the Self*, 390, 393, 413, 495, 503–4, 507.

27. Cf. Taylor, *Sources of the Self*, 503.

28. Glas, 'Geloofszekerheid,' 33.

Von Münchhausen? Is it possible to free the self from expressivism born out of self-justification, to receive a new, healed identity in Christ?

Charles Taylor emphasises in his analysis that the self has to live in a framework, a moral space. Loss of identity and loss of orientation are inseparable. The self, personal identity, and moral convictions belong together.[29] He mentions four terms that are interconnected: 'not only (a) our notions of the good, (b) our understanding of self, but also (c) the kinds of narrative in which we make sense of our lives, and (d) conceptions of society, i.e., conceptions of what it is to be a human agent among human agents.'[30] Consequently, to free the sinful subject from his disconnectedness and self-righteousness, a saving concept of 'being in Christ' that offers hope, must take all these four terms into consideration. It has to offer a notion of the good, an understanding of the self, a narrative to live in and a concept of community. When a concept of 'being in Christ' succeeds in offering this it will promise a future, and give hope in the present context. This research is a quest for such a hopeful concept.

1.1.3 THEOLOGICAL ONTOLOGY

To be or not to be—in Christ, I wrote. Then the question is, whether 'being in Christ' is only imaginative, or a non-fiction reality.[31] According to Taylor, the articulation of the framework surrounding the self may take the form of ontology. 'Ontological accounts have the status of articulations of our moral instincts. They articulate the claims implicit in our reactions.'[32] When developing not a 'hermeneutics of the self,' as Taylor does,[33] but a concept of 'being in Christ,' could such a concept consist in an articulation of the ontological implications of 'being in Christ'?

In recent theological discussions, the development of a theological ontology is an important issue. The rehabilitation of the doctrine of the Trinity has led to an ever growing literature on 'Trinitarian ontology,' 'relational ontology' and an 'ontology of the person.'[34] This literature sig-

29. Taylor, *Sources of the Self*, 25–52; Kreuzer, *Kontexte des Selbst*, 96–111.

30. Taylor, *Sources of the Self*, 105.

31. Cf. Garcia,'Imputation and the Christology of Union with Christ,' 224–26.

32. Taylor, *Sources of the Self*, 8.

33. Kreuzer, *Kontexte des Selbst*, 109.

34. See e.g. the work of Gerhard Ebeling, Colin Gunton, Wilfried Härle, Wilfried Joest, Eberhard Jüngel, John Milbank, Christoph Schwöbel, Miroslav Volf, John Zizioulas.

nals a theological quest for a post-metaphysical and (post-)critical realist elaboration of the perspective which the Christian faith offers on the reality we live in. In this investigation I want to participate in this quest, and I presuppose that the quest for a theological ontology is both possible and useful. This implies a choice of some form of (post-)critical realism. This choice is soteriologically motivated: if the Christian faith is really about *salvation*, a non-realist interpretation of the language of the Christian faith is excluded, for it leaves unclear how God can act to save us.[35] It is not language that creates and saves reality, however constructive it might be, but God who creates and recreates the world.

The question is, however, how this theological ontology should be elaborated. The starting point for this investigation is not the Trinity but our 'being in Christ.' Pursuing this theme, I will try to articulate the ontological implications of 'being in Christ.' My aim is not to give a complete account of a theological ontology, but to sketch some lines for a Christian understanding of reality and hence for such a theological ontology.

In conclusion, sufficient justification can be given from the theological climate and the cultural-philosophical context to study afresh the theme of 'being in Christ.' Interestingly, these reflections should provide opportunity to contribute to the development of a theological ontology.

1.2 Method

1.2.1 REFLECTION ON THE PRACTICE OF THE CHURCH

Theology is critical reflection on the practice of the church aimed at helping to communicate the gospel of Jesus Christ as clearly as possible and to enable the members of the church to live in Christ and in the Spirit in communion with God and with each other to the glory of God.[36] Methodologically, this study builds on the concept of theology as described in *Gereformeerde theologie vandaag*: a concept of theology in the Reformed tradition, in which the Holy Scriptures are central. The concept starts from the perspective of the Christian faith coloured by the Reformed confessional tradition, and in the community of the church.

Barth's theology stimulated this quest, cf. Jenson, *Systematic Theology. Volume 1*, 21.

35. Cf. Patterson, *Realist Christian Theology in a Postmodern Age*, 43, 45.

36. Cf. Jenson, *Systematic Theology. Volume 1*, 5, 11–12, 14–17.

It is practically oriented, hermeneutically sensitive and contextually relevant. In this concept, theology reflects primarily on the practice of the church and the Christian faith, and not on religion in general.[37] However, theology and church do not live in splendid isolation. Theology has her place in the university, the church in the public sphere of society, the Christian faith in the daily life of individuals. Church, society and university together constitute the context of theological reflection.[38]

It is presupposed in this study that theology is a complex hermeneutical movement, an ongoing circle from ecclesial practice to the reading of the Scriptures and systematic reflection and back to practice, comprising (a) interpretation of the empirical reality of the church and her context, (b) reflection on the tradition of the church to understand how the church arrived at its present position, (c) careful exegesis of the Holy Scriptures to renew the church's understanding of the Scriptures, (d) systematic reflection on the content of the gospel and the view of reality that the Christian faith implies in relation to questions of the context the church lives in,[39] and (e) practical recommendations for the daily life of the church. Hence, systematic theology is a part of this hermeneutical movement. At the same time, this whole movement from empirical reality of the church, reflection on the tradition of the Church, reading of the canonical texts, systematic reflection on the content of the Christian faith and practical recommendations can also be present in systematic theology itself.[40]

37. See esp. De Bruijne, 'Gereformeerde theologie vandaag,' 11–29. Together with the renewed emphasis on theology as science of religion (see e.g. the work of Ulrich Barth, Falk Wagner or Johannes van der Ven), this concept emphasises the difference between theology as second order activity and the first order life of the church. Further, it is emphasised that theology has to reflect on the empirical reality of the practice of the Christian life, see De Bruijne, 'Gereformeerde theologie vandaag,' 26–27; cf. Falk Wagner's criticism of 'Theologentheologie,' Wagner, 'Religion der Moderne—Moderne der Religion,' 17–19. Cf. 1.2.4.

38. Cf. Van den Brink, *Een publieke zaak*, 353–60.

39. Kamphuis, 'Systematische theologie,' 62–64.

40. De Bruijne, 'Gereformeerde theologie vandaag,' 21–22; cf. Browning, *A Fundamental Practical Theology*, 5–9, 42–44, 49–54, 58–59, 223–42. For a comparable practice-oriented concept of theology, see Bayer, *Theologie*, 18, 395–407, 426–32. A practice-oriented concept of theology does not necessarily exclude reflection on questions regarding ontological implications, cf. the combination of theology as practical and speculative in Jenson, *Systematic Theology. Volume* 1, 11–14.

In this investigation part of this movement will be made. I will start with the problem that in the empirical reality of the church there seems to be an inclination towards neglecting the position of Christ in pursuit of the relation with God (see 1.1.1), as well as the postmodern situation of the subject (see 1.1.2), without doing further empirical research on this. Most work will be done in part I *Reformed tradition—Perspective* on (b), in part II *Bible—Canonical Scriptures* on (c) and in part III *Reality—Ontological Implications* on (d). The concept of 'being in Christ' that will be developed has practical implications that could be worked out in a fifth step to a set of practical recommendations. However, this will not be done for my focus will be on the concept itself and on its ontological implications.

In the following sections, I will deal with methodological issues related to the different moments of the hermeneutical movement (1.2.2–4). Further I will answer the question of how theology can be *critical* reflection (1.2.5). Finally I will close with the hypothesis of the inquiry (1.2.6).

1.2.2 REFORMED PERSPECTIVE

Although the Holy Scriptures should have the decisive voice in theology, I start in part I with an evaluation of the Reformed tradition. In this section I will explain why. Doing this, I will deal with the related problem of perspectivity.

Systematic theology is a human activity, and as such tied to human finitude. This finitude has a creational aspect, for human beings are created bodily, speaking and living in the plurality of time and space. To be human is to be a perspective and to live within a plurality of perspectives. Sin made this finitude problematic, bringing death, brokenness, and frustration into the world; conflict and a plurality of languages; lies, ambivalence, misunderstanding and forgetting; blindness, lovelessness, unwillingness, and misuse of power. In the Christian tradition this problem shows itself in the conflicts within the tradition itself between different churches and their subsequent traditions. The hermeneutic problem reminds theology of its human, finite and perspectival character, a finitude that has a creational and a hamartiological aspect.[41]

41. Marquard sees human finitude as a central problem, posing the question to which hermeneutics is the answer. In this finitude he sees three aspects: finitude in relation to God, to space and to time. However, he concentrates on finitude in relation to time as mortality. See Marquard, 'Frage nach der Frage, auf die die Hermeneutik die Antwort ist,' 120–22.

It is important not to deny the creational aspect of our finitude. Further, the inevitability of death cannot be denied when striving at a God-like immortal epistemological position. This happened, in fact, in the quest for a 'God's eye point of view' and the negative view of tradition, authority and prejudice that characterizes modernity. Gadamer's hermeneutic is a plea for a rehabilitation of tradition, authority and prejudice (or pre-judgment)[42]. To be human is to be historically situated within a horizon. It is an illusion to try to overcome the fact that we are located at a particular time and place.[43] (However, 'the rightness and wrongness of what we say is not *just* for a time and place.'[44]) Prejudices can be negative but also positive. More fundamental however is his insight that prejudices are a requirement for understanding.[45] Understanding has a circular structure: interpretation begins with 'fore-conceptions' that are challenged by the subject-matter itself to be corrected and replaced by more suitable ones.[46] The tradition of effective-history makes the text familiar, but at the same time openness to the strangeness of the text is necessary to come to a new understanding.[47] Gadamer reminds theology of what it is to exist bodily, living in time as mortal beings and speaking different languages.

However, his hermeneutics have been criticised. First, his resistance to method leads to a position in which the critical potential of a rational

As a result the hermeneutical problem only receives a negative character. The positive aspect of our finitude is forgotten. However, it is a gift to be a real human human being, desiring no longer to be like God having a God's eye point of view and accepting our finitude as created beings. Jenson gives a more positive reflection on the hermeneutical problem, starting with the historical character of the gospel itself, see Jenson, *Systematic Theology. Volume* 1, 14–16.

42. According to Thiselton, 'pre-judgments' is a better English translation of the German 'Vorurteile,' see Thiselton, *The Two Horizons*, 321.

43. Gadamer, *Hermeneutik I. Wahrheit und Methode*, 307; cf. his critique of historism, 222–46; see also Grondin, *Einführung in die philosophische Hermeneutik*, 143–46; Thiselton, *The Two Horizons*, 302. See also McGrath, *The Genesis of Doctrine*, 92–102.

44. Hilary Putnam, cited in Patterson, *Realist Christian Theology in a Postmodern Age*, 27. Cf. McGrath, *The Genesis of Doctrine*, 102.

45. Gadamer, *Hermeneutik I. Wahrheit und Methode*, 281–95; Thiselton, *The Two Horizons*, 305–6.

46. Gadamer, Hermeneutik I. *Wahrheit und Methode*, 270–81; Thiselton, *The Two Horizons*, 304.

47. Gadamer, *Hermeneutik I. Wahrheit und Methode*, 273, 297–300. See also McGrath, *The Genesis of Doctrine*, 172–200.

(scientific) method cannot be applied. As Ricoeur and others have shown, understanding of truth (verstehen) and explaining by method (erklären) do not exclude each other as Gadamer seems to think.[48] According to Ricoeur, structuralist hermeneutics demonstrates that method belongs not only to the natural sciences, but also to the *Geisteswissenschaften*.[49] Further, the need for openness to the text indicates a problem. Understanding is determined by questioning, but our questioning is influenced by our own sinful interests and unwillingness. The hermeneutical problem is deeply influenced by human sin. Gadamer's position has been criticised because of its lack of critical potential against ideological distortion and its own totalitarian character.[50] The 'masters of suspicion' and postmodern hermeneutics emphasise this problematic aspect of hermeneutics, in which Christians can recognise (the consequences of) human sin. Hence the process of understanding implies a moment of connection as Gadamer's hermeneutics make clear, and a moment of distance, as his critics affirm. Hermeneutics must do justice to both moments: understanding as well as explaining; a hermeneutic of retrieval (characterized by the willingness to listen) as well as a hermeneutic of suspicion (characterized by the willingness to suspect).[51] These two couples, paralleling the two abovementioned criticisms of Gadamer, display that the moment of distance has two aspects: the aspect of the analysis of the structure of the texts and the aspect of suspicion.

This has methodological implications for the present investigation First, a human perspective excludes objectivity or neutrality in the absolute sense that the Enlightenment searched for, but honesty remains a scientific virtue. Therefore I want to be clear about the starting point that determines my perspective on 'being in Christ': my own Christian faith, the membership of a Reformed church confessing its faith in the Belgic Confession, the Heidelberg Catechism and the Canons of Dordt, and the

48. Grondin, *Einführung in die philosophische Hermeneutik*, 160–73; Ricoeur, 'Explanation and Understanding,' 71–88; Ricoeur, 'The Hermeneutical Function of Distanciation,' 75–88; Ricoeur, 'What is a text?', 105–24; Thiselton, *New Horizons in Hermeneutics*, 329–30.

49. Ricoeur, 'Explanation and Understanding,' 80–88; Ricoeur, 'What is a text?', 112–17.

50. Grondin, *Einführung in die philosophische Hermeneutik*, 167–78; Thiselton, *New Horizons in Hermeneutics*, 329–30.

51. A distinction of Ricoeur used by Thiselton in Thiselton, *Interpreting God and the Postmodern Self*, 69.

problems I see as formulated in 1.1 leading to the present investigation of 'being in Christ.' To characterize a Reformed perspective in terms of its specific content is not easy.[52] In the research-programme of which this investigation is a part, the following characteristics are given:

a. The intention to practice theology in a Trinitarian way and hence giving attention to the full breadth of God in creation and new creation;
b. The wish to do justice to the entire scriptures of Old and New Testament as the Word of God;
c. The awareness of the central meaning of reconciliation in Christ and communion with Him;
d. The conviction that as a result of the depravity of the human being as well as for our theological thinking, we are entirely committed to God's election and grace in Christ and to the illuminating work of the Holy Spirit;
e. Attention to covenant and church.

Second, the combination of a creational and a hamartiological aspect of the hermeneutical problem implies that tradition is an ambivalent phenomenon, both enabling and hindering understanding of the gospel of Jesus Christ. The perspective of one's own tradition is on the one hand a gift, enabling some form of understanding of the gospel and the Scriptures, which cannot be transcended but must be used as optimally as possible. On the other hand, it limits one's understanding by the weaknesses of the conceptualities developed within the tradition. Hence a critical evaluation of the reflection in the Reformed tradition on 'being in Christ' is necessary, both to appreciate the truth of its understanding of the Gospel of Jesus Christ and to learn from it in the search for the treasures present within this tradition. Critical evaluation is also necessary to see the limits of the conceptual structure developed within the Reformed tradition, its conceptual price, and to search for the things left unsaid. This is a precondition for a new reading of the biblical texts referring to 'being in Christ.' Therefore I start my investigations not with a reading of the Scriptures, but with a critical evaluation of the Reformed tradition.

52. For a discussion of the characteristics of the Reformed tradition, see Brinkman, 'De toekomst van de Gereformeerde theologie,' 138–56; Klooster, 'The Uniqueness of Reformed Theology,' 32–54; Alston Jr., Welker (Eds.), *Reformed theology*, 2003.

Third, it is important to acknowledge the brokenness of the church and the factual plurality of often conflicting Christian perspectives on the church, the gospel and the Christian faith. Therefore, we need a catholic and ecumenical intention to learn from other Christian traditions.[53] Hence, the voices heard in part III stem from other Christian traditions.

Fourth, the brokenness of the church and the hermeneutical problem cannot be understood entirely without mentioning human sin. Openness cannot be guaranteed theoretically and the intention to be open is not enough. The consequences of sin cannot be transcended by human beings; God must save us from sin and its consequences. Therefore, faith in God who saves in Christ and in the Spirit, and the prayer for the guidance of the Holy Spirit into the truth to renew our understanding, are always necessary.[54] The Spirit must enable again and again a new and fresh understanding of the gospel and the Scriptures,[55] and Scripture itself must form the reader.[56]

In conclusion, theological reflection has a perspectival character and is bound to tradition. This situation has a positive creational aspect as well as a negative hamartiological aspect. Methodologically, it implies that honesty about perspective is necessary, as well as a critical evaluation of the understanding of 'being in Christ' in the Reformed tradition. Accordingly, the investigation starts in part I with the Reformed tradition.[57] Because it is important to learn from other Christian traditions, in part III two theologians from other traditions will be studied. Finally,

53. Cf. Kamphuis, 'Systematische theologie,' 68.

54. Cf. Bayer, 'Wer ist Theologe?,' 208–13; Jenson, *Systematic Theology. Volume* 1, 25–26, 41.

55. Cf. Van Bruggen, 'The Authority of Scripture as a Presupposition in Reformed Theology,' 83.

56. See Wall, 'Reading the Bible from within Our Traditions,' 91–96.

57. According to theologians like Wagner the premodern 'Theologentheologie' is no longer relevant to the modern individual religious subject. But how important it may be to do justice to the empirical reality of the individual believer, the individual is part of a community and a tradition. More important than such post-liberal arguments is the soteriological argument: through community, tradition and bible, the individual is brought into contact with a reality which remains crucial to the modern religious individual: the saving act of the triune God in Jesus Christ. Against Wagner, 'Religion der Moderne—Moderne der Religion'; Wagner, *Metamorphosen des modernen Protestantismus*, 7–52, 70–74, 191–240. See further two works of U. Barth, *Religion in der Moderne*, and *Aufgeklärter Protestantismus*.

prayer for the guidance of the Holy Spirit has to accompany the research-practice to enable real openness for the truth.

1.2.3 BIBLICAL THEOLOGY

After a critical evaluation of the Reformed tradition, I continue with biblical-theological reflections on 'being in Christ' (part II). Biblical theology is the third moment of the hermeneutical movement of which this conversation is a part. In the tradition of Christian theology, usually the practice of the church was followed to read the Scriptures as canonical. It is also the intention of this study to remain faithful to the teaching of the apostles, testing critically the language of 'being in Christ' in systematic theology by investigating the way the expression 'in Christ' is used in Paul and John. Scripture should have the decisive voice to enable theology to develop a concept of 'being in Christ,' which stimulates the church to speak in such a way that it gives access to a life in Christ, as the apostles of Christ (the first ones who knew this reality) referred to it.[58] Consequently, I will give a systematic reading of Paul and John from a theological perspective, guided by an interest in the theme of 'being in Christ.' If necessary, based on this investigation proposals for improvement of the language of 'being in Christ' will be given.

However, in modern academic theology biblical studies and systematic theology became more and more separate. According to Brevard S. Childs, 'an iron curtain separated Bible from theology.'[59] This brought him to a new emphasis on the Bible as canon. In recent discussions attempts have been made to unite Bible and theology again, often following Childs in using the concept of canon.[60] But using the Bible as canon means intending to give the Scriptures a decisive voice in theology. Is it possible to give the Scriptures such a decisive voice or do the Scriptures consist of

58. Cf. Jenson, *Systematic Theology. Volume* 1, 30–33. The theological position of this study is characterized by the judgment that the Scriptures give access to a life in Christ, shaping Christian existence in accordance with the triune act of God. See Kelsey, *Proving Doctrine*, 205–16.

59. Childs, *Biblical Theology of the Old and New Testaments*, xvi; see also Green, 'Scripture and Theology,' 23.

60. Childs, *Biblical Theology of the Old and New Testaments*, 55–94; Scalise, 'Canonical hermeneutics: Childs and Barth,' 61–88; Scobie, *The Ways of our God*, 34–40, 49–76. In German discussions, an important essay stimulating a canonical approach is Gese, 'Erwägungen zur Einheit der biblischen Theologie,' 11–30.

a choir of dissonant or cracked voices making it impossible to regard the Scriptures as a decisive canon?

Recent justifications for giving the voice of the Scriptures a normative and decisive role in systematic theology often start with the church: it is the practice of the church to read the canonical Scriptures as the Word of God. Christian theology follows this practice.[61] This practice of regarding the Scriptures as the Word of God can be understood with the help of distinguishing the many modes of discourse, as Nicholas Wolterstorff does in his *Divine Discourse*. He mentions, a. Double agency discourse: if a secretary writes a letter for his superior, this text counts as a speech-act of the superior only if the superior signs it. b. Deputised discourse: someone can authorize someone else to speak on her behalf, for example an ambassador is authorised to speak in the name of his head of state. Likewise, a prophet can be deputised by God to speak in His name and a message can be given to be communicated by the prophet. c. Appropriated discourse: by saying 'I share those commitments' a person can appropriate the words of someone else. In this case, the content of the appropriating speech is identical with the content of the appropriated speech. The Bible can be understood in terms of divinely appropriated human discourse.[62] As a consequence, according to Wolterstorff a given text can be used to say different things to different addressees in different situations or even in the same situation.[63] The concept of appropriated discourse is central to his book. In the church, the books of the Scriptures are read as human discourse appropriated by God, and hence as his appropriating discourse. When the church reads the books of the canon, it is read as the one Word of God and as one book. This does not necessarily imply that the appropriated human discourse is a harmonious unity. It implies only that, to distinguish God's appropriating discourse, the appropriated human discourse must be understood within the whole of the

61. Childs, *Biblical Theology of the Old and New Testaments*, 70–79; Johnson, 'Fragments of an Untidy Conversation,' 276, 281–83, 285–89; Scobie, *The Ways of our God*, 40–42.

62. This raises the question how Wolterstorff deals with the historical development within the canon. And how is the figure of Jesus Christ related to this history and to the totality of the scriptures? Because this investigation focuses on Paul and John, these questions need not to be solved here.

63. Wolterstorff, *Divine discourse*, 37–57.

canon, because God does not contradict himself according to believers.[64] To ascribe 'wholeness' to the canon is not the same as ascribing 'unity' to the canon in the sense of 'a coherence or even a consistency among its contents. . . . It is not logically necessary that the canon actually exhibits such 'unity' in order for it to be construed as some kind of a 'whole.'"[65] Hence, contradictions within the appropriated human discourse do not make this practice impossible. In this weak justification, the practice of the church to read the Scriptures as the Word of God is to be followed in theology,[66] but this justification does not imply consistency within the contents of the canon.

Nevertheless, the fact is that the question of whether the canon is a unity is answered divergently within Christianity. For Wolterstorff this is not really a problem, for this problem is solved in the practice of reading the Scriptures as canonical with the help of the belief that God cannot contradict Himself. But others see the lack of unity in the canon as a justification for the diversity in the church. Because the canon itself contains mutually excluding perspectives, within the church also diverse and even conflicting readings of the Scriptures will be found. The canonical diversity of Christianity must be respected, it is said.[67] For this investigation, this implies an urgent problem: if the canon contains in Paul and John two or even more conflicting perspectives on 'being in Christ,' how can a systematic theological concept of 'being in Christ' be developed and the

64. Wolterstorff, *Divine discourse*, 202–22 and 314 notes 5–6.

65. Wolterstorff, *Divine discourse*, 314 note 5.

66. Wolterstorff himself gives a sketch of a historical justification of this practice of the church. See Wolterstorff, *Divine discourse*, 288–96. Cf. Balla, *Challenges to New Testament Theology*, 86–146; Van Bruggen, *Het kompas van het Christendom*, 9–54.

67. See e.g. Dingemans *De stem van de Roepende*, 460–62; Dunn, *Unity and Diversity in the New Testament*, 376–78; Johnson, 'Fragments of an Untidy Conversation,' 276–89; Käsemann, 'Begründet der Neutestamentliche Kanon die Einheit der Kirche,' 214–23. Cf. for a moderation of this position Link, 'Der Kanon in ökumenischer Sicht,' 82–96; Welker, 'Biblische Theologie,' 1552.

According to A. van de Beek, the Bible will function as a canon only if the book is read in a context determined by confession, ministerial office, and sacrament. See Van de Beek, 'Een aantrekkelijke kerk—maar voor wie?', 25. Cf. Jenson, *Systematic Theology. Volume* 1, 26–28.

Herms finds the unity of the canon in the historical reality the scriptures tell about, the movement of the life of the faith in the God of Israel and in Jesus Christ. See Herms, 'Was haben wir an der Bibel?', 133–48. For a comparable position see Schnackenburg, 'Neutestamentliche Theologie im Rahmen einer gesamtbiblischen Theologie,' 31–47.

question of its ontological implications be answered? Is the intention to give the Scriptures the decisive voice in theological reflection on 'being in Christ' meaningful?[68]

It is not surprising that in other justifications for canonical use of Scriptures in theology and in the church the unity of the content of the Scriptures is a central theme. This unity can be presupposed because of beliefs regarding the Scriptures as the revealed and inspired Word of God, or shown as a result of a comparison between the different voices in the Bible (or the New Testament).[69] In this 'stronger' justification, the unity of the canon plays an important role in justifying the decisive role of the Scriptures in theology.

However, taking this 'stronger' justification as a methodological starting point means that we presuppose that Paul and John cannot contradict each other, and that within Pauline or Johannine literature itself also no contradictions can be found. Methodologically I will not presuppose this unity, for even if it is presupposed nevertheless it must be shown how a Pauline and a Johannine perspective on 'being in Christ' are compatible.[70] Therefore I will restrict myself to Wolterstorff's justification. Although theologically more must be said about the Scriptures than Wolterstorff as a philosopher of religion does, methodologically his position suffices to justify a use of Scripture in theology as canonical and decisive voice. The emphasis on the unity of the canon however, inspires me not to capitulate too fast to the claim of contradictions but to search for compatibility.[71] It must become clear during the investigation whether

68. Cf. Carson, 'Unity and Diversity in the New Testament: the Possibility of Systematic Theology,' *Scripture*, 65–69.

69. See e.g. Carson, 'Unity and Diversity in the New Testament,' 65–95; Gaffin, 'The Vitality of Reformed Dogmatics,' 29–30, 43; House, 'Biblical Theology and the Wholeness of Scripture,' 269–70; Kamphuis, *In dienst van de vrede*, 43–44, 50–67; Köstenberger, 'Diversity and Unity in the New Testament,' 144–58; Wenham, 'Appendix: Unity and Diversity in the New Testament,' 684–719.

70. Cf. Balla, *Challenges to New Testament Theology*, 4, 35; Ridderbos, 'De theologie van het Nieuwe Testament,' 173, 184–87.

71. Cf. the work of P. Stuhlmacher, who sees it as an important task of biblical theology to search for the coherence of the canon. See Stuhlmacher, *Biblische Theologie des Neuen Testaments, Band 1*, 2–4, 12, 38; Stuhlmacher, *Wie treibt man Biblische Theologie?*, 15–26; Stuhlmacher, *Biblische Theologie des Neuen Testaments, Band* 2, 287, 302–21; Stuhlmacher, 'My Experience with Biblical Theology,' 174–91, esp. 175.; cf. Balla, *Challenges to New Testament Theology*, 45, 207–9 (and further 145–207); Ridderbos, 'De theologie van het Nieuwe Testament,' 184–87.

or not the Bible can have the decisive voice in the development of a concept of being in Christ.

A justification of a decisive biblical-theological moment in systematic theology is only preliminary for methodological explanation. Methodologically more must be said. I have been dealing already with the problem of perspectivity. For biblical theology this implies that the Scriptures have to be read within the perspective of the church, within a tradition and in accordance with the rule of faith.[72] Unfortunately, the Rule of faith exists as various "rules of faith" that according to Robert Wall 'bear a striking family resemblance to each other.'[73] That my starting point is a Reformed rule of faith does not contradict my intention of reading with as much openness as possible, to remain faithful to the Word of God according to the catholic ecumenical Rule of Faith.[74] Two steps will be taken.

The first step consists in a historical reconstruction of the Pauline and Johannine perspective on 'being in Christ' in so far as these perspectives became canonical.[75] This first step is historical but differs from a religious-historical approach in so far as it is based on the canonical texts only.[76] As a result, the reconstruction of the Pauline and Johannine perspectives can be no more than partial. The reading of the Pauline and Johannine texts will be guided by the systematic question regarding 'being in Christ,' not

72. Van de Beek, 'Een aantrekkelijke kerk—maar voor wie?', 25; Van Bruggen, 'The Authority of Scripture as a Presupposition in Reformed Theology,' 64–65, 73, 79; Jenson, *Systematic Theology. Volume 1*, 26–28; Stuhlmacher, *Wie treibt man Biblische Theologie*, 68; Wall, 'Reading the Bible from within Our Traditions,' 88–107; Wolterstorff, *Divine discourse*, 206–7, 218–22. Cf. also Mildenberger, 'Biblische Theologie als kirchliche Schriftauslegung,' 151–62.

73. Wall, 'Reading the Bible from within Our Traditions,' 102.
In accordance with this position, the diversity of confessions is not primarily a diversity within the canon, but a diversity of different perspectives on the canon as a whole.

74. Cf. Wall, 'Reading the Bible from within Our Traditions,' 102.

75. Balla, *Challenges to New Testament Theology*, 211–15; Carson, 'Unity and Diversity in the New Testament,' 91; Ebeling, 'Was heißt "Biblische Theologie"?', 69, 86; House, 'Biblical Theology and the Wholeness of Scripture,' 274; Stuhlmacher, *Biblische Theologie des Neuen Testaments, Band 1*, 12.

76. Balla, *Challenges to New Testament Theology*, 45–47, 85, 144–46; Scobie, *The Ways of our God*, 58–76; Wall, 'Reading the Bible from within Our Traditions,' 91–93; Wall, 'Canonical Context and Canonical Conversation,' 165–66. For an alternative religious-historical approach, see Räisänen, *Neutestamentliche Theologie?*. Cf. for a critical discussion with Räisänen Balla, *Challenges to New Testament Theology*.

only focussing on the use of the expressions 'ἐν Χριστῷ' and 'ἐν ἐμοὶ,' but also on surrounding images and expressions that colour the use of these expressions. The aim of this reading is to explicate the implied perspective on 'being in Christ' as it is present in the different texts.

It can be asked whether such a reconstruction is possible. Does a Pauline or Johannine perspective exist, or do we have to face the existence of different Pauline and Johannine perspectives? Do historical development and differences within the letters make this first step impossible? The presupposition of this investigation is that we do not need to let Paul or John crumble to pieces in a postmodern anti-systematic mood.[77] With regard to Paul, with N.T. Wright we can discern a worldview within Paul's letters 'behind, or above, or beneath the things that are actually said on any one particular occasion' or, in the words of Christiaan Beker, at 'a subtextual level.'[78] Although it cannot be denied that 'synthetic proposals are not neutral accounts of Paul's thought,' as Richard Hays writes, these proposals are all we have. With regard to John, I will follow Jörg Frey, who writes that the differences between the gospel and the first letter of John are not too big for a synthesis of the gospel and the letter to be made.[79] According to Hays, the value of proposals of synthesis can be tested only through the execution of concrete attempts. The value of a proposal is determined by the test of satisfaction: does it make informed readers say: 'Yes, that is a good reading of the texts'?[80] Let the quality of the reconstruction settle the discussion on the possibility of making such a reconstruction.

The result of this first step will consist in the reconstruction of a Pauline and Johannine perspective on 'being in Christ' in so far as these

77. The work of Räisänen is an example of this postmodern mood. See e.g. Räisänen, *Neutestamentliche Theologie?* For a critique of the work of Räisänen with regard to Paul see Van Spanje, *Inconsistency in Paul?*

With regard to Paul, J. van Bruggen has a remarkable position. On the one hand he opposes to a specific theology of Paul because he does not want Paul to be played off against the other apostles. They agree with each other and Paul does not have an *own* system of thinking. On the other hand he has something of the same reservation with respect to a systematic reconstruction of a theology of the apostles. See Van Bruggen, *Paulus. Pionier voor de Messias van Israël*, Kampen 2001, 156–62.

78. Wright, *The Climax of the Covenant*, 259–60; Beker, *The Triumph of God. The Essence of Paul's Thought*, 134.

79. Cf. Frey, *Die johanneische Eschatologie. Bd. III*, 465–66.

80. See Hays, 'Crucified with Christ,' 229–31.

perspectives became canonical. They will be regarded as decisive voices in the conversation on 'being in Christ.'

The second step consists in the search for compatibility of these two reconstructions.[81] Here it will be decided whether these two perspectives are compatible and hence be decisive, or whether they contradict each other and so make any further conversation on "being in Christ" very difficult. For the sake of clarity: the aim is not to show that religious-historical reconstructions of Johannine and Pauline perspectives do not contradict each other (this might be the case),[82] but only that these perspectives in so far as they became canonical are compatible.

To summarize, in the biblical-theological part of this study the canonical voice of the Scriptures will be heard. Here theology follows the practice of the church in reading the canonical Scriptures as the Word of God. The Scriptures will be read within the perspective of the church, within a tradition and in accordance with the rule of faith. The aim is to reconstruct the Pauline and Johannine perspective on 'being in Christ' in so far as these perspectives became canonical.

1.2.4 SYSTEMATIC THEOLOGY AND PRACTICE

Asking in this study for theological concepts and even for their ontological implications in part III, the question is raised whether it is possible to combine this with the practical concept of theology as given in 1.2.1. Is it possible to prevent an isolation of concept and reflection on their ontological implications from the practice of the church?

In the last decades, the influence of the 'linguistic turn' after Ludwig Wittgenstein, the speech-act theory of J.L. Austin, and more theologically, book of George Lindbeck's *The Nature of Doctrine* led in theology to a focus on the speech-acts of the church and a high estimation of the metaphor of 'grammar' for the activity of theology.[83] Austin's theory of speech-acts enriched the understanding of language, showing that language does

81. Carson, 'Unity and Diversity in the New Testament,' 91; House, 'Biblical Theology and the Wholeness of Scripture,' 278; Stuhlmacher, *Biblische Theologie des Neuen Testaments, Band 1*, 12.

82. It is obvious in the New Testament that at least the perspectives of Paul and Peter conflicted, at least on practical questions, see Gal. 2:11–14; cf. 2 Pt. 3,15. Consequently, also differences of insight between Paul and John cannot be excluded.

83. See as an example of a concept of theology influenced by Austin also Bayer, *Theologie*, 439–48.

more than represent reality. Building on Austin, Brümmer distinguishes (a) constatives, asserting that certain state of affairs exist in reality, (b) expressives, containing an expressive load, (c) commissives, committing to some specific future act(s) and (d) prescriptives, laying upon a hearer the obligation to adopt a certain attitude or follow a certain line of action.[84] Further, Brümmer shows that the model of *names* is inadequate to explain the relation between words, things and concepts. Instead, he proposes the model of *tools* in which words are regarded as tools used to perform speech acts in relation to things.[85] Consequently, theology should not only focus on content but acknowledge the diversity of speech acts and the rhetorical aspect of the Christian language game.

An enrichment of the understanding of doctrine in theology, comparable with this enrichment of the understanding of language, can be offered building on Lindbeck's theory of religion and doctrine. In his 'cultural linguistic' view of religion, Lindbeck offers a multi-dimensional view of religion, wanting to get past the dilemma of a cognitive-propositional account of religion and a experiential-expressive account. A cognitive-propositional account of religion focuses on cognitive aspects of religion, seeing doctrines as informative propositions or truth claims about objective realities, whereas in an experiential-expressive account doctrines are viewed as the expression of inner feelings, attitudes or existential orientations.[86] Instead, religion must be seen as a cultural-linguistic framework, a comprehensive interpretative scheme, embodied in myths or narratives and rituals. Doctrines are grammatical rules for structuring religious language.[87] His view of doctrine has been criticised as reductionist, for he minimizes the referential function of doctrines, concentrating on certain functions of doctrines but neglecting their *content*.[88] However, his cultural-linguistic approach can be extended 'to encompass not only

84. Brümmer, *Theology & Philosophical Inquiry*, 16–25.

85. Brümmer, *Theology & Philosophical Inquiry*, 35–55.

86. Lindbeck, *The Nature of Doctrine*, 16.

87. Lindbeck, *The Nature of Doctrine*, 79–84.

88. Van den Brink, *Almighty God*, 30; McGrath, *The Genesis of Doctrine*, 26–32; Jenson, *Systematic Theology. Volume* 1, 18–20; McGrath, 'An Evangelical Evaluation of Postliberalism,' 33–39; Milbank, *Theology and social theory*, 382, 385–86; Patterson, *Realist Christian Theology in a Postmodern Age*, 43–44, 51; Van Veluw, *De straf die ons de vrede aanbrengt*, 21–22. According to Jeffrey Hensley, Lindbeck's antifoundationalism is not antirealist, although he is often interpreted as antirealist, see Hensley, 'Are Postliberals Necessarily Antirealist?' 69–80.

vocabulary (i.e. the stories, concepts, rites, symbols etc. of a religion) and grammar (i.e. the rules for interrelating vocabulary), but also implicit and explicit truth claims.'[89] In such a 'complex pragmatic realism'[90] the integrative capacities of his cultural-linguistic theory can be exploited more than he himself does.[91] A presupposition of this study is that we need such a complex pragmatic realism.

Further, the relation between theological concepts and the practice of the church can be understood. It can be shown that doctrinal statements are 'closely bound up with the *praxis pietatis*.'[92] Doctrine is multifunctional, firmly rooted within the practice of the church. One of the functions of doctrine is a referential one. Theological concepts regulate the speech-acts of the church, order the content of the faith of the church and are a fruit of further reflection on its content.

Reading and retelling the narratives of the history of Israel and of Jesus Christ is a central element in the practice of the church. The relation between doctrine or concepts and the practice of the church as unfolded above has consequences for the relation between doctrine or concepts and the biblical narratives. Although the history of salvation and, as a consequence, narrative are essential for Christian theology, it is difficult to see how theology could be practised only in a narrative form. The presupposition in this study is that theology has tasks beyond the narratives of the history of salvation.[93] The narrative should be really 'foundational for the dogma'[94] and not just illustrative, but the doctrine and the con-

89. Van den Brink, *Almighty God*, 31, following Van den Brom in Van den Brom, 'Hermeneutics as a Feedbacksystem for Systematic Theology,' 178–82. Cf. also the four functions of doctrine McGrath mentions: (1) doctrine functions as a social demarcator; (2) it is generated by, and subsequently interprets the Christian narrative; (3) it interprets experience; (4) it makes truth claims, see his *The Genesis of Doctrine*, 35–80.

90. A term used by Patterson to describe the position of David Ford and her own postliberal Wittgensteinian programme, see Patterson, *Realist Christian Theology in a Postmodern Age*, 51.

91. Van den Brink, *Almighty God*, 31.

92. Van den Brink, *Almighty God*, 30.

93. Here I follow e.g R.B. Gaffin, E. Jüngel, Th.L. Hettema and J. Goldingay. According to Gaffin, systematic theology is 'one large-scale 'plot-analysis'' of the 'massive epic drama' of redemptive history. This analysis cannot itself be narrative. See Gaffin, 'The Vitality of Reformed Dogmatics,' 29. See further Jüngel, *Gott als Geheimniss der Welt*, XVII; Hettema, *Reading for Good*, 347–57; Goldingay, 'Biblical Narrative and Systematic Theology,' 123–42.

94. Holwerda distinguishes between a use of the history of salvation in preaching as

cepts the narrative generates and that subsequently interpret the narrative, cannot themselves be entirely narrative.[95] In systematic theology, we need conceptual thinking as well. This conceptual thinking is necessarily coloured by the language, concepts and questions of the context of the systematic theologian him- or herself.

The choice of some form of (post-)critical realism for soteriological reasons, asking for ontological implications (see 1.1.3), and this presupposition that conceptual thinking and a practical concept of theology can be combined, leave open methodological questions related to ontological reflection. What does this imply for the question regarding ontological implications of 'being in Christ'? These methodological questions will receive further discussion in part III.

In conclusion, it has been shown that it is possible to construe a concept of theology that is fully practical but also leaves room for conceptual thinking. In a comparable way, the relation between narrative and conceptual thinking can be understood. Further methodological questions regarding ontological reflection will be discussed in part III.

1.2.5 CRITICAL REFLECTION

Having made some methodological remarks on the second, third and fourth moments of the hermeneutical movement that this study focuses on, I return to theology as a whole. Systematic theology is critical reflection on the practice of the church. What can be said about the critical potential of systematic theology? Traditionally in Reformed theology the emphasis lies on the Scriptures as the ultimate normative source for theology. Nevertheless, although the Reformed watch-word '*Sola Scriptura*' declares that the Scriptures have the final word in theology, according to Van Bruggen it implies no complete hermeneutic.[96] In the hermeneutic

---

'dogma-funderend' and 'dogma-illustrerend,' see B. Holwerda, 'De Heilshistorie in de prediking,' 88, 94. Cf. De Bruijne, 'Navolging en verbeeldingskracht,' 214.

95. McGrath, *The Genesis of Doctrine*, 37, 52–66.

96. Van Bruggen, 'The Authority of Scripture as a Presupposition in Reformed Theology,' 63.

According to Van de Beek and Jenson, the *sola scriptura* is impossible, see Van de Beek, 'Een aantrekkelijke kerk—maar voor wie?,' 25; Jenson, *Systematic Theology. Volume* 1, 26–28. In my view, it is only possible to maintain the *sola scriptura* if it is understood as an implication of the *solus Christus* (we read the Scriptures because we believe in Jesus Christ), and in combination with the *sola fide* (faith as the perspective of reading) and the movement of theology, more is done than just reading the Scriptures. Apart from the Bible, context, tradition, and the practice of the church also play a role in theology. What does this imply for the critical potential of systematic theology?

In my view, the critical moment of systematic-theological reflection lies in the aim of theology: that the gospel of Jesus Christ is communicated as clearly as possible and that the members of the church in Christ and in the Spirit live in communion with God and as a result with each other to the glory of God. This means that the critical question is: does the church clearly proclaim the gospel and do the members of the church live in the reality determined by the saving acts of the Triune God, Father, Son and Spirit, of which the gospel speaks?[97] Does the church live in the reality of faith that ultimately cannot be seen now, the reality the texts of the Scriptures refer to?[98]

More must be said to make these questions methodologically manageable for doing theology,. Building on Brümmer[99] and Van den Brink,[100] and in continuity with the hermeneutical movement of theology as sketched above, the following criteria can be given. Good systematic theology should

a. react adequately to the demands of context. In the practice of the church and the world surrounding the church, specific problems occur that hinder a good understanding of the gospel and a Christian life in communion with the Triune God. Theology should react to

---

sola gratia (understanding as a gift from the Holy Spirit).

97. Cf. Jenson, *Systematic Theology. Volume* 1, 11,14–17.

98. Central in the hermeneutics of Van Bruggen is his conviction that exegesis as real theology has to do with the meaningful reality 'behind' the text of the bible, determined by who God is in His acts; a reality that cannot be seen. Ricoeur however is especially interested in the reality 'before' the text. Biblical texts project possible worlds and change our view. The theme of 'being in Christ' shows exactly the relation between the reality 'behind' (God and the history of salvation, culminating in Jesus Christ) and 'before' the text (God who in Christ and the Spirit uses the text to act in the life of the church and its members). See Van Bruggen, *Het kompas van het Christendom*, 81–82, 172–75; Thiselton, *New Horizons in Hermeneutics*, 363, 365, 369–72.

99. Brümmer gives four criteria: consonance with tradition, comprehensive coherence, adequacy to the demands of life and personal authenticity. See Brümmer, *The Model of Love*, 22–29.

100. Van den Brink lists three criteria: harmony with the tradition, comprehensive conceptual coherence, and adequacy to the demands of life. See Van den Brink, *Almighty God*, 33–40.

these problems and try to offer alternatives to enable a better understanding of the Scriptures and a more integral life in the reality determined by God's saving acts.

b. stand in continuity with the tradition. Tradition offers a starting point and a perspective that should not be neglected, but be used as optimally as possible. Through the tradition we stand in contact with the Scriptures and in the tradition we find a treasure of theological reflection from the past. Theology should not break down this effective history, but build on it (cf. 1.2.2).
c. do justice as comprehensively as possible to the relevant biblical material. Tradition is important, but not as decisive as the Holy Scriptures, which have a canonical value the tradition does not have. As a consequence, Scripture should have the decisive voice in theology. In 1.2.3 I dealt with the question whether Scripture can have this decisive voice. Further, systematic theology should do justice not to some biblical texts, but to as much relevant biblical material as possible.
d. be conceptually coherent and as consistent as possible. Theology is human knowledge. Theological knowledge has the character of a vast but frayed network with great holes. It deals with the whole of reality but has at the same time a fragmentary character. Although we must strive for coherence and consistency, at the same time the fragmentary character of theological knowledge must be respected.
e. result in recommendations for the practice of the church. Here the practical aim of theology again gives the focus. Good theology should stimulate the proclamation of the gospel and a life of the members of the church in accordance with the gospel to the praise of God. To be able to do so, the personal integrity and the authenticity of the theologian is crucial.[101]

To conclude, in this conversation theology is understood as critical reflection on the practice of the church. The critical moment lies in the goal for which theology strives. To make this critical moment manageable for the practice of theology, five criteria have been given corresponding to the five moments of theology's hermeneutical movement.

101. Cf. Bayer, 'Wer ist Theologe?', 208–13.

1.2.6 HYPOTHESIS FOR THE INVESTIGATION

The concept of 'being in Christ' I will develop in conversation with six thinkers, two theologians of the Reformed tradition, two writers of biblical texts and two contemporary theologians. The hypothesis for the investigation is that a systematic-theological concept of 'being in Christ' can be developed using the concepts 'representation' and 'participation': Christ is representative, believers participate in Christ. Representation is the Christological concept, Christology being understood as referring to Jesus Christ. Participation is the soteriological concept. I define soteriology as the part of theology that deals with the impact of salvation on the life of the believer.

To test this hypothesis two other concepts will be used. The first is the concept of 'substitution.'[102] It is possible that the concept of representation in Christology is kept in equilibrium by the concept of 'substitution.' Where the concept of representation refers to the inclusivity of Christ, the concept of substitution refers to the exclusivity of Christ. This evokes the question whether the concept of substitution is also needed to develop a systematic-theological concept of 'being in Christ.' A problem is how we should conceive the moment of exclusivity. It can be understood in relation to the question 'What did Christ do?' but also to another question: 'Who is Christ?' Hence I will distinguish between

- work-substitution: answering the question 'What did Christ do?': Christ did something instead of us, something we cannot do for ourselves. He goes where we cannot go.[103]
- person-substitution: answering the question 'Who is Christ?' Christ is exclusive because he includes all believers. His exclusivity consists in his universal inclusivity.[104]

I will not decide now which concept of substitution is the best, or whether a distinction between work and person is fruitful, but leave it open during the investigation. If work-substitution is a better concept

102. See for substitution, representation, and participation e.g. McGrath, *Christian Theology*, 402–3.

103. This concept of substitution can be found e.g. in Gestrich, *Christentum und Stellvertretung*, 389; Gunton, *The Actuality of Atonement*, 163–67; Packer, 'What did the Cross achieve?', 85–123.

104. See for this concept of substitution e.g. Jüngel, *Das Evangelium von der Rechtfertigung des Gottlosen als Zentrum des christlichen Glaubens*, 128–29.

than person-substitution, the distance to representation is greater than if substitution were to be understood as person-substitution.

The second is the concept of 'union' that refers to the moment of contact between Christ and the believer, comparable with concepts like 'incorporation,' 'inhabitation' or 'communion.' This concept will also be used to test the hypothesis. Is it possible to develop a systematic-theological concept of 'being in Christ' without a separate concept of 'union,' or do we necessarily need this concept of 'union'?[105]

Summarizing, these four concepts refer to four moments:

Two Christological concepts:

- substitution: the moment of exclusivity of Christ
- representation: the moment of inclusivity of Christ

Two soteriological concepts:

- union: the moment of contact between Christ and the believers
- participation: the moment of the believers' sharing in Christ

I will investigate how these four moments are present in the respective theologies I will deal with, and how these moments influence the understanding of 'being in Christ' and whether the concepts of representation and participation suffice to develop a systematic-theological concept of 'being in Christ.' As it has been said already, I will not only focus on the use of the expressions 'ἐν Χριστῷ' and 'ἐν ἐμοι.' Moreover I will deal with Christological concepts, images, and the significance of the story of Jesus Christ, as told by the gospels, for creation and salvation. Further the images for union with Christ will be investigated. And finally, soteriological concepts and images will be examined. Based on the result of these investigations, the question regarding the ontological implications of 'being in Christ' will be answered.

Summarizing, the hypothesis for the investigation is that a systematic-theological concept of 'being in Christ' can be construed with the help of two concepts, representation and participation. To test the hypothesis, two other concepts will be used, substitution and union.

105. Lehmkühler wants to rehabilitate the concept of inhabitation, see Lehmkühler, *Inhabitatio*.

1.3 Outline of the Inquiry

The aim of this study is to develop a concept of 'being in Christ' with special consideration of its ontological implications. This concept will be developed testing the hypothesis as sketched in 1.2.6 and in dialogue with six thinkers. In accordance with the hermeneutical movement as explained in 1.2.1, two voices of the Reformed tradition will be heard, as well as two canonical voices of the Scriptures that will be especially decisive, and two contemporary voices.

From the Reformed tradition I chose John Owen and Herman Bavinck. John Owen is important for several reasons. He has been chosen as an English 17th century Puritan because of the growing interest in Dutch Reformed circles in the Anglo-Saxon Puritan heritage. Themes like union and communion with Christ are important themes in his work, making him a good dialogue-partner. Herman Bavinck represents the heritage of the Dutch 'afgescheiden' and Neo-Calvinist tradition, which constitutes my own background. Of this tradition, he is the one that wrote the most independent systematic theology, still worth reading. Further, the theme of the mystical union with Christ is a central one in his work, a theme that will be important in conversation with him. I will start with Owen (Ch. 2) and Bavinck (Ch. 3) to be able to create a fairly representative image of the perspective of the Reformed tradition on 'being in Christ.' In Ch. 4 I will give a first and critical evaluation of this Reformed position.

The choice of Paul and John has obvious justification. The expression 'ἐν Χριστῷ' is used in the New Testament by Paul, the other 'ἐν ἐμοι' is used by John. I concentrate on those books that are relevant for a reconstruction of their perspectives on 'Being on Christ.' For Paul I will deal with 1 and 2 Corinthians, Galatians and Romans, and Colossians and Ephesians. For John both the gospel and the first letter are the important books. After the chapters on Paul (Ch. 5) and John (Ch. 6) a subsequent chapter will answer the question whether their perspectives are compatible and thus can be decisive in the development of a systematic-theological concept of 'being in Christ.'

In a third part of this study, two contemporary voices will be heard. The first is Ingolf U. Dalferth, a German theologian in the tradition of Luther, Barth and Bultmann. He reflects on problems regarding ontological reflection and draws a sketch of an eschatological ontology (see Ch. 8). The second is Oliver O'Donovan. O'Donovan is an Anglican, English theologian developing a moral ontology (Ch. 9). Their contributions will be used to reflect further on the ontological implications of 'being in Christ,' in the direction of moral life and eschatology.

Finally in the concluding Chapter 10 the question of the present investigation will be answered, giving an evaluation of the hypothesis and a proposal of a systematic-theological concept of 'being in Christ,' developed in dialogue with the Reformed tradition (John Owen and Herman Bavinck), the canonical Scriptures (Paul and John) and contemporary theology (Ingolf U. Dalferth and Oliver O'Donovan). I will deal especially with its ontological implications, and answer the question of what this concept means for the Reformed tradition.

2

JOHN OWEN

LOVING THE PRIESTLY BRIDEGROOM

2.1 Introduction

John Owen (1616–1683) is one of the greatest representatives of English Puritanism,[1] as the growing interest of the Anglo-Saxon world in Owen's theology indicates.[2] According to Sebastian Rehnman, he was

1. For Puritanism in general, see Van Asselt, 'Puritanism Revisited,' 221–32; Packer, *A Quest for Godliness*; Van 't Spijker et al., *Het puritanisme*; Van 't Spijker, 'Puriteinen op de agenda,' 233–45; De Vries, *"Die mij heeft liefgehad,"* 33–66.

For discussions regarding Owen's place within Puritanism, whether Owen was a Puritan or a Pietist and whether he was a mystic or not, see King, 'The Affective Spirituality of John Owen,' 223–33, who opposes Packer, *A Quest for Godliness*, 204 and Ferguson, *John Owen on the Christian Life*, 224.

2. See e.g. Oliver (Ed.), *John Owen—the man and his theolog.*; Rehnman, *Divine Discourse*; Troxel, "'Cleansed Once for All,'" 468–79, esp. 468; C.R. Trueman, *The Claims of Truth: John Owen's Trinitarian Theology*, Carlisle, Cumbria 1998, 1, 8; De Vries, *"Die mij heeft liefgehad,"* 15–16. For the Anglican Theologian J. I. Packer Owen is of great importance, as he writes in *A Quest for Godliness*, 12.

'one of the intellectual lights of his time.'[3] Since unity with Christ has been called the 'existential nerve of puritan piety,'[4] it is not surprising that, as we shall see in this chapter, unity and communion with Christ is also a central theme in Owen's thinking.[5]

The struggle for the further Reformation of the Church of England was very important in Owen's life. Born in 1616, he studied from 1628 to 1637 in Oxford, but decided to terminate his studies because of the growing influence of the High-Church party, making it difficult for people with non-conformist and Puritan ideas. But the tide changed and during the reign of Oliver Cromwell Owen became very influential, having good contacts with Cromwell himself. The tide changed again between 1656 and 1660. He lost his contacts with Cromwell; and after the restoration of the monarchy, as well as the victory of the Anglican party, Owen retreated from public life. He wrote more than half of his works after 1660. Owen wrote many books—his Works contain 23 volumes—although he did not write a systematic theology.[6]

To understand Owen's theological context, several parties must be mentioned. First of all the Arminians, followers of the Dutch theologian Jac. Arminius. According to Owen, he reduced salvation to the purchase of salvability and broke down the unity of the work of Christ. Second, the Socinians who denied the satisfaction of Christ and moralised salvation. Third, Richard Baxter must be mentioned. He was a leftwing Puritan who, in line with the theology of Saumur, tried to avoid the pitfalls of the Arminians as well as the in their eyes deterministic and antinomian rightwing orthodox Calvinists. Owen himself followed the lines drawn by the Synod of Dordt (1616–1618). In these discussions themes like the universality or particularity of atonement, satisfaction, effectual

3. Rehnman, *Divine Discourse*, 15. According to Trueman, Owen was 'by any standard one of the most influential men of his generation,' see Trueman, *The Claims of Truth*, 8.

4. Jones, 'Union with Christ,' 186–208; cf. De Vries, "*Die mij heeft liefgehad,*" 21–24.

5. De Vries, "*Die mij heeft liefgehad,*" 25; Won, *Communion with Christ*, 264–65.

6. Owen's works have been used in the following edition: Goold (Ed.), *The Works of John Owen*.

For Owen's life, see Oliver, 'John Owen—his life and times,' 9–40; Toon, *God's Statesman*, and De Vries, "*Die mij heeft liefgehad,*" 67–121. For an introduction to Owen's theology, see Trueman, *The Claims of Truth* and Ferguson, *John Owen on the Christian Life*. Although from the perspective of the Calvin—Calvinists debate, Randall Gleason offers a short but helpful survey of recent research on Owen in Gleason, *John Calvin and John Owen on mortification*, 26–33.

calling and regeneration, the intercession of Christ and the relation between justification and works were important issues; issues also central in Owen.[7] Another issue is the discussion between Presbyterians and Congregationalists. Owen chose the Congregationalist party in 1646.

Owen's theology can be characterized as scholastic and Puritan, as Trinitarian and Christocentric. Just as were all his contemporaries, Owen, educated at Oxford University, was a scholastic theologian.[8] But he was also a Puritan writing with a strong existential and practical interest.[9] Owen wanted to be a catholic theologian: he knew and used the church fathers. Owen's theology is obviously Trinitarian structured, as Trueman has shown.[10] The balance between the attention paid to the Father, the Son and the Spirit is carefully maintained. From the centrality of the

7. Cf. Boersma, *A Hot Peppercorn.*; Dekker, *Rijker dan Midas*; Graafland, *Van Calvijn tot Barth*, 85–256.

In his doctrine of atonement, Baxter defended the position of Hugo Grotius against Owen's attack. Grotius developed a modified idea of satisfaction in reaction on the criticisms of Socinus. See on Grotius' doctrine of atonement Schaede, *Stellvertretung*, 410–56. For other contemporary orthodox reflection on notions like representation and satisfaction, see also Schaede, *Stellvertretung*, 457–547.

8. For the intellectual background of Owen, see Rehnman, 'John Owen: A Reformed Scholastic at Oxford,' 181–203; Rehnman, *Divine discourse*, 21–44. According to Rehman, Owen 'is firmly rooted in Renaissance scholasticism and modified Thomism with a stricter Augustinian and Scotist orientation in the context of his Reformed theology,' see Rehnman, *Divine discourse*, 45. See further Trueman, 'John Owen as a theologian,' 43–68.

Clifford, *Atonement and justification* seems to blame Owen for using scholastic categories. Trueman has rightly shown that even Owen's opponents were scholastics. One could even ask whether Owen's scholasticism was the less dangerous form compared with the scholasticism of his opponents. See Trueman, *The Claims of Truth*, esp. 34–44, 227–45; Trueman, 'John Owen's *Dissertation on Divine Justice*,' 87–103; and Trueman, 'A Small Step towards Rationalism,' 181–95. Trueman follows Richard Muller's plea for rehabilitation of scholasticism as the usual method of the *schola*, see Muller, *Scholasticism and Orthodoxy in the Reformed Tradition*. This rehabilitation nonetheless does not take away the need for an evaluation of the conceptual price of the used scholastic categories. This means that after having shown that for Owen exegesis is more important than Aristotle, the question returns whether his exegesis to some extent is determined by Aristotle.

9. De Vries, *"Die mij heeft liefgehad,"* 63 writes that Trueman is justified in calling for the scholastic element in Owen, but that he underscores the Puritan element. De Vries sees Owen as a Pietistic Puritan. According to Won however, Owen's approach is 'less emotional, less applicatory, and more scholarly' than other Puritans, Won, *Communion with Christ*, 258.

10. Trueman, *The Claims of Truth*; De Vries, *"Die mij heeft liefgehad,"* 27, 169, 402, 408. For Owen's doctrine of the Trinity, see Spence, 'John Owen and Trinitarian Agency,' 157–73.

work of and community with Christ Owen's theology also has a strong Christocentric flavour.[11] The form of this Christocentric aspect is influenced by two books of the Bible, the Song of Songs and Hebrews, which were very important to Owen.[12] From Hebrews Owen takes the idea of the unity of the ministry of Christ as high priest in both his oblation, dying for our sins, as well as his supplication, praying in the heavenly sanctuary;[13] the Song of Songs Owen uses to interpret the community with Christ as a marital relation.[14] Furthermore, pneumatology is another important aspect of Owen's theology.[15] The overarching structure binding these themes together is as follows: God and his councils; Christ and his atoning work in the Spirit; the Holy Spirit and the appropriation of salvation given on Christ's supplication.[16]

Regarding what I call 'being in Christ,' this structure is important, for related to this threefold structure of his theology, a story with three episodes can be distinguished within the relation of believers with Jesus Christ. The first episode takes place in God's councils, the second in the life of Jesus Christ and the third is the renewal of our life. Further, several notions are used by Owen: e.g. representation, head and body, union and communion. Christ represents his own in Gods decrees and in his work of salvation. In his life he is formed as head of the new creation. The Holy

11. Ferguson, 'John Owen and the doctrine of the person of Christ,' 69–100, esp. 75; Trueman, 'John Owen's *Dissertation on Divine Justice*,' 87–103; Trueman, *The Claims of Truth*, 75, 127, 138, 172; De Vries, *"Die mij heeft liefgehad,"* 147, 156, 169, 172, 233, 243.

12. See Ferguson, *John Owen on the Christian Life*, p. 78. See for the Song of Songs Won, *Communion with Christ*, 116–31, 266–69, 294, 331–44.

13. Owen wrote between 1668 and 1684 a very large exposition of the Epistle to the Hebrews (*Works*, Vol. I8–23).

14. See Owen's *Meditations and Discourses on the Glory of Christ* (*Works* Vol. I, 314–19, 349–50, 360, 377, 409) and *Of Communion with God the Father, Son and Holy Ghost* (*Works* Vol. II, 40–51, 54–58, 71–78, 125–32).

15. Between 1674 and 1693 Owen wrote his works on Pneumatology (*Works* Vol. III and IV). The Dutch Neo-Calvinist theologian Abraham Kuyper starts his own *Het werk van den Heiligen Geest* praising Owen for his pneumatology, still being the great standard work on the Holy Spirit and his work, see *Het werk van den Heiligen Geest*, 5–6, 21; cf. Ferguson, 'John Owen on the Spirit in the Life of Christ,' Ferguson, 'John Owen and the doctrine of the Holy Spirit,' 101–30.

16. De Vries characterizes the structure of Owen's theology as God and His decrees; Christ and His atoning work; the Holy Spirit and the appropriation of salvation, De Vries, *"Die mij heeft liefgehad,"* 25. But then the strong 'pneumachristological' element in Owen is forgotten, as is his accent on the heavenly intercession of Christ, still being active for the salvation of His own.

Spirit unites us with Christ as head and body and makes us partakers of his benefits. And being united with Christ we enjoy our marital communion with him. In my rendering of Owen, I will follow this structure.

In what follows I will give an overview of Owen's thinking as far as it is useful for the development of a concept of 'being in Christ.' The different notions and the three episodes of the story will be investigated, with special attention paid to the two central concepts of the hypothesis (representation and participation) and the two other concepts to test the hypothesis (substitution and union). First, the relationship between Christ and the believers will be investigated within God's councils and the covenants (2.2 God's Councils and the Covenants). Second, I will deal with his Christology (2.3 Christology) and thirdly with his soteriology (2.4 Soteriology). Third, the question will be asked: according to Owen, what are the ontological implications of 'being in Christ' (2.5 The Reality of 'Being in Christ')? Finally, some conclusions will be formulated in 2.6.

2.2 God's Councils and the Covenants

To understand Owen's teaching on 'being in Christ' within the context of God's councils, something must be said about the doctrine of the covenant. Like other Puritans, Owen differentiated between the covenant of works, the covenant of the mediator and the covenant of grace. The covenant of works was established with Adam and in Adam with humanity.[17] This covenant serves as the necessary background of the covenant of grace to make the position of Christ as second or last Adam understandable. The covenant of grace is the covenant in which God restores his relation with fallen humanity. It has its roots in eternity, in the intratrinitarian covenant between the Father and the Son, the covenant of the mediator.[18]

Representation is an important concept that Owen uses to say something about 'being in Christ.' The concept of representation is very open. An image represents an original. Man created in God's image represented

17. Owen does not deal with the covenant of works apart from the other covenants and does not offer a separate doctrine of creation.

18. For a more general overview of the relation between union with Christ and the covenant according to the Puritans, see Jones, 'Union with Christ,' 194–208. On the covenants of works and the covenant of grace, see Ferguson, *John Owen on the Christian Life*, 22–25; Rehnman, *Divine Discourse* , 167–77; De Vries, *"Die mij heeft liefgehad,"* 186–88, 192–201.

God. Adam is representative of the old humanity. Christ is God's representation to mankind. Christ represents the new mankind in God's councils. And the Holy Spirit represents Christ to believers. In this section, I will concentrate on Christ as representative or head of the new humanity. If Christ is seen as representative of the church a relation between them is presupposed that parallels the relation between Adam and his descendants. These ideas of representation and head must first of all be understood in the context of the doctrine of the covenant.

First, this use of the concept of representation is related to the covenant of works. Adam is head and representative of humanity. Humanity is fallen in Adam. As head or representative Adam is a public or common person.

Second, it is related to the covenant of grace. Christ as second or last Adam is also a public or common person, acting as guarantee and mediator on behalf of the others he is representing. As Christ does not represent all but only the elect, his mediation has significance for the elect alone. Representative, head, public or common person are related ideas here.[19]

Third, this idea of representation cannot be separated from the covenant of the mediator. Here, in Owen's discussion of the covenant of the mediator, problems regarding the relation between election, covenant and Christ are solved. Owen did not like speculations about the ordering of God's decrees and wanted to concentrate on the work of Christ as the content of God's councils, but he did make some distinctions.[20] In the covenant of the mediator the following takes place. Father and Son agree that the Son will be sent to save the elect.[21] The Son is appointed as head of the elect, as surety (guarantee) and mediator of the covenant of grace, and the

19. See for Adam and Christ as public or common person Owen, *Works*, Vol. II, 177–78, 202; Vol. V, 260; Vol. X, 354–55, 358–60. For Adam and Christ as second Adam, see *Works*, Vol. I, 171, 199, 208, 353; Vol. II, 65, 177, 202, 281–82; Vol. III, 168, 286, 414; Vol. V, 169, 323; Vol. X, 72, 355. Christ as surety or guarantee, see *Works*, Vol. I, 357–58; Vol. V, 196, 258. The new covenant established in Christ with the elect only, see *Works*, Vol. X, 236.

20. On Owen and speculation, see Trueman, *The Claims of Truth*, 52, 110, 128, 138, 194, 196 and Trueman, 'A Small Step towards Rationalism,' 193–94. On faith and reason, see Rehnman, *Divine discourse*, 109–28.

21. This has implications for intertrinitarian relations, because the subordination of the Son to the Father results according to Owen from this covenant and not from differences within godhead. As God, the Son is involved in the decree. See Trueman, *The Claims of Truth*, 133–35, 163–64.

elect are given to the Son.[22] The assumption of human nature is designed and the Son becomes an object of predestination: 'The Lord Christ, as unto the nature which he was to assume, was hereon predestinated unto grace and glory.'[23] The promise of eternal blessedness is given to the Son and in him to all whom he represents. The Son also received the gift of the Holy Spirit. The position of the Son as representative of believers thus is rooted in eternity. This position of the Son in the councils of God forms the first origin and cause of the unity of Christ and the church, presupposed in the imputation of our sin to Christ and his righteousness to us.[24]

Owen never completely identified the covenant of the mediator (with the Son on behalf of the elect) and the covenant of grace (with the elect on behalf of the Son), probably for exegetical reasons. But his systematic theological concept does not really differ from theologians who did identify both covenants.[25]

This way of conceptualising the Son as representative in the covenant of the mediator results in the following:

a. the priority of the love of the Father;

b. a Christocentric view of election and covenant;

c. an emphasis on the unity between Christ and the elect;

d. the possibility of stressing the unconditional testament-character of the covenant of grace because of the strong bond between the covenant of the mediator and the covenant of grace, although Owen also speaks of conditions;

e. a very close relation between the themes of covenant and election and thus particular atonement.[26]

22. The eternal election must be distinguished although not separated from the covenant of the mediator. Further, for the gift of the elect to the Son different passages in John are central, e.g. John 10:29 (Owen, *Works*, Vol. II, 139; Vol. X, 292), John 17:6 (Owen, *Works*, Vol. I, 357, 365; Vol. II, 23, 177; Vol. V, 180; Vol. X, 64, 92, 292, 355).

23. Owen, *Works*, Vol. V, 179.

24. Owen, *Works*, Vol. I, 352; Vol. II, 177–80; Vol. V, 179–81; Ferguson, *John Owen on the Christian Life*, 25–27; Trueman, *The Claims of Truth*, 130–40; De Vries, *"Die mij heeft liefgehad,"* 175, 178, 181–82, 188–89.

25. De Vries, *"Die mij heeft liefgehad,"* 190–91.

26. Owen, *Works*, Vol. X, 236; De Vries, *"Die mij heeft liefgehad,"* 181, 184–85, 192–200; Trueman, *The Claims of Truth*, 128, 135, 139.

Seen against the background of Owen's theological context, this means that the positions maintained by Arminians, Saumur and Baxter become impossible. According to the Arminians, God only decrees so save individual people after he appointed Christ as mediator and after his decision to receive in favour all who repent and believe in Christ. Furthermore, this election takes place on the basis of God's foreknowledge. Hence the relation between Christ and the believers only came into existence due to God's foreknowledge that a person would believe. For Owen this destroyed the unity of the work of Christ in both oblation and supplication. By binding Christ and his own together from eternity he guarded against this position. The theologians of Saumur and Baxter wanted to maintain the tension they saw between universality and particularity. Instead of a particular atonement they first of all saw a decree of universal salvation in Christ, and only secondarily a decree of election specifying emptiness in the first decree. The unity between Christ and his own is not seen as clearly as in Owen's theology. Baxter denies that Christ can be seen as the actual representative of human beings; he does not know what to do with the concept of the mystical union between Christ and the believers. Owen instead wants to maintain the relation between Christ as saviour and the persons he saves from eternity to eternity.[27]

This all may seem fairly supralapsarian and determined by election. Owen's identification of election and covenant may seem deterministic, while the dynamic of history seems to disappear. But for Owen it is the free offer of grace that conceptually safeguards the dynamic of history, and not the concept of the covenant, as it is in many other Reformed theologians.[28] Furthermore it is good to mention that Owen himself developed his position from a more supralapsarian to a more infralapsarian one. This is connected to a development in Owen's doctrine of atonement. In his earlier days he stressed more strongly the absolute freedom and sovereignty of God: God was free to choose the way of forgiveness. Later, Owen relates the necessity of satisfaction with God's nature. This strengthens his concentration on Christ. If one compares e.g. Owen's speaking on unity with Christ in *the Death of Death* (1647) and in *The*

27. Trueman, *The Claims of Truth*, 131, 135, 242–44; De Vries, *"Die mij heeft liefgehad,"* 227. See further for the Arminians and Saumur Graafland, *Van Calvijn tot Barth*, 85–121 and 181–98. For Baxter see Boersma, *A Hot Peppercorn*, 232–41; Packer, *A Quest for Godliness*, 156–60.

28. De Vries, *"Die mij heeft liefgehad,"* 183, 209.

Doctrine of Justification by Faith (1677) one sees a greater stress on the unity with Christ.[29]

It may seem that to Owen the first episode of our relationship with Jesus Christ, made in God's councils, can be sufficiently clarified with the concept of representation or head as has just been explained and that the other concepts he uses, union and communion, are not used to understand this first episode. This would mean that Christ represents the church, but that he is not already united with the members of his body. However, this is not totally true. Although the mystical union between Christ and the Church through the Spirit is not actually consummate without the Spirit binding Christ and the church together, still this union is active *before* the actual consummation because in God's councils the church was designed to be the spouse of Christ. As God gave the elect to his Son, the mystical union began to be active.[30]

Analysing Owen's reflection on 'being in Christ' within the context of the covenant of the mediator using the concepts of the hypothesis as described in 1.2.7, the following can be said. The moment of representation is present. First, because the Son receives the position of representative. Second, because the Son is predestined to grace and glory, a destination in which the elect will share. This inclusive moment cannot be found in election, for the Son becomes representative of the elect given to him and election itself is, according to Owen, not a participation in the election of the Son.[31] The moment of participation is present in so far as the destination of the Son to grace and glory will have its impact on the elect in accordance with the covenant of the mediator. Regarding the concept of substitution, person-substitution as well as work-substitution can be found. In the covenant of the mediator, the person of Christ is designed. He is unique, for he is the Son of God who will assume human nature, and further because of the position He receives as head or representative of the elect who are given to him. Finally, he is personally unique because the Son is appointed as guarantee and mediator of the covenant of grace. This immediately implies the second form of work-substitution: he will do something on behalf of the elect given to him. The moment of union

29. De Vries, *"Die mij heeft liefgehad,"* 179, 230–34; Trueman, *The Claims of Truth*, 106–9; Trueman, 'John Owen's *Dissertation on Divine Justice*.'

30. Owen, *Works*, Vol. I, 357.

31. On the role of the Son in election, see Trueman, *The Claims of Truth*, 163–64.

is present in so far as the mystical union began to be active already before its active consummation.

To summarize, the central concept Owen uses for reflecting on the relationship between Christ and the believers in the context of the councils of God is the concept of representation, rooted in the covenant of the mediator. This concept of representation is related to the concept of headship. Further, the exclusive moment can be found in two forms, as person- and work-substitution. Finally, the moments of union and participation begin to be present as well. Consequently, both the concepts of representation and participation are helpful to analyse Owen within this context.

2.3 Christology

This first activity of the mystical union just mentioned is only an activity in God's councils. And God is not interested in his councils per se, but intended a new creation in which his image in man is restored. As long as the substance of this creation is not really formed as the mystical body of Christ, it is imperfect. God designed to communicate his goodness, grace, life and light for the new creation through Christ as the head of this new creation. From him all these things necessary for the new creation should be communicated to his mystical body, the church.[32]

To do this, two things must happen: Christ must be formed as head of his body first, and second his body must be formed in unity with him. Hence the story of union with Christ which started in God's eternal councils, receives a second and a third episode in history. In the first episode in eternity, the Son received his position of representative. But as representative, he must be formed in history as the first part of the formation of the new creation and as necessary precondition for the consummation of the union between the Son and the church. I will deal with this second episode in this section. The third episode of the story of union with Christ is the subject of the next section, 2.4 Soteriology. In this section the formation of the body of the new creation and the actual consummation of the mystical union as Owen sees them will be investigated. In the present section first the union will be investigated together with related concepts as head and representation, and other concepts as mediator and surety (2.3.1 Relevant Christological Concepts). Second I will show which mo-

32. Owen, *Works*, Vol. I, 357, 362–63.

ments of the story of Jesus Christ have significance for us according to Owen (2.3.2 Significance of the Story of Jesus Christ). Finally, I will analyse how the moment of inclusivity and exclusivity are both present (2.3.3 The Inclusive and the Exclusive Moment).

2.3.1 RELEVANT CHRISTOLOGICAL CONCEPTS

To understand Jesus Christ and his significance for our salvation the concepts of representation, head and union are central in Owen. To see how Owen uses these concepts, it is important to notice that he wrote a lot of books on similar subjects, more than once writing books on themes related to the concepts of representation, head, and union.

The first book I want to mention is Owen's ΠΝΕΥΜΑΤΟΛΟΓΙΑ (1674).[33] Owen sees here the work of the Spirit in the perspective of the new creation. Within the work of the Spirit with respect to the new creation, Owen distinguishes between the work of the Spirit to the head of the new creation and to the members of the body whereof Christ is the head. For this sub-section, the first aspect is important. Owen offers a complete 'pneumachristology' and shows the work of the Holy Spirit in the beginning of the life of Jesus, in his preparation for his work, when Jesus was anointed with the Spirit; in his work and in his obedience and offer at the end of his life; and finally in his resurrection and glorification. When dealing with the work of the Spirit in the life of Jesus Christ, Owen speaks about Christ as head of the new creation. Owen makes very clear that any renewal of our lives, whether in the form of regeneration or sanctification, is impossible without the work of the Spirit to the new creation in the life of Jesus Christ.[34]

In *The Doctrine of Justification by Faith* (1677) Owen deals with themes such as imputation of sin and righteousness, justification, faith

33. Owen, ΠΝΕΥΜΑΤΟΛΟΓΙΑ, in *Works*, Vol. III, 2–651; and Vol. IV, 1–520). Owen himself regarded this ΠΝΕΥΜΑΤΟΛΟΓΙΑ as his special contribution to the Christian church; see Owen, *Works*, Vol. III, 7; Ferguson, 'John Owen on the Spirit in the Life of Christ,' 10; De Koeyer, "Pneumatologia," 229.

34. Owen, *Works*, Vol. III, 159–88. For Owen's 'pneumachristology,' see Ferguson, 'John Owen on the Spirit in the Life of Christ'; Ferguson, 'John Owen and the doctrine of the Holy Spirit,' 107–15; Spence, 'Christ's Humanity and ours,' 74–94; Trueman, *The Claims of Truth*, 177–78. And further Gunton, *Theology through the Theologians*, 192; Gunton, 'Election and Ecclesiology in the Post-Constantinian Church,' 222.

and works.[35] Central in this book on the doctrine of justification is the idea of a mystical person. Christ and the church are together one person through the Holy Spirit: not a natural, legal or political person, but a mystical person. It is difficult to understand what a mystical person is, but according to Owen, the Holy Spirit uses a variety of images to clarify its nature: the unity of man and woman, exemplified in Adam and Eve; the union of a head and members of a natural and of a political body; a vineyard and its branches. Further the relation between Adam and his posterity explains it. These variety of resemblances makes is necessary to show the different aspects of that this union. As head of the mystical person Jesus Christ bore the church in all he did as mediator and suffered in their place. On the foundation of Christ and the church being together one mystical person, all the sins of the church were imputed to him.[36]

In *Meditations and Discourses on the Glory of Christ* (1684), Owen presents Christ to his readers as a glorious person to evoke affections of love.[37] He also writes about the glory of Christ in His great and intimate conjunction with the church. In this book, Owen sees three conjunctions: natural, mystical and federal. There is a natural conjunction between Christ and the church because he came to take our nature in the incarnation. Second, there is a mystical conjunction; because of the designed unity between Christ and the church in God's councils this conjunction was active before consummation through the Holy Spirit in our lives. This is a real conjunction as between head and body; vine and branches, or a moral and real conjunction as between husband and wife. And third, a federal conjunction, completing the mystical. Christ agreed to be guarantee and sponsor for the church, 'to do and answer what on their part is required of them for attaining the ends of the covenant.'[38]

Before I further investigate the different concepts, it is important to see how Owen draws two different lines. On the one hand, Owen argues in line with classical incarnation Christology: the pre-existent Son having assumed human nature has a human and a divine nature, hypostatically united. This human nature is anhypostatical.[39] As God incarnate the Son

35. Owen, *The Doctrine of Justification by Faith*, in *Works*, Vol. V, 1–400.

36. Owen, *Works*, Vol. V, 175–79, 196, 208, 214.

37. Owen, *Meditations and Discourses on the Glory of Christ*, in *Works*, Vol. I, 274–415.

38. Owen, *Works*, Vol. I, 356–57.

39. Owen, ΧΡΙΣΤΟΛΟΓΙΑ, in *Works*, Vol. I esp. 222–35; *Meditations and Discourses*

is the essential image of the Father, the true representative of God.[40] On the other hand, Owen's Trinitarian intention makes him direct attention to the work of the Holy Spirit in the life of Jesus Christ, preparing the head of the new creation.[41] Owen does not see an opposition between these two lines of a classical incarnation Christology and a 'pneumachristology,' while the *opera trinitatis ad extra indivisa sunt*, and the Spirit proceeds from the Son also. The Son assumes the human nature; the Spirit forms it.[42]

Common in both lines is the perspective of the new creation. The goal of the new creation is the restoration of the image of God. Jesus Christ as God incarnate is the true representation of the Father. His human nature is the start of the restoration of the image of God in humankind, providing the pattern for the regeneration of our nature. As incarnate Son, Jesus Christ is the foundation of the new creation. Without the formation of the image of God in Jesus Christ, the restoration of the image of God in humanity would be impossible. Now salvation can be wrought in the nature that had sinned. Because Christ has never been in Adam, he is without sin and as such able to restore humanity. The incarnation also gives the relationship between God and humanity a stable foundation. This foundation is constituted by the hypostatical union of divine and human nature, the one person who is at once representative of God and of the new humanity.[43] Seen from the 'pneumachristological' perspective, the new creation cannot exist without the existence of its head. The renewal of creation begins with the work of the Holy Spirit in the human nature of Christ. As his human nature was the same as our nature and the Spirit was working on his human nature, so he will do for ours, our entire human nature will be saved.

---

on the Glory of Christ, in *Works*, Vol. I, esp. 323–33; *Of Communion with God the Father, Son and Holy Ghost*, in *Works*, Vol. II esp. 59–78. See further Ferguson, 'John Owen and the doctrine of the person of Christ'; Trueman, *The Claims of Truth*, 154–60; De Vries, *"Die mij heeft liefgehad,"* 214–16.

40. Owen, *Works*, Vol. I, 65–67, 71–72, 78–79, 144, 146, 173, 175, 218–19, 294, 298; De Vries, *"Die mij heeft liefgehad,"* 215.

41. Owen, ΠΝΕΥΜΑΤΟΛΟΓΙΑ, in *Works*, Vol. III, 160–83. See further footnote 33.

42. Owen, *Works*, Vol. I, 225; Vol. II, 66; Vol. III, 160–62; Vol. X, 174–79. See further Trueman, *The Claims of Truth*, 173–79.

43. On the incarnation and its meaning for salvation, see Owen, *Works*, Vol. I, 45, 48, 63–64, 86–88, 169–71, 197, 200–202, 206–18, 276, 310; Vol. II, 51, 66; Vol. V, 180.

In 2.2 we saw already that Owen uses the concepts of representation, head, common or public person, and mystical union. Here the concept of headship returns, in the ΠΝΕΥΜΑΤΟΛΟΓΙΑ together with the concept of body in an organic model, in *The Doctrine of Justification by Faith* combined with the concept of a mystical person. I start a further discussion of these concepts saying something on the relations Owen distinguishes between Christ and the church, His body, to clarify the relations between these concepts and to clarify the concepts also.

We saw that Owen distinguishes three conjunctions: natural, mystical and federal. Natural and federal conjunctions exist between Adam and his posterity, as well as between Christ and believers, although in different ways. The natural and federal conjunction between Adam and humanity exists, because we are all humans sharing the same human nature and Adam is the head of the covenant of works. The believers also have a natural and federal conjunction with Christ, but their origin differs. The federal conjunction between Christ and the church is rooted in the covenant of the mediator and not in creation; and the natural conjunction also did not start in creation, but in incarnation. Nevertheless, the relation between Adam and humanity and between Christ and the church are alike in that a natural and a federal conjunction exists. Especially the mystical conjunction marks the difference between the relation with Adam and with Christ. Between Christ and the believers a mystical conjunction exists that does not exist between Adam and his posterity. Therefore in *The Doctrine of Justification by Faith* the relation between Adam and his posterity is only one of the relations that explain the relationship between Christ and his own.

The mystical conjunction marks a difference between the concepts of representation and head, and within the concept of headship. Representation implies a federal conjunction, head a natural and federal conjunction (both with Adam and Christ) or even a mystical conjunction (with Christ alone). Because this mystical conjunction is caused by the Holy Spirit, at the same time the work of the Holy Spirit marks these differences. The concept of representation is not related to the work of the Holy Spirit, the notion of head can be. This leads to a difference within the concept of headship, a difference between head as representative or common person without a mystical conjunction, and head including a mystical conjunction as head of a mystical body or a mystical person. As far as the headship of Christ is seen parallel with Adam as representative and common person, the work of the Holy Spirit is not mentioned. But the whole of the headship of Christ as head of the mystical person or the mystical body is impossible without the work of the Holy Spirit. Therefore the concept of headship is related to the concept of representation (Christ as common person; federal conjunction; without mentioning of the Holy Spirit) as well as to the concept of mystical union (Christ and the church as mystical person; mystical conjunction; necessary to mention the work of the Holy Spirit).

In 2.2 we discussed the concepts of head and representation within the covenantal context. Now more can be said on the concept of headship in so far as the mystical conjunction is concerned. Owen speaks of a mystical union, a mystical person and a mystical body. We saw that the mystical union was already active before the actual consummation in God's councils. That this is the case can also be seen in the concept of 'mystical person.'[44] This concept is used only in *The Doctrine of Justification by Faith*. It is noteworthy that Owen uses it in this context where the notion of imputation is very central. That Christ and the church are one mystical person is the foundation of imputation. This mystical person was designed in the council of Father and Son and made effectual by the Holy Spirit.[45] This concept allows Owen to make it understandable that the all sins of the church were imputed to Christ and that he died for their sins, even before their existence and before an actual consummation of a mystical union with him; the elect were already in Christ. The function of the concept of mystical person is to clarify imputation, even before the actual consummation of the presupposed mystical union.

The concepts of 'head' and 'mystical body' are not used for this purpose. The image of head and body is used to clarify imputation only in quotations from church fathers. Remarkably Owen himself never does so independently of these quotations, due to the conceptual apparatus of his doctrine of justification.[46] If Owen uses the concepts of head and mystical body, they refer to a concrete existing head and concrete exist-

44. Owen, *Works*, Vol. V, 176, 178, 196, 200, 209, 214, 218, 222, 351. Cf. the concept of 'mystical Christ' in Vol. X, 598; it is used 6 times in Owen's *Works*, but not in Vol. I–V and only once in Vol. X.

45. Owen, *Works*, Vol. V, 176, 179.

46. See Owen, *Works*, Vol. V, 176–77. The concept of 'mystical body' is used often in Vol. III. See further Vol. I, 130, 259 (2), 268, 269, 343, 362, 363 (2); Vol. II, 284, 313, 334, 348; Vol. V, 196, 209, 218, 344.

ing members of the body. This existence of head and body presupposes the twofold work of the Holy Spirit in the new creation: his work in and on the human nature of Christ and in respect of the members of the body. The Son received his position as representative in the covenant of the mediator, but in a second episode the Son takes our human nature in hypostatical union with himself. Hence the concept of headship is a dynamic one, including the dynamics of Owen's 'pneumachristology.' This second episode presupposes the third episode, taking place if Jesus gives the believers his Spirit. The second and the third episode presuppose each other: the incarnation has no saving significance without the inhabitation of the Spirit in the believers and the union with Christ through the Spirit has no saving significance without the union of divine and human nature in Christ.[47] In the work of the Spirit in the head of the new creation, the relation to the body of the new creation is presupposed already. Therefore the concept of headship presupposes a work of the Holy Spirit, uniting Christ and the church, making imputation of our sin to Christ possible and making Christ's work meaningful for the church. This makes clear that although the union between Christ and the believer comes fully into existence through the regenerating work of the Spirit and through faith as we shall see below (see 2.4), still some conjunction, not only natural and federal, but also mystical exists. The concept of headship implies this conjunction, related to the work of the Holy Spirit on the new creation.[48]

It is this presupposed union that enables Owen to use the concept of a 'mystical person.' The mystical union that the Holy Spirit creates and that is designed in the covenant of the mediator is already active. Therefore the sins of the believers can be imputed to Christ.

47. Gleason, *John Calvin and John Owen on mortification*, 90; De Vries, *"Die mij heeft liefgehad,"* 216.

48. According to De Koeyer, Owen gives the union with Christ in his ΠΝΕΥΜΑΤΟΛΟΓΙΑ too small a place. Owen concentrates too much on the work of the Spirit and the concept of *habitus*. See De Koeyer, "Pneumatologia," 244. He is justified in signaling problems in Owen, especially in relation to the concept of *habitus*, but he seems to overlook the function and the relational impact of the concept of head in the ΠΝΕΥΜΑΤΟΛΟΓΙΑ. De Vries corrects de Koeyer (De Vries, *"Die mij heeft liefgehad,"* 26, 306), but he does not see the importance of Owen's 'pneumachristology' and of the concept of head in Owen's *Pneumatology* (cf. De Vries, *"Die mij heeft liefgehad,"* 214–17).

Summarizing, the relation between the different concepts can be seen in this table:

Concept	Refers to	Context	Presupposes
Representative, common or public person	Adam, Christ alone	Covenant	Federal (and natural) conjunction
Mystical person	Christ and the elect	Imputation	Design of mystical union in God's council and (future) actual consummation of this union
Head	Adam, Christ alone	Covenant	Federal (and natural) conjunction
	Christ alone	Work of the Holy Spirit	Mystical conjunction, incarnation and inhabitation

To understand these concepts, it is important to see again the function they have in Owen's historical context. The relation between Christology and pneumatology was unclear in the theology of Arminians and Socinians, according to Owen. Jesus Christ was one, our faith another thing. Arminians saw satisfaction as universal, Socinians even denied satisfaction by the work of Christ and saw the idea of imputation as problematic as they also did the Trinity and the godhead of Jesus Christ. The idea of satisfaction contradicts God's free forgiveness in their opinion. Both thought the moral capacities of man great enough to say that moral persuasion was sufficient to bring a sinner to faith. The relation between the work of Christ and our good works, our sanctification, was unclear or absent. The active obedience of Christ during his life had no significance for our lives. Reformed theology after Dordrecht alleged that the Arminians believed that God enabled man to save himself in Christ, while making salvation a possibility instead of an actual reality. Christ, as seen by the Socinians, could not provide the salvation as needed according to the Reformed theologians.

For Owen the following interests are central: the work of Christ in his oblation and his intercession in heaven is essentially one, as we have seen already; the work of the Son and the work of the Spirit are one, while the *opera trinitatis ad extra* are undivided; justification is impossible without imputation and satisfaction; faith is a gift of the Spirit, actual faith even the gift of a new ability; sanctification is a fruit of the work of Christ. With the help of these concepts of representation, common and mystical person, and head Owen keeps Christology and pneumatology together and gives his doctrine of imputation a foundation. He also creates the possibility of making the entire life of Christ significant for the entire renewal of our lives, including faith and our good works, thus excluding moralistic soteriologies. Salvation is not a matter of moral reformation but of new creation.

These interests, together with his doctrine of election and his construction of the relation between the covenant of the mediator and the election, bring him to the opinion that Christ is representative and head of the elect, doing his work for the elect only; Christ is no half saviour. His death was of sufficient value for the redemption of all and everyone, but it was effective as a ransom only for the elect. Owen's defence of limited atonement is in line with these interests and the whole of his theology. As Trueman has shown, it is too easy here to blame Owen for using Aristotelian categories and ignore him further.[49]

In summary, central concepts in Owen's Christology are representative, common or public person, mystical person and head. These concepts indicate aspects of the union between Christ and the elect: a natural, federal and mystical conjunction. The concept of mystical person is used especially to clarify imputation. The concept of headship is indissolubly connected with Owen's 'pneumachristology' and hence with the work of the Holy Spirit. These concepts enable Owen to maintain the unity of Christology and pneumatology and give his doctrine of imputation a foundation.

2.3.2 SIGNIFICANCE OF THE STORY OF JESUS CHRIST

According to Owen, different moments of the story of Jesus Christ have significance for our salvation and not only his death on the cross. I will work this out through several points: incarnation, the life and obedience

49. For Owen's defence of limited atonement see *Works*, Vol. X. This contains his *Salus Electorum, Sanguis Jesu*. Clifford is, in his *Atonement and justification*, very critical on this book of Owen's, but according to Trueman Clifford jumps to conclusions too rapidly; see Trueman, *The Claims of Truth*, 185–97, 233–41. See further Packer, *A Quest for Godliness*, 125–45, who stresses the organic whole of the five points of Dordt, intending to show that God saves sinners.

of Christ, and the everlasting significance of the work of Christ for the whole of creation.

The first point has become clear already: Jesus Christ has a soteriological significance for us because of his incarnation. He is the essential representation of the Father, furthermore he is the foundation of the new creation, the hypostatical union of human and divine nature in his person gives the relation of God and man a stable foundation, and his incarnation is the first part of our union with Christ. Apart from this I want to mention that the Father appointed the Son as heir of all things. As in creation, the Father wanted to work through the Son in the new creation and the whole new creation had to exist in him. So he decided to communicate all the goodness, grace, life, light, mercy and power necessary for recreation only through his Son. As St. Paul writes in Col 2:9 that in Christ all the fullness dwells bodily, Owen sees this caused in incarnation: to communicate his fullness through Christ to the church God first of all communicated his fullness to Christ. As he was constituted as head of the new creation God made him a repository and treasure of all goodness, grace, life, power and mercy, necessary for the constitution and preservation of the new creation.[50] This communication of all the fullness to Christ cannot be understood without mentioning the work of the Holy Spirit. It is the Spirit who anointed Jesus for his ministry. So since the assumption of human nature into personal union with the Son of God, all the fullness dwells in him bodily. Owen sees the office of Christ as 'the way appointed in the wisdom of God for the communication of the treasures of grace which were communicated unto his person' unto the church.[51] It will be very clear now that for Owen the incarnation is fundamental, although at the same time De Vries is right in stating that the significance of cross, resurrection and ascension dominate in Owen's spirituality of the glorified Christ.[52] In incarnation, the fullness of grace is communicated to Christ to be communicated to the church.

The second point concerns the life of Jesus Christ on earth. Here the obedience of Christ is a central notion. Within Owen's historical context, the distinction was made between the active and passive obedience of Christ. Some theologians said that only the passive obedience of

50. Note the anti-roman formulations: in Jesus Christ, the high priest, the treasure can be found.

51. Owen, *Works*, Vol. I, 362.

52. De Vries, "*Die mij heeft liefgehad*," 163.

Christ—his obedience in his suffering at the cross giving his life as a sacrifice—rendered satisfaction and was imputed. The imputation of Christ's active obedience would imply antinomianism. His active obedience only had significance for Jesus himself.

For Owen and other theologians Christ's active obedience also had soteriological significance, as not only his sacrifice but his entire lifetime on earth had a meaning for soteriology. Of course, his sacrifice was important. As high priest Christ offered himself as a perfect sacrifice, bearing the punishment and the curse of the law in our stead. From his 1652 *Dissertation on Divine Justice*, Owen saw the death of Christ even as an absolute necessity and not only as willed by God. [53] But apart from his rendering passive satisfaction he rendered active satisfaction too, living a perfectly righteous life by obedience to the law. He satisfied our disobedience as well as he fulfilled the law. His active obedience also is imputed to believers. This resulted in the reproach of Baxter and others that Owen was an antinomian theologian. Owen denied this and indeed he cannot be seen as antinomian. Central to Owen's theology is the renewal of our life in the restoration of the image of God through the infusion of a new principle of life (regeneration) and the preservation and growth of this principle (sanctification).

It is noteworthy that Owen does relate the obedience of Christ to the imputation of his righteousness in justification, but not to regeneration and sanctification. This does not mean that Owen does not relate regeneration and sanctification to the work of Christ, rather, he relates them very obviously. But he relates them with the help of other ideas, as the work of the Holy Spirit on the human nature of Christ, the internal grace and holiness of Christ, or the restoration of the image of God in His human nature, giving the earthly life of Jesus a meaning from another perspective.[54] Just as obedience, fulfilment of the law, satisfaction and imputation are related notions, so are internal grace and the holiness of Christ, renewal of the image of God in the human nature of Christ, and the infusion of a new habit or principle of life. These notions form two different conceptual fields, standing against the background of the Aristotelian

53. Owen sees here three different models: 1. the payment of the price, resulting in redemption; 2. the bringing of a sacrifice, resulting in atonement and reconciliation; 3. the bearing of the punishment in our place, Owen, *Works*, Vol. II, 165–67.

54. See for the significance of the life of Christ in 'pneumachristological' perspective Ferguson, 'John Owen and the Doctrine of the Holy Spirit,' 108–15.

distinction between *habitus* and *actus*. As Owen uses this distinction of *habitus* and *actus*, the earthly life of Jesus Christ has a soteriological significance both in his *habitus* and *actus*. The soteriological significance of his habitual being is explicated along pneumatological lines with notions such as regeneration in the sense of the infusion of a new principle of life, the soteriological significance of Christ's actual obedience with the help of ideas as atonement and justification. This results in the following two conceptual fields:[55]

Conceptual fields	**Actual obedience**	**Habitual being**
Concepts	*Actus*	*Habitus*
General field	Justice, obedience, acts	Being, habit, principle of life
	Juridical	Physical
Ideal	Fulfilment of the law	Image of God
Sin	Disobedience, guilt	Pollution, defilement of God's image
Saviour	Satisfaction Fulfilment of the law Active / passive obedience	Renewal of God's image in Christ Internal grace, internal holiness God's fullness in Christ
Salvation	Justification: imputation of Christ's righteousness	Regeneration: infusion of a new principle of being, or a new habit; communication of Christ. Sanctification

It is noteworthy that Christ in both lines can be seen as head; both fields presuppose the work of the Holy Spirit in the second episode of the union, the formation of the head. But further, the conceptual field

55. For the first field of actual obedience see Owen's doctrine of atonement, satisfaction and obedience see Owen, *Works*, Vol. I, 189–206, 339–42; Vol. II, 96–98, 135, 153, 155–68, 170, 173–76; Vol. V, *The Doctrine of Justification by Faith* esp. 124–52, 163–75, 205–22, 251–75; and also the entire Vol. X, containing *A Display of Arminianism*, (esp. 88–100), *Of the Death of Christ, the Price He Paid and the Purchase He Made* and *Salus Electorum, Sanguis Jesu*. On Owens *Dissertation on Divine Justice* see Trueman, 'John Owen's *Dissertation on Divine Justice*,' 87–103.

For the other field of habitual being see Owen, *Works*, Vol. I, 169–71, 180–84, 365–67; Vol. II, 156, 158, 171, 199–201; in Vol. III ΠΝΕΥΜΑΤΟΛΟΓΙΑ, esp. 162–69, 208–24, 316–37, 386–87, 414–22, 472, 513–16.

of justice and obedience and the conceptual field of the renewal of being are not directly related in Owen's theology for two reasons: justification is not caused by the renewal of our being (against Rome), and habitual renewal does not follow the actual moral improvement of being, but the habitual renewal by the Holy Spirit precedes our acts (against Arminians and Socinians). This makes a direct reference to the obedience of Christ when dealing with our obedience not very obvious; the relation instead is an indirect one: Christ's obedience shows the habitual renewal of human nature in him, and this renewal results in a habitual renewal of our being, leading to our actual obedience. Christ is still the pattern and example of the renewal of God's image in us. And the whole of his life of habitual righteousness and actual obedience on earth has a saving significance for our life. Everything he did as mediator, 'he did for them whose mediator he was, or in whose stead and for whose good he executed the office of a mediator for God.'[56]

The third point where it becomes clear that different moments of the story of Jesus Christ are important (and not only the sacrifice of Christ), is his glorification and exaltation. In his glorification, the completing act of laying the foundation for the church, Jesus Christ's human nature has received all the glory and perfection of which it is capable. This means that, according to Owen, human nature is not deified and does not share in the essential divine glory; it does not lead to the destruction of his being. Because Jesus Christ is saviour and as such God and man, he also shares in the essential divine glory and is exalted as mediator. This means that there is a difference in kind and nature between his glory and the glory we shall receive, but the believers will share in the substance of this glory, as he is the pattern for our glorification.[57]

As exalted mediator, he is still active for our salvation. As a king he preserves and rules his church; as a priest he is in God's heavenly sanctuary. There he makes his atonement effective, intercedes and prays for his church. He gave the saints who lived before him full access to the glory of God, something which they did not have before. He further represents the church on earth and makes acceptable her worship, so giving access to the Father. He gives his Holy Spirit, who lives in him, and now comes to live in the church. He communicates himself to his body through the

56. Owen, *Works*, Vol. II, 160; and further Vol. I, 169–71.

57. Owen, *Works*, Vol. I, 236–47, 343–47; Vol. III, 181–82; Vol. X, 179.

Holy Spirit to bring his members to conformity with the head. For in him is all the fullness of the divine grace, goodness, light, life etc. that the Father through him communicates and applies by the Spirit to the church to form a new creation. Against the background of the discussions with the Arminians the priestly work of Christ has a special significance for Owen: because Owen is convinced that Christ in heaven is still working for the same persons that he died for, Christology and pneumatology are strongly linked together and the work of Christ in the past concerns our salvation in the present. We are not united with someone from the past, but with the living Lord. In the unity of the work of Christ in his oblation and intercession, Owen finds an important argument for his doctrine of limited atonement.[58]

So the glorification and exaltation of Christ has a twofold soteriological significance: it is a pattern and example of our future glorification and as exalted mediator Christ is still active for the benefit of the church.

The story of Jesus Christ never ends, according to Owen. Furthermore, his person and work not only have significance for human nature, but for the whole of creation. God created heaven for the family of angels and the earth for the family of man. For their continuance of being, both families were dependent on God as their head. As sin disturbed this unity and order, God wanted to bring them all together in one family under one head. Jesus Christ, the incarnate Son of God is the one head wherein God gathered all and reconciled all things in heaven and earth in him to himself. All God's communication of virtue, power, grace and goodness to all things comes immediately from this head. 'In Him they all consist, on Him do they depend, unto Him are they subject; in their relation unto Him doth their peace, union, and agreement among themselves consist.'[59] So in the recapitulation of all things, everything on heaven and earth is gathered in Jesus Christ, the Son of God. He is active in the new creation in the same way as he was active in creation as the wisdom and the power of the Father. This activity shall never end. Christ will give up his kingdom to the Father, but Christ in and by his human nature shall forever be the head of the new creation. We shall never lose our relation with him

58. Owen, *Works*, Vol. I, 247–72, 343, 360–66; Vol. X, 176–87.

59. Owen, *Works*, Vol. I, 371.

and he shall forever be the way of communication between God and the glorified saints.[60]

Owen thus shows that it is not only the incarnation and sacrifice of Jesus Christ that are important. His entire human life as a life of obedience, his glorification, his mediatorial work in heaven and his everlasting significance for the entire creation all receive attention. Owen's way of conceptualising all these aspects is among other factors dependent on the Aristotelian distinction between *habitus* and *actus*. The concept of act is central in a conceptual field consisting in obedience, satisfaction and justification; the concept of habit in a more pneumatological field consisting in renewal of being, restoration of the image of God and regeneration.

2.3.3 THE INCLUSIVE AND THE EXCLUSIVE MOMENT

It has been shown how Owen uses the notions of representation, mystical person and head, and how he succeeds in working out the significance of the entire story of Jesus Christ as relevant to soteriology. However, further analysis is necessary. Is the inclusive moment (representation) enough to develop a concept of 'being in Christ' building on Owen's views, or is also the exclusive moment necessary? And how do the inclusive and the exclusive moment relate?

It is clear that the inclusive moment is present. Christ is representative and head of the elect, of the mystical person, and of the mystical body. The inclusive moment is elaborated with the help of the conceptual field of habitual being and Owen's 'pneumachristology': in the human nature of Jesus Christ the renewal of the image of God in mankind has begun. It will lead to the glorification of the believers, participating in the glory of Jesus' human nature.

The exclusive moment is also present. First the aspect of work-substitution in the work of Christ is important: His entire actual obedience resulting in satisfaction for our sins with as its climax Christ's oblation as high priest, and His intercessory prayers in heaven. A second aspect is the person-substitution. Obviously, this is an aspect of the concepts of representative and head. The representative and head is not identical with the persons represented or the body, but has a unique place. Moreover Jesus Christ is unique because of his divine nature. However, more can be said; to understand better this aspect of person-substitution and its

60. Owen, *Works*, Vol. I, 48–49, 62–63, 209–11, 213–15, 265, 271, 361–62, 367–74.

relation to the inclusive moment, I will discuss Owen's use of the concept of surety or guarantee.[61]

To understand this concept something more must be said of Owen's theological context. According to the Arminians, Christ is the cause of election. Christ and faith in Christ precede the act of election. The work of Christ is the meritorious cause of election, and the Trinitarian aspect of election is neglected. God loves the elect only in Christ and for Christ's sake.[62] The Socinians said that Jesus Christ only guarantees the love of God, making the covenant sure. They denied the godhead of Jesus and the satisfaction of his death, affirming that Jesus Christ as a prophet made clear the will of God, assuring his love towards man. Being glorified he now is king and priest, reconciling God and man. He was only a surety for God before us, securing the covenant. We do not give Christ as a sacrifice to God.[63]

Against these two positions Owen uses the concept of surety in a different way. Opposing the Socinians, Owen wants to make clear that Christ is a surety for us before God. He does not assure us of the love of God, but he safeguards our position before God by his obedient sacrifice bringing the necessary satisfaction for our sins.[64] Christ is our representative, and his sacrifice has a substitutive value. However, the position of the Arminians is also excluded. Christ is our representative, but this does not imply, according to Owen, that we give Jesus Christ as a surety or guarantee to God or move God to love us. It was by free assent that the Son of God willingly decided to be our surety.[65] The priority of the love of the triune God is safeguarded by the covenant of the mediator.[66] It is not the sacrifice of Christ that moved the Father to love us for the love of God precedes the covenant and the sacrifice of Christ. Sacrifices do not secure the covenant; so Christ's sacrifice did not secure the new covenant, but yet he was in his person, mediation, life and death ,the only cause and means whereby the whole grace of the covenant is made effective for us.[67]

61. See on the concept of surety in Reformed orthodoxy Schaede, *Stellvertretung*, 533–39.

62. Dekker, *Rijker dan Midas*, 204–5; Graafland, *Van Calvijn tot Barth*, 99–102.

63. Owen, *Works*, Vol .V, 182–83.

64. Owen, *Works*, Vol. V, 182–89.

65. Owen, *Works*, Vol. I, 352–53, 357–58; Vol. V, 183–84, 187.

66. Owen, *Works*, Vol. V, 179–81, 189–91.

67. Owen, *Works*, Vol. V, 190–91, 193–96.

Moreover, according to Owen, it is not true that Christ's satisfaction is so imputed to us as if we had done or suffered ourselves in him. 'For we do not say that God judges or esteems that we did and suffered in our own persons what Christ did and suffered; but only that he did it and suffered it in our stead.'[68] Until the satisfaction of Christ is imputed to us no one can be said to have suffered in Christ or have any interest in his satisfaction. Notwithstanding the full satisfaction made once by Christ all men are by nature children of wrath apart from imputation. If we are not actually inserted into Christ we have no interest in his satisfaction.[69] Although Owen does not use the distinction between substitution and representation, his position is the same as that of theologians who use the idea of substitution together with representation to prevent the thought that we in Christ did ourselves what he did for us. Over against the Socinians, Owen emphasises representation and work-subsitution, over against the Arminians person-substitution and the work of the triune God in Jesus Christ. The exclusive and inclusive moment are both needed to balance each other.

It must be said that there is a tension in Owen here. On the one hand we do not give Jesus Christ as a surety, so we have no interest in him before the imputation of righteousness. Here the point at issue is salvation as a gift of God, who gave Christ as our guarantee. Owen emphasises person-substitution and the work of God in Christ. On the other hand, in his *Of the Death of Christ*, one of his earlier writings (1650) Owen stresses other aspects. Christ is made ours before we believe and made the righteousness of God for us. He does see a difference between Christ made ours before and after believing: 'He who is made ours in an act of God's love, that for him we may have faith, may be found and made ours in a promise of reconciliation by believing.'[70] Here the point at issue is the interest the elect have in salvation before believing. Owen says this to maintain again that salvation remains a gift of God and even faith is a gift of God resulting from the merit of Christ.[71] Now the inclusive moment is emphasised: the elect are included in Christ, even before they believe. But in saying this it becomes difficult to maintain that we have no interest in

68. Owen, *Works*, Vol. V, 210.

69. Owen, *Works*, Vol. V, 209–10, 216–18, 220.

70. Owen, *Works*, Vol. X, 470.

71. Owen, *Works*, Vol. X, 465–71.

Christ before imputation. A comparable thing can be said if Owen deals with the imputation of our sins to Christ related to the concept of mystical person in *The Doctrine of Justification by Faith*. The mystical union is the foundation for imputation. Here the influence of the moment of union is already present. Below I shall go further into this (see 2.4.1).[72] This tension shows how difficult it is to maintain the equilibrium of the exclusive and the inclusive moment[73].

To conclude, both the exclusive and the inclusive moment are present, balancing each other. The concept of surety is used to maintain on the one hand the satisfaction for our sins by Christ as our head; on the other hand the free decision of the Son in the covenant of the mediator to be surety for the elect avoids the idea of 'Umstimmung' as well as the idea that we are presenting ourselves to God in Christ, and gives the love of God primacy. Different interests make it difficult to maintain the equilibrium between the inclusive and the exclusive moment: it must be God who saves us in Christ (the exclusive moment; person-substitution); the sins of the elect must be imputed to Christ (the moment of union); the elect have an interest in Christ before believing, for even faith is a gift (the inclusive moment); and the elect have no interest in Christ before believing, for the believer is justified by faith alone (the exclusive moment; work-substitution). For a concept of 'being in Christ' in accordance with Owen this implies that the inclusive moment is necessary but alone does not suffice: the exclusive moment as person-substitution is necessary to balance the inclusive moment.

72. Here Owen's development is important: in his earlier writings as *Of the Death of Christ* Owen is more speculative and supralapsarist than in his later writings as *The Doctrine of Justification by Faith* (1677) and *Meditations and Discourses on the Glory of Christ* (1684) cited in footnote 59.

73. According to Boersma, Owen's concept of a mystical union makes it impossible to differentiate between the person of Christ and a person united with Him. Further in fact this concept makes a doctrine of imputation and forensic justification impossible. However, Boersma refers only to *Of the Death of Christ* that is more supralapsarian than his later writings. In his later writings, Owen differentiates more between Christ and the believers, using concepts like mystical person and mystical union. Boersma fails to see which possibilities the different concepts create, enabling Owen to distinguish between the position of Christ in the covenant of redemption, in the work of atonement, and in the actual consummation of the union. That for Owen the mystical union was the foundation of imputation does not exclude the difference between head and members. Further it is important to note that for Owen different problems were central: not only how the justice of Christ could be imputed unto the believers, but also how the sins of the elect could be imputed unto Christ. See Boersma, *A Hot Peppercorn*, 107–8.

2.4 Soteriology

Christ is our representative and our head. We saw that in the covenant of the mediator a first step is made. In a second episode the Son assumed the human nature and by the Spirit was formed as the head of the body of the new creation. To complete the mystical union a third step must be made. The story of Jesus Christ continues in the lives of the believers: as the heavenly high priest He gives His Spirit and makes His obedience and oblation effective for the elect. In this section I will deal with the third episode of the story of union with Christ.

We saw in 2.3.2 that two conceptual fields can be distinguished in Owen: the field of *actus*, justice, obedience, satisfaction and justification, as well as the field of *habitus*, being, image of God, regeneration and sanctification. The differences between these two must not be exaggerated. As Owen differentiates between personal grace—the grace that makes Jesus Christ excellent, comely and desirable—and purchased grace—the grace by Christ purchased for us—the grace of justification and sanctification together with the grace of privilege are taken as purchased grace.[74] Both lines do not stand unrelated beside each other. On the other hand, Owen wrote books concentrating on one of the two different lines: in his ΠΝΕΥΜΑΤΟΛΟΓΙΑ the line of *habitus* and being dominates, in his works on atonement and justification, as *the Death of Death in the Death of Christ* and *The Doctrine of Justification by Faith* the line of justice and *actus* dominates.[75]

For a further analysis of the conceptual structure of Owen's theology as far as it is relevant for the development of a concept of 'being in Christ' building on his theology, I will first describe how exactly the relationship of these both lines must be conceived in the light of the problem of the place of justification in Owen's soteriology (2.4.1). In 2.4.2 I will continue the discussion of these two lines, dealing with the relation between, on the one hand justification and, on the other hand regeneration and sanctification. In a third sub-section I will concentrate further on the mystical union itself (2.4.3). Fourth, I will deal with some aspects of the order of salvation in relation to 'being in Christ' (2.4.4). Finally, I will again discuss the hypothesis regarding 'being in Christ' (2.4.5).

74. Owen, *Works*, Vol. II, 47–78, 154–55.

75. De Vries is right in denying that regeneration dominates justification (De Vries, *"Die mij heeft liefgehad,"* 259 footnote 25). Both themes belong in different conceptual lines, and both lines receive enough attention.

2.4.1 DIFFERENT CONCEPTUAL FIELDS 1: THE PLACE OF JUSTIFICATION

The place of justification in Owen's theology is not totally clear. Owen does not deal with justification in his pneumatology and does not give any reasons for failing to do so. De Vries sees as a possible reason that according to Owen the ground for justification is not in us, but *extra nos*.[76] Hence in his pneumatology Owen does not offer much material to reconstruct the relation between both conceptual fields or to say something on the place of justification in his soteriology.

Besides the question of the relation of the two conceptual fields, a second and related point makes the question of the place of justification in Owen's theology an important one. The story of union with Christ has different episodes: the second is the incarnation, the third the work of the Spirit uniting us with Christ. The question of the place of justification in Owen can be reformulated as: how does the justification relate to the unifying work of the Spirit and regeneration as well as faith resulting from this work? There are two possibilities: justification precedes regeneration and faith, or justification follows regeneration and faith. It seems that both options are present in Owen.

According to De Vries it is important to see development in Owen: De Vries sees a difference between his earlier works and his 1677 *The Doctrine of Justification by Faith*. In his earlier works, Owen gave Baxter reasons to reject in his *Confession* (1655) a justification from eternity or on Golgotha, opposite to Owen. Nevertheless Owen denies in *the Death of Death in the Death of Christ* (1647) a justification from eternity and writes in *Of the Death of Christ, the Price He Paid and the Purchase He Made* (1650) that there is no justification on Golgotha.[77] In *Of the Death of Christ* Owen distinguishes between a '*ius ad rem*' and a '*ius in re*.' Before believing the elect have a '*ius ad rem*' and '*sub termino*' on the good things purchased by the death of Christ, like the prodigal son had

76. De Vries, *"Die mij heeft liefgehad,"* 25, 259–60. He sees as another part of a possible explanation that for Owen Christology and pneumatology were more independent than in Calvin. I don't agree with the thesis that in Owen Christology and pneumatology are independent of each other, for in his pneumatology the 'pneumachristological' element is present and important. The problem is not the independence of Christology and pneumatology, but the independence of the two different lines of *actus* / justification related with the obedience of Christ and the line of *habitus* / being related with the 'pneumachristology.'

77. Owen, *Works*, Vol. X, 276–77 and 465; Boersma, *A Hot Peppercorn*, 55; De Vries, *"Die mij heeft liefgehad,"* 273–75.

on the inheritance before his father died. The elect have not yet an '*ius in re*' before believing. The *ius in re* is based on faith; the *ius ad rem* is based on the covenant of the mediator and the merit of Christ. Because in the death of Christ the conditions of the covenant of the mediator are completely fulfilled, the elect for whom Christ died have an actual right to salvation. It is important to Owen not only that, if the ransom is paid, the person for whom the ransom is paid has a right to his liberty by virtue of that payment, but also that faith is a gift of God given for the sake of Christ. He cannot conceive 'how any thing should be made out to me for Christ, and Christ Himself not be given to me, He being "made unto us of God, righteousness," 1 Corinthians 1:30.'[78] So Christ is made ours before believing, although there is a difference between the way He is made ours before and after believing: before believing He is made ours in an act of love in a promise of reconciliation by believing. Owen further suggests that the absolution of guilt may precede our actual believing as this could perhaps be the justification of the ungodly by reckoning of Christ to the sinner in heaven and thus absolving him, and then bestowing him with faith. This would mean that justification could be seen as a process, beginning in heaven and terminating in the conscience. 'Absolution in heaven, and justification, differ as part and whole.'[79] It cannot be denied that here lines can be seen to the English Hypercalvinists who taught a justification from eternity. If justification is seen as a process in this way, it precedes regeneration and faith as well as following both of them.

According to De Vries, Owen is less speculative in his later works. Already the title of his *The Doctrine of Justification by Faith, through the Imputation of the Righteousness of Christ* (1677) suggests the central place of faith in justification, as does the fact that the first three chapters deal with faith. Owen wants to make clear that righteousness is a gift of God, not caused by any formal cause within us, be it obedience, the renovation of our nature, inherent habits of grace, good works or faith. Therefore he strictly distinguishes between justification as a forensic act of acceptance by the imputation of the righteousness of Christ and sanctification as an infusion of inherent grace. Our inherent righteousness resulting from this infusion is no ground for justification like it is for Rome. Central in his thought is what St. Paul writes in Rom 4:5 that God justifies the ungodly.

78. Owen, *Works*, Vol. X, 470.

79. Owen, *Works*, Vol. X, 470. And more generally 465–71; Boersma, *A Hot Peppercorn*, 105–8; De Vries, '*Die mij heeft liefgehad*,' 272–74.

It is important to see that Owen has what appears to be, at first sight, two colliding interests. The first is that justification is justification by faith; hence justification follows the unifying work of the Spirit and the gift of faith. But Owen's second interest is that God justifies the ungodly by the Holy Spirit, so that sanctification and even regeneration and renewal are not necessary for justification. (Moreover already the imputation of their guilt to Christ presupposes the uniting work of the Holy Spirit.) Owen's solution is a distinction between an order of nature and a chronological order. In the order of nature justification follows union with Christ and faith. This can be seen very clearly in the continuation of justification: it is justification by faith alone, faith being the instrumental cause of justification. But chronologically the moment of regeneration and the gift of faith, as well as the moment of the first justification take place at the same instant. When God justifies the ungodly and imputes the righteousness of Christ to him, 'he does at the same instant, by the power of his grace, make him inherently and subjectively righteous or holy.'[80] Hence both are true: justification by faith alone—faith receiving the justification—and justification by the Holy Spirit—faith being faith in the God who justifies the ungodly.[81]

The question is now whether Owen has really changed his position with respect to his earlier works. De Vries suggests this, saying that Owen is less speculative drawing different lines in making clear that justification is justification by faith alone. At first sight Owen's book suggests that justification follows faith. But still two options are present in Owen: a. justification follows regeneration and faith as well as b. a version of the option that justification precedes regeneration and faith, modified with the help of the idea of simultaneity: regeneration, the gift of faith and justification take place simultaneously. Owen has changed his position in this sense, that he needs no speculations on faith preceding justification and finds it possible to say that justification follows faith in the order of nature. But he stayed true to his earlier position in this sense that it is not the pious believer but the ungodly that is justified.

The complexity of his position is caused by the complexity of his story of the union with Christ. Already the work of Christ presupposes the moment of union: the sins of the elect are imputed to Christ and Christ

80. Owen, *Works*, Vol. V, 126.

81. Owen, *Works*, Vol. V, 7, 9, 126–27, 132–33, 151, 158, 212, 232, 316, 317, 339, 353.

dies for the elect. Even the gift of faith shows the influence of this moment of union. At the same time this work of Christ is characterized by its exclusivity (work-substitution). The believers participate in the righteousness of Christ only by faith, not by works. In the perspective of the work of God, the moment of union is active before faith. In the perspective of the believer, the moment of union results from faith.

Concerning the relation between the two conceptual fields, the work of the Holy Spirit can be seen in both fields. When God justifies the ungodly and imputes the righteousness of Christ, the Holy Spirit is active in it. And at the same instant the Holy Spirit gives a new spiritual nature, inherently righteous and holy. The significance of the work of Christ can be seen in both fields too: the obedience of Christ is imputed and the elect derive a new spiritual nature from him. Both fields are related in the order of nature as justification follows regeneration and faith. At the same time the independence of both fields is maintained where the first moment of justification and the gift of a new nature take place simultaneously and thus both presuppose different acts of God.[82]

To conclude, in Owen a development can be seen from a more speculative position in which justification is a process, beginning before believing and preceding regeneration as well as faith, and terminating after regeneration and the gift of faith in conscience. In his later work Owen is less speculative, stating clearly that one is justified by faith alone. However, the problem that the moment of union is active before the actual consummation of the union and that faith is a gift, is solved by stating the simultaneity of the gift of faith and the act of justification. At this moment the activity of the Holy Spirit in both conceptual fields relates those fields.

2.4.2 DIFFERENT CONCEPTUAL FIELDS 2: JUSTIFICATION, REGENERATION AND SANCTIFICATION

To say more about the relation between both fields more has to be said on the relation between, on the one hand, justification and, on the other hand, regeneration and sanctification. Doing this, it will become increasingly clear how Owen thinks the third step of the story of our union with Christ takes place.

82. De Vries, *"Die mij heeft liefgehad,"* 128.

The difference between justification and regeneration/sanctification can be characterized in various ways. The first is moral, the second real; the first concerns status, the second being; justification is acceptance, regeneration and sanctification making acceptable; the first is forensic, the second physical.[83] Justification is acceptance through imputation of the active and passive obedience of Christ, regeneration the infusion of a new spiritual principle, the gift of a new spiritual nature. In both of them the work of God is vital: it is God who imputes and it is God who gives new life. Faith does not receive as much attention as the work of God does, although the perspective of the participating human person is not absent in Owen (see below, 2.5.1).

Both justification and sanctification are related to the union of the believer with Christ and hence to the work of the Spirit. It may seem that when dealing with justification Owen mentions especially the second episode of the story of our union with Christ, the incarnate Son who is our head and representative, while when dealing with sanctification he mentions especially the third episode, the inhabitation and unifying work of the Holy Spirit. A few examples: In *Meditations and Discourses on the Glory of Christ* (1684) Owen deals in a chapter with the conjunction between Christ and the church. Here the themes concern the second episode of the story of the union, satisfaction and—briefly—forgiveness. In a following chapter concerning the communication of Christ to the believers the concepts he uses are creation, being, the gift of the Spirit, mystical union, the formation of a new nature, implantation in himself—the third episode of the story of the union. In *Of Communion with God the Father, Son and Holy Ghost* (1657) when Owen deals with the grace Christ purchased for us, he mentions three graces: justification, sanctification and the grace of privileges. Themes related to justification are: acceptance, removal of guilt and sin, imputation of righteousness, obedience of Christ, effectiveness of his death, satisfaction, Christ as common person and the place of our obedience. Among them are themes related to the second part of the story of the union and the work of Christ. In dealing with sanctification Owen speaks about removal of defilement, habitual cleansing, bestowing of cleanness, the purifying blood of Christ, habitual grace, habit, spiritual principle, inhabitation, Christ's mediation, Christ communicating him-

83. See Owen, *Works* Vol. II, 169–73; Vol. III, 630; Vol. V, 270; Ferguson, *John Owen on the Christian Life*, 33; De Vries, *"Die mij heeft liefgehad,"* 220.

self, mystical union. Among these concepts, we find ideas related to the third episode of the story of the union with Christ.[84]

This makes clear that Owen often relates justification more explicitly with the second episode of the story of the union, and sanctification more explicitly with the third episode, and furthermore relates justification with concepts of the field of justice and obedience and sanctification with concepts of the field of habitual being. According to De Vries, this leads to a relative independence of justification and sanctification.[85]

But he can also do things differently, relating justification with the third episode sanctification with the second episode. For example, in his ΠΝΕΥΜΑΤΟΛΟΓΙΑ (1674) Owen deals extensively with the work of the Spirit. Christ is seen as head of the new creation. Owen writes further on regeneration and sanctification. If he deals with justification it is for three reasons: to prevent our good works that result from the sanctifying work of the Spirit, from receiving a place in our justification, to state that justification does not take away the necessity of doing good works, and to mention the work of the Holy Spirit in a believer as including our justification. Here both episodes of the union are mentioned, but regarding the second episode Owen focuses on the human nature of Christ and not on incarnation, while the third step is central as it is effected by inhabitation and regeneration. So he concentrates on the field of being and habit, but he needs both of these episodes of the story of the union and thus relates both to sanctification. It is remarkable that he relates Christology and regeneration or sanctification by dealing with both in one book, whereas he never explores the relation between them apart from mentioning the activity of the same Spirit. While it is the same Spirit active in the head and the body of the new creation, the relation between head and body seems self-evident. His substantialist frame of reference presumably did not provide him with the relational concepts necessary for reflecting on this relation. Therefore R.W. de Koeyer sees a tension between relational and substantialist lines of thought.[86]

In *The Doctrine of Justification by Faith* (1677) Owen is very clear about the fact that imputation of guilt and righteousness presupposes the

84. For the passages in *Meditations and Discourses on the Glory of Christ* see Owen, *Works*, Vol. I 352–67; for the passages in *Of Communion with God the Father, Son and Holy Ghost* see Owen, *Works*, Vol. II, 196–207.

85. De Vries, "*Die mij heeft liefgehad*," 286.

86. See Owen, *Works*, Vol. III; De Koeyer, "Pneumatologia," 244.

unifying work of the Spirit. The foundation of the imputation of guilt to Christ is that Christ and the church were a mystical person in God's design by the Spirit inhabiting both head and body. So Christ bore the person of the church in what he did as mediator. As they actually coalesce in this state through the uniting efficacy of the Holy Spirit also Christ's righteousness is imputed to the believers. Here the justification is related to the second and third episode of story of the union, both presupposing the unifying work of the Spirit and thus the conceptual field of being.[87]

The lines of thought differ and yet offer parallels. Reflecting on justification, the emphasis is laid on the prevenient obedience of Christ that is imputed to us (the exclusive moment: work-substitution; participation as imputation) and the activity of the moment of union before its actual consummation (imputation of our guilt, faith as a gift). Reflecting on sanctification, the renewing work of the Spirit is emphasised—we are sanctified because we are members of Christ (participation in terms of being) and because Christ is our head (the moment of representation). However, both in justification and in sanctification, a movement can be seen from the second episode to the third episode of the story of our union with Christ, as well as the activity of the Holy Spirit. This movement starts in the Spirit forming Jesus as head of the church (person-substitution). This movement comes to its end if Christ and the individual believer are really united by inhabitation and regeneration, his righteousness is imputed and our life renewed. This movement of acceptance towards ungodly sinners originating in God's electing love must be seen also behind the idea of a justification in heaven before faith of the early Owen. Whilst this movement can be conceptualised in different semantic fields it is at the same time this movement of our union with Christ that unites both fields.

In conclusion, although both lines emphasise different moments of the relation between Christ and the believers—justification emphasises work-substitution and participation as imputation, sanctification stresses representation and participation in terms of being—they show the same movement from the second to the third episode of the story of the union with Christ.

87. Owen writes: 'The principal foundation hereof is, — that Christ and the church, in this design, were one mystical person; which state they do actually coalesce into, through the uniting efficacy of the Holy Spirit. He is the head, and believers are the members of that one person, as the apostle declares, 1 Corinthians 12:12, 13.' Owen, *Works*, Vol. V, 176. And further 196, 209.

2.4.3 MYSTICAL UNION

The relation between the different conceptual fields has been clarified; now more has to be said about the mystical union itself. In the New Testament, different images are used to make this mystical union with Christ understandable. Owen mentions the following images: body with head and members, vine and branches, husband and wife, and house with stones and a cornerstone. Central in Owen's thoughts are the image of the head and members, the image of vine and branches and the image of husband and wife. The image of head and members is crucial in his pneumatology and his doctrine of imputation, the image of vine and branches makes clear that Christ communicates real life to us, while the image of husband of wife, coloured by the Song of Songs, serves to evoke love for Christ, the glorious husband, although it also clarifies imputation.[88]

Beneath the surface of these metaphors with different functions lie different concepts: the concept of union with the second and third episode of its story, and the concepts of communion, communication and participation. I shall start the investigations of these concepts with the concept of union, especially with the third episode of the story of this union.

Owen uses the different images in the context of the second as well as the third episode of the mystical union with Christ. As has been shown he needs the intimate conjunction of Christ with his church to make clear that the imputation of our sins to Christ was possible, that Christ is the head of the new creation and that Christ bore the church in his meditorial work.[89] But this second episode aims at the designed third episode. The third step of the story of the mystical union is the proper act of God making us really one with Christ. It is the arrival of the electing God in the life

88. Owen, *Works*, Vol. I, 356; Vol. II, 281; Vol. III, 521; Vol. V, 179. The image of head and members is central in *The Doctrine of Justification by Faith* (Vol. V) and in Owen's ΠΝΕΥΜΑΤΟΛΟΓΙΑ (Vol. III). The image of husband and wife against the background of the Song of Songs is important in *Meditations and Discourses on the Glory of Christ* (Vol. I) and in *Of Communion with God the Father, Son and Holy Ghost* (Vol. II). See also Gleason, *John Calvin and John Owen on mortification*, 91–92.

In a different context Owen writes on metaphors that we do not always know which speech is metaphorical and which not. The Holy Spirit has chosen Himself expressions to teach the church, hence 'it is most safe for us to adhere unto the expressions of the Holy Spirit, and not to embrace such senses of things as are inconsistent with them, and opposite unto them' (*Works*, Vol. V, 291).

89. Owen, *Works*, Vol. I, 356; Vol. V, 179.

of an individual believer and the starting point of the life with God as a person recreated in God's image. Hence the concept of union refers to the starting point of the actual consummation of the relation with Christ, the other concepts (communion, fellowship etc.) refer to its continuance and increase.[90] Without this unifying work of Christ and His Spirit, we have no communion with him.[91]

Seen from the perspective of the glorified Christ acting in heaven, according to Owen, it can be said that he does three things to communicate himself to believers: a. He gives the Holy Spirit. Thence there follows an 'ineffable union' between Christ and the believer; the Spirit who comes to live in us is the same Spirit living in Christ. b. He forms a new nature, his own nature in us so that 'the very same spiritual nature is in him and in the church'; c. He actually implants or engrafts us in himself.[92] This all takes place simultaneously. Here Owen uses different images: inhabitation of the Spirit (a.), creation of a new nature (b.), vine and branches. Maybe here also a reference can be heard to the engrafting of branches in the olive root of Rom. 11 (c.). But Owen also uses the image of marriage: 'Christ gives himself to the *soul*, with all His *excellencies*, righteousness, preciousness, graces, and eminencies, to be its Saviour, head and husband,' and he makes us his own.[93] The substantive concept of the creation of the new spiritual nature is embedded in relational elements: the imagery of marriage, devotion of the glory of Christ, communion with the triune God, the gift of the Spirit and the incorporation in Christ.

Seen in the light of the acting of the Holy Spirit, Owen says similar things. It is the Spirit who unites us with Christ; he has implanted us into the body and united to the head. By the Spirit Christ lives in us. This inhabitation of the Spirit effects our regeneration. In the same instant 'wherein anyone is united unto Christ, and by the same act whereby he is so

90. De Vries, *"Die mij heeft liefgehad,"* 126.

91. Owen, *Works*, Vol. I, 357; II, 203; the treatment of regeneration in Vol. III as the new creation of spiritually death people, Vol. III, 207–337.

92. Owen, *Works*, Vol. I, 365–67. Cf. *Works*, Vol. II, 197–203, where Owen, dealing with communion with Christ in the purchased grace of holiness, describes how the Lord Jesus acts to bring us into communion with himself: 1. His intercession with the Father, praying to bestow them with the Holy Spirit; 2. The actual sending of his Spirit; 3. The creation of habitual grace.

93. Owen, *Works*, Vol. II, 56–57.

united, he is really and habitually purified and sanctified.'[94] Regeneration is a work of the Spirit, an immediate act. It is a new creation, a physical act and more than a moral act resulting from moral suasion. It is 'the infusion of a new, real, spiritual principle into the soul and its faculties, of spiritual life, light, holiness, and righteousness, disposed unto and suited for the destruction or expulsion of a contrary, inbred, habitual principle of sin and enmity against God, enabling unto all acts of holy obedience, and so in order of nature antecedent unto them.'[95] This new principle is the new man, created in righteousness and holiness in God's image. In regeneration, heart, mind, will and affections of a believer are renewed.

Apart from regeneration, Owen uses the images of vine and branches, of head and body and of inhabitation. Hence, relational as well as substantive elements are present in his pneumatology. He can say that believers have the fountain and principle of the new life not in themselves, 'but in Him, as one common head,'[96] but also that they like trees and plants 'have the principle of their growth in themselves,'[97] although they must be watered from above. Originally and efficiently the inhabitation of the Spirit is the cause of our union with Christ, 'but formally this new principle of grace is so.'[98] When dealing specifically with regeneration he uses less relational images fitting his more substantialist language with words like habit, principal, infusion. Very important is the Old Testament image of the renewal of the heart as used in Deut 30:6, Jer 31:33, and Ezek 11:19 and 36:26.[99] It is remarkable that Owen when citing St. Paul's images, which are often more relational and indirect as they relate our renewal with Christ, always interprets St. Paul in the light of the Old Testament image that is more direct and substantive. Presumably this fits better his Aristotelian conceptual framework, in which the idea of habit is a central one. This results in an interpretation of the indirect and Christological images, like the putting off the old man and putting on the new man (the image of dress and undress), the image of dying and rising in Christ, Christ living in us and being a new creation in Christ, in the light of the

94. Owen, *Works*, Vol. III, 517.

95. Owen, *Works*, Vol. III, 218–19.

96. Owen, *Works*, Vol. III, 286.

97. Owen, *Works*, Vol. III, 396.

98. Owen, *Works*, Vol. III, 478.

99. Owen, *Works*, Vol. III, 222–23, 323–25, 335, 476–77, 484.

direct and non-Christological image of the gift of a new heart and of the infusion of a new habit or life principle.[100] So Owen uses, in pneumatological contexts, the images for mystical union of vine and branches, body and members. But by his identification of the unifying work of the Spirit with substantialist thought regeneration, the Old Testament image of the gift of a new heart becomes central in his thinking on the work of the Holy Spirit. He uses relational metaphors, yet the philosophical concepts he has available are primarily substantialist, and influence his thinking in a substantialist direction. Again a tension can be seen between a substantialist frame of reference and a relational one.[101]

In this light what Owen does in *A Vindication of some passages in a Discourse concerning Communion with God* (1674) is noteworthy. Here he defends his *Of Communion with God the Father, Son and Holy Ghost* against his critics. Trying to show that his position is not a Puritan novelty but that he wrote in line with the church, he cites a famous Anglican writer, Richard Hooker (± 1554–1600). Hooker uses concepts like representation and participation, and the citation has a strongly relational tone. It is remarkable to see that although Owen agrees with Hooker, still his own reflections are less relational and dynamic. Maybe here the influence of the concept of habit can be seen.[102]

In conclusion, with regard to the third episode of the story of the union it can be said that, both in Christological and pneumatological contexts, Owen distinguishes the inhabitation of the Spirit, the renewing of our nature in regeneration and the unification with Christ, all taking place simultaneously. A strong emphasis is placed on the substantive renewal in regeneration presumably due to the Aristotelian concept of habit, but relational elements also find a place.

100. Citing e.g. Col 2:11 on 335 Owen links, as Paul does, the circumcision of the heart with the putting off the body of sin. But he seems to forget that Paul also mentions dying with Christ in baptism and being resurrected by faith in God. For a few other examples of Owen's dealing with St. Paul, see the interpretation of 2 Cor 5:17 in the light of regeneration see Owen, *Works*, Vol. III, 214, 220, 321, 386 and 477; for Gal 2:20 see 256, 286, 292, 393, 522; for Eph 4:24 see 101, 221, 222, 255, 260, 286, 330, 419, 437, 477, 478.

101. Owen, *Works,* Vol. III, 207–28, 297–337, 386–404, 516–20. See further Ferguson, 'John Owen and the doctrine of the Holy Spirit,' 115–19; De Vries, *"Die mij heeft liefgehad,"* 126–28, 295–305.

102. Owen, *Works,* Vol. II, 276–364. The Hooker-citation is written on 280–85. See also De Vries, *"Die mij heeft liefgehad,"* 125.

This relational aspect can be seen in Owen's use of the concepts of communion or fellowship, communication and participation.

In unity with Christ Owen sees a difference between union and communion, as we have seen. A Christian *is* united to Christ, but *has* communion with Christ. Communion presupposes mutuality between Christ and the believer united with him. God communicates himself to us and we in return give our lives to God.[103] According to Owen we can have communion with the Father, the Son and the Spirit, as his book *Of Communion with God the Father, Son and Holy Ghost* makes very clear, but for this investigation communion with the Son is most important.[104] However, to guard against losing sight of the Trinitarian framework of Owen's theology it is necessary not to forget that we have also communion with the Father in his love and with the Spirit who makes us believers and consoles us by giving the privileges of the death and purchase of Christ. To distinguish the Father, the Son and the Spirit, Owen characterizes the Father's communication of grace with original authority, the Son with purchased treasury and the Spirit with immediate efficacy.[105] According to Owen we have communion with the Son especially in grace. Within this grace he sees a difference in personal grace and purchased grace. The personal grace of Christ is the grace of his person as mediator in his fitness to save, his fullness to save and his excellency to endear. The purchased grace of Christ is the grace he purchased by his obedience, his suffering and his intercession: the grace of justification, sanctification and privilege. An important image in this context is the image of bride and bridegroom. This communion is a conjugal relation attended with suitable conjugal affections as described in the Song of Songs. Owen tries to make the excellency of Christ as clear as possible to strengthen our hearts, but also makes clear what the saints have to do to keep communion with Christ. We have communion with both the Son and the Spirit; hence it is possible to distinguish between the communion we have with Christ and our union with him through the Spirit he sends us.[106]

103. Owen, *Works*, Vol. II, 8–9.

104. Owen, *Works*, Vol. II, 5–276.

105. Owen, *Works*, Vol. II, 11–17, 21. See further Beeke, *Assurance of Faith*, 220–37; Ferguson, *John Owen on the Christian Life*, 74–98.

106. Owen, *Works*, Vol. II, 40–222. And further Beeke, *Assurance of Faith*, 226–30; Ferguson, *John Owen on the Christian Life*, 77–92; De Vries, *"Die mij heeft liefgehad,"* 124, 280.

Owen furthermore uses the word 'communication.' As has been shown above, according to Owen God has communicated all grace, goodness, life, light, benevolence and power necessary for new creation to Christ, making him repository and treasure of all this. In him all fullness dwells bodily. In his ministry Christ communicates this fullness to the church, his body. This communication shapes our union and communion with Christ. Owen parallels imputation and communication; imputation standing in the conceptual field of justice and actual obedience, communication in the field of habitual being. He speaks of a mystical communication of Christ with the church in which Christ gives Himself to the church; this communication can also be understood pneumatologically, as it is through the Spirit that Christ communicates Himself. The central image here is the image of the vine and the branches. There must be a real conjunction of Christ and his church, of head and members, as the church, for its being, is dependent on the communication of a new nature, life, grace, sanctification, purification etc. through which Christ nourishes her. He supplies spiritual life, sustentation, motion and power in grace and perseverance. This spiritual nourishment is the emanation of the person of Christ and the communication of that grace is necessary for holiness and evangelical obedience. So the Spirit gives us all grace renewing our lives in regeneration and sanctification.[107]

Owen often speaks of participation and of the believers being partakers of something or someone. Joint participation in something gives communion. According to Owen believers participate in the benefits of Christ as fullness of grace, purchased grace, the blood of Christ, righteousness, holiness, the new creation, the gracious work of the Spirit, consolation, joy, certainty and a new saving supernatural light.[108] Believers are also partakers of the Holy Spirit.[109] Participation is, furthermore, the reverse of representation, which is indicated by the fact that human beings participate in Adam.[110] Hence believers participate in Christ and in different aspects of the life of Christ, as his life, the unction of Christ with the Spirit, the inhabitation of the Spirit, his sufferings, the sacrifice of Christ,

107. Owen, *Works*, Vol. I, 271, 360–67, 371–74; Vol. II, 68; Vol. III, 414, 515–21; Vol. V, 222.

108. Owen, *Works*, Vol. I, 171, 178, 397, 399; Vol. II, 154, 175; Vol. III, 157, 190, 221, 370, 414, 442, 469, 473, 560–61 ; Vol. IV, 388–89; Vol. V, 193, 208, 314, 344, 371.

109. Owen, *Works*, Vol. I, 357; Vol. III, 226; Vol. IV, 409–11; Vol. V, 104.

110. Owen, *Works*, Vol. I, 199.

his death, his position as Son and finally the glory and inheritance of Christ.[111] This participation in Christ leads to greater and greater conformity with Christ.[112] In everything Christ is the pattern and example of the renewal of the image of God in believers.[113] It is the Spirit who makes us like Christ.[114]

Two aspects of this participation deserve more attention: the participation in His suffering and death, and the participation in his glorification. Generally the fellowship in the sufferings of Christ and the conformity to his death (Phil 3:10) can be an aspect of the general head of Owen's treatment of our communion with Christ in purchased grace.[115] Here the exclusive moment plays a role: in his suffering and death, Christ purchased grace for the believers. But also the inclusive moment is present in the participation in his sufferings and death, in three aspects: the aspect of the mortification of the flesh, the aspect of Christ who suffers with us as we suffer, and the aspect of suffering for Christ, following his example.[116] Two passages are especially noteworthy. First in his ΠΝΕΥΜΑΤΟΛΟΓΙΑ Owen writes, when dealing with afflictions, 'as the Lord Christ being the head of the covenant, all the afflictions and persecutions that befall his members are originally his, Isa 53:9, Acts 9:5, Col 1:24; so they all tend to work us unto a conformity unto him in purity and holiness.'[117] Further

111. Participation in Christ: Owen, *Works*, Vol. II, 280–82; Vol. III, 286, 414; his unction with the Holy Spirit, Vol. IV, 393–94, 409–11; for his sufferings and death, see footnote 116; his resurrection, Vol. III, 561; Vol. X, 251; his hiddenness in God, Vol. IV, 388–89; his heritage, Vol. I, 171, 177, 215–16; Vol. II, 173, 218–19, 245, 246; Vol. III, 518; Vol. IV, 410–12; Vol. V, 142, 144; his glorification, Vol. I, 241; Vol . II, 173.

112. Owen, *Works*, Vol. I, 365–66.

113. Owen, *Works*, Vol. I, 65, 79, 118, 168–77, 245, 343, 392–93; Vol. II, 222; Vol. III, 183, 561, 584, 648–49; Vol. V, 180.

114. Owen, *Works*, Vol. I, 172; Vol. III, 157, 183, 190, 561; Vol. IV, 389.

115. Owen, *Works*, Vol. II, 48, 154, 206.

116. Mortification: Owen, *Works*, Vol. I, 174, 177; Vol. III, 540–41; 560–61; Christ suffering with us if we suffer, often referring to Hebr 4:15: Vol. I, 117; Vol. II, 140–42; Vol. III, 447; suffering for Christ's sake and following his example: Vol. I, 116–18, 176; Vol. III, 371, 648–49; Suffering with Christ: Vol. I,177. On mortification, cf. Gleason, *John Calvin and John Owen on mortification*, 127; De Vries, *"Die mij heeft liefgehad,"* 310.

It is remarkable that Owen often refers to Phil 1:29, but always to prove that faith is a gift and never to say something about suffering with Christ, see Vol. II, 483, 486; Vol. II, 18, 153, 201; Vol. III, 323 (2x); Vol. IV, 50, 428; Vol. X, 101, 108, 123, 136, 159, 235, 257, 288, 397, 453, 469, 470.

117. Owen, *Works*, Vol. III, 447. Cf. Vol. II, 222: 'Christ is not ashamed to call us brethren: fellowship in sufferings.'

in *The Doctrine of Justification by Faith* he quotes Augustine: 'The church suffered in Him when He suffered for the church; as He suffers in the church when the church suffers for Him.'[118] Although the exclusiveness of the work of Christ was important for Owen, nevertheless he could also maintain participation in his suffering and death.

A second aspect is the participation in his supernatural life. The believers are made partakers of the divine nature in Christ by the love of the Father and the communion of the Holy Spirit.[119] Owen more than once writes that we are partakers of the divine nature, as Peter writes in 2 Pet 1:4.[120] This does not mean that we cease to be human. After his glorification even Jesus Christ remained human, for his being is not destroyed by his glorification. His human nature did not receive any essential property of the divine nature, and was not deified. As there is a difference between the glory of Christ and the glory we shall receive, although we in the highest participation with Christ will share in that glory and honour that our natures are capable of, we shall not be deified either.[121] According to Owen, there is no talk of the divine nature because we receive the essential nature of God, but because we receive a divine holy habitual principle worked by God in us who bear his image. This habitual principle is created, and hence different from the Holy Spirit living in the believer. Still the new creation is a divine nature.[122]

The ideas of union, communion and participation may remind one of medieval mysticism. This impression is strengthened by the fact that Owen uses words such as purgation and illumination, and furthermore uses the Song of Songs for what may seem a form of mysticism reminiscent of that of Bernard of Clairvaux. The Puritans deliberately returned to Bernard's mysticism and so showed themselves to differ from Reformation theologians. It is obvious that Owen uses the Song of Songs in a way reminiscent of Bernard, making the spiritual continuity explicit. I do not intend

118. Owen, *Works*, Vol. V, 176. Cf. the quotation of Eusebius on 177: In this passage Owen primarily wants to say something on the suffering of Christ, while Augustine also says something on the suffering of the church. However, the impact of these words—if Christ suffers, the believers suffer and if the believers suffer, Christ suffers—is not stated often but also not denied.

119. Owen, *Works*, Vol. I, 366; Vol. II, 19, 281; Vol. III, 469, 473.

120. Owen, *Works*, Vol. I, 366, 440; Vol. III, 221, 578; Vol. V, 430.

121. Owen, *Works*, Vol I, 238–42, 344–45; Vol. IV, 411.

122. Owen, *Works*, Vol. I, 366; Vol. II, 200; Vol. III, 221, 469, 473, 478; Vol. V, 430.

to solve the problem whether or not John Owen can be labelled a mystic, but I do want to note that there is an important difference setting Owen apart from medieval kinds of mysticism. The traditional mystical way is *purgatio, illuminatio, unio*. In Owen's use of these words the theology of the Reformation has changed the order, and in that way fundamentally changed medieval mysticism. Owen does not start with *purgatio*, but with *illuminatio* because of sin: man is not able to purify himself, but has to be illuminated first by the Spirit to be able to receive Christ. After this first *illuminatio* he secondly places union and regeneration (in 2.5.1 it will be shown that the preparation of the regeneration creates new problems, but this does not alter the fact that Owen's theology of grace fundamentally changed medieval mysticism). It is the Spirit who unites us with Christ; we do not have to ascend ourselves through the human nature of Christ to His divine nature. As Jones says, union with Christ is not an achievement of a few heroic souls, but a divine gift received by all true Christians. The foundation of this union is the obedience, sacrifice and intercession of Jesus Christ. After the unifying work of Christ or the Spirit we have communion with Christ in receiving His new life. This new life consists in continuing illumination as our mind is renewed, purgation as our life is sanctified and also in a remaining communion with the triune God, Father, Son and Spirit. This communion brings with it participation in the divine nature, but unlike in mysticism this participation does not mean deification. Although there may be spiritual continuity, the theology of grace has fundamentally altered the medieval mystical order.[123]

To return to communion, communication and participation: these concepts give the relational element a place and also make clear the place of faith in Owen's theology. It may seem until now that Owen is focussed on the divine actions in Christology and soteriology; and it is true that for Owen the work of God in the covenant of the mediator and election, in the incarnation, the obedience, oblation and intercession of Christ, and in regeneration, justification and sanctification is central. In his ΠΝΕΥΜΑΤΟΛΟΓΙΑ he does not give separate attention to faith. Due to this neglect, the relative independence of the two lines of *actus* /

123. See Jones, 'Union with Christ,' 191–92; De Vries, *"Die mij heeft liefgehad,"* 159–60, 213. According to King, 'The Affective Spirituality of John Owen,' 226, 232 it is not possible to make a clear-cut distinction between Owen's Puritanism and mysticism or pietism, as Ferguson suggests. He speaks of a Puritan affective mysticism. See further footnote 1.

justification / obedience of Christ and of *habitus* / being / 'pneumachristology' is maintained. As faith is the means that unites us with Christ more reflection on faith would have led to more reflection on the relation between both lines.[124] Here again it seems that in Owen's frame of reference the concept of the new habit was very central, leading sometimes to a neglect of the conceptualisation of the relational element yet present in his thinking through images. Furthermore, his theological interests over against Arminians and Socinians brought him to his focus on the divine work. Although the substantive element seems to have the primacy, the relational element is also present, as the ideas of communion, communication and participation make clear. As communion presupposes mutuality, communication presupposes a receiving instance and participation a human involvement, all these concepts presuppose faith and a believing person. However, this relationality has a secondary character, following the primacy of the substance of the concept of habit.

There is no misunderstanding possible for Owen: faith is a gift of God. If the Spirit comes and lives in a person, giving a new habit of grace, also faith is given, while the gift of the new habit implies the gift of faith: the new habit is the power of believing, the 'habit of faith.'[125] Regeneration and the gift of faith thus take place simultaneously. Owen characterizes faith as instrumental cause: of justification and sanctification; but also of our union and communion with Christ, and of participation and communication. It is by faith that we are united with Christ and have communion with Him. Without faith in Christ we will not receive Him and His benefits. If Christ communicates Himself we receive Him by faith.[126]

Summarizing, as union with Christ is the substance of the Christian life, the third step of the story of the union makes a real enjoyment of this union possible. The concepts of communion, communication and participation are used by Owen to refer to the completion of this mystical union. Central to Owen's conceptual framework is the substantive gift of

124. De Vries does not distinguish between these two lines but between Christology and pneumatology as we saw (see footnote 76). However, his observations are similar here; see De Vries, *"Die mij heeft liefgehad,"* 259–60.

125. Owen, *Works*, Vol. II, 347; Vol. III, 409; Vol. V, 354; Vol. X, 135.

126. Owen, *Works*, Vol. I, 85, 169, 178, 240, 364–66, 396, 413, 446; Vol. II, 153, 172, 200; Vol. III, 157, 292, 320, 375, 414, 436, 443, 446, 562; Vol. IV, 53; Vol. V, 108–10, 116–17, 144, 218, 222, 292; Vol. X, 252.

the new habit. However, the relational element is also present in his theology, although systematically it has a secondary character.

2.4.4 ORDER OF SALVATION

During the analysis of our union and communion with Christ according to Owen, a lot has already been said regarding the different aspects of the order of salvation. For Owen this is an order of nature, consisting in work of the Spirit preparatory to regeneration, calling and regeneration, faith, justification, adoption, sanctification and glorification. Seen chronologically regeneration, the gift of faith and imputation of Christ take place simultaneously. Some things still need to be said about justification, adoption and sanctification.

Because for Owen justification, on the one hand, and, on the other hand, the second episode of the story of the union and the work of Christ in his obedience and sacrifice, are closely related, it is not surprising that his stress lies on justification once and for all. Over against Baxter and Rome Owen maintained that justification is one and at once full and complete. We are accepted as Christ is imputed to us. But this does not mean that chronologically sanctification only follows justification because justification is completed at once. We are still sinners and sins cannot be actually pardoned before they are actually committed, so there is a continuation of justification. But this continuation is not dependent on our works as Baxter and Rome said, but only on faith. The continuation of our justification is dependent on the same causes as our justification itself. Owen compares Christ to a refiner's fire and to priests adding sweet incense to our works. 'Whatever is of the Spirit, of himself, of grace,—that remains; whatever is of self, flesh, unbelief (that is, hay and stubble),—that he consumes, wastes, takes away.'[127]

According to such critics as Baxter and Clifford, Owen's theology had antinomian tendencies. They see the problem in the imputation of the active obedience of Christ. When Christ fulfilled the law and his ac-

127. Owen, *Works*, Vol. II, 171. And further Vol. V, 137, 140, 143, 146–48, 152. Clifford creates an oppostition between Calvin who sees justification, according to Clifford, as ongoing process and his reconstruction of Owen's view of justification as a single moment once for all. However, this criticism of Owen is too easy, as De Vries has also shown, De Vries, *"Die mij heeft liefgehad,"* 267, Clifford, *Atonement and justification*, 173–75. For Baxter and the context of Owen's doctrine of justification see Packer, *A Quest for Godliness*, 149–62 and Boersma, *A Hot Peppercorn*.

tive obedience is imputed to us, why should we still do good works? It seems that for these critics the only ethical question is whether the law is fulfilled or not. For Owen this is not the one and only question; the commands of God are not the only reason for doing the good. Everything Christ did, including his active obedience, he did for us, but not only to justify, as if salvation and justification were identical. Christ was united to us to restore the image of God and renew humanity. He came not only to do good to us, but also to make us to do the good. By his separation of the conceptual fields of justice and actual obedience, on the one hand, and, on the other hand, of habitual being, Owen unfortunately was not able to relate the active obedience of Christ to our good works, as the image of putting on Christ suggests. But he did relate our habitual renewal, our faith, sanctification, and our resulting good works with the habitual being of Christ. While humanity was recreated in Christ, the head of the church, so our being could be renewed in the image of God. We are not accepted because of our good works, but in regeneration a new principle of life is given that must lead to good works. In a (maybe voluntarist) climate focussed on the law as willed by God Owen's position of a fulfilled law and imputation of Christ's active obedience without any relation to our obedience may be open to misunderstanding; but only for persons who do not see other reasons for doing good and who do not see that Christ came to make us able to live a holy and righteous life.[128]

In his soteriology, Owen deals not only with the soteriological images of justification and sanctification, but also with the image of adoption. Sometimes Owen sees adoption as a part of justification, for both presuppose a forensic act.[129] Sometimes he distinguishes justification and adoption, because justification is the grace of being accepted and adoption is the grace of privileges; adoption is 'the head, the spring and fountain whence they all arise and flow.'[130] Adoption 'is the authoritative translation of a believer, by Jesus Christ, from the family of the world and Satan into the family of God, with his investiture in all the privileges and advantages of that family.'[131] It is a forensic act, in which the person is

128. See Clifford, *Atonement and justification*, 12, 188, 190. For the reasons Owen gives for holiness see Owen, *Works*, Vol. III, 566–651.

129. Owen, *Works*, Vol. I, 177; Vol. V, 125, 142.

130. 'They' refers to the innumerable privileges we enjoy in Christ. See Owen, *Works*, Vol. II, 207; and further 173; Vol. V, 194; Vol. X, 159.

131. Owen, *Works*, Vol. II, 207.

freed from all the obligations towards his or her old family and invested with all the rights and privileges of the new family: liberty, title and right to a room in the house of God and to a future fullness of the great inheritance of glory.[132] We have adoption also by the Spirit, for he is called the 'Spirit of adoption': as Sons the believers are adopted by God's Spirit.[133] As adopted persons believers participate in the heritage of the Son.

To conclude, Owen's emphasis on the once-for-all character of justification does not make him an antinomian theologian. Although even the active obedience of Christ is imputed and at a conceptual level is not related to the obedience of believers, nevertheless the habitual renewal of believers excludes antinomianism. Apart from justification and sanctification, Owen gives separate attention to adoption as the grace of privileges.

2.4.5 'BEING IN CHRIST': FOUR MOMENTS?

In a final analysis of the third episode of the story of the union with Christ, I will discuss which of the four moments are necessary for a concept of 'being in Christ,' in continuity with Owen's theology: representation and participation, or also substitution and union?

At first sight it seems that the exclusive and the inclusive moment can be related to, respectively, the conceptual field of actual obedience and habitual being. The exclusive moment results in justification and imputation, the inclusive moment in sanctification and participation. However, Owen's thinking is more complicated. First, the image of adoption does not fit this reconstruction. Adoption is a forensic act and is related to justification, but it implies participation in the position of Christ, the Son. Second, justification, adoption and sanctification all are graces purchased by the obedient life of Jesus Christ. This second point indicates how problematic the conceptualisation in two different lines is. In Owen's conceptual framework, the obedience of Christ must be placed within the first field of actual obedience. However, obedience plays a role in the second line, for the habitual renewal is purchased by the obedience of Christ. And where it might play a role (believers participating in the obedience of Christ as a result of the habitual renewal) Owen's conceptual framework makes it impossible to say so. Owen can do justice to the exclusive moment in the obedience of Christ, but not to its inclusive mo-

132. Owen, *Works*, Vol. II, 207–22.

133. Owen, *Works*, Vol. II, 249.

ment. Remarkably he does so regarding the suffering of Christ: both the exclusive aspect of the suffering and death of Christ as well as its inclusive aspect—the believers participating in the suffering of Christ—are present in Owen. This indicates the inevitable intertwining of both moments. Person-substitution is the presupposition of work-substitution, leading to purchased grace (justification, adoption and sanctification), but it is also the presupposition of representation leading to participation. For a concept of 'being in Christ' this implies that in Owen work-substitution makes 'being in Christ' possible, but it does not play a role in 'being in Christ' itself. Person-substitution in so far it is together with representation another side of the one coin, is important for 'being in Christ,' as is the inclusive moment (representation).

A concept of 'being in Christ' building on Owen must do justice to the moment of union. According to Owen, no participation in Christ is possible without Christ who as high priest in heaven unites us with himself by giving us His Holy Spirit. This gift results in the indwelling of the Spirit, the habitual renewal of our nature and our engraftment into Christ. In this way the third step of the story of the mystical union is completed. In the moment of union different things take place simultaneously: seen from the conceptual field of justice and actual obedience this is the moment of justification by imputation of the righteousness of Christ; seen within the conceptual field of habitual being a new habit is given in regeneration that grows further in sanctification aimed at the restoration of the image of God. Unification with Christ, imputation of justice, habitual renewal and the gift of faith all take place at the same moment. The difference Owen draws between union and communion shows that the moment of union has two aspects: the aspect of unification and incorporation which is the beginning of the actual union with Christ, and the aspect of the ongoing communion with Christ and with the grace He gives. Therefore the moment of union in both its aspects is a necessary precondition for 'being in Christ.' It can even be said that the moment of union itself is 'being in Christ,' if 'being in Christ' is understood as a mystical union with Christ.

It is noteworthy that Owen's use of the concept of habit results in a substantialist understanding of the first aspect of the moment of union, the aspect of unification. Although he uses relational images such as the vine and the branches, head and body, a marriage and relational concepts such as communion, communication and participation, the substantialist concept of habit dominates his reflection. Thinking about regeneration as it relates to the image of the renewal of the heart leads to a more substantive interpretation of passages in St. Paul than necessary.

Finally, the moment of participation plays a role in Owen's thinking on 'being in Christ.' Its place is especially within the conceptual field of habitual renewal, parallel to imputation in the conceptual field of actual obedience. However, we saw that Owen does see a participation in the position of Christ as Son and heir. We participate in the inclusiveness of the person and work of Christ, not in His exclusiveness. This can be seen in the participation in the suffering and death of Christ. However, Owen has no place for a participation in the obedience of Christ.

To conclude, the hypothesis that a concept of 'being in Christ' can be developed using the concepts of representation and participation is not adequate in so far as Owen is concerned. Building on Owen, apart from the concepts of representation and participation, concepts such as union (referring to the moment of union in its aspect of unification) and communion (referring to the ongoing relation with Christ) are also necessary. Further representation and person-substitution are reverse sides of the one coin, and work-substitution is not a part of 'being in Christ' itself, but in Owen it is a precondition. Again we see that the concept of substitution balances the concept of representation.

2.5. Reality of 'Being in Christ'

Until now a sketch of Owen's theological perspective on what I call 'being in Christ' has been given. Before evaluating Owen's position, we need to look further at the reality of this 'being in Christ.' First I will discuss the perspective on this reality (2.5.1) and, second, its reality (2.5.2).

2.5.1 PERSPECTIVE

First, it is important to see the perspective that gives access to this reality. It is very clear to Owen: we need the eye of faith to see the glory of Christ. We need the divine revelation of the Scriptures as the only foundation and reason of faith. Our mind needs to be illuminated to understand the mind of God. Against the position of Rome, Owen denies that we can trust the infallibility of the church. In reaction to the collectivism of Rome he states that all individual believers have their own duty and right to understand the mind of God as the Spirit is given to all believers. The Spirit, as principal efficient cause of our understanding, needs to communicate spiritual wisdom, light and understanding to the understanding of believers enabling them to discern and apprehend the mind of God in His word and the mysteries of the heavenly truth in the internal work of illumination. Continual prayer, meditation and study of the Word are required to be taught meekness and humility by the Holy Spirit. It is important to see that although it is the Spirit who teaches us to understand the mind and will of God in the Scripture and although Owen opposes Rome, Owen does not forget the means the Spirit uses, not even the church. The means the Spirit uses are not enthusiasm, any pretended infallible church or infallible inspirations, but the reading of the scriptures and the doctrine of the gospel. It is the doctrine of the gospel that destroys and takes away the veil covering our understanding. Means to understand the Scripture are first of all diligent reading of the Scripture and secondly, to improve our understanding, spiritual means like prayer, openness, practical obedience, the desire to grow in love and knowledge, and spiritual worship. Furthermore Owen mentions means found in common arts and sciences, like knowledge of languages, history, geography, chronology as well as ways and methods of reasoning; and finally ecclesiastical means: the catholic or universal tradition, the consent of the fathers and the endeavours of any person holy and learned before us. This all makes clear that for Owen the perspective that gives access to the reality of Christ is the perspective of revelation, faith and active involvement in the life with God and in the church.[134]

The fact that Owen sees the perspective of the human participant as being very important accounts for the fact that he is praised as an 'experimental theologian.'[135] Although for him the work of God in Christ and the Holy Spirit is decisive, he again and again makes clear that human beings can do more than just wait for God doing nothing. He calls for attention to repentance, prayer, and reading of the scriptures, meditation, spiritual decay, mortification, vivification and obedience. Our search for 'being in Christ' in the description of Owen until now has been focussed

134. Owen, *Works*, Vol. I, 160, 164, 169; Vol. IV, *The Reason of Faith* (1677), esp. 53, 55, 57, 60, 72; ΣΥΝΕΣΙΣ ΠΝΕΥΜΑΤΙΚΗ (1678), esp. 121–42, 145, 152, 154, 199, 201, 209–11, 219, 223, 226.

135. Beeke, *Assurance of Faith*, 264.

on the perspective of the acting triune God, but the reverse side of the other perspective must not be forgotten.

It is interesting that because of the decisiveness of God's work he writes on the time before and after conversion, but not on conversion itself as this is the reverse of regeneration. In reaction to Arminians and Socinians saying that moral suasion evokes faith he stresses that there is only faith where God physically works something new. Saying that God does more than morally and rhetorically persuade people, this leads to a concentration on the work of the Spirit although admitting that the word is the instrumental cause. Thus faith is seen more as given by the Spirit than as a reaction to God's promise. Although he mentions the effective calling and the word of God he focuses on the Holy Spirit. This results in a less developed reflection on conversion in the perspective of the participant, or better: there is more attention given to the preparation of regeneration, self reflection, human activity and the principal efficient cause—the work of the Spirit, than to the instrumental cause—the *promissio* that confronts us with God's grace, and the human reaction to this *promissio*.[136] Owen's attention has shifted from the concept of effective calling implying a thinking together of the principal cause and the instrumental cause, to the concept of regeneration, in which the principal cause obviously is implied but the instrumental cause and the human reaction to it can be forgotten. This has a place in a theology in which act and being are two different conceptual fields, standing relatively independently beside one another.[137]

136. Comparably, in his doctrine of the sacraments Owen emphasised the role of faith and under-emphasised the Spirit's role in the reception of the sacraments. Further he highly valued the preparation for the Lord's Supper; see Payne, *John Owen on the Lord's Supper*, 49, 53–59.

137. It seems that to Owen the effective calling was unproblematically presupposed, although he does not very often use the words 'effectual calling' (Owen, *Works*, Vol. I, 486; Vol. X, 154, and never in Vol. II–V). It is present in the background of this thinking, as he mentions the word as *causa instrumentalis* (Vol. III, 231; Vol. IV, 94, 145; Vol. V, 118, 292; cf. Vol. III, 351); God uses the word (Vol. III, 213, 347). But it is remarkable that although Owen mentions the calling or vocation in his ΠΝΕΥΜΑΤΟΛΟΓΙΑ several times (Vol. III, 349, 362, 367, 504, 564, 573, 592, 596, 620) he does not reflect on it. Also in Vol. I, II, V and X it is mentioned but it does not receive separate attention except in his Catechism (Vol. I, 17, 54, 64, 80, 486; Vol. II, 281, 285; Vol. V, 131 (3x); Vol. X, 64, 411, 436). It seems to be unproblematic background knowledge. What this implies for his thinking on assurance of faith I dare not say. In any case, Beeke shows that Owen places a pneumatological emphasis making assurance less problematic than other puritan and reformed theologians. But he does not give the impression that for Owen the *promissio*

2.5.2 REALITY

Second, the question is: according to Owen, what is this reality of 'being in Christ'? What is its nature? A lot has been said on this already. Union with Christ is a mystical union that has a mysterious character although its character can be clarified with different images. The union is a real one, as the Spirit who unites us with Christ is real and divine. A real communication of spiritual nourishment is possible. This reality is a mystical and spiritual one, dependent on pneumatogical activity. Seen in the conceptual field of justice, the imputation of Christ is important. Seen in the conceptual field of habitual being, this union consists in the gift of a new, supernatural divine principle of life or habit. This habit is created, and implies no deification although it can be said that we are partakers of the divine nature. It is thus a supernatural being. It is a being dependent on Christ as the head of the new creation and on the Spirit, the bond between Christ and the church, but at the same time the habit of new life has a certain independence.

The first and principal cause of this reality is the work of the triune God, acting in his councils—the covenant of the mediator and election—in the work of Christ and in the work of the Spirit. This results in a modest attitude, while we in the work of God again and again are confronted with a mystery; Owen wants to respect these mysteries of the work of God. Our union with Christ is a mysterious reality according to Owen.[138]

Seen in relation to the original creation, union with Christ and regeneration consist in the restoration of the image of God as has been shown. This motive of restoration is central to Owen. Union with Christ leads to a restoration of the originally good created being. But in Christ, God renewed human nature 'with an addition of many glorious endowments which Adam was not made partaker of.'[139] Thus besides the dominant restoration-motive the motive of elevation is also present. This new being has to be glorified beyond simple restoration of original created being.[140]

---

was very important in his reflection on assurance. See Beeke, *Assurance of Faith*, 213–66. See further Ferguson, *John Owen on the Christian Life*, 35 who signals a shift in Owen's thinking from effectual calling to regeneration.

138. Owen, *Works*, Vol. I, 51, 76, 85, 232, 242, 309, 360, 365, 372; Vol. II, 90, 120, 182; Vol. III, 211, 320, 371, 372, 396, 402; Vol. IV, 125, 394, 395; Vol. V,. 178.

139. Owen, *Works*, Vol. I, 170.

140. See furthermore Ferguson, *John Owen on the Christian Life*, 65, 218; Gleason, *John Calvin and John Owen on mortification*, 108–29; De Vries, *"Die mij heeft liefgehad,"* 166.

This restoration (and elevation) is not complete yet for sin remains and believers fall into sin every day. Where there is twofold life, in Adam and in Christ, both the principles of sin and of grace are present in a Christian and he has to fight against the principle of sin and the principle of grace must be nourished and stimulated. Still a justified believer is not *simul iustus et peccator*. Owen sees 'ungodly' as an ontological qualification that cannot characterize the life of a Christian although sin is still present. In the light of the presence of both principles in a believer it is noteworthy that Owen distinguishes between sanctification and salvation, suggesting that (redemption and) sanctification precedes salvation. Although Owen concentrates himself on the present situation of the believer he says something on the difference between now and the future in *Meditations and Discourses on the Glory of Christ*, reflecting on the differences between our beholding the glory of Christ by faith in this world and by sight in heaven. There are differences as a result of different natures and actings of those means and instruments whereby we apprehend the glory of Christ. Now we see images and shadows, in darkness and indirectly; then we see immediately and directly. Our mind has to be freed from darkness, a light of glory will be planted in us and our body and senses will be glorified. Furthermore we do not always see the glory of Christ, and he sometimes withdraws and hides from us. Then he shall be with us and frequently communicate spiritual refreshment. Then there will be no internal defects or temptations. Now we gather impressions one by one and try to get a picture of the whole; in the vision above the whole glory of Christ will be at once represented to us and we shall be enabled, in one act, to comprehend it. There the vision will be perfect, absolutely transforming and beatifical. Now we are being sanctified but we wait still for our salvation; hence our present union with Christ is incomplete. But for Owen the presence of the reality is more central in his reflections than its future.[141]

The importance of the presence of this reality comes out in the importance of 'visible saints' for Owen's ecclesiology. The members of a local church have to be visible saints. They have to be recognisable in confession and life as members of Christ, but for Owen it is important that God's knowledge of the heart and his judgment of love remains decisive. The Lord's Supper was celebrated only within the circle of visible saints and Owen even only baptised children of the members of the communion of

141. Owen, *Works*, Vol. I, 52, 62–63, 64, 85, 374–414; Vol. III, 286; De Vries, "*Die mij heeft liefgehad,*" 265–66.

visible saints. So on the one hand, it is an invisible reality while people can profess something falsely and lie in their words and acts, but on the other hand it is a visible reality, because someone who is united with Christ cannot remain invisible.[142]

Finally, there is a question of whether union with Christ is an individual or a collective reality. For Owen the Congregationalist, the church is there where individual believers come together and establish a covenant to form a church. Seen from his ecclesiological practice and from his ideas of the work of the Spirit the union of the believer with Christ seems to be an individual reality for Owen. Owen is thinking more individualistically in his ecclesiology than the Reformers, as De Vries writes.[143] Sometimes Owen sees the bride in the Song of Songs as the church, but mostly it is the individual believer. Although the images he uses might suggest otherwise (like the body with a head and members, the vine and the branches), in Owen's thinking the notion that union with Christ establishes a community is not central. According to Colin Gunton, Owen sees the Spirit too little as the creator of community. A relation can be seen between Owen's ecclesiology and his pneumatology. De Vries sees the problems in ecclesiology and not in pneumatology, but he is too kind. He does not seem to see, first, that for Owen the Spirit is primarily a creator of a new habit of faith and not of community, and secondly that the collective images Owen used do not result in a conceptualisation of the collective intention of these images; thus this collective intention is lost, as Owen's ecclesiology shows. For Owen our being with Christ is mainly conceptualised as an individual reality.[144]

To conclude, Owen's understanding of the reality of 'being in Christ' is greatly determined by the concept of habit. This habit is mysteriously

142. De Vries, *"Die mij heeft liefgehad,"* 354, 387–88. See for more about John Owen and the Lord's Supper Payne, *John Owen on the Lord's Supper*.

143. De Vries, *"Die mij heeft liefgehad,"* 190 note 100, 390.

144. Gunton, *Theology through the Theologians*, 194–96; Ferguson, *John Owen on the Christian Life*, 154–201; De Vries, *"Die mij heeft liefgehad,"* 160, 190 note 100, 342, 352, 354, 390, 392, 405, 407.

Colin Gunton is very positive about Owen's ecclesiology, because according to Owen the church as a community is called to echo the kind of being in relation and communion that God is eternally. He is further very positive about Owen's concept of freedom because community and freedom do not exclude each other for Owen. But by not controlling his notion of freedom pneumatologically Owen's concept of freedom is in danger of collapsing into individualistic autonomy.

created by God. The gift of this habit consists in the restoration of the image of God. Hence the believer is not at the same time totally sinner and justified believer. Although sin is still present, the Christian cannot be characterized as 'ungodly.' The gift of a new habit must become visible and result in visible holiness. Finally, the individual character of the concept of habit is the starting point of Owen's ecclesiology.

2.6 Conclusion

In the preceding sections, Owen's view of the story of the mystical union with Christ has been investigated. We saw that it is a story with three episodes: the first in God's councils, the second in the life of Jesus Christ, and the third in the life of the believer. In the first episode the decision is taken that the Son is the head and representative of the elect. In the second episode this head and representative is formed as human being. Two conceptual fields are used to develop the significance of Jesus Christ. In the first field of actual obedience the sins of the elect are imputed to Christ which is possible because of the natural, federal and mystical relations between the elect and Christ as common or mystical person. Christ gives satisfaction for their sins in his entire life in active and passive obedience. In the second field of habitual being the humanity of Christ is understood 'pneumachristologically.' In the third episode the actual consummation of the mystical union with Christ has its place. Because salvation is anchored in election and in Christ, active both in oblation and in supplication, faith and justification are a gift: it is the ungodly who are justified. In the same moment the believer is united with Christ by the Spirit, a new habit is created and the justice of Christ is imputed to the believer. This concept of habit is central in Owen's understanding of the mystical union, although also relational metaphors and concepts play their role.

Representation and participation are both useful concepts for the development of a concept of 'being in Christ.' However, other moments are important: work-substitution is the presupposition of 'being in Christ'; person-substitution and representation are reverse sides of the one coin; and without the moment of union in both its aspects of a first unification, and following ongoing communion no participation in Christ is possible. If 'being in Christ' is understood as mystical union, it can even be said that the moment of union is identical with 'being in Christ.' According to Owen, the believers participate in Christ and in different moments of his story. Believers do not participate in his election and in his obedience, but they do participate in his Spirit, suffering, death and resurrection, and in his glorified position as Son and heir. In this participation, it can often be seen that believers participate in so far as the inclusive moment of Christ's person and work is concerned, but not with regard to the exclusive moment. Summarizing, for a concept of 'being in Christ' in continuity with Owen, the moments of representation, union and participation are necessary, whereas the moment of substitution is necessary as its presupposition.

Regarding the reality of 'being in Christ,' first, its perspectival character is emphasised: it is only available for participants. Second, it has a mysterious character, depending on the work of God in Christ and in the Spirit. Third, in referring to the new being in Christ, Owen uses as a central concept the concept of habit: a new supernatural habit that is created in the moment of regeneration by which we become partakers of the divine nature.

3

HERMAN BAVINCK

MYSTICAL UNION WITH THE HEAD OF THE ORGANISM

3.1 Introduction

HERMAN BAVINCK (1854–1921) IS one of the two great theologians of so-called Neo-Calvinism, the younger contemporary of Abraham Kuyper (1837–1920). His magnum opus is the four volume *Gereformeerde Dogmatiek*,[1] the first edition of which was written between 1895 and 1901. These volumes in particular make him a theologian still worthy of attention.[2] An important motif in his theology is the *unio mystica*; according to Gleason, it is even *the* central motif in Bavinck's theology.[3]

1. Bavinck, *Gereformeerde Dogmatiek* (*GD*).

2. Bavinck's *Gereformeerde Dogmatiek* is being translated into English. According to Gleason, Bavinck is 'one of the greatest theologians Holland ever produced,' Gleason, 'The Centrality of the *Unio Mystica*,' 44.

3. Gleason, 'The Centrality of the *Unio Mystica*,' 1; cf. 38, 45, 117–18. Regarding this theme in Neo-Calvinism, Abraham Kuyper is also worth looking at. Important ideas

After his study at the University of Leiden (1874–1880), he became professor of dogmatics in Kampen at the Theological School (1883–1902) and in Amsterdam at the Free University (1902–1921).[4] Together with Abraham Kuyper, Bavinck wanted to revitalise Dutch Reformed theology. They offered an alternative to the modern and 'ethical' theology—the Dutch version of German Vermittlungstheologie following Schleiermacher—in line with the Reformed theology of Calvin and the Reformed scholastics. But they saw it as their task to bring Reformed theology 'in rapport met de tijd,' in connection with their own time. They were Reformed theologians of the nineteenth century. Bavinck had an irenic nature and always looked for things he and his opponents had in common; always intending to do justice to them.[5]

For the historical background of Bavinck's ideas about being in Christ, nature and grace, it is important to note that he came out of a group of pietistically influenced Reformed people, who had some separatist tendencies. Bavinck wanted them to become less afraid of art, science and politics. The entire world is God's creation. As he wrote often, 'grace does not abolish nature, but renews and restores it.'[6] That is why he

---

in Kuyper are e.g. the organism of the new humanity with Christ as its head and the so-called palingenesis. See Kuijpers, *Abraham Kuyper over de mens,* Ch. X, XI and XII; Vree, 'Organisme en instituut,' 86–108; Vree, 'Tegen de evolutie de palingenesie,' 149–64; Douma, *Algemene genade*, 48, 54, 64–66.

See further on this theme in K. Schilder's theology Veenhof, 'Jezus Christus de plaatsbekleder,' 76–83.

4. For Bavinck's life, see the biography of Bremmer, *Herman Bavinck en zijn tijdgenoten*. For an introduction in his theology, see Bremmer, *Herman Bavinck als dogmaticus.* For a survey of Bavinck-research, see Gleason, 'The Centrality of the *Unio Mystica*,' 2–46. For the relation between Bavinck and Kuyper, see, besides Bremmer's books, Bolt, 'The Imitation of Christ Theme.' On different subjects related to Bavinck, see also Harinck, Neven (red.), *Ontmoetingen met Bavinck.*

5. For a comparison of Bavinck and the 'ethische' (ethical) theologians, see Veenhof, *Revelatie en inspiratie*. See further Bremmer, *Herman Bavinck als dogmaticus*, 65–114.

6. According to different Bavinck-researchers—John Bolt, Eugene Heideman and Jan Veenhof—this motif of nature and grace is the central theme of Bavinck's theology. Hielema and Gleason deny it is the central theme. See Bolt, 'The Imitation of Christ Theme,' 162–63; Gleason, 'The Centrality of the *Unio Mystica*,' 7–44; Hielema, 'Herman Bavinck's Eschatological Understanding of Redemption,' 171–99; Veenhof, *Revelatie en inspiratie*, 345–46; Veenhof, *The relationship between nature and grace according to H. Bavinck*, 1.

did not like dualism, something he found in different forms in Roman Catholic theology, in Pietism, Kant and Schleiermacher.[7]

The doctrine of the Trinity is very important for Bavinck, as Bolt and Bremmer emphasise again and again[8]. Bavinck can even write that every error comes out of or can be reduced to a deviation in the doctrine of the Trinity.[9] 2 Cor 13:14 is often quoted: 'May the grace of the Lord Jesus Christ, and the love of God, and the fellowship of the Holy Spirit be with you all.'[10] Regarding 'being in Christ' it must not be forgotten that Bavinck's thoughts of creation, sin, nature and grace, Christology and soteriology stand within a Trinitarian context. Further the love of the Father, creator of heaven and earth, is essential to understand Christology and soteriology. It is God's love that comes out in election and in the gift of his Son, so it was not the Son who caused this love. Consequently, Bavinck is very clear in rejecting the idea of an 'Umstimmung' of the Father by the Son. Christ's sacrifice seen as *satisfactio*, does not stand in contradiction to the love of God, for it was the loving Father who gave his Son to reconcile our sins.[11] The love of God in Christ is so great that only together with all the saints we can grasp how wide and long and high and deep this love is (Bavinck often refers to Eph 3:18).[12]

Bavinck is a Trinitarian theologian, but also a Christocentric thinker. However, unlike many other nineteenth-century theologians, as a Calvinist, Bavinck does not start methodologically with the historical person of Jesus Christ but with the Triune God and therefore with the eternal

7. See, for a short overview of Bavinck's interlocutors, Veenhof, *Revelatie en inspiratie*, 400–404. He mentions medieval and Roman-catholic scholasticism, reformed scholasticism, pietism, rationalism, supranaturalism, Kant and Schleiermacher, Ritschl, Hegel, naturalism and evolutionism, Ritschl's scholars and the Religionsgeschichtliche School. See further Veenhof, *Revelatie en inspiratie*, 11–140.

8. See Bremmer, *Herman Bavinck als dogmaticus*; Bolt, 'The Imitation of Christ Theme,' 162–256. Cf. Gleason, 'The Centrality of the *Unio Mystica*,' 22, 32, 35, 66, 99.

9. Bavinck, *GD* Vol. II, 255.

10. Bavinck, 'De Huishouding Gods,' *Kennis en leven*, 98–106, esp. 105; Bavinck, *De katholiciteit van christendom en kerk*, 15–16; Bavinck, *De algemene genade*, 14, 47; Bavinck, *De offerande des lofs*, 57; Bavinck, *Wijsbegeerte der openbaring*, 170.

11. Bavinck, *GD* Vol. II, 364–65; Vol. III, 380; and Yoo, *Raad en daad*, 93.

12. See Bavinck, *Kennis en leven*, 105; *De katholiciteit van christendom en kerk*, 15–16; *De algemene genade*, 14, 47; *De offerande des lofs*, 57; *Wijsbegeerte der openbaring*, 163, 170; *Modernisme en orthodoxie*, 34.

See for the references to Eph 3:18 *Kennis en leven*, 85, 103, 206; *De offerande des lofs*, 66; *Godsdienst en godgeleerdheid*, 59; *GD* Vol. I, 59.

and incarnate Son of God. This will become clear in his Christology and soteriology, but also in his doctrine of creation. In the *Gereformeerde Dogmatiek* we find the following structure: revelation and scripture, doctrine of God, creation and fall, person and work of Christ (including the covenant of grace), benefits of the covenant of grace, church and means of grace, and finally eschatology.

In my description of Bavinck, I will follow this structure. Regarding 'being in Christ' the mystical union with Christ is a central theme. With Gleason, the mystical union can be seen as an eternity-time-eternity relation: Christ's work is prepared in eternity and reaches its goal in eternity.[13] God's eternal council is realised objectively in the life of Jesus Christ and subjectively in the life of the believer.[14] Bavinck deals with God's eternal council and election in his doctrine of God, but the *pactum salutis* as the eternal spring of the mystical union is discussed in his doctrine of the covenant as its eternal foundation and hence after the doctrine of creation. For the Neo-Calvinist Bavinck, the identity of Christ cannot be understood without saying something about creation and about Adam. So I will say something about his doctrine of creation and sin in Adam, and because of the structure of Bavinck's theology, I will do this before a discussion of the *pactum salutis*. When dealing with Christology, I will deal also with the *pactum salutis*, and, in kind of a 'flash back,' also with election.

In what follows, I will give an overview of themes in Bavinck that are important for developing a concept of 'being in Christ.' The reality of 'being in Christ' has implications for both Christology and soteriology. Who is Christ that we can be in him—the Christological question. And how do we participate in Jesus Christ—the soteriological question. Answering these questions, I will search for the four moments to test the hypothesis of 1.2.6. I will start with saying something about creation, Adam and sin. (3.2). Secondly I will describe Bavinck's Christology (3.3). I continue thirdly with his soteriology (3.4). Fourthly I will investigate in which way this 'being in Christ' is a reality according to Bavinck (3.5). Finally I will draw some conclusions (3.6).

13. Gleason, 'The Centrality of the *Unio Mystica*,' 38.

14. Bavinck, *GD* Vol. III, 519–20, 599; Vol. IV, 100.

3.2 Creation and Sin

To understand the identity and soteriological significance of Jesus Christ according to Bavinck's theology, something more must be said about the position of the *logos asarkos* in creation (3.2.1) and about the position of Adam within humanity (3.2.2).

3.2.1 THE *LOGOS* AS CREATION MEDIATOR

Jesus Christ is the incarnate *Logos*. The *Logos* is eternal, for he is himself God, generated from eternity.[15] The *Logos* is God's wisdom and self-knowledge, the absolute true revelation of God and the true image of the Father. God reveals himself through the *Logos*.[16] With Augustine and Neo-Thomism Bavinck uses the Platonic idea-doctrine to understand these divine thoughts.[17] According to Bavinck God is unchanging being, whereas creation is becoming.[18] The entire world rests on the divine thoughts. The Father speaks out all his thoughts in the Son and thinks the world-idea. In the Son, the Father sees the world. The Son is the *Logos*, and the world is the realisation of God's thoughts.[19] So God revealed himself in the *Logos* and created by the *Logos*; creation is a kind of revelation. God creates,

15. Bavinck, *GD* Vol. II, 275–77.

16. Bavinck, *GD* Vol. II, 237–242.

17. For Bavinck's *logos*-doctrine, see Bremmer, *Herman Bavinck als dogmaticus*, 157–60, 192–96, 199, 328–31, 370; Yoo, *Raad en daad*, 77–79. Van der Walt and Veenhof have given an analysis of Bavinck's philosophy, see Van der Walt, *Die Wijsbegeerte van Dr. Herman Bavinck*; Veenhof, 'De God van de filosofen en de God van de bijbel,' 219–33.

Regarding Bavinck's relationship to Neo-Thomism, Bremmer mentions Matteo Liberatore's Neo-Thomist *Die Erkenntniss-Theorie des heiligen Thomas van Aquin* as an important source for Bavinck's own philosophical reflections (328–30).

Bavinck developed his *Logos*-doctrine together with Abraham Kuyper and Jan Woltjer, both teaching at the Free University in Amsterdam. See for their *Logos*-doctrines Klapwijk, 'Honderd jaar filosofie aan de Vrije Universiteit,' 530–46; Van der Walt, *Die Wijsbegeerte van Dr. Herman Bavinck*, 37–49.

18. Bavinck, *GD* Vol. II, 171–74; Bavinck, *Christelijke wereldbeschouwing*, 37, 45, 59; Bavinck, *Wijsbegeerte der openbaring*, 66–67, 91; Bremmer, *Herman Bavinck als dogmaticus*, 188–96, Jansen, *Relationality and the concept of God*, 40–53.

19. The doctrine of God's council is transitional from the doctrine of God to the doctrine of the works of God. However, God's council is not realised of necessity, but because of God's sovereign will. Further, Bavinck explicitly denies that the Son as the *Logos* can be seen as an intermediary between God and the world, between being and becoming. See Bavinck, *GD* Vol. II, 387; and further Bremmer, *Herman Bavinck als dogmaticus*, 198–99.

sustains, reigns and renews through his Word.[20] The *Logos* is not only the image of the Father; he is also the firstborn of creation, who existed before creation. As the firstborn of creation, the Son is the one who bears up the creation. Because the Son is Mediator of Creation from the beginning, he is also Mediator of Salvation, the incarnate *Logos*. As the first, he is *archè*, *causa exemplaris*; as the second he is also the *causa finalis* of creation. The world is created by the *Logos*, but also for him. He is the head of the new creation.[21] This explains why, in his exegesis of Colossians 1, Bavinck sees the *Logos* at the beginning of creation and at the end of creation.[22] Apart from Augustinian and Neo-Thomist Platonism the idea of creation mediatorship, based on John 1 and Colossians 1, plays an important role in his *Logos*-doctrine.

The *Logos* is mediator of creation and of re-creation. Only the One through whom God created the world, could be the mediator of re-creation.[23] In classical Reformed tradition the incarnation is only an answer to sin and guilt. Likewise in Bavinck's view incarnation is not necessary to perfect creation, but to remove sin—the special revelation, including incarnation, has a soteriological character[24]. Sometimes it seems that Bavinck saw incarnation differently, as an ontological necessity or as necessary because Christ is the head of the covenant. Bavinck writes that re-creation was already planned for in creation; creation prepares re-creation and Adam was a type of Christ already before the fall. The entire creation must be thought of infralapsarian, for before the fall, God planned Christ and the covenant of grace. Bavinck sees a line from eternal generation, revelation and creation to the special soteriological revelation with the incarnation as its centre. The Son was coming from the beginning of the

20. Bavinck, *Kennis en leven*, 208–9; Bavinck, *De offerande des lofs*, 29; Bavinck, *GD* Vol. II, 173–74, 207, 239, 387–89; Bavinck, *Christelijke wereldbeschouwing*, 28–29, 55–57; Bavinck, *Wijsbegeerte der openbaring*, 22–23 Bremmer, *Herman Bavinck als dogmaticus*, 209.

21. Bavinck, *Kennis en leven*, 101–2, 208–10; Bavinck, *De offerande des lofs*, 69; Bavinck, *GD* Vol. II, 239–42, 388–89; Vol. III, 259; Bavinck, *Wijsbegeerte der openbaring*, 22–23, 170, 267; and further Bremmer, *Herman Bavinck als dogmaticus*, 209.

22. For Bavinck's exegesis of John 1 and Colossians 1 see Bavinck, *Kennis en leven*, 101–2, 208–10; Bavinck, *GD* Vol. I, 316, 556; Vol. II, 241, 387, 389.

23. Bavinck, *GD* Vol. III, 450.

24. Bavinck, *Kennis en leven*, 210; Bavinck, *De algemene genade*, 41–42; Bavinck, *GD* Vol. I, 317–19, 329, 344; Vol. III 254–55, 259; Bavinck, *Christelijke wereldbeschouwing*, 89; Bavinck, *Verzamelde opstellen op het gebied van godsdienst en wetenschap*, 148.

times, preparing his incarnation and ultimately arriving to stay with humanity forever. The Christological teleology of creation is in tension with the contingent, soteriological character of the incarnation. As a result the unique character of the incarnation as an answer to sin and guilt seems to disappear, although Bavinck does not want this.[25]

In conclusion, according to Bavinck the Son of God is the mediator of creation as well as the mediator of re-creation. Bavinck's *Logos*-doctrine here plays an important role in the background. The combination of the *Logos*-doctrine and the Christological teleology of creation makes it difficult to avert the disappearance of the soteriological necessity of the incarnation that comes to be replaced by an ontological necessity. However, Bavinck maintains that the incarnation is soteriologically motivated.

3.2.2 ADAM AND HUMANITY

Because of the parallel between Adam and Christ it is important to see how Bavinck deals with the figure of Adam. To understand the fall of humanity in Adam, two related themes in Bavinck are important: a. humanity is an organism with a head and b. the covenant of works.

Adam, father and head of humanity, represents as *persona publica* the whole of humanity. This marks the difference between spiritual beings like angels and human beings: humanity is an organic unity, not an aggregate of unrelated individuals. God wanted no separate individuals, but an entire organism of humanity as his image and likeness.[26] God made a covenant with Adam, the covenant of works, and in him with all other human beings.[27] According to Bavinck, religion always has the character of a covenant, even before the fall. The covenant of works had as its purpose that humanity should reach its destination.[28]

25. Bavinck, *GD* Vol. II, 353–54, 425, 522, 525; Vol. III, 210, 258–61. And further for similar criticisms Bolt, 'The Imitation of Christ Theme,' 240–51; Jansen, *Relationality and the concept of God*, 47; Veenhof, *Revelatie en inspiratie*, 300–309, 406–15 (Veenhof 411–12 shows the differences and similarities with Karl Barth); Yoo, *Raad en daad*, 96–102.

To nuance this criticism Bolt and Yoo both mention Bavinck's view of the unity of God's eternal council, see Bolt, 'The Imitation of Christ Theme,' 245–51; Yoo, *Raad en daad*, 101–2.

26. Bavinck, *GD* Vol. II, 423–24, 487, 538–41, 549–50; Vol. III, 52, 80–82; Bavinck, *Bijbelsche en religieuze psychologie*, 17–18.

27. Bavinck, *GD* Vol. II, 512 549–50 ; Vol. III 84–85; Bavinck, *De offerande des lofs*, 14.

28. Bavinck, *GD* Vol. II, 525–26, 530, 532–33 . See for the covenant of works in Bavinck Hoekema, 'Herman Bavinck's Doctrine of the Covenant,' 70–103.

The relationship between Adam and other human beings is characterized by different bonds: physical and ethical-covenantal-juridical. Merely physical bonds would be insufficient: blood relationship does not make a unity, as comparison of humanity with animals evidences, and with Christ believers have no blood relationship although he assumed human nature. Still he is their head. Based on the physical relationship we need ethical, covenantal or juridical relationships.[29] What exactly is meant with an ethical relationship is not described. In Bavinck's days 'ethical' was a very common expression, meaning something like existential or personal. Human beings are organic parts of a greater whole, but as persons they do have their own responsibility. It is the ethical-covenantal unity with its head that makes humanity truly an organic whole.[30]

The character of the relationship between Adam and other human beings receives more clarity if one considers the spread of sin.[31] According to Bavinck, the generality of sin is in Genesis 3 inferred from the fall of the first man. Sin and death came to dominion in Adam, says Bavinck with Paul in Rom 5:12 and 1 Cor 15:22.[32] Here we see again that a realistic, physical interpretation of the organic unity of mankind in its head does not suffice. Also the idea of solidarity between humans is not sufficient. Maybe we suffer for the sake of our parents' evil, but that does not automatically make us sinners; a judgment of God precedes. From this judgment, our sin and death are derived. So there are here two moments of importance: a. in a certain way, all human beings are included in Adam; b. by a judgment of God, all human beings are sinners, who die in fact.[33] A strict realist and traducianist perspective does not suffice to understand

29. Bavinck, *GD* Vol. II, 540–41, 548–49; Vol. III, 80–84; Bavinck, *Bijbelsche en religieuze psychologie*, 128.

30. Bavinck, *GD* Vol. II, 549–50; Vol. III, 81. It is in line with this position, that Bavinck in his anthropology is a creatianist and not a traducianist, (see *GD* Vol. II 541–50) and in the field of original sin not a realist but a covenantalist (see *GD* Vol. II ,548; Vol. III 80–82, 96–97).

31. To understand original sin is one of the most difficult problems of theology, according to Bavinck. Bavinck, *GD* Vol. III, 78–79. Cf Bavinck, *Bijbelsche en religieuze psychologie*, 140.

32. Bavinck, *GD* Vol. III, 59, 79–80; Bavinck, *Bijbelsche en religieuze psychologie*, 128–29. According to Bavinck, it is firstly Paul who explains the generality of sin from Adams fall, see *GD* Vol. III, 59.

33. Bavinck, *GD* Vol. II, 549–50; Vol. III, 59–62, 80–85, 89.

this. Physical and hereditary factors do play a role, but we cannot omit ethical and covenantal factors to explain original sin.[34]

Without this organic unity of humanity, there would be no salvation in Christ, for a parallel exists between Adam as the head of the covenant of works and Christ as the head of the covenant of grace. Both covenants rest on the same ordinances, so Christ and the covenant of grace could immediately replace Adam and the covenant of works. We as human beings have the same relationship to both of them, excepting the physical relationship.[35] Adam and Christ both took an exceptional place within humanity for which we have only analogies. We need to see the special ordinance and judgment of God that gave them their special position. We cannot understand Adam and Christ from humanity, but we can only understand humanity if we understand them, for they constitute and establish humanity. Humanity is not a unity at once, but only if it is taken together in its head. It was God's ordinance and judgment that humanity is unclean and dying in Adam and justified and sanctified to eternal life in Christ. Death and resurrection have in the same way their respective causes in Adam and Christ.[36]

However, the Christological teleology complicates the parallel.[37] Because of the unity of the covenant, the Son has a place in both the covenant of works and the covenant of grace. In the covenant of works he is mediator of unity, in the covenant of grace mediator of salvation. Bavinck writes further that Christ was already planned for in the creation of Adam.[38] This leads to a tension between an Adam-Christ parallel and an Adam-Christ difference. On the one hand Christ does what Adam failed to do, bringing creation to its destination by obedience. 'And further it may not be forgotten that Christ obtained not only what Adam lost, but also what Adam would have obtained in the way of obedience,' Bavinck

34. Bavinck, *GD* Vol. II, 549–50; Vol. III, 80–85, 96–97.

35. Bavinck, *GD* Vol. II, 423–24, 487, 525–26, 540, 549–50; Vol. III 52, 60–61, 84.

36. Bavinck, *GD* Vol. II, 504, 539–40; Vol. III 59–62, 84–85, 397.

37. This Christological teleology is caused among others by Colossians 1, which inspires Bavinck to see Christ as final cause of the world. See footnote 21 and 22.

38. Bavinck, *GD* Vol. II, 354, 423–24, 525, 532. For the Logos as *Mediator unionis*, see e.g. Bavinck, *De algemene genade*, 40; Bavinck, *GD* Vol. II, 520; Vol. IV, 667. However, Bavinck also writes that we are not created unto Christ, Vol. II, 516.

writes.[39] On the other hand, Christ is more than Adam and gives more than Adam could ever give.[40]

Summarizing, we can say that Bavinck sees structure in humanity. God ordained humanity as an organism with a head. The covenant of works and the covenant of grace both are made with the head of humanity. The head as a public person acts on behalf of the remaining organism, representing it. Adam was such a head, and Christ fits into these ordinances. Physical relations do play a role, but are not sufficient to understand this headship: we need ethical-juridical-covenantal relations based on physical relations to understand it. God's judgments regarding Adam concern the whole of mankind. Between Adam and Christ a parallel can be drawn, but at the same time Christ exceeds Adam.

As a result of this discussion of Bavinck's doctrine of creation it can be concluded that Bavinck's doctrine of creation has a strong Christocentric flavour. Bavinck's doctrine of the mystical union with Christ cannot be understood without this Christocentric background in his doctrine of creation. The first sub-section of this section already signals the exclusiveness of Christ: he is the incarnate *Logos*, who is the mediator of creation; the second section shows that Christ, like Adam, is representative of believers, implying both the exclusive moment of person-substitution and the inclusive moment.

39. 'En dan mag ook niet vergeten, dat Christus niet alleen verwierf, wat Adam verloor, maar ook wat Adam in den weg der gehoorzaamheid verworven zou hebben.' Bavinck, *GD* Vol. II, 504; cf. 525–26; 534.

This is important for an evaluation of the thesis of Hielema, that grace not only restores nature but also elevates it, and that Bavinck's understanding of redemption is an eschatological one. Already creation and the covenant of works in Adam implied an eschatological elevation of creation, if creation would come to its destiny. Restoration of creation includes the elevation of creation that was intended in the original creation. Hielema is right in emphasising the teleological structure of creation and the emphasis in Bavinck on elevation, but he undervalues the fact that for Bavinck this is included already in the covenant of works with Adam. As a consequence, the opposition between an eschatological and a creational view of redemption is not so great as it seems in Hielema's argument. See Hielema, 'Herman Bavinck's Eschatological Understanding of Redemption,' 4–6, 72, 88–92, 114, 120–199.

40. Bavinck, *GD* Vol. II, 522, 525, 535; Vol. III, 60, 397; Bavinck, *De algemene genade*, 43.

3.3 Christology

From creation, Adam, and sin, we now turn to Christology. In this section I will discuss the person and work of Christ in so far as is relevant for the understanding of the objective realisation of the mystical union with Christ. In the first sub-section I will start with the concept of 'head' to indicate the position of Jesus Christ (3.3.1). I will continue with an analysis of the Christological aspect of the concept of mystical union, discussing its objective realisation (3.3.2). Moreover I will discuss aspects of salvation in Christ, where Bavinck emphasises again and again that Christ is our salvation, in his person (3.3.3). Finally I will analyse how the inclusive and the exclusive moment are present in Bavinck's Christology, and at the same time show that Bavinck uses two groups of concepts (3.3.4.).

3.3.1 CHRIST AS HEAD

We concluded in 3.2.2 that according to Bavinck the new humanity stands in a comparable relation to Christ in the covenant of grace as the old humanity stands to Adam in the covenant of works. In this section I will analyse how Bavinck in different contexts uses the concept of head referring to Jesus Christ, in successively God's election, the *pactum salutis*, the covenant of grace, humanity, and the church and the world.

First, the Son is head in predestination and election. He is elected and predestined to be the mediator but also to be the head of the covenant of grace and of the church. Further, believers are elected and predestined to be members of Christ. Because Christ is predestined to be the head of the church, Bavinck denies that the election of believers precedes logically the election of Christ. Instead, Christ is also the object of election and his election precedes logically the election of believers, as it is the first benefit given to believers in communion with Christ. The object of election is a perfect organism, consisting of Christ as its head and the church as his body. Bavinck can say that the proper object of election is the mystical Christ. This means that Christ is not just a means to realise the goal of election although election is realised in and through Christ. Election is election in Christ, organic participation in the election of Christ as object of God's eternal love.[41] However, it is important to note that, according to Bavinck, emphases in election differ from emphases in the covenant of

41. Bavinck, *GD* Vol. II, 352–53, 365–69; Vol. III, 259, 277. See moreover Bremmer, *Herman Bavinck als dogmaticus*, 207–8; Yoo, *Raad en daad*, 92–95.

grace. Although the elect are elected in Christ and constitute an organism with him as its head, the 'in Christ' is not at the foreground. In election the salvation of individual persons is anchored, resulting in an emphasis on individuals and not on organic, collective, historical processes, following the generations.[42] Nevertheless, Christ is elected to be head of the elect, and believers are elected together with Christ, as head and members of an organism.

Secondly, God's Trinitarian life is a covenantal life, in which lies the eternal foundation of the covenant of grace: the *pactum salutis* between Father, Son and Spirit concerning the salvation of the human race. The Father gives individuals to the Son to save them, even an exchange of place comes into being.[43] In the *pactum salutis*, the Son is guarantee and head of the elect; he is the mystical Christ who cannot be seen apart from his own, although the *pactum salutis* is not made with them. They are included in him as their head.[44]

Thirdly, Christ is head in the covenant of grace, to which the *pactum salutis* extends. They can be distinguished (and Bavinck lists several differences), but these differences may not obscure the coherence and unity of both.[45] In all the various historical divisions of the covenant of grace, Christ was the head of the covenant and in him the covenant has the character of an unbreakable testament. Also in the covenant of grace believers are never separate from Christ and he is the mystical Christ.[46]

42. Bavinck, *GD* Vol. III, 210, 212–13; and further Bavinck, *De offerande des lofs*, 20; Bremmer, *Herman Bavinck als dogmaticus*, 245–46 Gleason, 'The Centrality of the *Unio Mystica*,' 135.

When Bavinck writes about the difference between emphasis on the organic character of election and covenant in Vol. III (212–13) he (almost) contradicts what he wrote about the organic character of election in Vol. II (365–69).

43. Bavinck, *GD* Vol. III, 192–95, 396, 520; Vol. IV, 197–98, 234–35; *Kennis en leven*, 103; *Roeping en wedergeboorte*, 108; and further Hoekema, 'Herman Bavinck's Doctrine of the Covenant,' 103–8; Bremmer, *Herman Bavinck als dogmaticus*, 244.

44. Bavinck, *GD* Vol. III, 208–10.

45. See for these differences Bavinck, *GD* Vol. III, 209; Hoekema, 'Herman Bavinck's Doctrine of the Covenant,' 109.

Hoekema wrongly states that Bavinck emphasises especially the difference between *pactum salutis* and covenant of grace. Bremmer, Yoo and Gleason rightly write instead that Bavinck emphasises their unity, see Hoekema, 'Herman Bavinck's Doctrine of the Covenant,' 109; and Bremmer, *Herman Bavinck als dogmaticus*, 247–48; Gleason, 'The Centrality of the *Unio Mystica*,' 137; Yoo, *Raad en daad*, 99–100.

46. Bavinck, *GD* Vol. III, 184, 206–7, 209–10; Hoekema, 'Herman Bavinck's Doctrine of the Covenant,' 109f, 157–60. It is remarkable that Bavinck, when listing the differences

That Christ is head of the covenant of grace is clear. However, Bavinck's use of the concept in this context is complex, for as head of the covenant of grace Christ is also head of mankind, of the church and of the world. Bavinck uses the concept for different aims. The following aspects can be distinguished.

a. According to Bavinck, Christ receives immediately after the fall the position of Adam as head of fallen humanity. Like Adam, he represents mankind. And immediately from the fall onwards it is Christ who appears as prophet, priest and king. Consequently, in all different covenants with Adam, Noah, Abraham, Israël and David, Christ is the proper party and head with whom the covenant is sealed. [47]

b. As head of the covenant of grace, Christ is representative and substitute. As representative and *persona publica*, Christ can be compared with Adam; as substitute, Christ is more than Adam.[48] Here a certain ambivalence can be found in Bavinck. On the one hand, Bavinck emphasises that because in salvation the righteousness of Christ that is given to believers is the righteousness of their head, it is only in a certain sense an alien righteousness. The concept of head implies representation and inclusiveness.[49] On the other hand, in discussion with subjective concepts of atonement emphasising the mystical union with Christ, Bavinck stresses the objective-juridical aspect of atonement: as head of the covenant of grace, Christ substitutes for his own in a covenantal-juridical sense. Here the concept of head implies work-substitution and exclusiveness, as distinct from mystical-organic notions.[50]

c. Further, Christ is more than Adam, because he is head of the new humanity and of the church. Using the concept of head in this con-

---

between *pactum salutis* and *foedus gratiae* writes that Christ is mediator in the covenant of grace (not writing that he is head), whereas he on the same page (and on many other pages) refers to Christ as head of the covenant of grace. See *GD* Vol. III, 209.

47. Bavinck, *GD* Vol. III, 195, 209, 277; Bavinck, *De offerande des lofs*, 14; Hoekema, 'Herman Bavinck's Doctrine of the Covenant,' 157–60.

48. Bavinck, *GD* Vol. III, 209, 365, 397.

49. Bavinck, *GD* Vol. III, 289, 372; Vol. IV, 198, 201.

50. Bavinck, *GD* Vol. III, 392, 396–97.

text, it is related both to organic (growth of the body) and hierarchic notions (reigning of the church).[51]

d. The word 'head' is used mostly as a concept. Sometimes it is used together with the body-metaphor as a metaphor for the mystical union with Christ, standing in an enumeration together with other images for the mystical union.[52]

e. Christ, the head and mediator of the covenant of grace is, according to Bavinck, also the head of the entire new creation. He, the *logos* and the mediator of creation, is the One by whom God recreates the universe. The entire new creation is an organism, of which Christ is the head and *telos*.[53]

Finally, it is important to see how Bavinck relates Christ as head of the covenant and believers he substitutes and represents. The covenant of grace is monopleuric, for its origin lies in God and in the Trinitarian *pactum salutis*. However, this does not imply that believers are excluded, effaced and destroyed. The covenant is destined to become dipleuric, to become willingly assented to and maintained by human beings in the power of God. What is realised objectively in the head of the organism has to be applied subjectively in the members of the body.[54]

Summarizing, we have seen that the concept of head indicates that the Son has the central place in election, in the *pactum salutis* and in the covenant of grace. Although in election the emphasis is on the resulting individual salvation, the elect constitute together an organism with Christ as its head; they participate in his election. In God's Trinitarian life the *pactum salutis* is made, the eternal foundation of the covenant of grace. Also in the covenant of grace the Son is head. He replaces Adam and is the proper party in all of the different divisions of the covenant of grace. In Bavinck's use of the concept, both the moment of representation and work-substitution can be found. Further Christ is head of the body of the

51. Bavinck, *GD* Vol. II, 368; III, 208, 213, 321, 352, 372, 462, 478, 481; Vol. IV, 264, 395, 310, 354, 356; Bavinck, *De wetenschap der H. Godgeleerdheid*, 10; Bavinck, *Kennis en leven*, 103; Bavinck, *De katholiciteit van christendom en kerk*, 33; Bavinck, *De algemene genade*, 51; Bavinck, *De offerande des lofs*, 68; Bavinck, *Wijsbegeerte der openbaring*, 228.

52. Bavinck, *GD* Vol. III, 321, 472; Vol. IV, 356, 543.

53. Bavinck, *GD* Vol. III, 213; Bavinck, *Kennis en leven*, 37, 103; Bavinck, *De zekerheid des geloofs*, J.H. Kok Kampen 1918, 103; Bavinck, *Wijsbegeerte der opennbaring*, 267.

54. Bavinck, *GD* Vol. III, 211–12, 492, 520, 599; Bremmer, *Herman Bavinck als dogmaticus*, 246–47.

church and the new creation. In the head, the members of the body are revived to live together with the head. As head Christ can further be seen together with the church as the mystical Christ.

3.3.2 *'UNIO MYSTICA'* 1

Another important concept is the concept of the mystical union with Christ. It is a concept with a Christological and a soteriological aspect. Gleason has shown that the *unio mystica* is a central concept in Bavinck's theology, especially in the order of salvation and the Lord's Supper, but he did not analyse Bavinck's use of the concept in his Christology.[55] Here I will describe the Christological aspect, but will inevitably say something here also about his soteriology. Bavinck never gives a precise description of his concept of *unio mystica*, but he uses it in different contexts. For now four contexts are important: the context of God's councils, of religion in general, of Christology, and of the Trinity. It is a complex concept, for it is used in different contexts with different interests.

In a 'flashback' again I start with the context of the councils of God. We have seen, in 3.3.1 that Christ as mystical Christ is head of the elect in election and the *pactum salutis*.[56] The bond between Christ and his people that existed already in election and the *pactum salutis* is described by Bavinck as a communion and a *unio mystica*. Believers have no communion with the benefits of salvation outside communion with Christ, Bavinck can be heard repeating often. Election already is a benefit, which is impossible without communion with Christ.[57] Further, Christ could not fulfil the law, bear the believers' guilt and by his obedience make satisfaction for them, if there was no mystical union between him and his people. Therefore in the *pactum salutis* a mystical union between Christ and his own is established. As a result, Christ stands in communion with them as their guarantee and mediator, their head and substitute, and they exchange places. Both representation and substitution have their origin in the mystical union established in the *pactum salutis*. Christ and his benefits are given to those the Father gave him, before they accepted him in faith. Their guilt is imputed to Christ and his righteousness is imputed

55. See Gleason, 'The Centrality of the *Unio Mystica*.'

56. For the concept of Christ as mystical Christ in election, see Bavinck, *GD* Vol. II, 368; in the *pactum salutis* and the covenant of grace, see Vol. III, 210.

57. Bavinck, *GD* Vol. II, 365–68; Vol. III, 212.

to them.[58] This means that the righteousness of Christ is only in a limited sense an alien righteousness; head and organism belong together from the beginning.[59] For the sake of clarity: this does not mean that we are justified from eternity; Bavinck explicitly denies this.[60] In conclusion, the *unio mystica* established in the *pactum salutis* is the presupposition of substitutionary atonement and justification, even of the obtaining and gift of all other benefits of salvation.

Secondly, the concept can only be understood in its Christological context if its background is seen in creation and in religion in general. Religion itself rests on a mystical union of God and man. This is no substantive communion, but an ethical ('ethische') relation. A human being can not be really human without the essence of religion: communion with God, which is a mystical union with God; a personal union with God, which is so intimate that it changes a human being according to the image of God and makes one a partaker of the Divine nature. This communion with God, essential to religion, is broken by sin but will be restored in Christ and in the Spirit. *Unio mystica* is in its proper sense a theological notion.[61]

Thirdly, the concept is used in a Christological context. The *unio mystica* in its theological use is the aim of salvation and the essence of religion itself, in its Christological use it is a means for the restoration of the relation with God and the mystical union as the essence of true religion. The broken communion with God had to be restored and reconciled. To restore the religious relation between God and humanity, a new beginning, a principle and objective realisation of this religious relation was necessary, according to Bavinck. This principle Bavinck finds in the incarnation of the *Logos*. In the incarnation, resulting in the *unio* of the divine and human nature of Christ, this relation was realised objectively. The natural Son and the image of God, guarantee and mediator of God's children, becomes flesh. In Christ, the head and representative of humanity, God and man are united again. As the second and last Adam, Jesus

58. Bavinck, *GD* Vol. III, 209, 520, 598–99; Vol. IV, 100, 197–98, 234–35; Bavinck, *De offerande des Lofs*, 17f; Bavinck, *Roeping en wedergeboorte*, 24–25.

59. Bavinck, *GD* Vol. IV, 198.

60. Bavinck, *GD* Vol. III, 589, 598–99; Vol. IV, 199–200. Bavinck does not refer to Kuyper who defended a justification from eternity, but Kuyper must be seen at the background here. Cf. Bremmer, *Herman Bavinck als dogmaticus*, 275.

61. Bavinck, *GD* Vol. I, 235; Vol. III, 288–89; Bavinck, *Roeping en wedergeboorte*, 28, 38; Bavinck, *Wijsbegeerte der openbaring*, 202–3.

Christ needed an impersonal human nature. This was necessary, because the union between God and humanity, and not just an individual human being, had to be restored. Humanity is so structured that in the incarnate *Logos* the whole of mankind is represented. Hence in his person, he establishes the unity of God and man. However, this *unio* of natures in the person of Jesus Christ is not itself a mystical union. The mystical union is a *unio personarum*, this union is a *unio personalis* and *substantialis.* The mystical union is a moral ('zedelijke') communion, this union a *unio naturarum*. Although the incarnation was necessary for the objective realisation of the *unio mystica*, it was not sufficient.[62]

The *unio mystica* was realised objectively in the earthly life, suffering, death and resurrection of Christ. During his life on earth, Christ was never alone but stood always in communion with humanity whose nature he assumed. As our backs bear the punishment for the crimes of our hands, so Christ has been punished for our sins, as one with us. The communion is no aggregated whole, but an organic whole which is included in Christ as her head. He acquired salvation for the ones with whom he stood in communion as head, guarantee, mediator and representative. As a result of this union, the entire church was objectively crucified, dead, resurrected, glorified and seated in the heavenly realms with him. Salvation and its benefits are present objectively and actively in the risen and glorified Christ. They are included in him and lie ready for the church. All the benefits of salvation presuppose this objective *unio mystica.*[63]

However, the ambivalence we noted in Bavinck's use of 'head' returns here. This is the case, if Bavinck discussing the doctrine of atonement, confronts himself with Christologies of the nineteenth century of the likes of Schleiermacher, German 'Vermittlungs'-theologians and Dutch Groninger and 'ethische' theologians, like Ritschl, Hofstede de Groot and Chantepie de la Saussaye. They made a *unio mystica* or an ethical community with Christ the central moment in their theories of the cross. Bavinck admits that mystical and ethical representations of atonement contain elements of truth. But according to Bavinck these theologians disconnected the mystical or 'ethical' union from its objective foundation in Christ's satisfaction. The concept of *unio mystica* was used as an alternative for substitution and juridical imputation of guilt. They exchanged a concept

62. Bavinck, *GD* Vol. III, 257, 288–290, 372.

63. Bavinck, *GD* Vol. III, 372, 396, 462–63, 519–20, 599; Vol. IV, 99–100, 234; Bavinck, *Roeping en wedergeboorte*, 25.

of atonement based on substitution and expiation, for a 'solidaristisch-reparatorisch' concept, objective atonement was turned into subjective atonement. Against these theories, Bavinck maintains that Christ took our guilt; that his death was necessary because of God's justice; that he made satisfaction by bearing the penalty of sin in a substitutionary way; and that he acquired the benefits of salvation which are given us freely for his sake. He raises the objection that in these theories Christ stands principally beside and not above us. We just have to follow him to be conformed to his example. Furthermore, the significance of the death of Christ and the relation between his death and forgiveness is obscured.[64] The mystical theory sees the essence of religion in the unity of God and man, but the theory cannot be used to say how the unity, distorted by sin, is restored. It is undeniable that subjective elements do play a role, but as long as the relationship with the death of Christ is not explicated it remains unclear how consciences are purified and feelings of guilt taken away. To conclude, 'the mystical and moral interpretation of Jesus' suffering and death cannot even be maintained if it is not previously acknowledged that he suffered and died for us in the legal sense of substitution.'[65]

In his own alternative, Bavinck distinguishes between two relations. The first is a federal relation in which Christ as head of the covenant in a legal sense substitutes for his own. Bavinck finds this relation in Romans 3–5. The second is the mystical union, which Bavinck finds in Romans 6–8. However, now the concept of mystical union is used in two different ways. On the one hand, the mystical union is the presupposition of the first, federal, relation. The *unio* is rooted in the *pactum salutis* and is the presupposition of the imputation of our guilt to Christ and hence of his legal substitution. Substitution is only possible if communion exists between him and us. On the other hand, the mystical union and the mystical benefits must be acquired first by Christ as our federal head. Consequently, now the first, federal, relation is the presupposition of the mystical union.[66] This conceptual unclarity is shown in the astonishing fact that Bavinck on one page writes about the realist-mystical idea of substitution ('plaatsvervanging'), implying that Christ has been punished

64. Bavinck, *GD* Vol. III, 334–44, 371–74, 381–82; Bavinck, *De theologie van prof. dr. Daniel Chantepie de la Saussaye*, 47–48; Bavinck, 'De theologie van Albrecht Ritschl,' 378–79.

65. Bavinck, *GD* Vol. III, 388.

66. Bavinck, *GD* Vol. III, 396, 466, 500.

for our sins, while he is one with us like we are punished on our back for what we did with our hand, and agrees with this idea. This means that the first relation is a mystical union. (Had he used this realist-mystical idea of substitution in his theory of atonement, the inconsistency of his use of the concept of 'mystical union' would have disappeared.) Nevertheless, later on the same page, he distinguishes the second relation as mystical union from the objective atonement based on the juridical relation.[67] Consequently, his use of the concept of mystical union is ambivalent.

This ambivalence returns when Bavinck writes about the objectivity of salvation in Christ. On the one hand, according to Bavinck salvation is objectively present in Christ. The mystical union implies that the community participates objectively in the story of Christ, for the mystical union has been realised objectively in his history: the church has been crucified, dead, resurrected, glorified and seated in heaven objectively with Christ; the mystical and the objective are identical.[68] On the other hand, in discussions concerning the atonement Bavinck differentiates between the mystical and the objective, relating the objectivity of the atonement with the forensic-juridical. In the world of justice, Christ has effected re-creation by the cross; salvation has been acquired objectively. This objective-juridical removal of the guilt of sin he distinguishes from the realistic-mystical interpretation of Christ as representative. This realistic-mystical interpretation implies that believers themselves have been crucified, dead, buried, raised and seated in heaven in mystical union with Christ. Bavinck calls these benefits mystical benefits, which must be distinguished especially from juridical benefits.[69]

To understand this, it is important to see that Bavinck used the concept with different interests in the contexts of discussions with different opponents. First, in the context of the *pactum salutis*, Bavinck maintains the particularity of atonement against the Remonstrants. The union with Christ from eternity is a precondition for imputation. Second, in the context of his theory of atonement Bavinck fears the risk of losing the objective-covenantal-juridical satisfaction against theologians that em-

67. Bavinck, *GD* Vol. III, 396. Gleason notes that Bavinck tied the concept of the 'religious-ethical' with the 'unio mystica,' see Gleason, 'The Centrality of the *Unio Mystica*,' 204.

68. Bavinck, *GD* Vol. III, 327, 372, 462, 520, 599; Vol. IV, 54, 100, 201, 422.

69. Bavinck, *GD* Vol. III, 327, 373, 377, 379, 396, 445–46, 450, 492, 500. Vol. IV, 21, 66, 99. Cf. Bavinck on Adam and objectivity, Vol. III, 153–54.

phasise the mystical union out of criticism of classical forensic theories of atonement. Here Bavinck stresses that the mystical union is a benefit that must be acquired first. Mystical is opposed to objective and juridical. Third, Bavinck wanted to prevent the foreign character of the righteousness of Christ and the *extra nos* of salvation against theologians that identified the story of Jesus Christ with our life. This is e.g. the case in Kaftan's theology where, according to Bavinck, justification is equated with atonement and regeneration with resurrection.[70] Now Bavinck maintains that the life of Jesus Christ and the reality of salvation in his person have their own objectivity in distinction from the subjectivity of our life and person. To summarize these different ways of using the concept in a scheme:

<table>
<tr><td colspan="5">Unio mystica</td></tr>
<tr><td>Context</td><td>Interest</td><td>Front</td><td>Contrasted with</td><td>Significance</td></tr>
<tr><td>Pactum salutis</td><td>Particularity of atonement, precondition of imputation</td><td>Remonstrants</td><td></td><td>Relatedness from eternity</td></tr>
<tr><td rowspan="3">Doctrine of the work of Christ</td><td>Safeguarding satisfaction</td><td>Theologians against satisfaction</td><td>Objective, juridical, covenantal</td><td>Benefit acquired by satisfaction</td></tr>
<tr><td rowspan="2">Safeguarding objective reality of salvation in Christ, extra nos</td><td rowspan="2">Theologians losing the distinction between objective and subjective</td><td rowspan="2">Subjective, application of salvation</td><td>Dying and rising with Christ, objective realised in his dying and rising</td></tr>
<tr><td>Benefit, objectively present in Christ</td></tr>
</table>

70. Bavinck, *GD* Vol. III, 599–600. It is likely that Bavinck sees here a comparable danger as he saw in the theology of Ritschl. In his theology, influenced by Neo-Kantianism, the question cannot be asked who God, Christ and the Spirit are by themselves. The central question is, who they are for us. As a result, the objective reality of dogmatic truths is obscured. See Bavinck, 'De theologie van Albrecht Ritschl,' 378–80, 383–85. Cf. Bavinck, *Kennis en leven*, 145–64.

Although these different opponents and interests clarify the ambivalence in Bavinck's use of *unio mystica* and 'objectivity,' it remains unfortunate that Bavinck uses the concept of *unio mystica* in these different ways and in these different combinations with 'objective.'[71]

Fourthly, we can have no communion with Christ's benefits unless we have communion through the Spirit with Christ himself, who is, in his person, our life. I will deal with this subjective side of the *unio mystica* in the next paragraph (see 3.4).

However, it is important to note that the concept of *unio mystica* also functions in a more Trinitarian context. Although the Son is the one who restores the relationship with God by his incarnation and work, there is no subjective union with Christ if not by the Holy Spirit, and so we have communion with none other than God himself who made himself known as loving Father. Here true religion is restored: by mystical union with Christ, believers are brought back into mystical union with God himself.[72]

I have shown how Bavinck uses the concept of the *unio mystica* in different contexts. First, the *unio mystica* originates in the *pactum salutis*, in God's eternal council. Second, the *unio mystica* is a theological concept that refers to the essence of religion: mystical union with God. To restore this mystical union is the aim of salvation. Thirdly, the mystical union is realised objectively in Christ as head and mediator, when he became man, died and rose again. The church suffered, was crucified, dead, buried, resurrected, glorified and seated in heaven together with Christ. Fourthly, the mystical union has to be applied subjectively through the Holy Spirit. Here we see that it is used in a Trinitarian context too.

Bavinck never formulated an all-encompassing definition of his concept of *unio mystica*. Maybe I do Bavinck most justice if I characterize it as a kind of narrative with three different moments: the *pactum salutis*

71. Gleason has investigated Bavinck's use of the concept of the religious-ethical. According to Gleason, the term encompassed both the *juridical* and *ethical* aspects of redemption and was tied with the *unio mystica*. However, Gleason only investigated the *religious-ethical* and not Bavinck's use of 'mystisch' in combination with 'ethisch.' Further he did not deal with Bavinck's theory of the death of Christ. As a result, he has overlooked these different ways in which he uses the concept, and the complicated relation between the juridical and the mystical union. Against Gleason, 'The Centrality of the *Unio Mystica*,' 190, 204.

72. Bavinck, *GD* Vol. I, 235, 539; Vol. II, 236, 279; Vol. III, 288–89, 501; Vol. IV, 66–67; Bavinck, *Roeping en wedergeboorte*, 38; Bavinck, *Wijsbegeerte der openbaring*, 202–3; Bavinck, *Verzamelde opstellen*, 10.

in God's eternal council, the objective realisation in the history of Jesus Christ and the subjective application in the life of the believer.[73]

Further we have seen that the tension we found in Bavinck's use of 'head' returns in his use of the concept of mystical union and in his idea of 'objectivity.' Bavinck uses the concept of mystical union as presupposition of imputation and atonement, but distinguishes also between the juridical and the mystical in the history of Jesus Christ. Here we sense his fear that the exclusive moment of (work-) substitution should disappear if the mystical union was emphasised too much.[74]

3.3.3 OUR SALVATION IN HIS PERSON

Bavinck often emphasises the fact that we have no communion with the benefits of salvation without communion with Christ.[75] Christ is our salvation, in his person, and his person and work cannot be separated.[76] Therefore, believers need communion with the entire Christ which we have in the mystical union, as Bavinck emphasises especially in his doctrine of the sacraments.[77] Christ is the totality of all his blessings, which are all included in his person. He is law and gospel, in his person, the absolute miracle. Righteousness and holiness are given us in his person. In his person, the covenant of grace, the mystical union, the imputation of guilt and righteousness are realised objectively.[78]

The person of Christ is important for Bavinck for at least two historical motives. Firstly, he emphasises again and again with John Calvin and the Reformed tradition, that communion with the person of Christ

73. Cf. Bavinck, *GD* Vol. IV, 100. In Bavinck's doctrine of justification, a comparable series occurs: imputation and the gift of Christ, see Vol. IV, 202.

74. Schaede shows how in the Reformed tradition the concept of satisfaction and the emerging concept of 'Stellvertretung' became competing motives. Something of this competition can be seen in Bavinck's difference of the juridical and the mystical; see Schaede, *Stellvertretung*, 543–44.

75. Bavinck, *GD* Vol. II, 368; Vol. III, 321, 501, 519–20, 522, 523, 599; Vol. IV, 100, 235, 250, 553; Bavinck, *Kennis en leven*, 117; Bavinck, *De offerande des lofs*, 17; Bavinck, *Roeping en wedergeboorte*, 24. See further Bremmer, *Herman Bavinck als dogmaticus*, 255–57; Gleason, 'The Centrality of the *Unio Mystica*,' 104, 109.

76. Bavinck, *GD* Vol. III, 348.

77. Bavinck, *GD* Vol. II, 525; Vol. III, 366; Vol. IV, 455, 468–69, 473, 534; Bavinck, *Kennis en leven*, 174–77.

78. Bavinck, *GD* Vol. III, 318–20, 327, 441, 520, 599; Vol. IV, 242. Cf. also Vol. III, 366.

precedes communion with his benefits.[79] Secondly, he has assimilated nineteenth-century concepts of Christology in which the person and personality of Christ were important, although he himself stays on the track of the classical two-nature Christology of Chalcedon. Christianity is not a question of metaphysics but of a personal relation to Jesus Christ.[80]

These two historical lines might seem to exclude each other, for the Reformed tradition in line with John Calvin affirms the Classic doctrine of atonement as *satisfactio vicario*, that many nineteenth-century Christologies criticised. At first glance, it seems that Bavinck uses two different mutually exclusive conceptions. On the one hand concepts like acquisition and distribution of benefits, obedience as earning of benefits, benefits as quasi substantive things. On the other hand he uses concepts like mystical union, communion, person. Here more personal language is used, combined with the emphasis on union. Moreover, the concept of the organic is central. However, in Bavinck's emphasis on the person of Christ, these different conceptualities come together.

This is made possible by Bavinck's way of using the metaphor of benefits. First these benefits are purchased by Christ, for according to Bavinck all benefits of salvation find their ground in the death of Christ.[81] Second, referring to individual benefits, Bavinck can say that they are realised objectively in his history.[82] Third, in his resurrection and glorification Christ took a treasure of benefits with him. These benefits are not to be separated from his person, but they are found in him and contain nothing less than the entirety of salvation.[83] As a result, he is our salvation, in his person. And fourth, by his Spirit Christ distributes and applies these benefits among his body, the church.[84] The precondition of this application of salvation is that the church lives in communion with the person of Christ, her head.[85] In this way the two lines can be combined.

79. Bavinck mentions also Owen as a source, Bavinck, *GD* Vol. III, 238.

80. Bavinck, *GD* Vol. I, 581, 583; Vol. IV, 70, 82, 88, 99, 109, 168; Bavinck, *Kennis en leven*, 221; Bavinck, *De algemene genade*, 39; Bavinck, *De offerande des lofs*, 56, 88; Bavinck, *Wijsbegeerte der openbaring*, 193. Cf. Bremmer, *Bavinck als dogmaticus*, 255.

81. Bavinck, *GD* Vol. II, 244; Vol. III, 195–96, 206, 209, 320, 327, 379–80, 522, 599, 441, 445, 462, 576, 578, 584; Vol. IV, 99–100, 202, 422.

82. Bavinck, *GD* Vol. III, 327, 462, 520, 599.

83. Bavinck, *GD* Vol. III, 327, 441, 519–20, 576, 599; Vol. IV, 99–100, 157.

84. Bavinck, *GD* Vol. I, 541; Vol. II, 244, 368; Vol. III, 196, 206, 209, 445, 450, 462, 520, 522, 576, 578, 584; Vol. IV, 99, 202, 242, 258, 422, 426, 544.

85. See footnote 75.

However, this central metaphor has some disadvantages. Apart from the fact that, where in the New Testament the metaphor of buying or paying is linked with persons who are set free, in Bavinck's use it refers to benefits bought, the substantilist character of the metaphor, and the distinction of purchase and application of benefits results in a neglect of the relational character of the mystical union and communion with the person of Christ. Another problem of the centrality of the metaphor of benefits is that it makes it more difficult to see the eschatological character of salvation. According to this metaphor, Christ distributes his benefits. However, we could also say that we participate in the new eschatological life of Christ as justified, sanctified children of God in Christ. This participation in the eschatological life of Christ cannot be expressed in terms of the metaphor of the benefits.

Because the entire Christ is our salvation, according to Bavinck, different aspects of the history of Jesus Christ have soteriological significance. We have seen already that in the eternal origins of the mystical union, the election of Christ and the election of believers are tied together, and discussing the objective realisation we saw the importance of the incarnation: in his person Christ established the unity of God and man (see 3.3.2). He came from outside humanity, but entered in. His entire life was an increasing identification with sinful humanity, in which Christ humiliated himself and moved away from the heavenly joy.[86] However, although he was really man, he was perfect and without sin because he became man by the Holy Spirit.[87]

During his entire life, Christ stood in communion with the humanity whose nature he assumed. He was representative, public person and head: the second and last Adam. As a result, his life has a substitutionary character. The importance of his entire life becomes clear in the fact that Bavinck emphasises the significance of both his active and passive obedience. Yet precisely the Reformed tradition, Bavinck claims, is able to do justice to the meaning of Jesus' entire life. Bavinck resists theologians rejecting the active obedience, as well as theologians rejecting the passive one. Jesus' life was a life of self-sacrifice and voluntary obedience, both active and passive. This obedience is his *satisfactio vicaria*. As a consequence, it is not only his suffering at the cross that is important. His entire person is safeguarding the totality of the salvation of man, humanity and

86. Bavinck, *GD* Vol. I, 351; Vol. III, 277, 372, 399.

87. Bavinck, *GD* Vol. III, 267, 274–77.

the world, albeit his suffering is important too. Jesus prayed for surrender in obedience to the Father and learned obedience in it. He was perfected in this way and sanctified himself for us. He took sin and its curse and in this way he took the death on himself, drinking the cup until the end.[88]

We have seen in 3.3.2 that Bavinck maintains a satisfaction-theory of atonement. It is clear that Bavinck struggled with critiques of traditional satisfaction-theories that judged it too juridical, as he found them in e.g Socinus, Schleiermacher, Chantepie de la Saussaye and Ritschl. Honoring their critiques of some defendants of a satisfaction-theory, Bavinck declines the idea of an 'Umstimmung' and emphasises that the Father gave the Son out of love. He directs attention to the many perspectives that the different authors in scripture gave. He notes that the Father was never angry with the Son. He maintains that the murder of Jesus was a crime. He does not speculate about the endless depths of Christ's suffering and stays modest in his speaking and resists calculations, which according to him do not belong to the Reformed tradition. God is not a vengeful God, wanting to see blood.[89] But this is first of all a correction of caricatures given of the idea of satisfaction. At the same time he regards a satisfaction-theory to be theologically more satisfying than the alternatives offered by the opponents who concentrate on the religious-ethical influence of Christ and try to reconstruct the doctrine of the work of Christ from an ethical or mystical perspective. These theories are not wrong, but insufficient. The Father indeed gave the Son out of love, but he did so justifying the sinner as well as remaining true to his law and nature. Even though the death of Jesus was a crime indeed and the necessity of his death was an ethical ('zedelijke'), historical or psychological one it was also a metaphysical necessity, demanded by God's justice. We cannot do without objective satisfaction, without a sacrifice for our sin, without Christ bearing our punishment, satisfying right and acquiring salvation. In all the diversity in the New Testament, all voices agree on this, that Christ died for our sins. His death is connected with our sin, has an objective meaning and is willed by God. We cannot miss the idea of *satisfactio vicaria*, which is according to Bavinck founded on the Scriptures.[90]

By his satisfaction as representative of humanity, Christ changed the relationship between God and man (forgiveness) and as a consequence

88. Bavinck, *GD* Vol. III, 327, 363–67, 372, 375–78, 382, 384–85, 391, 398–99.

89. Bavinck, *GD* Vol. III, 353–55, 370–72, 374, 378, 380, 384, 389 and 391–93.

90. Bavinck, *GD* Vol. II, 328, 335–37, 371, 374, 378–81, 383 and 388.

other relationships, too (liberation). The significance of his cross and resurrection is more than satisfaction and atonement: the benefits he acquired are juridical, mystical, ethical, moral, economical, and physical. Christ gives more than Adam lost, but brings humanity to the end of the way Adam had to go.[91]

Bavinck's emphasis on the entire Christ has another background. Christ is more than a person in the past: the entire Christ is also the glorified Christ in heaven. Bavinck's Christology is a Christology of the present Christ, resurrected and glorified. According to Bavinck, it is the same person in his two natures who is humiliated and glorified, so that he sees a bodily identity between the resurrected One and the Jesus who suffered. In his glorification, Christ received what he earned for himself in his humiliation: not his divinity, but the public glorification in which also his human nature shares and the position he received at the right hand of God as Son of God, Lord, King and Mediator. In this way he became who he is for us now: a life giving spirit, in whom all benefits of salvation are included. This glorification consists in resurrection, ascension, the new position at God's right hand and his return to judge the living and the dead.[92]

The resurrection has a clear relevance for the believers' lives. It is, as Bavinck lists it, a proof of Jesus' messiahhood, the seal of his being the Son, the divine approval of his work, the beginning of his glorification, the guarantee of forgiveness and justification, a fountain of spiritual blessings, the principle and deposit of our resurrection and finally the foundation of Christianity.[93] This list shows first that the resurrection does not add something to the earning of salvation, but has significance for our justification. This becomes clear in Bavinck's exegesis of Rom 4:25 (Christ was delivered for our sins and raised for our justification) in the *Gereformeerde Dogmatiek*: he acquired justification by his death and made us partakers by His resurrection.[94] However, Bavinck writes also in the *Dogmatiek* that in death and resurrection 'the entire body of His communion objectively has died and raised, reconciled and justified.'[95] In *Magnalia Dei*, Bavinck ties the Divine revision of the sentence on Jesus in the resurrection to our justification, referring to Rom 4:25. Our justification is the cause of his

91. Bavinck, *GD* Vol. III 320–21, 372, 384, 445–46.

92. Bavinck, *GD* Vol. III, 351, 422, 425–28, 436, 441, 472.

93. Bavinck, *GD* Vol. III, 435.

94. Bavinck, *GD* Vol. IV, 99, 200–201.

95. Bavinck, *GD* Vol. IV, 201.

resurrection. We are justified in him and with him. Nevertheless, based on Rom 5:9, 19 Bavinck maintains that Christ acquired our justification by his death and not by the resurrection.[96] It is most likely best to interpret Bavinck in the sense that the justification is caused juridically by Christ's death and mystically also by his resurrection. Second, it shows that the believers' resurrection is related to Christ's resurrection.

Bavinck sees a comparable relation between the ascension of Jesus Christ and the ascension of believers. His ascension prepares their ascension; he precedes but they will follow.[97] Further, the relevance of the glorification becomes clear in the mystical benefits: the church is raised, glorified and seated in heaven together with Christ.

After his resurrection and glorification, Christ remains active as saviour, distributing his benefits by his Holy Spirit and praying for those for whom he died.[98] Here the Reformed anti-remonstrant motive returns: the glorified Lord is no half saviour, but a real one. He does not only create the possibility of salvation, but really saves his people.[99] In line with this position Bavinck maintains particular satisfaction and renounces universalism.[100] Furthermore, Bavinck emphasises the necessity of the glorification for Christ's work. This shows the eschatological drive of Bavinck's Christology. Christ has to prepare a place for his own and to fill them with his fullness by his Holy Spirit. His work is not complete until he hands over the kingdom to the Father (cf. 1 Cor 15:24). Until then his work as mediator of salvation is not finished.[101]

Summarizing, Christ is, in his person, our salvation. Person and work cannot be separated, for in his person all his benefits are included. The metaphor of benefits makes it possible to combine a classic doctrine of satisfaction with an emphasis on the person of Christ. However, the substantialist benefit-metaphor has some disadvantages. Bavinck further stresses that the entire Christ is important for salvation. Hence more than one moment of the story of Jesus Christ is soteriologically relevant: incarnation, his entire life in (passive and active) obedience, death, resur-

96. Bavinck, *Magnalia Dei*, 415–16.

97. Bavinck, *GD* Vol. III, 437.

98. Bavinck, *GD* Vol. III, 462, 470–81; Vol. IV, 356, 408, 550, 618.

99. Bavinck, *GD* Vol. III, 463, 520; Vol. IV, 232.

100. Bavinck, *GD* Vol. III, 464–66 (and more general 450–66); Vol. IV, 5.

101. Bavinck, *GD* Vol. III, 480–81, 520.

rection and glorification. Christ remains active as mediator until he has handed over a saved people to his Father.

3.3.4 THE EXCLUSIVE AND THE INCLUSIVE MOMENT

To conclude this discussion of Bavinck's Christology, more has to be said on representation and substitution, the inclusive and the exclusive moment. It may be evident, based on the foregoing, that both moments are present in Bavinck's Christology.

The importance of the exclusive moment for Bavinck is obvious. This moment appears first as person-substitution. Jesus Christ is the *Logos*, the eternal Son of God who assumed our human nature and became a person in two natures. His person is the divine person of the Son, the second person of the Trinity, for his human nature is an impersonal human nature; his human nature has no individual personal existence apart from the *Logos*.[102] In the *Logos* the totality of humanity is represented. Jesus Christ is the head of the organism of humanity; he is guarantee and mediator of his people. He is their substitute and took their place, for according to Bavinck in the *pactum salutis* an exchange of places already occurred.[103] The resurrected and glorified Christ is, in his person, our salvation, in Him all the benefits of salvation are included objectively. The objectivity of salvation in Christ is very important for Bavinck, emphasising the *extra nos* of salvation in Christ.

Second, the exclusive moment is present as work-substitution. Central is the metaphor of acquisition and distribution of the benefits of salvation. Christ earned salvation by his active and passive obedience, fulfilling the demands of the covenant of works where Adam failed. As the church's substitute, he made satisfaction for her. Bavinck emphasises the importance of the federal-juridical over against Christologies of the nineteenth century that judged classical Christology too juridical.

The inclusive moment is present from eternity together with the exclusive moment. From the *pactum salutis* on, Christ is head of the covenant of grace. As head, he is representative and public person. The election of the church is a participation in the election of Christ. From

102. Bavinck, *GD* Vol. III, 290.

103. Bavinck, *GD* Vol. III, 520. For the concept of substitution: Bavinck often uses words like 'plaatsvervanger,' 'plaatsvervanging,' 'plaatsvervangen,' see Bavinck, *GD* Vol. III, 365, 385, 388, 390, 393, 397, 466, 520.

eternity, a mystical union exists between Christ and the church, his body. This mystical union is a precondition for the imputation of our guilt unto Christ and righteousness unto us, and hence for satisfaction, atonement and justification. During his life on earth, his suffering, death and resurrection, Christ never was alone but stood in communion with humanity, whose nature he assumed. By the mystical union, the church participated in his history, and suffered, died, was buried, resurrected and seated in heaven together with Christ. Christ was raised for our justification, which is understood by Bavinck in this sense, that Christ was raised to make us partakers of the righteousness he earned for us. His ascension is to be followed by our ascension. All benefits of salvation were realised objectively in his history and they are included in his person. To conclude, the inclusive moment is present also, related to the concepts of head and mystical union.

For Bavinck the exclusive and inclusive moment belong together, for it is clear that they are intertwined. The exclusiveness of Christ is a precondition for His inclusiveness. Bavinck judged it insufficient to see salvation in terms of religious, ethical, mystical or psychological terms alone. He tried to show that the juridical elements were not just formal, cold categories but essential: without objective and juridical dealing with sin and guilt, there would be no new life, no ethical or mystical union, no religious influence of a religious personality worth of attention. On the other hand the inclusive moment is a precondition of the exclusive moment. The *unio mystica* with Christ established in the *pactum salutis* is a precondition of imputation of guilt and righteousness, of atonement and justification.

It is important to note that Bavinck uses the concept of unio mystica to refer to two moments in my own model: the inclusive moment, for the mystical union results in death, burial, resurrection and ascension with Christ; but also the moment of union, for it is a union between head and body of an organism. This moment of union also can be found in the concept of 'mystical Christ.'

However, the moments of exclusiveness and inclusiveness being intertwined also leads to problems in Bavinck's theory of atonement.

Bavinck uses the concept of *unio mystica* in two different ways: as a precondition for imputation in the context of the *pactum salutis*, and to distinguish the inclusive moment—to which he refers with the concept of *unio mystica*—from the exclusive moment—to which he refers with words as objective, juridical, federal. As a result, he distinguishes seemingly between two different compartments in the death of Christ: a compartment of satisfaction and the purchase of the benefits of salvation, and a compartment of dying and rising with Christ. This re-occurs in his distinction between mystical benefits and objective-juridical benefits.[104] Is it necessary to distinguish a separate layer of benefits? Are we e.g. not justified in Christ and is not our right to eternal life the same as being glorified with Christ? Was the problem of e.g. Schleiermacher's Christology that he started with the mystical, or that he did not see the juridical implications of it? Bavinck was anxious that emphasis on the mystical would obscure the objective, the juridical, the extra nos, the *satisfactio vicario*. Many nineteenth-century-Christologies were deficient here, but Bavinck's attempt to solve that problem was not a good solution, separating the mystical from especially the juridical aspect of the work of Christ.

Nevertheless, what Bavinck's solution makes clear, is that the inclusive moment (the *unio mystica*) needs to be balanced by the exclusive moment, and that the risk of emphasising the *unio mystica* is that the exclusive moment is forgotten. His central motive is an important one: to maintain the foreign character of the righteousness given in Christ, the *extra nos* of salvation. According to Bavinck, no 'being in Christ' is possible without person- and work-substitution.

Summarizing, the inclusive and the exclusive moment are both present in Bavinck's Christology: representation, work-substitution and person-substitution. They are intertwined, balance each other, and even precondition each other. Furthermore the moment of union is present; remarkably the concept of *unio mystica* refers both to the inclusive moment and the moment of union. The moment of union can be found further where Bavinck uses the concept of 'mystical Christ.' Bavinck especially wants to maintain the exclusive moment over against Christologies of his nineteenth-century context, but he sees also the truth of these Christologies emphasising the *unio mystica*. As a result, he separated the inclusive and exclusive moment in his theory of atonement, as can be seen in his use of the concept of mystical union and his idea of mystical benefits. His solution is not satisfactory, but the central interest of Bavinck must not

104. Bavinck, *GD* Vol. III, 445. On page 500 Bavinck identifies mystical and ethical benefits (sanctification), distinguishing them from the objective juridical benefit of forgiveness.

be forgotten: without the exclusive moment, without work- and person-substitution no 'being in Christ' is available.

3.4 Soteriology

After Christology and its objectivity, the soteriology and its subjectivity follows. The benefits of salvation, acquired by Christ must be applied in the life of the believer. In this section I will first analyse how Bavinck uses the concept of the *unio mystica* in the soteriological context. Doing this I will also draw more general conclusions regarding this concept (3.4.1). In the following sub-section, I will investigate Bavinck's order of salvation to see how he uses different soteriological images (3.4.2). Finally, I will return to the different moments of union and participation, to see which are present and which we need for the development of a concept of 'being in Christ,' to test the hypothesis formulated in the first chapter (3.4.3).

3.4.1 MYSTICAL UNION WITH CHRIST THROUGH THE HOLY SPIRIT

Christ is our salvation, in his person, in whom all benefits of salvation are included. The mystical union with Christ precedes the remaining part of soteriology: we cannot share in Christ's benefits unless we have communion with the person of Christ himself.[105]

Bavinck makes an important remark regarding differences between the Lutheran and Calvinistic tradition as he sees them in his time, which helps us to understand Bavinck's own soteriology. According to Bavinck, the Calvinistic tradition has a theological perspective on the mystical union. Calvinists see the *unio mystica* rooted in the eternal council of God and worked out by the Holy Spirit. Lutherans however see the *unio mystica* from an anthropological angle and place it after justification and regeneration. In this tradition penance, faith and justification precede the *unio mystica*. This position has a double danger: passivity in an emphasis on the powerlessness of the sinner; synergism where attempts are made to mitigate the formed fault. In the Reformed tradition where the *unio mystica* in the *pactum salutis* precedes the *ordo salutis*, all the benefits follow this union, even faith, conversion and penance.[106] This theologi-

105. See footnote 75, 77 and 78.

106. Bavinck, *GD* Vol. III, 517–20, 522, 525; IV, 234–35. Bavinck more often judges that the Lutheran tradition has an anthropological perspective, whereas the Reformed

cal perspective determines Bavinck's way of dealing with the *ordo salutis*, as it does for Reformed orthodoxy. As the reason for his choice of this theological perspective, Bavinck gives his belief that Christ in heaven continues his work as mediator of salvation. He works as saviour, as we have seen, until he can hand over the Kingdom to the Father.[107]

This theological perspective has several implications.

First, the imputation of Christ and his benefits precede the entire order of salvation, including the gift of the Holy Spirit.[108] In the *pactum salutis* Christ is imputed to his body together with his benefits.[109] If Christ was not given to the community, the Holy Spirit, the grace of regeneration and the gift of faith—all benefits acquired by Christ—could never be received by believers, who are Christ's own.[110] Although Bavinck denies a justification from eternity, he writes that it is possible to say that justification precedes faith.[111] The imputation and gift of Christ is an act of the eternal God, as is regeneration. Justification takes place 'ideëel' in the decree already from eternity, and is realised objectively in Christ's incarnation, death and resurrection; it is the substance of the word of the gospel; it is individually applied and distributed in the *vocatio interna*, and passively accepted in regeneration.[112] Or as he writes elsewhere, justification takes place principally in the decree, virtually in the resurrection of Christ, is contained objectively in the gospel, takes place subjectively in the consciousness of the believer (which is the most important), and is settled fully at the last judgment.[113] Nonetheless, it is a juridical act, a judgment of forgiveness that is completed in one moment.[114] It is of interest to note how the terms Bavinck uses describing the union with Christ, are influenced by the Reformed doctrine of justification. We are given to Christ so that his benefits are given and imputed to the church. The *solus*

tradition has a theological one; see Vol. I, 151; Vol. II, 212–13, 317, 534. He sees the biographical differences between Luther and Calvin as its explanation, see Vol. III, 522.

107. Bavinck, *GD* Vol. III, 483. According to Bavinck, all the good of the anthropological perspective is taken up in the theological perspective, see Vol. III, 577.

108. Bavinck, *GD* Vol. III, 522.

109. Bavinck, *GD* Vol. III, 396, 598.

110. Bavinck, *GD* Vol. III, 599; Vol. IV, 100.

111. Bavinck, *GD* Vol. IV, 99; see further footnote 59.

112. Bavinck, *GD* Vol. IV, 100.

113. Bavinck, *GD* Vol. IV, 202; cf. Vol. III, 589.

114. Bavinck, *GD* Vol. IV, 233.

Christus is very clear. A movement of love, coming from God and out of which Christ is given, precedes the mystical union.

Second, the gift of the Holy Spirit is the first benefit Christ gives after his glorification.[115] The Spirit applies the benefits of salvation, acquired by Christ.[116] It is not sufficient that believers are seen to be together with Christ because of the unity in God's council and the objective realisation of this union during Jesus' lifetime: we need the gift of the Holy Spirit, who unites us with Christ and with his benefits. By the Spirit the believer is united personally with Christ in a mystical union.[117] In the Spirit, Christ comes to his own, binding them together as a body and giving them his benefits.[118] The Spirit can do this, because in resurrection and ascension he became the property of Jesus Christ, so that Christ can be identified with the Spirit as 'lifegiving Spirit.'[119] The gift of the Spirit, and the resulting mystical union with Christ, are the precondition of the gifts of other benefits.[120]

The Spirit works with Word and sacrament. The Holy Spirit connects our soul to Christ in a *unio mystica*, but for our consciousness there is no communion with Christ other than by a communion with the word of the apostles.[121] The sacraments of baptism and the Lord's Supper follow the word of the gospel. They give the communion with the whole Christ in his full richness through the Spirit.[122] Baptism is the sacrament of the incorporation, the Lord's Supper the sacrament of the growth in the communion with Christ.[123]

115. Bavinck, *GD* Vol. III, 321, 493; Vol. IV, 100, 242.

116. Bavinck, *GD* Vol. II, 244; Vol. III, 195, 206, 210, 483, 571–72, 575–76, 598; Vol. IV, 242; Bavinck, *De wetenschap der H. Godgeleerdheid*, 10.

117. Bavinck, *GD* Vol. I, 539; Vol. II, 236, 279, 288–89; Vol. III, 500; Vol. IV, 21, 65–67, 70, 235, 242, 272, 534, 533, 554; Bavinck, *Kennis en leven*, 178–82; Bavinck, *Roeping en wedergeboorte*, 25.

118. Bavinck, *GD* Vol. III, 501; Vol. IV, 21; cf. Bavinck, *De katholiciteit van christendom en kerk*, 15.

119. Bavinck, *GD* Vol. III, 294–95.

120. Bavinck, *GD* Vol. III, 521–22; Vol. IV, 100.

121. Bavinck, *GD* Vol. I, 442, 538–39; Vol. IV, 312, 497; Bavinck, *De zekerheid des geloofs*, 75. Cf in terms related to jusitification *GD* Vol. III, 520, 599; Vol. IV, 100, 202.

122. Bavinck, *GD* Vol. IV, 21, 456, 497, 510, 534, 543; Bavinck, *Kennis en* leven, 174–79.

123. Bavinck, *GD* Vol. IV, 555.

That the mystical union is itself complex, becomes evident when Bavinck tries to describe the *unio mystica*. Because it is difficult to describe the union, Bavinck refers to different images used in the New Testament to clarify what he means. He often mentions several images together: a bridegroom and bride, a vine and its branches, head and body, and a cornerstone with a building; images that recur in his ecclesiology.[124] Referring to John 6, Bavinck writes that the Lord's Supper shows what the union is: we eat the body of Christ and drink his blood. [125] Because Bavinck often uses organic thinking, images like vine and branches, head and body, nurturing, food, eating, growth, development, and life are central to him. Once Bavinck starts writing about this communion of life believers have with Christ, many different New Testament passages are quoted, among which Romans 6—8 and Gal 2:20 are important:[126] Christ lives in believers and they live in him;[127] believers are crucified, buried and resurrected with Christ.[128] Sometimes Bavinck uses the image of clothing oneself with Christ.[129] Bavinck refers to these images because the mystical union is a reality that can be hardly expressed in words.[130] The supernatural life believers receive is hidden from the world and partly also from believers themselves.

Nevertheless, Bavinck tries to say more. The union is a very close communal life, profound, spiritual, everlasting and indissoluble.[131] Christ and his community cannot be separated and are nothing without each other,

124. Bavinck, *GD* Vol. III, 462, 472 (see also 320–21 where the same images are used to refer to Christ only); Vol. IV, 70, 73, 235, 238, 240, 282 (church), 356 (church), 543, 553; Bavinck, *De wetenschap der Heilige Godgeleerdheid*, 10, 46, 49; Bavinck, *Kennis en leven*, 36, 37, 177, 220; Bavinck, *De katholiciteit van christendom en kerk*, 15, 52; Bavinck, *De offerande des lofs*, 35, 65, 66, 103, 108; Bavinck, *Roeping en wedergeboorte*, 38, 56, 170; Bavinck, *Wijsbegeerte der openbaring*, 228.

125. Bavinck, *GD* Vol. IV, 543, 552, 557; cf. 553; Bavinck, *Kennis en leven*, 174–81.

126. For references to Romans 6—8 see Bavinck, *GD* Vol. III, 321, 396, 445, 462, 501; Vol. IV, 21, 65–67, 73, 218, 234, 481, 496; to Gal 2:20 see Vol. III, 321, 396, 445, 501; Vol. IV, 21, 66, 73, 234–35, 242.

127. Bavinck, *GD* Vol. IV, 65, 73, 235.

128. Bavinck, *GD* Vol. III, 396.

129. Bavinck, *GD* Vol. IV, 66, 481.

130. Bavinck, *GD* Vol. IV, 543, 553; Bavinck, *Kennis en leven*, 177. This corresponds with the fact that the reality of faith itself and its power are wonderful, mysterious and difficult to describe. See Bavinck, *GD* Vol. I, 469, 541; Vol. IV, 66, 462.

131. Bavinck, *GD* Vol. III, 437; Vol. IV, 66, 70, 543, 553.

but Christ must fill his body more and more.[132] Conceptually however it is easier to say what it is not. The *unio* is not magical, physical, and natural. It implies no pantheistic or theosophical change.[133] It is no pantheistic mixture or identification, no overflowing of substances, no perichoretic unity as in the Trinity, and no personal unification of two natures as between the two natures of Christ.[134] It is not an immediate union, but a communion by the Holy Spirit and by faith. It is no substantive communion with God and implies no essential deification or eternalisation, although in this communion believers participate in the divine nature.[135] Nonetheless, although grace is existential ('ethisch') and not physical, it does not follow that the mystical union is merely a personal communion in will and inclination. It also includes essence and nature.[136] This becomes clear where Bavinck enters into a discussion with Ritschl and Herrmann concerning the mystical union. Where Ritschl sees the *unio mystica* as impossible or just a union in attitude and acts, Bavinck maintains that it is a real personal life-communion. The union is a *unio personarum* between the person of Christ in body and soul and the person of the believer in person and soul.[137] It is a mystical union with Christ who is in heaven but also present, not physically or limited by bread and wine or by the Word, but by his Spirit,.[138]

Bavinck's use of the concept shows that it refers to an encompassing reality. Bavinck does not distinguish between union—referring to the moment of unification with Christ, the engrafting in Christ—and communion—referring to the ongoing intimate and personal relationship with Christ. The mystical union is the ongoing communion with the entire person of Christ, the continuous presupposition of soteriology. However, two slightly different distinctions seem to be implied in his use of the concept of *unio mystica*.

First, the difference between the juridical and the mystical returns in the soteriology, together with an ambivalence comparable with the

132. Bavinck, *GD* Vol. III, 471–72.

133. Bavinck, *GD* Vol. IV, 70.

134. Bavinck, *GD* Vol. IV, 553; Bavinck, *Kennis en leven*, 177.

135. Bavinck, *GD* Vol. I, 235; Vol. II, 157, 500, 503; Vol. III, 234, 255, 289, 581–82; Vol. IV, 69.

136. Bavinck, *GD* Vol. IV, 235, 553.

137. Bavinck, *Kennis en leven*, 177, 182–83; Bavinck, 'De theologie van Albrecht Ritschl,' 378–79 ; see further Bavinck, *GD* Vol. III, 447, 460; Vol. IV, 235.

138. Bavinck, *GD* Vol. IV, 554–55.

ambivalence we saw in 3.3.2. On the one hand Bavinck emphasises that the mystical union precedes the entire order of salvation. In this sense it is the first and fundamental benefit of salvation.[139] This use of the concept is comparable with the *unio mystica* as precondition for imputation of guilt and righteousness. On the other hand, the mystical union is one of the mystical-ethical benefits. Bavinck distinguishes between the objective-juridical benefits and the mystical-ethical benefits, and draws two different lines: of forensic imputation (justification, adoption and forgiveness) and of organic renewal (regeneration and sanctification). In the second line of the organic renewal, many different New Testament metaphors are listed, all showing that believers receive new life in Christ. Within this complex the mystical union is one metaphor together with the mystical benefits of death, burial and resurrection with Christ, reciprocal inhabitation, regeneration, Christ living in believers and they in him, the end of the old creation, living in the Spirit etc. This complex is distinguished from metaphors like atonement, forgiveness, justification and adoption; the 'objective juridical benefit of forgiveness' 'is followed by the ethical and mystical benefit of sanctification.'[140] This second use of the concept has to be paralleled with Bavinck's use of the concept of mystical union in his discussion of the objective-juridical significance of the death of Christ.[141]

Second, Bavinck deals with the *unio mystica* in his doctrine of the order of salvation and in his sacramentology, especially when discussing the Lord's Supper. Bavinck wrote an article about Calvin's doctrine of the Lord's Supper. This study of Calvin has influenced him deeply, as Gleason has shown.[142] As in Calvin, the mystical union with Christ is central to Bavinck's view of the Lord's Supper. It is the Holy Spirit who makes this union possible. Although Christ is in heaven and although his true human body is not with us on earth, our hearts are taken up to Christ. As a result, we have not just communion with his Spirit and his benefits, but really with Christ himself, his flesh and his blood.[143] Here

139. Bavinck, *GD* Vol. III, 522; Vol. IV, 100, 198, 235.

140. Bavinck, *GD* Vol. III, 500.

141. Bavinck, *GD* Vol. III, 396, 445, 500–1; Vol. IV, 21, 65–66. Cf. Vol. III 520, where the mystical union follows on reconciliation, forgiveness and justification.

142. Bavinck, *Kennis en leven*, 168–83; Gleason, 'The Centrality of the *Unio Mystica*,' 264–93.

143. Bavinck, *GD* Vol. IV, 551, 553–55; Bavinck, *Kennis en leven*, 171, 174–78, 181–82.

we find the problem whether the celebration of the Lord's Supper influences the mystical union with Christ or not. On the one hand, Bavinck maintains the normal Reformed order of Word and sacrament; the Word has the primacy, the sacrament is the *appendix*. The sacrament does not give anything that the Word does not give. He even denies that in the sacrament the community with Christ is a different or higher community than the union already given in the Word. The Lord's Supper just signifies and seals a union also given in the Word.[144] On the other hand, the Lord's Supper seems to have an intensifying impact as if celebrating the Lord's Supper makes the subjective mystical union more intense. It is more than sharing in Christ's benefits; by the Spirit there is communion with Christ himself. Although this communion does not come into existence through the Lord's Supper, it is given 'illustrius,' sealed and confirmed. It is spiritual nourishment, resulting in a very close community, like that of bread and wine to the body.[145] The new spiritual life has to be nourished and maintained.[146] According to Gleason, there is 'a slight tension' in Bavinck here just as I described it. The union is an abiding reality indeed. At the same time, where both in baptism and in the Gospel we do not receive Christ totally but only partially, the Lord's Supper gives him more clearly. The participation in Christ is more than cognitive, emotive or volitional, but deeper and more intimate than man can ever imagine. The *unio* is one where growth and progression are realities. The previously established union with Christ through faith grows and is nourished.[147]

We have seen first that Bavinck uses the concept of *unio mystica*, referring to a fundamental benefit that precedes the remaining part of soteriology, but at the same time as referring to a benefit that is not really distinguishable from mystical-ethical benefits, benefits that belong only in the line of organic renewal by sharing in the life of Christ and not in the line of juridical imputation. Second, in his treatment of the Lord's Supper Bavinck writes that the sacrament gives nothing that the Word does not give, whereas he at the same time suggests that it has an

144. Bavinck, *GD* Vol. IV, 457, 543, 554; Bavinck, *Kennis en leven*, 170.

145. Bavinck, *GD* Vol. IV, 534, 542–43, 553.; H.Bavinck, *Kennis en leven*, 170–71, 174, 177–78.

146. Bavinck, *GD* Vol. IV, 73.

147. Gleason, 'The Centrality of the *Unio Mystica*,' 272–74, 277–78, 279, 292; cf. Bavinck, *Kennis en leven*, 170–71.

intensifying effect. This again shows the complexity of Bavinck's view of the *unio mystica*.

Analysing the concept of mystical union we have seen now that Bavinck uses the concept in different contexts. By 'context' I mean semantic contexts of different language fields. In Bavinck's use of the concept, three different lines of thought come together: the line of satisfaction and the acquiring of benefits (*unio* as acquired benefit), the line of personal language (*unio* as personal communion), and the line of organic language and biological concepts like engrafting, nurturing, and growth (*unio* as communion of head and body, vine and branches).

But apart from these different semantic contexts it is used also in different theological contexts. First in the context of the *pactum salutis*, where the mystical union is established. The second is the moment of the acquiring of the benefit of mystical union in the satisfaction, and the objective realisation in the life, death and resurrection of Christ. Bavinck goes further with the third context, where Christ as the glorified one applies the mystical union subjectively in the life of the believer. In the present sub-section, we saw that this third context can be divided in three sub-contexts: a. the context of the first benefit, the gift of the Holy Spirit who establishes a mystical union by the word of the gospel, a benefit which precedes the soteriology; b. the context of the organic renewal by sharing in the life of Jesus Christ; c. the context of the sacraments, especially the Lord's Supper. Apart from these soteriological contexts, we have seen already that Bavinck uses the concept of mystical union also in a more general, theological sense: the mystical union is the essence of true religion.

Seeing this complexity, the concept of mystical union can be interpreted as a story with a sequence of events; as a narrative concept. Understanding it as a narrative, especially the relationship between the theological and the Christological contexts must be explained. Maybe we could best reconstruct Bavinck as follows. Originally in creation man lived in mystical union with God, the creator. This mystical union is the essence of religion. However, by sin man lost communion with God. Nevertheless, from eternity God worked to restore this mystical union. To restore this mystical union *with God*, God gave Christ and the church to each other. This mystical union *with Christ* exists in God's eternal council from eternity and is realised objectively during the earthly lifetime of Jesus Christ. In Christ, the mystical union between mankind and *God* is restored objectively. As this mystical union *with Christ* is applied subjectively by the Holy Spirit in the life of believers, this union *with Christ* is growing existentially more and more. At the same time by the Spirit of Christ, God Himself lives in the believer again. In this way the mystical union of the believer *with God* in Christ is restored more and more subjectively.[148]

In a table:

<table>
<tr><td colspan="4">Bavinck's narrative concept of unio mystica</td></tr>
<tr><td>Union with</td><td colspan="2">Context</td><td>Event in the story</td></tr>
<tr><td>God</td><td colspan="2">Creation</td><td>Originally in creation: union with God as the essence of religion</td></tr>
<tr><td rowspan="9">Christ</td><td>Origin in Eternity</td><td>Pactum salutis</td><td>Mystical union established</td></tr>
<tr><td rowspan="5">Objectivity—Christology</td><td>Incarnation</td><td>God and man united in Jesus Christ</td></tr>
<tr><td>Death</td><td>Acquiring of mystical union, mystical benefits</td></tr>
<tr><td>Death, resurrection, glorification</td><td>Objective realisation of mystical union</td></tr>
<tr><td rowspan="2">From glorification on</td><td>Objective reality of mystical benefits in the person of Christ</td></tr>
<tr><td>Distribution of benefits</td></tr>
<tr><td rowspan="3">Subjectivity—Soteriology</td><td>Gift of the Holy Spirit</td><td>Subjective application of mystical union; first benefit of salvation</td></tr>
<tr><td>Distribution of mystical-ethical benefits</td><td>Organic renewal by sharing in the life of Jesus Christ</td></tr>
<tr><td>Lord's Supper</td><td>Sacrament gives nothing that the Word does not give, at the same time it has an intensifying effect</td></tr>
<tr><td>God</td><td colspan="2">Re-creation</td><td>Union with God restored in Christ and by the Spirit</td></tr>
</table>

148. For a comparable narrative given by a Neo-Calvinist in 1930, see Post, 'De Unio Mystica,' 23–26.

3.4.2 *ORDO SALUTIS*

After this analysis of Bavinck's use of the concept of *unio mystica* in his soteriology, I will further investigate Bavinck's order of salvation to see how he uses different soteriological images.

Bavinck's dealing with the *ordo salutis* is determined by the continuing work of Jesus Christ as glorified Lord, the work of the Spirit applying the benefits of salvation and hence the concepts of *unio mystica* and benefit, but also by organic categories like germ of new life, nurturing and growth. Before discussing some items I want to recall that we have seen that election is organic participation in the election of Christ (3.3.1).

First I want to deal with Bavinck's treatment of regeneration. Bavinck saw regeneration, with Kuyper, and in line with Reformed Scholasticism, as the infusion of a new substance, worked immediately by the Spirit and giving the ability of faith (*potentia* in Aristotelian terms; 'geloofsvermogen') in Jesus Christ. Regeneration is the implantation of a germ of new life that has to grow. Again we find organic language. The central interest of this concept of regeneration is anti-Remonstrant: the genesis of faith can not be understood with the help of rhetorical, ethical or psychological categories, for faith is a gift of the Spirit.[149] However, his solution has several problems:

a. The relation between regeneration and the Word. In Bavinck's time, the Reformed churches of the Secession of 1834 had a dispute with Kuyper and his followers. Theologians of the Secession emphasized the priority of calling for regeneration, while Kuyper saw regeneration as the infusion of a new substance, worked immediately by the Spirit. Bavinck tried to mediate in his book *Roeping en wedergeboorte*, maintaining both the objective priority of calling for regeneration, and at the same time that regeneration is a precondition of the hearing of the Word, implying that the work of the Spirit in working the germ of the new life precedes the Word. Nevertheless, this solution does not solve the problem. Further, although Bavinck says he sees the Word as the seed of regeneration, he sees the gift of this germ of new life too greatly disconnected from the word of the gospel. How the Word can be the seed of regeneration, he cannot make clear, for

149. Bavinck, *GD* Vol. IV, 24, 53, 56f, 73, 100f, 111, 610; Bavinck, *Offerande des Lofs*, 37; Bavinck, *Roeping en wedergeboorte*. See further Bremmer, *Herman Bavinck als dogmaticus*, 261–72.

stressing the need for more than rhetorical and moral persuasion he does not reflect on the impact of the content of the gospel or its rhetorical character as promise.[150]

b. The relation between regeneration, faith and Jesus Christ. It is not easy to determine when a person can be called a believer: how can one determine whether someone has made the transition from a person without faith to a person with faith? But in Bavinck this problem is doubled unnecessarily, adding another transition: when does a person make the transition from a not regenerated to a regenerated person? Bavinck is aware of the fact that in the New Testament and in John Calvin regeneration is not a fixed concept; it is the beginning of the new life as well as the moral renewal of the believer and the restoration of the whole world in her original perfection. But he still takes over from Reformed scholasticism a more fixed substantialist concept of regeneration, interpreted in terms of the metaphor of the organic: regeneration as the gift of the germ of the new life. In this way the new life of the believer is seen too much as a substance and made independent of Jesus Christ and the Holy Spirit, leading to unfruitful discussions about the timing of regeneration. This concept does not resist introspection about the question 'Am I a regenerated person or not?' apart from Jesus Christ who is our life.[151]

In this concept, regeneration becomes a substantial benefit that has lost its relational character as participation in the new life of Jesus Christ, in spite of the organic language Bavinck uses. Further, the metaphorical character of regeneration is obscured in the conceptualisation of the image as gift of a germ of life or *potentia*.

Second, I want to make a remark on dying and rising with Christ. The spiritual life, implanted in regeneration, is developed in conversion. Bavinck mentions that according to Calvin, conversion is both mortification and vivification, tying conversion to the cross and resurrection of Christ.[152] However, although he mentions Calvin's view, Bavinck himself does not use these words in his own positive discussion of conversion. Bavinck only refers to dying and rising with Christ in his discussion of

150. Bavinck, *GD* Vol. IV, 2–3, 100–101, 610; Bavinck, *Roeping en wedergeboorte*.

151. Bavinck, *GD* Vol. IV, 17–31, 40–42, 71–72; Bavinck, *Offerande des Lofs*, 37; Bavinck, *Roeping en wedergeboorte*.

152. Bavinck, *GD* Vol. IV, 133.

regeneration and baptism.[153] It seems that these mystical benefits refer especially to the beginning of the Christian life. Again we see that the position of mystical benefits remains unclear. Sometimes Bavinck speaks of the mystical-ethical benefit of sanctification, identifying mystical and ethical benefits;[154] sometimes it seems that the mystical benefits are given in regeneration; and sometimes regeneration and sanctification are ethical benefits that must be distinguished from the mystical benefits.[155] As a result, the possibility of exploring narrative relations between the history of Christ and the life of the believer is only used as far as the beginning of the Christian life is concerned. Maybe Bavinck was afraid that in doing this the distinction between objective and subjective soteriology would disappear, as he saw happen in the theology of Kaftan.[156] Because he limited the dying and rising with Christ to the beginning of the Christian life, possibilities present in the Reformed tradition are not used by Bavinck.

Third, something must be said on justification. We have seen already that according to Bavinck the righteousness of Christ is only in a certain sense an alien righteousness because of the *unio mystica* between Christ and his own (3.3.1); further that justification is an act of the eternal God in which the righteousness of Christ is given, showing a movement of love out of which Christ is given (3.4.1); and finally that Bavinck clearly distinguishes between the two different lines of forensic imputation and organic renewal (3.4.1). In discussion with Rome, Bavinck maintains justification apart from works. It is not an ethical but a juridical deed; a judgment, which implies a change in attitude towards an individual, for it really gives the righteousness of Christ.[157] This entails that we participate in the position of Christ, for justification implies also adoption as children, the gift of entitlement on eternal life and the heavenly heritage.[158]

Fourth, sanctification. Bavinck states that Christ is our sanctification. Christ does not rest before he has made us fully participate in his

153. Bavinck, *GD* Vol. IV, 21, 218, 481, 496. Gleason does not distinguish between Bavinck writing about Calvin in the historical parts and Bavinck's own position. Hence he did not see that Bavinck writes about mortification and vivification only in the context of his description of Calvin. See Gleason, 'The Centrality of the *Unio Mystica*,' 183–84.

154. Bavinck, *GD* Vol. III, 500.

155. Bavinck, *GD* Vol. III, 445.

156. Bavinck, *GD* Vol. III, 599–600.

157. Bavinck, *GD* Vol. IV, 188–91, 196–98, 202, 208–9.

158. Bavinck, *GD* Vol. III, 445; Vol. IV, 208–9.

holiness. The holiness in which believers will share rests completely ready in Christ. Sanctification is an ethical process, in which the righteousness of Christ becomes more and more the personal, ethical possession of the believer.[159] In this process of sanctification, we have to imitate Christ; not in his suffering, but in his obedience.[160] The purpose of sanctification is that believers are conformed to the likeness of the Son.[161]

Summarizing, if Jesus Christ applies the benefits of salvation by the Holy Spirit, first a germ of new life is given; a substantialist concept that has some problems, for it obscures the relation of regeneration with the Word and with Jesus Christ. In the way Bavinck uses the language of dying and rising with Christ, he relates this especially to the beginning of the existence of the believer, to regeneration and baptism. In the forensic act of justification, Christ's righteousness is imputed apart from works and, as a result, believers participate in the position of Christ. In the ethical benefit of sanctification, this righteousness of Christ becomes more and more the possession of the believer, leading to conformity to Christ.

3.4.3 UNION AND PARTICIPATION?

At the end of our discussion of Bavinck's soteriology it is now time to evaluate the hypothesis. Is it possible to develop a concept of 'being in Christ' building on Bavinck, using the concept of participation? Can we find a moment of participation in Bavinck, or do we need a moment of union?

It is evident that the moment of union is important for Bavinck, as his concept of *unio mystica* underlines. The mystical union with the person of Christ in whom our salvation is an objective reality, is fundamental for Bavinck's soteriology. This union is possible by the Word (*vocation externa* end *interna*), the Holy Spirit, regeneration and faith. Organic imagery is central to Bavinck's view of this mystical union: vine and branches, head and body, the eating of the body and the drinking of the blood of Christ in the Lord's Supper; but also other images like building and cornerstone, and husband and wife. Bavinck does not use

159. Bavinck, *GD* Vol. IV, 232–34.

160. Bavinck, *GD* Vol. III, 363; Bavinck, *Kennis en leven*, 115–45, esp. 133; see further Bolt, 'The Imitation of Christ Theme,' and Bolt, 'Christ and the law in the ethics of Herman Bavinck,' 45–73.

161. Bavinck, *GD* Vol. IV, 237.

a concept of 'being in Christ,' but if he had developed such a concept, it would probably have been similar to his concept of mystical union, hence including a moment of union.

But can we say the same concerning the moment of participation? In election, the election of believers is election in Christ, in organic participation with his election.

In his soteriology, it seems more complicated. First, his soteriology has four central moments: calling and the gift of a germ of new life (regeneration), faith and conversion, forensic imputation of the righteousness of Christ (justification) and organic growth making the righteousness of Christ the existential possession of the believer (sanctification and glorification).[162] Both the more organic line of the gift of a substance of new life and its growth, as well as the juridical line of forensic imputation do not immediately evoke associations with a moment of participation. Second, central to his soteriology is the image of benefits, acquired by Christ, present in his person, and distributed and applied in the Spirit. This imagery is important for Bavinck, for it secures the moments of work- and person-substitution and prevents a melting of objective and subjective doctrines of salvation, which Bavinck feared, as his use of the concept of mystical union in his theory of atonement indicates. This imagery of benefits also does not primarily suggest the importance of a moment of participation, for this image emphasises the difference between Christ (acquiring and distributing benefits) and believers (receiving them).

Nonetheless, the moment of participation can be found in several places of his soteriology, and it can be used to solve some problems in Bavinck's soteriology. It can be found first in Bavinck's doctrine of justification. As a result of the forensic act of justification, believers participate in the position of Christ: righteous children of God, entitled to eternal life and the heavenly heritage. Justification leads to participation in the position and identity of Christ. Second, it can be found in the organic imagery. Believers share in the supernatural life of Jesus Christ, they follow him in his obedience, and the process of sanctification leads to conformity to him. Third, Christ is given to believers as wisdom, righteousness, holiness and redemption, and these benefits that Christ embodies must become increasingly the personal possession of believers. Participation in the position of Christ, organic participation in his supernatural life and a process of growing conformity leading to the presence of the person of

162. Bavinck, *GD* Vol. III, 603.

Christ and his benefits in the person of the believer all suggest the necessity of this moment.

Different problems in Bavinck's soteriology can be solved with more emphasis on this moment. First, his concept of regeneration is too substantialist. When regeneration is understood as participation in the new life of Christ, more justice should be done to the relational character of regeneration. Furthermore the significance of the resurrection for our justification is neglected because Bavinck stresses the death of Christ as the acquiring of benefits. With the help of the moment of participation our justification can be seen more as participation in the vindication of Christ. Finally, Bavinck gives too limited an elaboration of our participation in the story of Jesus Christ: he limits the dying and rising with Christ to the beginning of the Christian life and is not clear about how he understands the mystical benefits. With the help of a concept of participation the narrative relations between the history of Jesus Christ and the life of the believer can become more elaborated. This improvement of Bavinck's position is only loyal to his theology if his fear that the exclusive moment would disappear is not forgotten. But it must be possible to do more with the moment of participation, without neglecting the moment of exclusivity.

Summarizing, the centrality of the concept of mystical union shows the importance of a moment of union for Bavinck. Without union with Christ, no participation in Christ is possible. If a concept of 'being in Christ' is to build on Bavinck, this cannot be neglected. Concerning the moment of participation, Bavinck's position is more complicated. It can be found in his theology, but he also uses concepts and metaphors (germ of life, forensic imputation, benefits) that evoke other associations. Important here is Bavinck's fear that objective Christology and subjective soteriology are fudged. However, when more place is given to the moment of participation, some problems and shortcomings in Bavinck's soteriology can be improved. Therefore a concept of 'being in Christ' can be developed containing a moment of participation and building on Bavinck, as long as the moment of exclusivity is not forgotten.

3.5 The Organic Reality of 'Being in Christ'

Until now we have investigated Bavinck's theology to see how a concept of 'being in Christ' could be developed building on his theology. In this section I want to go into the question what kind of reality this 'being in Christ' is, if Bavinck were able to answer this question. We have seen when discussing his concept of mystical union that Bavinck cautiously tries to describe it, although it is very difficult to answer this question, as this union is a mystery.[163] Further, we have seen here that Bavinck denies that the mystical union implies deification (see 3.4.1). In this section I want to go into an important concept that Bavinck uses to clarify the reality of being in Christ: the concept of organism.

The concept of organism was an important concept in the Neo-Calvinist theology of Abraham Kuyper and Herman Bavinck; Veenhof calls it a 'Schlagwort' of Neo-Calvinism.[164] For their use of organic categories different sources have been mentioned, especially in nineteenth-century German theology and philosophy. In connection with Bavinck, Veenhof mentions theologians like Bengel, Böhme, Oetinger and Beck; and philosophers like Schelling and Hegel.[165] However, in the preface of his *Het werk van den Heiligen Geest* (1888), Kuyper relates how important John Owen's pneumatology was to him.[166] Regarding the work of the Spirit in re-creation, Owen's pneumatology is structured by the image of head ('pneumachristology') and body (soteriology). This reminds one of the idea of the 'organism of new creation' or 'organism of the church' with head and body we find in Neo Calvinist organic thinking, indicating that it also has its roots in John Owen. Organic thinking was developed in opposition to modernist, individualist and mechanical thinking, supporting revolution, arbitrariness and the idea of feasibility. Characteristic features of organic thinking are biological metaphors, development, historicity, growth, self-organisation, process-character, teleology, and holism.[167] Because Bavinck's organic thinking has been investigated already, I concentrate on aspects relevant for 'being in Christ' and use the characteristics Bavinck gives himself in *Christelijke wereldbeschouwing*.[168]

163. Hielema has shown how this notion of mystery is important for Bavinck's theological method in general. As Hielema schematises Bavinck's method, step one is the assertion that the subject under discussion is characterized by mystery, see Hielema, 'Herman Bavinck's Eschatological Understanding of Redemption,' 15.

164. Veenhof, *Revelatie en inspiratie*, 250.

165. Veenhof, *Revelatie en inspiratie*, 259, 361–62.

166. A. Kuyper, *Het werk van den Heiligen Geest*, 5–18.

167. For an overview of the history of the concept of organism see Ballauf et al., 'Organismus'; Moxter, *Güterbegriff und Handlungstheorie*, 137–76.

168. Bavinck, *Christelijke wereldbeschouwing*, 50–68. See further Gleason, 'The

1. In an organism, development is teleologically structured.[169] Because creation is an organism, it has a teleological definiteness.[170] According to Hielema the organic is characterized by an eschatological teleology.[171] Here we face again the same problem of the relation between creation and re-creation as we found discussing the Christological teleology: how is the relation between the teleology of creation and of re-creation, between the work of the *Logos* in creation and in re-creation?[172] But apart from this problem, it may be clear that the organism of re-creation has a teleological, eschatological structure.

This eschatological nature of the organism of re-creation indicates that the concept of the organic refers to 'relations which have been broken by sin but reconciled through the cross of Jesus Christ.'[173] According to Bavinck, it is possible to restore relations broken by sin, because sin and grace have an ethical and not physical character. Redemption reaches as far as sin does, and a real restoration is possible.[174]

Centrality of the *Unio Mystica*,' 117–30; Hielema, 'Herman Bavinck's Eschatological Understanding of Redemption,' 59–72; Veenhof, *Revelatie en inspiratie*, 250–68; and moreover Kamphuis, *In dienst van de vrede*, 27–35, 61–65; Yoo, *Raad en daad*, 76 note 23.

169. Bavinck, *Christelijke wereldbeschouwing*, 57–58.

170. Bavinck, *Christelijke wereldbeschouwing*, 60, 67–68.

171. Hielema, 'Herman Bavinck's Eschatological Understanding of Redemption,' 62.

172. This is related to the problem of the relation between nature and grace in Bavinck's theology. See on this theme Bremmer, *Herman Bavinck als dogmaticus*, 219–27; Veenhof, *Revelatie en inspiratie*, 346–65; Veenhof, *The relationship between nature and grace*.

173. Hielema, 'Herman Bavinck's Eschatological Understanding of Redemption,' 59; cf. 62, 65.

174. Bavinck, *Gereformeerde Dogmatiek*, Vol. III, 94, 212, 583; Vol. IV, 418; Bavinck, *De katholiciteit van christendom en kerk*, especially 10–11, 29–30, 32; Bavinck, *De algemeene genade*, 46–47.; Bavinck, *Roeping en wedergeboorte*, 149; Bavinck, *Christelijke wereldbeschouwing*,. 86, 89; Bavinck, *Wijsbegeerte der openbaring*, 93–94, 197, 229–30.

Conceptually, Bavinck clarifies this position in the *Gereformeerde Dogmatiek* with the help of the scholastic thesis that sin has no substance. Sin as *privatio boni* has no substance of its owen and means no essential, only an accidental, change from the matter God created. Had there been an essential, substantial change, sin would have a substance, independent from God, the creator. Now, although the influence of sin is deep, it is not so deep that it becomes impossible to remove sin and restore the creation, which means that re-creation does not bring a new substance. What is formed can be deformed but also be reformed. See Bavinck, *GD* Vol. II, 505, 508–9, 512–14; Vol. III, 39–40, 45, 86, 106, 116, 118–20, 162, 583; Vol. IV, 68–69.

2. In an organism, development is determined by a fixed starting point: its nature, the principle and radix of all its properties and activities.[175] Concerning the reality of 'being in Christ,' this is elaborated in two ways:

a. Christ is the head of the organism of re-creation. If Christ, the head of the body, is in organic terms seen as the one who determines the body as its principle it can be understood how he is decisive for his body. He is the source of new supernatural life and of growth; the believer has to grow together with Christ in one life.[176] Re-creation here parallels creation, for it is the idea and hence the *Logos* that animates and determines the organism of creation.

Bavinck also elaborates the primacy of Christ on the body using the distinction between the juridical-objective and the ethical-subjective. Objectively salvation is reality in Christ; subjectively it has to become reality.[177] In Bavinck objective generally means 'independent of the subjective human consciousness.' Thus the thesis that salvation is an objective reality in Christ means that the reality of salvation exists before the activity of our subjectivity. Bavinck is very clear about this. Christ is the objective realisation of religion. All benefits are objectively contained in his person. He has changed the relationship between God and mankind objectively. His death had an objective meaning. The entire church is objectively crucified, dead, resurrected and glorified. Believers are objectively justified in Christ's resurrection. In short, grace is revealed objectively in Christ.[178] This objectivity must be understood first as juridical. At the cross re-creation is accomplished objectively and principally in the sphere of right.[179] So at least being in Christ as an objective reality is a juridical reality. This is understandable if we see Christ as head of the covenant, acting on behalf of its members. But at the

175. Bavinck, *Christelijke wereldbeschouwing*, 59.

176. Bavinck, *GD* Vol. III, 84, 213–14, 463; Vol. IV, 356, 618.

177. Meijers has analysed objectivity in Bavinck, but did so focussing on revelation and scripture and on the opposition between objectivity and existentiality. As far as I have seen he is not of help for an answer on the question of the reality of being in Christ. See Meijers, *Objectiviteit en existentialiteit*, 35–148.

178. Bavinck, *GD* Vol. III, 289, 327, 378, 446, 449, 462, 492, 500, 520 589; Vol. IV, 54, 99, 100, 422.

179. See Bavinck, *GD* Vol. III, 446, 450, 500.

same time it is more than juridical as the mystical benefits, the organic language, and the image of head and body indicates. However, Bavinck is not very clear about what he sees as the reference of the concept of 'mystical benefits.'

b. In the believer, re-creation starts with the gift of a new principle, a new germ of life. The Holy Spirit infuses this principle in the believer in regeneration. This principle determines the existence of the believer and has to grow out as it is the rule in the organic life: become what you are.[180]

3. In an organism, the whole precedes the parts and unity precedes diversity.[181] This is a characteristic that follows from the second. If the head determines the body, the parts of the body are determined by the body and the entire body is more than the totality of the different members. If the church constitutes together with Christ an organic whole, that is included in him, the individual believer is primarily part of a larger whole.[182] As a result, this organic reality is a collective reality. A danger in theology in the line of the Reformation is to see the believer too much as an individual standing alone, but Bavinck does not risk this individualism in his soteriology.[183] Christ is the head of the organism of the new humanity that has to grow up until it becomes mature, reaching the whole measure of the fullness of Christ. Christ is formed as head of the community; now the community has to be formed as the body of Christ. Christ, the covenant, and the organism of the new creation in Christ precede the individual.[184]

180. Bavinck, *GD* Vol. IV, 240; cf. Vol. I, 62: 'In het nu ligt wat worden zal.'

181. Bavinck, *Christelijke wereldbeschouwing*, 59–60, 62–63.

182. Bavinck, *GD* Vol. III, 462–63, 521; Vol. IV, 264, 286.

183. In his epistemology, Bavinck does risk individualism, analogous to his concept of regeneration. He uses the autopistie of Scripture to prevent this danger. See Van der Kooi, 'Het beroep op het innerlijk getuigenis van de Geest,' 256–60; Van den Belt, 'De autonomie van de mens of de autopistie van de Schrift,' 293–301.

184. Bavinck, *De wetenschap der Heilige Godgeleerdheid*, 10, 46; Regarding contemporary discussions on community and Trinity, it is important to note how Bavinck brings in the social element: this is related to the covenant. Humanity has a covenantal structure as organism with a head. This structure of humanity is an image of the Trinity; the Trinity also is a covenantal life as is seen in the *pactum salutis*. It is noteworthy that for Bavinck the image of God is not a matter of individual humans, but of humanity in general, Bavinck, *GD* Vol. II, 538–39.

4. Organic thinking respects the rich diversity of creatures and does not force individual instances in a predetermined system.[185] Within an organism, all different members receive a place and can grow and flourish, whereas the organism as a whole does not constitute a threat for the individual. According to Hielema, the organic 'describes how one reality can serve as organ of another reality while retaining its own inherent value.'[186]

   This goes together with Bavinck's emphasis on the 'personal' and 'personality.' The reality of 'being in Christ' does not threaten or destroy personal identity. Personality and character are not wiped out by regeneration, but they are sanctified.[187] In the mystical union the personalities of Christ and believers are maintained.[188] The Holy Spirit uses no coercion in regeneration.[189]

5. The development of an organism has a hidden character.[190] This is also the case with the new supernatural life that Christ gives. Bavinck often elucidates its influence with the image of the leaven that works through the dough.[191] Furthermore, it is a life given by the Holy Spirit, who blows like the wind. This spiritual life is wonderful in its essence and working. It will stay a mystery as long as

---

Note moreover that Bavinck does not bring in this collective aspect with the help of the church, for fear of making the institute of the church necessary for salvation as Roman-Catholic theology does. It is not the church that distributes grace, but it is the Holy Spirit, who applies Christ's benefits to the members of the body. For this reason he places his section on ecclesiology after his soteriology, even though he admits that a reverse order as found in some reformed theologians is possible; the organism of the church is mother of the believers. See Bavinck, *GD* Vol. III, 584–85, 598–99; Vol. IV, 313.

185. Bavinck, *Christelijke wereldbeschouwing*, 60–61, 63–64.

186. Hielema, 'Herman Bavinck's Eschatological Understanding of Redemption,' 59; cf. 65, 69.

187. Bavinck, *GD* Vol. IV, 619.

188. Bavinck, *GD* Vol. IV, 553.

189. Bavinck, *GD* Vol. III, 577.

190. Especially Hielema has emphasised this hidden character of the organic, see Hielema, 'Herman Bavinck's Eschatological Understanding of Redemption,' 59, 62–63, 65.

191. For the image of the leaven, see: Bavinck, *GD* Vol. III, 225, 491; Vol. IV, 376; Bavinck, *Kennis en leven*, 40, 47; Bavinck, *De katholiciteit van christendom en kerk*, 21, 30; Bavinck, *De zekerheid des geloofs*, 52, 102; Bavinck, *Christelijke wereldbeschouwing*,. 95; Bavinck, *Wijsbegeerte der openbaring*, 231; Bavinck, *Verzamelde opstellen*, 146–47.

the life of believers is hidden in God with Christ. It is not a human work, but a result of God's recreating acts.[192]

6. That salvation is realised in an organic way implies growth and progress, and progress implies change over a period of time. As a result, the reality of salvation is not the only reality in the life of believers. The germ of new life grows, but for re-creation is complete, sin is still a reality too, even in the life of believers. Consequently, a believer is simul iustus et peccator.[193]

7. The reality of salvation concerns the reality determined by the work of Jesus Christ and the Holy Spirit, the reality of the new creation. This is a reality that it not generally available but only for those who believe. Even then, it is only partly available because of its hidden character. Even growth of knowledge of it is a fruit of the mystical union with Christ.[194]

Summarizing, an important category to understand Bavinck's view of (in my terms) the reality of 'being in Christ' is the organic, an important concept in Neo-Calvinism with roots in German theology and philosophy, but also in John Owen. First, in organic thinking, the teleological development of re-creation is emphasised. Second, where the development of an organism is determined by the nature or *forma* of the organism, Christ determines the development of the organism of re-creation. Another distinction to make the position of Christ understandable is that between objective (juridical) and subjective (ethical). Further, the new germ of life determines the existence of the Christian. Third, as in organic thinking the whole precedes the parts, the reality of 'being in Christ' is a collective reality. But, fourth, this does not imply that organic thinking does not respect individuality. Instead, it acknowledges the factual plurality of creatures. Fifth, the development of an organism has a hidden character; so has the development of the new life in Christ. Sixth, the organic development of new life implies progress in time and incompleteness until the end. And finally, it is a reality that exists together with the reality of sin and that is available only in the perspective of 'being in Christ' itself—by faith.

192. Bavinck, *GD* Vol. IV, 65–68, 482.

193. Bavinck, *GD* Vol. III, 538, 602; Vol. IV, 175–76, 202, 209–10, 246–50, 418, 496–97.

194. Bavinck, *Kennis en leven*, 220, 234.

3.6 Conclusion

In this chapter we have investigated Bavinck's theology to see how a concept of 'being in Christ' could be developed building on his thinking. We have seen that for the Neo-Calvinist Bavinck the doctrine of creation was important, resulting in his *Logos*-doctrine and the emphasis on the Christ-Adam parallel that constitute the décor of his reflections concerning 'being in Christ.' The organism of creation is characterized by a Christological teleology.

Dealing with his Christology, we have investigated several concepts; first the concept of head. As head the Son has the central place in election, in the *pactum salutis* and in the covenant of grace. Moreover, Christ is head of the church and the organism of the new creation. Second, the concept of the mystical union has been analysed in different Christological contexts. Especially interesting was that to maintain the exclusive character of the work of Christ, Bavinck's use of the concept has some ambivalences in his doctrine of atonement. We concluded that the concept can be interpreted as a narrative with different events, recounting the everlasting union between Christ and his own, from eternity to eternity. Third, we have seen that Christ is our salvation, in his person. With the emphasis on the person of Christ Bavinck combines different conceptual lines, to which the metaphor of benefits enables him. Nevertheless, the substantial character of this metaphor has also some disadvantages. Because Christ is our salvation, in his person, also different moments of the story of his life have soteriological significance.

Also in the context of his soteriology we discussed the concept of mystical union, resulting in a reconstruction of its narrative. The mystical union with Christ is fundamental for the further application of salvation in the life of the believer, but Bavinck also uses a concept of regeneration, implying the gift of a new principle of life, substantialistically conceived, that obscures the relation with Christ and with his Word. Furthermore, we have seen that Bavinck is not very clear about what he sees as mystical benefits, and refers to dying and rising with Christ only in the context of regeneration and baptism. In justification and sanctification, believers receive a sharing in the position of Christ and a growing conformity to Christ.

Regarding a concept of 'being in Christ,' first of all Bavinck emphasises the importance of the work-substitution of Christ as its presupposition. Bavinck is anxious not to lose the exclusive character, stressing the objectivity of salvation in Christ. Apart from the moment of work-substitution, the moments of representation and person-substitution are both present, intertwined and balancing each other. However, stressing the moment of work-substitution Bavinck separated the inclusive and the exclusive moment too much as his use of the concept of mystical union in his theory of atonement shows. Furthermore, the moment of union is very important to Bavinck. A concept of 'being in Christ' building on Bavinck must give the mystical union with Christ a central place. This union is even more important than participation. Concerning the moment of participation, Bavinck's position is rather complicated. The centrality of the metaphor of benefits, the concept of regeneration and imputation suggest other ideas. However, it is clear that we participate in Christ, in his election, in his position and become more and more conformed to his likeness. And finally, using the concept of participation some shortcomings of Bavinck's soteriology can be solved. Summarizing, work-substitution is a precondition of 'being in Christ'; and in a concept of 'being in Christ' we need not only the moments of representation and participation, but also person-substitution and union.

The reality of 'being in Christ' must be characterized as an organic reality: teleological, determined by Christ and the germ of new life, social and collective but also respecting the individual personality, hidden, progressive in time and finally only available in the perspective of the participating believer.

4

CRITICAL EVALUATION OF THE REFORMED TRADITION

4.1 Introduction

In the hermeneutic movement, in which this systematic theological conversation consists, I started with the Reformed tradition; on the one hand, to utilize the treasures of the understanding of the gospel concerning 'being in Christ' present in this tradition; on the other hand, to discover problems in the tradition that have to be solved or weaknesses that hamper a reading of the New Testament to make space for a renewed understanding of this New Testament regarding 'being in Christ.' After an investigation of the theologies of John Owen, representing the Puritan part of the Reformed tradition, and of Herman Bavinck, representing Dutch Neo-Calvinism, it is time to assess its results in a critical evaluation. The character of this evaluation will not be historical, but primarily systematic in line with the position sketched in Chapter 1. I start with two important and valuable issues: the love of the Triune God as starting point of reflection on 'being in Christ' (4.2) and the centrality of the mystical union in the Reformed tradition (4.3). Next, two more critical issues will be dealt with: firstly the relation between the theological reconstruction of 'being in Christ' in the Reformed tradition and the speech acts of saying the gospel in the practice of the church (4.4); and secondly the way in which the Reformed tradition uses different images concerning 'being in Christ (4.5). Moreover I will give a first evaluation of the hypothesis concerning the two moments of a concept of 'being in Christ': representation and participation (4.6). In a next section I will deal with the question concerning the reality of 'being in Christ,' according to Owen and Bavinck (4.7). And finally I will formulate some conclusions (4.8).

4.2 God's Love as Starting Point

The love of God and the Trinitarian framework it includes is important in the theologies of Owen and Bavinck.

The eternal love of God the Father has the primacy. According to the Remonstrants, the decree to save all who would believe in Christ precedes the election of the believers.[1] Owen and Bavinck both state that neither faith in Christ nor the work of Christ determine God's love. It is not the Son who moves his Father to love us, but the Father sends his Son out of love; God's love for us cannot and must not be earned of bought. Neither Owen's nor Bavinck's their doctrine of satisfaction does imply an 'Umstimmung.' The Father himself gave his Son as high priest and sacrifice out of love for ungodly sinners. God's love does not depend on anything outside God, and the election of the believers is not caused by something else than God's love.

Owen and Bavinck differ on the relation between Christ and the believers in election; according to Bavinck, Christ and the elect are chosen together as one organism, whereas in Owen the relation between Christ and the elect is not yet established in election. But they agree on the primacy of the love of God the Father. Probably Bavinck's position would have reminded Owen too much of Arminius. Unfortunately, the Remonstrant position made it difficult for their Reformed opponents to see election really as election in Christ. The lack of Trinitarian reflection in Arminius—the work of the Son is seen in isolation from the love of the Father and the Son as *fundamentum electionis* moved his Father to

1. Graafland, *Van Calvijn tot Barth*, 95–96, 99–102, 104–5, 108; Dekker, *Rijker dan Midas*, 204–5.

love—resulted in a new Trinitarian shortage in his opponents—the election of the believers is seen in isolation from the love of the Father for his elected Son, and the Son threatens to become only *primum medium electionis*.[2] Happily after centuries it became possible again to understand election in Christ as participation of the elect in the election of Christ, as Bavinck did.[3]

It is not only the Father who is involved in God's eternal love, but also the Son and the Spirit, for God's love is a Trinitarian love. Owen and Bavinck use here the concept of the *pactum salutis*, in which the Son is appointed as head and representative of the elect as well as as their guarantee and mediator.[4] The concepts of headship and representative refer to the inclusiveness of Christ, guarantee and mediator to his exclusiveness. The roots of the mystical union with Christ can be found here, in the Trinitarian life of God, for in the *pactum salutis* this mystical union is established in principle: the elect are given to the Son.[5] The establishing of the union between Christ and the elect is crucial both for Owen and Bavinck, because in their view, firstly, no imputation of the guilt of the elect to Christ would be possible without this union. Secondly, the righteousness of Christ, the Holy Spirit, regeneration and faith can be given to the elect only because of this union. The emphasis on the justification of the ungodly and on the gift of faith in regeneration creates here a tendency towards justification from eternity. In the early works of Owen

2. In this way, God's election is not coloured from the beginning by the love of God, risking the impression of divine arbitrariness. If Gunton's analyses are correct, here the influence can be seen of the lack of Trinitarian reflection in western theology. According to Gunton, the absolute will of God to create is conceptualised individualistically in western theology, and not as the will of a Trinitarian community of love of Father, Son and Spirit. As a result, this divine will is not conceptualised from the beginning as a loving will and becomes vulnerable to the idea that God's will is arbitrary and rootless. See Gunton, *The One, the Three and the Many*, 54–55, 119–21. As an alternative, election could be conceptualised as the participation in the love of the Father for his Son. See further Douma, *Algemene genade*, 302–3.

3. Cf. Berkouwer, *De verkiezing Gods*, 150–99; Douma, *Algemene genade*, 302–4; Trimp, *Tot een levendige troost zijns volks*, 115–17.

4. See for an evaluation of the doctrine of the *pactum salutis* Loonstra, *Verkiezing—verzoening—verbond*.

5. The appeal to John 10:29 and 17:2, 6, 11, 24 is decisive here for Owen and Bavinck. In this light it is remarkable that discussions on the Reformed doctrine of predestination often concentrate on Paul (Romans 9—11; Eph 1:4). Reading the Pauline letters, one would never develop a position as we find it in the Canons of Dordt. The gospel of John is necessary to understand the genesis of this document.

this justification from eternity can be found, the later Owen and Bavinck focus on justification by faith alone, rejecting speculations about justification from eternity.

For the development of a concept of 'being in Christ' it seems vital not to give up this starting point in the Trinitarian love of God. God is love in himself. It is not something outside God that moves him to love and justify the ungodly. Instead, the love of the Father for the Son in the Spirit is the source of his love for us, as it is expressed in election, the gift of atonement, and union with Christ.

4.3 Centrality of Mystical Union with Christ

What I hold as valuable in Owen and Bavinck as Christocentric theologians is the centrality of the mystical union with Christ in their theologies. The believers are united with the person of Christ. According to Owen and Bavinck, this does not imply a union with the divine nature. This union has a creational character.

According to both, the mystical union has a history, and consequently their concepts of mystical union can be interpreted as narrative concepts. We have seen in 4.2 that this story starts with the love of God and in God's eternity, especially in the covenant of the mediator.

Its second part concerns the history of Jesus Christ. This history is soteriologically significant for 'being in Christ,' because Christ is the second and last Adam, public person, head and representative of humanity. Firstly, this significance concerns the incarnation and the human life of Christ. Here Owen is especially important because of his 'pneumachristology.' It is important that as a result of the incarnation God and man are united again (as Bavinck emphasises), but moreover that in Christ the head of the organism of the new creation is formed, a precondition of the formation of its body. Owen and Bavinck furthermore both stress the soteriological importance of the active obedience of Christ during his lifetime. Secondly, its significance concerns his death understood as making atonement by satisfaction. Here the mystical union guarantees that Christ really dies for the believers, in line with the particularity of atonement.[6] Thirdly, the resurrection and glorification of Jesus Christ guarantee the resurrection and glorification of the believers. However,

6. Again the gospel of John plays a crucial role (John 10:27, 28).

although neither restricts the soteriological significance of the history of Jesus Christ to his death, still his sacrificial death is the central moment in their soteriologies.

The third part of the story concerns the life of the believers. Both Owen and Bavinck emphasise that Christ is not a half saviour, but that he really saves his own. He does not create the possibility of salvation, leaving it to the decision of the believers whether this possibility is realised or not, but continues his work as saviour in heaven for his people he died for, until he can hand over the kingdom to his Father. In line with this anti-Remonstrant emphasis the mystical union with Christ is fundamental to redemption. By the Holy Spirit the elect are united with Christ and only as a result of this union can the members of the body of the new creation grow and mature, until full conformity to Christ is reached.

Calvin's emphasis was on the mystical union with Christ as fundamental for salvation. This mystical union is central to the Lord's Supper.[7] The seventeenth century Puritans emphasised furthermore the communion with Christ, a devotion to the person of Christ which was very attentive to its emotional and affective aspects. At the same time, because of the stress on regeneration and visible saints the Lord's Supper became less central to their spirituality.[8] In Calvin the emphasis is more on faith, in the Puritans the emphasis on love, which we find in Bernard of Clairvaux, is taken up.[9] Owen obviously was a seventeenth century Puritan with the attention he paid to communion with Christ characteristic of them. Bavinck is more in line with Calvin, focussing on the mystical union and not on communion with Christ, although he—like Calvin—sees the mystical union with Christ as the centre of the Lord's Supper.[10]

7. Baars, *Om Gods verhevenheid en zijn nabijheid*, 405–7, 436–37; Kolfhaus, *Christusgemeinschaft bei Calvin*, 24–85, 116–22; Van 't Spijker, *Gemeenschap met Christus*, 59–63; Tamburello, *Union with Christ*, 84–93; Wallace, *Calvin's Doctrine of the Christian Life*, 14–27; Won, *Communion with Christ*, 14–19, 43–68.

8. De Vries, *"Die mij heeft liefgehad,"* 387–88; Won, *Communion with Christ*, 313–20, 326–31.

9. Tamburello, *Union with Christ*, 85; Won, *Communion with Christ*, 25–29, 313–19, 331–44.

10. Remarkably the Puritans reflected on the communion with Christ outside the context of the Lord's Supper, whereas Calvin (and Bavinck) did not reflect on communion, althought the union with Christ in the Lord's Supper was very important to them. Cf. Won, *Communion with Christ*, 319–20.

Owen and Bavinck both favour organic images to refer to the mystical union with Christ. Owen's pneumatology (as far as re-creation is concerned) is structured by the image of head and body, but he also refers often to the image of vine and branches. In Bavinck organic thinking stimulated the use of these images. Further for Owen the image of husband and wife was essential, stimulated by his reading of the Song of Songs that was so important for reflection on communion with Christ. Another image that is mentioned by both is a building (or a temple) with a cornerstone. Remarkably an image that we still find in Calvin is forgotten by Owen and only mentioned by Bavinck apart from the list of images for the mystical union: the image of clothing oneself with Christ.[11]

To conclude, this central emphasis on the mystical union shows that a concept of 'being in Christ' can build well on the Reformed tradition. For the Reformed tradition the effectiveness of the work of Christ as real saviour is tied indissolubly to the mystical union with him. A concept of 'being in Christ' could very well contain narrative elements, for the union itself has a narrative structure. Moreover many moments of the history of Jesus Christ are soteriologically important, and not just his death. Furthermore, the continuing effect (growth) of the union in the life of the believer has narrative implications. Finally, the Reformed tradition contains important images for communion with Christ, among which organic images (head-body and vine-branches) but also other images (husband-wife), some of which are somewhat neglected (house-cornerstone, clothing).

4.4 Speech Act and Theoretical Theology

Despite the valuable starting point of God's electing love and the centrality of the mystical union with Christ, problems have been risen in the Reformed tradition, as can be seen in Owen and Bavinck. Especially stimulated by opponents, Reformed theologians continued reflecting on election and related themes.[12] At several points this leads to theoretical reconstructions of God's acts that could easily undermine the practice of the proclamation of the Gospel and the perspective of the participating believer. This concerns questions like: has the covenant to be divided in

11. See e.g. Calvin, *Institutes of the Christian Religion*, Philadelphia, Book III, 1, 537, 541.

12. Graafland, *Van Calvijn tot Barth*, 593–95.

an internal and external covenant, is God's promise really to be trusted, what is the significance of baptism, how to attain assurance of faith?[13] As far as 'being in Christ' is concerned, the following three problems are important, related to the three parts of the story:

a. Both Owen and Bavinck saw a close relation between the covenant of the mediator and the covenant of grace. Christ is head of the elect and head of the covenant of grace. As a result, election and covenant are closely tied together. Its positive and intended effect is the stress on the solidness of the covenant, as can be seen in its testament-character. The conceptual price of this solution is that election becomes central, which can undermine the free offer of salvation.[14] Although Owen teaches a free offer of grace and Bavinck stresses the centrality of calling, conceptually election dominates.
b. Owen and Bavinck, following the Canons of Dordt, want to prevent the unity of the work of Christ (in his sacrifice and his intercession in heaven) and of the work of God (in Christ and in the Spirit) from breaking. This leads to the thesis that the sacrifice of Christ only becomes effective for the elect; Christ dies for his own to save them. But how does someone know that Christ really died for him? Is it possible to maintain the particularity of atonement without undermining the universality of the call and promise of the gospel?[15]
c. The concept of regeneration Owen and Bavinck use has no intrinsical relation to Christ and to the word, and differs from the concept used by Calvin, Beza and Perkins who understood regeneration as effectual calling, implying an essential relation to the word of the gospel understood as calling.[16] As a result, the work of God in the sinner is emphasised; God even gives the ability of faith. Further it is made clear that a real ontological change has been made in regeneration. The conceptual price is that the shift from unbelief to belief is doubled, for it is accompanied by the shift from the old

13. Cf. Trimp, *Tot een levendige troost zijns volks*, 154–62.

14. Cf. Van Genderen, *Covenant and election*, 1–37; Graafland, *Van Calvijn tot Barth*, 601–2; Veenhof, *Prediking en uitverkiezing*.

15. Cf. Boersma, *Violence, Hospitality and the Cross*, 53–73; Douty, *Did Christ Die Only for the Elect?*; Graafland, *Van Calvijn tot Barth*, 601; Kennedy, *Union with Christ and the Extend of the Atonement in Calvin*; Thomas, *The Extent of the Atonement*.

16. See on the use of the image of regeneration 4.5.

> life to the gift and resulting presence of a new principle of life. This new principle of life is the presupposition of the shift from unbelief to belief. Hence the emphasis lies on the immediate work of the Holy Spirit, whereas the sinner is not directed to the word of the gospel—passively waiting or uncertain whether the gospel will be given to him of not.

What happens in fact is that the effective character of the speech act of the promise of the gospel in which Christ is offered as Christ *pro nobis*, and which the Holy Spirit uses, is forgotten. More and more a theoretical reconstruction is given of the work of the eternal God in the ungodly, abstracting from the concrete speech acts of the saying of the gospel and of doxology. The communicative character of the mystical union, promising, inviting, giving, is at least partly replaced by theological concept of a mystical union active from the *pactum salutis* on. The emphasis on the work of God leads to a neglect of the rhetorical aspect of the gospel, which risks a change into a mere description of the work of God. Significant expressions that semantically relate Christ and the contemporary person are translated into theoretical, theological concepts. In this light it is significant that, whereas for Luther the *promissio* was the central category, the Reformed tradition dealing with salvation speaks from 'calling'—the promising, inviting, giving character has been lost at least at terminological level.[17]

The tradition of the Dutch Secession of 1834 has, through ongoing struggle over the place of election in the preaching of the gospel, emphasised the importance of calling, shifting to a more experiential level.[18] Abraham Kuyper however reintroduced the theoretical heritage of the Reformed tradition. In the 'Liberation' of 1944 again the solidness of the promise given in baptism was emphasised.[19] Starting with baptism, an attempt was made to shift from a theoretical perspective to a perspective of the participant. C. Trimp, building on Luther, made important steps here,

17. In this light it is a question whether Bavinck's interpretation of the difference between Lutheran and Calvinist theology as anthropological and theological is right. Maybe this difference is the difference between two theological perspectives, a perspective starting with the *promissio* and a perspective with a greater theoretical interest. Cf. also Berkouwer, *Geloof en rechtvaardiging*, 55.

18. See on this development Veenhof, *Prediking en uitverkiezing*; Faber, *American Secession theologians on covenant and baptisms*.

19. See Kamphuis, *Een eeuwig verbond.*

emphasising the promise-character of the gospel.[20] Further, the relation between election and covenant was loosened, denying that Christ is head of the covenant.[21] In the Dutch Christian Reformed Church a comparable development took place in discussion with G.H. Kersten, minister in the *Gereformeerde Gemeenten.*[22]

These developments remind one of the importance of the perspective of the participating believer. The saying of the gospel and the doxology in the practice of the church have to be stimulated by theology, not undermined. Therefore especially the speech acts of the New Testament, documenting the original saying of the gospel, have to be investigated, to see what the church has to say. In the light of these speech acts also the relation between Christ and the believers from eternity, the significance and effectiveness of the death of Christ, and the gift of faith have to be rethought.

4.5 Use of Images

Due to theological history, some New Testament images have become central to Reformed tradition, others not. The selection of images is determined by theological interests and the selected images are often used as theological concepts, leading to a loss of their metaphorical (and less determined) character

This is the case with images referring to the mystical union with Christ. In particular, images that fit within an organic thought-pattern are used often: head and body, vine and branches. Especially, 'head' is used also as an important concept with the sense of representative, public person. The image of husband and wife is further used often by Owen, stimulated by his use of the Song of Songs. But the images of clothing, and building with cornerstone are neglected.

Regarding soteriological images, especially justification, sanctification and regeneration have become important as central concepts. The image of justification is used as a concept referring to the gift of a new identity and a restored relation with God; the image of regeneration becomes a concept referring to the gift of a new being; and the image of

20. Trimp, *Klank en weerklank*, 52–64.

21. Kamphuis, *Een eeuwig verbond*, 84–89.

22. Van Genderen, Velema, *Beknopte Gereformeerde Dogmatiek*, 506–9; Van der Schuit, *Het verbond der verlossing*.

sanctification refers as concept to the process of renewal that follows on regeneration.

However, these combinations of images with theological concepts evoke some questions. Firstly, these questions concern the use of the image of justification. What is justification if it does not result in righteous acts?[23] Why should the image of justification by faith not include a righteous life? What does justification consist in as long as the effects of the unrighteous act are still visible? Is justification possible without a complete re-creation? It is a possibility that the separation of the justified status and righteous acting is stimulated by a voluntaristic climate, which it self may have perpetuated. With voluntaristic climate I mean a way of thinking, in which the divine or human (moral) will has become isolated from reason or being, and the spheres of justice and ontology split further and further apart. Especially in Owen's theology the line of forensic imputation (*actus*-obedience) is separated from our being (and resulting acts). It is clear that this separation of the two lines of forensic imputation (*actus*-obedience) and organic participation (*habitus*-being) is determined by theological interests.[24] However, is it also possible to justify this separation in reference to the New Testament? As a result of this separation, Owen and Bavinck see no relation between justification and participation. But does this correspond to the use of the image of justification in the New Testament? Furthermore, evidently it is said in the New Testament that the believer *is* justified. But it is also said that the believer *is* sanctified. Why has the gift of a new identity and the restored relation to be expressed in juridical terms and not in e.g. cultic terms, whereas the process of renewal is expressed in juridical terms instead of cultic terms (you are sanctified—you are being justified)? Is it really necessary

23. If the justifying judgment is effective, this judgment not only implies forgiveness and restoration of the relation with God, but also re-creation and renewal. In Martin Luther's theology, the justifying word is effective, effecting what came to be called regeneration and sanctification; see Luther, *Tractatus de libertate christiana*, 51, 53–56, 61–62, 65–66; Peters, *Rechtfertigung*, 39, 59; cf. Jüngel, *Das Evangelium von der Rechtfertigung des Gottlosen als Zentrum des christlichen Glaubens*, 180, 182. Berkouwer wants to maintain the declarative character of justification, which guarantees the *extra nos* of salvation, but resists the idea that justification by faith and acts of faith are opposed or should exclude each other; see Berkouwer, *Geloof en rechtvaardiging*, 75–78, 91–94, 98, 100, 106–11.

24. Cf. Schaede, *Stellvertretung*, 542. See on the two lines (a line of justification and a line of regeneration) further McCormack, 'What's at Stake in the Current Debates over Justification?', 84–106.

to relate the images of justification and sanctification with the theological concepts as has happened in the history of theology?

The position the image of justification received as a central concept has to be understood against the background of medieval theology and spirituality. Within medieval spirituality the sacrament of penance played a central role. Penance is a sacrament that evokes problems with a forensic character, related to introspection, satisfaction, contrition, and reconciliation.[25] In connection with this sacrament, and especially for the doctrine of justification, ambiguities occurred., e.g. in the theology of Gabriel Biel.[26] Hence it was in the sphere of right that the saving word was necessary: 'You are righteous' as effective judgment in the present tense which creates a new reality.[27] Further, this context made it impossible for the Reformed tradition to say things about justification as a process, the not yet-character of justification, or about justification as participation in Christ. This would all seem to give room again to self-righteousness. It was exactly a part of the problem that in penance the believer participated in the satisfaction made by Christ.[28]

However, we have lost this late medieval background, and are confronted with new questions, related to nihilism and voluntarism, or to the relation between atonement with God and reconciliation between human beings.[29] Therefore, it is good to investigate again how the image of justification is used in the New Testament and how it is related to participation in Christ. In this way we will be able to distinguish better the imagery as used in the New Testament and the concept it comes to be related to (the gift of a new identity and a restored relation with God).

Still, the image of justification is an important image, related to central concerns: salvation has a forensic aspect, God's judgment saves, and God justifies the ungodly. Many problems attend the idea of a justification from eternity as Owen defended it in his early years, but it is a Reformed

25. See on penance, its place and development during the Middle Ages: Angenendt, *Geschichte der Religiosität im Mittelalter*, 35, 39, 626–58; Pelikan, *The Christian Tradition*, Vol. 1, 147, 330; Vol. 3, 32, 143; Vol. 4, 95, 129–38; Vol. 5, 51–52.

26. Oberman, *Spätscholastik und Reformation. Bd.* 1, 139–75, esp. 167; Pelikan, *The Christian Tradition*, Vol. IV, 145–46, 253.

27. Cf. Bayer, *Promissio*; Bayer, *Martin Luthers Theologie*, 46–53.

28. Cf. Angenendt, *Geschichte der Religiosität im Mittelalter*, 647.

29. See e.g. Boersma, *Violence, Hospitality and the Cross*; Volf, *Exclusion & Embrace.*

attempt to remain loyal to the discovery of the Reformation: God's judgment saves in Christ.

The image of regeneration also came into use as a theological concept, due to the discussion with the Remonstrants. As a concept it referred to the beginning of the new life of the believer. Subsequently, it lost its metaphorical character. Further the concept threatens to become substantiated as a habit, which obscures the relation to Christ.[30] This substantialist understanding of salvation was more dangerous in a Reformed context, in which the relation with God was central, than in a Roman-Catholic context, which focused on the sacraments.[31] Consequently, the use of this metaphor and its relation to 'being in Christ' has to be investigated also, to distinguish the use of the metaphor of regeneration as concept in the Reformed tradition from its use in the New Testament.

In the Reformed tradition, New Testament images like justification and regeneration were used as theological concepts in soteriology. Consequently, a discussion within this tradition about images in the New Testament is at the same time a discussion about concepts, and the New Testaments is easily read with dogmatic spectacles. In the order of salvation the only images to recur are those used as theological concept; other images are forgotten. In the case of the image of adoption both possibilities are realised: in Owen's theology it becomes a theological concept and a distinct moment in soteriology, in Bavinck's theology the image is not conceptualised and receives almost no separate attention.

Apart from images for union with Christ and soteriological images, Paul in particular relates the story of Jesus Christ to the story of the believers (dying and rising with Christ). Owen and Bavinck give these relations between two lives a place in their theologies only to a meagre extent.[32] Firstly, both Owen and Bavinck let their interpretation of these narrative relations be determined by their concept of regeneration as the gift of a

30. *Acta of Handelingen der Nationale Synode* 1618 *en* 1619, 469–532 768–846; Berkouwer, *Geloof en heiliging*, 67–99; Graafland, *Van Calvijn tot Barth*, 63–66, 73; Van Ruler, *De vervulling van de wet*, 205–6, 210–21; Toon, *Born Again*, 89–107, 118–48.

Berkouwer wants to maintain the relation to Christ and emphasises the radicality of the renewal of the sinner, while preventing an isolation of the beginning of sanctification as a distinct habit.

31. Graafland, *Gereformeerden op zoek naar God*, 162–63.

32. A table of the English Puritan William Perkins (1558–1602) shows that they could have done otherwise. In this table all relations between the life of Jesus Christ and the life of the believer are explored; see Graafland, *Van Calvijn tot Barth*, 73.

new principle of life. Secondly, such narrative relations are never set out in the context of the doctrine of justification. Again we see the influence of the separation of justification and participation—but is this separation justified? Thirdly, Bavinck conceptualises these narrative relations as mystical benefits. However, these mystical benefits remain vague, due to his emphasis on objectivity. Fourthly, the relation between the suffering of Christ and our suffering as we find it in the New Testament can only to some extent be found in Owen and Bavinck, because they see his suffering specifically in relation to satisfaction.[33] Nevertheless, for a concept of 'being in Christ' this participation in the story of Christ could be very important. As a result, it is necessary to investigate these relations anew.

To conclude, if theology (at least partly) can be understood as a grammar of the use of e.g. soteriological images, theology has to be conscious of what happens when images are used as theological concepts, and when as a result some images are privileged over others. It must not stimulate the use of dogmatic spectacles when reading the Bible. Instead, theology has to clarify the use of images in the Bible and prove itself in reading. Therefore it is good to regain the metaphorical character of several images that came to be used as theological concepts. Further, neglected images deserve to be given more attention. Thus it is important to investigate anew the use of several images and especially the relation between these images and 'being in Christ.' This concerns images for union with Christ (organic images, but also other images), soteriological images (justification, regeneration and sanctification, but also adoption etc.) and narrative relations between the history of Jesus Christ and the biography of the believers.

4.6 'Being in Christ': Two Moments?

Important in this investigation is the question whether it is possible to develop a concept of 'being in Christ' in continuity with the Reformed tradition, using the concepts of 'representation' and 'participation.' Do these two concepts suffice, or do we also need the moments of substitution (understood person- and/or work-substitution) and union—as far as the Reformed tradition, exemplified in Owen and Bavinck, is concerned (cf. 1.2.6)?

33. Cf. Calvin, *Institutes of the Christian Religion*, Book III, 8; Douma, *Grondslagen christelijke ethiek*, 191–93; Harmannij, *Jezus leed wat wij nu lijden*, 111–14.

Firstly, I start with the Christological concepts. Concerning work-substitution, this concept is necessary for 'being in Christ,' but only as its precondition. Work-substitution made 'being in Christ' possible, but it is characteristic of work-substitution that this moment refers to the exclusive work of Christ. It refers to something Christ did for the believers, but in which the believers were not participating actively. However, without this exclusive work of Christ no believer would ever be in Christ.

The moment of inclusiveness is clearly present. Christ is the second and last Adam, head and representative, public person.[34] He represents and includes the new humanity, i.e. the church, the elect, the believers. Further, Christ is the head of the organism of new creation, of which the church is the body. This relation of inclusiveness may be present already in election (Bavinck) or only since the covenant of the mediator (Owen), nevertheless the source of the inclusiveness of Christ is in God's eternal council. This does not mean that the historical life of Jesus Christ was superfluous, for in his life the head of the new creation was formed (Owen's 'pneumachristology') and the mystical union was realised objectively (Bavinck). His human life has an inclusive quality. The same is the case with his resurrection and glorification, for these events show the destiny of the persons he includes. So far as atonement and justification are concerned, Owen and Bavinck see inclusiveness regarding imputation of guilt and righteousness, and the gift of faith, but not regarding satisfaction (work-substitution). This inclusive moment cannot be separated from the reverse side of the one coin: person-substitution. We have seen that in Bavinck, as well as in Owen, representation and person-substitution are intertwined and balance each other. As the representative, Christ is unique. And he can only be our representative, because he is unique, God and man in one person. To be in Christ is to be in the person who is exclusive in his inclusiveness.

Secondly, something has to be said about the soteriological concepts. The moment of union is important to the theologies of both Owen and Bavinck. Their concept of *unio mystica* refers partly to the inclusiveness of Christ (as far as imputation is concerned), partly to a moment of union. Without union with Christ no salvation is possible, no new life is given. The organic images clarify this well: a body cannot live without a head, as

34. According to Loonstra, the concept of representative has to be preferred to the concept of head. The concept of representative implies a relation to the history of salvation and to Israel; see Loonstra, *Verkiezing—verzoening—verbond*, 296–97.

is also the case with a branch and a vine. Owen makes a distinction that Bavinck does not make between union and communion, referring to the image of husband and wife. Both agree that union (communion) with Christ is the presupposition of the further order of salvation. To be in Christ is to be mystically united with Christ.

The concept of participation is less evidently present in Owen and Bavinck. Because of the emphasis on the once and for all character of satisfaction, justification cannot be seen as participation but as imputation. Because of the emphasis on the divine work of salvation, regeneration is seen as the gift of a new life principle. The soteriological images are at first sight more used in a way that excludes participation and those images that exclude it receive the primacy. The medieval background makes this especially understandable: participation would imply self-justification. However, in the organic line of thought participation is present. Further, maybe the concept of participation can be used to solve some problems and to reinforce the Reformed position, e.g. concerning the problem of 'mystical benefits' in Bavinck, and the separation of forensic imputation and organic participation. Understanding 'to be in Christ' as 'to participate in Christ' therefore implies an apposition of the Reformed tradition, but if the exclusiveness of the work of Christ is not undermined it might imply an improvement. [35]

Summarizing, building on the Reformed tradition, to be in Christ without work-substitution must be regarded as impossible. However, work-substitution is a presupposition of being in Christ, not a moment of the concept itself. Person-substitution and representation are both necessary, for to be in Christ is to be in the person who is exclusive in his inclusiveness. In addition to the original hypothesis, a moment of union has to receive a place in a concept of 'being in Christ.' Finally, understanding 'being in Christ' as participation in Christ implies partly an alteration but—as yet has to be investigated—also an improvement of the Reformed tradition.

35. If Trevor Hart is right, reasons for this improvement can be found in the theology of Calvin, one of the founders of the Reformed tradition. See Hart, 'Humankind in Christ and Christ in Humankind,' 67–84.

4.7 Reality of 'Being in Christ'

Concerning the reality of 'being in Christ,' the following can be said, based on Owen and Bavinck.

a. It is a reality determined by Christ, by his person and his work. In his life, he became, in his person, our salvation. His sacrificial death paved the way towards this new reality in Christ. Resurrected and glorified, he is the beginning of the new creation, the head of the organism of the church. As head or as vine, he is the source of new supernatural life. Further, Owen stresses the work of Christ as high priest in heaven. Bavinck moreover emphasises the objectivity and forensic character of its reality in Christ. It will be worth trying to express the ontological implications of the heavenly presence of Jesus Christ for the earthly believers in contemporary categories.

b. Believers participate in this reality by the Holy Spirit, who unites them mystically with Christ. This mystical union is difficult to describe, but it nevertheless results in a ontological new beginning in the believer. A new principle of life is given. Therefore, 'being in Christ' has ontological implications, for it implies an ontological change. This idea of regeneration results in some problems as we have seen. Therefore, the challenge is to rethink this reality as less substantive or separate from Christ, and more in relation to Jesus Christ and to the word.

c. This reality is only partly available and knowable for those who believe. A participant's perspective is required to experience its reality. As a consequence, it has a hidden and secret character, even to the believers, for ultimately it is a reality hidden in God. Nevertheless, according to Owen, it has to become visible now already. Central to Owen's ecclesiology are the 'visible saints': a renewed sinner must become visible by his different confession and life.

d. Bavinck and Owen do not agree on the question whether it concerns primarily an individual or a collective, social reality. For Owen, the concept of habit given to the individual is decisive. As a result it is primarily an individual reality. Bavinck does not deny this individual character, but due to his organic thinking he emphasises its collective and social character. The images for union with Christ can also be used as images for the church. Consequently, it is an open question whether 'being in Christ' is an individual or a social reality.

e. The new being in Christ is involved in a process of maturation and growth. Until the resurrection of the dead, it will be imperfect and defective. The believers are being sanctified and sin still lives within them. Where Owen and Bavinck agree to this point, they disagree on the problem whether the qualification *simul justus et peccator* applies to a believer. According to Owen, this is not the case, according to Bavinck it is. But the question is whether this shibboleth is more than a difference in language (and resulting spirituality). Does it really imply a difference at an ontological level?

f. The final end of the process of sanctification is a restoration of the original creation, of the original image of God as Owen especially emphasises. However, it is more, for Christ gives more than Adam lost. Human nature will be glorified and become partaker of the divine nature without losing its created human finite character. Therefore both Owen and Bavinck reject the idea of deification.

To conclude, Owen and Bavinck agree on many aspects of the reality of 'being in Christ': it is a reality determined by Christ and by the Spirit who gives a new principle of life resulting in an ontological new beginning; it is a hidden reality which even the believers can comprehend only in part; and it is involved in a process of growth until, in resurrection and glorification, conformity to Christ is given. Owen and Bavinck differ on the question whether it concerns an individual reality as Owen thinks, based on the centrality of the concept of habit, or, without denying the individual aspect, that it concerns more a collective and social reality, as Bavinck affirms. Owen especially emphasises that it must become a visible reality, corresponding with his denial that the believer is *simul justus et peccator*. The main challenge is to rethink the reality of 'being in Christ' without a substantialist principle of new life, but in relation to the word of the gospel and to Jesus Christ.

4.8 Conclusion

As a first result of this conversation, some conclusions can be formulated. It seems vital not to give up the starting point of Reformed theology in the love of the Triune God. Furthermore, the centrality of the mystical union remains important. Where the Reformed tradition, reflecting on the mystical union, risks giving a theoretical reconstruction of the acts of God that undermines the proclamation of the gospel, it is important to develop a concept of 'being in Christ' that respects and even stimulates the speech acts of the church in the saying of the gospel and in doxology. Because theology can be conceived of as grammar all the images that might be relevant to 'being in Christ' must be investigated anew, focussing on their relationship to 'being in Christ,' without giving some the primacy in advance. This concerns especially the images of justification and regeneration in their relation to 'being in Christ.' Moreover some images and the narrative relations between the life of Christ and of the believer need to be rehabilitated. For a concept of 'being in Christ' to be developed in line with the Reformed tradition the following moments are important in ordering the diversity of images: representation and person-substitution as reverse sides of the one coin, and union. The moment of participation is less evidently present. Using it would not only imply an apposition but hopefully also an improvement of Reformed theology. Finally, concerning the reality of 'being in Christ' many valuable elements have been found. However, we need to try to rethink the reality of 'being in Christ' as more relational without a substantialist concept of regeneration.

5

PAUL

PARTICIPATION IN THE STORY OF CHRIST

UNTIL NOW I HAVE assumed that the concepts of representation and participation give good access to theological reflection on the theme of 'Being in Christ.' But the important question is whether this assumption fits with the canonical scriptures of the New Testament. The apostles Paul and John are the most important sources for in Christ-language, both with a decisive voice in this investigation. In this second part we turn to Pauline and Johannine literature, starting in this chapter with an analysis of the Pauline texts. The aim is to give a biblical-theological reconstruction of a Pauline perspective on 'being in Christ' (see further 1.2.3).

5.1 Introduction

The Jew Paul of Tarsus was the last of the apostles of Jesus Christ, 'abnormally born' when Christ appeared to him in the outskirts of Damascus.[1]

1. For general introduction on Paul, see: Becker, *Paulus*; Beker, *The Triumph of God*; Van Bruggen, *Paulus*; Dunn, *The Theology of Paul the Apostle*; Gnilka, *Paulus von Tarsus*;

Converted from a persecutor of Christians to a missionary of Jesus Christ, he travelled around in the Greek-Roman world, spreading the good news of the resurrection of Jesus Christ. As a missionary, he kept in contact with local churches by writing them letters.

In these letters, the gospel of Jesus Christ is unfolded and defended in the face of threats from Jewish or Hellenistic camps. Paul was a creative writer, reacting to his readers and their problems. As a result, each letter highlights its own aspects of the salvation in Christ or voices similar aspects in a particular way as it fits best within that specific letter.

In this chapter I concentrate on six letters (although I will also refer to the other letters). They constitute three pairs of letters in which Paul deals with similar themes. To list them chronologically: 1 and 2 Corinthians, Galatians and Romans, Colossians and Ephesians.[2]

In the Corinthian correspondence, Paul defends the foolishness and weakness of the cross and his own person against Hellenistic and Jewish wisdom. Christ as our wisdom is to be preferred to that wisdom. Because this implies a participation in the suffering and weakness of Christ, Paul exhorts his readers in the first letter not to strive for power and acceptance in the surrounding Hellenistic world. They live in an eschatological time: this age with its rulers is going to disappear and the new world of the kingdom of God is coming. In the second letter the theme of weakness returns in a different way. Paul does not exhort the Corinthians to share in this weakness. Instead, his own weakness is a weakness in favour of the Corinthians, who remain strong. In a situation of conflict, he makes himself as small as possible so that the power of God and the well-being of the Corinthians may be central. Everything is made subordinate to the ministry of reconciliation.

In Galatians and Romans, Paul gives an exposition of the gospel in relation to the Jewish law. In Galatians salvation is pictured as liberation, including liberation from the power of the law, resulting in the freedom of the children of God. God justifies by faith and not by works of the law. God is consistent in so doing, Paul demonstrates, by showing that the promise is older than the law. A central problem in the letter to the Romans is the

---

Ridderbos, *Paulus*; Wright, *What Saint Paul Really Said*.

See further for recent discussions in Pauline Theology the four volumes *Pauline Theology*: Bassler (Ed.), *Pauline Theology. Vol.* 1; Hay (Ed.), *Pauline Theology. Vol. II*; Hay, Johnson (Eds.), *Pauline Theology. Vol. III*; Johnson, Hay (Eds.), *Pauline Theology. Vol. IV*.

2. Concerning the chronological ordering, I follow Van Bruggen, *Paulus*.

place of the Jewish people as God's covenant people and God's faithfulness to his covenant. Romans places all human beings, whether Jew or Gentile, as sinners before the coming judgment of God. Only through the sacrificial death and resurrection of Christ can justification of the wicked be found. This might suggest that God changed his mind and yielded to sin. Paul shows this is not the case. He hopes that the new life of the gentile believers might arouse his own people to envy.

Colossians and Ephesians display the universal impact of Jesus Christ. Colossians is written in reaction to a Jewish Hellenistic syncretism that is difficult to identify.[3] It seems that (some among?) the Colossians wanted to reach divine fullness by observing religious rites, trying to court the favour of the cosmic powers. But Christ has triumphed over the powers and in him divine fullness is given. Christ's universal significance is explained in more ecclesiological terms in the letter to the Ephesians. Christ is head of the church and in him everything is given to the praise of God.

To understand the New Testament usage of 'ἐν Χριστῷ,' it is necessary to deal also with these last two letters, whether they are genuinely Pauline or deutero-Pauline. We will see that differences exist between Colossians and Ephesians and the other letters, e.g. in respect to the in Christ-language. Consequently, I will deal with them as a special subcategory, the 'later letters.' Whether they represent a final phase in Paul's theology or a post-Pauline theology does not really matter for this investigation. As canonical scriptures, they have to be read and used in this systematic-theological investigation, while at the same time the differences within the corpus of Pauline literature have to be respected. However, it is my conviction that these two letters are genuine Pauline letters.[4]

The central question in this chapter is whether a reading of Pauline literature justifies the choice of the concepts representation and participation to construct a systematic-theological concept of 'being in Christ.'

In literature on Paul it does not seem to be questioned whether the concepts of representation and participation are helpful. Many authors

3. This Colossian syncretism can e.g. be identified as Jewish-apocalyptic influenced (Dunn, *The Epistles to the Colossians and to Philemon*) or as strongly influenced by Greek cosmological speculation (Van Kooten, 'The Pauline Debate on the Cosmos').

4. Here I follow e.g. Van Bruggen, *Paulus*; Ridderbos, *Paulus* (for both letters); O'Brien, *Colossians, Philemon*, and Witkamp, *Kolossenzen* for Colossians; and O'Brien, *The Letter to the Ephesians*, for Ephesians. See on pseudepigraphy Baum, *Pseudepigraphie und literarische Falschung im frühen Christentum*.

use the concept 'representation' more or less with approval.[5] D. G. Powers for example agrees with Margaret Thrall that 'the idea that Christ "acted representatively on behalf of the whole human race" seems . . . to be "the key principle of Paul's theology."'[6] Some of them prefer representation to substitution.[7] Others use the concept while noticing that we also need other words, because representation alone does not suffice.[8] The way in which Christ is a representative seems unclear, it is said.[9] The concept of participation is also used, because it can be the reverse of representation, and increasingly in the so-called new perspective on Paul.[10] E. P. Sanders made participation in Christ the central theme in his reconstruction of Pauline soteriology.[11] Traditionally, the metaphor of justification received a lot of attention together with the righteousness of God, although in some Paul-interpretations the in Christ-language received a central place.[12] Sanders took up this second line, following the analysis of Albert Schweitzer that the doctrine of justification is a 'Nebenkrater' besides the mysticism of 'being in Christ.'[13] This contributed to the discussion in the newer research about the centre of Pauline theology. However, participation in Christ remains a theme that has received relatively little attention, although recently some literature on the theme of participation in

5. For example Ridderbos, *Paulus*, 54; 431; Wedderburn, 'The Body of Christ and related concepts in 1 Corinthians,' 1, 79, 88–89, 94–95; Wedderburn, 'Some Observations on Paul's use of the Phrases 'in Christ' and 'with Christ,'' 91; Wedderburn, *Baptism and Resurrection*, 358, 396; Wright, *The Climax of the Covenant*, 34–35, 151, 213; Wright, 'Romans and the Theology of Paul,' 34.

6. Powers, *Salvation through Participation*, 61.

7. Dunn, *The Theology of Paul the Apostle*, 223; Hooker, *From Adam to Christ*, 51; Powers, *Salvation through Participation*, 58, 60, 70, 76, 103, 104, 130, 151, 233.

8. Dunn, *The Theology of Paul the Apostle*, 223; Fatehi, The *Spirit's Relation to the Risen Lord in Paul*, 266, 274; Son, *Corporate Elements in Pauline Anthropology*, 64.

9. Barcley, "*Christ in You*," 113.

10. See on the 'new perspective' Noordegraaf, 'Paulus' spreken over rechtvaardiging,' 4–26; Westerholm, *Perspectives Old and New on Pau*; and also Van Bruggen, 'Kingdom of God or Justification of the Sinner?' 253–67.

11. Sanders, *Paul and Palestinian Judaism*, 441, 458–61, 463–68, 520–23.

12. E.g. the Christ-mysticism in the interpretations of Deissmann and Schweizer, see Deissmann, *Die neutestamentliche Formel "in Christo Jesu"*; Deissmann, *Paulus*; Schweitzer, *Die Mystik des Apostels Paulus*.

13. Sanders, *Paul and Palestinian Judaism*, 441, 458–61, 463–68, 520–23; cf. Schweitzer, *Die Mystik des Apostels Paulus*, 220.

Christ has been published.[14] In 1998, Dunn wrote: 'In comparison with the amazingly vigorous contemporary debate on justification by faith, interest in our present theme, even the thoroughly and distinctive Pauline "in Christ" and "with Christ" motifs, has been modest and marginal.'[15] It is a wish of many Paul-scholars that renewed study of these motifs be undertaken.[16] The importance of the theme is clear, for even if it is denied that participation in Christ is *the* centre of Paul's thinking, what Dunn writes may be true: 'study of participation in Christ leads more directly into the rest of Paul's theology than justification.'[17]

This short survey of recent discussions shows that although representation and participation seem useful concepts, open questions remain. Consequently, it is still an important question whether we need the concepts representation and participation to understand Paul's in Christ-language. To test the hypothesis formulated in 1.2.6 I will also investigate whether we need the concepts of substitution and union to reconstruct a Pauline perspective on 'being in Christ.'

To see whether the two (or four) moments these concepts refer to are present within Pauline thinking, it is insufficient to concentrate on the expression 'ἐν Χριστῷ. Paul has a dynamic and metaphorical style of writing. As a consequence, regarding 'being in Christ' and these two (or four) moments a lot of motifs and expressions are important, each contributing to the colour of the Pauline perspective. We need to discern

14. For the theme of 'in Christ,' see apart from the work of Deissmann and Schweitzer: Wikenhauser, *Die Christusmystik des hl. Paulus,*; Neugebauer, *In Christus. En cristw. Eine Untersuchung zum Paulinischen Glaubensverständnis*, Göttingen 1961; Bouttier, *En Christ*; Reid, *Our Life in Christ*; Ridderbos, *Paulus*, 56–63; Smedes, *Union with Christ*; Wedderburn, 'Some Observations on Paul's use of the Phrases 'in Christ' and 'with Christ'; Seifrid, 'In Christ.'

And more recently: Gnilka, *Paulus von Tarsus*, 255–60; Dunn, *The Theology of Paul the Apostle*, 390–412; Barcley, "*Christ in You*," 105–37; Fatehi, *The Spirit's Relation to the Risen Lord in Paul*, 263–74; Son, *Corporate Elements in Pauline Anthropology*, 7–39.

On the theme of participation, see further Powers, *Salvation through Participation*; Schnelle, 'Transformation und Partizipation als Grundgedanke paulinischer Theologie,' 58–75; Smedes, *Union with Christ*, 93–109; Reid, *Our Life in Christ*, 89–94.

15. Dunn, *The Theology of Paul the Apostle*, 395.

16. See besides Dunn e.g. Wedderburn, 'Some Observations on Paul's use of the Phrases 'in Christ' and 'with Christ,' 83. Cf. Son, *Corporate Elements in Pauline Anthropology*, 6.

17. Dunn, *The Theology of Paul the Apostle*, 395. See further Schnelle, 'Transformation und Partizipation als Grundgedanke paulinischer Theologie,' 70.

how Paul speaks of Christ, how he uses expressions like ἐν Χριστῷ, ἐν κυρίῳ, Χριστὸς ἐν ὑμιν, ἐν πνεύματι, σὺν Χριστῷ, εἰς Χριστόν and several συν-compounds; images like body and head, building, house and temple, marriage and the union between man and wife, new clothing, as well as the Christ—Adam parallel.

In this chapter I will now give a reconstruction of an aspect of Pauline theology. The central question will be whether we need the concepts of representation and participation to reconstruct Paul's thinking on the relationship between Christ and believers. Are they necessary and do they suffice, or do we also need the concepts of substitution and union? Furthermore I will concentrate on the reality of what I call 'being in Christ.'

I will deal with representation (and substitution) and participation (and union) in two different sections. Because Paul's Christology was deeply relational, this separation is artificial, but for the sake of clarity it is necessary. In reading Paul, it is remarkable how for him these two sides of the coin were always together. For a good impression of Paul's Christology and soteriology, both sections must be read.

Following the order of Ch. 2 and 3, I start in 5.2 with the position of the Son in election and creation. In 5.3 I will deal with the relation between Christ and the new humanity from a christological perspective, concentrating on the exclusive and the inclusive moment. 5.4 concerns this relation in a soteriological perspective, concentrating on the moments of participation and union. Finally in 5.5 the question addressed is of what can be said on the reality of 'being in Christ.'

5.2 Election and Creation

Paul's thinking is strongly christologically and soteriologically motivated. But although Paul occupies himself less with questions concerning eternal election and the relation between the Son of God and creation than the Reformed tradition does, he still writes something on these subjects. Both the themes of election and creation place us before the one and true God, creator of heaven and earth. In the gospel of Jesus Christ we meet the eternal One who has his plans and his purposes with his creation and its history. Paul clearly stands in continuity with motifs in Jewish monotheism.[18] I want to mention four passages here: two passages regarding the relation between Christ and election, Rom 8:29, 30; Eph 1:4, 5, 11; and two passages concerning the relation between Christ and the first creation, 1 Cor 8:6 and Col 1:15–17. I am especially interested in the presence of the four moments in these passages, and in their rhetorical and theological function.

If the eternal God loves us, he does so with eternal love. This brings a believer to the discovery that the story of salvation starts in eternity, as Paul tells this story in Rom 8:28–30. This chain of salvation expresses a great assurance and feeling of safety, for if the eternal One begins something, he will finish it too. This can evoke nothing but adoration and praise of God. Only in the letter to the Ephesians, the last of Paul's letters, is the full impact of this eternal election worked out in the theocentric and universal first chapter. Before the creation of the world, God decided to choose the church and to make its members holy and blameless as adopted sons, to the praise of his gracious love. Nothing in the elect forced God to do this, but his aim is clear and believers are involved in this aim: to be holy and blameless—which has moral implications—to the praise of his glory. The genre of these passages is not theoretical or kerugmatic, but doxological and hymnal. Further, the election-theme does have an impact on daily life practice.

Both in Romans 8 and in Ephesians 1 the relation of the elect to Christ is mentioned. In Romans 8 conformity to the image of Christ is the purpose of election. He must become the firstborn among many brothers. The many are to share in his destiny, his resurrection and glorified life. In Eph 1:4 Paul writes that believers are elected ἐν αὐτῷ, in Christ. According to Best, Christ is viewed here as representative or inclusive figure, but he also sees the possibility of an instrumental interpretation of 'in Christ.' Election and predestination here do not concern individual salvation, but God's purpose.[19] O'Brien also sees corporate elements, but does not want to play off individual and corporate election against each other. He is right in noting that, although the focus is primarily ecclesiological, still some of the divine gifts mentioned are personal and individual (like salvation, forgiveness and sealing with the Spirit).[20] Somehow

18. See Dunn, *Romans 1–8*.

19. Best, *A Critical and Exegetical Commentary on Ephesians*, 119, 121.

20. O'Brien, *The Letter to the Ephesians*, 99.

Christ and the persons he saved cannot be separated, but this does not imply a real pre-existence of believers.[21] Christ therefore can be seen as a representative figure, in whom election takes place, but also as the purpose of predestination to whom the elect will be conformed as they come to participate in his position. In both passages the moment of person-substitution is also present: Christ is firstborn (Rom 8:29) and head (Eph 1:10). We find here the moments of representation, person-substitution and participation.

Secondly we turn to the relation between Christ and creation. In 1 Cor 8:6, Paul is dealing with questions concerning the eating of food sacrificed to idols. He writes that there is but one God, although there are so-called gods. For Christians there is but one God and one Lord, Jesus Christ. The cosmological and soteriological roles of Christ are combined. Paul assigns to Christ a function in the creation of the world as well as in the salvation of the creation. According to Wright, Paul here refers to the *shema* and in consequence places Christ within the monotheistic confession.[22] Christology receives a cosmological dimension. Δι' αὐτοῦ all things came into existence and we live δι' αὐτοῦ. Paul does not reflect on how a pre-existent divine person could be involved in creation before his incarnation and at the same time be an incarnate divine saviour. However the practical implications of his beliefs are very obvious: an idol is nothing and we are no worse or better if we eat.

The second passage is Col 1:15–20. Paul here struggles with a syncretistic cosmology and the religious practices this cosmology brings. He makes very clear that all cosmic and angelic powers the Colossians venerate are created ἐν αὐτῷ, in Christ, δι' αὐτοῦ καὶ εἰς αὐτὸν, by him and for him—just like all other things. He is before all things and he gives coherence to the entire cosmos. Here is an example of what has been described as Paul's Wisdom-christology. Paul is using the tradition of Jewish wisdom literature and identifies Christ with divine wisdom.[23] This not only means that Jesus Christ embodies the powerful action of God expressed by the Wisdom-metaphor as Dunn says, opposing a literal read-

21. So Schnackenburg, *Der Brief an die Epheser*, 51.

22. Wright, *The Climax of the Covenant*, 129, 131.

23. Dunn, *The Epistles to the Colossians and to Philemon*, 91; O'Brien, *Colossians, Philemon*, 43–46. See also Dunn, *The Theology of Paul the Apostle*, 272–77; Wright, *The Climax of the Covenant*, 107–13.

ing of the metaphor.[24] The strength of the argument, placing Christ over all creation, depends on some ontological continuity between the person Jesus Christ and the personified Wisdom of God active in creation.[25]

The supremacy of Christ can be seen in relation to creation (1:15–17) as well as to salvation (1:18–20). He is 'the firstborn of all creation' (1:15) but also 'the firstborn from among the dead' (1:18). He is 'before all things' (1:17) and has become the supreme one (1:18). All things 'were created by him and for him' (1:16) and all things were reconciled 'through his blood' (1:20). This suggests that as mediator of creation he was exactly the right one to be the mediator of salvation.

Furthermore, as the firstborn of creation as well as among the dead, he is related to creation as the first to the many who follow him. His destiny will be the destiny of creation, created εἰς αὐτὸν. He is the first representing creation which will follow him. In this light it might be significant that Paul never in a context like this one uses ἐν αὐτῳ immediately together with δι' αὐτοῦ and εἰς αὐτὸν, or ἐξ αὐτοῦ (Rom 11:36 and 1 Cor 8:6). Dunn and Van Kooten show that such use of prepositions like 'from,' 'by,' 'through,' 'in,' 'to,' etc. was widespread in talking about God and the cosmos; Van Kooten calls it 'propositional metaphysics.' [26] But in the ancient examples they mention, 'in' is used together with the other propositions and not, like here in Col.1:16 separated from the other propositions. Maybe this ἐν αὐτῳ is separated deliberately, having a locative flavour and hence reinforcing the representative connotation of 'firstborn.' In any case, apart from having a role in creation, Christ has a representative position towards creation, which is to share in his destiny.

Paul's interest, however, is not primarily metaphysical, but practical, and the passage is not theoretical but hymnal. He wants to make clear that Christ is above all other cosmic powers. Christ as the image of the invisible God gives access to the fullness of God and the revelation of

24. Dunn, *The Epistles to the Colossians and to Philemon*, 91.

25. Reitsma is right in emphasising that the αὐτός refers to the concrete person Jesus Christ. However, claiming that we can only refer to the beginning from the end, he downplays the activity of he who is now known as Jesus Christ in creation, binding creation too closely together with the cross and resurrection of Jesus Christ. See Reitsma, *Geest en schepping*, 128, 149–52.

26. Van Kooten, 'The Pauline Debate on the Cosmos,' 111–14; Dunn, *The Epistles to the Colossians and to Philemon*, 91.

mysteries and not the veneration of other cosmic, angelic powers or the observation of specific religious rites.

Having seen these four passages we can conclude two things: Firstly, already in relation to election, predestination and creation regarding Jesus Christ the line of representation and participation is emerging. Jesus Christ can be seen as representative, opening the door for the participation of many others. As a result, a moment of person-substitution can also be found.

Secondly, these themes might evoke metaphysical speculations, but this is not the case with Paul. He refers to these themes only in a doxological context or with a specific practical interest. This does not mean that he does not make implicit ontological claims, for the strength of his arguments depends on these implicit claims. However, it is still significant that Paul does not give a treatment of these themes in a detached and theoretical way. Even in the preaching of the gospel these themes seem to have a secondary character.

5.3 Christology: Representation

Before dealing with questions regarding representation, some preliminary remarks must be made on the eschatological character of Paul's Christology. A lot of Paul-scholars have paid attention to this aspect of Paul's thinking although they have done so in different ways.[27] With N.T. Wright the eschatological character of Paul's thinking can be seen as follows. Faced with the fact of the resurrection of Jesus, Paul came to a reworking of the traditional model of Jewish apocalypse. He saw the bodily resurrection of Jesus Christ as the real return from exile. The Age to Come, the *eschaton* of Jewish expectation, had already arrived. This meant that the Age to Come was arriving in two stages. The end *has already* happened in the resurrection of Jesus, but at the same time *is still* to happen when all the people of Jesus are raised to life. Paul is living

27. For example Beker, *The Triumph of God*, 19–39, 61–80; Gaffin, 'Resurrection and Redemption,' 128, 209–21 (cf. Gaffin, 'The Vitality of Reformed Dogmatics,' 30–35); Ridderbos, *Paulus*, 40–55; Reitsma, *Geest en schepping*, 69–120; Schweitzer, *Die Mystik des Apostels Paulus*, 54–101; Versteeg, *Christus en de Geest*, 2–3, 381–95; Wright, *What Saint Paul Really Said*, 49–52.

between the end and the end.[28] As a result, Christology and eschatology are identical.

Further it is important to be aware of the Jewish context of Jesus Christ and its meaning for the concept of representation. Wright makes clear that Jesus was representative exactly as *Messiah,* Christ. As the Christ he was the true representative of Israel and the just remnant, in his person. As such he is the eschatological Israel. Because Israel is the true humanity, Christ as the last Adam represents the new humanity. Paul hence gives a retelling of the story of Israel. Where Israel saw itself 'as the people through whom the sin of Adam would be finally defeated,' in the view of Paul it is 'in Christ, not in national Israel, that Adam's trespass is finally undone.'[29] According to Wright, the use of Χριστός is incorporative. 'The king and the people are bound together in such a way that what is true of the one is true in principle of the other.'[30] Hence the concept of representation is related closely to the ministry of Jesus as Christ. I will deal with this further in 5.4.1 and 2, related to expressions like ἐν Χριστῷ and σὺν Χριστῷ.

In this sub-section I will focus on the relation between Christ and the new humanity in a christological perspective, concentrating on representation (the inclusive moment) as well as on substitution to test the hypothesis. Different notions will be investigated to answer the question whether we need a concept of representation of Christ to understand Paul, maybe together with a concept of substitution. Attention will be paid to the sending of Christ and his identification with humanity (5.3.1). Moreover I will deal with expressions clarifying the relation between Christ and believers, like Christ as Adam (5.3.2), the first one (5.3.3), and head (5.3.4). Further I will deal with questions concerning the decisiveness of Christ (5.3.5) and the concept of substitution (5.3.6). The section closes with a conclusion (5.3.7).

28. Wright, *What Saint Paul Really Said*, 49–51. Cf. Dunn, *The Theology of Paul the Apostle*, 461–66; Holleman, *Resurrection and Parousia.*

29. Wright, 'Romans and the Theology of Paul,' 46.

30. Wright, *The Climax of the Covenant*, 46; see further 26, 28, 34, 35, 151, 213; Wright, *What Saint Paul Really Said*, 51–55; Wright, 'Romans and the Theology of Paul,' 34.

5.3.1 IDENTIFICATION WITH HUMANITY

In the background of Paul's Christology stands a process of the identification of the Son of God with humanity, fallen in sin. This can be sketched as a succession of sending and incarnation, obedient living in the reality of sin, curse and law, culminating in the condemnation of sin and Christ becoming a curse.

The first stage of this process we find in Rom 8:3 where Paul writes that God sent his own Son 'in the likeness of sinful flesh' (KJV). Moo and Dunn both insist that the ὁμοιώμα in Rom 8:3 must not be read too weakly, in a docetic way; a full participation in sinful flesh is intended. This evokes the question whether Paul says here something with reference to the sinlessness of Christ. Dunn doubts this is the case here, although he admits that Paul does speak of it in 2 Cor 5:21 where the apostle writes that God made Christ who had no sin to be sin for us. However, it seems to me that Moo and Van Bruggen are right if they say that ὁμοιώμα expresses some distance, implying that Christ did not identify himself with sin.[31] This sending in the human condition is also stated in Gal 4:4 where Paul writes: 'God sent his Son, born of a woman, born under law.' This 'born of a woman, born under law' is a description of human and Jewish life.[32] Here preexistence may be present in the background according to Bruce—Paul believed in preexistence, so why could it not be the case here?—although this does not need to be the case necessarily.[33] Although in different words, both passages state that God sent his Son into the human condition.

As a human being the Son lived a life of obedience, culminating in a full identification with our problems. Paul writes in another letter, that Christ humbled himself and became obedient to death—even death on a cross (Phil 2:8). In different letters Paul makes clear in different ways that Christ identified himself with us. In Romans, sin and flesh being the problems of us humans, God sent his Son into the sinful flesh to condemn sin in sinful man (Rom 8:3). In Galatians the law is the problem. Paul writes that God sent his Son, born under law. He came to share in slavery 'to re-

31. Van Bruggen, *Romeinen*, 114–15; Dunn, *Romans 1–8*, 421; Moo, *The Epistle to the Romans*, 479.

32. Van Bruggen, *Galaten*, 118. It does not just refer to human life, as Betz writes, Betz, *Galatians*, 207.

33. Bruce, *The Epistle of Paul to the Galatians*, 195.

deem those under law' (Gal 4:3–5). As the law brings a curse to 'everyone who does not continue to do everything written in the Book of the Law,' humanity is cursed. But Christ 'redeemed us from the curse of the law by becoming a curse for us' (Gal 3:10, 13). Or, with 2 Cor 5:21: to reconcile sinful man to God, 'God made him who had no sin to be sin for us.' Again and again Paul states that Christ fully identified himself with our problems and, although he had no sin, fully participated in our existence.

This process of identification culminated in his death on the cross, but it is not right to say that he identified himself *by* dying on the cross. At the same time, the identification cannot be reduced to the moment of incarnation. Then the identification of Christ with humanity is seen too statically, instead of as a more dynamic movement with a climax.[34]

As we will see more extensively later, Paul sees two realms of reality: the realm of God and the realm of man, enslaved to the powers of death, law, sin and the other cosmic powers. God sent his son into the realm of slavery to live here and to deal within this realm of slavery with these enslaving powers. He became one of us, identifying himself with our problems to redeem us from our slavery. Therefore, we could say, he made himself our representative. A process can be seen of Christ becoming our representative.

5.3.2 CHRIST AND ADAM

That Paul sees Christ as *last Adam* is important for understanding Paul's Christology and seeing its inclusive moment. This notion has a place within what has been called Paul's Adam-christology, which has a traditional Jewish background. The Adam-Christ parallel is a central line in Paul's thinking. At the same time, Fatehi observes that the Adam-Christ analogy is only partial, because 'it is Adam who is a foil for Christ rather than the other way round.'[35] In any case, just as Adam was for the old

34. If his identification with sinful humanity is a movement, starting with his birth and ending in his death at the cross, on the one hand this identification cannot be understood exclusively in terms of work-substitution. Therefore, Bouttier is not right if he writes: 'Par sa mort substitutive, . . . le Fils de l'Homme s'est identifié à nous pour nous associer à lui': he equates identification with work-substitution and with the death of Christ. See Bouttier, *En Christ*, 45, 132. Wedderburn on the other hand disturbs the dynamics relating identification exclusively with incarnation; see Wedderburn, 'The Body of Christ and related concepts in 1 Corinthians,' 90.

35. Fatehi, *The Spirit's Relation to the Risen Lord in Paul*, 272.

humanity, Christ is decisive for the new humanity. It is not easy to understand *how*, according to Paul, Adam and Christ were decisive. To clarify this, scholars have recently used concepts like representation, solidarity, comprehensiveness, inclusiveness and corporateness.[36] I will deal with the conceptual clarification of this relationship later (see 5.5.2). Here I will concentrate on the three passages where Paul mentions Adam, 1 Cor 15:21—22:45 and Rom 5:12–21.

In 1 Cor 15:21—22:45 Paul shows that the acts of two human beings had an immense impact with regard to death and resurrection. Death came through a man, but also resurrection comes through a man. Paul uses here διὰ, indicating the decisiveness of their respective acts.[37] At the same time these two men, Adam and Christ, each represent an entire era, an era of dying and an era of life: an age in which all men die ἐν τῷ Ἀδὰμ, and an age in which all will be made alive ἐν τῷ Χριστῷ.[38] Paul writes πάντες twice, which gives rise to the question whether really all man, believers or not, will be made alive. According to Sanders, Paul means neither 'all . . . all' or 'many . . . many,' but 'all . . . many.' Unfortunately 'the Adam/Christ analogy does not permit this formulation.' He meant to write 'all who are in Christ will be made alive,' for all who are without Christ will be destroyed according to Paul.[39] But I think this is more than a slip of the pen forced by the expressions used. The Adam—Christ parallel indicates the universal impact of the work of Christ: Christ brings new

36. For Paul's use of the Adam-motif and its Jewish background see Dunn, *The Theology of Paul the Apostle*, 79–101, 199–204, 241–42; Son, *Corporate Elements in Pauline Anthropology*, 39–82; Wright, *The Climax of the Covenant*, 18–40. Barcley and Son both call attention to the fact that Paul does not explain *how* Adam and Christ determined humanity, Barcley, "*Christ in You*," 113; Son, *Corporate Elements in Pauline Anthropology*, 64. For the different concepts used to clarify this relation see e.g. Hooker, *From Adam to Christ* (representation, solidarity, interchange); Park, *Die Kirche als "Leib Christi" bei Paulus*, (representation, comprehensiveness); Powers, *Salvation through Participation* (corporateness, solidarity, participation); Ridderbos, *Paulus* (corporate personality, representation); Son, *Corporate Elements in Pauline Anthropology* (corporateness, solidarity, comprehensiveness, inclusiveness); Wedderburn, 'The Body of Christ and related concepts in 1 Corinthians' (representation, solidarity).

37. Bouttier, *En Christ*, 33.

38. Ridderbos, *Paulus*, 55, 59. Bouttier notes that this is the only place in Paul's letter that he combines the ἐν (τῷ) Χριστῷ formula with a futurum, Bouttier, *En Christ*, 120.

39. Sanders, *Paul and Palestinian Judaism*, 473. This implies that Schrage is right in noting a tension here, but he does not see that the Adam—Christ parallel with its universal impact causes this tension, although he mentions the fact that the resurrection has a cosmic dimension, see Schrage, *Der erste Brief an die Korinther*, Bd. 1, 163–64.

humanity to existence, and the question is whether one belongs to this new humanity or not. As for the old humanity death was unavoidable, so for believers the resurrection is unavoidable, as Fee says.[40]

The second time Paul mentions Adam in 1 Corinthians 15 is in verse 45. Paul deals here with the different bodies of human beings in Adam and in Christ. Paul cites Gen 2:7: Adam became a living being. To underscore the difference between those in Adam and those in Christ, he continues: the last Adam became 'a life-giving spirit.' Four things must be noticed here. First, Paul speaks of the first and the last, ἔσχατος, Adam. Christ is not just a second figure in the history of creation, he is the final and ultimate human being; an eschatological figure.[41] Secondly, as Adam, representative of humanity, he is more than just a representative. He becomes a life-giving spirit and accordingly, the source of spiritual life. Thirdly, Paul does not say that Christ becomes the last Adam in his resurrection, but that the last Adam becomes a life-giving spirit in his resurrection.[42] Adam indicates his human nature, although it is the nature of a person with an impact on the whole of humanity. Still this Adam has a history, in becoming a life-giving spirit. And finally, it becomes clearer here that Adam and Christ cannot be paralleled. Whereas Adam was a living being, Christ became a life-giving spirit. Adam was of the dust of the earth and had a natural body; Christ is from heaven and gives us a spiritual body (1 Cor 15:47). Christ is more and gives more than Adam was.

Finally Paul writes about Christ and Adam in Rom 5:12–21, in a context dealing with sin and righteousness. Through Adam sin and death came to reign, but through Christ the gift of grace and righteousness is received. Just as in 1 Corinthians, a parallel is drawn between Adam and Christ, but the contrast is even bigger.[43] Both Adam and Christ are human beings whose acts have universal impact. At the same time they differ: trespass is contrasted with the gift of grace. One trespass brought condemnation, but the gift of grace brings the justification of many tres-

40. Fee, *The First Epistle to the Corinthians*, 751.

41. See Schrage, *Der erste Brief an die Korinther*, Bd. 1, 305; Collins, *First Corinthians*, 549.

42. According to Ridderbos Christ becomes the last Adam in the resurrection, see Ridderbos, *Paulus*, 54. Wright is right in opposing this opinion; see Wright, *The Climax of the Covenant*, 33.

43. Van Bruggen emphasises especially the differences, see Van Bruggen, *Romeinen*, 84–85.

passes. Adam caused humanity to be sinful, ruled by the king of death; Christ makes humanity itself reign as kings. That Paul mentions Christ's act of righteousness, referring to the obedience of Christ until death on the cross, makes clear again that Christ was like Adam already before his resurrection.[44] Beyond the similarities with 1 Corinthians, differences can also be seen. Where Paul in Corinthians deals with death and resurrection, he relates Adam and Christ in Romans to sin and righteousness, although death and life are also mentioned in a consequential way. Another difference with 1 Corinthians 15 is, that Paul only refers to *acts* of Adam and Christ—one trespass and one act of righteousness. Accordingly Paul only uses διὰ (5:12, 16, 17, 18, 19, 21) and not, as he does in 1 Corinthians, formulae like ἐν τῷ Ἀδὰμ or ἐν τῷ Χριστῷ.[45] In the letter to the Romans Paul starts to use the in Christ-language in chapter 6. In chapter 5 the two decisive acts of these two men receive all the attention.[46] The underlying assumption regarding the relation between Adam and Christ on the one hand and humanity on the other remains implicit. Paul does not even call Christ ὁ ἔσχατος Ἀδὰμ. But nevertheless the life of Jesus was 'Adamic in character,' having some representative quality.[47]

Ridderbos stressed that Paul related Adam and Christ both to a different aeon in a salvation-historical way.[48] Wright emphasises another aspect of Paul's Adam-christology. It is based on the Jewish view of Israel as Adam that had to annul the consequences of sin. However, Israel was not able to do this; only the representative of Israel could do what was required: being obedient until death to save the old humanity and give an abundance of life resulting from subsequent exaltation. Consequently sin and its effects 'are thus undone and God's original intention for humanity is thus restored in the age to come, which has already begun in the work of Jesus Christ.'[49] Nevertheless it is important to see that Paul makes another contrast, as Hooker indicates. Besides the contrast between Adam and Christ Paul makes the contrast between what humans do and what God does. Christ indeed has Adamic qualities, but it is also God who acts

44. Wright, *The Climax of the Covenant*, 39.

45. Son, *Corporate Elements in Pauline Anthropology*, 64.

46. Bouttier states that διὰ Χριστοῦ indicates often the objective and decisive character of the work of Christ. See Bouttier, *En Christ*, 33, 85.

47. Dunn, *The Theology of Paul the Apostle*, 203.

48. Ridderbos, *Paulus*, 59.

49. Wright, *The Climax of the Covenant*, 39; see further 36–40.

in Christ. 'God's act of vindication in rising Christ from the death stands over against the initial transgression.'[50]

In conclusion, Adam-christology stresses the importance of the humanity of Christ but also the special position of Christ within humanity. This Adam-christology has a Jewish background. Like Adam, Christ has a representative position with a universal significance. He did not become a figure like Adam through his resurrection, but his being like Adam made what he did universally significant. Christ has a special position within humanity because he is like Adam, but moreover because, as *eschatos* Adam, he is more than Adam: in him God has shown his gracious love, annulling the trespasses of humanity in Adam. Consequently, the moment of representation (his inclusiveness), the moment of person-substitution (his exclusive position) and maybe even of work-substitution (his acts; see 5.3.6) all are necessary to understand Adam-christology.

5.3.3 THE FIRST ONE

Paul uses metaphors like firstfruits and firstborn to indicate the impact of the person and work of Christ.

The first one, firstfruits (ἀπαρχὴ), is used in 1 Cor 15:20, 23 to show the connection between the resurrection of Christ and the future resurrection of believers. Paul writes that Christ has been raised from the death as 'firstfruits of those who have fallen asleep.'[51] Just as Christ is risen, so those who belong to him will be raised when he comes. With ἀπαρχὴ not only the sequence of time is meant, but at the same time the constitutive (causal or organic) relation.[52] Jesus' resurrection is a guarantee of the future resurrection of the believers.[53] The resurrection expected by Israel had bifurcated.[54] Jesus resurrection is the beginning of the eschatological resurrection; the eschatological resurrection of the believers is a participation in Jesus' resurrection. The believers, who are in Christ, will

50. Hooker, *From Adam to Christ*, 31.

51. For the original agricultural context of the firstfruits-metaphor, see Williams, *Paul's Metaphors*, 40.

52. Park sees the relation as causal, Gaffin as organic. Gaffin, 'Resurrection and Redemption,' 32–33; Park, *Die Kirche als "Leib Christi" bei Paulus*, 139; cf. Schrage, *Der erste Brief an die Korinther*, Bd. 4, 159–60.

53. Wright, *The Climax of the Covenant*, 27.

54. Wright, *The Climax of the Covenant*, 29.

be raised at the *parousia* of Christ as a result of their unity with him. Once it is believed that Christ has been raised, it is also to be believed that all Christians will be raised.[55] Christ as *eschatos* Adam is standing at the end of humanity, bringing humanity to its eschatological *telos* and making it bear fruit in the eschatological harvest.

The second metaphor, firstborn (πρωτότοκος), is used in Rom 8:29 and in Col 1:15 and 18. In Romans 8 Paul writes that God predestined those who he foreknew to be conformed to the image of his Son, that he might be the firstborn among many brothers. In this verse, the notion of firstborn is related to several other motifs. First, Paul uses the expression συμμόρφους, one of the συν compounds that he uses to indicate the intimate relationship between Christ and believers (see on this subject 5.4.2). Secondly, the many brothers will be conformed to the *image* of the Son. According to Dunn, it is almost certain that Paul has Adam in mind once again, man created in the image of God. He writes: 'The Adam-christology involved is clear: Christ is the image of God which Adam was intended to be, the Son as the pattern of God's finished product.'[56] Thirdly, 'firstborn' refers to the resurrection of Christ from the dead. Because Paul has in mind the risen Christ, it is the eschatological outcome of God's creative purpose with creation which Paul has in mind here, as Dunn continues. Hence Paul does not speak here of a return to original state, but of an eschatological purpose.[57] And finally, Paul pictures Christ as the firstborn of many brothers. He is the eldest son, being the first of many other brothers (and sisters), who together with him will form the family of God the Father. This third and fourth point again make clear that Christ was not just like Adam, but that as *eschatos* Adam, he was greater than the first.

The metaphor πρωτότοκος returns in Col 1:15 and 18. I have already dealt with 1:15 (see 5.2); here I concentrate on 1:18. Just as Christ was supreme in creation, he is in new creation. Paul writes that Christ is 'the head of the body, the church; he is the beginning and the firstborn from among the dead, so that in everything he might have the supremacy.' According to Dunn this shows that Adam-christology and Wisdom-christology are complementary: both emphasise the supremacy of Christ over creation,

55. See for a extensive treatment of the relation between the resurrection of Jesus Christ and the resurrection of those who belong to him, Holleman, *Resurrection and Parousia*, esp. Part III and IV; Gaffin, 'Resurrection and Redemption.'

56. Dunn, *Romans 1–8*, 483.

57. Dunn, *Romans 1–8*, 483–84.

in 1:15 in terms of creation (Wisdom), in 1:18 in terms of new creation (last Adam).[58] In 1:18 the relation between the metaphor πρωτότοκος and the resurrection from the dead is made explicit. Christ is seen as the beginning of the new humanity and the guarantee of the resurrection of those who follow him.[59] He is born *from* death, showing his solidarity and identification with our mortality.[60] Further it is remarkable that Christ as Adam and therefore as human being cannot be separated from Christ as the one in who God himself acts: Christ is not only supreme because of his being the firstborn among the new humanity, but also because God was pleased to have all his fullness dwell in him (verse 19).

Both expressions make clear that the resurrection of Christ has to be followed by the resurrection of the many that belong to him. The image of firstfruits has connotations with harvest, the image of firstborn with the family, but both make clear that the resurrection of Christ has the status of a 'to be continued.' An inclusive moment (the many will follow) as well as an exclusive moment (his is the first) are necessary here.

5.3.4 HEAD

Next, an important expression is the head-metaphor (κεφαλὴ). It can be found in 1 Corinthians 11 and in the later letters to the Colossians and Ephesians. Again, the question is, whether 'head' can be understood in a representative sense, as is the case according to Ridderbos: Christ is the first one, having a dominating position by his decisive dealing with our problems. He is head in an including and representing sense.[61] Is he right?

In 1 Corinthians 11 Paul merely writes that Christ is the head of every man (11:3). He uses this within a complex argument regarding women covering their heads. The relation between Christ and every man is paralleled not only with the relation between husband and wife, but also with the relation between God and Christ. In all of these relations a certain hierarchy seems present, but the relations Paul mentions also have an aspect of intimacy. In any case, a relation of the metaphor of head with the field of marriage is present from the beginning. This is

58. Dunn, *The Epistles to the Colossians and to Philemon*, 99.

59. O'Brien, *Colossians, Philemon*, 51–52.; Gaffin, 'Resurrection and Redemption,' 40.

60. Gaffin, 'Resurrection and Redemption,' 38.

61. Ridderbos, *Paulus*, 427, 431–32.

not the case with the metaphor of body. It is not the place here to deal with the body-metaphor (see 5.3.4), but it is still important to observe that in 1 Corinthians the body-metaphor and the image of the head are both present, although unrelated. In Romans the image of the body is present, whereas the head-metaphor is entirely absent. Consequently, in 1 Corinthians and Romans, the images of head and body are not related. In conclusion: in 1 Corinthians, the head-metaphor suggests a relation of hierarchy and intimacy, but not representation.

In the epistle to the Colossians, the head-metaphor occurs three times, in 1:18 and in 2:10 and 19.

Col 1:18 is the second part of the so-called Christ-hymn (1:15–20). Whereas 15–17 voice the relation between Christ and creation, in 18–20 the relation between Christ and the new creation is voiced. Apart from ἀρχή and πρωτότοκος ἐκ τῶν νεκρῶν, Christ is called ἡ κεφαλὴ τοῦ σώματος τῆς ἐκκλησίας, head of the body of the church and not head of the cosmos.[62] Paul creatively combines two metaphors, the metaphors of head and body.[63] However, the body of the church is seen in cosmological perspective. This justifies speaking here of a new *creation*. But the idea of head is also associated with other notions. The second part of verse 18 relates the notion of head to supremacy and to the idea that he is the first, while others will follow. In verse 19 it becomes clear that behind this the divine fullness must be seen, wanting to reconcile the cosmos with

62. According to Dunn and Walter, the words τῆς ἐκκλησίας are added, but by the author himself. He revised an original hymn, expressing a common view in Greek cosmology of the cosmos as body, by adding the words τῆς ἐκκλησίας; see Dunn, *The Epistles to the Colossians and to Philemon*, 94–95; Walter, *Gemeinde als Leib Christi*, 175–76; O'Brien (O'Brien, *Colossians, Philemon*, 48–49) and Van Kooten, however, see these words as original. Van Kooten even sees no reason to see here a critical revision of an older hymn. According to him the author of Colossians himself 'is to be credited with the entire introductory prayer in Col 1:9–23'; Van Kooten, 'The Pauline Debate on the Cosmos,' 108. See also 104.

63. With Dunn and Walter I see the head-body combination as a later development of the body-metaphor, see Dunn, "The Body of Christ in Paul," 152–53; Walter, *Gemeinde als Leib Christ*, 175, 197. Stuhlmacher makes some interesting observations, showing how this development of the head-metaphor makes it possible to take together at once different motifs already present within Paul and to clarify further the relation between Christ and the church, see Stuhlmacher, *Biblische Theologie des Neuen Testaments, Band* 2, 31.

G. Howard (Howard, 'The Head / Body Metaphors of Ephesians,' 350–56) H. Ridderbos (*Paulus*, 425–26), and D.J. Williams (*Paul's Metaphors*, 90), emphasise the independence of the metaphors of body and head, although they can occur together.

himself through Christ. In conclusion, here the notion of head stands in a context consisting first of all in the body of the church. The metaphor contains notions of supremacy, of the first followed by others, and of the divine fullness.

The second time the word κεφαλὴ is used, is in 2:10. Here Christ is called ἡ κεφαλὴ πάσης ἀρχῆς καὶ ἐξουσίας. In Colossians Paul reacts on a Colossian 'philosophy,' in which cosmic or angelic powers as these ἀρχῆς and ἐξουσίας were very important. It has already been said that these powers were created in Christ (1:16), now it is stated explicitly that Christ is head of these powers. A few verses further on in the text, the author writes that Christ has triumphed over them. Although there seems to have been a period of cosmic disorder, now the order has been restored by Christ. Here, κεφαλὴ has a clear hierarchical meaning: Christ stands above and rules over the cosmic powers. Again, the metaphor of κεφαλὴ is associated with the idea of divine fullness in the preceding clause. All the divine fullness lives in Christ and fullness has been given them in Christ (2:9–10). A relation seems to be suggested between this participation in the divine fullness in Christ and Christ as head. Finally, a direct link with the body-metaphor is absent here, although Paul plays with the word σῶ μα. Hence Van Kooten sees a relation with this metaphor, because in 2:9 it is written that the divine fullness lives in Christ σωματικῶς, but together with Dunn and O'Brien I tend to see this as referring to the historical body of Christ (see also the discussion of the body-metaphor, 5.4.3).[64] Consequently, the metaphor of κεφαλὴ has a hierarchical meaning here, and is related to the notion of divine fullness just as in 1:18, yet differing in that the body-metaphor is absent.

Thirdly the head-metaphor occurs in 2:19. Here Paul warns against practices resulting from the Colossian philosophy that lead to a loss of connection with Christ, the head of the body. I will confine myself to some observations now and continue in 5.4.3. First, the head-metaphor is used again together with the body-metaphor. Secondly, for the body the head is the source of divine growth. Thirdly, the words κεφαλὴ, σῶμα, ἁφή, συνδέσμος, and αὔξησις used together, evoke the idea that Paul, although referring implicitly to antique cosmology that saw the cosmos as a

64. See Van Kooten, 'The Pauline Debate on the Cosmos,' 17–19; Dunn, *The Epistles to the Colossians and to Philemon*, 152; O'Brien, *Colossians, Philemon*, 112–13. Walter just reads 2:10 as body-metaphor, without dealing with the absence of the word body; Walter, *Gemeinde als Leib Christi*, 182–83.

body, uses the model of the human body here. Cosmology and ecclesiology seem to interfere. Hence I do not agree that the model of a human body would be absent here, as is the consequence of the opposition of Ridderbos and Van Kooten to a physiological interpretation of verse 19.[65] Fourthly, the connection with the head is related to obedience and not participating in wrong practices. This implies that some hierarchical flavour is also present in this head-metaphor. Consequently, in this verse the head-metaphor is used in a physiological context. The head is primarily seen as source of growth, but hierarchical and moral connotations are also present.

To conclude, in Colossians the head-metaphor is a living metaphor used in different ways. Christ can be seen as head of the cosmos and as head of the church. The head-metaphor is used without, but also, together with the body-metaphor. The combination with the body-metaphor can stand against the background of the model of the human body. The head-metaphor has different connotations: the head as the first to be followed by others, as the one having authority and hierarchical superiority, and finally as source of growth. Finally, in two of the three cases the head-metaphor is associated with divine fullness. The metaphor emphasises especially the exclusiveness of Christ, in 1:18 and maybe in 2:19 also his inclusiveness.

Besides the letters to the Corinthians and the Colossians, the head-metaphor is used in the letter to the Ephesians. In this letter the metaphor occurs three times, in 1:22, 4:15 and in 5:23.

Eph 1:22 is a part of the longer sentence in verse 20–23 that describes the exaltation of Christ. God 'raised him from the dead and seated him at his right hand in the heavenly realms,' placed all things including the cosmic powers under his feet and gave him as head to the church. The head-metaphor is combined with two other metaphors, the metaphor of all things being placed under his feet, referring to Ps 8:7, and the metaphor of the church as his body. This makes very clear the vividness of Paul's writing and living character of the head-metaphor: Paul is playing with words. Best and Walter read the head-metaphor from the clause following in verse 23 and stress that head, body and church form one group.

65. See Van Kooten, 'The Pauline Debate on the Cosmos,' 44–48; Ridderbos, *Paulus*, 424, 426. See in favour of my conclusion Dunn, "The Body of Christ' in Paul,' 152; Walter, *Gemeinde als Leib Christi*, 186–90; and for similar conclusions regarding parallels in Ephesians Dawes, *The Body in Question*, 164.

Hence they see here an organic relation between Christ and the church.[66] Syntactically speaking, however, there is more reason to connect the head-metaphor primarily to the feet-metaphor. The text actually says: 'And he subjected all things under his *feet* and gave him as a *head* over all things to the church.' Only then is the body-metaphor mentioned in a dependent clause, 'which is his *body*.' Howard shows this, but does not reflect further on the relation between the head- and body-metaphor.[67] Dawes and O'Brien better succeed in combining both the feet- and head-metaphor with the body-metaphor. Although the head- and body-metaphor were used originally independent of each other, they are used together later. According to Dawes, this shows that the church has a relation with Christ which the cosmos does not have.[68] In this special relation to the church, according to O'Brien, Christ as head is 'inspiring, ruling, guiding, combining, sustaining power, mainspring of its activity, centre of unity, seat of its life.'[69] Nonetheless, the head-metaphor here has especially a sense of authority, as Christ is head over everything.

The second time the head-metaphor is used in this letter is in 4:15. This verse strongly resembles Col 2:19. The head-metaphor is combined with the verb αὐξάνω, and the words σῶμα, ἁφή and other words, all together evoking the image of a growing organic whole, or in short, a living body. Just as in Col 2:19 the model of the human body is present here. This means I agree with Dawes, who opposes Ridderbos' rejection of the idea of a composed head-body-metaphor. According to Dawes, the head-metaphor means in 4:15 that Christ is the source of growth of his body.[70] An organic, life-giving unity exists between Christ and his

66. Best, *A Critical and Exegetical Commentary on Ephesians*, 182; Walter, *Gemeinde als Leib Christi*, 210–11.

Walter locates the body between head and feet, concluding that the body participates in the authority of Christ. However, the syntactical construction relates the authority with the head, and less obviously with the feet; see Walter, *Gemeinde als Leib Christi*, 212.

67. Howard, 'The Head / Body Metaphors of Ephesians,' 353–54.

68. Dawes, *The Body in Question*, 141; see also 139–40.

69. O'Brien, *The Letter to the Ephesians*, 148; see further 141–47.

70. Dawes, *The Body in Question*, 145; see also Ridderbos, *Paulus*, 422–23 and Howard, 'The Head / Body Metaphors of Ephesians,' 355. Ridderbos separates the two metaphors from each other too strictly; see Dawes, *The Body in Question*, 119–21, 164.

body.[71] Physiological language is used metaphorically here.[72] Howard and Van Kooten interpret the headship of Christ against the background of Christ's cosmic headship.[73] According to them, the church can grow in everything because Christ is head over all things. In the preceding verses this cosmological emphasis is present by the ascension of Christ (4:7). At the same time, the focus is on the ecclesiological body (4:4, 12), evoking a more physiological interpretation. Cosmology and ecclesiology are intertwined here, with an emphasis on ecclesiology. In conclusion, the headship of Christ is focussed here on the church as his body. Body and head easily combine, evoking together the model of a human body as an organic whole. The head is source and destiny, which might imply inclusiveness but emphasises in any case the exclusiveness of Christ.

The third passage where the head-image is used is Eph 5:23. In the surrounding verses, 5:22–33, Paul uses the relation between Christ and the community as an example for the relation between man and woman within marriage. Husbands are exhorted to love their wives as Christ loved the community. Within this context both Christ and the husband are referred to as head; Christ as head of the church and the husband as head of his wife. A much debated question is, whether κεφαλὴ has a sense of authority or of source of life. Dawes has shown convincingly that because a metaphor can have different meanings in different contexts, we cannot decide this question in general. In this verse the notion of head is placed within an exhortation to submission, so that is has here primarily the meaning of 'authority over.'[74] Still the possibility that this authority could become tyrannical is avoided, by pointing to the love of Christ.[75] Christ is the saviour of the church. Also in this verse the body-metaphor is mentioned: Christ is the head of the church, his body. However, it seems that this does not solely happen against the background of the model of a

71. Dawes, *The Body in Question*, 146–47; cf. Walter, *Gemeinde als Leib Christi*, 227.

72. O'Brien, *The Letter to the Ephesians*, 314.

73. Howard does so asking attention for the relation with the notion of τὰ πάντα. He resists an adverbial interpretation of τὰ πάντα and translates 4:15b as 'let us cause all things to increase unto him.' See Howard, 'The Head/Body Metaphors of Ephesians,' 355; cf. Van Kooten, 'The Pauline Debate on the Cosmos,' 173.

74. Dawes, *The Body in Question*, 122–37.

75. Dawes, *The Body in Question*, 138; Schnackenburg, *Der Brief an die Epheser*, 252.

human body as Dawes claims, but also of the model of marriage.[76] Again, the exclusiveness of Christ is stressed, not his inclusiveness.

In summary, in this letter also, the metaphor is a living one used in different ways. The first time the metaphor is combined with the submission of everything under the feet of Christ, the second time explicitly with the model of a human body and the third time the model of a marriage seems present. Twice the metaphor has the meaning of authority over, the other passage uses it more in the sense of source of life and growth. Still it is remarkable that in all passages the word σῶμα is present, be it more at a distance, be it nearer. Concerning representation and substitution, again the emphasis is on person-substitution. Maybe in 4:15 also a hint of representation might be discovered.

To conclude, the head-metaphor deserves separate attention apart from the body-metaphor. It is used as a living metaphor so that it is not possible to see a general concept of headship behind its use. Within Pauline thinking, the following development can be seen. In the earlier letters it is only used in 1 Cor 11:3, independently of the body-metaphor but related to the field of marriage. In Colossians and Ephesians the head-metaphor is used more frequently and gives expression to the position of the exalted Christ. Broadly speaking, it is used with two senses: 'authority over' and secondly 'source of the body's life and growth.'[77] The first sense of 'authority over' can refer to the supremacy of Christ over the entire cosmos, as is the case in Col 2:10 and in Eph 1:22. However, it can also refer to the specific relation Christ has with the church as in Eph 1:22. If this is the case, the model of marriage can be present, as in Eph 5:23. Here we see continuity with the use of the metaphor in 1 Corinthians 11. The second sense of 'source of the body's life and growth' evokes further the model of the human body. This is very obviously the case in Col 2:19 and in Eph 4:15 and less clear in Col 1:18 and Eph 1:22. Both letters give the metaphor a specific colour, related to the specific character of the letter. In Colossians, two of the three occurrences combine the head-metaphor with the notion of the divine fullness, in Ephesians the metaphor is always combined with the word σῶμα. In summary, the head-metaphor is related to three different fields of meaning: the field of authority ('under

76. Dawes, *The Body in Question*, 116. Park emphasises this model of marriage very strongly, see for his exegesis of this passage Park, *Die Kirche als "Leib Christi" bei Paulus*, 245–52.

77. Dawes, *The Body in Question*, 148.

his feet'), the field of marriage and the field of the human body and has two senses: 'authority over' and 'source of the body's life and growth.'

With regard to the moments of representation and person-substitution, we saw that the moment of person-substitution is especially present in the use of the head-metaphor. In Col 1:18 and maybe in Col 2:19 and Eph 4:15 a representative flavour can be discerned. In the sense of 'authority over,' κεφαλή seems closer to κύριος, and hence, with Dunn, a relation can be seen to Kurios-christology.[78] This is more difficult where head has the sense of 'source of the body's life and growth.' Still the conclusion must be that 'head' cannot directly be understood in the sense of 'representative' as Ridderbos argues.

5.3.5 DECISIVENESS OF CHRIST: INCLUSIVENESS

Until now we have seen firstly an ongoing movement of identification: the Son of God identifies with humanity during his life, culminating in his death. Further, we have seen that the use of several metaphors shows the presence of a moment of inclusiveness in Paul's Christology, but also a moment of person-substitution. In relation to the acts of Christ as last Adam maybe we could even discern a moment of work-substitution.

In the two last sub-sections of this section I want to investigate further the question concerning representation and substitution. Evidently, in the life, death and resurrection of Christ something decisive happened for believers. But what is the character of this decisiveness? Does it have an inclusive or an exclusive nature? In which sense did Jesus' death have a special meaning? In this sub-section I will concentrate on the moment of representation, in the next sub-section on the moment of work-substitution (5.3.6).

I distinguish these two moments as follows. Representation means that Christ enables us to go after him—we will go where he went. Work-substitution means that Christ did something we could not do—he went where we will not go.[79]

This distinction corresponds to a remarkable feature of Paul's theology. On the one hand we find positive semantic relations between events in the history of Jesus Christ and events in the life of believers, e.g. he

78. Dunn, "The Body of Christ' in Paul," 159. See further Dunn, *The Theology of Paul the Apostle*, 244–52.

79. Cf. Gunton, *The Actuality of Atonement*, 166; see also 1.2.6.

died—we have died; he lives—we live. These semantic relations affirm the inclusiveness of the story of Jesus Christ: we will go where he went. We need a concept of representation to understand them. On the other hand we find negative semantic relations, e.g. he died—we have not died, but live. Or we discover that no positive relations are laid, e.g. he died. . . . To understand this second kind of semantic relation, we need a concept of work-substitution: he went where we will not go.[80]

In 5.3.5 and 6, I will concentrate on the christological side of this medal. In 5.3.5 we now turn to several passages where a moment of inclusiveness can be distinguished, in 5.3.6 we will search for a moment of exclusivity. Of course, the concept of representation demands its reverse in a concept of participation. In 5.3 I will focus on what *he did*, in 5.4 I will deal with where *we (will) go*.

In the second letter to the Corinthians, Paul tries to convince the Corinthians that he aims at their well being. He does so, following God 'who reconciles us to himself through Christ and gave us the ministry of reconciliation.' Explaining this reconciliation, Paul writes that he is convinced that one died ὑπὲρ πάντων. His conclusion is remarkable: 'therefore all died,' (2 Cor 5:14). How should we understand this conclusion and the implied relation between the death of Christ and the death of all? First of all, it is important to notice with Sanders that Paul does not conclude 'therefore all have had their sins expiated,' but 'therefore all died.'[81] Secondly, Paul also writes about the resurrection of Christ and relates the resurrection of Christ with new life in Christ. With this context in mind, it is noteworthy that the final clause of 2 Cor 5:15, τῷ ὑπὲ ρ αὐτῶν ἀποθανόντι καὶ ἐγερθέντι, can be translated in two ways: 'for him who died and was raised for them' or 'for him who died for them and was raised.' Grammatically, it is not clear whether the ὑπὲρ αὐτῶν is related to ἐγερθέντι or only to ἀποθανόντι. Seen in context, the first option is more plausible.[82] Therefore, it seems right to conclude that Paul

80. Reid makes a similar distinction, dealing with participation. On the one hand we participate in benefits won by Christ which he did not need himself. Here a rule of contrariety operates: Christ dies, we live. On the other hand Christ confers benefits upon us which he himself may be said to enjoy. Participation now is subject to a different rule of correspondence. See Reid, *Our Life in Christ*, 90–91; cf. Thiselton, *New Horizons in Hermeneutics*, 303.

81. Sanders, *Paul and Palestinian Judaism*, 464.

82. See Martin, 2 *Corinthians*, 132; Powers, *Salvation through Participation*, 57.

here affirms the inclusiveness of both the death and the resurrection of Christ for all. Powers sees in the background the idea that Christ acted representatively for humanity.[83] The question in which sense 'all died' is another one, which will be dealt with later (see 5.4.2). In any case the moment of inclusiveness seems present here. Therefore it is not right to read the ὑπὲρ πάντων in this verse primarily in the sense of exclusivity and of substitution.[84]

In the letter to the Galatians, Paul argues that man is not justified by works of the law, but by faith in Jesus Christ. In Gal 2:19 he then writes: 'For through the law I died to the law.' At first sight, this might seem a passage mentioning an event in the life of Paul and not in the earthly life of Jesus Christ. It might then refer to Paul's conversion or baptism. But then it has to be explained how the law caused Paul's death to the law. This might refer to the *usus elenchticus* of the law, but it is difficult to see how this idea fits within the letter to the Galatians.[85] In Galatians, the law is an enslaving power. Christ redeemed from the curse and the power of the law, by being born under law and becoming a curse himself (Gal 3:13, 23; 4:3–5). Because Christ died, condemned by the law as a blasphemer making himself the Son of God, and because in Gal 2:20 Paul continues with the motif of being crucified with Christ, it is more fitting to see this verse as referring to the death of Christ. He died through the law and is free now from the power of the law, raised from the dead. The fact that Paul writes 'through the law I died to the law' makes clear that the dying of Christ had an inclusive character. Through the law he himself has died to the law, because through the law Christ died to the law (cf. Rom 7:4, 6).[86]

83. Powers, *Salvation through Participation*, 61.

84. Contra Ridderbos, *Paulus*, 206–7; Martin, 2 *Corinthians*, 129–30.
In *Zijn wij op de verkeerde weg?* Ridderbos reads 2 Cor 5 in the light of the concept of corporate personality, doing more justice to the inclusive moment. See Ridderbos, *Zijn wij op de verkeerde weg?* 24.

85. Bruce suggests the possibility that Paul's personal experience might be present also. His zeal for the law brought Paul to sin in prosecuting the body of Christ. Although this is true, still it is not clear how this fits within the letter to the Galatians. The *usus elenchticus* might be present in Rom 7:8–11. See Bruce, *The Epistle of Paul to the Galatians*, 143.

86. Cf. Bruce, *The Epistle of Paul to the Galatians*, 143; Martyn, *Galatians*, 257; Tannehill, *Dying and Rising with Christ*, 58–59. Van Bruggen emphasises that the 'I' is Paul in discussion with Peter. Nevertheless, this supports my exegesis: if Paul dies together with Jesus, who was executed legally, Jesus' death was an inclusive death, liberating from the plights of the law. See Van Bruggen, *Galaten*, 93–94.

This inclusive character of the death and resurrection of Christ implies that he has a certain representative position causing this inclusiveness.

In the letter to the Romans, three passages deserve our attention. Firstly Rom 4:25, where Paul finishes an exposition arguing for the continuity between the justification of Abraham and the justification of a Christian. Paul returns to what he said in 3:21–30.[87] He finishes with Christ, 'who was delivered διὰ τὰ παραπτώματα ἡμῶν and raised διὰ τὴν δικαίωσιν ἡμῶν.' Paul relates Christ's deliverance to death with our salvation from sin and the resurrection of Christ with our justification. Hence Hooker and Powers both affirm the inclusiveness of what Christ experienced: we participate in the fate of the representative who participated in our fate.[88] Han sees the death of Christ as 'the pointed manifestation of his solidarity in condemnation,' and 'his resurrection is the pointed manifestation of this solidarity in justification.'[89] It is undeniable that the inclusiveness of the work of Christ is present here: as he is vindicated and justified in the resurrection as the 'firstfruits,' so we will be justified with him. This is important, because traditionally the soteriological significance of the resurrection is underestimated.[90] It is also undeniable that the death of Christ can be seen as a sharing in our death. But Paul does not say in this verse that we die with Christ—what would affirm the inclusiveness—but that he was given over to death 'διὰ τὰ παραπτώματα ἡμῶν.' In what sense did our sins make God deliver Christ over to death? It is right that the notion of representation is present here, but does that necessarily imply that the notion of substitution is absent here as Powers claims?[91] I will deal with these questions below (see 5.3.6). For now it suffices to see in Rom 4:25 the inclusiveness of the work of Christ as our representative.

The second passage in Romans is Rom 5:18–19, a part of the section where Paul deals with the Adam-Christ parallel. Above we have already seen that this parallel implies that Christ can be seen as representative (see 5.3.2). Christ's act of obedience and righteousness will make the new

87. Cf. Van Bruggen, *Romeinen*, 73.

88. Hooker, *From Adam to Christ*, 39–41; Powers, *Salvation through Participation*, 130.

89. Han, *Raised for our Justification*, 238.

90. The soteriological significance of the resurrection is affirmed by Dunn, *Romans 1–8*, 225; Han, *Raised for our Justification*, 238–39; Hooker, *From Adam to Christ*, 40–41; Moo, *The Epistle to the Romans*, 290; Powers, *Salvation through Participation*, 131.

91. Powers, *Salvation through Participation*, 130.

humanity righteous. This act of obedience will refer to his obedience to death, 'even death on a cross' (Phil 2:8). Although Paul does not start to use the expression 'in Christ' until Rom 6 and writes here 'δι' ἑνὸς δικαιώματος' and 'διὰ τῆς ὑπακοῆς τοῦ ἑνὸς,' still the notion of representation is present here, for this constitutes the parallel between Christ and Adam. The justice of the one will make the many just. But again a question arises: does the fact that Christ acted as representative imply the absence of the notion of substitution? Wherein consisted the decisiveness of his act as righteous representative? Although the inclusiveness is present here, maybe the exclusivity is not absent, but I will return to this subject below (see 5.3.6).

Finally Rom 7:4 deserves attention. In this verse the bond between husband and wife that is released by the death of one of them is compared with the bond between law and man, released by the death of Christ. Remarkably, Paul does not make the following comparison: the dying of the one—the husband or Christ—releases the other—the wife or the sinner—from the law. He only says that the fact of dying loosens the bond of the law.[92] Through the body of Christ two things obtain: the death of the Christian to the law and a new life for God under the lordship of the resurrected Christ. Implied is a change of Lordship: Lord Law is exchanged for Lord Jesus Christ. In this complex passage Paul has intertwined two motifs: the motif of marriage and man and wife being one body or one flesh, with the motif of dying with Christ and living a new life under his reign (cf. Rom 6). Therefore it may be clear that 'the body of Christ' does not refer to the ecclesiastical or eucharistical body, but the human body of Jesus of Nazareth, who died on the cross.[93] Paul expresses ideas comparable to Gal 2:19. That the death of Christ implies our death to the law, implies a relationship between Christ and believers. In some sense he

92. See Baarlink, *Romeinen* 1, 99; Dunn, *Romans 1–8*, 368–69; Park, *Die Kirche als "Leib Christi" bei Paulus*, 256; Tannehill, *Dying and Rising with Christ*, 44–45.

The absence of the complete parallel could be understood in the light of the difference between the relation that a Jew had with the law, and the relation between Christians from the gentiles and the law. Strictly spoken, the gentiles never were under the law. Cf. Van Bruggen, *Romeinen*, 100–101.

93. See Van Bruggen, *Romeinen*, 100–101; Dunn, *Romans 1–8*, 362; Moo, *The Epistle to the Romans*, 417; Tannehill, *Dying and Rising with Christ*, 45–46.

H. Lichtenberger rejects an ecclesiological interpretation and understands 'the body of Christ' as the death of Christ, but sees influence from the Eucharistic liturgy; see Lichtenberger, *Das Ich Adams udn das Ich der Menschheit*, 118.

is our representative and his death as well as his resurrection implies our death to the law and our new life for a new Lord. The inclusiveness is very clear, as it is in the direct context of this passage (6:1—7:6). Within 7:1–6 this inclusiveness is painted in a special colour as it is suggested that this inclusiveness is to be compared with the inclusiveness of marriage, where a wife is included in her husband.

In conclusion, these passages in 2 Corinthians, Galatians and Romans make clear again that Paul's writings presuppose a moment of inclusiveness that necessitates the use of a concept of representation to understand his view of the work of Christ. Paul establishes a semantic relation between events in the life of Jesus and events in the life of believers, suggesting a positive relation between what happens in his and our lives (he died—we have died; he lives—we live). The passages in Romans 4 and 5 evoke the question whether Paul distinguished clearly between representation and substitution when dealing with the death of Christ. It might be that both ideas are present at the same time. Therefore it is necessary to deal again with these texts and see whether we also need a concept of substitution to reconstruct Paul's thinking. To this we turn now.

5.3.6 DECISIVENESS OF CHRIST: SUBSTITUTION

After having investigated the inclusive side of the decisive history of Jesus Christ, we now turn to its exclusive side. I will investigate several passages to answer the following question: do we need a concept of work-substitution to understand Paul's letters? This concept refers to the moment of exclusivity. In the preceding sub-section I described this exclusive moment as characterized by negative semantic relations (e.g. he died—we have not died, but live), or by the absence of a positive relation (e.g. he died . . .).

To this I want to add something. If Paul speaks about acts of God in Jesus Christ I understand this also as substitution: not just because *God* acts, but because God acts *in Christ*. The acts of God in Christ give Jesus Christ his exclusive character. Of course, this does not necessarily imply work-substitution. In any case it does imply person-substitution. If it is said that God acts in him, Jesus Christ is not only a human representative, but a person with a special significance.

The first passage is 2 Cor 5:15–21. It is already clear that in these verses Paul emphasises the inclusive character of the work of Christ and that we need a concept of representation to understand them. However,

Paul writes in 5:18 that God reconciled us to himself 'διὰ Χριστοῦ.' What did God do in Christ that was reconciling? Did he let Christ die and rise for all to make all die and rise, as he writes in 5:14–15? But why then does Paul write in 5:21 that God made him, who had no sin, to be ἁμαρτία for us, so that in him we might become the righteousness of God? The inclusiveness is clearly present with regard to the righteousness we receive, but is this inclusiveness also present with regard to the death of Christ as ἁμαρτία for us? Hooker and Powers suggest that Christ participated in our experience to make us share in his experience and in his destination. They oppose the idea that we need the concept of substitution to understand Paul.[94] Christ did identify himself with us and he did share our experience as became clear above. By his death and resurrection, 'the old has gone, the new has come' (5:17). However, what did he do as our representative when he died on the cross? We do not need to solve the question whether 'to be made ἁμαρτία for us' means to be made an offering for sin or not[95], to see that his death did something special to our sin. He was identified with sin to deliver us from sin. And this gave his death an exclusivity that justifies the 'διὰ Χριστοῦ' in 5:18.[96] This makes clear that representation and substitution do not exclude each other in these verses.[97] On the contrary, as our representative Christ did things we

94 Hooker, *From Adam to Christ*, 26, 42; Powers, *Salvation through Participation*, 74, 76.

95. Powers denies this, see Powers, *Salvation through Participation*, 11. Others who deny this are Lambrecht and Thrall, see Lambrecht, *Second Corinthians*, 101; Thrall, *A critical and exegetical Commentary on the Second Epistle to the Corinthians* (Vol. 1), 441.
Stuhlmacher sees it as a good possibility but leaves it open, Stuhlmacher, *Biblische Theologie des Neuen Testaments, Band 1*, 291, 296. Han does the same, see Han, *Raised for our Justification*, 53. Dunn relates it to the *function* of the sin offering, Dunn, *The Theology of Paul the Apostle*, 217.

96. Bouttier states that διὰ Χριστοῦ indicates often the objective and decisive character of the work of Christ. See Bouttier, *En Christ*, 33, 85. And Wedderburn writes: 'Perhaps the difference is that in Paul's usage *ἐν can* carry with it a sense of togetherness, association (σύν) with the agent of reconciliation, an idea that is not present in διά as such,' see Wedderburn, 'Some Observations on Paul's use of the Phrases 'in Christ' and 'with Christ,' 90.

97. Cf. Sanders who sees a mix of juridical and mystical elements in 5:17, see Sanders, *Paul and Palestinian Judaism*, 460. Lambrecht speaks of inclusive substitution and representation as complexes of thought which are not mutually exclusive, see Lambrecht, *Second Corinthians*, 105. Martin also sees Christ as a representative, whereas his death was substitutive, see Martin, *2 Corinthians*, 143. Ridderbos writes about a combination of the corporate thought and forensic imputation, Ridderbos, *Zijn wij op de verkeerde weg?* 24–25.

could never do and do not have to do anymore. This is expressed by Paul, when he contrasts Christ, being made sin(-offering), with righteousness. Although this does not imply a simple exchange—only *in* Christ may we become righteousness—the fact remains that Paul makes this contrast. To understand what Paul says in this passage about the things Christ did as representative we need the concept of work-substitution. Furthermore, when we see Jesus Christ merely as a human representative we fail to see that *God* acts in Christ. The concept of substitution helps to make clear that God made Christ to be (a) sin (offering) for us.

The second passage is to be found in Galatians 3. Discussing the curse of the law, in 3:13–14 Paul pictures Christ as redeeming from the curse of the law in order that Abraham's blessing might come to the Gentiles through Christ Jesus. Christ redeemed us from the curse of the law by becoming a curse for us, dying a cursed death hanging on the cross. He became a curse; the blessing comes to us. Wright shows that the difference between Israel and Gentiles make it impossible to treat the passage 'simply as a *locus classicus* of Paul's atonement-theology.'[98] How then should we understand Paul here? Israel lived with the law and the curse of the law. The covenant-breaking Israelite was a cursed Israelite. Christ identified himself with the people of Israel under the law who broke the covenant, and became their representative (Gal 4:4–5). As their representative he became a curse but made them also share in his position as son. Israelites are involved directly in this event, the Gentiles who were excluded by the law indirectly. By redeeming from the curse of the law, Christ opened the new covenant for both covenant breaking Jew and Gentile, hence giving them the blessing of Abraham.[99] Consequently, Hooker rightly denies that 3:13f can be understood as a simple exchange.[100] But I do not see why this implies that we do not also need the concept of work-substitution to understand what happened when Christ died.[101] The concept of substi-

98. Wright, *The Climax of the Covenant*, 138.

99. Cf. Van Bruggen, *Galaten*, 103–4; Wright, *The Climax of the Covenant*, 137–56. Dunn suggests a more direct relation between the death of Christ and the Gentiles, for according to him the covenant-breaking Israelite thus cursed is placed in the same position as the Gentile, the one already outside the covenant. See Dunn, *The Theology of Paul the Apostle*, 225–27.

100. Hooker, *From Adam to Christ*, 13–16. Cf. Sanders, *Paul and Palestinian Judaism*, 466.

101. Hooker claims that we cannot use the concept of substitution because she identifies substitution and exchange. See Hooker, *From Adam to Christ*, 42. However, this

tution makes clear that he bore the curse so that we would never more be cursed. The exclusivity becomes clear in the contrast that Paul makes between curse and blessing. We need the concept of work-substitution to understand the meaning of the horrible death of Christ on the cross. It is not just that Christ also opened the covenant for the Gentile; his horrific death was necessary also for the Jews to redeem them from the curse of the law. The curse requires more than just the death of the sinner; it has a meaning that Christ did not die a natural death, but that he died a cursed death.[102] Again, the concept of substitution and the concept of representation do not exclude each other. Exactly as representative Messiah, Jesus died the death of a cursed one on the cross.[103]

The letter to the Romans contains several passages that deserve our attention. The first of these is Rom 3:21–26. In the chapters preceding this passage Paul has built up an immense tension: both Gentile and Jew are under God's wrath. Even by observing the Jewish law no one will be declared righteous. Nobody can escape God's judgment. But now, χωρὶς νόμου, apart from the law, δικαιοσύνη θεοῦ has been made known.[104] Observing the law includes the offerings of the law—these were insufficient because the law brought no justification (3:20). But the law (and the prophets) testifies to this other δικαιοσύνη θεοῦ (3:21). This new road, buying captives freeing from God's wrath through payment of a ransom, is the way of faith in Jesus Christ as ἱλαστήριον (3:25).[105] Stuhlmacher has shown that it is impossible to understand the meaning of ἱλαστήριον against the background of the Maccabean martyr-theology.[106] The Old Testament theology of sacrifices centred in Lev. 16 offers a better background to understand the meaning of this ἱλαστήριον; the exact meaning is not important now.[107] By interpreting the death of Jesus on the cross

identification of substitution with exchange is not necessary.

102. Ridderbos, *Zijn wij op de verkeerde weg?* 28–30.

103. Cf. Wright, *The Climax of the Covenant*, 151–53.

104. The importance of the χωρὶς νόμου is emphasised by Seifrid, *Justification by Faith*, 220. See also Van Bruggen, *Romeinen*, 63.

105. Van Bruggen emphasises that ἀπολύτρωσις in 3:24 should be understood in its literal sense; Van Bruggen, *Romeinen*, 64.

106. See Stuhlmacher, 'Zur neueren Exegese von Röm 3,24–26,' esp. 121–32.

107. According to Baarlink and Stuhlmacher ἱλαστήριον means *kapporet*, the Mercy seat or atonement cover on the ark. See Baarlink, *Romeinen* 1, 64; Stuhlmacher, 'Zur neueren Exegese von Röm 3,24–26,' 131–32. Williams states that Paul not compares Christ with a piece of furniture, but he does see Lev 16 as possible background and

as a ἱλαστήριον, Paul makes clear that Jesus' death did what the complex of sacrifices prescribed by the law could not do. Faith in Jesus Christ, his death as ἱλαστήριον, his blood save from the impasse of Jewish history and from the judgment of God. He saves both Jew and Gentile. This might sound strange to Jewish ears: how could God be righteous and justify a sinful Gentile (cf. 3:28–30)? Can God be righteous and justify apart from observing the law? According to Paul, the cross proves that God *is* righteous. This must imply that the death of Jesus on the cross has an atoning effect on human sin, giving the justification of even the gentile sinner a juridical ground.[108] Otherwise God could not be faithful to his covenant.[109] And this again implies that, where the death of Jesus did what

---

translates with 'a propitiatory sacrifice,' see Williams, *Paul's Metaphors*, 247. Dunn gives 'means of expiation' and 'medium of atonement' as possibilies, see Dunn, *Romans 1–8*, 171 as well as 'expiation,' see Dunn, *The Theology of Paul the Apostle*, 213. Moo opts for 'sacrifice of atonement,' see Moo, *The Epistle to the Romans*, 237. Piper translates 'propitiation,' see Piper, *The Justification of God*, 115; Piper, 'The Demonstration of the Righteousness of God in Romans 3,25.26,' 4; Ridderbos gives 'zoenmiddel,' 'means of atonement,' Ridderbos, *Zijn wij op de verkeerde weg?* 35.

For two different interpretations of the theology of sacrifices and of Lev 16 see e.g. Gese, 'Die Sühne,' 85–106; eleborated by Janowski in *Sühne als Heilsgeschehen*; and Kiuchi, *The Purification Offering in the Priestly Litterature*. In the interpretation of Gese, the figure of the priest is not a central one. Kiuchi offers an interpretation making the figure of the priest more important. Cf. Exod 28:38.

108. For this idea of a juridical ground for justification, see Stuhlmacher, *Biblische Theologie des Neuen Testaments, Band 1*, 297, 334.

109. The so-called 'new perspective on Paul' sought attention for the Jewish character of Paul's theology and the problem of the relation between Jew and Gentile within the early church. This new perspective might question the German exegesis of Rom 3:21–26 in the line of Kümmel and Käsemann. According to Kümmel, Käsemann (and Stuhlmacher) ἔνδειξις means an active showing rather than a factual proof. In the past God showed his saving justice by forgiving, in the present by justifying the ungodly. Against the background of the gap between Jew and Gentile, and of God's covenant with Israel, 'proof' gains more plausibility. From a Jewish perspective, that God is righteous comes to light exactly in judging the gentiles to save his people, whereas his justification of the Gentiles by faith questions God's righteousness and his loyalty to Israel. It is an open question whether God is righteous if he justifies ungodly Gentiles. By presenting Jesus Christ as a ἱλαστήριον, God proves that he *is* righteous even if he justifies those who have faith in Jesus Christ.

Moreover, the interpretation of God's righteousness as 'covenant loyalty' has its problems in this light. God is not unjust in bringing his wrath on us (Rom 3:5). If God proves to be righteous in saving both Jew and Gentile by presenting Jesus Christ as ἱλαστήριον, and if he remains loyal to his people Israel, the justice shown in Jesus Christ has to be understood also as retributive justice and as loyalty to his creation (cf. Van Bruggen, *Romeinen*, 65).

the sacrifices could not do, his death had also an atoning effect on Jewish sin. In the death of Jesus Christ, God gave an offering for sin to atone sin and bring reconciliation for both Jew and Gentile. Hence we need the concept of substitution to understand the interpretation of the death of Jesus Christ that Paul gives here in Rom 3:21–25. For as a ἱλαστήριον, the death of Jesus Christ has its exclusivity: he did what we did not do and will not do (work-substitution). Further, Paul is clear about God's action in the death of Jesus.

The second is a passage we have been dealing with already, Rom 4:25. We have seen that the aspect of inclusiveness is present, but the question is whether the aspect of exclusiveness is also present in this passage. What happened in the death of Christ with our sin that makes it possible for us to say: Christ was delivered διὰ τὰ παραπτώματα ἡμῶν? The sequence of deliverance to death for our sins and resurrection to life for our justification suggests a negative moment of deliverance from sin, and a positive moment of a new beginning. Seen against the background of the preceding 3:21–26 (and Gal 3:13) this negative moment includes a moment of exclusivity. Not in the sense of a simple exchange (he died—we live), but in a more complex movement of identification of Christ with us, resulting in his life, death and resurrection in our place, and of our identification with Christ. We identify with Christ and share in his death and resurrection.[110] But our dying with Christ does not mean a complete identity of our death with his death. We die with him for sin, but in his death the negative moment is still stronger. Our death is no longer the death of a cursed one, our death cannot be seen as a ἱλαστήριον, but his death was. His death διὰ τὰ παραπτώματα ἡμῶν is different from our dying to sin.[111] To indicate this difference, the concept of work-substitution is necessary. As our representative he died our death, but in dying our death for our sins he

For a critical analysis of this German exegesis from another point of view see Piper, 'The Demonstration of the Righteousness of God in Romans 3,25.26,' or Piper, *The Justification of God*, 115–30. See further Käsemann, 'Zum Verständniss von Römer 3,24–26,' 96–100; Stuhlmacher, 'Zur neueren Exegese von Röm 3,24–26.'

110. That is the moment of truth in the exegesis of Hooker in *From Adam to Christ*, 39–41 and Powers in *Salvation through Participation*, 124–31.

111. The difference between his death and our death with him is reinforced, if the 'handed over'-motif refers to Isa 53, as Dunn claims. See Dunn, *Romans 1–8*, 241. Hofius sees also a relation between Isa 53 and Rom 4:25, see Hofius, 'Das vierte Gottesknechtlied in den Briefen des Neuen Testaments,' 121. Powers doubts whether such a relation between Isa 53 and Rom. 4:25 exists, see Powers, *Salvation through Participation*, 125–27.

changed the meaning of our death. Both his resurrection *and* death give our justification a juridical ground.[112] Therefore we need the concept of representation as well as the concept of work-substitution to understand this verse. The exclusivity of the death of Jesus may be expressed in the difference of his deliverance and our sin, and of his resurrection and our justification.[113] Moreover, God is the subject of the deliverance and not humanity, which indicates another aspect of this exclusivity.[114]

Now we turn to Romans 5, starting with the first part of this chapter, verses 1–11. Paul writes about the assurance we can have in faith, because God has demonstrated his love for us in Christ. In 5:9–10 Paul wants to make clear that where God was able to accomplish 'the extremely difficult and unlikely act of justifying and reconciling agonistic sinners,' he will also accomplish 'the relative easy act . . . to grant salvation at the last day to believers,' as Powers observes.[115] However, I do not see how this contrast between what has been and will be accomplished excludes the distinction between effects of Christ's death and of his resurrection, as Powers claims.[116] Paul may see the death and resurrection of Christ as 'inseparably connected';[117] still he does distinguish twice between the effects of death and resurrection in 5:9–10. He distinguishes between on the one hand justification and reconciliation, and on the other hand salvation (from God's wrath). Justification and reconciliation are connected with the blood of Christ and the death of the Son of God, salvation with Christ and the life of Christ. According to Powers, Paul is 'talking about the believers' participation in the death and resurrection.'[118] He interprets 5:9–10 solely in terms of inclusiveness. Nevertheless, in relation to the death of Christ Paul chooses words emphasising the exclusivity of the death of Christ. Paul does not say that we now have *died* by his death,

112. Cf. Moo, *The Epistle to the Romans*, 290. See further Stuhlmacher, *Biblische Theologie des Neuen Testaments, Band 1*, 297, 334.

113. Cf. Stuhlmacher, *Biblische Theologie des Neuen Testaments, Band 1*, 334–35: 'Existenzstellvertretung und Sühne durch Jesu Kreuzestod lassen sich bei Paulus nicht trennen, sondern bilden gemeinsam den von Gott selbst gelegten geschichtlichen Rechtsgrund für die den Glaubenden zuzusprechende Rechtfertigung.'

114. Stuhlmacher, *Biblische Theologie des Neuen Testaments, Band 1*, 294; cf. Rom 3:25.

115. Powers, *Salvation through Participation*, 95.

116. Powers, *Salvation through Participation*, 95.

117. Powers, *Salvation through Participation*, 96.

118. Powers, *Salvation through Participation*, 100.

hence laying a positive semantic relation between Christ's death and ours, affirming the inclusiveness. On the contrary, he writes that 'we have now been *justified* by his blood' (5:9), and 'were *reconciled* to him through the death of his Son' (5:10), emphasising the difference between what happened to Christ and what happens to us. Further, he mentions the blood of Christ, a sacrificial term emphasising the exclusivity of the death of Christ.[119] Moreover, where he speaks of future salvation ἐν τῇ ζωῇ αὐτοῦ, using the proposition ἐν, which can be interpreted in terms of participation in the life of Christ,[120] he speaks of justification and reconciliation διὰ τοῦ θανάτου τοῦ υἱοῦ αὐτοῦ. The preposition διὰ also could emphasise the exclusivity of the death of Christ.[121] Therefore we need the concept of work-substitution here to understand the special nature of the death of Christ. In the light of this interpretation the death of Christ ὑπὲρ ἡμῶν (5:8) can be seen in terms of work-substitution as well as of representation.[122]

Paul continues in the second part of chapter 5 with the comparison between Adam and Christ. We have seen already that we need a concept of representation to understand this passage, but also that it is a question whether this implies the absence of an exclusive moment (see 5.3.2 and 5.3.5). Against the background of 5:1–11 it is at least plausible that the 'δι' ἑνὸς δικαιώματος' and the 'διὰ τῆς ὑπακοῆς τοῦ ἑνὸς' imply also the notion of exclusivity, again affirming the impression that for Paul representation and substitution, inclusiveness and exclusivity do not exclude each other.

The fifth passage in Romans is Rom 8:3. In Romans 8 Paul returns to his explanation of the message of the gospel as freedom from condemnation, after having dealt with the problem of sin in Romans 6 and the problem of the law in Romans 7. He contrasts the powerlessness of sinful human nature with God's salvation in Christ. Although Rom 8:3 is a

119. Powers identifies the 'ἐν τῷ αἵματι αὐτοῦ' in 5:9a with the 'through him' and 'through his life' in 5:9b and 5:10, hence disturbing the parallelism identified between 5:9–10.

120. The preposition ἐν can have an inclusive meaning as is the case in this clause, but also an instrumental one, as is the case in ἐν τῷ αἵματι αὐτοῦ, which affirms the exclusivity.

121. See footnote 96.

122. As in other places, Powers interprets this *Sterbensformel* exclusively in terms of representation and participation, not seeing that representation and substitution do not exclude each other. See Powers, *Salvation through Participation*, 101–5.

classical proof text for the substitution theory, Sanders and Hooker claim that there is no question of substitution.[123] Hooker is right in so far as she means that there is no question of substitution seen as a simple exchange. In Romans 8 Paul states that Christ shared our sinful existence to make us share in his resurrected existence as Son of God. The more complex movement Paul has in mind can be labelled interchange as Hooker has done.[124] However, does this concept of interchange have as a consequence that a concept of substitution affirming the exclusivity of Christ is not necessary to understand Rom 8:3? This moment of exclusivity can be found at different points. Firstly, Paul writes that God sent his Son περὶ ἁμαρτίας. According to Stuhlmacher, Williams and Dunn this περὶ ἁμαρτίας has to be translated as 'sin offering' as in the LXX περι ἁμαρτίας is used to translate taJ'x;.[125] The interpretation of the death of Jesus as sin offering emphasises the exclusive meaning of his death. But even when this has to be translated as 'for sin,' a second point can be seen. Paul writes that God 'condemned sin in sinful man.' He used juridical language suggesting that something special happened in Christ's life and death: the condemnation of sin. If Paul only means that Christ was sent περὶ ἁμαρτίας in the sense of 'for sin,' even then this special juridical character remains. The power of sin is broken.[126] Thirdly, the semantic relation between events in the life of Christ and in the life of believers is a negative one: God dealt with sin in Christ; the law is fulfilled in us, who do not live 'according to the sinful nature but according to the Spirit' (8:4). To these arguments can be added that Paul contrasts the capacities of the law and human nature with what God does by sending Christ. The emphasis on God's acts in Christ reinforces the moment of exclusivity. In conclusion, although substitution in the sense of an isolated exchange is not a Pauline idea, we still need

123. Sanders, *Paul and Palestinian Judaism*, 466; Hooker, *From Adam to Christ*, 18, 42, 60.

124. See Hooker, *From Adam to Christ*, ch. 1–4.

125. Stuhlmacher, *Biblische Theologie des Neuen Testaments, Band 1*, 291; Williams, *Paul's Metaphors*, 247; Dunn, *Romans 1–8*, 439; Dunn, *The Theology of Paul the Apostle*, 216.

126. Cf. Van Bruggen, *Romeinen*, 115; Stuhlmacher, *Biblische Theologie des Neuen Testaments, Band 1*, 299; Dunn, *Romans 1–8*, 422, 440; Moo, *The Epistle to the Romans*, 480. Ridderbos, *Paulus*, 181.

the concept of (work-)substitution to understand what Paul means.[127] The acts of the representative comprise a moment of exclusivity.[128]

In the letter to the Colossians, two passages deserve attention. First Col 1:20–22. When Paul is dealing with the headship of Christ, he relates how Christ obtained his position as head in the new creation by the cross. Paul writes about a cosmic reconciliation making an end to the alienation of the Colossians. This reconciliation is achieved by the blood of Christ, shed on the cross, and 'the body of his flesh' (KJV). It is important to see that God dwells in Christ, hence taking over the place of the Jewish temple. What is especially of interest now is the blood-language, evoking the interpretation of the death of Christ as a sacrifice for sin. The blood of Christ brings the cosmos back in its order of *shalom*. He dies and gives his blood, we receive peace and reconciliation. With Stuhlmacher, the Old Testament tradition of atonement is to be seen in the background of this passage.[129] Furthermore, this passage presumes that the supremacy of the image of God over the cosmic powers, the 'θρόνοι εἴτε κυριότητες εἴτε ἀρχαὶ εἴτε ἐξουσίαι' (1:16), was somehow lost. The sacrifice of Christ restores his supremacy over the cosmic powers and is the moment of his triumph over these powers.[130] Finally, it is *God* who acts to reconcile through Christ. These elements suffice to see the element of exclusivity in the death and resurrection of Christ, which shows the necessity of the concept of substitution.

Another important passage in the letter to the Colossians is 2:14–15. Paul tells how God has made the Colossians alive with Christ and forgiven all their sins. Then he continues saying two things about the cross: a. God took away the χειρόγραφον that with its regulations was against us, by nailing it to the cross, and b. he disarmed τὰς ἀρχὰς καὶ τὰς ἐξουσίας and triumphed over them by the cross. On the one hand an incriminating and condemning document is taken away, a handwritten document of human guilt or a signed acknowledgement of our indebtness before God.[131]

127. Cf. Moo, *The Epistle to the Romans*, 481.

128. Cf. Wright, *The Climax of the Covenant*, who notes here that the incorporative and juridical language of Paul cannot be separated and belong together, 213.

129. Stuhlmacher, *Biblische Theologie des Neuen Testaments, Band* 2, 10.

130. Cf. Dunn, *The Epistles to the Colossians and to Philemon*, 102–5; O'Brien, *Colossians, Philemon*, 53–58.

131. For the meaning of χειρόγραφον see Dunn, *The Epistles to the Colossians and to Philemon*, 164–66; O'Brien, *Colossians, Philemon*, 124–25.

On the other hand the threatening powers are disarmed and defeated. By nailing the body of Christ to the cross the powers lose their weapon and their influence, and hence Christ triumphed over them. The cross as place of destruction becomes a place of triumph. He dies on the cross; we are liberated from the enslaving powers by his triumph over them. We could say that we do not need the concept of substitution to understand this passage, because the inclusiveness of the death and resurrection of Christ offer enough possibilities to understand what is said here. Furthermore, in the immediate context the idea of dying and rising with Christ is obviously present: circumcision in Christ (2:11), burial with Christ (2:12), resurrection with Christ (2:12) and dying with Christ (2:20). But in 2:14, the cross is not interpreted as the death of the sinner or criminal. Something was taken away, that was testifying against us. Paul's language is metaphorical and he does not use exact terms to make clear how this took place precisely, but it is clear that something unique happened with juridical consequences. Moreover, the powers are not disarmed and defeated by our dying with Christ—by our faith or by our baptism—but by the cross. Again, the death and resurrection of Jesus Christ have exclusivity that makes the use of the concept of work-substitution necessary. At the same time, we see in this passage that the concepts of substitution and of representation do not exclude each other.

Finally turning to the letter to the Ephesians, firstly Eph 1:7 is noteworthy. Here it is written: 'in him we have redemption through his blood, the forgiveness of sins, in accordance with the riches of God's grace.' Redemption and the forgiveness of sins are somehow related to the blood of Christ, referring to the interpretation of the death of Christ as a sacrifice.[132] The 'ἐν ᾧ' can be interpreted to be instrumental or inclusive. In the second case, the inclusive and the exclusive moment are again found together. In any case, we need the concept of work-substitution in this verse.

Secondly Eph 2:13–16. Here Paul is dealing with the difference between Jews and Gentiles. The Jews were in the covenant, but the Gentiles were foreigners, without hope and without God, far away. But the μεσότοιχον τοῦ φραγμοῦ, the dividing wall causing this separation, is taken away by Christ (2:14). In his flesh, which means in his bodily existence, he somehow abolished the law (2:15). Both were reconciled

132. O'Brien, *The Letter to the Ephesians*, 106.

to God through the cross (2:16). Paul refers to the blood of Christ that brought the ones who were far away near (2:13). Again, a concept of representation is not enough to understand this passage, although this idea is present in the new man that Christ made out of the two (2:15).

To conclude, the concept of work-substitution is necessary to understand Paul's reflection on the meaning of the death of Christ. This concept of work-substitution is not to be interpreted in the sense of an isolated exchange, but constitutes a moment of exclusivity within a more complex movement. In order to indicate this moment of exclusivity, the concept of substitution is necessary. The concepts of substitution and representation do not exclude each other but are intertwined. The motif of triumph, especially in Colossians, is remarkable in giving a perspective on the exclusivity of the death and resurrection of Christ other than the juridical or sacrificial images.

5.3.7 CONCLUSION

The central question in section 5.3 has been whether the concept of representation is necessary to describe Paul's Christology and which motifs give expression to the inclusive moment to which this concept refers. Jesus is the Messiah, having a position comparable to Adam but doing more than Adam. It is important that he is human, because he has a special position within the whole of humanity. As Christ, he represents Israel that again represents humanity. As last Adam, he brings humanity to its fulfilment, not only cancelling the trespasses of Adamic humanity, but also giving eternal life as life giving Spirit. Besides the Adam-motif, Paul uses other motifs indicating the position of Christ and fleshing out the concept of representation: firstfruits and firstborn, indicating that he receives as the first one what the many will receive by faith in him. The image of head however, traditionally understood as having a representative meaning, does not have the meaning of representative.

Apart from these different words, something more general must be said about Christ as representative, more precisely about how he is our representative. His significance as our representative cannot be understood in terms of a simple exchange, as if Christ took our place, whereby we receive his place. A more complex movement can be seen, described by Hooker as 'interchange.' He became one of us, identifying himself with sinful humanity, without becoming a sinner himself. This identification was that far reaching, that Jesus died the death of a cursed sinner, a blasphemer. What he experienced has a meaning for what we experience. At more than one moment, Paul can state a positive semantic relation between what he experienced and what we will experience. He suffered—we suffer with him. He died—we die with him. He rose from the death—we will rise from the dead with him. He is our representative; we participate in his fate.

However, this 'interchange' does not exclude the necessity of the concept of substitution to understand what Paul writes about Christ, as Hooker and Powers claim. Although every concept has its limitations[133] and although the concept of substitution is not useful if understood as isolated exchange, the concept of substitution has its function to do justice to the element of exclusivity in the work and person of Christ. This exclusivity can be seen at different moments. First, Paul states a negative semantic relation between what Christ did and what we do. He died; we are justified and live. Second, the sacrificial language and the interpretation of the death of Jesus Christ as a sacrifice for sin cannot be understood within the perspective of representation alone. Thirdly, the moment of exclusivity is found in the motif of Christ bearing the curse of the law and the motif of triumph over the powers. We need these motifs and the moment of exclusivity to understand the horrific character of the death of Jesus on the cross. Within the whole of representation and interchange, there is a moment of exclusivity, a depth in the death of Jesus that we do not have to experience.[134] He did something for us we could not do. But he did it, to save our life—dying on the cross, bearing the curse of the law, and encountering the wrath of God. Apart from these grounds for the necessity of a concept of work-substitution, the exclusivity of Jesus Christ has to be emphasised because God acted in Christ to save us from sin, death and the devil.

This implies that representation and substitution are concepts that we both need and that cannot be easily separated. Only if Christ is seen as

133. Cf. Dunn, *The Theology of Paul the Apostle*, 223. He writes that 'substitution' tells 'only half the story.' That is right, but if not interpreted as exchange (as he does), it still is necessary to tell this part of the story.

134. This does not mean that the concept of substitution alone suffices to understand the death of Christ. Instead, we need the whole of representation, interchange and substitution. Bouttier e.g relates the death of Christ and the concept of substitution too exclusively, see Bouttier, *En Christ*, 45, 115.

our representative can the moment of substitution be prevented from being understanding in terms of exchange. Only with the help of the concept of substitution can the position of Christ as representative be prevented from understanding humanity as saving itself.[135] Paul writes that Christ died 'for us' and 'for our sins.' This has to be understood with the help of the concept of representation as well as with the concept of substitution.[136] A separation of the so called juridical and mystical, the juristic and participationist, the exclusive and the inclusive, is not possible; they are intertwined and belong together.[137]

5.4 Soteriology: Participation

In section 5.3 I concentrated on the concept of representation within the whole of Paul's Christology, in this section the concept of participation within the whole of his soteriology is central. Paul uses a lot of different images to unpack the complexities of salvation in Christ. Reconciliation, liberation, redemption from slavery by paying a ransom, freedom, righteousness of God, inclusive 'Stellvertretung' resulting in death, atonement, justification, new creation, grace, triumph of enslaving powers, sonship, gift of the Spirit as guarantee, and inheritance.[138] Paul also frequently uses the language of 'ἐν Χριστῷ' and 'σὺν Χριστῷ.'

In this section we ask whether the diversity of this soteriological language has to be interpreted in terms of participation in Christ, and whether the concept of participation needs to be used when developing a concept of 'being in Christ' based on Paul. First, the in Christ-language receives attention together with related expressions like ἐν κυρίῳ, Χριστὸς ἐν ὑμιν, ἐν πνεύματι, εἰς Χριστόν (5.4.1). Secondly, I will concentrate on

135. Cf. Reid, *Our Life in Christ*, 89–93; Thiselton, *New Horizons in Hermeneutics*, 301–3.

136. Against the thesis of Powers, who claims that this must be understood in terms of representation alone, see his *Salvation through Participation*.

137. Cf. Beker, *The Triumph of God*, 93; Bouttier, *En Christ*, 132; Gaffin, 'Resurrection and Redemption,' 201–6; Schnelle, 'Transformation und Partizipation als Grundgedanke paulinischer Theologie,' 74; Stuhlmacher, *Biblische Theologie des Neuen Testaments, Band 1*, 334; Tannehill, *Dying and Rising with Christ*, 123; Wright, 'Romans and the Theology of Paul,' 66; Wright, *The Climax of the Covenant*, 213.

138. See Becker, *Paulus*, 433–37; Beker, *The Triumph of God*, 114; Dunn, *The Theology of Paul the Apostle*, 328–33; Gnilka, *Paulus von Tarsus*, 248–55; Ridderbos, *Paulus*, 171–223.

the motifs of dying, suffering, resurrection and glorification σὺν Χριστῷ and the συν-compounds Paul uses (5.4.2). Thirdly, several images indicating the unity of the believers with Christ, as body and head, temple and building, marriage and the union between man and wife, new clothing, will receive attention (5.4.3). Fourthly, I will give attention to different soteriological metaphors such as justification, sonship and sanctification (5.4.4). The section closes with a concluding sub-section (5.4.5).

5.4.1 ἐν Χριστῷ

The formula ἐν Χριστῷ is used by Paul often and in different ways.[139] Since Deissmann, it is often understood in the sense of Christ-mysticism. However, his mystical interpretation has been criticised for several reasons.[140] Firstly, he was wrong in identifying 'in Christ' with other expressions, like 'Christ in you' and 'in the Spirit.'[141] Secondly, he interpreted the 'in Christ' exclusively as a locative, whereas sometimes an instrumental sense is obvious.[142] Consequently, he was criticised for his philological presumption that the formula always means the same thing.[143] Thirdly, he was too restrictive in interpreting 'in Christ' only in subjective, individual and mystical terms. The ecclesiological character of Paul's thinking does not fit with his individualism.[144] Fourthly, interpretations in his trail failed to do justice to the eschatological or salvation-historical character of Paul's thinking or created an incorrect opposition between eschatology and mysticism, e.g. Albert Schweizer's interpretation.[145]

139. For an exact enumeration of all passages, see Neugebauer, *In Christus*, 65–72; Son, *Corporate Elements in Pauline Anthropology*, 187–90.

140. The mystical interpretation of Wikenhauser is less vulnerable to these criticisms. He emphasises the person of Christ determining the new sphere of life, stresses the ecclesiological and sacramental origin of the mystical union, and maintains the future being with Christ. See Wikenhauser, *Die Christusmystik des hl. Paulus*, esp. 27–35.

141. Barcley, "*Christ in You*," 5, 6, 9, 13; Bouttier, *En Christ*, 62–63; Neugebauer, *In Christus*, 31; Son, *Corporate Elements in Pauline Anthropology*, 17–19

142. Barcley, "*Christ in You*," 6; Bouttier, *En Christ*, 25–27

143. Neugebauer, *In Christus*, 20

144. Barcley, "*Christ in You*," 6; Fatehi, *The Spirit's Relation to the Risen Lord in Paul*, 273; Neugebauer, *In Christus*, 29; Son, *Corporate Elements in Pauline Anthropology*, 16.

145. Neugebauer, *In Christus*, 27, 148.

The influence of the salvation-historical approach is very clear in the interpretation offered by Neugebauer.[146] But he compared the expression 'in Christ' only with the expression 'in the Lord' and 'in the Spirit,' identifying 'in Christ' with the indicative, 'in the Lord' with the imperative and 'in the Spirit' with both. Other expressions, like Χριστὸς ἐν ὑμιν, εἰς Χριστόν, and σὺν Χριστῷ and the συν-compounds, were neglected. Furthermore, he separated the expressions 'in the Lord' and 'in Christ' too rigidly.[147] Consequently, I will not deal with the expression 'ἐν κυρίῳ' separately.

Bouttier and recently Son investigated the expression ἐν Χριστῷ within the whole of Pauline expressions. Their investigations show that for an adequate understanding of ἐν Χριστῷ, it is fruitful to analyse the other expressions as well.

The formula has been classified in different ways. Son has made the most extensive classification, based on grammatical criteria concerning subject, (implied) verb and object[148]:

1. The involved subject is personal	
a. with a verb denoting a being	(A is in Christ)[149]
b. with a copulative verb, denoting a status or state	(A is *x* in Christ)[150]
c. with an action verb, denoting an activity	
i. without object	(A does in Christ)[151]
ii. with a non-personal object	(A does *x* in Christ)[152]
iii. with a personal object	(A does to B in Christ)[153]

146. Smedes, Reid and Versteeg stand in line with Neugebauer, see Smedes, *Union with Christ*, 65–66; Reid, *Our Life in Christ*, esp. 30–31; and Versteeg, *Christus en de Geest*, 340–43.

147. Son, *Corporate Elements in Pauline Anthropology*, 9. Cf. the treatment of Dunn of 'ἐν Χριστῷ' and 'ἐν κυρίῳ'; Dunn, *The Theology of Paul the Apostle*, 397–99.

148. Son, *Corporate Elements in Pauline Anthropology*, 11–17. Sometimes I differ with Son about the classification of specific passages.

149. Rom 8:1; 16:7; 1 Cor 1:30; 2 Cor 5:17; 12:2; Gal 1:22; Eph 1:1; Phil 1:1; Col 1:2; 1 Thess 1:1; 2:14; 2 Thess 1:1.

150. Rom 6:11; 12:5; 16:3; 16:9; 16:10; 1 Cor 3:1; 4:10; 4:17a; Gal 3:26; 3:28; Eph 2:21; 3:6; Col 1:28; Phlm :23.

151. 1 Cor 15:19; 2 Cor 13:4 (ἐν αὐτῷ); Eph 1:12; Phil 3:3; Col 2:6 (ἐν αὐτῷ).

152. Rom 9:1; Eph 1:13a (ἐν ᾧ); 3:12 (ἐν ᾧ); Phlm :8; :20b.

153. 1 Cor 4:15a; 2 Cor 2:17; 12:19; Phil 2:21.

iv. with God as subject	(God does in Christ)[154]
v. with an action verb in passive, often God as implied subject and emphasis on the status as result of the action	(A is [*verb*]-ed in Christ)[155]

2. The involved subject is non-personal

a. with a verb denoting a being	(something is in Christ)[156]
b. with a copulative verb, denoting a status or state	(something is *x* in Christ)[157]
c. with an action verb, denoting an activity	(something does in Christ)[158]

Having classified different usages of the formula does not mean that we *understand* how Paul uses it. I will deal with several issues to clarify Paul's usage, concentrating my attention on themes important for 'being in Christ' understood with the help of the concepts of representation and participation. I will concentrate on the most important passages. I will not deal with passages focussing on the activity of God in Christ or passages where 'in Christ' can just be translated with 'christian.'[159]

The first question is whether there is a relation between the formula ἐν Χριστῷ and the concept of representation. To start very basically, the observations of Weddenburn are important. He compares 'in Christ' and 'with Christ' with 'in Abraham' and 'with Abraham' in Galatians 3. Paul

154. 2 Cor 1:20 (ἐν αὐτῷ); 2:14; 5:19; Eph 1:3; 1:4; 1:6 (ἐν τῷ ἠγαπημένῳ); 1:10; 1:20; Eph 2:6: 2:7; 2:16 (ἐν αὐτῷ); 4:32; Phil 4:19; 2 Tim 1:9.

155. 1 Cor 1:2; 1:5 (ἐν αὐτῷ); 15:18; 15:22; 2 Cor 5:21 (ἐν αὐτῷ); Gal 2:17; Eph 1:11; 1:13b; 2:10: 2:13; 2:22 (ἐν ᾧ); 4:21a (ἐν αὐτῷ); Col 2:7 (ἐν αὐτῷ); 2:10 (ἐν αὐτῷ); 2:11 (ἐν ᾧ).12 (ἐν ᾧ); 1 Thess 2:14; 2 Thess 1:12 (ἐν αὐτῷ).

156. Rom 3:24; 8:39; 15:17; 1 Cor 4:17b; 16:24; Gal 2:4; Eph 1:7 (ἐν ᾧ); 1:9 (ἐν αυ'τῷ); 3:11; 3:21; Phil 1:13; 2:1; 2:5; 3:14; Col 1:4; 1:14 (ἐν ὧ); 2:3 (ἐν ᾧ); 1 Tim 1:14; 3:13; 2 Tim 1:1; 1:13; 2:1; 2:10; 3:15.

These passages include several places with the expression 'faith in Christ Jesus,' Col 1:4; 1 Tim 3:13; 2 Tim 3:12.

157. Rom 6:23; 2 Cor 1:19 (ἐν αὐτῷ); 1 Thess 5:18.

158. Rom 8:2; 2 Cor 1:4; 3:14; Gal 3:14; Phil 1:26; 4:7; Col 1:16 (ἐν αὐτῷ); 1:17 (ἐν αὐτῷ); 1:19 (ἐν αὐτῷ); 2:9 (ἐν αὐτῷ).

159. Although 'in Christ' can sometimes be translated as 'christian,' it must not be done too easily, because then 'the formula loses a sense of personal connection with the historical Christ which the phrase ἐν Χριστῷ retains,' Son, *Corporate Elements in Pauline Anthropology*, 13.

mentions that Scripture says that all nations will be blessed in Abraham (Gen 12:3 and 18:18). With Abraham, believers will be blessed (Gal 3:8–9). The blessing that was promised in Abraham, came in Christ (3:14). In the case of Abraham, it is impossible to understand the expressions 'in him' and 'with Abraham' in the sense of spatial and ontological categories. Hence he tends to interpret the ἐν Χριστῷ and σὺν Χριστῷ in an instrumental, causal sense, although he leaves room for an inclusive or local sense. Both 'Abraham and Christ are viewed as representative figures through whom God acts towards the human race: he acts towards them 'in' those figures and they are caught up 'with' them in that divine initiative of grace.'[160] Given this Jewish background, Weddenburn argues against a background of the 'in Christ'-formula in Hellenistic mystery-cults.[161]

This parallel signalled by Weddenburn must make us cautious with regard to speculative interpretations of 'in Christ.' At the same time, it is a question whether the figure of Christ has its own singularity, making the impact of the Abraham-parallel less important. The totality of Paul's language must be decisive.

In the light of Weddenburn's observation it is important that Paul only once writes 'in Jesus,' viz. in Eph 4:21: '(ἀλήθεια) ἐν τῷ 'Ιησοῦ.' In every other case Paul writes 'in Christ,' 'in Christ Jesus,' or 'in the Lord.' Remembering that Wright sees the Messiah as a representative figure, it is possible to understand this aspect of Paul's usage: not as ordinary human being, but as Messiah—Christ—and as Lord is Jesus the one in whom we are.

Together with the observations of Weddenburn, this makes clear that it is impossible to understand the 'in Christ'-formula without the concept of representation.

A second point concerns the question whether the 'in Christ' can be understood in locative sense.

The expression 'ἐν Χριστῷ' can be understood as dative, in a locative or instrumental. Often it is difficult to determine whether locative or instrumental is intended. For the discussion regarding participation

160. Wedderburn, 'Some Observations on Paul's use of the Phrases 'in Christ' and 'with Christ,' 91. See further 88–90; Wedderburn, 'The Body of Christ and related concepts in 1 Corinthians,' 86–90.

161. Wedderburn, 'Some Observations on Paul's use of the Phrases 'in Christ' and 'with Christ,' 91; Wedderburn, *Baptism and Resurrection*, 342; 357–59; 393–96. Cf. Van Bruggen, *Romeinen*, 94.

and inclusiveness, it is especially important to determine whether the ἐν Χριστῷ can have a locative meaning. To settle this discussion, Son made his classification as given above. His analysis of this classification brings Son to the following conclusions: 'There are instances in which Paul clearly uses the formula in a locative sense' and 'Throughout all the instances, whether the verb denotes a status/state or an activity in Christ, a locative sense still remains. Even in the instances where an instrumental sense dominates, one cannot completely eliminate a locative sense.'[162] Other scholars share the conclusion that a locative sense and an instrumental sense are both present in Paul's usage of the expression.[163]

This impression of a locative is confirmed in dealing with the expression εἰς Χριστόν. This expression is used several times in the context of baptism and together with the verb πιστεύειν. Regarding baptism, it is significant that Paul never connects βαπτίζειν with ἐν Χριστῷ but with εἰς Χριστόν.[164] To be baptised seems to mean to be transferred in a sphere or space determined by Christ, in Christ as a space or sphere.[165] As Dunn writes, 'it is difficult to avoid the basic sense of *eis* as movement into a location.'[166] Regarding the verb πιστεύειν, whereas Paul connects πίστις with ἐν Χριστῷ, he always connects the verb with εἰς Χριστόν;[167] Col 2:5 is the only exception. Again, a sense of movement into a place or sphere seems present.[168]

Another indication of a locative sense is given by expressions paralleling 'in Christ': 'in Adam,' 'in the flesh,' 'in the body' and 'in the world.' The old humanity is the humanity in Adam, the new one the humanity in Christ (1 Cor 15:21—22:45). Paul writes about being in this world,

162. Son, *Corporate Elements in Pauline Anthropology*, 16.

In the case of some usages, it is according to Son difficult to determine whether Paul used a locative or an instrumental. The following cases are concerned: 1 c i, ii, iii, iv and v. In other cases the instrumental is according to Son rarely present although not impossible: 1 b. In some cases the locative seems dominant according to Son: 1 a; see Son, 11–17.

163. Barcley, "*Christ in You*," 110–11; Dunn, *The Theology of Paul the Apostle*, 400; Fatehi, *The Spirit's Relation to the Risen Lord in Paul*, 263–74.

164. Rom 6:3; Gal 3:27; cf. 1 Cor 10:2; 12:13.

165. See Dunn, *The Theology of Paul the Apostle*, 404–5; Bouttier, *En Christ*, 36–38; Son, *Corporate Elements in Pauline Anthropology*, 22–23.

166. Dunn, *The Theology of Paul the Apostle*, 404.

167. Rom 10:14; Gal 2:16; Phil 1:29.

168. Bouttier, *En Christ*, 36; Son, *Corporate Elements in Pauline Anthropology*, 22.

'ἐν τῷ αἰῶνι τούτῳ' or 'ἐν τῷ νῦν αἰῶνι.'[169] Further he writes about our still being in the flesh, 'ἐν τῇ σαρκί,' which is at the same time the place where God has redeemed us.[170] All these expressions indicate a sphere or place opposed to the sphere or place 'in Christ'; an old aeon and a new one.[171]

I have not mentioned 'in the Spirit' yet. Deissmann paralleled this expression with 'in Christ,' but he has been criticised for doing so.[172] Analysing Paul's use of 'ἐν πνεύματι' with the same categories as 'ἐν Χριστῷ,' Son found the following results:

- apart from Rom 8:9 Paul does not speak of the believers indwelling or state / status in the Spirit
- Paul refers often to the Spirit's indwelling in believers, but here Paul does not use the expression 'in the Spirit';[173]
- mostly Paul employs an action verb, denoting some kind of activity in the Spirit;[174]
- when Paul refers to an objective act of redemption, he uses a passive voice with a more instrumental ἐν.[175]

Paul uses 'in the Spirit' in a more limited way than 'in Christ.' He speaks only once of being in the Spirit and further of actions 'in the Spirit'

169. 'ἐν τῷ αἰῶνι τούτῳ' (1 Cor 3:18); 'ἐν τῷ αἰῶνι τούτῳ ἀλλὰ καὶ ἐν τῷ μέλλοντι' (Eph 1:21); 'ἐν τῷ νῦν αἰῶνι' (1 Tim 6:17); 'ἐν τῷ νῦν αἰῶνι' (Titus 2:12).

170. For our being in the flesh, see Rom 7:5; 8:8–9; 2 Cor 10:3; Gal 2:20; Phil 1:22, 24; Col 2:1; Phlm :16. For God acting in the flesh see Rom 8:3; 1 Tim 3:16.

171. That I mention also the old and new aeon indicates that I see no real opposition between a locative and salvation-historical interpretation. In a salvation-historical interpretation, a 'geschichtlich' understanding is favoured sometimes in opposition to the spatial understanding of Deissmann. See Neugebauer, *In Christus*, 148; Versteeg, *Christus en de Geest*, 342–43. A spatial understanding that obscures the salvation-historical and eschatological-temporal dimension of 'in Christ,' fails to do justice to Paul. A localising interpretation however, can do justice to the salvation-historical dimension as well as to spatial dimensions—the space determined by Christ, the representative. Cf. Bouttier, *En Christ*, 27–28, 35–38, 85–86, 93, 98, 133–34; Smedes, *Union with Christ*, 65–92; Son, *Corporate Elements in Pauline Anthropology*, 23–37, 58–65, 178–80.

172. Bouttier, *En Christ*, 62–63; Son, *Corporate Elements in Pauline Anthropology*, 18–19.

173. Rom 8:9, 11; 1 Cor 3:16; 6:19; 2 Tim 1:14.

174. Rom 9:1; 14:17; 1 Cor 12:3; 14:16; Eph 6:18; Col 1:8; 1 Thess 1:5.

175. Rom 2:29; 15:16; 1 Cor 12:9, 13; Eph 2:22; 3:5; 4:30; 5:18; 1 Tim 3:16. See Son, *Corporate Elements in Pauline Anthropology*, 20.

and our salvation being present in our lives in or by the Spirit. Bouttier has analysed how Paul uses 'in the Spirit' compared to how he uses 'in Christ.' Historical salvation in Christ arrives in our personal lives in the Spirit.[176] Anyway, regarding Rom 8:9 and our actions in the Spirit, a locative sense is present.

As far as the 'being in Christ' of persons is concerned, two passages that contain this locative very strongly deserve our attention: 2 Cor 5:17 and Rom 8:1.[177]

In 2 Corinthians, Paul writes to the church in Corinth in a tense situation. He makes clear that he tries to reach them as a minister of Christ. The love and death of Christ determine even his way of knowing people: no longer regarding man after the flesh—'from a worldly point of view' (5:16), but as someone living for Christ (5:15). Because, 'if anyone is in Christ, he is a new creation. The old things have gone, the new have come' (5:17). All have died with the death of Christ, making the old things disappear. But he rose for them and consequently, they should live for him. With his resurrection the new things have come. All who are in him are included in this new creation. Paul does not say that they are resurrected, although they have died and live for him. They are not a new creation of themselves; they are only a new creation *in Him*. They live in Christ, their representative. The locative sense is very clear.

In Rom 8, Paul returns to Rom 5 after having dealt with the problem of sin and the problem of the law. There is no condemnation. Now in Rom 8:1 he voices this freedom from judgment as follows: there is no condemnation for 'τοῖς ἐν Χριστῷ Ἰησοῦ.' In Christ Jesus, the representative Christ, no condemnation should be feared. What matters is belonging to the age of Christ and identification with his death and resurrection.[178] This 'in Christ' resounds against the background of the 'in the flesh' (7:5; 8:8–9) and the 'in the Spirit' (8:9). Believers no longer live in the flesh but in the Spirit, given as firstfruits (8:23), and in Christ. As chapter 8 makes

176. Bouttier, *En Christ*, 61–69.

177. Another text that could be mentioned here is 1 Cor 1:30. Unfortunately, there is a problem. Paul opposes here the wisdom of the Jews and Gentiles with the foolishness of God. But for believers, the foolishness of God is wisdom. Christ became their wisdom from God. Paul contrasts worldly with godly existence. Now it depends on whether we should translate 'You are from God, in Christ Jesus' or 'It is from God that you are in Christ Jesus.' In the second case a strong locative sense is present, in the first case there is not.

178. Dunn, *Romans 1–8*, 415.

clear, salvation has not been achieved fully yet, but it is present in the Spirit and in Christ. The presence of salvation in Christ is that decisive so we can be full of hope.[179] The 'in Christ' locates us in the realm of this salvation.

In Christ, salvation is already present—be it described as new creation (2 Cor 5:17) or in more juridical terms as freedom from condemnation (Rom 8:1). At least in some passages the locative sense of in Christ is very clear as we have seen. In many others it is less explicit but still present, more or less together with an instrumental sense. The 'in Christ'-formula has its own intriguing ambiguity.

Thirdly, I will concentrate on the perspective the 'in Christ'-formula offers on the tension between the already and not yet. Dealing above with 2 Cor 5:17 and Rom 8:1 we have seen that salvation is present already in Christ, the representative Messiah, although believers wait for a more complete participation in Christ's salvation.

This tension between the already and not yet becomes clear, furthermore, in Rom 6. Having shown the justification by faith alone, Paul asks whether we shall go on sinning. Answering this question, it becomes clearer in which sense according to Paul, salvation was already achieved and in which sense not. We died with Christ to sin (6:2—8:11). Our new life together with the resurrected Christ retains a future aspect (6:5–8). But for the present it must be clear: 'count yourselves dead to sin but living to God in Christ Jesus' (6:11). The future aspect related to resurrection is not present regarding our being alive in Christ. In Christ is already present what will become full reality in the future.[180] In this passage, Paul says again that in Christ, our representative, we have new life already, in which we will participate in a fuller sense later.

Whereas the earlier letters say that we live in Christ to God, but will be made alive in the future resurrection together with Christ, the later letters to the Colossians and Ephesians differ from Rom 6. In Christ, believers are 'raised with him' (Col 2:12), or seated 'with him in the heavenly realms in Christ Jesus' (Eph 2:6). Analogous to the other letters, it is said that we have salvation in Christ (Col 1:14; Eph 1:7); that we are circumcised in Christ in the putting off of the body of the flesh (Col 2:11) and are created in Christ Jesus. But more than in the other letters it is said:

179. Dunn, *Romans 1–8*, 435.

180. Cf. Bouttier, *En Christ*, 46.

in Christ, the representative Messiah we are even raised from death and glorified in heaven. This does not mean that the future aspect disappears in Colossians and Ephesians: Christ still has to appear in glory (Col 3:4) and the day of redemption still has to come (Eph 4:30). Moreover, we are raised through faith in the power of God (Col 2:12).

These differences can be understood in the light of the context of the different letters. Where in Corinthians people thought that no future resurrection would happen and salvation was totally realised in the present, Paul is forced to emphasise the future aspect. But in Colossians, where people tried to climb towards Christ by observing religious practices forgetting that Christ has related us to himself, the present aspect of salvation is emphasised. Maybe moreover Paul's personal situation as a prisoner brought him to this emphasis. Van Bruggen writes that where Paul has become the victim of the powers of this world, he stresses that Christ stands above these powers.[181] Again the expression 'in Christ' is used differently, but the tension between present salvation in Christ and future salvation remains.

In conclusion, the formula 'in Christ' often makes clear how salvation is a present reality and is therefore in those cases characterized by the tension between already and not yet.

This tension brings us to the fourth point: how is a more intensive participation in Christ realised?

Here the expression 'Christ in you' deserves attention, used six times by Paul.[182] A complete reciprocity between 'in Christ' and 'Christ in you' as Deissmann saw, is impossible. 'In Christ' is broader that 'Christ in you.'[183] Recently Barcley investigated Paul's use of 'Christ in you' as an important Pauline concept. He claims that this expression is used primarily to stress the individual, personal side of the relationship with Christ. It points back to the basis of the life of faith, it indicates an ongoing transformation in the life of the believer and points to the goal of maturity, when believers will be fully transformed to conformity to Christ's image.[184] However, some critical questions must be faced. Firstly, it is a question whether 'Christ in

181. Van Bruggen, *Paulus*, 124.

182. In 2 Cor 13:5; Gal 2:20; 4:19; Rom. 8:10; Col 1:27; and 3:11. Cf. 2 Cor 13:3. See on this expression Barcley, "*Christ in You*"; Bouttier, *En Christ*, 82–85; Smedes, *Union with Christ*, 129–38; Son, *Corporate Elements in Pauline Anthropology*, 17–20.

183. Barcley, "*Christ in You*," 112; Son, *Corporate Elements in Pauline Anthropology*, 18.

184. Barcley, "*Christ in You*."

you' can be treated as a concept. The passages differ in character and deal with critical self-examination regarding the indwelling of Christ (2 Cor 13:5; Rom 8:10); the indwelling of Christ in Paul (Gal 2:20); a growing conformity to Christ (Gal 4:19);[185] the proclamation of Christ among the gentiles (Col 1:27) unity in Christ, who is all and in all (Col 3:11). If the use of the words 'Christ in you' is the only connection between these passages, the argument for speaking of a concept becomes very thin. Secondly, it is a question whether can be said that 'Christ in you' is the basis for 'being in Christ' as Barcley claims. Paul's message of the gospel does not start with 'Christ in you.' We are saved by Christ—the moment of exclusivity. We are saved in Christ—the moment of inclusiveness. God's acting in Christ is fundamental to our salvation and to our being in Christ. The saving acts of God in Christ precede the presence of Christ by the Spirit in our lives. Therefore I cannot agree with Barcley if he makes 'Christ in you' the basis for 'in Christ.' In conclusion, the idea of a fundamental concept of 'Christ in you' in Paul is not convincing.

Still, two passages deserve our attention: Gal 2:20 and Rom 8:10. In Gal 2 Paul is very clear about the impossibility of justification by works of the law. As a sinner, Paul even does not exist any more. He died through the law to the law, being crucified with Christ (2:19). Yet he lives, but that is Christ who lives in him. Although he still lives in the flesh, faith in Christ is everything (2:20). The statement concerns primarily the absolute impossibility of any self-justification. However, the statement implies a presence of Christ in the life of Paul. Christ is his life. And as long as he lives in the flesh, he lives by faith in him. How Christ is present in his life is not said because it has only a secondary interest regarding the problem Paul is dealing with. In any case, this presence has to do with the death and resurrection of Christ, seen as an event that includes Paul.[186] Christ is not only the representative Messiah, in whom Paul is; Christ is also present in Paul.

In Romans 8 Paul distinguishes between, on the one hand, those who walk and live 'κατὰ σάρκα,' and, on the other hand, believers who walk and live 'κατὰ πνεῦμα' (8:4–5). Death stands against life and peace. Someone is in the Spirit and not in the flesh if the Spirit of God lives in

185. In Gal 4:19, the formation of Christ in you indicates more the growth of a Christian character than the indwelling of Christ himself; cf. Son, *Corporate Elements in Pauline Anthropology*, 17.

186. Cf. Bouttier, *En Christ*, 82.

that person. Writing about the Spirit living in believers (8:9), Paul writes in 8:10: 'If Christ is ἐν ὑμῖν, the body is dead because of sin, but the Spirit is alive because of righteousness' (my translation). The inhabitation of the Spirit can be expressed as Christ's presence in us.[187] This presence of Christ enables Paul to bring two things together: the body is dead; the Spirit is alive. The Spirit is life and peace, opposed to death, flesh, and hostility to God. Still living in the body before the *parousia* we meet both realities. By putting the inhabitation of the Spirit unusually into words such as 'Christ in us,' Paul creates new possibilities: this idea enables Paul to mention both flesh and Spirit in a way related to salvation in Christ, hence enabling life with both. The step from Christ in us to dying and rising with Christ is made easily. This verse makes clear two things: the inhabitation of the Spirit can be seen as 'Christ in you'; and by the inhabitation of the Spirit the death and resurrection of Christ are somehow present realities in the life of the believer.

In conclusion, Paul's use of the expression 'Christ in you' in these two verses indicates the presence of Christ in the life of believers and their participation in his death and resurrection. Hence it makes clear that Christ is more than a representative. We are included in Christ, but this inclusion has consequences in the direction of a more intense participation in Christ. It could be that Paul uses 'Christ in you' where he normally refers to the inhabitation of the Spirit, where his argumentation demands the notions of dying and rising with Christ.

To this point we have seen that 'in Christ' is an expression used in different ways. The notion of Christ as representative Messiah is important to understand Paul's use of this formula with regard to 'being in Christ.' God has acted in Christ to save us, we are in Christ and salvation is in Christ. Beyond an instrumental sense, the 'in Christ' can further have a locative sense. It is not only Paul's use of the formula that indicates this, but also the expression 'εἰς Χριστόν' and other expressions as 'in the flesh,' 'in the world' and 'in the Spirit.' These all indicate two different spheres or aeons, an old one existing in Adam and a new one existing in Christ. Being in Christ, the believer lives in a new aeon as a new creation. In Christ, salvation is present. Still, the story of salvation did not start with 'being in Christ,' nor is it finished with it. 'Being in Christ,' the localisation in the representative, is only one of the first results of God's act in Christ

187. Versteeg, *Christus en de Geest*, 361–67.

for us, and awaits further participation in the Christ-event. This growing participation is indicated by the expression 'Christ in you,' but also by the 'with Christ'-expressions. To these I turn now.

5.4.2 σὺν Χριστῳ

To understand the 'with Christ' motif it is first of all important that Paul used not only the expression 'σὺν Χριστῳ,' but moreover about forty σὺν-compounds. He uses them both to describe the participation in the death and life of Christ as well as the common reality of the believers.[188] I concentrate on the first category, although Dunn very properly observed that 'the two uses were no doubt linked in Paul's mind': the communality of believers is 'rooted in its dependence upon their common experience of participation in Christ.'[189]

Furthermore, we have already seen with regard to 'ἐν Χριστῷ' that in the later letters to the Colossians and the Ephesians relatively more emphasis is laid on the present character of salvation. This is the case also with regard to 'σὺν Χριστῳ' as will become clear later on in this sub-section.

Regarding the background of Paul's use of 'with Christ' the work of Weddenburn deserves attention. He has shown that it has an Old Testament background. Gal 3:9 shows that an analogy exists between 'with Christ' and 'with Abraham.' Because Abraham cannot be seen as a mystery-god, the background in antique mystery-cults becomes less plausible. Moreover, there is no parallel for the 'with Christ'-expression in the mystery-cults.[190]

The expression 'σὺν Χριστῳ' makes it possible to relate semantically different moments in the history of Jesus Christ with the life of believers: suffering with Christ, being crucified with Christ, dying with Christ, rising with Christ, appearing with Christ, being heir with Christ, being glorified with Christ, living with Christ and being seated with Christ in heaven. In what follows I will deal with the different moments in the order of the

188. Dunn gives a list of these σὺν-compounds, see Dunn, *The Theology of Paul the Apostle*, 402–3. For another list, see Son, *Corporate Elements in Pauline Anthropology*, 20–21. Cf. further Douglas J. Moo, *The Epistle to the Romans*, 391–92.

189. Dunn, *The Theology of Paul the Apostle*, 402–3.

190. Wedderburn, 'Some Observations on Paul's use of the Phrases "in Christ" and "with Christ,"' 88–91; Wedderburn, *Baptism and Resurrection*, 342, 357–58, 393.

story of Jesus Christ: suffering and crucifixion, death and burial, resurrection and glorification and his second coming.

Christ has suffered and we suffer with Christ. This reality is indicated in Rom 8:17 by the σὺν-compound 'συμπάσχομεν.' Paul is dealing here with the present condition of believers, living in the Spirit and waiting for the future salvation of the body. The sharing in the suffering of Christ is a present reality as Paul pictures it. This is confirmed by two other passages about participation in the suffering of Christ where he does not use 'σὺν Χριστῷ' or a σὺν-compound, 2 Cor 1:5 and Phil 3:10. During their earthly life, Christians share in the suffering of Christ. This seems to be a necessity. We need to identify ourselves with the suffering of Christ and share in his sufferings to participate in his glory.[191] In Romans 8 this surprisingly seems to imply that all our experiences of suffering can be seen as a sharing in his sufferings, and not only our suffering for Christ's sake. Maybe Paul, Christ having identified himself with our condition of suffering, saw all our suffering as henceforward indissolubly connected with his suffering.[192] Hence we may interpret all our suffering as a participation in his sufferings. And the suffering of an apostle can be a suffering for other people (cf. 2 Cor 4:12).[193]

This raises the question whether the work of Christ loses its exclusivity. Does this imply that our suffering has a substitutionary character? One might get this impression when reading Paul in Col 1:24: 'Now I rejoice in what was suffered for you, and I fill up in my flesh what is still lacking in regard to Christ's afflictions, for the sake of his body, which is the church.' Further, in the second letter to the Corinthians it is clear that Paul's suffering is for the sake of the Corinthians (2 Cor 4:12). But Van Bruggen has shown that although an analogy is made between the experiences of suffering of Christ and of believers in this world, never has

191. Dunn, *Romans 1–8*, 456; Moo, *The Epistle to the Romans*, 505; Tannehill, *Dying and Rising with Christ*, 114.

192. Tannehill, *Dying and Rising with Christ*, 114. Hooker confirms this impression in relation to Paul's writing about his suffering in 2 Corinthians. Paul does not distinguish between suffering due to his apostolic call and his 'other' suffering. All suffering can be transformed by the experience of interchange as a participation in the suffering of Christ. See Hooker, *From Adam to Christ*, 52. Cf. Rom. 8:22; Siber, *Mit Christus leben*, 157–59, 167, 180.

193. For participation in the suffering of Christ within the Corinthian correspondence, see Hafemann, *Suffering and the Spirit*; more general Gorman, *Cruciformity*; and Hays, 'Crucified with Christ.'

an analogy been made between the death of Christ as an act wherein he gave his body and blood for us. It is not the sacrificial death of Christ that is filled up, but his suffering for the sake of his people and humanity.[194]

To conclude, believers participate in the sufferings of Christ. Their suffering with him is a continuing reality as long as this world has not yet been saved. It seems that the identification of Christ with us and of us with Christ goes that far, that we can see all our suffering as participation in Christ's suffering.

Christ's suffering culminated in his crucifixion. Twice, Paul relates the crucifixion to our lives with the help of the verb συσταυρόομαι, a passive perfect in Gal 2:19 and a passive aorist in Rom 6:6 (cf. Gal 5:24). Whereas participation in the suffering of Christ is a present reality, participation in his crucifixion is a past reality underlying the present. Crucifixion with Christ marks in Galatians 2 the radical rupture between a life under the law and a life for God with Christ. Participation in the crucifixion of Christ is a presupposition for the present life in Christian freedom. The same is the case in Romans 6. Freedom from sin and liberation from the body of sin are achieved by the crucifixion of the old self. Paul does not analyse when this happened—in the crucifixion of Christ, in conversion, in baptism[195]—but the impact of the image is very clear: 'Crucifixion with Christ is conceived as neither self-induced nor a prolonged activity. It is a once-for-all act that God has already performed for the believer, although he continues to benefit from its results.'[196] Being crucified once for all with Christ in the past, we are free in the present.

On the cross, Christ died; and we died with Christ according to Paul. We have discussed already 2 Cor 5:14 and Gal 2:19 (see 5.3.5), where this death with Christ is expressed without a σὺν-compound. Further it is an important motif in Romans 6. After having dealt with justification apart from the law, Paul asks in Romans 6 whether we shall go on sinning or not. The answer is no, because we died to sin. This death to sin is a consequence of our dying with Christ. In 6:8 it is said the most clearly: ἀπεθάνομεν σὺν Χριστῷ, we died with Christ. This dying with Christ implies a change of Lord. Sin was our king, but now we serve God. But the next question is, in which sense it can be said that we died with Christ. This can be clarified

194. Van Bruggen, *Paulus*, 131. Cf. De Ru, *Heeft het lijden van Christus aanvulling nodig?*

195. Cf. Moo, *The Epistle to the Romans*, 372.

196. Han, *Raised for our Justification*, 274.

by reading 6:3–6 carefully. Baptism into Christ brings us into the sphere of Christ, liberating us from the dominion of sin.[197] Baptised believers are 'in Christ.' But for Paul it is evident: we can only come into Christ through *death*. We must be baptised, immersed, into his death. Hence he died in a way we do not have to die. He really died on the cross—we are united together with τῷ ὁμοιώματι, the likeness, of his death. There is some distance between his death and our sharing in his death.[198] Nevertheless, the reality of Christ's 'sin's-dominion-breaking death, in its outworking in the here and now' can be experienced and is effective.[199] We are united with his death—a unity comes into existence that did not exist before. We are united by our faith: the Christ-event touches *me*, as it is made manifest in Christian baptism.[200] Paul does not distinguish between the Christ-event, faith and baptism. But it is evident: this Christ-event—faith—baptism-complex concerns me.[201] We believe that in this complex something very real has happened: our old self died. We are no longer who we were before our conversion as a human being in Adam.[202] This death of our old self implies that it can be said now: you died with Christ (6:8); you are free from sin (6:7); count yourselves dead to sin (6:11). Here in Rom 6, having died with Christ and being crucified with Christ are synonyms. It is a past reality, causing liberation from the reign of sin and underlying the present as freedom in Christ. But the question when and how this death with Christ took place—at Golgotha, in conversion, by faith, in baptism—is not answered explicitly. It is important that we died with Christ, not when we died. Nevertheless, the fact that Paul writes 'σύμφυτοι γεγόναμεν,' we are united, indicates that the idea that we all died at Golgotha is too static and does not do justice to the existential impact of Christ's death on the

197. Tannehill, *Dying and Rising with Christ*, 8–10, 21.

198. Cf. Van Bruggen, *Het diepe water van de doop*, Kampen 1997, 39–41; Van Bruggen, *Romeinen*, 90, 92. With him I do not see a necessity to add ὁμοίωμα in 6:5b to make a complete parallel between our death and resurrection with Christ. We share in his death indirectly in experiencing its consequences, but really share in his life. A similar asymmetry can be found in Phil 3:10–11. Against Dunn, *Romans 1–8*, 317; Han, *Raised for our Justification*, 268–72; Moo, *The Epistle to the Romans*, 370.

199. Dunn, *Romans 1–8*, 317. Cf. Moo, *The Epistle to the Romans*, 370.

200. The unity with the death of Christ is not primarily a sacramental unity, but a unity by faith and by God's saving acts. Cf. Han, *Raised for our Justification*, 261–62; Siber, *Mit Christus leben*, 221.

201. Siber, *Mit Christus leben*, 224–26.

202. Cf. Dunn, *Romans 1–8*, 318–19.

believer.[203] In conclusion, 'having died with Christ' means: we believe that the person we were as slave of sin no longer exists. We will see below that this does not mean that we do not exist and lose ourselves: we have a new identity in Christ and we shall receive this new life in Christ if we rise from death in our resurrection with him.

In Romans 6 Paul needs our dying with Christ as a past event to underline his call to live a new life. Nevertheless, in 2 Corinthians 4 where he wants to interpret his own weakness in the light of the story of Christ, he uses communion with the death of Christ in a different manner. According to 2 Cor 4:10–12 the death of Christ is something present in his life as apostle. He carries the death of Jesus around in his body, he writes. But he does not speak of 'dying with Christ.' Furthermore, in Rom 8:13 Paul speaks of putting to death the deeds of the body by the Spirit, a passage comparable to Col 3:5. This shows Paul's flexibility: on the one hand, the believer died with Christ, on the other hand the Spirit still has 'a killing function.'[204]

Similar ideas to those in Rom 6 return in the later letter to the Colossians, in Col 2:20 and 3:3. To prevent the Colossians from living according to the powers of this world, Paul emphasises the death of the Colossians with Christ. Earthly things have lost their importance, the 'στοιχεῖα τοῦ κόσμου' have lost their power, because of this death with Christ.

In summary, just as Paul can say that we are crucified with Christ he can write that we died with Christ. We no longer exist as persons under the dominion of powers of the old aeon. Baptism makes manifest that the death of Christ concerns me as believer. Nevertheless, Paul has the flexibility of thinking to see his participation in the death of Christ in a different way: his own weakness is a sharing in the death of Christ.

As Christ was buried, it can be said that we have been buried with Christ. This idea can be found in the same letters where we find the idea of our death with Christ: in Rom 6:4 and in Col 2:12. The expressed ideas are the same. We are buried with him through baptism (Rom 6:4) or buried with him in baptism (Col 2:12). In both passages the verb συνθάπτομαι, be buried together with, is used.

203. Gaffin, 'Resurrection and Redemption,' 50–51, 53.

204. Tannehill, *Dying and Rising with Christ*, 128.

After three days, Christ rose from the death. Paul uses different words to relate Christ's resurrection to our existence: συνεγείρω (raise together with; Col 2:12; Col 3:1; Eph 2:6), συνζωοποιέω (make alive together with; Col 2:13; Eph 2:5), συζάω (live with; Rom 6:8; 2 Tim 2:11), ζάω σὺν αὖ 'τῷ (live with him; 2 Cor 13:4; 1 Thess 5:10) and ζάω ἐν Χριστω 'Ιησοῦ (live in Christ Jesus; Rom 6:11; 2 Tim 3:12). Furthermore, he uses these words sometimes to say something about the Christian hope, sometimes to refer to the Christian existence in the present. I will deal with these texts more closely now to determine how Paul relates the resurrection of Christ to believers.

To start with the earlier letters, I return to Romans 6. In this chapter Paul mentions our death and burial with Christ, but moreover he mentions our new life together with the resurrected Christ. We have seen that there is a tension here between the already and the not yet. Paul encourages the Romans to stop sinning and live a righteous life. He does this with the help of the resurrection of Christ. However, his writing implies a distinction between, on the one hand, 'walking in newness of life' (6:4; KJV) and being 'alive to God in Christ Jesus' (6:11), and, on the other hand, our future unity with Christ's resurrection (6:5) and living with him (6:8). In the present we have life *in* Christ, in the future we will rise *with* Christ and live *with* him. 'While the resurrection with Christ lies in the future, there is a sense in which we already share in his resurrection life, because we are in him.'[205]

A comparable impression is given in 1 Thess 5:10 and 2 Tim 2:11. Our living with Christ concerns a future, eschatological reality. Further, this impression is confirmed in 2 Cor 4:14,[206] although the question here is whether we should read with Nestle-Aland ἐγείρω συν or δια 'Ιησου

205. Hooker, *From Adam to Christ*, 44. See further Bouttier, *En Christ*, 45–46; Dunn, *Romans 1–8*, 315–16, 318, 322, 324; Hooker, *From Adam to Christ*, 43–44; Moo, *The Epistle to the Romans*, 367, 371, 377, 380; Powers, *Salvation through Participation*, 157–61; Sanders, *Paul and Palestinian Judaism*, 468; Siber, *Mit Christus leben*, 212–13, 237–46; Stuhlmacher, *Biblische Theologie*, Bd. 1, 347; Tannehill, *Dying and Rising with Christ*, 10, 12

Against Ridderbos, *Paulus*, 230; Han, *Raised for our Justification*, 254–55, 266, 277; Gaffin, 'Resurrection and Redemption,' 52–56, 59.

According to Van Bruggen, 6:4 refers also to our future participation in the resurrection of Christ, see Van Bruggen, *Romeinen*, 91–94.

206. Tannehill, *Dying and Rising with Christ*, 88; Thrall, *A critical and exegetical Commentary on the Second Epistle to the Corinthians*, 343.

with Hodges-Farstad. Nevertheless, in 2 Corinthians it becomes clear also that the life of Christ was already present in the apostolic ministry of Paul. Apart from 4:10, 12 this is the case in 13:4, where Paul writes that he and his co-workers are weak in Christ, but they will live with Christ by the power of God—'ζήσομεν σὺν αὐτῷ.' This cannot concern a future life with Christ, because as the aim of this life he mentions that they want to serve the Corinthians. This makes clear again that Paul was flexible in using words. Still, it remains true that resurrection with Christ is primarily a matter of a future participation in his resurrection.[207]

At first, the later letters to the Colossians and the Ephesians offer a different picture. Here we find the verbs συνεγείρω and συνζωοποιέω, used by Paul together in Col 2:12–13 and Eph 2:5–6 and in Col 3:1 (συνεγείρω). In all these passages it is written in the aorist that God has made us alive with Christ (Col 2:13; Eph 2:5) and raised us with him (Col 2:12; Eph 2:6; Col 3:1). It might seem that these letters have a more realised eschatology than the earlier ones: whereas the earlier ones say that we will rise with Christ in the future, the later letters say that we have already been raised with Christ. However, the differences are not that great. First, Paul's use of 'with Christ' in the other letters is not static. Although he normally uses 'live with Christ' with regard to our life with Christ after resurrection, in 2 Cor 13:4 he deviates from this use. At least in Colossians reasons can be given for deviating from Paul's earlier ideas on resurrection with Christ. The Colossians forgot that Christ had conquered the cosmic powers, liberating them from any reason to reckon with these powers or observe rituals. To correct the Colossians, Paul emphasises the present reality of salvation. Second, in Col 2:12 and in Eph 2:6 Paul mentions that this resurrection with Christ has taken place only *in* Christ. Third, the future aspect of salvation remains present (Col 1:23; 3:4; Eph 4:30). Fourth, the 'resurrection' with Christ took place through faith in the power of God (Col 2:12). Although the difference with Romans is clear—we have been raised with Christ already in Colossians and Ephesians, whereas this is not the case yet in Romans—at a deeper level the picture is the same: in the present we already partly participate in the new life of Christ, in the future we will fully participate in his new life, including its glory.

Resurrected from the death, Christ is glorified and receives the inheritance of God. Rom 8:17 states that we are συγκληρονόμοι δὲ Χριστοῦ,

207. Cf. Rom. 8:11; Holleman, *Resurrection and Parousia*; Powers, *Salvation through Participation*, 162–67.

co-heirs with Christ. We will συνδοξασθῶμεν, share in his glory.[208] This is a matter of the future, just as is our resurrection with Christ.

In heaven he sits at the right hand of God. Ephesians gives a similar picture as with regard to the resurrection, emphasising the present reality of salvation: God seated us with Christ in heaven in Christ Jesus (2:6). Paul uses here the verb συγκαθίζω.

Finally, Christ will return and appear in glory. As we are hidden with Christ in God in heaven according to the letter to the Colossians, we will appear in glory together with Christ: καὶ ὑμεῖς σὺν αὐτῷ φανερωθήσεσθε ἐν δόξῃ (Col 3:4).

We have followed the different moments of the story of Jesus Christ to see how Paul relates these moments semantically to our life. Moreover, we have seen now how Paul uses the different expressions: ἐν Χριστῷ, εἰς Χριστόν, ἐν πνεύματι, Χριστὸς ἐν ὑμιν and σὺν Χριστῷ (including the σὺν-compounds). Now it is time to draw conclusions.

1. Differences can be seen between the order of the moments of the story of Jesus Christ and the chronological order of moments within the life of the believer. In the life of Christ, it is suffering—crucifixion—death—burial—resurrection.

   Within the life of the believer it is:

   a. past: crucifixion & death & burial—

   b. present: suffering & dying & new life (resurrection)—

   c. future: resurrection.

   The chronological order within Jesus' life disappears if the different moments in his story are related semantically to the story of the life of the believer.

2. Some moments of the story of Jesus Christ can be combined with ἐν Χριστῷ, others with σὺν Χριστῷ (or a σὺν-compound), and several with both:

208. Cf. Phil 3:21.

Suffering		With Christ
Crucifixion		With Christ
Death		With Christ
Burial		With Christ
Resurrection	In Christ	With Christ
Being made alive	In Christ	With Christ
Life	In Christ	With Christ
Being	In Christ	
Being a new creation	In Christ	
Being seated in heaven	In Christ	With Christ
Being glorified		With Christ
Inherit		With Christ
Being hidden in God		With Christ
Appearance in glory		With Christ

Moo rightly writes that it is not true to say that 'with Christ' concerns past and future, whereas 'in Christ' concerns the present.[209] So does Bouttier, who sees dying with Christ and resurrection with Christ as two banks of a river, and 'in Christ' as the bridge between them.[210] 'With Christ' does not only concern the past and the future, but also the present: we suffer with Christ in the present and it can be said that we live with Christ. Further the letters to the Colossians and Ephesians frequently use 'with Christ' for the present. Nevertheless, the formula 'in Christ' is used always for the present; this is only not the case if an action verb is used and God is the (implied) subject. In all the other cases, the 'in Christ' indicates a participation in Christ that is only partial and waits for a fuller participation, indicated by 'with Christ.'

3. Being ἐν Χριστῷ presupposes baptism εἰς Χριστόν and crucifixion (death) and burial σὺν Χριστῷ.

4. To this point, I have distinguished between substitution (the moment of exclusivity) and representation (the moment of inclusiveness) on the basis of the semantic relation between Christ and the

209. Moo, *The Epistle to the Romans*, 393. See further Son, *Corporate Elements in Pauline Anthropology*, 21.

210. Bouttier, *En Christ*, 53.

believer. In the case of a positive relation (e.g. he died, we died) the moment of inclusiveness is present; in the case of a negative relation (e.g. he died, we live) or the absence of a relation (e.g. he died, . . .) the moment of exclusivity is present.

Now we see that in the case of a positive relation another distinction must be made. We can say 'he suffered—we suffer with him' and 'he was crucified—we are crucified with him.' But the first is a present reality, the second a 'past' reality. We continue to suffer with Christ, but we do not continue to be crucified. Moreover, we have seen that in Rom 6 we participate indirectly in the death of Christ, whereas we will really participate in the resurrection of Christ. This makes clear that the death of Christ contains a moment of exclusivity. Consequently, it does not suffice to distinguish between substitution and representation on semantic grounds. Doing so, we only discover that Christ experienced something we will not experience. However, regarding our participation in a moment of the history of Christ, it is also necessary to distinguish between an inclusive aspect in which we participate and an exclusive aspect in which we do not participate.

5. A basic structure can be seen within the thinking of Paul. Our created reality became the reality of sin and death, separated from God's reality. But Christ was sent by the Father into our reality and identified himself fully with sinful humanity, without sinning himself. He completely shared our experience and became our representative Messiah. Finally he died for us on the cross. To understand this death, we do not only need the concept of representation, but also substitution: he did what we could not do, and we participate only indirectly in this death. He rose from the dead and was glorified. Where he identified himself with us, he now made it possible for us to identify ourselves with him. He shared our experience, now we share his experience. He is our life in which we participate. To echo Irenaeus: 'Christ became what we are in order that we might become what he is.'[211]

   In a scheme:[212]

211. *Adversus heareses* 5 preface, cited in Dunn, *The Theology of Paul the Apostle*, 204.

212. This scheme must be read as a movement: Christ comes the reality of God (above in the scheme) into our reality (below in the scheme), to bring us from flesh and

Story of Jesus Christ	Sending	Birth and baptism	Death	Since resurrection and glorification	Future
Reality of God and the new creation	Election in Christ God sends his Son			Christ resurrected and glorified We live in Him (/with Him)	Christ and we resurrected and glorified with him.
Reality of sin, flesh and death	We in the flesh, in Adam	Christ becomes one of us	Christ dies for us We die with him	We in the flesh Christ in us Gift of the Spirit Suffering with Christ	

6. This structure determines Paul's use of the different expressions. As a result, a 'basic grammar' can be made (see table on page 224).

5.4.3 IMAGES FOR UNION WITH CHRIST

The communion between Christ and the believers is indicated by expressions like 'in Christ' and 'with Christ' as we have just seen. But furthermore Paul uses several images to voice this unity: body with or without the image of head, temple or building, marriage and the union between man and wife, and new clothing. What light do these images shed on the main question concerning the necessity of participation in understanding Paul's writings? Does their use imply the need of a moment of union apart from representation and participation?

Body

When dealing with the image of head, already some observations were made regarding the body-image (see 5.3.4). In 1 Corinthians and Romans,

sin (below) in God's reality of the new creation (above).

Story of Jesus Christ	Sending	Birth and baptism	Death	Since resurrection and glorification	Future
Reality of God and the new creation				• ἐν Χριστῷ • ἐν κυρίῳ Col / Eph: • συνεγείρω, συνζωοποιέω • κέκρυμμαι σὺν τῷ Χριστῷ ἐν τῷ θεῶ • ἐν Χριστῷ	• συζάω • ζάω σὺν αὐτω συγκληρονόμοι Χριστοῦ • σὺν αὐτῷ φανερόομαι ἐν δόξῃ
Reality of sin, flesh and death	We: • ἐν τῇ σαρκί • ἐν νόμῳ • ἐν τῷ Ἀδὰμ	Christ: • ἐν ὁμοιώματι σαρκὸς • ἁμαρτίας • γενόμενον ἐκ γυναικός, γενόμενον ὑπὸ νόμον • ἁμαρτίαν ποιέω	Christ: • ὑπὲρ ἡμῶν • ὑπὲρ τῶν ἁμαρτιῶν ἡμῶν We: • σὺν Χριστῷ • συσταυρόομαι • βαπτιζω- εἰς Χριστὸν Ἰησοῦν	We: • ἐν τῇ σαρκι • ἐνδημέω ἐν τῷ σώματι, ἐκδημέω ἀπὸ τοῦ κυρίου • Χριστὸς ἐν ὑμῖν • Spirit as ἀρραβῶν • ἐν πνεύματι • συμπάσχω	

the images of head and body are not related. In Colossians, these two images occur sometimes together. If this is the case, the model of the human body stands in the background. In the letter to the Ephesians, the body-metaphor is always present—be it more at a distance or closer—if the head-metaphor is used. Once the image of body and head are obviously used against the background of the model of the human body. Now I will deal with this metaphor more closely.[213]

In the first letter to the Corinthians, Paul often refers to the body, and also to body in relation to Christ. He does so in different ways, related to different fields of meaning: sexuality, inhabitation by the Spirit, the Lord's Supper and the church.

The first time this happens in 1 Corinthians 6. Because it is not obvious that the image of body and its members in this passage has a collective meaning, I will deal with this passage in relation to the image of marriage.[214]

First Corinthians 10 is the second passage. Dealing with the problem of food sacrificed to idols, Paul compares the idol feasts and the Lord's Supper. If idols were real, eating sacrifices offered to an idol would result in κοινωνία with these idols (10:19–20). Similarly, eating the bread and drinking the cup at the Lord's Table is (somehow) a participation with Christ; more specifically, it is a κοινωνία in the blood and the body of Christ (10:16). In addition Paul relates the one bread with the ecclesiological community as one body (10:17). Some exegetes have suggested an identification of the sacramental body of Christ and the ecclesiological body of Christ, implying that the church is literally the body of the resurrected Christ. I see no reasons to do so. The bread as κοινωνία τοῦ σώματος τοῦ Χριστοῦ is primarily combined with the cup of thanksgiving as κοινωνία τοῦ αἵματος τοῦ Χριστοῦ. Consequently, Paul refers

213. For the body metaphor, see Dawes, *The Body in Question*; Dunn, "The Body of Christ' in Paul'; Dunn, 'The "Body" in Colossians'; Gundry, *Sōma in Biblical Literature*; Howard, 'The Head / Body Metaphors of Ephesians'; Van Kooten, 'The Pauline Debate on the Cosmos,' 3–48; Park, *Die Kirche als "Leib Christi" bei Paulus*; Ridderbos, *Paulus*, 404–41; Son, *Corporate Elements in Pauline Anthropology*, 83–120; Walter, *Gemeinde als Leib Christi*; Wedderburn, 'The Body of Christ and related concepts in 1 Corinthians.'

214. Fatehi and Park do think that a collective interpretation is possible, Fatehi, *The Spirit's Relation to the Risen Lord*, 270; Park, *Die Kirche als "Leib Christi,"* 219, 223, 231. Fee, Hollander, Schrage and Wedderburn deny this, Fee, *The First Epistle to the Corinthians*, 258–59; Hollander, 1 *Korintiërs I*, 103–4; Schrage, *Der erste Brief an die Korinther* Bd. 1, 25–26 Wedderburn, 'The Body of Christ and related concepts in 1 Corinthians,' 75.

in 10:16 to the body as the historical body of Christ, given in the death for us.[215] However, in 10:17 'body' denotes the communion of the church. Note that Paul does not say that the church is the body *of Christ*, he only emphasises their unity as ἓν σῶμα.[216] Nevertheless, it is still remarkable that Paul, playing around with words, uses both the sacramental and the communal concept of body.[217] At least he suggests a relation between communion with Christ and his (historical) body and the communion of the church as one body.[218] The corporate communion of the believers, participating in Christ, is connected with a moment of (Eucharistic) union with Christ. This suggests the importance of a concept of union to refer to this moment. The ecclesiological use of the body-metaphor however says more about the corporate nature of the church than about union with Christ, although this corporate nature results from union with Christ.

In 1 Corinthians 11 Paul returns to the theme of the Lord's Supper. It is used in an unworthy manner: some remain hungry while others get drunk. The Corinthians did not eat together and despised the church of God. The problem is clear: a malfunctioning community. Within this context referring to the Lord's Supper, Paul emphasises that we should διακρίνειν τὸ σῶμα (11:29).[219] In 11:23–28 Paul refers to eating the bread and drinking the cup. As a consequence, it is reasonable that διακρίνων τὸ σῶμα refers to the bread in the preceding verses as sacramental body of Christ. However, the logic of the entire passage 11:17–34 necessitates that διακρίνων τὸ σῶμα refers also to the ecclesiological body. It is undeniable here that Paul again plays with words and uses διακρίνων τὸ

215. Cf. Gundry, *Sōma in Biblical Literature*, 238; Park, *Die Kirche als "Leib Christi" bei Paulus*, 276–80; Ridderbos, *Paulus*, 417–19.

216. Dunn emphasises that it is not at first sight clear that Paul is saying here that the church is the body of Christ, see Dunn, "The Body of Christ' in Paul,' 151.

217. According to Walter, the sooma-concept oscillates semantically between a real and metaphorical meaning, see Walter, *Gemeinde als Leib Christi*, 113.

218. Cf. Park, *Die Kirche als "Leib Christi" bei Paulus*, 279–80. According to Wedderburn it is difficult 'to regard the idea of the Church as the Body of the risen Christ as prior to, or independent of, that of the Christians sharing in the death of Christ,' see Wedderburn, 'The Body of Christ and related concepts in 1 Corinthians,' 76; cf. Stuhlmacher, *Biblische Theologie des Neuen Testaments*, 364. Nevertheless, it is impossible for us to determine how the use of Stoic ideas regarding 'body' within the Christian community has developed. We can only conclude that this development has taken place.

219. Or διακρίνων τὸ σῶμα τοῦ κυρίου according to the Majority text.

σῶμα deliberately in an ambiguous way, hence relating the historical or sacramental body of Christ with the ecclesiological body.[220] He sticks these two concepts of the body of Christ together on purpose. Laying this semantic relation by deliberate wordplay, he makes clear that those having communion with Christ by eating his body form together at the same time the body of Christ. [221] Again we find a moment of union with Christ. Now the corporate union of the church and the union with Christ are related more explicitly.

The fourth passage in 1 Corinthians is 1 Cor 12:12–27. In chapters 12–14 the gifts of the Spirit are the subject. To clarify the diversity of gifts and the common aim of all these gifts, Paul uses the image of the body. A body has different members with different functions, but together they are one body, in need of each other. What interests us most is the relation between Christ and believers. This relation remains unclear. Paul refers to the one Lord (12:5), but mostly to the Spirit.[222] Nevertheless, in 12:12 Paul equates Christ with the body, and in 12:27 he speaks of the σῶμα Χριστοῦ. A comparable passage is Rom 12:4–8. Here Paul writes we are one body ἐν Χριστῷ. Paul is not concerned here with the precise relation between Christ and the church as one body. What matters, are the paranetical consequences he gives to the image of the church as one body.[223] Therefore, Dunn speaks of 'metaphorical imprecision.'[224] Paul is mainly concerned with the relations *within* the body. Nevertheless, the relation with Christ and the Spirit is somehow constitutive for the church as one

220. Collins, *First Corinthians*, 563–64; Fee, *The First Epistle to the Corinthians*, 439; Park, *Die Kirche als "Leib Christi" bei Paulus*, 297–98; Schrage, *Der erste Brief an die Korinther*, Bd. 3, 51; Walter, *Gemeinde als Leib Christi*, 122–23; Wedderburn, 'The Body of Christ and related concepts in 1 Corinthians,' 77.

221. Stuhlmacher and Wedderburn even see a causal relation: *through* the Lord's Supper the Christians are knit into one collective body, see Stuhlmacher, *Biblische Theologie des Neuen Testaments*, Bd. 1, 364; Wedderburn, 'The Body of Christ and related concepts in 1 Corinthians,' 77.

222. Dunn and Fatehi emphasise the work of the Spirit for the unity of the body, Dunn, "The Body of Christ' in Paul,' 149; Fatehi, *The Spirit's Relation to the Risen Lord in Paul*, 270–71. Therefore Dunn critisises Ridderbos for creating too large an opposition between the unity as caused by the Spirit or caused by redemptive-historical realities, see Dunn, *Romans 9–16*, 724; cf. Ridderbos, *Paulus*, 415, 419.

223. Gundry, *Sōma in Biblical Literature*, 232; Ridderbos, *Paulus*, 412; Walter, *Gemeinde als Leib Christi*, 147.

224. Dunn, "The Body of Christ' in Paul,' 151. Van Bruggen still understands the body as on by incorporation in Christ, see Van Bruggen, *Romeinen*, 185.

body. Whether this relation has to be understood as a union with Christ remains unclear in both passages.

We have seen already that in Colossians the body-metaphor occurs twice together with the head-metaphor, in Col 1:18 and in 2:19.

The first time the body-metaphor is used in Colossians is in Col 1:18. Here the relation between Christ and the new creation is concerned. Christ is called head of the body of the church.[225] That the church functions within a cosmological perspective is noteworthy. The emphasis has shifted from the local church to the universal church, but σῶμα still has an ecclesiological meaning. New, with respect to the earlier letters, is the combination of the image of head and body as we saw. To distinguish this new combination from the earlier use of the body-metaphor, Dawes distinguishes between 'unitive' and 'partitive' use of the body metaphor. Used unitively, Christ and his body are inseparable. If the metaphor is used partitively, Christ as the head and the church as his body are distinguished.[226] The more 'head' has to be understood in the sense of 'source of the body's life and growth' and the model of the human body is presupposed (see 5.3.4), the more a moment of union is present in this verse.

The ecclesiological meaning returns in 1:24, where Paul says he is doing something for the sake of Christ's body, the church. The relation between Christ and his body remains relatively unclear in this short statement. The metaphor is used unitively here.

The body-metaphor returns in 2:17 and 19. In the immediate context (2:6–23), Paul exhorts the Colossians not to lose their life in Christ by observing non-Christian religious rituals. Doing so would mean that they live again according to this world, having lost connection with Christ. Encouraging the Colossians to stay in Christ, Paul places Christ above ancient cosmology. Christ is head of the cosmos and its powers, although it is still possible to return to the old world. The confrontation between ancient cosmology and Christ introduces within this cosmology the tension between the new reality in Christ and the reality of this world with its powers. He does so against the background of Jewish eschatology (cf.

225. See footnote 62 on the question whether the words τῆς ἐκκλησίας are original.

226. Dawes, *The Body in Question*, 248.

τα μελλόντα in 2:17).[227] To clarify further the relation of the Colossians with Christ and the cosmological importance of Christ within the new creation, Paul plays with the word σῶμα. In 2:9 he starts with the historical Christ, in whom all the divine fullness lived σωματικῶς.[228] But the Colossians themselves got involved in God's salvation: in Christ they put off their σῶμα τῆς σαρκός (2:11). But Paul furthermore needs to show that even the cosmic powers are under Christ and that Christ's work has a cosmological impact. Therefore he refers implicitly to ancient cosmology, which saw the cosmos as stable σῶμα, bound together (συνδεῖν) with bonds (δεσμοί) (2:19).[229] The true reality is not found in the rituals related to the syncretistic cosmology, but only in Christ: τὸ δὲ σῶμα τοῦ Χριστου (2:16–17).[230] Consequently, the cosmological σῶμα must be interpreted ecclesiologically, just as in 1:18 cosmology and ecclesiology were intertwined.[231] Paul thus views the church in terms referring to cosmology, but at the same time, referring to growth, he returns to the more organic metaphors used in 2:6–7 indicating the relation with God in Christ. This evokes the model of a human body: Christ as head and source of growth, the community of the new creation as his body. The combination of κεφαλὴ, σῶμα, ἁφή, συνδέσμος, and αὔξησις evokes the model of a human body too strongly to interpret 2:19 only in cosmological and not in physiological terms. Playing with words, cosmology and physiology interfere, just as do cosmology and ecclesiology.[232] In

227. See Dunn, *The Epistles to the Colossians and to Philemon*, 176–77; O'Brien, *Colossians, Philemon*, 140.

228. Dunn, *The Epistles to the Colossians and to Philemon*, 152; O'Brien, *Colossians, Philemon*, 112–13. To interpret this with Van Kooten as a reference to some cosmological body of Christ would disturb the careful construction of this passage, see Van Kooten, 'The Pauline Debate on the Cosmos,' 17–18.

229. For an investigation of antique cosmology, see Van Kooten, 'The Pauline Debate on the Cosmos,' esp. 10–48.

230. Walter hears an allusion to the Eucharistic body in 2:17, related to the eating and drinking in 2:16, see Walter, *Gemeinde als Leib Christi*, 184.

231. According to Walter, Paul re-uses 1:18–19 in 2:9–10, see Walter, *Gemeinde als Leib Christi*, 182f.

232. Van Kooten interprets this passage strictly against the background of ancient cosmology and focuses strongly on the word σῶμα. However, he does not reflect on the question regarding the modification of ancient cosmology by Christology and of the eschatological tension between old and new creation. Nevertheless, the evidence of the use of cosmological material is too great to interpret 2:19 strictly in ecclesiological terms as O'Brien does. Dunn better sees the richness of Paul's play with the term. See Dunn,

doing so, Paul has forged a new concept of the church, combining two metaphors separate in his earlier letters and using the body-metaphor partitively: the church as a living human organism with Christ as its head in heaven and the church as his body on earth.[233] This makes possible the warning that although reality is found in Christ, we can lose connection with the head (2:19). For ongoing growth this connection with the head is essential.[234] Consequently, in this new combination of metaphors especially the moment of union is highlighted, although the moment of participation is also present.

Themes comparable to Paul's use of the body-metaphor in 1 Corinthians 12 and in Romans 12 return in Col 3:15, which is an example of unitive use of the body-metaphor. Again the relation with Christ remains implicit.

The body-metaphor returns in the letter to the Ephesians, firstly in Eph 1:22–23. We have already seen that the head- and body-metaphor are used here primarily independently of each other.[235] The entire cosmos is placed under Christ as its head, but within this cosmos the church has a special place as the body of Christ.[236] The cosmological background of the notion of πληρὸω τὰ πάντα indicates that in this passage ecclesiology is viewed in a cosmological perspective.[237] The universal church as beginning of the new creation does not enclose the entire cosmos yet. What is of interest now, is the relation between Christ and the church, his body. Paul's combination of the head with, on the one hand, the feet of Christ, referring to Ps 8:6, and, on the other hand, the body-metaphor shows that although both 'belong to the same metaphorical complex, on

---

The Epistles to the Colossians and to Philemon, 185–87; Dunn, 'The "Body" in Colossians'; Van Kooten, 'The Pauline Debate on the Cosmos,' 4–48; O'Brien, *Colossians, Philemon*, 146–47.

233. Ridderbos sees the head and body metaphor in Col 2:19 still as two seperate metaphors; see Ridderbos, *Paulus*, 424–25. Cf. Dawes, *The Body in Question*, 119–21, 164.

234. Walter, *Gemeinde als Leib Christi*, 186–87, 190.

235. See 5.3.4; Howard, 'The Head / Body Metaphors of Ephesians,' 353–54.

236. Dawes, *The Body in Question*, 139–41; O'Brien, *The Letter to the Ephesians*, 141–47.

237. Van Kooten gives evidence for this cosmological background, see Van Kooten, 'The Pauline Debate on the Cosmos,' 146–53.

this occasion they do not form a consistent model.'[238] Whether σῶμα is used unitively or partitively in 1:23, is not totally clear. A problem for the clarification of the relation between Christ and the church is the interpretation of τὸ πλήρωμα τοῦ τὰ πάντα ἐν πᾶσιν πληρουμένου that raises many questions.[239]

Is it an accusative referring to αὐτόν and κεφαλήν in v. 22 following the αὐτοῦ, or does it refer to the church, τὸ σῶμα? In the first case Christ is the fullness of God who filling τὰ πάντα ἐν πᾶσιν (in the table nr. 1); in the second case the church is the fullness of τοῦ τὰ πάντα ἐν πᾶσιν πληρουμένου (nr. 2–6). Next, it is not clear who is the subject of the πληρουμένου. Grammatically, different possibilities exist: is it the church, Christ or God? Seen within the whole of the letter (cf. Eph 3:11; 4:15–16) and taking into account that in ancient cosmology it is the divine power filling everything, it is not reasonable to see the church as subject of the filling (nr. 4). The theocentrism of Eph 1 supports an interpretation with God as subject of the filling, Eph 3:11 and the headship of Christ an interpretation with Christ himself as subject. Because of the unclarity of the voice of πληρουμένου—passive, middle, or middle with an active sense—both are possible: Christ can be the one being filled (by God; passive; nr. 2, 3), but also the one filling for himself (middle with an active sense; nr. 5, 6). Finally, it is a question whether τὸ πλήρωμα has an active sense ('that which fills'; nr. 3, 4, 5) or a passive ('that which is filled'; nr. 2, 6)?

Given these questions, το πλήρωμα τοῦ πληρουμένου can be interpreted in different ways:

238. Dawes, *The Body in Question*, 157. Walter reads this passage as if it presents a consistent picture of Christ as head with the powers under his feet and the church between head and feet, participating indirectly in the power of Christ; Walter, *Gemeinde als Leib Christi*, 211–12.

239. For an extensive treatment of this passage and the different possibilities, see Best, *A Critical and Exegetical Commentary on Ephesians*, 183–89; Dawes, *The Body in Question*, 237–48.

	P/A	to πλήρωμα	Subject	του πληρομουμένου	Interpretative translation
1		the fullness (reference: Christ)	God	of the filling one	Christ, the fullness of God who fills
2	P	that which is filled (ref.: the church)	God	of the one being filled	The church as that which is filled by Christ, being filled by God
3	A	that which fills (ref.: the church)	God	of the one being filled	The church as that which fills Christ, being filled by God using the church
4	A	that which fills (ref.: the church)	Church	of the one being filled	The church as that which fills Christ who is being filled (by the church)
5	A	that which fills (ref.: the church)	Christ	of the filling one	The church as that which fills Christ who is filling himself
6	P	that which is filled (ref.: the church)	Christ	of the filling one	The church as that which is filled by Christ who is filling for himself

Possibility 4 is not reasonable; the other 5 are possible interpretations. The majority of the exegetes rejects the first possibility. Nr. 3 and 5 fit within a catholic understanding of the church as completing Christ, nr. 2 and 6 fit more within a protestant ecclesiology of a *solus Christus*.[240]

The next question is the interpretation of τὰ πάντα ἐν πᾶσιν and the relation between the filling of το πλήρωμα and the filling of τοῦ τὰ πάντα ἐν πᾶσιν πληρουμένου. Is the filling of the church completed, and followed by the filling of everything? Or is the filling of the church part of the filling of τὰ πάντα ἐν πᾶσιν, or is the cosmos filled by filling the church?

It is impossible to solve all these problems here. In any case, it is clear that God in Christ fills and gives growth, and that the church as body of Christ has a special position within this process of filling.[241] The relation between Christ as head and the church as body of Christ is a relation of πληρόω. The emphasis lies, in this chapter, on what God does in Christ,

240. Dawes, *The Body in Question*, 250.

241. Dawes, *The Body in Question*, 141, 157.

not on what the church does. Therefore, as Lord and head of the cosmos and the church Christ is the 'inspiring, ruling, guiding, combining, sustaining power, mainspring of its activity, centre of unity, seat of its life.'[242] Nevertheless, this does not solve the ambiguity of πλήρωμα: is Christ completing the church or is the church completing Christ? Eph 4:12, 13, and 15 leaves open the possibility that Christ, by giving growth to his church, is 'completing' himself. It might be the case that Paul's formulation is deliberately ambiguous; it does not really matter whether *God* is filling (in Christ) or whether the divine *Christ* is filling. The ambiguity of πλήρωμα might also be deliberate. Were this the case, it can reflect the ambiguity in Paul's use of σῶμα that we have seen: it is used unitively and partitively.[243] A partitive reading with Christ as subject of the filling implies the presence of a moment of union, in the case of a unitive reading with God as subject the relation between Christ and his body remains implicit. Evidently a moment of participation is also present, although it can be understood differently: in a protestant reading the church participates in the life and fullness of Christ, a catholic reading the church participates also in the filling.

The body-metaphor is also found in 2:16. Here the motif of unity of Jew and gentile in Christ (cf. Gal 3:28) is creatively combined with the body-metaphor.[244] Paul uses the semantic possibilities offered by the σῶμα-metaphor to relate Christ and the church closely, even suggesting that the church is incorporated in Christ.[245] Whether σῶμα refers to the crucified or the ecclesiological body of Christ, in both cases the relation between Christ and the church remains implicit.[246]

242. O'Brien, *The Letter to the Ephesians*, 148.

243. Dawes, *The Body in Question*, 248.

244. Best mentions that it is the first time that these motifs are combined, Best, *A Critical and Exegetical Commentary on Ephesians*, 265. Cf. Dunn, "The Body of Christ' in Paul,' 149.

245. Cf. Dawes, *The Body in Question*, 173; Schnackenburg, *Der Brief an die Epheser*, 115–17.

246. Some exegetes see the ecclesiological interpretation as more likely. Best, *A Critical and Exegetical Commentary on Ephesians*, 265; Dawes, *The Body in Question*, 159–60; Schnackenburg, Der Brief an die Epheser, 117. According to Ridderbos it is difficult to decide whether an ecclesiological or a historical reference is to be chosen, see Ridderbos, *Paulus*, 421. And Dawes concludes, that although the immediate referent is the church, 'in this context the Church is not distinguished from Christ. Rather it is identified with him,' see Dawes, *The Body in Question*, 159–60.

In a comparable way, Paul shows how Christ brought Jew and Gentile together in Eph 3:6 using a συν-compound: σύσσωμα. The Gentiles are heirs together with the Jews and share in the promise of Christ. They are also 'σύσσωμα,' members of the same body. Any reference to the head is absent here, which suggests a unitive meaning of body. Again the relation with Christ remains implicit.

The next time Paul uses the body-metaphor in Ephesians is in chapter 4, in the verses 4, 12, and 16. This passage resembles 1 Corinthians 12 and Romans 12, as comparable themes are touched upon: the unity of the body and the gifts for building it up. In 4:4 and 12 the use of the image is unitive with an ecclesiological referent. The relation with Christ remains implicit until 4:13–16. In these verses Paul elaborates what the upbuilding of the body of Christ consists in. Its goal is 'unity in the faith and in the knowledge of the Son of God,' maturity, growing up into Christ, the head. Hence the body is seen here as something in need of growth and maturation. What is the relation between head and body? First, the head is the goal of the growth (4:15). The aim is a complete incorporation of the church in Christ.[247] Second, indirectly the head is viewed as cause of unity and source of growth; indirectly, for the 'ἐξ οὗ' at the beginning of 4:16 refers to ὁ Χριστός and not to ἡ κεφαλή.[248] Nevertheless, as Christ is the head this indirectness must not be overstated. Third, it is not clear whether 'πᾶν τὸ σῶμα' refers to the body inclusive of the head or not. Is 'σῶμα' used unitively or partitively? For Ridderbos this is a reason to see head and body as two separate metaphors.[249] Dawes has a better solution. He sees in 4:16 a clash between the unitive and partitive use of 'σῶμα' in the letter to the Ephesians.[250] Paul's use of different metaphors together results in a whole constituted by the different parts of this passage that are held in tension: the body of Christ, Christ as measure and stature of maturity, Christ as head, growth into Christ.[251] But although it remains visible through this tension that the creative combination between the more hierarchical metaphor of head and the corporate body-metaphor is secondary, nevertheless the different metaphors evoke the image of or-

247. O'Brien, *The Letter to the Ephesians*, 312.

248. Best, *A Critical and Exegetical Commentary on Ephesians*, 410; Howard, 'The Head / Body Metaphors of Ephesians,' 354; Walter, *Gemeinde als Leib Christi*, 227.

249. Ridderbos, *Paulus*, 425.

250. Dawes, *The Body in Question*, 165.

251. Cf. Dunn, "The Body of Christ' in Paul,' 152.

ganic growth and the model of the human body. Paul pictures an organic, life-giving unity between Christ, the head, and the body.[252] Consequently, a moment of union is present together with a moment of participation.

Finally we turn to Ephesians 5, where the body-metaphor is found in verse 23 and 30. In Ephesians 5, motifs already present in 1 Corinthians 6 return. The body-metaphor is combined with the image of marriage. Paul parallels a marriage between husband and wife with the relation between Christ, the head, and his body (5:23). The love and care husbands have for their body and their wives is compared with the love of Christ for his church, caring for her and feeding her (5:29). Whereas Paul writes in 1 Cor 6:15 that we are members of Christ, he now writes: 'we are members of his body.' Both husband and wife have this in common.[253] This body-metaphor is in addition interpreted from the perspective of Gen 2:24 as comparable with being one flesh in marriage. The model of the human body (the unity of head and body) and the model of marriage (husband and wife being one flesh) are both present in the background. Consequently, this passage again shows the creativity of Paul and the richness of the possibilities offered by the body-metaphor. The combination with marriages makes it possible to integrate a unitive and a partitive use. In marriage, the two become one. This makes clear that the distinction between unitive and partitive use of 'body' is not sufficient. Even if it is used partitively, two different models can be evoked: the model of one human body, within which head and body are distinguished; and the model of marriage, within which two persons, man and wife are distinguished as head and body, who are at the same time united as one flesh.[254] Consequently, the moment of union is evident here.

Having seen all these different usages of the body-metaphor it is time to look back. The metaphor is used within different fields of significance and with different referents. The different kinds of usage, the different combinations and semantic fields and the different combinations are

252. Dawes, *The Body in Question*, 163–64.

253. Best, *A Critical and Exegetical Commentary on Ephesians*, 552; Dawes, *The Body in Question*, 155–56.

254. In his interpretation of the body-metaphor, Park focuses too much on one of these two models, the model of marriage. Hence he interprets the body-metaphor against the background of Paul's Adam-Christology and the one flesh-unity between man and wife as it existed between Adam and Eve. He ignores the presence of the second model, the model of the human body. See Park, *Die Kirche als "Leib Christi" bei Paulus*.

shown in the next table. This table ignores the fact that Paul by wordplay often relates different references and semantic fields.

Paul uses 'body' metaphorically and literally, referring to a historical human body or to the historical body of Christ. It is used by Paul to relate semantically different referents. Always it reveals some kind of unity, be it a unity within the church, be it a unity between Christ and the church. Dunn gives a list of the different kinds of unity, indicated with the help of the metaphor: a eucharistic unity, a charismatic unity, a unity of Jew and Gentile, a unity of faith and a unity like that between husband and wife.[255] The body-metaphor always implies a certain corporateness, showing that the Christian existence is not an individual one. In the earlier letters the referent of the body is the local church, in the later letters the referent is the universal church. Cosmology and ecclesiology become intertwined, with Colossians focussing on cosmology, Ephesians on ecclesiology. The motif of the new creation in the earlier letters now receives a place within ecclesiology.

<table>
<tr><th></th><th>Use</th><th colspan="2">Combination with</th><th>Semantic field</th><th>Referent</th></tr>
<tr><td rowspan="8">Σῶμα</td><td>Literally</td><td colspan="2">Σαρξ, cross and resurrection</td><td>-</td><td>Crucified, historical body</td></tr>
<tr><td>Metaphorical/ sacramental</td><td colspan="2">The Lord's Supper</td><td>Bread as sign of Christ</td><td>Sacramental body</td></tr>
<tr><td rowspan="3">Metaphorical/ unitive</td><td colspan="2" rowspan="2">Diversity of gifts</td><td rowspan="2">Unity in diversity</td><td>Local ecclesiological body (seen together with Christ)</td></tr>
<tr><td rowspan="2">Universal ecclesiological body (seen together with Christ)</td></tr>
<tr><td colspan="2">Jew and Gentile</td><td>New and unthought unity</td></tr>
<tr><td rowspan="3">Metaphorical/ partitive</td><td rowspan="3">Κεφαλη</td><td rowspan="2">Model of human body</td><td>Organic relation</td><td rowspan="3">Universal ecclesiological body (as distinct from Christ)</td></tr>
<tr><td>Hierarchical relation</td></tr>
<tr><td>Model of marriage</td><td>Marital unity (one flesh)</td></tr>
</table>

255. Dunn, "The Body of Christ' in Paul," 150.

With regard to the question concerning a possible moment of union in the relation between Christ and believers, the metaphorical-sacramental use and the metaphorical-partitive use are especially important. In the unitive use the relation with Christ remained implicit until the metaphorical-unitive use was combined with the metaphorical-sacramental. The combination with the head-metaphor made it possible that relation between Christ and the church became clearer. Both the metaphorical-sacramental and the metaphorical-partitive use of the body-metaphor imply a moment of union between Christ and the church.

Building and Temple

The next image that needs to be dealt with is the image of a building (οἰκοδομή) or temple (ναός).[256] 'When used in connection with the temple in Jerusalem, ναός served to distinguish the sanctuary from the larger precinct (the ἱερόν).'[257] This imagery is used less often than the image of body. It occurs only in the Corinthian correspondence and in the letter to the Ephesians. However, it is important to see that οἰκοδομή means building as well as upbuilding. In this second sense, Paul uses it in Romans and not just in the aforementioned letters.[258] Consequently, the imagery of building is broader than the passages I focus on now. Further, the metaphor of body is used several times together with the building/temple-metaphor or with οἰκοδομή in the sense of upbuilding; in 1 Corinthians 6, in Ephesians 2 and 4. It is possible that the images of body and temple are related, maybe caused by (reflection on) the word of Jesus about his own body 'Destroy this temple, and I will raise it again in three days.'[259]

256. For these images, see Strack, *Kultische Terminologie*, 221–72; 321–53; Son, *Corporate Elements in Pauline Anthropology*, 121–46; Williams, *Paul's Metaphors*, 14–19, 245–47.

257. Williams, *Paul's Metaphors*, 245.

258. οἰκοδομή in the sense of 'upbuilding' is found in Rom 14:19; 15:2; 1 Cor 14:3, 5, 12, 26; 2 Cor 10:8; 12:19; 13:10; Eph 4:12, 16, 29. In the sense of 'building' it is found also in 2 Cor 5:1.

259. Matt. 26:61; 27:40; Mark 14:58; 15:29; John 2:19–21; Acts 6:14. According to Park this relation is not necessary. Paul makes this relation possible, see Park, *Die Kirche als "Leib Christi" bei Paulus*, 202, 222–24. Son writes that the concept of the church as the body of Christ is 'closely related' with the designation of the church as temple or building, see Son, *Corporate Elements in Pauline Anthropology*, 119.

The first time it is found in 1 Corinthians 3. Paul shifts in 3:9 from agricultural imagery to more architectural images: 'you are God's field, you are God's οἰκοδομή.' Then he continues, exploring the possibilities of this imagery. The foundation of the building is Jesus Christ himself (3:11). The Corinthians, as well as the apostles, can build on this foundation with different quality. In 3:16f the metaphor is transformed pneumatologically into the metaphor of a temple. The metaphor of the building pictures the relation between Christ and his church as a relation between foundation and building, indicating a moment of union.

In 1 Corinthians 6 the temple-metaphor is used to emphasise the holiness of the body of an individual Christian (6:19). Paul makes clear that, although the physical body will perish, its actions are not morally indifferent. The temple-metaphor is used together with the idea that our bodies are members of Christ. Nevertheless, the body-metaphor concentrates in this passage more on the relation with Christ, the temple-metaphor on the relation with the Spirit.

Paul also views the church as God's temple in 2 Cor 6:16. Because he does not refer to the relation with Christ I will not deal with this passage further.

Finally we find the metaphor in Eph 2:20–21. After having written about the unity of Jew and Gentile in the one body of Christ, Paul further elaborates the togetherness of Jew and Gentile, using the images of a household (2:19) and a building (2:20–21). It is made to become a temple where God lives by his Holy Spirit (2:22). Different from 1 Corinthians 3, the foundation of this building consists of the apostles and prophets, while Jesus is the ἀκρογωνιαῖος. Literally ἀκρογωνιαῖος means 'lying at the extreme angle.' With our present knowledge it is not clear to what kind of stone this expression exactly refers; cornerstone, capstone, keystone? Anyway, it is a very important stone within the building, more important than the apostles and prophets.[260] The stone seems vital for the foundation.[261] Then in 2:21 the suggested position of Christ within the image changes: the building is joined together 'in him' and it grows to become a holy temple 'in the Lord.' According to Best, it is most convincing to interpret this as corporate or local, because of the corporate nature

260. Best, *A Critical and Exegetical Commentary on Ephesians*, 284.

261. O'Brien, *The Letter to the Ephesians*, 217.

of the image.[262] This change of the position of Christ shows Paul's creative use of imagery, but also that for him it is impossible to conceptualise the relation between Christ and his church in one systematic, fixed way. The complexity of this relation seems to necessitate flexibility of imagery. The moments of exclusivity and union are clearly present in this image.

These passages show that the image of building which has a christological colour can be used together with the pneumatologically coloured image of the temple. It can have a corporate as well as in an individual emphasis. The image has its own possibilities, showing that Christ came not for the sake of himself but to restore the relation between God and his people. The relation between Christ and the building can be seen in different ways: as most important stone, as foundation or as the one 'in whom' the building exists and grows. This makes clear the complexity of the relation between Christ and his church, necessitating flexible dealing with imagery. This image emphasises the exclusive moment but indicates also the moment of union.

Marriage

Now we turn to the image of marriage.[263] Park as well as Muller call attention to this image again, according to Park, a forgotten image.[264]

Paul uses this image for the first time in 1 Cor 6:15–17. Dealing with Corinthian sexual immorality, he parallels the one flesh unity with a prostitute with the unity of a believer with Christ as his member. It is impossible to be at the same time a μέλος, member of Christ and a μέλος of a prostitute (6:15). In addition, Paul places the sexual one flesh / one

262. Best, *A Critical and Exegetical Commentary on Ephesians*, 287.

263. For the image of marriage, see. Batey, 'The MIA ΣΑΡΞ Union of Christ and the Church,' 270–81; Dawes, *The Body in Question*, Part Two; Park, *Die Kirche als "Leib Christi" bei Paulus*, 163–259; Muller, *Trinity and Marriage in Paul*; Son, *Corporate Elements in Pauline Anthropology*, 147–77; Williams, *Paul's Metaphors*, 51–56.

According to Williams, it is possible that Paul draws the designation of the Spirit as ἀρραβών (2 Cor 1:22; 5:5; Eph 1:14) from the rite of betrothal, although this word had a wide commercial application. In this case the Spirit would be portrayed as 'the token of our "betrothal," given in anticipation of our "marriage" at the return of Christ,' see Williams, *Paul's Metaphors*, 53.

264. Park, *Die Kirche als "Leib Christi" bei Paulus*, 161.

Muller and Park both see coming from Gen 2:21–24 a relation between the church as bride of Christ and Christ as Adam. Just as Eve was in Adam and was given to Adam as bride, so the church is in Christ and is given to Christ as his bride. Muller, *Trinity and Marriage in Paul*, 79–80; Park, *Die Kirche als "Leib Christi" bei Paulus*, 230–32.

body unity ('κολλώμενος'; 6:16) next to the unity with the lord in the Spirit (6:17). Being one body is interpreted as being one flesh, referring to Gen. 2:24. A real and comparable unity exists (κολλώμενος is used twice), influencing or even excluding the other union. This unity reaches into our bodily existence, for otherwise sexual immorality would be no problem.[265] At the same time, differences exist between sexual unity with a prostitute and unity with Christ. The dissimilarities are caused by the more complex character of the relation between a believer and Christ, apart from the contrast between a sinful and a holy relation.[266] This unity is no bodily union as sexual union is, but a unity ἓν πνεῦμά, in the Spirit.[267] The unity with Christ is a unity between a human being and a divine-human being, in which a second divine person, the Holy Spirit also has a place. Consequently, this image shows the presence of a moment of union, and further clarifies a little bit the nature of this union: real, and comparable with a sexual union in marriage, but more complex, for Christ and the Holy Spirit both play a role in it.

Echoes of Gen 2:24 can also be found in 2 Cor 11:2 where we again find the image of marriage. Paul pictures himself as the friend of the bridegroom, who promised the church in Corinth to their future groom, Jesus Christ. According to Williams, this reflects the Jewish marriage customs.[268] During the time between betrothal and marriage, the friend of the bridegroom had to 'ensure that the bride came to her wedding as a *virgo intacta*.'[269] This has implications for everyday life: loyalty to Christ,

265. Versteeg, *Christus en de Geest*, 190, 192, 197.

266. Park and Son seem not to see this complex character. Park interprets everything in the perspective of the Adam-christology: as Eve was in Adam and one flesh with him, so the church is in Christ and one with him. Son wants to see a corporate personality everywhere: constituted by Christ and the church or by husband and wife. Hence they minimize the difference between the sexual *one flesh* union with a prostitute and the union with Christ in the *Spirit*. See Park, *Die Kirche als "Leib Christi" bei Paulus*, 219–20; Son, *Corporate Elements in Pauline Anthropology*, 167–68.

Gundry stresses the importance of the *sinful* character of the relation with a prostitute for the contrast between both relations, see Gundry, *Sōma in Biblical Literature*, 68.

267. Versteeg, *Christus en de Geest*, 192, 195f. Gundry and Versteeg are correct in emphasising that Paul does not make a contrast between a lower bodily existence and a higher spiritual existence. That was exactly what the Corinthians did and caused their immorality. Gundry, *Sōma in Biblical Literature*, 65–68; Versteeg, *Christus en de Geest*, 193, 197.

268. Williams, *Paul's Metaphors*, 53–54.

269. Williams, *Paul's Metaphors*, 54.

the bridegroom. It is important to note, that in 1 Corinthians 6 the image focuses on the relation between Christ and an individual, whereas Paul focuses in 2 Corinthians 11 on the relation between Christ and the church as collective. In conclusion, Christ and the church are portrayed here as a betrothed couple not married yet, awaiting their marriage when Christ comes again. Consequently, the moment of union receives an eschatological flavour.

A passage where Paul might refer to the relation between Christ and believers as a relation between married people is Rom 7:1–4. It is clear that Paul uses the bond between husband and wife in Rom 7:1–3. The question is however, whether the change caused by the dying to the law διὰ τοῦ σώματος τοῦ Χριστοῦ results in a change (εἰς τὸ γενέσθαι ὑμᾶς ἑτέρῳ) of husband, continuing the imagery of 7:1–3, or a change of lord, returning to the imagery Romans 6. According to Moo we need to focus on the delivery of the law; Van Bruggen and Dunn also write that Paul returns to the idea of transfer of lordship.[270] Other exegetes however, still see a continuation of the marriage-metaphor.[271] The problem is the complexity of the comparison Paul makes and the dense combination of different imagery. We have seen already that in this passage Paul has intertwined two motifs: the motif of marriage and man and wife being one body or one flesh and the motif of dying with Christ and living a new life under his reign.[272] Consequently, Tannehill writes 'No example will quite fit what Paul wishes to say . . .'[273] Hence it seems impossible to solve the question whether Paul intended the marriage-metaphor to be continued or not.

Finally the marriage-metaphor is found in Ephesians 5. In verse 22 the relation between husband as head and wife is paralleled with the relation between Christ as head and the church, his body. In Eph 5 the relation obviously is not a relation between Christ and an individual soul, but between Christ and the church as collective. Moreover in verse 31 just like in 1 Corinthians 6 and 2 Corinthians 11 Gen. 2:24 is used. Hence the

270. Van Bruggen, *Romeinen*, 100; Dunn, *Romans 1–8*, 362 ; Moo, *The Epistle to the Romans*, 413, 416. Cf. Williams, *Paul's Metaphors*, 55.

271. Park, *Die Kirche als "Leib Christi" bei Paulus*, 257–58; Seifrid, *Justification by Faith*, 228; Wright, *The Climax of the Covenant*, 196, 217.

272. See 5.3.5; Tannehill, *Dying and Rising with Christ*, 45–46; Williams, *Paul's Metaphors*, 55.

273. Tannehill, *Dying and Rising with Christ*, 45.

one body unity is interpreted by wordplay as one flesh unity. As Dawes puts it, 'the phrase μία σάρξ has a double reference. On the level of the marriage paranesis it refers to the union between wife and husband; on the level of the christological and ecclesiological paradigm it refers to the union of Christ and the Church.'[274] Paul mentions that this is a mystery (5:32).[275] The moment of union hence has a mysterious character.

To conclude, the metaphor of marriage is used to portray the relation between Christ and a believer (to exclude fornication), or between Christ and the church. The emphasis does not lie on the relation between Christ and the soul, but between Christ and the collective of the church or a bodily existing person. The one flesh-relation in marriage can be compared with the relation between Christ and the church. At the same time, the fact that the Spirit has a place within this relation shows that the relation between Christ and the church is more complex than a marital relation. The image is used in a flexible way: sometimes the marriage has not occurred yet (2 Cor 11), sometimes marriage between husband and wife and between Christ and the church are just paralleled, without asking the question when marriage took place. In any case, this image very clearly indicates the presence of a moment of union, a moment with a complex and mysterious character.

Clothing

Finally we turn to a fourth metaphor, the metaphor of clothing and ἐνδύω (dress, clothe).[276]

Within the Corinthian correspondence, the image is used referring to the resurrection. In 1 Corinthians 15 Paul writes about the perish-

274. Dawes, *The Body in Question*, 169.

275. The question is, whether the mystery is that this parallel exists or that this unity between Christ and the church, comparable with the unity between husband and wife, has a mysterious character. In any case, a sacramental interpretation of marriage grounded on this passage must be excluded. See Best, *A Critical and Exegetical Commentary on Ephesians*, 557; Dawes, *The Body in Question*, 181–84; O'Brien, *The Letter to the Ephesians*, 430–33; Park, *Die Kirche als "Leib Christi" bei Paulus*, 247; Schnackenburg, *Der Brief an die Epheser*, 260–61.

276. The metaphor receives only marginal attention in studies on Paul. Becker, Dunn Gnilka, Ridderbos and Sanders mention the metaphor, see Becker, *Paulus. Der Apostel der Völker*, 414, 444; Dunn, *The Theology of Paul the Apostle*, 194, 453; Gnilka, *Paulus von Tarsus*, 276; Ridderbos, *Paulus*, 447; Sanders, *Paul and Palestinian Judaism*, 459. See further Williams, *Paul's Metaphors*, 92–95. Kim's study might inaugurate a change in this neglect; see Kim, *The Significance of Clothing Imagery in the Pauline Corpus*.

able that 'must clothe itself with the imperishable' (1 Cor 15:53–54). In 2 Corinthians 5 comparable thoughts are found, as Paul writes that he does not want to be found naked 'but to be clothed with our heavenly dwelling' (2 Cor 5:3–4). But here the swallowing up of death by life is concerned (1 Cor 15:54; 2 Cor 5:4) and it is not used as an image for union with Christ. Hence I will not deal further with these passages.[277]

In the letter to the Galatians, the image returns (Gal 3:27). Exploring the purpose of the law, Paul seems to refer to a Roman practice, the change of the *toga praetexta* for the *toga virilis* when a boy grew to manhood. As children, boys were under control of a παιδαγωγός and wore a *toga praetexta*. The change of clothing brought freedom from the παιδαγωγός and the change of a slave-like position to a new position as responsible citizen.[278] No difference exists between a slave and a future heir as long as the heir is a child (4:1). Now Christ has come and the believers have clothed themselves with Christ, they have become adults with him, heirs according to the promise (3:29) and no longer slaves but free sons of God. Clothing yourself with Christ results in sharing in his position: a free son of God, whatever was one's position before (3:28). The metaphorical interpretation of baptism as a clothing with Christ shows the total involvement of a believer in Christ.[279] The believer is identified with Christ, sharing in his position, in his identity. Hence the image of clothing makes clear the union between Christ and the believer who is in Christ.

The image in Galatians shows the new position that Christians have in unity with Christ, in Romans 13 the metaphor has a moral significance. The moment of dawn is evoked. The present time is the time that 'the night is nearly over; the day is almost here' (13:12). Consequently, Paul urges the Romans to live as in daytime, putting on (ἐνδύω) the armour of light (13:12). In 13:14 he continues: rather, ἐνδύσασθε the Lord Jesus Christ. What exactly does Paul mean with 'clothe yourselves with Jesus Christ'? The preceding verses make clear that it refers to behaviour and hence to imitation of Christ, resulting in conformity to him. However, within the whole of Paul's thinking, it should not be to seen as mere moral improvement. Hence, Thompson suggests it is more: the meaning of 'putting on

277. See on these passages Kim, *The Significance of Clothing Imagery*, 192–223.

278. Van Bruggen, *Galaten*, 113; Kim, *The Significance of Clothing Imagery*, 92–95; Williams, *Paul's Metaphors*, 94.

279. See on the relation between the metaphor of clothing and baptismal practices Kim, *The Significance of Clothing Imagery*, 96–101; and further 112–28.

Christ' 'surely points to adoption of his mind, character and conduct.' It corresponds to 'taking care to discern and fulfil the θέλημα of God, as Jesus did.'[280] Again, the image indicates the firm union between Christ and the believer, but now seen more in its moral consequences.[281]

The image returns in Colossians 3 and Ephesians 4. Paul summons the Colossians to put to death the earthly members and to stop sinning, ἀπεκδυσάμενοι the old man with its practices (3:9). This taking off of the old man is followed by the reverse: dressing (ενδύω) with the new man (3:10). The old man is a human being in Adam, the new man is not Christ himself but the human being in Christ;[282] being renewed in knowledge after the image of his Creator. This dressing with the new man is paralleled with another version of the metaphor: 'clothe yourselves with compassion, kindness, humility, gentleness and patience'(3:12). We find the image in Ephesians 4 used in a comparable way. Paul reminds the Ephesians that they were taught to put off the old man (4:22) and to put on (ἐνδύσασθαι) the new man (4:24). The image of putting on the armour of God (Eph 6:10–18) is comparable to Col 3:12. Consequently, in these two letters, the emphasis has shifted with regard to Galatians 3 and Romans 13. The relation with Christ is seen only indirectly, as the new man is the human being in Christ. Nevertheless, although the emphasis is not on the relation with Christ, something is presupposed that came into existence with Christ, the new man (cf. Eph 2:15); something just as available for the believer as their clothes.

To conclude, the metaphor of clothing is a metaphor for salvation. It can be used to refer to the resurrection (Corinthians), to the old and new man (Colossians and Ephesians), to virtues (Col 3:12), but also to Christ himself (Gal 3:27; Rom 13:14). In the second case, the relation with Christ is viewed only indirectly but this relation is presupposed as the source of life of the new man. In the fourth and last case, it refers to the firm unity existing between Christ and the believers: he determines their identity and existence in every respect. Here a moment of union is indicated.

In conclusion, Paul uses these four images—body, building and temple, marriage and clothing—with creativity and flexibility. Sometimes

280. Thompson, *Clothed with Christ*, 158.

281. Cf. Kim, *The Significance of Clothing Imagery*, 147–50.

282. Kim, *The Significance of Clothing Imagery*, 162–67, 180–84; O'Brien, *Colossians, Philemon*, 190, 192; Best, *A Critical and Exegetical Commentary on Ephesians*, 439–40; O'Brien, *The Letter to the Ephesians*, 328–32.

these images are used with a focus on the individual (marriage, clothing), in other passages they have a more corporate focus (body, building, marriage). In the case of the unitive use of the body-metaphor the emphasis is on the union between believers and not on the union between Christ and the church. This relation remains implicit, apart from cases where it is used in combination with the sacramental use of the body-metaphor. In other cases of the use of these four metaphors, a moment of union is always present. This indicates the necessity of a concept of union in order to understand Paul's Christology and soteriology.

5.4.4 METAPHORS FOR SALVATION

In this section on Paul's soteriology, we now finally turn to three different metaphors for salvation: justification, sonship and sanctification. I will investigate these images to see what we receive in Christ. Again I focus on the moments of participation and union, to see whether we need concepts of union and participation to understand Paul's writings. Regarding another metaphor for salvation, election, we have already seen in relation to Eph 1:4 that the church is chosen in participation with Christ, the chosen One (see 5.2).

Justification

Justification is one of the metaphors for salvation. Δικαίωσις is a juridical metaphor, belonging to words like δικαιόω, δίκαιος, and δικαιοσύνη. With regard to justification, we have seen already that the separation of the so-called juridical and mystical, the juristic and participationist is impossible, for they are intertwined and belong together.[283] The scholarly debate on the relation between these two aspects is related with the problem of the centre of Paul's thinking. The discussion on the question of whether justification is the centre of Paul's theology or not, was roused by Sanders, who reminded his readers of Schweitzer's thesis that the doctrine of justification is only a 'Nebenkrater' of Paul's theology and not the centre.[284] Within the debate after Sanders, the place of justification within Paul is a much-debated problem.[285] Moreover, his separation of

283. See 5.3.7 and footnote 135.

284. Sanders, *Paul and Palestinian Judaism*, 434–35; cf. Schweitzer, *Die Mystik des Apostels Paulus*, 220.

285. For the recent discussion on justification, see e.g. Dunn, *The Theology of Paul*

justification and participation evoked the question regarding the relation between justification and participation. I will concentrate on this now, for this concerns the central question of this section.

Starting with the Corinthian correspondence, 1 Cor 1:30 and 2 Cor 5:21 are important. In 1 Corinthians 1 Paul opposes the wisdom of the world with the foolishness of the cross. However, for those whom God has called, Christ is God's wisdom (1:24). And in 1:30 Paul writes that Christ became for us wisdom from God. This wisdom consists in δικαιοσύνη, holiness and redemption.[286] Consequently, Paul says that Christ is given to us as righteousness. He is our δικαιοσύνη, as he is also our holiness and our redemption. In translating the first clause of the verse two possibilities exist: 'You are from God, in Christ Jesus' and 'It is from God that you are in Christ Jesus.' In the second case the relation between justification and union with Christ or participation in Christ is even stronger: we are in Christ, who is our righteousness. But also in the first case, if Christ is our righteousness, the relation between (union with or participation in) Christ and justification is obvious.

We now turn to 2 Cor 5:21. We saw that in 2 Cor 5:15 the inclusiveness of both the death and rising of Christ for all is affirmed. Moreover, in 2 Cor 5:17 it is said that 'if anyone is in Christ, he is a new creation'; the 'in Christ' is used here clearly with a locative meaning.[287] Hence, in the preceding verses Christ is viewed as representative, in whose dying and resurrection believers participate. Now the question is whether something similar is the case in 5:21. Paul says that the sinless Christ was made sin, and in him we might become righteousness. This can be interpreted as a 'simple' exchange: Christ takes our position; we take his. In this case the 'in Christ' is used instrumentally. But seen within the context of the preceding verses and my reconstruction of Paul using the concept

the Apostle, 334–89; Kim, *Paul and the New Perspective*; Noordegraaf, 'Paulus spreken over rechtvaardiging'; Seifrid, *Justification by Faith*; Stuhlmacher, *Biblische Theologie des Neuen Testaments, Band 1*, 234–43, 312–49; Westerholm, *Perspectives Old and New on Paul*, esp. 352–407; Wright, *What Saint Paul Really Said*, 113–34. See also Van Bruggen, *Paulus*, 192–223.

286. Fee and Schrage both emphasise that Paul opposes Christ as true wisdom over against the Corinthian wisdom, whereas the three metaphors elaborate this wisdom. We must not see the three metaphors and the wisdom in line as four concepts of salvation. See Fee, *The First Epistle to the Corinthians*, 86; Schrage, *Der erste Brief an die Korinther*, Bd. 1, 215.

287. See 5.4.1.

of representation, these words could be understood differently. It can be understood this way, that Christ identified himself with us including with our sin, and being united with us he was justified by God, who raised him from the dead. He was affirmed innocent, vindicated, and restored in his right. Being united with Christ we share in his righteousness, hence becoming δικαιοσύνη θεοῦ ἐν αὐτῶ.[288] This second interpretation is more plausible, because it fits better within 2 Corinthians 5 and within Paul's thinking as a whole. Consequently, for Hooker, 2 Cor 5:21 is one of the important passages that voice what she calles 'interchange' of experience: 'Christ became what we are, in order that, *in him*, we might become what he is.'[289] To conclude, this verse shows the relation between our justification and our participation in Christ.

It might seem, based on the Corinthian correspondence, that a relation exists between being in Christ and justification, but is not this relation found to be lacking in the letters to Galatians and Romans? In Galatians 3 and Romans 4, Paul writes about Abraham's faith, about God who ἐλογίσθη αὐτῷ εἰς δικαιοσύνην (Gal 3:6; Rom 4:3). He writes about justification ἐκ πίστεως (Gal 3:24; Rom 5:1) and the problem of the law and works of the law. God is acting, with Abraham, with believers, he justifies by faith, crediting faith as righteousness. Nothing is said about union with Christ, until at the end, in Rom 4:25: Christ 'was raised to life for our justification.' Comparably, only after dealing with justification in Gal 3:6–14 does Paul mention Christ, writing about the promise given to Abraham and his seed, Jesus Christ. What this promised salvation consists of becomes clear in Gal 3:26–27. These verses can be interpreted also as a passage concerning justification, although this word is not mentioned. Clothed with Christ we receive justification. Consequently, in Rom 4:25 and in Gal 3:26–27 the relation between justification and Christ at once is mentioned.

Before dealing further with these passages, we need to understand better why Christ is not mentioned earlier. In Galatians 3 as well as in Romans 4 Paul stresses that our works of the law do not bring us justification before God. In both chapters, the problem is that it seems that God has changed. Does God change his attitude towards man after Christ? Paul wants to make clear that this is not the case. Therefore he goes back

288. Powers, *Salvation through Participation*, 75–80; Thrall, *A critical and exegetical Commentary on the Second Epistle to the Corinthians*, 444.

289. Hooker, *From Adam to Christ*, 42; cf. 17, 26, 59.

to someone who lived before the gift of the law at Sinai: Abraham. Paul stresses that God did not change his attitude towards man, for in the case of a believer nothing is different from the case of Abraham. We live from faith in the promise, and this faith is credited as righteousness. To underline this continuity, he refers to several places in the Old Testament, trying to show the continuity in God's acting towards believers in Old and New Testament, and to deal with the problem of the law.[290] It is impossible to mention Christ as long as Paul deals with Abraham. Abraham never knew the historical figure of Christ, but nevertheless God justified him by faith, just as he does with those who believe in Christ.

Once Paul no longer deals with the continuity between God's dealing with Abraham and with believers in the present, the picture changes as we see in Rom 4:25 and Gal 3:26–27.

In Rom 4:25 Paul writes that Christ was delivered to death for our sins and was raised again for our justification. How must this contribution of Christ's resurrection to our justification be seen? Is it only necessary to understand Jesus' death not as the death of a martyr, but as an effective sacrifice, providing an eschatological breakthrough?[291] Or should we conclude with Hooker that Christian theology often gave no place to resurrection, and so leave more place for a relation between justification and resurrection?[292] Rom 4:25 can be interpreted along this line, showing the soteriological significance of the resurrection for justification. The resurrection was the vindication of the one condemned as a blasphemer: he was declared to be the Son of God by his resurrection (Cf. Rom 1:4). Injustice is undone. Just as Christ participated in our unrighteousness, we now participate in his vindication and become justified. Our justification is a gracious participation of the ungodly in the vindication of Christ.[293] In 4:25 a moment of participation is evidently present.

Nevertheless, the picture is more complex. Rom 4:25 shows a relation between resurrection as vindication of Christ and our justification.

290. Gen 15:6 in Rom 4:3, 9 and Gal 3:6; Ps 32:1–2 in Rom 4:7–8; Gen 17:10–11 in Rom 4:11; Gen 17:4–6 in Rom 4:13 and Gal 3:29; Gen 17:5 in Rom 4:17; Gen 15:5 in Rom 4:18; Gen 12:3 in Gal 3:8; Deut 27:36 in Gal 3:10; Hab 2:4 in Gal 3:11 and Rom 1:17; Deut 21:23 in Gal 3:13.

291. Dunn, *Romans 1–8*, 241.

292. Hooker, *From Adam to Christ*, 38.

293. Cf. Han, *Raised for our Justification*, 238; Gaffin, 'Resurrection and Redemption,' 201–3, 205–6; Hooker, *From Adam to Christ*, 39–40; Powers, *Salvation through Participation*, 129–31.

We participate in Christ as representative and inclusive figure. Hence he was raised and vindicated for our justification. But we have seen already that, apart from this inclusiveness we need the concept of substitution to underline the exclusivity of the work of Christ. Consequently, he died for our justification. This can be seen in Rom 5:9–10, where both the exclusive and the inclusive aspect is found. On the one hand Paul writes that 'we have now been justified by his blood' (5:9). This shows the exclusivity of the sacrifice of Christ, taking away our guilt. In so far as 'διὰ' indicates also the exclusivity, this reinforces the emphasis on the exclusive moment. On the other hand he writes that we will 'be saved through his life' (5:10). This can only be understood as participation in the resurrection of Christ, a participation that saves from the ὀργή (5:9). Paul uses juridical language: we will be saved from God's wrath. Here the inclusive moment is voiced. Obviously, Paul's concept of justification is a flexible one: he can relate our justification with the death of Christ as well as with the resurrection of Christ.[294]

Justification further has a past and a future aspect. We were justified by his blood, but we will be saved from wrath. Comparably, Paul sees righteousness as a future gift in Rom 5:17. This shows the eschatological tension present in Paul's doctrine of justification: we have received justification *in Christ*, we will be saved from God's future judgment. To conclude, we need a concept of substitution to understand justification, as well as a concept of participation (together with representation). Both do not exclude each other, for they can both be found in Rom 5:9–10.

In Galatians 3, Paul explains how faith in Jesus Christ brought justification (as well as sonship). This new position he combines here with baptismal language. Baptised εἰς Χριστὸν, we have clothed ourselves with Christ. Clothing ourselves with Christ, we receive a new identity including justification. Although Paul does not use the language of justification in Gal 3:26–27, nevertheless these verses have their implication for the idea of justification. Again we see that the relation between justification and union with, or participation in, Christ is evident: he is around us like our clothing.

Elaborating the soteriological significance of the gift of Christ, Paul's use of the metaphor of justification has its own aims and possibilities.

294. Cf. Powers, *Salvation through Participation*, 95–96.

1. It uses juridical language and deals with the problem that all human beings once need to face individually: the inescapable judgment of God (Romans 1–3).[295]

2. Christ is given as righteousness to the ungodly (Rom 4:5). Faced with the judgment of God, works of the law do not matter any more. Consequently, the passivity of man and the activity of God in justification is emphasised. This gives the doctrine of justification a relevance transcending the idea of a contingent 'Kampfeslehre.'[296]

3. The doctrine of justification is used to show the continuity in God's dealing with believers in Old and New Testament and thus his loyalty to his covenant. [297] This makes it useful for handling the problem of the law.[298] In cases concerning the continuity is it impossible to mention Christ. A believer is justified by faith, just like Abraham; faith is credited as righteousness.

4. Justification is related with the death as well as with the resurrection of Christ. The relation with death is based first on the exclusive character of the work of Christ: he took away our sins; second, it is based on the inclusive character of his work: we participate in his history and thus in his vindication. The relation with his resurrection and vindication is based on the inclusive character of the work of Christ: participating in his history, we share also in his justification.[299]

5. The theme of the judgment of God has an eschatological character. Therefore, we can find an eschatological tension in Paul's doctrine of jus-

295. Wright concentrates on the ecclesiological (coventantal) character of the doctrine of justification. Hence he thinks that justification concerns the vindication of the true people of God and denies that justification concerns individual salvation. 'It wasn't so much about soteriology as about ecclesiology.' I do not see how this can be combined with Romans 1–3. See Wright, *What Saint Paul Really Said*, 119, 131; Stuhlmacher, *Biblische Theologie des Neuen Testaments, Band 1*, 309, 340.

296. See Seifrid, *Justification by Faith*, 249, 255; cf. the emphasis on the doctrine of justification in Stuhlmachers *Biblische Theologie des Neuen Testaments, Band 1*, 231, 241, 294, 312, 340, 391.

297. Cf. the coventantal reading of Paul's doctrine of justification according to Wright: this doctrine deals with the continuity of the covenant. See Wright, *What Saint Paul Really Said*, 117, 131–32.

298. On this problem of the law, see Van Bruggen who shows that this problem was not a central problem in Paul's thinking: Van Bruggen, *Paulus*, 192–223.

299. Cf. Gaffin, 'Resurrection and Redemption,' 201–5; Schnelle, 'Transformation und Partizipation als Grundgedanke paulinischer Theologie,' 72, 74; Han, *Raised for our Justi-fication*, 231–48, 328–29

tification: we are justified, but we shall be saved from God's wrath (Rom 5:9).[300] This can be understood analogously to the participation in the resurrection of Christ: we are raised in Christ and live in him, but we will rise with him. Likewise, we are justified in him and will be justified with him. That this eschatological tension does not receive much attention in Romans 4 and Galatians 3 is not surprising, because of the centrality of the figure of Abraham.

6. Where Paul in Galatians 3 and Romans 4 deals with Abraham, the word 'λογίζομαι' plays an important role.[301] This is due to the fact that it is used in the OT-citations. Remarkably, λογίζομαι is used as long as Christ is not mentioned, once he is mentioned Paul does not use λογίζομαι. Paul never uses this verb where he deals with the gift of salvation in explicit relation to Christ.[302] Once Christ is mentioned, we can say more directly: Christ is the righteousness of the believer (1 Cor 1:30; 2 Cor 5:21), or, the believer participates in the justification of Christ (cf. Rom 4:25).

In the Protestant doctrine of justification, however, the emphasis is on the *imputation* of righteousness. Together with this emphasis the idea of justification by imputation became separated from participation or mystical categories. Further the role of resurrection in justification was often neglected. As a result, the relation between Christ and the believer with regard to justification was often seen more indirectly than in the case that our justification can be seen as participation in the justification of Christ. This is partly due to the fact that the proper issue of Galatians

300. 'This declaration, this verdict, is ultimately made at the end of history. Through Jesus, however, God has done in the middle of history what he had been expected to do—and indeed, will still do—at the end; so that the declaration, the verdict, can be issued already in the present, in anticipation. The events of the last days were *anticipated* when Jesus died on the cross, as the representative Messiah of Israel, and rose again.' Wright, *What Saint Paul Really Said*, 131; see further 117–19. And also Stuhlmacher, *Biblische Theologie des Neuen Testaments, Band 1*, 334, 340.

Dunn gives his treatment of justification in a chapter on the Beginning of Salvation. Hence he emphasises the present character. Consequently, the eschatological tension seems to disappear too much. See Dunn, *The Theology of Paul the Apostle*, 317, 335–89.

301. Rom 4:3.4.5.6.8.9.10.11.22.23.24; Gal 3:6.

302. The verb is used in passages concerning someone not counting the evil of a person (1 Cor 13:5; 2 Cor 5:19; 2 Tim 4:16). Further, in Rom 6:11 it is used in relation to life in Christ, but here it is not God who counts (λογίζεσθε) someone as alive in Christ, but the believer. And in Rom 9:8 Paul writes about the children of the promise who are regarded (λογίζεται) as Abraham's offspring. Again the relation with Christ is not mentioned.

3 and Romans 4 is neglected: the demonstration of God's continuity in dealing with Abraham and with believers of the new covenant.

However, the verb λογίζομαι is used because it has a prominent role in the OT-citations, where the relation with Christ cannot be mentioned. Further it is not related exclusively with justification and does not exclude the idea of participation. It is possible to say that one is regarded as a participant in Christ, by God or by oneself.[303] Finally, it is not necessary to use the verb λογίζομαι if Christ can be mentioned directly. Therefore it is remarkable that the concept of imputation became so central to the understanding of justification, at least in the light of the Pauline texts. Justification and participation are not opposed. Where this opposition disappears, in the doctrine of justification a place can also be left for the significance of participation in the resurrection.

Adoption

The soteriological significance of the gift of Christ is explicated with the help of the idea of justification, but also with the idea of sonship. Which view offers the idea of sonship on being in Christ?

For this theme two passages are important: Gal 3:26–4:7 and Rom 8:14–23.

In Galatians 3 and 4, Paul might refer to two different customs. The first is the exchange of the *toga praetexta* for the *toga virilis* on the threshold of manhood, as we saw in 5.4.3. The second custom Paul might refer to is the adoption of a child by another family.[304] The idea of a παιδαγωγὸς (3:24–25), and the fact that Paul mentions that an heir as child 'is no different from a slave' (4:1), point at the first custom; the redemption of those under the law (4:5), however does not. It seems that Paul shifts from image, both images being related to υἱοθεσία.[305] Both customs led

303. In Rom. 6:11 the readers are summoned to count themselves as alive in Christ. And in Rom. 9:8, Paul writes that 'it is the children of the promise who are regarded as Abraham's offspring.' To be Abraham's seed is to participate in Christ (cf. Gal 3:16).

304. For these customs, see Kim, *The Significance of Clothing Imagery*, 92–94; Williams, *Paul's Metaphors*, 64–66 and 94.

305. According to Betz, Bruce, Reitsma and Van Bruggen υἱοθεσία means 'adoption' here in stead of sonship. Williams chooses the other option. If Paul shifts from image, we would do better not to choose. See Betz, *Galatians*, 208; Bruce, *The Epistle of Paul to the Galatians*, 197; Reitsma, *Geest en schepping*, 83–84; Williams, *Paul's Metaphors*, 94. Van Bruggen mentions both images, see Van Bruggen, *Galaten*, 113–19. Ridderbos sees the background in the Old Testament-idea of the acceptance of Israel as God's son, Ridderbos, *Paulus*, 215.

to the acquiring of υἱοθεσία, and in both cases almost only *boys* were involved. Several things deserve attention. First, the change from slave (-like child) to adult son takes place by Jesus Christ: baptism is seen as clothing with Christ (3:27) and God sent his Son to redeem the slaves and give them υἱοθεσία, sonship or adoption. Second, being a son of God results in the gift of the Spirit of *the* Son of God.[306] Third, being a son implies being a heir (3:29; 4:7). To understand what is said here, we must not translate υἱός too fast as child; in contrary, according to Hooker we need the 'sexist' language of υἱός and υἱοθεσία.[307] First of all because of the fact that only boys were involved in the described customs. The position we receive in Christ as a position of responsibility, adulthood and being an heir was a male position. Nevertheless, both male and female believers receive this position. Consequently, there is no male or female in Christ (3:28). Second, because we are sons of God only in unity with *the* Son of God, who is explicitly mentioned in 4:4, 6. Our sonship is a participation in the position of the Son of God. In Christ, the Son of God, we are sons of God. And by the Spirit of the Son we call God 'Abba, Father' (4:6).[308] Consequently, the idea of sonship presupposes, in this passage, our unity with Christ, as well as our participation in his position, in him and by his Spirit.

In Romans 8 no reference to a change of toga and becoming an adult is found. Here the inhabitation of the Spirit is the starting point: 'those who are led by the Spirit of God are sons of God' (8:14). This Spirit is the Spirit of υἱοθεσία (8:15). The Spirit marks a contrast, between slavery and anxiety on the one hand, and, on the other hand, sonship and calling God 'abba, father' (8:15). This Spirit testifies with our spirit that we are τέκνα θεου, children of God (8:16); Paul does not use the word υἱὸι. Correspondingly, the relation between the sonship of the Son and our sonship is less clear in these verses than in Gal 3 and 4.[309] The Son is not mentioned as υἱός before 8:29, where he is seen as πρωτότοκος ἐν

306. It is most likely to translate 'Oτι δέ ἐστε υἱοί' (4:6) with 'because you are sons.' See Betz, *Galatians*, 209; Ridderbos, *Paulus*, 217.

307. Hooker, *From Adam to Christ*, 61.

308. Hooker, *From Adam to Christ*, 18–19, 61; Stuhlmacher, *Biblische Theologie des Neuen Testaments, Band 1*, 290, 355.

309. According to Van Bruggen, the use of the word 'abba' refers implicitly to Jesus who called God 'abba.' This shows that we call upon God together with Jesus; see Van Bruggen, *Romeinen*, 120.

πολλοῖς ἀδελφοῖς, firstborn among many brothers. As a consequence, the relation between the Son and our position as sons or children is seen less directly here, although the Spirit is called the Spirit of υἱοθεσία. How can this be understood? The problem in Romans 8 is not our position in Christ, but the tension between the already received gift of the Spirit and the not yet received redemption of our bodies (8:10, 11, 13, 19, 21–25). Therefore, Paul is not interested here in what we share with Christ but in what we do not share with him yet. The gift of the Spirit is only an ἀπαρχή, the firstfruits (8:23). We received the Spirit of υἱοθεσία, but we wait until we see that we are children of God: together with the creation we expect the revelation of the sons of God (8:19); remarkably we even wait for our υἱοθεσία that is equated by Paul with the redemption of our bodies (8:23) and the receiving of glory (8:21). To conclude, Paul is interested, in Romans 8, in what we will receive later. And it is evident that we receive this together with Christ, for we are his συγκληρονόμοι, co-heirs, sharing in his heritage. Hence the participation in Christ is presupposed in the future position we will receive as glorified children of God. For the present, this participation in Christ is seen less directly in the gift of the Spirit of υἱοθεσία as firstfruits. As a consequence, whereas the gift of the Spirit is, in Galatians 4, based on our being children, in Romans 8 the gift of the Spirit is an anticipation of our being children of God. The emphasis here is on the future participation in Christ.

To conclude, the metaphor of sonship offers a perspective on an aspect of the identity we receive in Christ: we share in his position as Son of God and in his relation with God as his Father. It is a metaphor, not a fixed concept, as the differences between Galatians 4 and Romans 8 show. In Galatians the gift of the Spirit follows the new identity that is a present reality, in Romans the gift of the Spirit is an anticipation of the identity we will receive fully in the future.[310] Especially important for this metaphor is the Holy Spirit who as Spirit of sonship lives in us, uniting us with the Son and saying 'Father' with our Spirit. As such the metaphor stands within a Trinitarian framework: by the Spirit we are united with Christ the Son and participate in his relation with the Father. Moreover, the metaphor is characterized by an eschatological tension. This is because of the relation between sonship and heritage. Only as children of God we receive the

310. In his treatment of the metaphor of adoption, Ridderbos tries to solve these differences without doing justice to the different rhetorical aims Paul has in Galatians and in Romans. See Ridderbos, *Paulus*, 214–22, esp. 217–18.

inheritance together with Christ. Clearly this metaphor presupposes a moment of participation and a (pneumatological) moment of union.

Sanctification

Thirdly, the soteriological significance of Christ is viewed in the light of the metaphor of sanctification. The language-field of sanctification has to do with the Holy Spirit, God's holiness, sacrifice, blamelessness, cleansing, all words related to the cultic sphere of the temple and of dedication to God. Believers are called ἁγίοι, saints.[311] Different elements of the life of a Christian believer are seen as holy.[312] Within the framework of sanctification believers are seen as both passive and active.

The passivity is related with the Holy Spirit[313] as well with Jesus Christ; this last one is of interest here. First, Paul writes about Christ, given as righteousness, ἁγιασμὸς and redemption in 1 Cor 1:30. We have dealed with this text already. It is important to notice here that Christ is given as sanctification also. Second, in the later letter to the Ephesians, Christ is mentioned as an actor in the sanctification of the church. In Eph 5:26 Christ, loving his church, is said to have given himself for his church to make her holy (ἁγιάζω). In the letter to the Colossians, sanctification is seen as the aim of the work of God by Christ. He wants to see us holy before him (Col 1:22). To conclude, within the work of Father, Son and Spirit for our holiness, both Christ as our holiness and the Holy Spirit have their place. This can be understood with the help of the concept of participation as a participation in the holiness of Christ by the Holy Spirit.

The activity of the believer is also mentioned. First this is the case in 2 Cor 7:1, where Paul writes that the Corinthians should purify themselves, perfecting ἁγιωσύνη, holiness. Moreover Romans 6 is important. Christians are set free and now serve righteousness (Rom 6:18–19). The fruit of this activity is ἁγιασμός, sanctification (Rom 6:19, 22). Thirdly, in the letter to the Ephesians Paul writes that the Ephesians should clothe themselves with the new man, created in righteousness and holiness (ὁσιότης).

311. Rom 1:7; 8:27; 12:13; 15:25, 26, 31; 16:2, 15; 1 Cor 1:2; 6:1–2; 14:34; 16:1, 15; 2 Cor 1:1; 8:4; 9:1, 12; 13:12; Eph 1:1, 15, 18; 2:15; 3:5, 8, 18; 4:12; 5:3; 6:18; Col 1:2, 4, 12, 22, 26; 3:12.

312. Cf. Rom 11:16; 12:1; 15:16; 16:16; 1 Cor 3:17; 7:14; 7:34; 16:20; 2 Cor 13:12; Eph 1:4; 2:21; 5:27; Col 1:22.

313. Rom 15:16.

Consequently, again an eschatological tension can be seen: Christ is given as holiness, but at the same time the Holy Spirit sanctifies us and we are urged to purify ourselves and perfect our holiness. This has an eschatological aim: to stand holy before God's face. Within this process of sanctification, Christ is our holiness, making us participants of this holiness by his Holy Spirit and by our own activity.

In 1 Cor 1:30 Christ is seen as righteousness, holiness and redemption. This third metaphor of salvation, ἀπολύτρωσις, does not really change the picture. Redemption is given in Christ (Rom 3:24) or in Christ by his blood (Col 1:14; Eph 1:7). This metaphor is a metaphor with a strong eschatological character: we wait for the day of redemption (Eph 4:30). Until this day, we receive the Spirit as ἀπαρχή, firstfruits (Rom 8:23); as ἀρραβών, guaranteeing deposit (Eph 1:14) or as seal (Eph 4:30).

We have now investigated different metaphors for salvation: justification, sonship, sanctification, and, briefly, redemption. These metaphors use different semantic fields: a juridical field, a field of slavery and family life, a religious field and a field of liberation. Within all of these fields different actors can be seen: God (the Father), Jesus Christ, the Holy Spirit and the believer. The field of justification emphasises the activity of God; the field of family pictures the believer as sharing in the position of Christ as Son of the Father by the work of the Son and the Holy Spirit; the field of sanctification sees at different moments these four actors acting; and viewed within the perspective of redemption God is redeeming us in Christ, giving the Spirit in advance. Although Father, Son and Spirit as three divine actors all are mentioned, Jesus Christ has a central position. He has died and is raised for our justification and is given as righteousness; we participate in his position as child of God; he is given as sanctification and as redemption. In different ways, these four metaphors show something of our salvation as participation in Christ. The union with Christ becomes explicit in relation to the image of clothing in Galatians 3, and further it might be seen in the work of the Spirit who unites us with our position in Christ.

Within this section on soteriology as participation in Christ, some attention could be given to the theme of πίστις χριστοῦ (Rom 3:22, 26; Gal 2:16, 20; 3:22). It is a matter of discussion whether this should be translated as 'faith in Jesus Christ' or as 'faith of Jesus Christ.' In the second case this might mean that we participate in the faith or faithfulness of Jesus Christ. Hence to believe would mean to share in the faith of Jesus

Christ himself. This might fit very well within the whole of my reconstruction of the thinking of Paul. Nevertheless, it is not clear yet whether this position is a possible one. Hooker and Hays defend this second possibility, whereas Dunn (and Van Bruggen) deny its truth. I will leave this open and will not try to decide this discussion. If Dunn is right, this is not a problem for the given reconstruction, if Hooker and Hays are right the given reconstruction stands even stronger.[314]

5.4.5 CONCLUSION

Within this section was the question: is the concept of participation in Christ necessary to understand Paul's soteriology? And do we also need a concept of union?

First Paul's use of the expression 'ἐν Χριστῳ' was investigated. We saw that it must be understood as a consequence of Paul's idea of the representative Christ. Among a diversity of uses, it can be used in a locative sense. This locative sense is further indicated by the idea of baptism 'εἰς Χριστόν.' Being in Christ bears itself a tension between the already and not yet. We are already in Christ, but salvation is more than being in Christ. Localised in Christ, we wait for a further participation in Christ. To understand the formula 'ἐν Χριστῳ' within this eschatological tension aiming at a more intensive participation in Christ, other expressions as 'Χριστὸς ἐν ὑμιν,' 'σὺν Χριστῳ' and different σὺν-compounds received attention. 'Χριστὸς ἐν ὑμιν' shows a reciprocity and a nearness of Christ living within us.

Second, we turned to 'σὺν Χριστῳ.' With the help of 'σὺν Χριστῳ,' Paul creatively established different semantic relations between the story of Jesus Christ and our life. We suffer now with Christ; we have been crucified with Christ; we died with Christ but at the same time we die with him now; we have been buried with Christ. With regard to our present life, differences exist between the earlier letters and the later letters to the Colossians and Ephesians. Whereas the earlier letters see us living *in* Christ now and living *with* Christ in the future, the later letters see more 'with-ness' realised in the present. Nevertheless, in all Pauline letters salvation is not fully accomplished yet: we will rise with Christ, we will

314. See Van Bruggen, *Galaten*, 91; Dunn, *The Theology of Paul the Apostle*, 379–85; Dunn, 'Once more, ΠΙΣΤΙΣ ΧΡΙΣΤΟΥ'; Hays, 'ΠΙΣΤΙΣ and Pauline Christology'; Hays, *The Faith of Jesus Christ*; Hooker, *From Adam to Christ*, 165–86.

inherit with Christ, we will appear with him in glory and live with him. By establishing many different semantic relations between the story of Christ and the story of our life, Paul makes it clear that according to him we participate in Christ. This participation in Christ can be understood as a sharing in the story of Christ. We saw that we do not fully participate within the death of Christ: his death contains a moment of exclusivity. Our participation in Christ's story goes together with flexibility in semantic relations and in chronological order. Within this whole, a movement can be seen of a double identification: Christ identified himself with us, becoming our representative. We may identify with the life of Christ as he lived it for us, hence participating in his story.

Investigating further our relation with Christ, we dealt with different images used for our union with Christ. The flexibility of Paul's use of images was astonishing. First we explored Paul's use of the body-image. This image indicates a moment of union when used in a sacramental context or against the background of two different models: the model of the human body with Christ as head and the church as body, and the model of marriage, with Christ as husband and the church as his wife. In other cases the relation with Christ remains implicit. The second image shows the exclusive position of Christ and the union of the church with him. This moment of union is also clearly present in the use of the image of marriage. Here again we found the model of marriage, with Christ as husband and the church as his wife. Often, these images suggest corporateness. More emphasis on the individual relation with Christ is laid in the image of clothing, which is used to picture Christ as our new clothing. These images make explicit what otherwise would remain implicit: the presence of a moment of union in the relation of the church with Christ. Hence a concept of union is necessary besides a concept of participation.

Finally we turned to metaphors for salvation. We saw that Christ is raised for our justification, letting us share in his vindication. Further, Christ is given to us as righteousness, sanctification and redemption. And we share in his position as child of God by the gift of the Spirit. More or less all these metaphors contained an eschatological tension. Furthermore, these metaphors for salvation showed that Christ is one of the three divine persons acting for our salvation. Paul's soteriology has a Trinitarian outlook, with our participation in Christ as its central moment. We participate in Christ's identity: that is our salvation. It is the Father who gives us this identity, the Son is our identity, and the Spirit is given as first downpayment of this identity. Consequently, the concept of participation is necessary to reconstruct a central element of Paul's soteriology.

5.5 The Reality of Being in Christ

Until now we have investigated Paul's writings to come to a reconstruction of his understanding of 'being in Christ.' We have discussed different formulas, expressions, metaphors and semantic relations. It is clear that Paul uses many different fields of language: juridical, cultic, family life, the human body, marriage, and architecture. Paul's use of these fields is highly flexible and creative. He easily combines metaphors from different fields. Obviously, he needed the total complex of formulas, expressions, metaphors and semantic relations to offer his readers a perspective on their involvement in Christ as Christian believers. Consequently, e.g. the juridical and the mystical must not be played off against each other.

We concluded that we need several concepts to structure Paul's use of different expressions and to reconstruct his view on 'being in Christ.' We saw that we need a concept of representation, referring to the inclusive moment of his Christology, and a concept of participation, referring to the moment of sharing in Christ to understand this notion. But we saw further that the inclusive moment cannot be separated from an exclusive moment, to which the concept of substitution refers, and that a moment of union, which remains implicit often, is indicated by several metaphors for union with Christ. Finally we saw that 'being in Christ' refers to an incomplete participation in the story of Jesus Christ, the representative. Being in Christ, a believer already participates in the first part of this story and he will participate in the final one.

In this last section I will deal with the question concerning reality. If someone believes 'I am in Christ,' which implications does this belief have for his self-understanding and his understanding of reality?

Answering this question is not easy. An important reason for this difficulty is the great complexity of this reality. First, this is the case with regard to Christ himself. When dealing with just one image, the image of building, Christ received two different positions: he was the ἀκρογωνιαῖος, but at the same time the building was joined together *in him*. Comparably, the body-metaphor can be used unitive and partitive. Christ lives within us, but is also our clothing. We discovered two different models, the model of the human body (with Christ and the church as one body) and the model of marriage (with Christ and the church as two different persons); but at the same time these models interfere. Second, this complexity is found with regard to the relation between Christ and the Spirit. Sometimes Christ lives in me, but it is also the Spirit who lives in me. It is important to note that when facing the reality of the church or a believer being in Christ, we see them related with God the Father by two divine persons, Jesus Christ and the Spirit. It is not surprising that this may cause some complexity. Third, the complexity is caused by the fact that individuals both as individuals and as part of a collective are involved. Fourth, 'being in Christ' is as we have seen characterized by an eschatological tension. And fifth, we are facing this reality not through the window of a theoretical treatise, but through the windows of different letters with different practical aims. These letters are written to historical churches that needed encouragement or correction in different respects, although in all these cases the ultimate aim was keeping them in union with Christ. The fact that the reality of being in Christ can be understood only within Paul's rhetorical structures, causes more complexity.

Due to this complexity it is not surprising that many different categories have been used to understand Paul's view of this reality: infusion of a substance of new life, organism, Christ mysticism, corporate personality, or Gnostic cosmic concepts. 'Being in Christ' is understood as a local, mystical, ecclesiological, existential, salvation-historical, corporate, forensic or pneumatological category.

This all is further complicated by the historical distance and the secularised culture in which we live, the disenchantment of our world. Therefore, Sanders writes:

> 'We seem to lack a category of 'reality'—real participation in Christ, real possession of the Spirit—which lies between naïve cosmological speculation and belief in magical transference on the one hand and a revised self understanding on the other. I must confess that I do not have a new category of perception to propose here.'

Nevertheless, he continues:

> 'This does not mean, however, that Paul did not have one.'[315]

315. Sanders, *Paul and Palestinian Judaism*, 522–23.

It is a pity that 'few NT scholars seem to ask how Paul and the other first Christians actually conceptualised the exalted Christ.'[316] Trying to understand Paul, it may be clear that both the idea of a magical transference and the idea of a revised self understanding do not suffice. We do not receive just a new *understanding* of being, but a new being has already begun in Christ.[317] We have to do with *reality*. My aim in this section is to understand how Paul understood 'being in Christ.'

In this section I will deal with several aspects of the reality of 'being in Christ.' First in 5.5.1 I start with the determining presence of Christ and the Spirit. In the next sub-section, an evaluation will be given of the concept of corporate personality (5.5.2). Another proposal, to understand it as a salvation-historical reality will be evaluated in 5.5.3. An additional aspect, the eschatological character receives attention in 5.5.4. In 5.5.5 I will continue with the perspective of faith. Finally the section closes with a concluding sub-section (5.5.6).

5.5.1 DETERMINED BY THE PRESENCE OF CHRIST AND THE SPIRIT

'Being in Christ' is a reality determined by the presence of Christ and the Spirit. This presupposes the reality of the bodily risen Jesus Christ as well as of the Holy Spirit. We saw 'the tremendous sense of "togetherness" implicit in Paul's language,'[318] indicating the presence of Christ: in Christ, in the Lord, with Christ, Christ in us, into Christ. We can be seen as located in Christ. The many semantic relations, laid between the story of Christ and our life-stories, make clear that we are closely related to Christ. We share in his story only because we share in him and in his life. The images for our unity with Christ show that Christ is present within our lives, uniting us with himself.

It is remarkable that these images and expressions only partly contain a suggestion of inwardness: the inhabitation of the Spirit, the body as temple of the Spirit, 'Christ in you,' together with the motif of the inner man (Rom 7:22; Eph 3:16), and of the heart.[319] Other images and expres-

316. Dunn, *The Theology of Paul the Apostle*, 409.

317. 'Nicht nur ein neues Seinsverständnis, sondern das neue Sein selbst hat in umfassenden Sinn bereits begonnen,' Schnelle, 'Transformation und Partizipation als Grundgedanke paulinischer Theologie,' 71.

318. Dunn, *The Theology of Paul the Apostle*, 404.

319. See e.g. Rom 2:29 (circumcision of the heart); Rom 5:5 (God has poured out

sions do not suggest this inwardness. Suggested are a localisation (in Christ, in the Spirit), a position within a larger corporate whole (body, building, temple), a cover including actions (clothing), and participation within a story (the semantic relations between the story of Christ and our biography). Hence, apart from inwardness we need concepts of positioning and relatedness to understand our being in Christ.

The presence of Christ is a presence which does not stand outside the eschatological tension. Often, Paul does not say that we are with Christ. We do not live at home, but away from the Lord (2 Cor 5:6, 9; cf. Phil 1:23; 3:20). At the same time, as Lord he makes the church participate in his life. He lives in the believers and gives them his Spirit.

Christ and the Spirit both realise the *eschaton*.[320] According to Bouttier and Ridderbos, Christ has the primacy. The Spirit is relative to Christ and the body of Christ: those who are united corporately with Christ receive the Spirit. The corporate body of Christ precedes the work of the Spirit.[321] Here the concept of corporate personality proves itself to be too static (see 5.5.2). Dunn and Fatehi state that it is the Spirit who incorporates into the body of Christ, and Smedes sees the Spirit with Calvin as Christ's creative agent.[322] In this way a more balanced view of the relation between Christ and the Spirit can be given. The Spirit is the power by which Christ reigns and incorporates us into his body. As Dunn puts it, Christ is the context and the Spirit is the power.[323] Consequently, Fatehi partly rehabilitates Deissmann's interpretation of 'in Christ' in terms of a pneumatic union between the risen Lord and the believer. Deissmann went wrong, according to Fatehi, by limiting its meaning to this aspect and in viewing this union as a mystical and subjective experience.[324] The

---

his love into our hearts by the Holy Spirit); Rom 10::8 (the word is in your heart); 2 Cor 1:22 (God gave us the Spirit in our hearts as a pledge); 2 Cor 3:3 (a letter from Christ . . . written . . . on tablets of human heart); 2 Cor 4:6 (God made his light shine in our hearts); Gal 4:6 (God sent the Spirit of his Son into our hearts); Eph 3:17 (Christ may dwell in your hearts).

320. Versteeg sees the relation between Christ and the Spirit as determined by the *eschaton*, see Versteeg, *Christus en de Geest*, 381–89.

321. Bouttier, *En Christ*, 113; Ridderbos, *Paulus*, 241–42, 415.

322. Dunn, 'The Spirit and the Body of Christ,' 344–48; Fatehi, *The Spirit's Relation to the Risen Lord in Paul*, 269–71, 273; Smedes, *Union with Christ*, 31, 46–51, 54.

323. Dunn, *The Theology of Paul the Apostle*, 408.

324. Fatehi, *The Spirit's Relation to the Risen Lord in Paul*, 273.

Spirit must be seen less subjectively, as the power of the new aeon and the new dominion: he is the Spirit of the risen Lord.[325]

To conclude, both Christ and the Spirit are important to understand being in Christ, for both realise the *eschaton*. Christ is risen from the dead and he incorporates us in his body by his Spirit. At the same time, Christ is raised by the Spirit, and the Spirit is the power who unites us with Christ. Christ has the dominion, the Spirit is the personal power determining the sphere of influence of this dominion. It is by the Spirit that Christ unites us with himself and his body.

5.5.2 CORPORATE REALITY

It has been proposed that the reality of 'being in Christ' be understood with the help of the concept of 'corporate personality,' referring to the idea of 'all-in-one' According to this concept the whole group functions as a single individual. This concept of corporate personality plays a central role in the Paul-interpretation of Ridderbos and, more recently, of Son.[326] But this concept has been widely criticised also.[327]

Problematic, firstly, is the concept of personality. The term 'corporate personality' is vague and can be used with different meaning. As Dunn puts it, 'evidently our contemporary concepts of personality are quite inadequate.'[328] But the problem is not only on our side and our concept of personality; he sees the concept as 'another twentieth-century amalgam of disparate ideas from the period.'[329] Evaluating the critique of the concept of 'corporate personality,' Powers also discards this idea of a corporate *personality*.[330]

325. Fatehi, *The Spirit's Relation to the Risen Lord in Paul*, 273; Ridderbos, *Paulus*, 89, 223, 242.

326. Ridderbos, *Paulus*, 33, 56–63; Son, *Corporate Elements in Pauline Anthropology*, 30, 63–65, 111, 178–84.

327. For a short survey of the history of the concept of corporate personality and its critique within Biblical Scholarship, see Powers, *Salvation through Participation*, 3–8. See further Gaffin, 'Resurrection and Redemption,' 69–72; Kamphuis, 'De kerk—een corporatieve persoonlijkheid?' 146–64.

328. Dunn, *The Theology of Paul the Apostle*, 409.

329. Dunn, *The Theology of Paul the Apostle*, 409.

330. Powers, *Salvation through Participation*, 7; cf. Fatehi, *The Spirit's Relation to the Risen Lord in Paul*, 273; Gaffin, 'Resurrection and Redemption,' 69.

Another problem is that reconstructions of Paul with the help of the concept of 'corporate personality' tend to emphasise the objectivity and realised character of the Christ event. Ridderbos for example often stresses the objectivity of the Christ-event.[331] This results in a static reconstruction of Paul, emphasising one moment of the Christ-event and neglecting the work of the Holy Spirit in the church and the life of believers. This reconstruction can also be found in Son, again under influence of the concept of corporate personality.[332] In this emphasis on the objectivity of the Christ-event, resulting in a static and realised reconstruction, the dynamics of Paul's soteriology are reduced. Moreover, Paul's eschatology is not a fully realised eschatology as the concept of corporate personality suggests.

The Christ event is decisive, but at the same time our participation in Christ is a real participation, taking place within our lives. We need to become σύμφυτοι with Christ (Rom 6:5). Furthermore, this participation is not fully realised yet, but is being realised until it is fully realised after our resurrection and glorification. We died with Christ, we suffer with Christ in the present and live in him, and in the future we will rise with him and live with him in glory. The gift of the Spirit is a first anticipation of our full participation in Christ. Our union with Christ is not a denial of our own history, although we share in his history. The concept of corporate personality elicits a reduction of this dynamic and this eschatological tension.

This criticism of the concept of 'corporate personality' does not justify a denial of the importance of an aspect of corporateness, inclusivity or solidarity within Paul. The presence of this aspect in Paul is evident. Consequently, other proposals have been made, such as 'corporate Christ'[333] or 'corporate unity.'[334] As long as these proposals do not result in a renewed denial of the dynamics of Paul's soteriology and the idea of participation, these proposals are useful. Moreover, the concept of corporate personality has been redefined as 'representation.'[335] Wright has empha-

331. Cf. Ridderbos, *Paulus*, 58, 61–63, 223–34, 241, 245.

332. Cf. Son, *Corporate Elements in Pauline Anthropology*, 180–82.

333. Dunn, *The Theology of Paul the Apostle*, 408–9.

334. Powers, *Salvation through Participation*, 6–8.

335. Fatehi, *The Spirit's Relation to the Risen Lord in Paul*, 265; cf. Ridderbos, *Paulus*, 33.

sised the importance of the concept of the 'representative Messiah.'[336] We already concluded that the concept of representation is very appropriate for understanding Paul. Hence an exchange of 'corporate personality' for 'representation' is a good step.

This concept of representation implies for an individual believer that he can never see himself as autonomous, but as someone not possessing himself, and receiving himself in Christ by the Spirit as anticipation; and only fully receiving himself in the resurrection. As a consequence, indirectness characterizes the self and identity of the individual believer. An individual believer receives himself only in Christ and by the Spirit.

Moreover, an individual always receives himself within a larger, corporate whole. The images of body, building and marriage all contain a collective aspect. In our individualistic times, and against the background of the emphasis on the personal within the Reformed tradition, this corporate aspect of 'being in Christ' deserves more attention.[337] Against the background of representation and corporateness, further critical questions must be posed to the Reformed, pietistic and evangelical stress on regeneration. Paul uses the image of regeneration only once (Titus 3:5), what makes it difficult to see regeneration as *the* central image for salvation. Further, the stress on regeneration may result in the idea that the born again Christian lives as a more or less autonomous individual, whereas corporate dimensions and the indirectness of 'being in Christ' are forgotten. Personal faith and personal involvement in salvation is important; but even then a believer exists only in Christ and within a corporate whole of the body of Christ.

Finally, the corporate existence of believers in Christ makes discrimination grounded on sex, social or racial position no longer possible with regard to our identity before God. In Christ is neither Jew nor Greek, slave nor free, male nor female (Gal 3:28; cf. Eph 3:6). What counts is to be or not to be—in Christ.

To conclude, 'being in Christ' is a *corporate* reality, constituted by Christ as representative Messiah. At the same time it is a *dynamic* reality, because of the tension of an incomplete participation in Christ, awaiting fuller participation.

336. Wright, *The Climax of the Covenant*, 46.

337. Cf. Dunn, 'The Spirit and the Body of Christ,' 344, 356.

5.5.3 SALVATION-HISTORICAL REALITY

Another proposed understanding of 'being in Christ' is made with the help of the history of salvation and the idea of different αἰῶνας, as can be found in Ridderbos and Tannehil.[338] The Christ event as objective event with a central position within the history of salvation has its implications within our lives. Christ died for the old aeon and he is raised in the new aeon. In him we have died and risen and live no longer in the old aeon, but in the new. This objectivity is related closely with the concept of corporate personality, to which I have already formulated my objections. It is important to see that God is acting to make us fully participate in Christ. We hope for a fuller participation in Christ.

However, with the cross and resurrection of Christ a new aeon has begun indeed. Jesus Christ has conquered the powers of the old aeon. The old aeon is characterized by expressions like 'in the law,' and 'in the flesh'; the new aeon by 'in Christ,' 'in the Spirit.' The question is, how Christ as representative of this aeon and how our participation in this aeon must be seen. Ridderbos and Tannehil argue using the concept of an objectively present Christ *event*. Fatehi, building on Wright, offers a different possibility that fits better with Paul's thinking.[339] Primarily Christ is seen as κύριος, Lord, reigning in the new aeon that came into existence with his resurrection. He reigns over us by his Spirit. We live in his sphere of influence already.[340] Furthermore, he is as representative the firstborn of many brothers, letting us participate in his position as the first new creature. We participate in this new aeon only *in* Christ as our representative. This means that he is the first human being living with a new spiritual body, the like we will shall only have later. In him the new creation has begun. We wait for the salvation of our bodies, when we will live no longer in exile and participate fully in the new aeon and live with Christ. Therefore, the Adam-Christ analogy is only partial: Adam has never been Lord like Christ.[341] Consequently, to be in Christ is to live within the sphere of influence of Christ, the Lord of the new aeon and the first human being

338. Tannehill, *Dying and Rising with Christ*, 70–75. For Ridderbos see 5.5.2 and footnote 326.

339. Fatehi, *The Spirit's Relation to the Risen Lord in Paul*, 266–69; cf. Wright, *What Saint Paul Really Said*, 39–62.

340. Cf. Gorman, *Cruciformity*, 36.

341. Fatehi, *The Spirit's Relation to the Risen Lord in Paul*, 272.

living in this new creation, working to make us participate in the position he has already, as our representative.

5.5.4 ESCHATOLOGICAL REALITY

This brings us to the *eschatological* character of the reality of being in Christ and the eschatological *tension* that marks this reality. We have seen already that Paul revised the Jewish apocalyptical scheme (5.3). With the death and resurrection of Christ, the Age to Come has begun. Christ, the *eschatos* Adam, died for the present age and lives as Lord of the Age to Come. The present age continues until the *parousia* of Christ. The Age to Come arrives in two stages: it has arrived in the resurrection of Jesus Christ; it will arrive when all Jesus' people are raised to life. Because Jesus is representative Messiah, he makes believers participate in his position. This implies, for the present, that believers have died with Christ, have been buried with him, live in Christ, suffer with Christ and, at the *parousia*, will be raised and glorified with Christ. The Spirit realises the *eschaton* together with Christ and is given as anticipation of our complete participation in Christ's position. Thanks to the first part of the movement of salvation, a movement that aims at a complete participation Christ, we have arrived at 'being in Christ.' We will arrive at living with him as children and heirs of God.

For the present, believers have to do with the old as well as the new aeon. This leads to suffering, temptation, struggle. We have seen that believers, according to Paul, suffer with Christ, although they at the same time live in Christ. But how does Paul see this tension exactly?

In 2 Corinthians, the ambivalence of our present bodily existence is obvious. Paul characterizes our bodies as 'jars of clay' (2 Cor 4:7) and 'mortal flesh' (2 Cor 4:11 KJV). We live not in a heavenly house, but in a tent; in our body living far from home (ἐκδημέω; 2 Cor 5:2, 4, 6). Nevertheless, 'if anyone is in Christ, he is a new creation; the old has gone, the new has come' (2 Cor 5:17). We still live in the flesh (i.e. in the body), but not according to the flesh (2 Cor 10:2–3 KJV). Flesh is used neutrally firstly, but secondly it refers to a sinful existence.

In Galatians we also find this tension. I am crucified with Christ, who lives in me. However, I still live in the flesh now, but in faith in Jesus Christ (Gal 2:19–20). Flesh is used neutrally, referring to our bodily existence. In Galatians 5 and 6 the eschatological tension returns as the opposition between Spirit and flesh, now referring to the power of sin. 'The flesh desires what is contrary to the Spirit, and the Spirit what is contrary to the flesh' (Gal 5:17; my translation). On the one hand the triumph of Christ is clear: 'Those who belong to Christ Jesus have crucified the flesh with its passions and desires' (Gal 5:24; my translation). On the other hand, it is necessary to keep warning: the one who sows to his flesh, will reap destruction from his flesh; the one who sows to the Spirit, will reap eternal life from the Spirit (Gal 6:8; my translation). Christ conquered the flesh, but the flesh is still present and can be stimulated.

In Romans, the eschatological tension is evident in Romans 6–8 .[342] In these chapters, Paul deals with the reality of Christians, living with the perspective of justification unfolded in Rom 3–5 . Grace reigns 'through righteousness to bring eternal life through Jesus Christ our Lord' (5:21). Several issues receive attention:

6:1–14	We receive grace; shall we go on sinning, so that grace may increase?
6:15—7:6	We are not under law but under grace. Shall we go on sinning?
7:7–25	Christ liberates from the law. Is the law the problem?
8:1–13	Life in Christ and in the Spirit, but still with a dead body
8:14–18	The hope of God's children, led by the Spirit
8:19–27	The longing of God's children and creation for salvation
8:28–38	The certainty of salvation in Christ

A much-discussed problem is the question whether the 'ἐγὼ' in 7:7–25 refers to a Christian believer or not. To understand the reality of 'being in Christ,' this is an important question. But before dealing with this problem I will concentrate on the perspective on this reality given by 6:1–7:6 and 8:1–27.[343]

Reality outside Christ is characterized as follows. It is a situation of mastery of the law and of sin (6:6, 7, 14). Hence, as slaves of sin we were

342. Dunn goes too far when he sees this eschatological tension as the central theme of these chapters. Van Bruggen shows that it deals also with a problem created by the manifestation of God's righteousness apart from law: is the Gentile way of life, a life in sin, the alternative to the Jewish way of life, the life of the synagogue and the law? In these chapters a third way is pointed out: a life determined by the risen Christ. See Van Bruggen, *Romeinen*, 88; Dunn, *Romans 1–8*, 302–3.

343. I have been dealing with these chapters already, see 5.4.1 and 2.

free from the control of righteousness (6:17, 19, 20). Law has authority over man (7:1–3). Being in the flesh, the law aroused the desires of sin (7:5). Consequently, the law could bring no righteousness (8:3). For the flesh was weak. Outside Christ people live according to the flesh with their minds set on the things of the flesh (8:4–5), with the mind of the flesh (8:6), and they are according to the flesh (8:8–9). The flesh is hostile to God and cannot please God, but leads to death (8:7–8). Creation is also bound up in sin, subject to futitily and enslaved to decay (8:20–21). It is important to note, that 'flesh' is not used neutrally now, referring to bodily existence, but morally, referring to the power of sin.

The present existence of a Christian is characterized by a. a participation in Christ's death; b. life in Christ and in the Spirit; c. hope for future redemption and resurrection with Christ; d. remaining presence of the body and e. the possibility of new life.

a. Christ brought first of all, a participation in his death. We died with Christ to sin (6:2, 11). We died through the body of Christ (7:4). Consequently, we were set free from sin (6:18, 22) and from the law (7:2—3:6), from the mastery of sin and law (6:6, 7, 14).

b. Secondly, Christ brought life in Christ and in the Spirit. We live in Christ (6:11). We have become slaves to righteousness and to God (6:18, 22). We belong to Christ, the raised One (7:4). In Christ is freedom from condemnation, from the law and from death (8:1–2). We walk according to the Spirit (8:4); we are according to the Spirit and have set our minds on the things of the Spirit (8:5); we have the mind of the Spirit (8:6); and are not in the flesh but in the Spirit—if the Spirit lives in us (8:9). The Spirit is life and Christ is in us (8:10). As children of God, we are led by the Spirit (8:14).

c. Third, Christ brought hope of a full participation in his new life in the future resurrection (6:5, 8). We hope for the resurrection of our bodies (8:11). We will share in the glory of Christ (8:17–18). Together with the creation, we hope for our liberation that we do not see yet (8:21–25). For if we receive glory together with Christ, creation will be liberated also (8:21). Even our sonship we do not see yet, but we hope for it: we have not received yet the redemption of our bodies (8:23).[344]

344. See on Rom 8:17–30 Siber, *Mit Christus leben*, 134–90; and on Rom 8:19—23:26 Reitsma, *Geest en schepping*, 89–117.

d. Fourth, although we live no more in the flesh, the flesh and our fleshly body are still present. The mortal body with its evil desires still exists (6:12); it is dead and mortal (8:10–11). Moreover, we still suffer from the weakness of our flesh (6:19; 8:23, 26). Consequently, it is still possible to offer our members to impurity and lawlessness (6:19) and to live according to the flesh (8:12). Our bodies are not redeemed yet (8:23), but still have actions that must be put to death (8:13). We share in the sufferings of Christ (8:17), and groan, together with creation (8:23–23).

e. Finally, it is possible to live a new life (6:4, 12–13), for the body of sin, although present, has lost its power over us (6:6). It is possible to exhort us to offer our members to righteousness leading to holiness (6:19). We live in the newness of the Spirit (7:6). Renewal starts in the mind and in the spirit (8:5, 6, 10; cf. Rom 12:2). We even have an obligation not to live according to the flesh. This implies struggle: putting to death the actions of the body (8:13). But where we have received the firstfruits of the Spirit (8:23), he testifies with our spirit that we are God's children (8:16), helps us and prays for us (8:26).[345]

Now it is clear that we live between dying with Christ and living with him. In the meantime, we live *in* Christ, but our fleshly and mortal bodies are still present and the deeds of our bodies must be put to death. To see more precisely how Paul understood this reality of being in Christ, we must deal further with Rom 7:7–25 and 8:4.

Rom 7:7–25 is a difficult passage.[346] To understand its place within Romans, it is important to note that Rom 8:1 takes up the line of 5:20–21 and 7:6. Romans 5 ends with justification. The following chapters deal with problems evoked by this justification. In Romans 6 the central questions are: shall we go on sinning, living under grace? Does grace promote lawlessness? The change of lord is clarified with an example in 7:1–6. But then the question rises: is the law the problem? If the law did not bring righteousness, does this mean that the law is sin? No, the law is good. When saying something about these issues, it is necessary to say some-

345. See on this renewal of man between old and new aeon Buchegger, *Erneuerung des Menschen*, 288–95.

346. Lichtenberger gives a history of the exegesis of Rom 7, see Lichtenberger, *Das Ich Adams und das Ich der Menschheit*, 13–105.

thing about the human soteriological capabilities. The law is not the real problem, but sin and flesh.

Referring to this real problem, Paul uses 'ἐγὼ' several times. The big question is now, to whom the 'ἐγὼ' refers. If it refers to a Christian believer, this is an important passage for the reality of 'being in Christ.' To solve the problem concerning the reference of 'ἐγὼ,' several observations are important.

1. Rom 7:7–26 can be seen as elaboration of 7:5, whereas Rom 7:6 is elaborated in 8:1–30.[347]
2. Rom 7:7–12 places the 'ἐγὼ' in a position apart from law, where the commandment came. The gift of the law resulted in desire and brought death. This refers to a pre-christian, Jewish or human confrontation with the law. The problem of the exact reference does not have to be solved, for 7:7–12 is not decisive for the identification of the 'ἐγὼ' in 7:14–26.[348]
3. Between 7:13 and 14 the tenses change. In 7:7–13 Paul uses the aorist, in 7:14–26 he shifts toward the present tense. This can indicate a change from narration of an event to description of a condition.[349] If 7:14–25 would refer to the past, this would be marked by time-indicators indicating a past reference. Instead, we only find present-time markers (7:14, 25).[350] This makes a present reference most likely.
4. 7:14–25 has its closest parallels in the penitential prayers and confessions of the Hebrew Bible and early Judaism. According to

347. Seifrid, *Justification by Faith*, 232; Stuhlmacher, *Biblische Theologie des Neuen Testaments, Band 1*, 282.

348. According to Van Bruggen, 7:7–12 tell about Paul's own experience with the law as a Jewish boy who became a 'son of the law.' Most other exegetes understand these verses as an identification of Paul with the history of Adam, or the history of Israel. Paul should see himself in solidarity with Israel and shows the hidden Adam in Israel. Lichtenberger reads 7:7–25 in the light of 7:7–11 where in his view the story of Adam in the paradise is re-used. The 'ἐγὼ' is every human being *remoto Christo*. Moo decides the identification of the 'ἐγὼ' based on 7:9–10. Dunn sees a change in the reference of 'ἐγὼ' in 7:14. See Van Bruggen, *Romeinen*, 106–7, 258; Dunn, *Romans 1–8*, 381, 387; Lichtenberger, *Das Ich Adams und das Ich der Menschheit*, 136, 160–66, 266–67; Moo, *The Epistle to the Romans*, 414. Cf. Seifrid, *Justification by Faith*, 228–34.

349. Seifrid, *Justification by Faith*, 234.

350. Seifrid, *Justification by Faith*, 231.

Seifrid, especially striking is the similarity between 7:14–25 and confessions in the Qumran *Hodayoth*. They share the concentration on the condition of the individual. 'The individual is described from the limited perspective of his or her intrinsic soteriological resources.'[351]

5. The 'ἐγώ' in Pauline letters always refers to Paul himself. More than once he gives an autobiographical description which offers an example for other Christians.[352]

6. Given this limited perspective it is not surprising that Paul does not give a complete treatment of the Christian existence. He does not mention our death with Christ, our being in Christ and in the Spirit, our hope on future salvation. Hence it is impossible to read Rom 7:7–25 as a complete treatment of Christian existence.[353]

   This limited perspective is enforced by the specific aim of Rom 7:7–26 within the letter to the Romans. It is its aim to say something about the law and about the human soteriological capabilities. He wants to make clear, why the law could not bring salvation. This ensures that anthropological questions are of secondary importance in Rom 7.[354] Romans 7 shows the absence of intrinsic soteriological capabilities, whereas salvation is entirely extrinsic as Rom 8:1–4 show.[355] This limited perspective and specific aim cause the difficulties in interpreting Romans 7.

7. We saw already, based on a reading of Romans 6 and 8, that the Christian existence is further characterized by an ongoing presence of the flesh and the mortal body, with its evil desires, weakness, and actions that must be put to death. Rom 7:14–25 concentrates on

351. Seifrid, *Justification by Faith*, 235; see also 234.

Remarkably, Lichtenberger deals only with parallels of 7:7–12 concerning Adam, coveting, and the meeting of a child with the law. But the most important question is not whether 7:7–12 refers to the history of Adam, but what this implies for the interpretation of 7:13–25. See Lichtenberger, *Das Ich Adams und das Ich der Menschheit*, 203–64.

352. Van Bruggen, *Romeinen*, 257.

353. Cf. Van Bruggen, *Romeinen*, 259; Dunn, *Romans 1–8*, 388.

According to Lichtenberger, 7:14–25 paints the conflict of the historical human being with himself a a creature, see Lichtenberger, *Das Ich Adams und das Ich der Menschheit*, 163.

354. Moo, *The Epistle to the Romans*, 409.

355. Seifrid, *Justification by Faith*, 235–37, 241–42.

this aspect of being human, saying things comparable to what we found in Romans 6 and 8. Sin lives within me and in my members (7:17, 20, 23) and evil desires are still present (6:12). The actions of the body must be put to death (8:13). I cannot carry out the desire to do what is good (7:17). Paul mentions several times the weakness of the flesh (6:19; 8:26). The big problem is the body of death (7:24; compare to the hope for the not yet achieved redemption of the mortal body, 6:12; 8:10—11:23).

8. A difference with Romans 6 and 8 is that in 7:14–25 a sense of imprisonment and powerlessness is voiced. 'I am fleshly, sold as a slave to sin' (7:14; my translation). I am made 'a prisoner of the law of sin, being in my members' (7:23; my translation). These phrases in particular bring exegetes to the decision that the 'ἐγὼ' cannot refer to a believer.[356] Can a Christian say these things? Or does his existence in Christ imply such a change in the presence of the flesh, that the 'ἐγὼ' must refer to a non-converted person, living in the flesh? To conclude, rephrasing the question, the problem is whether the 'ἐγὼ' refers a. to a person living according to the flesh or b. to the Christian, as far as the flesh is still present within his life.

9. Romans 7 presupposes a Christian perspective. The view of the law as 'spiritual' (7:14), the distance made between a 'self' not mentioned and the flesh (7:18) and sin living in me (7:20), all necessitate such a perspective.[357] Moreover, this self not mentioned is mentioned in 7:22: the 'inner man,' delighting in God's law. This presupposes a renewal of the mind or the spirit, worked by the Spirit. Further, in the end Paul writes about his hope, which lies in a future salvation from 'this body of death' (7:24–25a). And finally, Paul writes that he is at the same time a slave to God's law and to the law of sin (7:25).

10. A problem for a past reference of 'ἐγὼ' in a biographical interpretation of 7:14 is that Paul nowhere is as negative about his unconverted existence as one would expect. The new, more positive perspective on Judaism made it more plausible that Paul's problem is not with unconverted Judaism, but with human flesh in general.[358]

356. Cf. Baarlink, *Romeinen 1*, 102–4; Lichtenberger, *Das Ich Adams und das Ich der Menschheit*, 161; Moo, *The Epistle to the Romans*, 448, 454; Ridderbos, *Paulus*, 134–38.

357. Dunn, *Romans 1–8*, 388.

358. Seifrid, *Justification by Faith*, 231–32.

These observations having been made, it is evident that the 'ἐγὼ' does not describe the complete Christian existence. The aim as far as it is anthropological is to show the impotence of human flesh to live according to the will of God. That this intrinsic impotence for a Christian is accompanied by the extrinsic salvation in Christ and in the Spirit, does not change this human impotence. The ongoing presence of the flesh and the mortal body in the Christian existence until the resurrection and the presupposed Christian perspective in Romans 7, bring me to the conclusion that the 'ἐγὼ' is a Christian believer as Paul was himself. This believer experiences the eschatological tension, living still in the mortal body with the presence of the flesh but with a renewed mind. However, Rom 7:14–25 does not give a complete description of this eschatological tension and of the Christian life. It describes the weakness of the flesh and the resulting struggle, but not the positive presence of the Spirit, enabling Christian freedom. Hence Rom 7:14–25 does not give a complete picture of the existence of a believer, but only one side of it.

The positive reverse of 7:14–25 is found in Rom 8:1–4, voicing the extrinsic character of salvation. Salvation is given in Christ to believers, walking according to the Spirit. Now is reached what the law could not achieve: 'that τὸ δικαίωμα τοῦ νόμου might be fulfilled in us, who do not walk according to the flesh but according to the Spirit' (8:4). This does not mean that our sinless and righteous life fulfils the law. Christian obedience remains imperfect. The emphasis is not on the law, but on the life that God gives in Christ. In Christ we receive what the law promised but could not give. Giving us Christ, the fulfilment of the law, God acheaves in us what the law could not do. The law is fulfilled by faith, not by our actions.[359]

Colossians and Ephesians do not really change the picture. At first sight, Colossians has a more realised soteriology. However, a very sharp word is written in Col 3:5: 'Put to death the members that are on earth' (my translation). The Colossians must clothe themselves with Christian virtues (3:12). Killing implies pain and struggle.

Finally, in Ephesians the church is in need of further growth and must be built up (Eph 2:21–22; 4:16). Maturity and fullness are not reached yet (4:13). Paul writes them to put off the old man, to be renewed in the spirit of their mind and to put on the new man (4:22–24). Obviously, the old man still is a present reality.

359. Cf. Dunn, *Romans 1–8*, 423–24, 440–41; Moo, *The Epistle to the Romans*, 482–84; Wright, *What Saint Paul Really Said*, 211–12.

The eschatological tension does not only concern the existence of the individual. Creation itself waits for liberation (Rom 8:19–22). In Christ, in his resurrected spiritual body living in the nearness of the Father, the new creation exists. This evokes the question concerning the relation between the old and the new creation. Old and new differ, as the old mortal body differs from the new spiritual body like earthly bodies differ from heavenly bodies. However, continuity exists, which is indicated by the image of seed. It is sown, growing out and becoming a plant (1 Cor 15:36–44). Paul does not offer an elaborated cosmology or metaphysics. However, the position of Christ within the new creation is comparable with his position within the old creation. The relation between the old and new creation is no issue, but it is clear that continuity exists in the person of Christ.

To conclude, the eschatological character of this reality and the eschatological tension of being in Christ have become evident. As long as our body is not redeemed, we have not reached perfection. Christians live in a certain sense outside themselves. They have died with Christ and live in him and in his Spirit. At the same time, they live far away from Christ, in their fleshly body. Paul even writes that we are of flesh. We live in the flesh (as referring neutrally to the body in 2 Corinthians and Galatians) as well as not in the flesh (as referring to a sinful life in Romans). We hope for salvation and grow toward Christ until we receive perfection at the *parousia*. Until that day, we share in his sufferings, whereas the Spirit helps us in our weakness. Jesus Christ guarantees continuity between the old aeon and the new creation.

5.5.5 PERSPECTIVE OF FAITH

'Being in Christ' is bound to a perspective, the perspective of faith. It is this perspective of faith that gives access to Jesus Christ as well as to 'being in Christ.' To be in Christ is to believe in Jesus Christ.

This has implications for the experience of the reality of 'being in Christ.' Its reality can be experienced only within the perspective of a participant, which is the perspective of faith. This perspective has to be lived actively. This existential involvement concerns first of all participation in the life of the church and the sacraments. We saw that 'being in Christ' is a corporate reality (5.5.2). Consequently, to be in Christ is to be a member of the body of Christ, a stone in the temple of the Holy Spirit built on Christ the cornerstone. A member of the body cannot say to another member 'I do not need you.' Nor is it possible to live a Christian life as an isolated member. The church celebrates the sacraments. Baptism and Eucharist make it possible to experience what it is to be in Christ. Baptism as baptism *into* Christ makes incorporation in Christ concrete and marks this incorporation symbolically. The Lord's Supper reminds us of Paul's wordplay with the image of the 'body of Christ.' To receive the bread and eat the body of Christ is related to living in the church and understanding it as Christ's body. Another image, the image of clothing, makes clear that 'being in Christ' has to do with our actions. Consequently, the life in the perspective of faith has moral implications. To be in Christ means not only to receive Christ as example to be followed by his imitators. It means primarily to receive Christ as clothing, i.e., in a certain sense to receive actions to enact like him. We receive Christ-likeness to enable us to act like him. We receive the new man to put off the old man and to put on the new. Eph 2:10 says: we are 'created in Christ Jesus to do good works, which God created in advance for us that we should walk in them' (my translation). Believers are called to mortify the members, which are upon the earth. We should offer our members in slavery to righteousness leading to holiness. 'Being in Christ' requires a life in the Spirit instead of a life according to the flesh. In such a life the fruits of the Spirit will grow, making us like Christ. Participating actively, in the church, in the sacraments and in moral life, the reality of 'being in Christ' becomes discernible.

The perspective of the participant is not only necessary to experience the reality of 'being in Christ,' but more fundamentally to be in Christ and to participate in him. Only believers share in Christ. 'The righteous will live by faith' (Rom 1:17).[360] This might seem to contradict the universal scope of the representation of humanity in Jesus Christ. However, no real contradiction exists. The scope of Paul's theology is universal, with a message destined for all Israel (Rom 11:26, 32) and all people (Gal 3:8). Paul's formulations are always very open and inviting. His message is a message of hospitality. Salvation in Christ concerns a new creation, a new human-

360. It is remarkable that the word 'πίστις' is not used in Romans 6–8. This might suggest that 'faith' is more directly related to e.g. the theme of justification than to participation. However, Gal 3:26 and Col 2:12 correct this impression. Further, in Rom 6:8 the verb 'πιστεύω' is used. Still it is remarkable that when dealing with subjects related directly to participation in Christ, Paul does not often use the word 'faith' or the verb 'believe.'

ity. However, his open formulations often also contain a limiting element: the whole body, all who believe, all who love our lord Jesus Christ, or all who call on the name of our Lord Jesus Christ.[361] Furthermore Paul often writes 'we,' 'us' or 'you all.' No one should exclude himself from the good news, but he who does not want to believe excludes himself.[362] The inviting character of his language does not exclude a call to faith, which is necessary to participate in Christ, the last Adam.

This evokes the question, how one becomes a believer who lives in this perspective of faith. If 'being in Christ' is a locative, a border is presupposed between not being in Christ and being in Christ. This border has a complex character, for it consists in acts of different actors. Someone's 'being in Christ' is determined by the acts of Jesus Christ and of the Holy Spirit; by acts of the church, which cannot be separated from simultaneous acts of God; by acts of the believer himself, which can also not be separated from simultaneous acts of God; and finally by the eternal choice of God. In a scheme:

<table>
<tr><th>Event</th><th colspan="2">Actor</th></tr>
<tr><td>Christ event—Gift of the Spirit</td><td colspan="2">God</td></tr>
<tr><td>Preaching of the Gospel—Baptism</td><td>the church</td><td rowspan="2">God</td></tr>
<tr><td>Conversion—Faith</td><td>the believer</td></tr>
<tr><td>Election in Christ</td><td colspan="2">God</td></tr>
</table>

In the history of the church all different moments of this complex have received emphasis: election in a part of the Reformed tradition, the eschatological Christ-event in the salvation-historical interpretation of Paul,[363] the gift of the Spirit in charismatic groups, conversion in certain evangelical circles, baptism in the roman-catholic tradition;[364] or, to mention another not very Pauline theme, regeneration in the pietistic and evangelical tradition. All these different emphases can find to a certain

361. The whole body (Col 2:19); all who believe (Rom 1:16; 3:22; 4:11; 6:3; 10:4, 11; 16:15; Gal 3:26), all who love our lord Jesus Christ (Eph 6:24), or all who call on the name of our Lord Jesus Christ (Rom 10:12, 13; 1 Cor 1:2).

362. Cf. Reid, *Our Life in Christ*, 139.

363. See e.g. Tannehill, *Dying and Rising with Christ*, 70–71.

364. Wikenhauser is an example of this sacramental interpretation of this border, see Wikenhauser, *Die Christusmystik des hl. Paulus*, 65–72.

extent a justification in Paul, but tend to distort a more relational and dynamic whole.[365] That this relational and dynamic complex was a reality to Paul can be seen in the semantic relations between different moments of this complex. Election is election in Christ; the Lord is the Spirit; baptism into Christ is related with dying and burial with Christ, or clothing with Christ. We need the entire complex to see God acting in Christ and by his Spirit to make us arrive at 'being in Christ.' Within this whole of divine acting, our acts as result of and answer to God's acts are included. To conclude, 'being in Christ' implies having received the gift of crossing the border subsisting in this complex.

A final question concerns the mystical interpretation. Does the fact that the reality of 'being in Christ' is bound to a participant's perspective leave open the possibility of a mystical interpretation of 'being in Christ'? First, an interpretation of 'in Christ' that is entirely mystical is excluded. Deissmann's mystical interpretation focussed on the nature of the relation and disregards the basis on which the relation, whatever its nature, alone rests.[366] Bouttier and Wikenhauser however do justice to the work of Christ in the past and to his future coming, and still speak of a mystical element in relation to the present.[367] Second, the answer depends on the concept of mysticism. Barcley and Smedes both reject a mystical interpretation. Doing this, they reject an absorption or loss of personality, a union with Christ as a goal in itself, an insight or vision not included in the word of the gospel, a perfectly cleansing of deification of the soul, a mystical union of a spiritually elite only, an anthropocentric theology of the pious or deified man, or an ecstatic escape from the world.[368] Wikenhauser however, defending a mystical interpretation, rejects the idea of a fusion of the personality of the believer with Christ's personality or an annihilation of the human.[369] In any case, the presence of Christ through his Spirit and even his inhabitation involves our subjectivity, too. 'Being in Christ,' union with Christ, and inhabitation of the Spirit result in subjective experiences, like gladness, peace (cf. Phil 4:7), love, comfort. Such deep subjective ex-

365. Gaffin, 'Resurrection and Redemption,' 197–200; Siber, *Mit Christus leben*, 224.

366. Reid, *Our Life in Christ*, 20, 30.

367. Bouttier, *En Christ*, 93, 98, 132; Wikenhauser, *Die Christusmystik des hl. Paulus*, 53–63.

368. Barcley, "*Christ in You*," 93, 140; Smedes, *Union with Christ*, 128.

369. Wikenhauser, *Die Christusmystik des hl. Paulus*, 54.

periences resulting from 'being in Christ' might be labelled as 'mystical,' if this does not imply the annihilation of human individuality.

5.5.6 CONCLUSION

To conclude, when talking about being in Christ with the help of the concepts of representation and participation we are dealing with reality. It is a complex reality. We live within the sphere of influence of Christ's reign through the Holy Spirit. 'Being in Christ' is an eschatological reality, which has come with the new aeon. This new aeon stands under the dominion of Christ, the Lord. Further, it is the Spirit who unites us with Christ. The Spirit is given as anticipation of our full participation in this new creation. Until then we live within the eschatological tension, still living with the fleshly and mortal body. Further, although the concept of corporate personality is better not used, 'being in Christ' is a corporate reality. Finally, we are involved existentially as active subjects, with our faith, living as members of the church, celebrating the sacraments and living a moral life in the Spirit, imitating Christ's example. This existential involvement results in subjective experiences that might be labelled as mystical.

6

JOHN

RECIPROCAL INHABITATION

6.1 Introduction

THE SECOND DECISIVE VOICE in this conversation on 'being in Christ' is the voice of Johannine literature. For Johannine literature the important documents concerning 'being in Christ' are the gospel and the first letter of John, traditionally ascribed to the apostle John, the son of Zebedee.[1]

1. The authorship of the gospel and first letter of John is much debated. Concerning the gospel of John, the identification of the apostle John of Zebedee as author represents a minority position within the recent research. Nevertheless, the old churchly tradition unanimously ascribes the gospel to the apostle John, son of Zebedee; see Van Bruggen, *Christus op aarde*, 52; Carson, *The Gospel according to John*, 68; Van Houwelingen, *Johannes*, 23–28; Schnackenburg, *Das Johannesevangelium*, Bd. 1, 63–76. Different authors working with the idea of a Johannine school, nevertheless still see a (close) relation with the apostle John, the son of Zebedee.

In recent research, synchronic approaches somewhat increased the plausibility of the traditional position with regard to authorship, see Anderson, *The Christology of the*

John

Before dealing with John some methodological issues must be dealt with. The first concerns the integrity of the gospel of John. A presupposition of my reading of the canonical text of the gospel is the integrity of this document, which gained renewed plausibility in recent research.[2]

Another methodological problem is caused by the fact that the gospel of John is a narrative with two layers: a layer of historical reference, telling about Jesus, his words and his audience; and a second layer of the audience of the writer of the gospel of John. Narrating the speech acts of Jesus is itself a speech act. Regarding the first layer it is important to see how Jesus, according to the narrative, reacted on his audience and what he said to his disciples; regarding the second layer it is important to ask why the writer says what he says in reaction to his readers' world.[3] The first is a pre-Easter perspective, the perspective of the audience of Jesus before his death; the second a post-Easter perspective, the perspective of the church. Because of these two layers, statements in the gospel must be understood against the background of two different contexts. Presupposed in this reading of John is the conviction that things go wrong if one of these layers is neglected.[4]

Fourth Gospel, 151, 165; Tovey, *Narrative Art and Act in the Fourth Gospel*, 270. See for a defence of the traditional position further Carson, *The Gospel according to John*, 68–81; Van Houwelingen, *Johannes*, 17–22.

With regard to the first letter of John, Guthry cautiously argues for the probability of seeing John the apostle as author, see Guthry, *New Testament Introduction*, 858–64. Lalleman defends that the author of the first letter of John, an eyewitness of Jesus, is the same as the author of the gospel, and identifies him as the apostle John, see Lalleman, *1, 2 en 3 Johannes*, 11–19.

2. Synchronic readings resulted in a criticism of the classic paradigm of literary criticism, and renewed pleas for the integrity of the gospel, cf. Anderson, *The Christology of the Fourth Gospel*, 163–65; Nielsen, 'Johannine Research,' 12–14; Popp, *Grammatik des Geistes*, e.g. 78, 80, 444, 457, 462–64, 479, 492–93; Scholtissek, 'Johannine Studies,' 227–59, esp. 226, 231; Stibbe, *John as Storyteller.*

3. Sasse, *Der Menschensohn im Evangelium nach Johannes*, 27; Stibbe, *John as Storyteller*, 58. See for this second layer e.g. Zumstein, *Kreative Erinnerung*, 31–45.

4. If John is read as only a document with historical reference, the specificity of Johannine thinking and theological impact of the text is missed; if it is only read as a theological document the historiografical intention it claims itself is not taken seriously. However, the difference between the two layers has not to be overstated, as if the gospel of John comprises two stories: the story about Jesus and the story about the Johannine community; cf. Hägerland, 'John's Gospel,' 309–22; Stibbe, *John as Storyteller*, 56–61.

The analyses of Stibbe and Tovey show that narrative critisism enables to do justice to the social function of the gospel, its narrative character, its theological meaning and its historical reference, see Stibbe, *John as Storyteller*, 50–94; Tovey, *Narrative Art and Act*

To understand the second layer a reconstruction of the Johannine community has been attempted.[5] This presupposes however, that this Johannine community lived in isolation from other parts of the church and that Johannine literature has no central place in the New Testament canon. In recent research this idea of an isolated communion has been challenged, and the hypothetical character of many reconstructions has been criticised. According to these critics, the theory of orthodox Johannophobia has proved to be a myth. Instead, the gospels are written for all Christians, and the gospel of John belongs in the heart of the canon. According to some, it presents a synthesis of the theology of the Pauline letters and the synoptic gospels.[6] This does not make the context of John irrelevant, but yet less specific.[7] However, the selection of material used in the texts does tell us something about controversies present in the context in which the gospel and the first letter were written.[8] Discussion with the synagogue seems important: the readers of John were expelled from it (cf. John 9:22; 12:42; 16:2).[9] Further discussions within the group of readers can be traced (1 John 2:18–27; cf. John 6:60–71; 8:31–59). Maybe other 'false prophets' appeared (1 John 4:1–6).[10] Some forms of early Gnostic thinking might be present in its context. A conflict with the sect of John the Baptist is also suggested.[11] Another important issue within the discussion was the origin and identity of Jesus.[12] Is he the Christ indeed, the

in the Fourth Gospel, 212–13, 222, 256–72.

5. Cf. De Ruyter, *De gemeente van de evangelist Johannes*.

6. See Bauckham (Ed.), *The Gospels for All Christians*,; Söding (Hg.), *Johannesevangelium—Mitte oder Rand des Kanons?*; Hill, *The Johannine Corpus in the Early Church*. See further also Lalleman, 1, 2 *en* 3 *Johannes*, 21–24.

7. Bauckham, 'For Whom Were Gospels Written?,' 46.

8. According to Stibbe, the only evidence that can be used to reconstruct this community must be internal to the gospel itself, see Stibbe, *John as Storyteller*, 64.

9. Lalleman, 1, 2 *en* 3 *Johannes*, 25; Nissen, 'Community and Ethics in the Gospel of John,' 196–98; Sasse, *Der Menschensohn im Evangelium nach Johannes*, 36–42; Stibbe, *John as Storyteller*, 57–60.

10. See for a possible identification of the opponents in the first letter Rusam, *Die Gemeinschaft der Kinder Gottes*, 170–209. Lalleman identifies the opponents with the help of the 'Acts of John,' a Gnostic text of the heirs of John's adversaries; see Lalleman, 1, 2 *en* 3 *Johannes*, 28–32; Lalleman, *The Acts of John*.

11. Sasse, *Der Menschensohn im Evangelium nach Johannes*, 47–49; Stibbe, *John as Storyteller*, 62.

12. Sasse, *Der Menschensohn im Evangelium nach Johannes*, 42.

fulfilment of the scriptures? Is he from above and did he really come in the flesh? John's story of Jesus reflects 'a community in crisis'[13] and its social function is to bring encouragement.[14]

For a systematic reconstruction of the Johannine perspective on 'being in Christ,' a third problem is the relationship between the gospel and the first letter of John. Scholars do not agree on the question whether the first letter must be read as a commentary on the gospel or whether the gospel builds upon the letter.[15] I will try to not solve this problem, but read both texts and do justice to the specific emphases of both documents.[16] Doing this, I will follow the canonical order, because of the uncertainties concerning the historical order.

Further, although the idea of 'Johannine literature' is not disputed, theological differences between the gospel and the first letter are signalled. A further presupposition of this chapter is, that these differences are not so big that a synthesis of the gospel and the letter cannot be made.[17] As with Paul, it must be said: let the quality of the synthesis decide the discussion on the possibility of making such a synthesis.

Just as in other chapters, the central question is whether the concepts of representation and participation are necessary to reconstruct

13. Stibbe, *John as Storyteller*, 61.

14. Stibbe, *John as Storyteller*, 61; Kowalski, *Die Hirtenrede (Joh 10.1–18) im Kontext des Johannesevangeliums*, 279–82.

15. Some scholars regard the gospel of John as earlier than the first letter, e.g. Frey, Knöppler, Schnelle and Stuhlmacher. See Frey, *Die johanneische Eschatologie*, Bd. III, 467; Knöppler, *Sühne im Neuen Testament*, 220; Schnelle, *Antidoketische Christologie im Johannesevangelium*, 65–75; Stuhlmacher, *Biblische Theologie des Neuen Testaments, Band* 2, 209.

Others see the first letter as a commentary on or a rereading of the gospel, e.g. Hays, Scholtissek and Zumstein. See Hays, *The Moral Vision of the New Testament*, 141; Scholtissek, *In ihm sein und bleiben*, 340–43; Zumstein, *Kreative Erinnerung*, 2.

For a survey of the discussion see Frey, *Die johanneische Eschatologie*, Bd. III, 53–60.

16. Frey arrives, only at the end of his study, at the conclusion that the letter has the primacy over the gospel. His methodological starting point is different: he leaves open the question regarding the relation between both and confines himself to a reading of the texts together, interpreting them in relation to each other. See Frey, *Die johanneische Eschatologie*, Bd. III, 59. According to Lalleman, the first letter presupposes acquaintance with the preaching of the message of Jesus Christ as it can be found in the gospel of John. It is possible that the gospel of John is written after the letter, but he regards it as likely that the gospel was already committed to paper. For reading the letter however, this question can be left open; see Lalleman, *1, 2 en 3 Johannes*, 12–13, 39.

17. Cf. Frey, *Die johanneische Eschatologie*, Bd. III, 465–66.

Johannine thinking. Regarding 'being in Christ,' the Pauline expression 'ἐν Χριστῷ' will not be found in John. Nevertheless, 'ἐν αὐτῷ' and 'ἐν ἐμοὶ' are used referring to Christ. These expressions will be investigated together with other images and themes related to being in Christ. I start with Christology (6.2), continue with soteriology (6.3) and the reality of 'being in Christ' (6.4) and finish with a concluding section (6.5).

6.2 Christology

John's Christology is rich and complex.[18] According to Anderson, it is a living Christology, having arisen out of encounter, with Jesus of Galilee as well as with the risen Christ. Anderson uses two models to clarify the character of John's Christology. First a developmental model for understanding the ways people mature in their faith and approaches to God. John represents stage 5, conjunctive faith. This stage 'holds apparently conflicting aspects of truth in tension and affirms a both/and approach to faith, rather than an either/or stance.'[19] Second, he uses a 'crisis' model, reconstructing how people react to a transforming spiritual encounter, a 'peak' experience. These models can help to understand the character of John's thinking.[20]

Narrative is a good means to expose this complex Christology. Loader offers the following reconstruction of the narrative structure of Johannine Christology:[21]

The Father
sends and authorises the Son,
who knows the Father,
comes from the Father,
makes the Father known,
brings light and life and truth,

18. Cf. much discussed the dilemma's like docetic Christology—anti-docetic Christology, exalted Christology—subordinated Christology, theology of glory—theology of the cross, and realised eschatology—futuristic eschatology.

19. Anderson, *The Christology of the Fourth Gospel*, 164. The five stages in J. Fowler's theory of faith development are: 1. Intuitive-Projective faith; 2. Mythic-Literal Faith; 3. Synthetic-Conventional faith; 4. Individuative-Reflective faith; 5. Conjunctive faith; see 142–44.

20. Anderson, *The Christology of the Fourth Gospel*, 163–65.

21. Loader, *The Christology of the Fourth Gospel*, 76. In this reconstruction, incarnation and cross are underplayed.

completes his Father's work
returns to the Father,
exalted, glorified, ascended,
sends the disciples
and sends the Spirit
to enable greater understanding,
to equip for mission,
and to build up the community of faith.

The divine character of the Son is very clear, as well as the fact that the Son represents his Father. Although John's Christology is anti-docetic, affirming the real humanity of Christ,[22] nevertheless it can be said that the true man Jesus Christ is almost taken up in the true God.[23] The post-Easter perspective colours the image given of Jesus Christ.[24] Whereas in literature dealing with Paul the idea of Christ as representative of humanity occurs often, this is not the case in literature dealing with John. Consequently, the question becomes pressing whether Christ can be seen as representative of Israel, believers or humankind. What is the soteriological significance of the incarnation and of the Son's being human? Does Christ only represent the Father, or does he also represent humanity?

I will start with the incarnation. Is Jesus as man representing mankind (6.2.1)? Next I will turn to the relation of Jesus with his Father. Does the designation of Jesus as 'Son of God' have representative connotations (6.2.2)? Further I will investigate the 'I am'-sayings on the inclusive moment (6.2.3). To see the importance of the inclusive moment the importance of the exclusive moment must also become clear. Therefore I will turn to John's view on the death of Jesus (6.2.4). I will continue investigating some passages expressing inclusivity (6.2.5). Finally the section will close with a conclusion (6.2.6).

22. See Schnelle, *Antidoketische Christologie im Johannesevangelium*, 249; Thompson, *The Humanity of Jesus in the Fourth Gospel*, 117–22.

23. Stuhlmacher, *Biblische Theologie des Neuen Testaments*. Bd. 2, 282.

24. Frey, 'Die "*theologia crucifixi*" des Johannesevangeliums,' 191, 226; Nielsen, 'John's Understanding of the Death of Jesus,' 254; Thompson, *The Humanity of Jesus in the Fourth Gospel*, 114, 122–26.

The post-Easter perspective can be used to relativize the value of John's gospel as historiography. This is not my intention. In this respect it is important that recent narrative criticism has increased the plausibility of seeing John as (some kind of) historiography. See Stibbe, *John as Storyteller*, 75; Tovey, *Narrative Art and Act in the Fourth Gospel*, 264–70.

6.2.1 INCARNATION: JESUS AS MAN

Searching for an answer to these questions I start with the incarnation and the humanity of Jesus. Is Jesus as man representing humanity? First I turn to the Prologue of the Gospel.

The prologue shows a relation, existing before the incarnation, between 'ὁ λόγος' and the entire creation. Through the λόγος 'all things were made; without him nothing was made that has been made' (1:3). The entire world, including humanity, is a creation of God by the λόγος.[25] Everyone has a relation with the λόγος: we are dependent on him for our being, for our life. In the prologue, the λόγος is identified as the divine source of life.[26]

Nevertheless, this relation with everyone, giving life and light (1:9) is not as such a relation of harmony. The astonishing fact is that the world, which was made through him, did not know him (1:10). This implies that, although the λόγος was involved in creation and the entire creation is somehow dependent on him in whom life is, the λόγος is not immanently present in the creation apart from incarnation and his coming into the world.[27] That which was his own, be it his own creation or his own people Israel, did not receive him (1:11).[28] By refuting the λόγος as their light (1:4), they made their home in darkness.[29] Apart from a new birth

25. Carson, *The Gospel according to John*, 118; Hofius, 'Struktur und Gedankengang des Logos-Hymnus in Joh 1.1–18,' 16; Van Houwelingen, *Johannes*, 45; Schnackenburg, *Das Johannesevangelium* , Bd. 1, 214; Marshall, *New Testament Theology*, 492; Schnelle, *Neutestamentliche Antropologie*, 134; Scholtissek, *In ihm sein und bleiben*, 176; Stuhlmacher, *Biblische Theologie des Neuen Testaments,* Band 2, 235.

Ridderbos surprises by denying an involvement of the Word in creation, see Ridderbos, *Het evangelie naar Johannes*, Dl. 1 51.

26. Endo, *Creation and Christology*, 210, 216–17, 228.

27. Scholtissek, *In ihm sein und bleiben*, 187–88; cf. Bergmeier, *Glaube als Gabe nach Johannes*, 236.

28. According to Hofius and Scholtissek οἱ ἴδιοι refers to his people, created in his image, see Hofius, 'Struktur und Gedankengang des Logos-Hymnus in Joh 1.1–18,' 20; Scholtissek, *In ihm sein und bleiben*, 179. Carson and Van Houwelingen think it refers to Israel, although according to Van Houwelingen it is a symptom of the reaction of the entire world; see Carson, *The Gospel according to John*, 124; Van Houwelingen, *Johannes*, 49–50. Schnackenburg thinks that the hymn originally referred to 'his created people,' but that the evangelist thought it referred to Israel, see Schnackenburg, *Das Johannesevangelium*, Bd. 1 235–36. Ridderbos leaves it open, Ridderbos, *Het evangelie naar Johannes*, Dl. 1, 60.

29. Scholtissek, *In ihm sein und bleiben*, 180.

'ἐκ θεοῦ' (1:13) nobody has a positive relation with the λόγος. We are unable to acknowledge our dependence on him as our source of life.

He came into the world, 'became flesh and made his dwelling among us' (1:14). This makes clear *that* the λόγος became flesh. He became a human being.[30] But why, according to the prologue, did the λόγος want to become *human*? An answer is not stated explicitly, but part of an answer can be given based on the prologue. On the one hand, we see the alienation of the world from the source of life (the darkness of the world, which did not recognise or receive him). On the other hand, the incarnate λόγος gave the ἐξουσία to become children of God (1:12); he gave grace upon grace from his fullness (1:16), grace and truth came through him (1:17) and finally he has revealed the unseen God, his Father (1:18). The λόγος became flesh to give somehow the relation between himself as source of life (1:4) and humanity a new quality, gracefully enabling those who received him to live as God's children.[31] Because in him the creation will of God is revealed, he enables a life conformed to the wisdom of the Creator.[32] Fullness of life, light, grace, truth and knowledge of God he made available for them. He embodied the presence of God on earth.[33]

To conclude, through the λόγος all things were made. He is the divine source of life. Nevertheless, an alienation existed between the λόγος and human beings. The λόγος became flesh to renew the relationship between human beings and himself as their source of life and to give their existence a new quality as children of God. His incarnation played a crucial role in this renewal, making his fullness available for human beings. The prologue gives no indication of Jesus Christ's humanity as somehow representative or inclusive.

In the Prologue it is said that the λόγος became σάρξ, in John 6 this 'σάρξ' returns. The day after Jesus has fed the 5000, he presents himself as the true bread from heaven and the bread of life. Teaching the Jews what it means that he is the bread of life, he says 'and the bread that I will give is my flesh, which I will give for the life of the world' (6:51c; my translation). The Jews, misunderstanding his words, ask 'How can this man give

30. Bergmeier, *Glaube als Gabe nach Johannes*, 219; Schnelle, *Antidoketische Christologie*, 247; Schnelle, *Neutestamentliche Antropologie*, 135; Thompson, *The Humanity of Jesus*, 40, 42, 48–49.

31. Schnelle, *Neutestamentliche Antropologie*, 137.

32. Schnelle, *Antidoketische Christologie*, 246.

33. Scholtissek, *In ihm sein und bleiben*, 190.

us his flesh to eat?' In verses 53–58 Jesus continues to speak on this theme of 'eating his flesh.' To understand the soteriological significance of the humanity of Jesus, it is necessary to see what 'σάρξ' denotes here. This confronts us with the problem whether 6:51–58 should be interpreted as a eucharistic passage with 'σάρξ' denoting the eucharistic bread.

When reading the text, several arguments against the sacramental interpretation can be given. First, the gift of Jesus' 'σάρξ' in 6:51 reminds one of John 10:15, 17–18, where Jesus says that he gives his 'ψυχή.' In John 10 this refers to his death on the cross.[34] Second, Jesus gives his flesh 'ὑπὲρ τῆς τοῦ κόσμου ζωῆς.' The preposition ὑπέρ with the genitive together with 'give' suggests a reference to Jesus' dying for others on the cross. This dying for other does not take place within the Eucharist.[35] Third, the use of 'flesh' does not fit within a sacramental context. Instead, one would expect 'body.'[36] Fourth, in the discussion with the Jews as John tells it, a reference to the Eucharist is difficult to understand. Only Christian believers, reading this story after Easter, can hear sacramental overtones, but this must not dominate the interpretation. The perspective of Jesus' audience within the narrative is forgotten within a sacramental interpretation.[37] Fifth, the reactions show the offensiveness of Jesus' words (6:52, 60). A sacramental gift of bread and wine is far less offensive than the gift of Jesus' own life. To argue for a sacramental interpretation of the 'drinking of the blood' because it was forbidden for Jews to drink blood, misses the offensiveness of Jesus' words and renders them harmless. But it is hard to understand that someone needs to die to give life to the world. The real offensiveness of Jesus' words lies within this paradox of the cross.[38] Sixth, as is often the case, the discussion is propelled along by misunderstanding

34. Thompson, *The Humanity of Jesus in the Fourth Gospel*, 46.

35. Frey, 'Die "theologia crucifixi" des Johannesevangeliums,' 218; Knöppler, *Die theologia crucis des Johannesevangeliums*, 203; Nielsen, 'John's Understanding of the Death of Jesus,' 243; Ridderbos, Het *evangelie naar Johannes*, Dl. 1, 277.

Van Bruggen emphasises that exactly *by* his dying Jesus becomes food for humanity, Van Bruggen, *Het evangelie van Gods Zoon*, 149.

36. Burge, *The Anointed Community*, 181. An alternative for this reason is offered by Popp, who sees an alternative eucharistic tradition behind this use of 'flesh'; Popp, *Grammatik des Geistes*, 356, 364.

37. Cf. Van Houwelingen, *Johannes*, 161; Wierenga, *Verhalen als bewijzen*, 213.

38. Van Houwelingen, *Johannes*, 159–60; Wierenga, *Verhalen als bewijzen*, 213. Against Burge, *The Anointed Community*, 182.

fuelling questioning leading to still further explanation.[39] It is important to note that this question (6:52) adds the theme of eating to the words of Jesus about the gift of his flesh. Jesus' words about the gift of his flesh for the life of the world can be understood without the notion of eating. Consequently, 6:51 cannot be understood sacramentally.[40] Seventh, the eating of his flesh and the drinking of his blood must not be understood primarily as sacramental. Especially when with Scholtissek 6:52–58 is seen as 'reécriture' of 6:24–51,[41] this eating and drinking builds on the coming to Jesus and the believing in him (6:35) and has to be interpreted figuratively at first.[42] The result of this coming is no more hunger, and of this believing is no more thirst. Eighth, the Son points at himself in 6:54, 56.[43] It is Jesus who will raise the believer on the last day (6:54). What matters is the reciprocal 'remaining in' of Jesus and the believer (6:56). The sacramental interpretation gives the Eucharist too absolute a meaning, whereas this passage gives this meaning to Jesus himself.[44] Ninth, Jesus speaks in 6:62 about his return to heaven. Given that, in John, this return is connected to his death on the cross, one would expect that the gift of his flesh would also refer to his death on the cross.

As additional evidence against a sacramental reading Anderson has shown that it is a mistake to think that the idea of 'medicine of immortality' found in the view of the sacraments of Ignatius of Antioch would offer reasons for a sacramental interpretation.[45] Further, Thompson offers convincing reasons against the interpretation of 'σάρξ' in 6:51 as entirely different from 'σάρξ' in 6:63.[46] Finally, in recent exegesis the idea of an eucharistic *interpolation* is left, whereas convincing reasons are given by Anderson and Popp for the unity of John 6.[47]

39. Cf. Popp, *Grammatik des Geistes*, 360; Scholtissek, *In ihm sein und bleiben*, 203. Wierenga, *Verhalen als bewijzen*, 213–14.

40. Scholtissek, *In ihm sein und bleiben*, 202.

41. Scholtissek, *In ihm sein und bleiben*, 200.

42. Thompson, *The Humanity of Jesus in the Fourth Gospel*, 47.

43. Thompson, *The Humanity of Jesus in the Fourth Gospel*, 46.

44. Carson, *The Gospel according to John*, 297; Van Houwelingen, *Johannes*, 162; Ridderbos, *Het evangelie naar Johannes*, Dl. 1 280.

45. Anderson, *The Christology of the Fourth Gospel*, 119–26.

46. Thompson, *The Humanity of Jesus in the Fourth Gospel*, 45–48.

47. See Anderson, *The Christology of the Fourth Gospel*; Popp, *Grammatik des Geistes*. Cf. also Scholtissek, *In ihm sein und bleiben*, 195–201.

To conclude, John 6:51–58 refers primarily to the gift of Jesus' life on the cross and to the communion of believers with the crucified Jesus Christ as their source of life.[48]

Undeniably John 6:51–58 has sacramental overtones.[49] It is hard to read this passage without having associations with the Lord's Supper. But the relation between John 6 and the Eucharist must be conceived differently. John 6 does not refer to the Eucharist, but the Eucharist refers to John 6 and the communion with the crucified Jesus Christ it describes.[50] The mystery of John 6 is represented in the Eucharist.[51] However, more must be said: the communion with Christ is described using words, which fit within a sacramental context themselves and immediately evoke sacramental associations.[52] As a consequence of what was said in the beginning of this chapter, an interpretation of John 6 must do justice to the perspective of Jesus' audience within the story (the Jews) as well as the perspective of the narrator's audience. For this second perspective, christological metaphors and eucharistic overtones interpret each other.[53]

Returning to 'σάρξ,' we can now conclude that 'σάρξ' in 6:51 denotes the human body of Jesus Christ. Consequently, the two times 'σάρξ' is used referring to Jesus Christ, it is used in relation to his incarnation and to his death on the cross. Hence, Popp sees an emphasis of both a theology of the incarnation and the cross, related to this word.[54] This seems to imply that for the gospel of John incarnation and death on the cross belong together. The word became flesh to die on the cross. What remains open in the prologue, is further explained in John: the fullness of life became available not only by the incarnation, but by the death of the incarnate λόγος as well. The λόγος became flesh to die and to give life to the world only in this paradoxical way. This interpretation of 'σάρξ' does not necessarily imply a notion of representation.

48. For a different interpretation, see Theobald, 'Eucharistie in Joh 6,' 178–257.

49. Even Anderson, arguing for a non-sacramental interpretation acknowledges this, Anderson, *The Christology of the Fourth Gospel*, 208.

50. Van Bruggen, *Het evangelie van Gods Zoon*, 149; Van Houwelingen, *Johannes*, 162.

51. Ridderbos, *Het evangelie naar Johannes*, Dl. 1 276.

52. Ridderbos, *Het evangelie naar Johannes*, Dl. 1 275.

53. Cf. Scholtissek, *In ihm sein und bleiben*, 199; see further the interpretation offered by Popp in *Grammatik des Geistes*.

54. Popp, *Grammatik des Geistes*, 355.

Still it is remarkable that the word 'σάρξ' is used to denote the humanity of Jesus Christ, for in John 1:13, 3:6, 6:63 and 8:15 'σάρξ' is not used neutrally, but contains connotations of sin and opposition to God. 'σάρξ' refers to 'the human realm in contrast to the divine and the natural existence in contrast to the life given by the Spirit.'[55] Further it implies being perishable and destined to death.[56] That the λόγος not just became man, ἄνθρωπος, but σάρξ indicates how deeply he became involved in our existence and how far he went in identifying with us. Hence it is not surprising that the confession that Jesus Christ came into the flesh was controversial (cf. 1 John 4:2).

Within the gospel, Jesus is further called 'Son of man.' Does this title imply representation?

The title Son of man has been interpreted in a way that implies representation. However, within the present state of the debate on this title, these interpretations have lost their plausibility, including the corporate interpretation.[57] A direct relation with Adam is not evident.[58] Burkett sees two alternatives that lie at the heart of the present debate: '(a) the Christian Son of Man tradition originated with Jesus in the use of *bar enasha* as a nontitular idiom (circumlocutional, generic, or indefinite); (b) it originated as a messianic title applied to Jesus either by himself or by the early church.'[59]

To see whether this title really has no representative implications, it is necessary to investigate briefly the way it is used within the gospel. The first time it is used in 1:52, where the Son of man is like Jacob's ladder, angels ascending and descending on him. He provides the point of contact between heaven and earth. In John 3:13 the Son of man himself descended from heaven and will ascend again. He will ascend, being lifted up like Moses' snake in the desert (3:14). This theme of lifting up in relation to the Son of man returns in John 8:28 and 12:32–34. The theme of ascending, the Son of man returning to where he was before, we find also in John 6:62. A comparable theme is the theme of glorification, occurring in John together with the title Son of man in John 12:23 and 13:31. The

55. Thompson, *The Humanity of Jesus in the Fourth Gospel*, 49.

56. Knöppler, *Die theologia crucis des Johannesevangeliums*, 52.

57. Burkett, *The Son of Man Debate*, 121.

58. Van Bruggen, *Het evangelie van Gods Zoon*, 96.

59. Burkett, *The Son of Man Debate*, 122.

Son of man further is the one who has authority to judge (5:27). Moreover, he gives the bread of life, his own flesh and blood (6:27, 53). Finally, he evokes controversy, making it necessary to ask: 'Do you believe in the Son of Man?' (John 9:35).[60] In conclusion, the Son of man is descended from heaven and ascended to where he came from; he is the one lifted up, glorified and crucified; he is the bread of life and the eschatological judge. As heavenly figure he evokes controversy and demands faith.

Some other observations can be made. The title 'Son of man' is not used within human messianic expectations, confessional statements or predications of the narrator outside the words of Jesus. It only occurs as a self-designation of Jesus.[61] Were it to bear representative connotations, one would expect the title also in confessional statements, expressing the belief in Jesus as someone's representative. Further the Son of man is an absolute figure, not standing within a dependency relation to God. He is heavenly and divine himself,[62] although he is controversial, being mere man.[63] Consequently, this designation functions within an immense tension: this human being is unique. This points more at exclusiveness than at an inclusive representation, but this exclusiveness is just the exclusiveness of a human being.

To conclude, the title 'Son of man' has no representative connotations, but emphasises the exclusiveness of Jesus. Consequently, it is related more to the idea of substitution. John's use of 'Son of man' confirms the earlier findings with relation to 'σάρξ.' The Son of man descended and came to die and give his life on the cross, hence giving life to the world.

6.2.2 RELATION WITH THE FATHER: JESUS AS SON

Several times, the gospel of John parallels the relation between the Father and the Son with the relation between the Son and believers.[64] 'The Father-

60. For a detailed survey of the different passages see Sasse, *Der Menschensohn im Evangelium nach Johannes*, 71–236 and 238–40.

61. Sasse, *Der Menschensohn im Evangelium nach Johannes*, 248–49. Van Bruggen also emphases that 'Son of man' is a self-designation, see Van Bruggen, *Het evangelie van Gods Zoon*, 85.

62. Sasse, *Der Menschensohn im Evangelium nach Johannes*, 259–60.

63. Van Bruggen stresses that the paradox between a descendant of a human being and the greatness of what he describes to himself lies at the heart of Jesus' use of 'Son of man.' Van Bruggen, *Het evangelie van Gods Zoon*, 97–99.

64. It must not surprise that this parallel is not drawn in the first letter as explicitly as

Son relation is the canon for the determination of the relation between the Son and the christians.'[65] Therefore, to understand the relation between the Son and believers, including the ἐν-language, something must be said about the relation between the Father and the Son.[66] I focus on the passages where an explicit parallel is drawn between the relation between Father and Son and relations with believers. For a good understanding of these passages, it is important to see that John in his gospel uses the title 'Son of God' only for Jesus Christ, the incarnate λόγος. It is Jesus, God and man, who is the Son of God. It is impossible to abstract the title 'Son of God' from Jesus Christ.[67]

The first time this parallel is drawn is in John 6:57. Jesus is speaking about himself as the living bread, being life for the one who eats his flesh and drinks his blood. Then he continues: 'Just as the living Father has sent me and I live by the Father, so the one who eats me will live by me' (my translation). This reminds one of John 5:26 (where the parallel is not found): 'For as the Father has life in himself, so he has granted the Son to have life in himself.' As believers are dependent on the Son with regard to their life, so the Son is dependent on his Father.[68]

In John 10 Jesus pictures himself as a good shepherd. The sheep follow the shepherd because they know his voice. At this point of knowledge, Jesus draws the parallel: 'I am the good shepherd; I know my sheep and my sheep know me—just as the Father knows me and I know the Father' (John 10:14–15). Knowing each other means finding community with a person and includes a close intimacy. It implies love and trust. This

---

in the gospel. In the gospel, it is always Jesus himself who parallels these relations. In the first letter, we find no speaking Jesus.

65. 'Die Vater-Sohn-Beziehung ist der Kanon für die Bestimmung des Verhältnisses zwischen dem Sohn und den Christen,' Scholtissek, *In ihm sein und bleiben*, 168, 209. Cf. Jerumanis, *Realiser la communion avec Dieu*, 409, 473; Popp, *Grammatik des Geistes*, 462; Crump, 'Re-examining the Johannine Trinity,' 401–3.

Malatesta does not parallel the Father-Son relation with the Son-disciples relation alone, but also with the Father-disciples relation, see Malatesta, *Interiority and Covenan*, 32, 35, 133, 323.

66. Cf. Jerumanis, *Realiser la communion avec Dieu*, 405.

67. Van Bruggen, *Het evangelie van Gods Zoon*, 128–29. Consequently, it is a deliberate choice to deal with the incarnation first and only secondly with the title 'Son of God.'

68. Cf. Scholtissek, *In ihm sein und bleiben*, 205: 'Die joh Übertragung des Vader-Sohn-Verhältnisses auf das Sohn-Christen-Verhältniss bewahrheitet sich auch bei der ζωή-Thematik.'

community of personal knowledge and intimacy between the Son and believers is grounded on the intimacy between Father and Son.[69]

After this passage about the good shepherd, John describes a discussion between Jesus and the Jews during the Feast of Dedication. Asked whether he is the Christ or not, Jesus refers to his works (10:25, 38). He summons the Jews to believe his works, 'that you may know and believe that the Father is in me and I in the Father' (10:38; my translation). The works of the Son and the works of the Father can be identified, and show a deeper unity that can be seen as reciprocal interiority or mutual indwelling.[70] This theme returns in 14:10–11. Philip wants to see the Father. Answering this question, Jesus refers to himself, pointing at the transparency of his words for the works of the Father. Their works and words again show a deeper unity, consisting in reciprocal interiority. The 'I am in the Father and the Father is in me,' (ἐγὼ ἐν τῷ πατρὶ καὶ ὁ πατὴρ ἐν ἐμοί (ἐστιν)) formulated as a question in 14:10 is repeated in 14:11. Further, it is said by Jesus that the Father stays in him (14:10; ἐν ἐμοὶ μένων). The Father is present in the Son, and the Son is totally in the Father, being an organ for his works and words.[71] In both passages we find the idea of a reciprocal interiority and a transparency of the works of the Son for the works of the Father.

It is remarkable that in 10:38 and in 14:10–11 the parallel is absent. Does this imply that a mutual indwelling, resulting in a total transparancy of Father and Son for each other has no parallel in the Son-disciples relation? However, in 14:20 the parallel of mutual indwelling is not absent.[72] On the day Jesus returns, they will know that he is in his Father and Jesus in them and they in him (14:20). The mutual 'being in' here is related to the disciples' increased knowledge concerning the relation between the Father and the Son and between Son and disciples. It is remarkable that the idea of total transparency is absent in 14:20, although an increased insight and a mutual 'being in' is mentioned. The interpretation of this verse depends on the moment of the return of Jesus: does this refer to his resurrection and the gift of the Spirit, or the *parousia*? I will discuss this

69. Carson, *The Gospel according to John*, 387–88; Van Houwelingen, *Johannes*, 222; Ridderbos, *Het evangelie naar Johannes*, Dl. 1 418–19; Schnackenburg, *Das Johannesevangelium*, Bd. 2 373–74; Scholtissek, *In ihm sein und bleiben*, 168–69.

70. Scholtissek, *In ihm sein und bleiben*, 326–27.

71. Scholtissek, *In ihm sein und bleiben*, 254–56.

72. Schnackenburg, *Das Johannesevangelium*, Bd. 3, 90.

later (see 6.3.1). For now it remains an open question whether a parallel can be drawn between the relation of the Father and the Son and the relation between the Son and believers also with regard to a mutual 'being in' that is so total as in 10:38 and in 14:10–11. Is this mutual indwelling only a matter of the eschata and not yet a reality?

The farewell discourses continue in John 15 with the image of the vine and the branches. In this context the 'μένειν ἐν' is used often: it is necessary that the branches stay in the vine to bear fruit. In 15:9–10 this 'remaining in' is worked out as remaining in someone's love: 'As the Father has loved me, so have I loved you. Remain in my love. If you keep my commands, you will remain in my love, just as I have kept my Father's commands and stay in his love.' The love of the Father for the Son is foundational for the love of the Son for his disciples.[73] But the parallel is threefold: not only the love of the Father for the Son is paralleled with the love of the Son for the disciples; further the remaining of the Son in his Father's love with the remaining of the disciples in the love of the Son; and the keeping of the commandments of the Father by the Son with the keeping of the Son's commandments by the disciples. Hence, the Son receives a double position: he is the loving one (like his Father) and he is the one remaining in someone's love, obeying someone's commands (like his disciples).

Finally some parallels can be found in the prayer of Jesus in John 17. Two types of parallels are drawn. The first type is like the parallels we have seen before: the Son is mentioned in both parts of the parallel. Parallels of this type can be found in 17:18, 22 and 23. Jesus says that he has sent his disciples into the world, like the Father has sent him into the world (17:18). He continues saying that he gave his disciples the glory that his Father gave him (17:22). And he says that he is in his disciples like his Father is in him (17:23). The second type is different: the unity between Father and Son is compared with the unity between the disciples among themselves. It is the prayer of the Son 'that they may be one as we are one' (17:11), that those who will believe in Jesus by the message of the disciples 'may be one . . . just as you are in me and I am in you' (17:21). And finally in 17:22: Jesus gave his glory to his disciples, 'that they may be one as we are one.' Nevertheless, it is important to see that now the Father is also involved directly in the relation with believers. In 17:21 Jesus prays that

73. Heise, *Bleiben*, 89; Scholtissek, *In ihm sein und bleiben*, 299.

they 'may be one . . . just as you are in me and I am in you, that they may be in us' (my translation). Further, the love of the Father for the Son is paralleled with the love of the Father for the disciples (17:23).

In John 17, the relation of Father and Son is characterized by unity springing from a mutual 'being in' and by the primacy of the Father, who sends the Son and gives him glory.[74] The first type of parallel indicates that the disciples receive a mutual 'being in' with the Son and that the Son sends them and gives them glory. The second type of parallel adds something new. The relation of Father and Son not only provides the model of the relation between the Son and the believers. It becomes the model and source also of relations between the disciples.[75] The focus here is on unity, a unity between persons, who remain distinct yet forming a unity.[76] Further, a new dimension is added in John 17 as the relation between Father and Son opens up for the disciples. The love of the Father for the disciples is mentioned and Jesus prays 'that they may be in *us*.' The relation itself is somehow open for others.

It is important to note that in John 17 the reciprocal 'being in' does not lead to dissolution of identity. The conformity of willing and acting of Father and Son does not imply a disappearance of the individual persons. Instead, according to Scholtissek, the inhabitation of the Father gives the Son his identity. The mutual 'being in' founds and determines personal identity and stability.[77]

To summarize, three types of parallels can be distinguished in these passages:

1. Parallels between the relation Father-Son and Son-disciples. Within this type, three subtypes can be seen: a parallel affirming dependency (living by, loving, sending, giving glory, 'being in'), a parallel stressing mutuality (knowing, 'being in') and a parallel emphasising

74. Scholtissek, *In ihm sein und bleiben*, 335–36.

75. Ridderbos, *Het evangelie naar Johannes*, Dl. 2, 217; Scholtissek, *In ihm sein und bleiben*, 332, 335.

According to Malatesta the Father-Son relation becomes 'the model and source of every other relationship,' see Malatesta, *Interiority and Covenant*, 32; and further 35, 133, 323. This is a statement too general. Malatesta does not distinguish sufficiently between the Father-Son relation and the Father-disciples relation; see 6.3.1.

76. Carson, *The Gospel according to John*, 567; Scholtissek, *In ihm sein und bleiben*, 335.

77. Jerumanis, *Realiser la communion avec Dieu*, 410, 473; Scholtissek, *In ihm sein und bleiben*, 274, 335–36, 339, 372.

human acts (remaining in the love, keeping the commands). Or formally:

- F > S // S > D
- F < > S // S < > D
- F < S // S < D

These parallels show that the Son is to the disciples what the Father is to him—a loving, divine source of life. The disciples are to the Son what the Son is to the Father—dependent, obedient beings.[78]

2. Parallels between the unity of Father and Son and the unity of the disciples among themselves. Two subtypes are to be distinguished: a parallel supposing the unity of Father and Son and a parallel supposing mutuality between Father and Son. Or formally:

   - (F—S) // (D—D)
   - F < > S // (D—D)

   These parallels show that the unity of Father and Son is source and model of the unity of the disciples among themselves

3. A parallel between the love of the Father for his Son and for the disciples, or formally:

   - F > S // F > D

   This parallel shows that the Father loves the disciples as he loves his Son.

4. A fourth relation does not presuppose a parallel: the disciples are in the Father and the Son:

   - (F-S) < D

   With regard to the central question, it is important to notice that these parallels do not necessarily imply that the Son must be seen as representative of the disciples, or that the disciples participate in his story. At the same time, these parallels do not exclude these ideas, although many parallels primarily focus on the exclusivity of the Son. In his relation with the disciples, he often seems to represent

78. Cf. Carson, *Divine Sovereignty and Human Responsability*, 160. See also Jerumanis, *Realiser la communion avec Dieu*, 405–11.

the Father, whereas in his relation with the Father he might be seen as representing the disciples. The following types might especially be important:

- F < > S // S < > D
- F < S // S < D
- (F—S) // (D—D)
- F < > S // (D—D)
- F > S // F > D
- (F-S) < D

Passage	Formal	Element	Father (F)	Son (S)	Disciples (D)
6:57	F>S S>D	Living by		The Son lives by his Father	The Christian lives by the Son
10:14–15	F<>S S<>D	Mutual knowing	The Father knows the Son	The Son knows the Father	
				The shepherd knows his sheep	The sheep know their shepherd
14:20	F<>S S<>D	Mutual 'being in'		Jesus is in his Father	
				Jesus is in the disciples	The disciples are in Jesus
15:9–10	F>S S>D	Loving	The Father loves the Son	The Son loves the disciples	
	F<S S<D	Remaining in the love		The Son remains in the Father's love	Remain in the love of Jesus
	F<S S<D	Keeping the commands		The Son keeps his Father's commands	Keep Jesus' commands
17:11	(F-S) (D-D)	Unity	as we are one		That they may be one
17:18	F>S S>D	Sending	The Father sends the Son into the world	The Son sends his disciples into the world	

Passage	Formal	Element	Father (F)	Son (S)	Disciples (D)
17:21	F<>S (D-D)	Unity Mutual 'being in'	just as you are in me and I am in you,		That they may be one,
	(F-S) <D	Being in Father and Son			that they may be in us.
17:22	F>S S>D	Giving glory	The Father gives glory to the Son	The Son gives glory to his disciples,	
	(F-S) (D-D)	Unity	as we are one		that they may be one,
17:23	F>S S>D	'Being in'	The Father is in the Son	The Son is in the disciples	
	F>S F>D	Loving	The Father loves the Son The Father loves the disciples		

The question is now, whether the Son in his relation with the Father can be seen as representing Israel, believers or humanity. Precisely with 'Son,' the uniqueness of the relation of Jesus Christ with his Father is indicated. It refers to the origin of this man Jesus—God is his father. Reactions of his audience show that the application of this title to Jesus was unique. The words of Jesus in his discussion with the Jews in John 10 even go so far that the Jews accuse Jesus of blasphemy, because he, a mere man, claims to be God (John 10:33; cf. 5:18). Jesus is God himself on earth.[79] At the same time, the Son is totally dependent on his Father. So we note his unity with his Father in willing, speaking, and acting. He has been sent by his Father and is as such part of the saving acts of God. Consequently, it is decisive for a human being, whether they believe that Jesus is the Son of God or not. As Son of God, he is seen within the divine perspective of salvation.[80] This is a first and important line of thought, affirming his exclusivity.

79. Van Bruggen, *Het evangelie van Gods Zoon*, 125–29. Cf. Jerumanis, *Realiser la communion avec Dieu*, 406.

80. Carson, *Divine Sovereignty and Human Responsibility*, 188; De Jonge, *Jesus*, 141–43; Sasse, *Der Menschensohn im Evangelium nach Johannes*, 258–60.

Moreover, several predications used for Jesus Christ can be applied to believers only after a comparable modification, as we shall see below (see 6.3.3). All these modifications show the difference between Jesus and believers, confirming the first line. Nevertheless, these modifications show that, although the Son is unique, the Son can be seen as representative. In some sense, he is like the believers. In his dependency, love and obedience to his Father, he is an example for his followers. Even more, he can be seen as representing them in this respect. Further it is important that the Son is always the *incarnate* λόγος—the Son is a human being. Some resonance of the Old Testament idea of Israel as (firstborn) son might be heard in this designation. As Son of God he represents Israel.[81] Although it cannot be denied that Jesus' audience did not react to this name as if it was a new application of a familiar metaphor,[82] this does not exclude that a second, thinner line of inclusiveness is drawn. To conclude, some space exists for the idea of representation, although this does not stand in the foreground.

Excursus: New Covenant?

This idea of representation is supported by the claim of Edward Malatesta that the Father-Son relation refers to the context of the covenant. Malatesta has studied εἶναι ἐν and μένειν ἐν in the First Letter of John resulting in his *Interiority and Covenant*. His thesis is that the interiority, indicated by these expressions, must be understood as fulfilment of the promise of the new covenant (Jer 31:33b and Ezek 36:26–27). They describe 'the interior nature of the New Covenant communion.'[83] Both incarnation and cross are important for this covenant, because the new covenant 'was first realised and continues to be realised in Jesus.'[84] 'The decisive moment for inaugurating the New Covenant was the Incarnation of God's eternal Word.'[85] In the person of Jesus 'a perfect reciprocity came to exist between man and God. . . . What was announced by Jeremiah was first and most perfectly realised in Jesus.'[86] The Paschal Mystery sealed the New Covenant

81. Exod 4:22–23; Ps 80:16; Hos 11:1.

82. Cf. Van Bruggen, *Het evangelie van Gods Zoon*, 126.

83. Malatesta, *Interiority and Covenant*, 24.

84. Malatesta, *Interiority and Covenant*, 147.

85. Malatesta, *Interiority and Covenant*, 308, 323.

86. Malatesta, *Interiority and Covenant*, 308.

by Jesus' blood.[87] That Jesus is the Son also must be understood within the context of the covenant. The dependency and obedience of the Son reveals a loyal covenant partner, referring with his entire life to his God. 'Christ is the Son par excellance who by His holiness realizes the Covenant most perfectly in Himself and by His sacrifice makes it possible for other sons to enter into the New Covenant relationship with the Father.'[88] To be in Christ is to discover and to live within the New Covenant communion.[89] In the view of Malatesta, Jesus Christ represents the New Covenant and we participate in him, becoming also members of this covenant.

According to Malatesta, it is not a problem that the word 'covenant' is not explicitly used or that Jeremiah and Ezekiel are not explicitly cited.[90] But this is exactly the weakness of his interpretation criticised by Scholtissek. The absence of the covenant-concept makes an immediate derivation of the interiority-language and theology from the Old Testament covenant-concept questionable.[91] Moreover, it is questionable whether the first letter presents Jesus Christ as representation of the New Covenant. We will be like Jesus Christ (1 John 2:8, 29; 3:2, 5, 6, 9) but that does not necessarily imply that John sees Jesus as the perfect covenant-partner. John could also mean that we will be like God, the Son being e.g. the perfect image of God. God sent his Son for us (1 John 4:9, 10, 14), but John does not say that the Son inaugurated or sealed the New Covenant. Finally, the use of 'Son of God' applied to Jesus is unique. Although God's people can be called 'his son' and the righteous 'his children' within the Old Testament, Jesus' audience did not react to this name as if it was a new application of a familiar metaphor as we saw above. Malatesta's interpretation focuses too much on the thinner line of inclusiveness and does not enough justice to the uniqueness of Jesus Christ as Son of God.

In conclusion, although it is attractive to follow Malatesta's interpretation, the weakness of his solution is the lack of evidence for it as well as his failure to see the uniqueness of the use of the title 'Son of God' as designation for Jesus Christ. The choice for the New Covenant as central

87. Malatesta, *Interiority and Covenant*, 252, 308, 323.

88. Malatesta, *Interiority and Covenant*, 250.

89. Malatesta, *Interiority and Covenant*, 323.

90. Malatesta, *Interiority and Covenant*, 22.

91. Scholtissek, *In ihm sein und bleiben*, 21.

category to interpret the thinking on interiority in the First Letter of John is not convincing.

6.2.3 'I AM'-SAYINGS: JESUS AS VINE

Important for the Christology of the gospel of John are the 'I am'-sayings.[92] In dealing with these passages I focus here on the position that Jesus Christ receives in relation to believers. Can he be seen as representative?

Passage	I am . . .	Relation	Believers
6:35	the bread of life	come	will never go hungry
		believe	will never be thirsty
6:48, 50	the bread of life	eat	will not die
6:51	the living bread	eat	will live forever
8:12	the light of the world	follow	will not walk in the darkness, but will have the light of life.
10:7, 9	the door of the sheep	enter through me	will be saved and will go in and out and find pasture
10:11	the good shepherd, who lays down his life for the sheep		
10:14–16		know, listen	will constitute one flock
11:25	the resurrection and the life	believe	will live, even if he dies
14:6	the way and the truth and the life		come to the Father through him
15:1, 2, 4	the true vine	remain in him and he in them	bear fruit
15:5	the vine	remain in him and he in them	branches, which bear much fruit

In the table the different passages can be found, showing what Jesus says about himself, the verb used for the relation between Jesus and the believer, and finally what is said about the believer. These passages display Jesus as the only one giving life[93] and light. They show that in Jesus the salvation creating reality of the only God has appeared once and for

92. See for the 'I am'-sayings generally Van Houwelingen, *Jezus stelt zich voor*; Stuhlmacher, *Biblische Theologie des Neuen Testaments*, Band 2, 228–32.

93. See for Jesus as source of life Frey, *Die johanneische Eschatologie*, Bd. III, 261–71.

all.[94] It is noteworthy that in most of the images used believers are rather different from Jesus. Instead of continuity between Jesus Christ and the believer, they affirm discontinuity: bread and a person eating bread; light and someone walking in the light; shepherd and sheep; the way, the life and a living person, the truth and the life as well as someone coming to the Father. These 'I am'-sayings do not evoke anything like an idea of representation, but the images emphasise Christ's uniqueness, expressing his divine authority.[95]

Is this also the case with the vine-metaphor? It is evident that the vine-metaphor emphasises the uniqueness of Jesus. He is not just *a* vine but *the true* vine. He is the source of the fruit-bearing of the disciples. At the same time, the question is whether Jesus as the true vine can be seen as the representative of the true Israel. It is undisputed that the vine-metaphor has an Old Testament-background: it is not only one of the symbols of a fruitful life, but it is used also as a metaphor for Israel.[96] Several times Israel is compared with a vine, planted by God but disappointing because of its (lack of) fruit.[97] Now it is crucial how Jesus as the true vine relates to Israel, the disappointing vine. John does not explicitly make a contrast, whereas he does make the contrast between the bread of life and manna, as well as between the good shepherd and the thief or the hired hand. Consequently, the contrast between Jesus and Israel does not play the main role.[98]

Instead, the vine-image shows more continuity between Jesus and his followers than the other metaphors. Jesus is the vine, his disciples the

94. Stuhlmacher, *Biblische Theologie des Neuen Testaments*, *Band* 2, 230.

95. Stuhlmacher, *Biblische Theologie des Neuen Testaments*, *Band* 2, 229. This does not necessarily mean that the 'I am'-sayings must be understood as *identification* of Jesus with God, referring to JHWH, the name of God in the Old Testament. Cf. Van Houwelingen, *Johannes*, 37; Schnackenburg, *Das Johannesevangelium*, Bd. 2 69. Leijgraaf does defend such an identification, see Leijgraaf, *Brood en wijn binnen de spanning van Gods verkiezing*, 39, 117.

96. Leijgraaf, *Brood en wijn binnen de spanning van Gods verkiezing*, 117–19. See further Carson, *The Gospel according to John*, 513; Dettwiler, *Die Gegenwart des Erhöhten*, 87–89; Van Houwelingen, *Johannes*, 309; Van Houwelingen, *Jezus stelt zich voor*, 59; Schnackenburg, *Das Johannesevangelium*, Bd. 3, 121; Scholtissek, *In ihm sein und bleiben*, 279–80.

97. Ps 80:9–11, 15–16; Isa 5:1–7; 27:2–6; Jer 2:21; 5:17; 6:9; 8:13; Ezek 15:2, 6; 19:10–14; Hos 2:14; 10:1; 14:8.

98. Van Houwelingen, *Johannes*, 309. Carson emphasises the opposition too much, suggesting a contrast and a replacement, see Carson, *The Gospel according to John*, 513.

branches, having much more in common than e.g a shepherd and his sheep, or bread and a person eating bread. Further Jesus does not replace Israel, Abraham's children, but enables them to bear fruit and do the works of Abraham (cf. John 8:40). Therefore the relation between Jesus and Israel might be representative. The absence of a salvation historical perspective[99] or an explicit reference to Israel does not contradict this possibility. It can be compared with Jesus as the fulfilment of the scriptures. John not only explicitly presents Jesus Christ as the fulfilment of the scriptures,[100] but he uses also more implicitly e.g. the rich symbolism of Jewish feasts to articulate his Christology.[101] In a comparable way the representative character of Jesus Christ might be suggested more implicitly with the vine-image. To conclude: given the Old Testament background of the image, it is plausible to see Jesus Christ as the true vine as the representative of the true Israel, in whom all believers are incorporated.[102] This means that the true Israel is christologically accentuated and concentrated in Jesus Christ.[103] Hence the vine-metaphor implies incorporation[104] and representation.[105]

Summarizing, the 'I am'-sayings emphasise the uniqueness of Jesus Christ. This is also the case with the vine-metaphor. Nevertheless, this image shows Jesus as the one representing the true Israel, enabling Israel to bear fruit. The vine-metaphor shows that the uniqueness of Jesus Christ can be combined with seeing Jesus as representative, incorporating believers. Exclusivity and inclusiveness do not exclude each other.

6.2.4 JESUS' DEATH: SUBSTITUTION?

Now I will investigate the meaning of the death of Jesus within Johannine thinking. What place does it have within Johannine thinking? Do we need

99. This makes Dettwiler hesitate to see Jesus replace Israel, see Dettwiler, *Die Gegenwart des Erhöhten*, 89.

100. John 1:23; 2:17; 6:31, 45; 10:34, 35; 12:13, 15, 38, 40; 13:18; 15:25; 19:24, 28, 36, 37; see further Obermann, *Die christologische Erfüllung der Schrift im Johannesevangelium.*

101. See Yee, *Jewish Feasts and The Gospel of John.*

102. Stuhlmacher, *Biblische Theologie des Neuen Testaments, Band* 2, 267.

103. Schnackenburg, *Das Johannesevangelium*, Bd. 3, 121; cf. Van Bruggen, *Het evangelie van Gods Zoon*, 163.

104. Carson, *The Gospel according to John*, 514; Ridderbos, *Het evangelie naar Johannes*, Dl. 2, 166.

105. Ridderbos, *Het evangelie naar Johannes*, Dl. 2, 166.

the concept of representation to understand the meaning of this death or the concept of substitution? Is the exclusiveness of this death emphasised or its inclusiveness? I start with the exclusiveness in 6.2.4, first in the gospel of John and second in the first letter. I will continue in 6.2.5 with its inclusiveness.

The composition of the gospel makes clear that the cross is an important moment, even the goal and climax of the narrative. Frey mentions five narrative means, used to give this death its central place. First, the farewell discourses prepare Jesus' departure. Second, the use of the idea of Jesus' hour indicates the decisiveness of the moment of the death of Jesus (esp. John 7:30; 8:20; 12:23, 27; 13:1; 16:32; 17:1). Third, the narrative tempo is adjusted to Jesus' hour; when this hour draws near, the tempo slackens. Fourth, proleptic hints at the death of Jesus are given throughout the whole narrative. And finally, commentary from the narrator shows that the death and glorification of Jesus is a central theme of the narrative.[106]

Several aspects characterize the view on Jesus' death. First, it is part of the mission of the Son (12:27). His death on the cross is God's will. He received the command from his Father (10:18; 14:31) and his Father gave him the cup to drink (18:11). Obediently the Son goes this way and freely accepts it. It is his food to do the will of Him who sent him (4:34; cf. 10:18; 18:11). He has to complete the work of his Father (4:34; 5:36; 17:4). Just before he dies, Jesus says 'It is finished' (19:28, 30), indicating that his mission is completed. Consequently, the importance of this death must be great.[107] This shows the uniqueness of the death of Jesus Christ, that is, not just of his person, but also of what he did.

Second, the death of Jesus has its place within the exaltation and glorification of the Son of Man. The Son of Man must be lifted up and will be glorified. The relation between a *theologia crucis* and a *theologia gloriae* has been much discussed.[108] However, these cannot be separated but are

106. Frey, 'Die "*theologia crucifixi*" des Johannesevangeliums,' 192–200. Cf. Knöppler, *Die theologia crucis des Johannesevangeliums*, 122–53.

107. Knöppler, *Die theologia crucis des Johannesevangeliums*, 174–83; Loader, *The Christology of the Fourth Gospel*, 94, 101; Nielsen, 'John's Understanding of the Death of Jesus,' 237–39; Stuhlmacher, *Biblische Theologie des Neuen Testaments*, 238–39, 241.

108. See Frey, 'Die "*theologia crucifixi*" des Johannesevangeliums,' 169–91, 228–36; Knöppler, *Die theologia crucis des Johannesevangeliums*, 6–25, 154–73; Loader, *The Christology of the Fourth Gospel*, 107–23; Nielsen, 'John's Understanding of the Death of Jesus,' 233–37; Stuhlmacher, *Biblische Theologie des Neuen Testaments*, Bd. 2, 240;

intertwined and belong together in John.[109] The lifting up of the Son of Man refers to his being lifted up on the cross as well as to his being lifted up into heaven, drawing all men to himself (3:14; 8:28; 12:32, 34).[110] The same is the case with his glorification: his glorification is associated with suffering and the cross (12:23) as well as with a return to the glory Jesus had before the world began (17:5).[111] Both the lifting up and the glorification of the Son of Man show his uniqueness, although his glorification also contains a moment of inclusiveness, as we will see below (see 6.2.5).

Third, the cross is a place of judgment over the world and the ruler of this world (ὁ ἄρχων τοῦ κόσμου). The moment of the cross, death and glorification is the moment of judgment and the moment that the ruler of this world is to be driven out (12:31). He came, but he had nothing in Jesus, for Jesus loved his Father and did exactly what his Father commanded him (14:30–31).[112] Jesus is from above and not from this world

---

Thompson, *The Humanity of Jesus in the Fourth Gospel*, 1–10.

109. Cf. Frey, 'Die "*theologia crucifixi*" des Johannesevangeliums,' 178; Knöppler, *Die theologia crucis des Johannesevangeliums*, vii, 269–78.

110. In 3:14, the lifting up on the cross must be the primary referent, because the lifting up is related to the snake on a stick in 3,14 identifying the exalted place of Jesus as a place on a stick, and to the love of God, who gave his one and only Son (3:16). The cross will be a place of divine healing and removal of a deadly plague. In this way, he has ascended into heaven (3:14). In 8:28, the Jews are the actors; unintended they exalt Christ, nailing him on the cross. By his cross, Jesus becomes a highly placed person. Then they will know that he is the one he claims to be. In 12:32–33, the 'ὑψωθῶ ἐκ τῆς γῆς' is ambiguous. It is interpreted in 12:33 as a hint of his death on the cross, but the context of glorification and the lifting up *from the earth* make clear that it also refers to Jesus' ascent into heaven. To conclude, a reference to the cross and a reference to the exaltation in heaven do not exclude each other but are both present.

See Carson, *The Gospel according to John*, 201–2; Frey, 'Die "*theologia crucifixi*" des Johannesevangeliums,' 228–31; Hofius, 'Das Wunder der Wiedergeburt,' 61–65; Van Houwelingen, *Johannes*, 98, 196; Knöppler, *Die theologia crucis des Johannesevangeliums*, 154, 158–65; Loader, *The Christology of the Fourth Gospel*, 117–23; Marshall, *New Testament Theology*, 498; Nielsen, 'John's Understanding of the Death of Jesus,' 248–50; Popp, *Grammatik des* Geistes, 150; Ridderbos, *Het evangelie naar Johannes*, Dl. 1, 162–63; Schnackenburg, *Das Johannesevangelium*, Bd. 1, 409; Stuhlmacher, *Biblische Theologie des Neuen Testaments*, Bd. 2, 240.

111. Knöppler focusses here on the cross too much, giving a forced exegeses of 11:4 and 17:5. Loader emphasises too much the return to the pre-existent glory, seeming not to see that the context of 12,23 is full of cross-related motives. See Knöppler, *Die theologia crucis des Johannesevangeliums*, 168–73; Loader, *The Christology of the Fourth Gospel*, 107–10.

112. Cf. Van Houwelingen, *Johannes*, 305.

(8:23); he has not sinned (8:46).[113] Consequently, the ruler of this world is judged (16:11) and Jesus has overcome the world (16:33).[114] The cross is the moment of judgment of Satan and this world, and Jesus' victory over these powers.[115] This motive of judgment and victory affirms the exclusivity of Jesus and of what he did.

Fourth, John the Baptist designated Jesus Christ as the Lamb of God (ὁ ἀμνὸς τοῦ θεοῦ) in 1:29 and 1:36. This designation has no parallel; consequently, the question which lamb is meant is much debated. It seems a creative combination of different Old Testament motives,[116] e.g. the lamb in Gen 22, the Paschal lamb in Exod 12, the goat in Lev 16, and the servant in Isa 53, who is willing, like a lamb.[117] Given this uncertainty concerning the background of this designation, the clause following on ὁ ἀμνὸς τοῦ θεου becomes important: who takes away the sin of the world (1:29).[118] Jesus is the unique lamb of God, given by God as atonement for sin. Jesus' death as Lamb of God brings comprehensive atonement.[119] This is confirmed by the narrative of the gospel, which emphasises that the death of the Lamb of God brings the end of the sacrificial cult in the

113. Cf. Carson, *The Gospel according to John*, 509.

114. Frey, 'Die "*theologia crucifixi*" des Johannesevangeliums,' 236; Loader, *The Christology of the Fourth Gospel*, 105–6.

115. Frey, *Die johanneische Eschatologie*, Bd. III, 188–89, 283, 288.

116. Cf. Frey, 'Die "*theologia crucifixi*" des Johannesevangeliums,' 211–12; Van Houwelingen, *Johannes*, 67; Schnackenburg, *Das Johannesevangelium*, Bd. 1 288; Stibbe, *John*, Sheffield 1993, 35. According to Wierenga, the metaphor is deliberately ambigeous; see Wierenga, *Verhalen als bewijzen*, 122–23.

117. Much discussed are especially the Paschal Lamb and Isa 53. For a survey of different Old Testament motives that could stand in the background of the Lamb of God-metaphor, see Carson, *The Gospel according to John*, 148; Van Houwelingen, *Johannes*, 66–67; Knöppler, *Die theologia crucis des Johannesevangeliums*, 83–87; Loader, *The Christology of the Fourth Gospel*, 96; Ridderbos, *Het evangelie naar Johannes*, Dl. 1, 88–91.

118. Both Van Bruggen and Frey follow this path, see Van Bruggen, *Het evangelie van Gods Zoon*, 144; Frey, 'Die "*theologia crucifixi*" des Johannesevangeliums,' 202. See also Marshall, *New Testament Theology*, 495–96.

119. Van Bruggen, *Het evangelie van Gods Zoon*, 144; Frey, 'Die "*theologia crucifixi*" des Johannesevangeliums,' 203, 208; Van Houwelingen, *Johannes*, 67–68; Knöppler, *Die theologia crucis des Johannesevangeliums*, 87–89; Knöppler, *Sühne im Neuen Testament*, 241, 244, 247; Nielsen, 'John's Understanding of the Death of Jesus,' 251–52; Ridderbos, *Het evangelie naar Johannes*, Dl. 1 91–92; Schnackenburg, *Das Johannesevangelium*, Bd. 1, 285.

temple.[120] According to Stibbe, the gospel has a Paschal-plot and the description of the death of Jesus has subtle Paschal overtones.[121] This may be the case e.g. in John 19:36, where we are told that according to the scriptures not one of Jesus' bones is broken. This was the case with the Paschal Lamb,[122] but also with the righteous man in Ps 34:20. To conclude, both the designation 'Lamb of God' and the narrative point at the exclusive character of Jesus' death as unique place of atonement.

Fifth, the death of Jesus is viewed as death for others. Several passages are important:

a. John 6:51. We have been dealing with this verse already (see 6.2.1). We saw that it refers to the death of Christ on the cross.[123] His death is interpreted within the imagery of the chapter as bread giving eternal life. On the cross, he gave his flesh 'ὑπὲρ τῆς τοῦ κόσμου ζωῆς.' It is stated *that* his death is a death for the life of the world and that his death is life for anyone who eats this bread; *how* this metaphor must be understood is not explained, apart from the sacramental associations it evokes. It might be the case that in 6:51 there resound associations with the Paschal Lamb and the divine Servant from Isa 52:13—53:12 as Popp claims, but this is disputed.[124] Very clear is the exclusive nature of his death. Semantically, no relation of continuity between Jesus and his followers is suggested. Instead, the relation is a relation of discontinuity: eating. His death is for food and for life.

120 Cf. Knöppler, *Sühne im Neuen Testament*, 247–48.

121. Stibbe, *John*, 35. Less certain is Loader, *The Christology of the Fourth Gospel*, 96.

122. Frey, 'Die "*theologia crucifixi*" des Johannesevangeliums,' 209–10.

123. A reference to the death on the cross is not disputed. A much-discussed question is, whether 6:51 also refers to the Eucharist or not. For now it is sufficient that the majority of the exegetes sees a reference to the death of Christ on the cross for others. See Anderson, *The Christology of the Fourth Gospel*, 207; Van Bruggen, *Het evangelie van Gods Zoon*, 149; Carson, *The Gospel according to John*, 295; Frey, 'Die "*theologia crucifixi*" des Johannesevangeliums,' 215; Van Houwelingen, *Johannes*, 159; Knöppler, *Die theologia crucis des Johannesevangeliums*, 202–3; Nielsen, 'John's Understanding of the Death of Jesus,' 243; Popp, *Grammatik des Geistes*, 356–57; Ridderbos, *Het evangelie naar Johannes*, Dl. 1, 277; Scholtissek, *In ihm sein und bleiben*, 202; Thompson, *The Humanity of Jesus in the Fourth Gospel*, 48.

Differently Loader, *The Christology of the Fourth Gospel*, 97.

124. See Popp, *Grammatik des Geistes*, 358–59. Knöppler sees here the idea of an atoning sacrifice, but Nielsen doubts whether Jesus' death is seen in this passage as a death of atonement, see Knöppler, *Die theologia crucis des Johannesevangeliums*, 202; Nielsen, 'John's Understanding of the Death of Jesus,' 243.

Consequently, this metaphor does not show an inclusive moment of the death of Jesus, but an exclusive moment only.

b. John 10:11, 15. Here Jesus as the good shepherd is contrasted with the hired hand. The good shepherd never leaves the sheep and runs away if his own life is in danger. Instead, he cares for the sheep and lays down his life (τὴν ψυχήν) for the sheep (ὑπὲρ τῶν προβάτων). He risks his life to allow the sheep to live safely. The shepherd not only risks his life but actually dies, for Jesus says repeatedly that he lays down his life (10:11, 15, 17, 18). Hence the death of Jesus on the cross is meant; a death according to the commandment of his Father as 10:17–18 makes clear. The perspective, offered on the death of Christ by this metaphor, is that Christ resisted the danger ('the wolf') and laid his life down instead of letting the sheep be attacked and scattered. His death protects the sheep from danger. What danger the wolf refers to, is not said, only that his death saves from this danger.[125] He is really a good shepherd. Further, the death of Jesus is somehow a precondition of the fellowship of Jesus and his sheep as Nielsen writes,[126] and apart from his death his resurrection is mentioned also (10:17–18). Again only the exclusive moment of Jesus' death is emphasised, but his death is not viewed as vicarious atonement.[127]

125. Kowalski thinks that the shepherd is associated with the Lamb of God. If that were true, the death of Christ would be seen here as a sacrificial death. However, in John 10 this relation is not laid. See Kowalski, *Die Hirtenrede*, 197–98, 205–6.

126. Nielsen, 'John's Understanding of the Death of Jesus,' 245. Carson refers to John 12:32 and concludes that Jesus by his death draws his sheep to himself. See Carson, *The Gospel according to John*, 386.

127. Cf. Dietzfelbinger, 'Sühnetod im Johannesevangelium?,' 67; Van Houwelingen, *Johannes*, 221–23; Knöppler, *Die theologia crucis des Johannesevangeliums*, 205; Loader, *The Christology of the Fourth Gospel*, 98; Marshall, *New Testament Theology*, 503; Ridderbos, *Het evangelie naar Johannes*, Dl. 1, 417–18, 419–20; Schnackenburg, *Das Johannesevangelium*, Bd. 2 370–72, 375; Thompson, *Humanity of Jesus in the Fourth Gospel*, 92–93.

According to Carson, the suggested interpretation of the death of Jesus is the interpretation of his death as sacrifice. As argument he gives the use of ὑπὲρ, that should be used always in a sacrificial context. But this is not the case: although a death ὑπὲρ others is a death for others, that does not make that such a death a is interpreteted as a *sacrificial* death in this passage (cf. 11:50–52; 13:37–38). See Carson, *The Gospel according to John*, 386–87.

c. John 11:50–52; 18:14. In John 11 the Sanhedrin decides to kill Jesus because he is a threat to their position. They fear the Romans might come and take away their place and their nation. According to Caiaphas, it is better to kill Jesus than to let the whole nation perish. Consequently, it is better that one man die 'ὑπὲρ τοῦ λαοῦ' (11:50). According to the narrator, these words have a deeper meaning: Caiaphas prophesied that Jesus would die for the nation and for the scattered children of God. This prophecy is referred to again in John 18:14. The mentioning of the scattered children of God suggests that the death of Christ creates a new fellowship. It is clear that this death is good for the nation, but it is not explained how this will be the case. According to Loader the notion of vicarious atonement might be present subordinately.[128] It might be significant that Caiaphas prophesied as highpriest, but this is not sure. Further, again the exclusive moment is emphasised: he dies instead of others, to prevent the whole nation from perishing and to gather the scattered children of God (cf. John 10:16).[129]

d. John 15:13. In John 15, Jesus introduces the metaphor of the vine and the branches. He goes on, elaborating the remaining in him as remaining in his love. He holds his own love for his disciples as an example for their love. Then he says: 'Greater love has no-one than this, that he lay down his life for his friends' (τὴν ψυχὴν αὑτοῦ θῇ ὑπὲρ τῶν φίλων αὑτοῦ; 15:13). This evokes the situation of someone, who protects his friends from something or gives them some benefits by dying for or instead of them. The love of Jesus Christ is emphasised here, manifest in his death. What his death acquires and how is not important now. Central is the love for friends, leading to the gift of someone's life for his friends. The emphasis is here on his death as a moral example, not on the inclusiveness or exclusivity of this death. Anyhow, no indication is given here of an inclusiveness as a dying with Christ.[130]

128. Loader, *The Christology of the Fourth Gospel*, 98.

129. Van Houwelingen, *Johannes*, 247–48; Knöppler, *Die theologia crucis des Johannesevangeliums*, 206–7; Nielsen, 'John's Understanding of the Death of Jesus,' 246.

130. Carson, The Gospel according to John, 521–22; Dettwiler, *Die Gegenwart des Erhöhten*, 98; Van Houwelingen, *Johannes*, 313; Knöppler, *Die theologia crucis des Johannesevangeliums*, 209–10; Loader, *The Christology of the Fourth Gospel*, 99; Nielsen, 'John's Understanding of the Death of Jesus,' 247–48; Ridderbos, *Het evangelie naar Johannes*,

To conclude, the death of Christ as death ὑπὲρ others brings food and life (John 6), protects his sheep from a certain danger (John 10), prevents the whole nation from perishing (John 11) and is a manifestation of his love for his friends and as such a moral example (John 15). *How* his death is a death for others is not elaborated. Twice it is suggested that the death of Christ creates a new, greater fellowship (John 10:16; 11:52). Sacrificial or judicial imagery is not used in these passages, so that these passages do not suggest a vicarious atonement, although it is possible that they implicitly presuppose it.[131] Dietzfelbinger and Loader both state that John presupposes the idea of a vicarious atonement and does not dispute it, but has his own agenda, showing other aspects of the death of Jesus Christ. The idea of vicarious atonement alone is not enough to understand the meaning of this death.[132] Instead, emphasis is placed on the paradox that his death gives life, the protecting effect of his death against danger and the moral content of his death as manifestation of love. Three times the exclusive moment of the death of Christ is emphasised, whereas the inclusive moment is not mentioned. Two times the death of Christ for others is given as a moral example. Consequently, this view of the death of Christ for others can be understood with the help of the concept of substitution and not with the concept of representation. The exclusivity does not concern only his person, but also his acts. However, in these passages the death of Christ is not seen as a sacrifice.

Until now we have seen that the gospel of John pictures the death of Jesus as a result of his mission from the Father, as part of his exaltation and glorification, as moment of judgment of and victory on the world and its ruler, as sacrifice of the Lamb of God, reinforced by the Paschal overtones of the narrative and as death for others. The uniqueness of the death of Christ is obvious within the gospel. Consequently, the concept of (work-)substitution is necessary to structure our understanding of John's vision of the death of Christ as he emphasises the exclusive moment of this death. It is noteworthy that this exclusiveness is broader than the idea

170–71; Schnackenburg, *Das Johannesevangelium*, Bd. 3, 124.

131. Although sacrificial imagery is not used (apart from the image of the lamb of God), the gospel of John uses a cultic image: Jesus replaces the temple (John 2:19–22); cf. Marshall, *New Testament Theology*, 519; Stuhlmacher, *Biblische Theologie des Neuen Testaments, Band 2*, 268; Yee, *Jewish Feasts and The Gospel of John*, 82.

132. Dietzfelbinger, 'Sühnetod im Johannesevangelium?,' 74–76; Loader, *The Christology of the Fourth Gospel*, 101–2.

of sacrifice. Although the idea of a sacrifice and a vicarious atonement is presupposed, John uses far more metaphors to speak about the soteriological meaning of the death of Jesus Christ.

Does the first letter of John change this picture?

In the first chapter, the author writes that God is light. To live in fellowship with God is to live in the light. Living in the light, fellowship with one another and forgiveness of sin presuppose each other. All this is preconditioned upon the blood of Jesus, the Son of God, which purifies from all sin (1 John 1:7). The effect of the work of Jesus is expressed in cultic metaphors: blood, purification; the crucifixion of Christ is interpreted in sacrificial terms.[133] Further, this blood makes fellowship possible. Next, John writes about sin. We have sinned and must confess our sins, for God is faithful and just and will forgive our sins. They need not despair if they have sinned because of Jesus, our παράκλητος with the Father (2:1). 'He is ἱλασμός for our sins and not only for ours, but also for the sins of the whole world' (2:2). Jesus is the atoning sacrifice and he intercedes for them with the Father.[134] Again, sacrificial terms are used. In both passages, the exclusivity of the work of Jesus is clear and it is expressed in sacrificial terminology. Jesus brings forgiveness of sins and fellowship with God and with one another.

In chapter 3, John writes that we are children of God and shall see the Son of God. Next the theme of sin returns. To have this hope in him means to purify oneself (3:3). For the Son of God 'appeared so that he might take away our sins' (3:5). How he did so is left unexplained, but it is clear that Jesus is opposed to sin. It might be significant that the verb αἴρω, to take away, is used also in John 1:29: the Lamb of God who takes away the sin of the world.[135] According to Strecker, the sinlessness of Jesus ('in him is no sin,' 3:5) evokes associations with a sacrificial lamb.[136] It is possible that John alludes to Jesus as the Lamb of God. Parallel to 3:5 again is said why the Son has appeared: sin is from the devil and the Son of God appeared 'to destroy the devil's work' (3:8). Again, how he did this

133. Knöppler, *Sühne im Neuen Testament*, 221–22; Lalleman, 1, 2 *en* 3 *Johannes*, 109, 138; Smalley, 1, 2, 3 *John*, 24–26.

134. Knöppler, *Sühne im Neuen Testament*, 223–26; Lalleman, 1, 2 *en* 3 *Johannes*, 109, 142; Marshall, *The Epistles of John*, 117–18; Smalley, 1, 2, 3 *John*, 38–40; Strecker, *Die Johannesbriefe*, Göttingen 1989, 93–94.

135. Lalleman, 1, 2 *en* 3 *Johannes*, 173; Marshall, *The Epistles of John*, 177.

136. Strecker, *Die Johannesbriefe*, 163; cf. Lalleman, 1, 2 *en* 3 *Johannes*, 173.

is left unsaid. The relation with his death and resurrection is not explicitly stated, but it is reasonable to presuppose this connection. Still the aim of John is not to say something about the 'how,' but to exhort them not to sin. Within this paranetical setting, what is said however in passing about the work of the Son displays the exclusive nature of his work. He took away sin and he broke the power of the devil.

In contrast to sin stands love. We know what love is by what Jesus Christ did: 'Jesus Christ laid down his life for us' (3:16a). Jesus' death is a death for us. In what sense this is the case is not elaborated, for now it is more important that his death demonstrates what love is. What matters is not that this death was an atoning sacrifice, but an act of loving self-renunciation.[137] In this way his death can serve as a moral example. We ought to lay down our lives for the brothers (3:16b).[138] When someone lays down his life for his brothers, he dies *instead* of them. Consequently, here the exclusive moment of the death of Jesus is implied, although it is used as a moral example.

In chapter 4 John returns to the theme of love and its demonstration in Jesus Christ. Now he focuses on God: he showed his love, sending his only begotten Son that we might live through him, as ἱλασμὸς περὶ τῶν ἁμαρτιῶν ἡμῶν (4:9–11). God sent his Son as saviour of the world (4:14). Like in 2:2 Jesus is viewed as the atoning sacrifice for sin.[139]

In the first letter of John, the death of Christ is seen as result of the divine sending of the Son, as atoning sacrifice taking away sins, as a moment of destroying the works of the devil and as a demonstration of love, for it was a death for his brothers. Within the letter sacrificial ideas are used more explicitly than in the gospel of John.[140] Other motifs were also found in the gospel. Just as in the gospel, the exclusivity of the death of

137. Lalleman, *1, 2 en 3 Johannes*, 178–79. Knöppler, Smalley and Strecker presuppose too much that the idea of a sacrifice is present here. His sacrificial death was a death for his brothers, demonstrating his love. But John 10:11, 15 and 15:13 show that in Johannine thinking the idea of a death ὑπὲρ others itself does not imply the notion of sacrifice. See Knöppler, *Sühne im Neuen Testament*, 227–28; Smalley, *1, 2, 3 John*, 194; Strecker, *Die Johannesbriefe*, 187.

138. Knöppler, *Sühne im Neuen Testament*, 227–28; Lalleman, *1, 2, en 3 Johannes*, 179; Marshall, *The Epistles of John*, 192–95; Smalley, *1, 2, 3 John*, 193–95; Strecker, *Die Johannesbriefe*, 186–88.

139. Knöppler, *Sühne im Neuen Testament*, 228–30; Lalleman, *1, 2, en 3 Johannes*, 109–10; Marshall, *The Epistles of John*, 214–15.

140. Knöppler, *Sühne im Neuen Testament*, 220; Smalley, *1, 2, 3 John*, 25.

Jesus is evident. My interpretation of the letter confirms the necessity of the concept of (work-)substitution.

6.2.5 THE INCLUSIVE MOMENT OF JESUS' DEATH AND RESURRECTION

It might seem that in Johannine thinking especially the exclusive moment of the death of Christ is present. But can we also find an inclusive moment? I will deal with some passages from the gospel.

First, John 12:23–26. Here Jesus says that the hour of the glorification of the Son of man has come. As an image for his coming death, he uses a kernel of wheat. If it does not fall to the ground and die, it remains a solitary seed. But its purpose is to produce many new seeds, by falling to the ground and dying. Life presumes death and death brings new life. Again we see the motif of the death of one, leading to many fruit: the death of Jesus creates a new fellowship. This returns in 12:32: being exalted, Jesus will draw all men to himself.[141] However, it is not the exclusive moment of Jesus' death that is stressed, but the dying kernel of wheat is used as a pattern, which his disciples need to follow. It is not said that the death of the disciples produces new life or a new fellowship, but the willingness to lose one's life, even to hate it in this world, is a presupposition of keeping it for eternal life (John 12:25). To serve Christ is to be prepared to follow him (12:27)—even in his death. Where Jesus is, there his servant will be. Hence, Jesus' story is not only a pattern to repeat, but his servants will also participate in his way and his destiny. To conclude, here we find a combination of the inclusive and exclusive moment, as well as the idea of a pattern to follow.

Second, John 14:2–6. After Jesus said that the disciples could not follow him (13:33, 36) he continues telling them that he goes to his Father's house to prepare a place for them there.[142] Then he will come back and take them to be with him that they may also be where he is (John 14:2–3). There is a consensus among the majority of exegetes that this is an element of a future eschatology.[143] These verses indicate how exclusiveness

141. Nielsen, 'John's Understanding of the Death of Jesus,' 239–40; Thompson, *The Humanity of Jesus in the Fourth Gospel*, 96–97.

142. Frey, *Die johanneische Eschatologie*, Bd. III, 154.

143. Carson, *The Gospel according to John*, 488; Dettwiler, *Die Gegenwart des Erhöhten*, 155–56; Frey, *Die johanneische Eschatologie*, Bd. III, 147–50; Van Houwelingen, *Johannes*, 292; Ridderbos, *Het evangelie naar Johannes*, Dl. 2, 136–38.

Van Hartingsveld's position is different: 14:3 refers to a return of Jesus after his and inclusiveness can occur together. Jesus Christ is unique: he is the one preparing a place in his Father's house. At the same time he makes us participate in his presence in his Father's house.

Third, John 14:19. Jesus says here that he will return to his disciples and that they will see him. This reunion has a double presupposition: Jesus lives and they will live. In the case of Jesus, the tense is present, in the case of the disciples future. This shows the relation between the life of Jesus and the life of his followers. They receive their life from the glorified Jesus Christ, the resurrected one who has life in himself.[144] He who is, in his person, our life came to make his followers participate in his life, being the resurrection for them.[145] The temporal difference shows that Jesus is unique, as the living one, who promises life to his disciples.[146] At the same time, semantically, continuity is clear: the same verb 'ζῶ' is used for Jesus as well as for the disciples.[147] When this will be the case—immediately after Jesus' resurrection or at the *parousia*—is less important now (see 6.3.1). They will see Jesus, for they will share in his life.

Finally the moment of inclusiveness is to be found in John 17. After having prayed for himself, Jesus prays for his disciples. The prayer shows similarities between Jesus Christ, his disciples and their followers. A similarity exists in their origin: they are both not 'ἐκ τοῦ κόσμου' (17:14, 16).[148] Further, they are both sent 'εἰς τὸν κόσμον' (17:18), although the Father gave the Son his mission, whereas the Son gave his disciples their mission. The Son remains unique, because he is the one sent by the Father and because he is the sender of his disciples. Whether they have the same mission or not is not made clear. Consequently, the uniqueness of the mission of the Son and the possible difference between their

---

departure to prepare a place during the lifetime of his disciples to bring them at home; Van Hartingsveld, *Die Eschatologie des Johannesevangeliums*, 106–10.

144. Frey, *Die johanneische Eschatologie*, Bd. III, 168; Schnackenburg, *Das Johannesevangelium*, Bd. 2, 89.

145. Dettwiler, *Die Gegenwart des Erhöhten*, 193f; Kammler, 'Jesus Christus und der Geistparaklet. Eine Studium zur johanneischen Verhältnissbestimmung von Pneumatologie und Christologie,' *Johannesstudien* , Tübingen 1996, 106.

146. Dettwiler, *Die Gegenwart des Erhöhten*, 194; Frey, *Die johanneische Eschatologie*, Bd. III, 168; Kammler, 'Jesus Christus und der Geistparaklet,' 107.

147. Rusam, *Die Gemeinschaft der Kinder Gottes*, 152.

148. Carson immediately adds the difference between the origin of Jesus and the origin of his followers. Elsewhere in the gospel this might be the case; here the similarity is expressed. See Carson, *The Gospel according to John*, 564.

missions is not emphasised, but the resemblance is stated clearly: both are sent into the world. Apart from these two similarities in origin and mission, the work of the Son has its inclusiveness. He prays: 'And for them I sanctify myself, that they also may be sanctified in truth' (17:19; my translation). The result of Jesus' sanctifying himself is not only that he is sanctified, but also that his followers are sanctified. The involvement of his followers in this sanctification is evident. His acting for his followers shows his uniqueness, whereas the result is shared. Sanctified, they will be sent into the world just as Jesus was sent.[149] Again we find a combination of substitution and representation.[150] Furthermore, the glorification includes a moment of inclusiveness. In 17:22 the Son says that he gave 'τὴν δόξαν ἣν δέδωκάς μοι' to his followers. And in 17:24 he prays that his followers may be where he is. Jesus makes his followers participate in his glorification.[151] Within this chapter, again and again a combination of the exclusive and the inclusive moment can be discovered.

To conclude, although the exclusiveness of Jesus Christ is evident within the gospel of John, the moment of inclusiveness is not denied. Instead, a careful reading of the gospel shows that this inclusive moment is present indeed. Not only do Jesus and his followers share the same pattern of life through death, also his way and destiny have its inclusiveness (John 12:23–26). The shared destiny we find further in 14:2–6: the Father's

149. Carson, *The Gospel according to John*, 566; Van Houwelingen, *Johannes*, 340f; W. Loader, *The Christology of the Fourth Gospel*, 100; Ridderbos, *Het evangelie naar Johannes*, Dl. 2, 211; Scholtissek, *In ihm sein und bleiben*, 332; Schnackenburg, *Das Johannesevangelium*, Bd. 3 211f.

150. See for the ὑπὲρ αὐτῶν further 6.2.4 . For 17,19 see Carson, *The Gospel according to John*, 567; Frey, 'Die "*theologia crucifixi*" des Johannesevangeliums,' 213; Van Houwelingen, *Johannes*, 341; Knöppler, *Die theologia crucis des Johannesevangeliums*, 210–15; Ridderbos, *Het evangelie naar Johannes*, Dl. 2, 212; Schnackenburg, *Das Johannesevangelium*, Bd. 3 212f.

151. Frey, *Die johanneische Eschatologie*, Bd. III , 223–31. Loader and Ridderbos distinguish between δόξα in 17:22 and 24: in 17:22 the glory associated with the revelatory work of Jesus Christ on earth, in 17:24 the heavenly glory of the pre-existent Jesus Christ. Van Houwelingen, Knöppler and Schnackenburg do not find this distinction here and identify δόξα as the heavenly divine glory. Nevertheless, both in 17:22 and in 24 the followers of Jesus participate in his δόξα (17:22) and in his heavenly place (17:24). Whether Loader and Ridderbos are right or Van Houwelingen, Knöppler and Schnackenburg does not change the fact that the moment of inclusiveness is present in both verses. See Loader, *The Christology of the Fourth Gospel*, 113; Van Houwelingen, *Johannes*, 344–45; Knöppler, *Die theologia crucis des Johannesevangeliums*, 62; Ridderbos, *Het evangelie naar Johannes*, Dl. 2, 220; Schnackenburg, *Das Johannesevangelium*, Bd. 3, 218.

house. John 14:19 shows the participation of believers in the life of Jesus. Finally John 17 point towards a similarity in origin, mission and glorified destiny, as well as an inclusive sanctification.

6.2.6 CONCLUSION

Do we need the concept of representation to understand the Christology of John?

To answer this question, I started with the incarnation. In the passages where 'σάρξ' is used designating Jesus, I found no representative connotations. Nevertheless, the use of this word indicates the deepness of his identification with sinful humanity. Further the word 'σάρξ' is used in relation to the cross, where he gave his flesh for us. The title 'Son of man' contained no representative connotations, either, but is used in passages expressing Christ's uniqueness. This is also the case in most of the 'I am'-sayings. Further the death of Jesus is mostly seen as unique and exclusive. This all leads to the conclusion that the exclusive moment is very important for John. The concept of substitution is useful in understanding John's Christology.

However, the inclusive moment is not absent and can be combined with the exclusive moment. More representative connotations were found in the vine-metaphor. They might be present in the designation of Jesus as 'Son of God.' Finally, we found some passages that clearly contain the inclusive moment.

To conclude, substitution is more important than representation for John, but we need both to understand John, and they do not exclude each other.[152]

6.3 Soteriology

Now I turn from Christology to soteriology. Of governing interest is the use of the expressions related to 'being in Christ,' and the question whether the concept of participation is necessary to reconstruct the Johannine view of soteriology. I start with the question how John uses expressions

152. Cf. the scheme Carson gives (Carson, *Divine Sovereignty and Human Responsibility*, 160):

GOD } *Over against man:* Jesus stands with God in
Over against God: Jesus stands with { JESUS } revelation and authority
man in obedience and dependence MAN.

like ἐν αὐτῷ and ἐν ἐμοι (6.3.1). Next I turn to images he uses for unity with Christ (6.3.2), and finally I search for other motifs in which the idea of participation can be found (6.3.3). 6.3.4 formulates the conclusions of 6.3.

6.3.1 COMMUNION: RECIPROCAL INTERIORITY

In 6.2.2 I investigated the parallels drawn between the relation Father-Son and the relation Christ-disciples concentrating on the Father-Son relation. We found that in the gospel a parallel is drawn with regard to the dependency of the Son on the Father for his life (6:57), the reciprocal intimate communion of knowing each other (10:14–15), the unity in works and words showing a deeper unity of reciprocal interiority (14:20; cf. 10:38; 14:10–11), the 'remaining in' as remaining in someone's love (15:9–10), the being sent into the world (17:18), the gift of glory (17:22) and the 'being in' (17:23). Further we found other parallels: the unity between Father and Son is parallel to the unity among the disciples (17:11, 21, 22), and the love of the Father for his Son is like the love of the Father for the disciples (17:23). Finally, it can be said that the disciples are in the Father and in the Son (17:21). Just as the Son is dependent on his Father—living by his Father, being loved by his Father, obedient to the sending of his Father, receiving glory from his Father, his Father being in him—the disciples are dependent on Jesus. The Son represents the disciples or the true Israel in his relation with his Father. At the same time he is the divine, loving source of life for his disciples. We saw that the mutual remaining or being in does not lead to dissolution of identity. Instead, the inhabitation of the Father in the Son gives the Son his identity.

Now I want to continue this investigation, concentrating on the relation Jesus Christ—disciples. I will investigate the use of the different expressions with ἐν as far as they are relevant for this project. Again a central question is whether the concepts of representation and participation are necessary to understand John's use of these expressions.

Within recent research with regard to the expressions with ἐν, these concepts do not play a central role.[153] Central in the interpretation of Heise is the speech of Jesus and the *place* it opens up. His speech, his imperative

153. For a more complete survey of recent research and the different positions within the discussion, see Scholtissek, *In ihm sein und bleiben*, 7–22. See futher also Crump, 'Re-examining the Johannine Trinity.'

to remain, opens up and secures a place of new being, resulting from the presence of God in Jesus Christ.[154]

Malatesta focuses on the fulfilment of the promise of the New Covenant (Jer 31:31–34; Ezek 11:19–20; 36:25–27). The interiority indicated by the expressions with ἐν must be understood against this background. The idea of representation does play a role. In Jesus the New Covenant is realised, he represents the covenant people. Nevertheless, the expressions with ἐν do not refer to a concept of representation, but of *interiority*. The interiority expressions are used 'as an especially apt manner of describing the interior nature of the New Covenant communion.'[155]

Jerumanis has investigated the communion with God in John, concentrating on believing, living and remaining. God has the initiative, but the human being also plays its role, believing and loving. The expressions with ἐν show some aspects of the mysterious communion with God. Hence *communion* is a central concept in his research.[156]

Scholtissek, finally, starts with the problem of the relation between transcendence and immanence. After a careful analysis of the language of 'Immanenz' he concludes that this problem is overcome by the *communio* opened by Christ. The language of reciprocal immanence refers to a relationality of reciprocal immanence, originally present within the relation Father-Son and graciously opened in the relation Father/Son-believers. It is this communion that results in identity. Here central concepts are *Immanenz* and *communion.*[157]

Before dealing with questions concerning the expressions with ἐν I give a classification of different expressions as far as they are theologically relevant:[158]

154. Heise, *Bleiben*, 173–74.

155. Malatesta, *Interiority and Covenant*, 24. See further 10–12. Problem with his interpretation is that an immediate derivation from the expressions with ἐν and the idea of the Old Testament concept of covenant cannot be proved from the text of the Johannine literature, for the word 'covenant' is not used. See the excursus 'New Covenant?' in 6.2.2.

156. Jerumanis, *Realiser la communion avec Dieu*, 408–11, 474, 495–96.

157. Scholtissek, *In ihm sein und bleiben*, 364–73.

158. This classification is made purely on grammatical grounds. I have drawn no distinction with regard to the non-personal objects between objects related to the sphere of God and to the opposite sphere, or between positive or negative statements in order to keep it brief.

For other overviews, see Jerumanis, *Realiser la communion avec Dieu*, 412–49; Malatesta, *Interiority and Covenant*, 24–36; Scholtissek, *In ihm sein und bleiben*, 151–61.

A. The subject is personal
1. God, He
a. with believers as personal object
- with the verb μένειν (God remains in believers)[159]
- without a verb (God in believers) [160]

b. with a non-personal object (God is in *x*)[161]

2. Father, You
a. with the Son as personal object
- with the verb εἶναι (The Father is in the Son)[162]
- with the verb μένειν (The Father remains in the Son)[163]
- without a verb (The Father in the Son)[164]

3. Son, I
a. with a personal object
i. Father
- with the verb εἶναι (I am in the Father)[165]
- without a verb (The Son in the Father)[166]

ii. Believers
- with the verb μένειν (The Son remains in believers)[167]
- without a verb (The Son in believers)[168]

b. with a non-personal object
- with the verb εἶναι (The Son was in *x*)[169]
- with the verb μένειν (The Son remains in *x*)[170]
- with another verb[171]

4. Spirit
a. with believers as personal object
- with the verb εἶναι (The Spirit is in believers)[172]

159. 1 John. 3:24 (2x), 4:12, 13, 15, 16.

160. 1 John 4:4.

161. In the light, 1 John 1:7.

162. John 14:10.

163. John 14:10.

164. John 10:38; 14:11; 17:21, 23.

165. John 14:10.

166. John 10:38; 14:11; 17:21.

167. John 6:56; 15:3, 5.

168. John 14:20; 17:23, 26.

169. In the world, John 1:10; 9:5.

170. His love, John 15:10.

171. ἔρχομαι in the world, John 12:46.

172. John 14:17.

5. Believers
   a. with a personal object
      i. God
         - with the verb εἶναι (Believers are in God)[173]
         - with the verb μένειν (Believers remain in God)[174]
      ii. Son, Jesus Christ, me
         - with the verb εἶναι (Believers are in the Son)[175]
         - with the verb μένειν (Believers remain in me)[176]
         - without a verb[177]
      iii. Father and Son, Us
         - with the verb εἶναι (Believers are in us)[178]
         - with the verb μένειν (Believers remain in Father / Son)[179]
      iv. indefinite divine object (God, Jesus Christ?)—Him
         - with the verb εἶναι (Believers are in Him)[180]
         - with the verb μένειν (Believers remain in Him)[181]
   b. with a non-personal object
         - with the verb εἶναι (Believers are in *x*)[182]
         - with the verb μένειν (Believers remain in *x*)[183]
         - with another verb (Believers do in *x*)[184]
   c. with a personal and a non-personal object
         - with another verb (Believers have *x* in Christ)[185]
6. Sinner
   a. with a non-personal object
         - with the verb εἶναι (Someone is in *x*)[186]

173. 1 John 5:20 (in him who is true).

174. 1 John 3:24; 4:13, 15, 16.

175. 1 John 5:20.

176. John 6:56; 15:3, 4, 6, 7; 1 John 3:6.

177. John 14:20.

178. John 17:21.

179. 1 John 2:24.

180. 1 John 2:5.

181. 1 John 2:6, 27, 28.

182. In the world, John 17:10; in the light, 1 John 2:9.

183. In my word, John 8:31; not in the darkness, John 12:46; in my love, John 15:9, 10; in the love, 1 John 4:16; in the light, 1 John 2:10.

184. περιπατέω in the darkness, 1 John 1:6; in the light 1 John 1:7.

185. ἵνα πᾶς ὁ πιστεύων ἐν αὐτῷ ἔχῃ ζωὴν αἰώνιον, John 3:15; ἐν ἐμοὶ εἰρήνην ἔχητε, John 16:33.

186. In the darkness, 1 John 2:9, 11.

- with the verb μένειν (Someone remains in *x*)[187]
- with another verb (Someone does in *x*)[188]

B. The subject is non-personal

a. with a personal object

i. God

- with the verb εἶναι (Something is in God)[189]
- with another verb (Something does in God)[190]

ii. The Son, me

- with the verb εἶναι (Something is in Christ)[191]
- without a verb (Something in me)[192]

iii. Believers

- with the verb εἶναι (Something is in believers)[193]
- with the verb μένειν (Something remains in believers)[194]
- without a verb (Something in believers)[195]
- with another verb (Something does in believers)[196]

iv. Sinner

- with the verb εἶναι (Something is in someone)[197]
- with the verb μένειν (Something remains in someone)[198]

b. with a non-personal object (Something is in something)[199]

187. In the death, 1 John 3:14.

188. ἀποθανῆσκω in sin, John 8:21, 24.

189. No darkness, 1 John 1:5.

190. Works done in God, John 3:21.

191. Truth, 1 John 2:8; life, John 1:4; 1 John 5:11.

192. Branch, John 15:2.

193. Light, John 12:35; my joy, John 15:11; σκάνδαλον ἐν αὐτῷ οὐκ ἔστιν, 1 John 2:10.

194. My words, John 15:7; the word of God, 1 John 2:14; that what you have heard from the beginning, 1 John 2:24 (2x); the anointing, 1 John 2:27; no sin, 1 John 3:5; his seed, 1 John 3:9.

195. Love, John 17:26.

196. τὸ ὕδωρ . . . ενήσεται ἐν αὐτῷ πηγη., John 4,14; ἔχωσιν τὴν χαρὰν τὴν ἐμὴ ν πεπληρωμένην ἐν ἑαυτοῖς, John 17:13; ἐν τούτῳ ἡ ἀγάπη τοῦ θεοῦ τετελείωται, 1 John 2:5.

197. Not the truth, 1 John 1:8; 2:4; not his word, 1 John 1:10; not the love of the Father, 1 John 2:15; no eternal life, 1 John 3:15.

198. Not his word, John 5:38.

199. John 1:5; 1 John 2:15; 4:18.

Having made this classification, I now want to deal more detailed with some issues related to 'being in Christ.'

Expressions with Believers as Subject and a Personal Object

The first concerns personal objects of expressions with ἐν with believers as subject (A.5.a). In whom are the believers?

In the gospel it is said that believers are in Jesus Christ. This occurs six times with 'me' referring to the Son, in combination with the metaphors of the living bread (John 6) and the vine (John 15), and in John 14:20. It is not said that the Spirit plays a role in this being in the Son, as it is never said that the believer is 'in the Spirit.'[200] In the prayer in John 17 a new possibility appears: Jesus prays that those who believe in Jesus through the word of his disciples 'may be in us' (17:21; my translation). The Father alone is never object, but now he becomes involved together with his Son. The Father lives in unity with his Son. When the disciples receive a unity among each other comparable with the unity of Father and Son, they receive at the same time their being in 'us,' referring to Father and Son. Consequently, in the gospel the being in the Son leads to and results in a being in Son and Father.[201]

In the first letter only a few passages are clear. The Son is mentioned several times together with God or the Father. In 2:24 the author writes that if what they have heard from the beginning remains in them, they will remain in the Son and the Father. Next in 1 John 5:20 we are told that the Son came and gave us understanding of ὁ ἀληθινὸς and that we are ἐν τῷ ἀληθινῷ ἐν τῷ υἱῷ αὐτοῦ Ἰησοῦ Χριστῷ. Although in the following clause Jesus Christ is identified with the true God, 'ὁ ἀληθινὸς θεὸς,' Jesus Christ is also seen as the Son of the true one who gave knowledge of the true one. Consequently, also in 1 John 5:20 it is said that we are in the Son as well as in God. But also: we are in the true God being in his Son. The being in the Son results in being in God.[202] Like in the gospel, the Spirit is never object in the first letter.[203] God is object twice in 1 John

200. Malatesta, *Interiority and Covenant*, 34.

201. Carson, *The Gospel according to John*, 568; Van Houwelingen, *Johannes*, 344; Ridderbos, *Het evangelie naar Johannes*, Dl. 2, 216.

202. Lalleman, *1, 2 en 3 Johannes*, 216; Malatesta, *Interiority and Covenant*, 274, 321–23; Smalley, *1, 2 en 3 John*, 306–7.

203. Malatesta, *Interiority and Covenant*, 34.

4:15, 16. Here remaining in God is related to the confession that Jesus is the Son of God and with remaining in the love.

Five other passages are less clear. In these passages where John writes seven times that we are or remain 'in him,' it is difficult to distinguish to whom John refers. The first concerns 1 John 2:5, 6. In 1 John 2, John starts writing about the Father and our advocate. He continues about knowing αὐτόν and about his commands (2:3 and again in 2:4). Against the background of chapter 1 it is reasonable to presuppose that knowing him (2:3) refers to knowing God,[204] but if 'αὐτόν' refers to the person mentioned last, Jesus Christ must be referent.[205] 'His commands' might refer to God's commands,[206] but in the gospel Jesus speaks from my commands (John 14:15, 21; 15:10). God is mentioned explicitly in 2:5 (the love of God), so that the being in him (2:5) could refer to being in God. Nevertheless, the sentence with the being in him (2:5) and remaining in him (2:6) closes with an example that must be followed: walk as 'ἐκεῖνος' has walked (2:6). The person's example that must be followed can only be Jesus' example, for in the first letter, 'ἐκεῖνος' always refers to Jesus.[207] Consequently, in 2:5 and 6 being and remaining in him can both be defended as referring to God and to Jesus Christ.[208]

The second passage is 1 John 2:27–28. In 2:24 John writes about being in the Son and the Father. Then we find a 'remaining in him' in 2:27. In this verse, we read about the 'χρῖσμα' that we received from 'him.' Did they receive the χρῖσμα from Jesus or from God? Subsequently, after continuing about the χρῖσμα that teaches, an imperative follows: remain ἐν αὐτῷ, which might refer to the χρῖσμα, to Jesus or to God. The first possibility is less plausible for we do not find it anywhere else in Johannine literature. Still it remains open whether the second or the third possibility

204. Malatesta, *Interiority and Covenant*, 120, 124.

205. Carson, *The Gospel according to John*, 122.

206. Malatesta, *Interiority and Covenant*, 124.

207. Lalleman, *1, 2 en 3 Johannes*, 108; S. S. Smalley, *1, 2, 3 John*, 52; cf. 1 John 2:6; 3:3, 5, 7, 16; 4:17.

208. Smalley leaves the reference open, see S. S. Smalley, *1, 2, 3 John*, 50. Carson sees a community with Father and Son, see Carson, *The Gospel according to John*, 127. Although this passage is ambiguous according to Malatesta, he finally chooses God as reference, just as Scholtissek does, see Malatesta, *Interiority and Covenant*, 123; Scholtissek, *In ihm sein und bleiben*, 353. Lalleman writes that it is plausible that in 2:3–5 is referred to God, and in 2,6 to Jesus, Lalleman, *1, 2 en 3 Johannes*, 143.

is intended.[209] In 2:28 again we find 'remain in him,' followed by a clause 'when he appears,' referring to the coming of Jesus at the *parousia*.[210] Consequently, 'remain in him' refers probably to Jesus.

The third passage is 3:6. This is relatively clear. In 3:3, 5, 7 we find again three times 'ἐκεῖνος,' which refers to Jesus.[211] Therefore, in 3:6 the being in him refers most likely to being in Jesus.

The last two are parallel passages, 3:24 and 4:13, both referring to the gift of the Spirit. In 3:21–23 God is subject and 'his commands' in 3:21–23a must be Gods commands. Hence it is plausible that in 3:23–24 also Gods commands are meant, although in 3:23 also 'his Son Jesus Christ' is mentioned. The keeping of his commands in 3:22 returns in 3:24. This is related to the remaining in 'him,' which consequently refers to remaining in God. The parallel in 4:13 reinforces this, for here it is clear that God is subject: this is explicitly the case in 4:12, so that the remaining in him refers to remaining in God. To conclude, in 3:24 and 4:13 the remaining in him is a remaining in God.[212]

We see that often the 'him' is ambiguous and the emphasis changes from an emphasis on God to an emphasis on Jesus and back again. In 2:5, 6 and 2:27 the referent is not clear, whereas in 3:6 and probably in 2:28 a reference to Jesus is found. In 3:24 and 4:13 the remaining in him is a remaining in God. This shows that in the first letter the emphasis has shifted in line with John 17. The Son brings us into communion with himself as well as with his Father. Or, if they are viewed together: he brings us into communion with God.

According to the gospel, believers are in Jesus Christ and 'in us,' referring to Son and Father. According to the first letter believers are in 'him,' which means in Jesus Christ or in God. This difference is caused by a difference in speaker. Within the gospel, the expressions with ἐν are words of Jesus himself. The Son refers to his 'Father,' to himself as 'me'

209. Accoring to Lalleman and Smalley this verse refers to remaining in Christ; Lalleman, *1, 2 en 3 Johannes*, 165; S. S. Smalley, *1, 2, 3 John*, 127.

210. Frey, *Die johanneische Eschatologie*, Bd. III, 83–85; Lalleman, *1, 2 en 3 Johannes*, 167; Strecker, *Die Johannesbriefe*, 142. Smalley also sees it as the coming of Jesus, but denies that this coming must be limited to the *parousia*, see Smalley, *1, 2, 3 John*, 132.

211. Lalleman, *1, 2 en 3 Johannes*, 173; Smalley, *1, 2, 3 John*, 148; see also footnote 207.

212. Lalleman, *1, 2 en 3 Johannes*, 182–83; Malatesta, *Interiority and Covenant*, 273–74; Scholtissek, *In ihm sein und bleiben*, 353; Smalley, *1, 2, 3 John*, 210; against Strecker, *Die Johannesbriefe*, 203.

and to his disciples, not to 'God.' In the first letter it is the author who utters them. He refers to God, to the Son or to 'him.'[213] Because God is God in Christ and Christ is God in unity with the Father, theology and Christology are not alternatives in the first letter. Consequently, John can easily shift from Jesus to God, making it difficult to discern, in several cases, whether a 'he' refers to God or to Jesus.[214]

Expressions with Believers as Object and a Personal Subject

Secondly, we need to deal with expressions with believers as object and a personal subject (A.1.a.ii; A.3.a.ii; A.4.a). Who is in believers?

In the gospel, apart from John 17:23, 26 these expressions with believers as object are all reciprocal expressions spoken by Jesus with the form 'he/ you in me, I in him / you.' We find the reciprocal expressions in John 6:56 (the living bread), in 14:20, and in 15:3, 5 (the vine). Further, in the gospel believers are object once with the Spirit as subject (John 14:17). In the gospel, it is the Son and once the Spirit who are in the believers, but never the Father or God.

In the first letter, the personal subject always is God. We find expressions with believers as object as non-reciprocal expressions (3:24; 4:4, 12), as reciprocal expressions of the form 'he in God, God in him' (3:24; 4:13, 16) and as a reciprocal expression of the form 'God in him, he in God' (4:15).

To conclude, in the gospel, it is the Son who is or remains in the believers, in the first letter, it is God. In both the Spirit at first sight does not play a central role; he is the subject only once in an expression with ἐν (Joh 14:17).[215] This difference can again be understood by the difference in speaker: in the gospel Christology is central because of the centrality of the words of Jesus who is speaking, in the first letter Christology and theology are not alternatives.

Reciprocal Expressions

Thirdly, the reciprocal expressions deserve our attention. It is important to see when expressions with ἐν are reciprocal and when not.

213. Malatesta, *Interiority and Covenant*, 33, 35.

214. Frey, *Die johanneische Eschatologie*, Bd. III, 90; Lalleman, *1, 2 en 3 Johannes*, 108; Malatesta, *Interiority and Covenant*, 124; Scholtissek, *In ihm sein und bleiben*, 358.

215. Cf. Malatesta, *Interiority and Covenant*, 33–35.

a. In the gospel we find four reciprocal expressions with Father and Son as the two subjects and two non-reciprocal expressions with the Father as subject and the Son as object (A.2, A.3.a.i). But these two non-reciprocal expressions follow immediately upon a reciprocal expression (14:10) or show how believers are involved in the communion of Father and Son (17:23). Consequently, the Father-Son relation is a relation of reciprocal being (or remaining, 14:10) in the other. With regard to the relation between the subjects, it is remarkable that the Son is never subject of a non-reciprocal expression, whereas the Father is subject twice (14:10; 17:23); further, twice it is said 'the Father is in me—I am in the Father' (10:38; 17:21) and twice 'I am in the Father—the Father is in me' (14:10, 11). I will deal with these four passages in more detail to see whether more can be said on the relation between Father and Son.

In John 10, the discussion is whether Jesus is allowed to say that he and the Father are one (10:30), that he is the Son of God (10:36) or does what his Father does (10:37). He claims to do works in the name of the Father (10:25) and that the Father gave him his sheep (10:29). Jesus makes decisive the question whether he does the works of his Father or not. If he does, then the Jews need to acknowledge 'that the Father is in me and I in the Father' (10:38). Here the primacy of the Father is very clear and consequently the order of 'the Father in me—I in the Father' understandable.

In John 17 again the primacy of the Father is very clear. The Son prays to his Father. The Father is the one who sent the Son (17:21, 23), who gave the Son his glory (17:22), who loved the Son (17:23, 24) and who gave things to the Son (17:24). Again the order of 'the Father in me—I in the Father' (17:21) is understandable.

In John 14 a different issue is at stake. The question is how Jesus is the way to the Father (14:6) and how it must be understood that to see and to know Jesus is to see and to know the Father (14:7–9). Now the order is the reverse: 'I am in the Father—the Father is in me' (14:10–11). The Son is the way to the Father because he is already in the Father and is going to the Father's house (14:2–4). Paradoxically this reverse order again shows the primacy of the Father: it is not that the Father is in Jesus and that consequently Jesus has the power to make the Father known. On the contrary, Jesus is already in his Father and it is not his activity that makes the Father known. The Father is the greater One and the place where he is has the primacy. It is the Father who does his works, remaining in Jesus (14:10).

To conclude with regard to reciprocal expressions with Father and Son as subject, the relation between Father and Son is a relation of reciprocal being in each other. The Father has the primacy in this relation, but depending on the context the order within a sentence may change. Consequently, the Son is never subject alone, whereas the Father is. The Son is the one who opens this reciprocal communion to believers.

b. Further we find in the gospel (A.3.a.ii; A.5.a.ii) four reciprocal expressions with the Son and the believers as subjects (6:56; 14:20;15:3, 5), two non-reciprocal expressions with the Son as subject (17:23, 26) and four non-reciprocal expressions with the believers as subject (15:4, 6, 7; 17:21).

In John 6 Jesus presents himself as the living bread, who gives his flesh to eat and his blood to drink (6:51, 53–54). Then he says in 6:56: 'Whoever eats my flesh and drinks my blood remains in me and I in him, ἐν ἐμοὶ μένει κἀγὼ ἐν αὐτῷ.' Jesus does not say that when we eat his flesh and drink his blood, he will remain in us and (consequently) we in him. It is not our eating and drinking that is decisive. For if we eat and drink and believe in him, first of all we remain in him and secondly he remains in us. He has the primacy, as 6:57 makes clear again: he who eats Jesus, will live because of him.[216]

The second passage is 14:20. Here Jesus elaborates what he said in 14:10–11.[217] At that moment the disciples might not understand that Jesus is the way to the Father and that to see and know Jesus is to see and know God, because the Son is in the Father and the Father in the Son. However, the day will come that they will know that Jesus is in his Father and the disciples in Jesus and Jesus in them (14:20). Just as the Son is at home with the Father, being in him, and just as the Father works in the Son, being in the Son, they will know 'ἐν ἐκείνῃ τῇ ἡμέρα' (see below) that they are at home with the Son, being in him and that the Son works in them, being in his disciples. The relation Father-Son is paralleled with the relation

216. Carson, *The Gospel according to John*, 299; Van Houwelingen, *Johannes*, 160; Schnackenburg, *Das Johannesevangelium*, Bd. II, 94.

217. Schnackenburg, *Das Johannesevangelium*, Bd. III, 90; Scholtissek, *In ihm sein und bleiben*, 260–61.

Son-disciples including its characteristics. Whereas in the first relation the Father has the primacy, in the second the Son is first.[218]

The third passage, where we find reciprocal and non-reciprocal expressions, is John 15:1–10. Jesus says he is the true vine. His introduction immediately makes clear what the emphasis of this metaphor is: that his disciples will be fruitful (15:2).[219] Presupposed is the fact that the disciples are already clean (15:3).[220] Because they are the branches and branches can bear no fruit unless they remain in the vine (15:4), the disciples are exhorted to remain in Christ.[221] Twice this exhortation is voiced with the help of a reciprocal expression: they must remain in Christ and he in them, 'ἐν ἐμοί κἀγὼ ἐν ὑμῖν' (15:4, 5). Whereas the Father-Son relation is a reciprocal relation wherein the reciprocal character is not threatened, this is not the case in the Son-disciples relation. Although the disciples are clean and although the Son has loved them (15:9), they do not automatically remain in him. This becomes very clear in the non-reciprocal exhortations in 15:4 and 6. Here the problem is not that the branches do not bear fruit because of a lack in the vine, but the danger is that the branches bear no fruit because they are separated from the vine.[222] Hence the 'κἀγὼ ἐν ὑμῖν' cannot be understood as if the disciples bring Christ to remain in them by remaining in Christ. Instead, it must be understood as a promise[223] and the remaining of Christ in them is presupposed as long as they do not separate themselves from Christ. The disciples have to keep the words of Christ within themselves (15:7) and remain in Christ's love (15:9).[224] If they do so, they will by doing so and asking whatever they wish (15:7) remain in Christ and he will remain in them. To conclude, Jesus has the primacy as source of life. The life-giving com-

218. Schnackenburg, *Das Johannesevangelium*, Bd. III, 90.

219. Carson, *The Gospel according to John*, 515.

220. Ridderbos, *Het evangelie naar Johannes*, Dl. 2, 167; Schnackenburg, *Das Johannesevangelium*, Bd. III, 111.

221. Carson, *The Gospel according to John*, 516; Van Houwelingen, *Johannes*, 311; Ridderbos, *Het evangelie naar Johannes*, Dl. 2 167–68; Schnackenburg, *Das Johannesevangelium*, Bd. III, 112.

222. Carson, *The Gospel according to John*, 517; Schnackenburg, *Das Johannesevangelium*, Bd. III, 114.

223. Schnackenburg, *Das Johannesevangelium*, Bd. III, 115.

224. Carson, *The Gospel according to John*, 517; Van Houwelingen, *Johannes*, 311–12; Ridderbos, *Het evangelie naar Johannes*, Dl. 2 169; Schnackenburg, *Das Johannesevangelium*, Bd. III, 115–16.

munion with him is threatened, for the branches risk the danger of being separated from the vine. As long as this exhortation is necessary, the Son-disciples relation does not have the character of a non-problematically reciprocal relation.

Finally John 17:20–26 is an important passage, although we do not find a reciprocal expression in these verses. Three non-reciprocal expressions are used with the Son or the believer as subject. The Father and the Son together form a communion of reciprocal 'being in' (17:21), of glory (17:22), of unity (17:21) and love (17:23). Within this communion the Father has the primacy as we have seen. The Son's prayer is that believers may participate to some extent within this communion. Because it is a complex passage, we need to read carefully to see what he prays. The Son says he gave the believers his glory (17:22) and prays that his Father makes evident that he loved the believers with the same love as he loved his Son (17:23). Further he prays that believers among themselves may have the same unity as Father and Son have together (17:21) and that they may be at the same place where he is to make them see his glory (17:24). He prays that the love of the Father for the Son may be in the believers (17:26).[225] The Son does not pray that believers may immediately become part of the unity of Father and Son, but that they all may have unity among each other as Father and Son are one (17:22) and as Father and Son are in each other (17:21, 23). Although the unity of Father and Son is distinguished from the unity of believers among each other, and the unity of Father, Son and believers is never spoken of,[226] at the same time the prayer of the Son is that the believers may be in us (17:21) and that he may be in the believers and the Father in him (17:23). Because these formulations follow on a prayer for unity, some relation exists between the unity believers have among themselves and their being 'in us' or the Son being in them and the Father in the Son.[227] In conclusion, the relation between Father and Son remains unique, the Son mediates the communion of believers with God and makes believers to some extent participate within his position,

225. Scholtissek, *In ihm sein und bleiben*, 332.

226. Ridderbos, *Het evangelie naar Johannes*, Dl. 2, 217; Scholtissek, *In ihm sein und bleiben*, 338. Against Schnackenburg, see Schnackenburg, *Das Johannesevangelium*, Bd. III, 217, 219–20.

227. Carson, *The Gospel according to John*, 567; Van Houwelingen, *Johannes*, 343, Ridderbos, *Het evangelie naar Johannes*, Dl. 2, 217–18, Schnackenburg, *Das Johannesevangelium* , Bd. III, 217, Scholtissek, *In ihm sein und bleiben*, 335.

consequently opening the communion of God's love to the same extent for believers.[228] Hence a communion—not a unity—is formed[229] in which the Father is the source of all and the Son is the source of all for the believers. This is not a communion of a reciprocal being in each other from two persons, but three: Father—Son—believers.

To conclude, in the gospel we find formulations of reciprocal being or remaining in not only with regard to Father and Son, but also with regard to the Son and the disciples.[230] The four passages where we find the second category give two different views. John 6 and 15 emphasise that without Jesus the believer has no life and bears no fruit. Hence the communion with Jesus must be maintained: the believer must remain in Christ and Christ in the believer. This communion is not a perfect reciprocal communion, but a threatened communion in need of the exhortation to believe and remain in Christ. John 14 and 17 show that believers will participate to some extent in the perfect communion of reciprocal 'being in' each other, which Father and Son have together. John 17, more than John 14 eleborates how believers, Son and Father will be related.[231] In both views the Son has the primacy.

c. In the first letter no expressions with ἐν are used to say something about the relation between Father and Son or about the Son being in the believers.[232] All expressions refer to the relation between God (A.1.a; A.5.a.i) or Jesus Christ (A.5.a.ii) and the believer. Four are explicitly reciprocal (3:24; 4:13, 15, 16). Three non-reciprocal expressions have God as subject (3:24; 4:4, 12), the other have the believer as subject (2:5, 6, 24, 27, 28; 3:6; 5:20).

The first two non-reciprocal expressions we find in 2:5–6. In the preceding verses Jesus Christ is presented as the righteous one and as atoning sacrifice. Next a criterion is mentioned to determine that we know Christ: if we obey his commands (2:3). This is elaborated in 2:4–6. We know that

228. Cf. the analysis of Wierenga, see Wierenga, *Verhalen als bewijzen*, 328–34.

229. According to Scholtissek we can speak from a *vita communis* in God, but not from a *unio christianorum cum deo et in deo*, Scholtissek, *In ihm sein und bleiben*, 338.

230. Jerumanis, *Realiser la communion avec Dieu*, 405.

231. According to Malatesta John 14:20 is unique within the gospel, speaking from a reciprocal being in of Son and disciples. He compares this verse with John 17:21 where is said that the believers may be 'in us.' This confirms that John 14:20 and 17:20–26 give an other view than John 6 and 15. See Malatesta, *Interiority and Covenant*, 35.

232. Scholtissek, *In ihm sein und bleiben*, 354.

we are in him, if we obey his word and the love of God is made complete in us (2:5).[233] Whoever claims to remain in Christ must walk as Jesus walked himself (2:6).[234] To know Christ, to be in Christ and to remain in Christ are used here as parallel expressions. The issue here is not our communion with Christ or his knowledge of us, but only our knowledge of him. Hence it is understandable that no reciprocal expressions are used. The issue here is the reliability of someone's claim to know Christ.

The second group of non-reciprocal expressions we find in 2:24–28. These verses follow a passage dealing with the antichrist. John reminds his readers of the anointing they received and their knowledge of the truth (2:20). He exhorts them to keep to their confession of the Son, to prevent them from losing Christ and the Father. What they have heard from the beginning must remain in them. If this happens, they will remain in the Son and in the Father (2:24). The anointing they have received also teaches them to remain in 'him' (2:27). Again the exhortation returns to remain in 'him' (2:28), referring to the coming appearance of Christ. In these verses the emphasis is on loyalty to the received anointing and teaching. Hence a non-reciprocal expression is logical. However, not only the human activity but also the divine is mentioned: the anointment and the received knowledge.

1 John 3:6 is a verse within the next section on the appearance of Christ and his righteousness. To not be ashamed at the coming appearance of Christ it is necessary to purify oneself from sin, for Christ came to take away sin and Christ is righteous. Because in Christ is no sin (3:5), no one who remains in Christ keeps on sinning (3:6). This expression is non-reciprocal, for the emphasis is on the human remaining and purifying. Nevertheless, the context mentions also the divine love, the birth of God, the adoption as God's children and the coming of the Son of God to take away sins.

The first reciprocal expression we find is in 3:24. For the first time it is not just said that whoever obeys God's commands remains in God, but also that God remains in him.[235] This verse is special for another reason, for it is the first time in the letter that God is subject of a (non-reciprocal)

233. Lalleman, *1, 2 en 3 Johannes*, 145–46; Marshall, *The Epistles of John*, 124; Smalley, *1, 2, 3 John*, 50; Strecker, *Die Johannesbriefe*, 96–98.

234. Lalleman, *1, 2 en 3 Johannes*, 147; Marshall, *The Epistles of John*, 126–28; Smalley, *1, 2, 3 John*, 52–53; Strecker, *Die Johannesbriefe*, 99.

235. Smalley, *1, 2, 3 John*, 210.

expression. Moreover, it does not give a criterion for our remaining in God (as was the case in 2:5, 6) but for God's remaining in us.[236] The criterion is the Spirit, given by God, mentioned now more explicitly than in 2:20, 27 where the Spirit was designated as 'anointment.' This first reciprocal expression concurs with more attention for God's activity toward us.

A second verse with an expression with ἐν and God as subject is 4:4. The theme here is the testing of the spirits whether they are from God or not. The readers of the letter are from God and they have overcome the false prophets of this world, for God is in them and he is greater than the one who is in the world. The presence of God makes the believers conquerors. The expression is not reciprocal in the strict sense of the word, but the idea is reciprocal: they are from God, God is in them.

A central passage is 4:12–16, where we find a non-reciprocal expression with God as subject and three reciprocal expressions. It starts in 4:7 with the admonition to love, for God is love. Love is a movement starting with God and not with us (4:10). If we love each other, God remains in us (4:12). This presupposes that God is already in us. John continues with a repetition of the criterion given in 3:24, but now in a reciprocal form. 'We know that we remain in him and he in us, because he has given us of his Spirit' (4:13; my translation). Further the idea of 2:22–24 is repeated but now also in reciprocal form, that God remains in the one who confesses Jesus as the Son of God and that he remains in God (4:15). And finally the identification of God as love results in the last reciprocal expression, that 'who remains in love, remains in God and God remains in him' (4:16; my translation). The order does not seem relevant now, for it can be said that remaining in love God remains in us (4:12) but also that we remain in God and God in us (4:16), and the order of reciprocal expressions changes within 4:13–16 three times. The love of God is fundamental, and has the primacy,[237] but this results in a reciprocal relation of love without fear.

Finally a non-reciprocal expression is used in 5:20. Here God and the world are contrasted (5:18–19). It is our life that we know the true God and that we are in this true God as well as in his Son. The emphasis lies here on knowing God and not being in the world, which lies 'ἐν τῷ πονηρῷ.' Believers are from God and they are in God. It is reasonable that here only a non-reciprocal expression is used.

236. Malatesta, *Interiority and Covenant*, 274.

237. Smalley, *1, 2, 3 John*, 247.

In the use of reciprocal and non-reciprocal expressions a development can be discovered, marking a development in the letter as a whole: from God as light (1:5) to God as righteous (2:29) and God as love (4:8, 16); from an atoning sacrifice for sins (2:2) to purification from sin (3:3) and confidence on the day of judgment and absence of fear (4:17–18); from being and remaining in God and in Christ (2:5, 6, 27, 28) to God being and remaining in us (3:24; 4:4, 12); from more paranetic and exhorting passages in the first chapters to affirming passages on the victory of faith (4:4; 5:4, 5). During the letter, God comes more and more near, in a threefold pattern of *illuminatio—purgatio—unio*, or forgiveness—purification—communion. This movement can be seen very clear in 3:24, the first reciprocal expression and the first passage where God is subject of the remaining in us. Summarizing, if we come closer to God, God comes closer to us.

To conclude, in the first letter, the choice of non-reciprocal or reciprocal expressions has to be understood against the background of the context. With regard to the reciprocal character of communion with God, two things must be said. On the one hand, it is God who has the primacy. He is light, he gives his Son, believers are born from God, he makes us his children etc. He intends a communion with the character of reciprocal being and remaining in each other. On the other hand, the letter shows a process in which God comes closer and closer, being mentioned in the later part of the letter more explicitly as loving subject acting to remain in us. The believer needs exhortation to remain in God and to live a life without sin, fitting with God and Jesus Christ. During the process of reading, the communion is seen more and more as a reciprocal communion of love. Love and the reciprocal character of this communion belong together.

μένειν **and** εἶναι

A fourth issue concerns the question whether the preceding observations are confirmed by the use of μένειν and εἶναι. Does μένειν signal a less stable character of a reciprocal relation, whereas εἶναι represents another, more stable view of this relation?

a. With regard to the relation Father—Son in the gospel (A.2; A.3.a.i), once a reciprocal εἶναι ἐν is used (14:10), once a non-reciprocal μένειν ἐν with the Father as subject (14:10), and further expressions have no verb (10:38; 14:11; 17:21, 23). The μένειν ἐν in 14:10 is used to emphasise that Jesus is the way to the Father. The Father never stops being in his Son. The verb μένειν here emphasises the duration in time.[238] However, the stable character of this relation between Father and Son of reciprocal being in each other is not contested.[239]

b. The following observations can be made with regard to the relation Son—believers in the gospel (A.3.a.ii; A.5.a.ii). If the Son is subject, the verb μένειν is used in John 6:56 and 15:3, 5. No verb is used in John 14:20 and 17:23, 26. If the believer is subject, the verb μένειν is used again in John 6:56 and in 15:3, 4, 5, 6, 7. No verb is used in 14:20 and the verb εἶναι (as being in us, in Son and Father) is used in 17:21.

   This confirms that we find two different views of this relation: John 6 and 15 emphasising the need of some effort to remain in communion with Christ, and John 14 and 17 showing the participation in the perfect stable communion of reciprocal being in each other of Father and Son. Although the Son-disciples relation is not stable yet, if these words are uttered by Jesus in the story of the gospel, it has a stable future.[240]

c. In the first letter, the relation between God and the believer is expressed six times with the help of the verb μένειν where God is subject (3:24 (2x); 4:12, 13, 15, 16), one time without a verb (4:4) and never with the verb εἶναι (A.1.a).

When the believers are subject, five times the verb μένειν is used with God as object (3:24; 4:13, 15, 16; A.5.a.i), once with the Son as object (3:6; A.5.a.ii), once with Father and Son as object (2:24; A.5.a.iii), and three times with an indefinite divine object (2:6, 27, 28; A.5.a.iv). The verb εἶναι is used once with the Son Jesus Christ as well as God as object (5:20; A.5.a.i and ii) and once with an indefinite divine object (2:5; A.5.a.iv).

Over against the threats of self-deception, antichrist and false prophets, the readers are encouraged with the message that God is not only in

238. Jerumanis, *Realiser la communion avec Dieu*, 470.

239. Jerumanis, *Realiser la communion avec Dieu*, 471.

240. Frey, *Die johanneische Eschatologie*, Bd. II, 293–94; Jerumanis, *Realiser la communion avec Dieu*, 443, 471, 480.

them, but that he remains in them. And the readers are exhorted not to break the communion, but to remain in God.[241] The two passages where εἶναι is used together with 1 John 4:4 constitute an extra encouragement. The future already determines the present.

To conclude, generally speaking the verb εἶναι is used more with regard to the relation of Father and Son, the verb μένειν is used more with regard to the relation between God or Jesus Christ and believers.[242] The absence of a verb is equal to the use of the verb εἶναι. The verb μένειν is used often in a paranetical context.[243] Hence the relation between Father and Son is seen as more stable, whereas the relation between God or Jesus Christ and the believer is more in need of the consolation that God or the Son remains in the believer and the exhortation to remain in God or in Christ. Nevertheless, John 14:20 and 17:20–26 offer a different more future oriented view of a stable communion between God and the believer. In the letter this is presented as an encouraging present reality (1 John 2:5; 4:4; 5:20).

Singular and Plural

To see how important the collective of believers is, it is important to investigate whether the expressions with ἐν are used with verbs in singular or plural. Singular forms we find 8 times,[244] plural forms occur 23 times.[245] Within the gospel, three passages with a singular say that (everyone) who believes, receives salvation in Christ (3:15; 4:14; 6:56). One singular expression is a negative one, written in a passage with, furthermore, only plurals (15:6). All four singular forms in the first letter are expressions voicing a criterion for communion with God, which makes the use of the singular understandable. To conclude, the majority of plural forms seems to indicate that the collective is important to John. At the same time, personal involvement is necessary.[246]

241. Malatesta, *Interiority and Covenant*, 32.

242. Scholtissek, *In ihm sein und bleiben*, 365–66

243. Scholtissek, *In ihm sein und bleiben*, 365.

244. John 3:15; 4:14; 6:56; 15:6; 1 John 2:6; 3:6, 24; 4:15.

245. John 8:31; 14:17, 20; 15:3, 4, 5, 7, 8, 9; 16:33; 17:21, 23, 26; 1 John 2:5, 8, 24, 27, 28; 3:24; 4:4, 12, 13, 16; 5:20.

246. Cf. Jerumanis, who states that both the collective and the personal aspect are important, see Jerumanis, *Realiser la communion avec Dieu*, 469–70.

Local and Communal Concepts

As a next issue, we have to face the question whether the expressions with ἐν have a local character. The preposition ἐν can be used locally (literally or figuratively), causally or instrumentally.[247] It is used with the verbs εἶναι and μένειν. Used in this combination, ἐν is used always in a local sense.[248] This results in a intriguing combination of local expressions and a personal relationship, as is indicated by the central concepts used by the different authors: interiority (Malatesta), communion and reciprocal inhabitation (Jerumanis, Scholtissek), and *Immanenz* (Scholtissek). The nature of the relation between Father and Son, Jesus Christ and the disciples, and God and the believers makes it possible to say that the Father is in the Son and the Son in the Father, that Jesus Christ is in the disciples and the disciples are in Jesus Christ, and that God is in the believers and the believers are in God.

Because this combination of spatial and communal language is used in these three different relations, it cannot primarily be understood with the help of the representation-concept. It might theoretically be possible to understand the ideas of being and remaining in Christ with it, but this is impossible concerning the two other relations: God cannot represent believers over against God, and the Father does not represent his Son. Consequently, the expressions with ἐν and a personal subject and object must refer to a personal communion. We need concepts like interiority, communion and reciprocal inhabitation to understand its nature.

'Coordinates' of Communion with Christ

Within Johannine literature, not only persons can be subject or object of expressions with ἐν. Non-personal subjects and objects are used which we can call the 'coordinates' of the personal communion. I concentrate now on coordinates related semantically to the personal communion.

First these coordinates consist in salvation, which is in Jesus Christ: life (John 1:4; 1 John 5:11), eternal life (John 3:15) and peace (John 16:33).[249]

A second coordinate is the word, 'that what you have heard from the beginning' (1 John 2:24). This word causes cleanness, for Jesus said his disciples were clean because of the word he had spoken to them (John

247. Scholtissek, *In ihm sein und bleiben*, 143.

248. Jerumanis, *Realiser la communion avec Dieu*, 443, 466–67.

249. Cf. Marshall, *New Testament Theology*, 520.

15:3). The spoken and believed word somehow causes them to be in Christ and he in them, for Jesus continues that they must now remain in him and he in them (15:4). Further Jesus said that the believing Jews would truly be his disciples, if they remained in his word (John 8:31). It is not only possible to be in the word of Jesus, but his word also can and must be in us. His words must remain in us (John 15:7; 1 John 2:24) and we must obey his word (1 John 2:5) and his commands (John 15:10; 1 John 3:24; cf. 1 John 2:3). Doing this, God's love is made complete in us (1 John 2:5), we remain in the Son and the Father (1 John 2:24), and in God and God in us (1 John 3:24). Consequently, the word causes somehow our reciprocal being in each other with Christ or God. Further it plays a role in maintaining this communion and even in intensifying it, if we keep this word and if this word remains in us.[250]

A third coordinate is love. The love of Jesus for his disciples, loving them like his Father loves him, causes them to be in his love, for now they are exhorted to remain in his love. They can do this by keeping his commands (John 15:9–10) and his command is that they love each other (John 15:12; cf. 1 John 3:16). Loving each other we remain in the love as well as in God, and God remains in us (1 John 4,16).[251] Besides the disciples being in the love, the love is said to be in them. Jesus makes his Father's name known to his disciples to let the Father's love be in his disciples, and Jesus himself in them (John 17:26). Love results in this love being in the disciples and even in Jesus himself being in them. Loving someone results in the lover being in the loved one.[252] Further, the perfection of the presence of this love within us can increase. If we keep his words and love each other, God's love is perfected in us. This perfection of God's love is directly related to our being in God and God's remaining in us (1 John 2:5; 4:12). To conclude, the love of God has a primacy on the reciprocal interiority, but at the same time the presence of God's love in us can be perfected. It seems that this perfection of God's love within us coincides with an intensification of the presence of Jesus and of God in us.

A fourth coordinate is confessed faith. Dealing with John 6:56 (see 6.2.1) we saw that eating Jesus' flesh and drinking his blood, resulting in the eater remaining in Jesus and Jesus in the eater, has to be understood

250. Cf. Malatesta, *Interiority and Covenant*, 160, 202, 225, 249.

251. Scholtissek, *In ihm sein und bleiben*, 312.

252. Jerumanis, *Realiser la communion avec Dieu*, 478.

as an expression of a relation of confessing faith. This relation receives visible form in the eating and drinking in the Eucharist. In 1 John 4:15 we find an explicit relation between confession of faith in Jesus Christ and a remaining of the confessor in God and God in the confessor: 'Whoever confesses that Jesus is the Son of God, God remains in him and he in God' (my translation; cf. 1 John 2:22–23; 1 John 4:2–3). Believing in Christ and expressing this faith, we maintain our communion with him and in him with God.[253]

A fifth coordinate, the Holy Spirit, is not really non-personal. Nevertheless I want to mention it here, because in the first letter the Spirit is pointed out with 'ἐν τούτῳ' as a criterion for reciprocal 'remaining in' in a way comparable to that in which other coordinates are indicated as criterion (1 John 3:24; 4:13; cf. 1 John 2:3, 5; 3:10, 16, 19; 4:2, 6; 5:2). The first time this happens, the presence of the Spirit is a criterion for God remaining in us (1 John 3:24). The second time the presence of the Spirit indicates both God's remaining in believers as well as the remaining of believers in God (1 John 4:13).[254] Further the metaphor of the 'anointing' remaining in them, refers to the Spirit (2:20, 27). This reminds one of the gift of the Spirit as promised in John 14:17, where it is said that the Spirit lives with the believers and will be in them.

Sixthly, I want to mention joy. Jesus speaks his words so that his joy may be in them (John 15:11). Further, he prays again that his joy may be in them (John 17:13). In the intermediate chapter, joy is also an important motive (16:20–24).

A final coordinate, related closely to love, consists of the acts of believers. Here an analogy exists with the relation between Father and Son. Just as the works of Jesus show that the Father is in him and he is in his Father (John 10:38; 14:10–11), in the same way the works of believers will show that they remain in Christ and he in them. Within the metaphor of the vine this is expressed as bearing fruit (John 15:4–6), within John 17 this theme returns as unity (John 17:21, 23). We find this also in the first letter. In 1 John 2:6 the claim to remain in Christ is directly linked with the critical question whether the one who claims this follows the example of Jesus and walks as he did. Further, this is expressed negatively in 1 John 3:6 where John writes that no one who remains in Christ keeps on sin-

253. Jerumanis, *Realiser la communion avec Dieu*, 477–78.

254. Malatesta, *Interiority and Covenant*, 277; Scholtissek, *In ihm sein und bleiben*, 355.

ning.[255] This shows that the expressions of reciprocal being and remaining in not only point towards a reality of salvation, but also towards conformity of acting as is the case with respect to the relation of Father and Son, too.[256] Hence theology and ethics are closely related in John.[257]

These positive coordinates are opposed to several negative coordinates, like darkness (John 12:46; 1 John 1:5, 6; 2:9, 11), death (1 John 3:14), and sin (John 8:21, 24; 1 John 3:5).

To conclude, the relation of reciprocal being and remaing in each other stands within a greater field, of which positive coordinates are salvation in Christ, the word, love, faith expressed in the Eucharist and the confession of faith, the presence of the Spirit, joy, and the works of believers. Most of these coordinates are criteria or identity markers of the reciprocal interiority.[258] Opposed to them are darkness, death and sin.

Primacy and Order

We have seen already that although the sequence of Father and Son and God or Christ and the believer might change in reciprocal expressions,[259] nevertheless the Father has the primacy in the relation Father—Son, as the Son has in the relation Son—believers.

According to Jerumanis, more can be said. He distinguishes two orders, an order of faith and an order of love, which are both not chronological but causal. In the order of faith the immanence of the disciples in Jesus precedes the immanence of Jesus in the disciples and the resulting reciprocity. Faith makes the disciple enter in Jesus. The order of love is a reverse one. In the order of love, Jesus establishes with the disciples a relation as close as a relation of immanence—Jesus in the disciples—and hence the disciples can remain in him, remaining in this love.[260] The order of faith focuses more on the establishment of the relation (a relation realised by the reception of Jesus' words), the order of love emphasises

255. Cf. Malatesta, *Interiority and Covenant*, 246.

256. Scholtissek, *In ihm sein und bleiben*, 274.

257. Scholtissek, *In ihm sein und bleiben*, 356; see also Hays, *The Moral Vision of the New Testament*, 142–44. The difficulty according to Hays is that formal assertions of Jesus as an ethical pattern still have to be unpacked in terms of specific behaviour (143).

258. Malatesta, *Interiority and Covenant*, 119, 121, 125, 160, 275, 276, 278, 290, Scholtissek, *In ihm sein und bleiben*, 355, 359.

259. Cf. Jerumanis, *Realiser la communion avec Dieu*, 476.

260. Jerumanis, *Realiser la communion avec Dieu*, 476–78.

the relation itself, realised by the ecstasy of love.[261] In both directions a dynamic circularity exists: the more the disciples believe, the more they remain in Christ, the more they also receive the love of God and hence Jesus himself. But the more the disciples receive this love and Jesus, the more they remain in him and in his love. In this way, the relation between Jesus and the disciples becomes more and more a relation of perfect reciprocity.[262]

Jerumanis' picture is even more complex. He distinguishes a third order, the order of mediation. This mediation consists of a descending and an ascending mediation. In the descending mediation, the Son mediates the love of the Father. This mediation consists in the following movement: the Father loves his Son, the Son loves his disciples, the disciples are in the love of the Son, and the Son is in the disciples by the ecstasy of love. In the ascending mediation, the Son is the way to the Father. The Son is in the Father. As a result, the disciples, being in the Son are enabled to be in God. In the order of love, the love of the Father enables the Son to love his disciples. Consequently, the Son lets the disciples live in his love and lives in them. But to receive this love, the disciples have to believe. And believing, they already 'enter' in Jesus. By love and faith, in this way the believer can 'enter' and live in God.[263] Consequently as far as love is concerned, a movement from the exterior to the interior can be seen: first the disciples are in the love of Jesus, second Jesus' love is present in the disciples, third by his love Jesus is present in them.

Looking to the other coordinates, a comparable movement can be seen with regard to the word: an external word is heard, the disciples are in this word (John 8:31) but more and more the word must remain in the disciples, and by his word Jesus remains in them; a comparable process of interiorisation. Also the Spirit is external but comes and remains with the disciples and will be in them.

Given this movement from the exterior to the interior, it must be asked whether Malatesta is right when he states that God's remaining in us is 'the ultimate reason for our remaining in Him.'[264] Malatesta is right in that the reason of our remaining in Christ and in God is (the work of)

261. Jerumanis, *Realiser la communion avec Dieu*, 478–79.

262. Jerumanis, *Realiser la communion avec Dieu*, 479–80, 482–81.

263. Jerumanis, *Realiser la communion avec Dieu*, 481–83.

264. Malatesta, *Interiority and Covenant*, 274.

God himself in Christ and not our obedience. However, it is too simple to identify this work of God with 'God remaining in us.' The primacy of God is not the same as the primacy of the interiority of God in us.

The following reconstruction can be made:

1. God comes with light and love, for Jesus, the incarnate word, comes as the one in whom life and salvation can be found. To be in him is to live.
2. Jesus speaks his word, presenting himself as the one in whom life and salvation can be found.
3. In a not further clarified secret and hidden way, by the complex of light, love, Jesus' word, and the Spirit (birth from above), faith comes into existence.
4. The believer believes and discovers himself to be in Christ, to be in his love, to be in his word, receiving life and salvation. At the same time, the mystery is true that to be in Christ is to be related with Christ that closely that Christ is in the believer, by the ecstasy of his love, by his word received in faith, by his Spirit.
5. The believer is exhorted to remain in Christ, in a process of perfecting the reciprocity of the relation and of interiorisation: remaining in the love and the love being perfected in the disciple, remaining in the word and the word remaining in the disciple, keeping Jesus' commands, eating and drinking the flesh and blood of Christ, loving each other, the Spirit being in the disciple, remaining in Christ and Christ remaining in the disciple, bearing fruit and following the example of Jesus, not sinning, and even remaining in God as well as God remaining in the disciple.

Consequently, the communion with Christ and God in a Johannine perspective is a dynamic process in which the believer 'absorbs' Jesus more and more, remaining in the thus obtained communion with Christ.[265] The gospel and the first letter of John both can be read as mystagogical works, initiating into the mystery of Christ. They bring the reader further and further along the road to perfect reciprocity with Christ and as a result with God.[266] The gospel starts from the beginning, whereas the first letter

265. Scholtissek, *In ihm sein und bleiben*, 365.

266. Cf. Popp, *Grammatik des Geistes*, 462, 469–71; Scholtissek, *In ihm sein und bleiben*, 379.

concentrates on the process implied in the fifth step, the exhortation to remain in Christ and in God. In the letter this fifth stap consists of a three-fold pattern of forgiveness—purification—communion, as we have seen.

John 14:15–23, The Eschatological Tension and the Holy Spirit

Finally, we turn to John 14:15–23. This is a crucial passage for two reasons. First, it is important with regard to the relation between the two views on the communion with Christ, which we found in the gospel of John. On the one hand, where the verb μένειν is used the union has a less stable character; on the other hand the use of the verb εἶναι suggests a perfect reciprocity. This will be a reality 'ἐν ἐκείνῃ τῇ ἡμέρα' (14:20). Consequently, this passage may clarify the relation between the two different views. Second, it explains the relation between Christ and the Spirit. It is a crucial question in the exegesis of this passage, how the return of Jesus after his departure to his Father's house (14:2—3:28), the coming of the Spirit (14:16), the coming of Jesus (14:18) and the coming of Son and Father (14:23) are related. Hence it might clarify the role of the Spirit within the communion with Christ according to Johannine thinking.

Regarding these problems, an ambiguous picture emerges when reading the following chapters of John. On the one hand, Jesus speaks about his departure again in John 16:16–33. In a little while they will see him no more, for he will leave the world, going back to his Father (John 16:16, 28). There he will receive his heavenly glory, as he prays (17:5). After his resurrection, Jesus still has to ascend to his Father (20:17). Consequently, it seems that Jesus' departure includes both his death and his ascension. At the end of the gospel, the return of Jesus still has to take place (John 21:22–23). On the other hand, in John 16:16 Jesus suggests that the time between his death and his return will be very short. Further, it is indeed said that Jesus came (John 20:19, 24, 26 and 21:13).[267] This suggests that Jesus departed in his death and returned in the Easter-appearances. Is Jesus departing in his death and resurrection, returning at the *parousia*, or did he depart in his death and return at Easter?

Even more complicating is the possibility that the return of Jesus may be understood as a coming in the Spirit. The Spirit represents Jesus Christ and seems to effect his presence (15:26; 16:14). Do we have to identify

267. Carson, *The Gospel according to John*, 501; Frey, *Die johanneische Eschatologie*, Bd. III, 165.

Christ and the Spirit and understand the return of Jesus as a return in the Spirit? Against this possibility speaks the coming of the Spirit that presupposes the departure and absence of Jesus (15:26; 16:7). The Spirit sent by Jesus, and Jesus sending the Spirit, cannot be identified. However the interpretation of 14:18 is decisive: does this refer to a coming in the Spirit? Hence John 14:15–20 may give more clarity if a plausible reading can be found.

We are warned already within the story that Jesus' words are confusing (16:17f, 25, 29). Their pragmatical intention is important. Jesus begins and ends this chapter with the exhortation 'Do not let your hearts be troubled' (14:1.27). He does not want to give an eschatological schedule, but announcing his departure, consoles his disciples with the threefold coming of Spirit, Son and Father.[268]

Two things are evident: Jesus departs and the Spirit comes. Jesus goes to his Father (14:2, 12, 28), and he will ask his Father to send ἄλλος παράκλητος (14:16). This presupposes that Jesus is a παράκλητος, and that the Spirit of Truth (14:17) is another παράκλητος.[269] This second παράκλητος somehow fills an absence caused by Jesus' departure. This is evident in 14:16, where Jesus promises to send another παράκλητος to stay with them and be in them.[270] And again in 14:25–26, where Jesus creates an opposition between this moment, on which he speaks to them while still with them, and the moment, on which the Spirit works, bringing the words of Jesus in remembrance. Consequently, it is impossible to identify Jesus, the one παράκλητος and the Spirit, the other. The same applies to the coming of the Spirit and the coming of the Son.[271] The gift of the Spirit follows on the departure of Jesus as a result of Jesus' presence

268. On the pragmatical intention, see Frey, *Die johanneische Eschatologie, Bd. III*, 131–34.

269. Bornkamm, 'Der Paraklet im Johannes-Evangelium,' 96–97; Carson, *The Gospel according to John*, 500; Crump, 'Re-examining the Johannine Trinity,' 405; Frey, *Die johanneische Eschatologie*, Bd. III, 160; Van Houwelingen, *Johannes*, 297–99; Kammler, 'Jesus Christus und der Geistparaklet,' 98; Schnackenburg, *Das Johannesevangelium*, Bd. 3, 84; Scholtissek, *In ihm sein und bleiben*, 257–58; Stuhlmacher, *Biblische Theologie des Neuen Testaments*, Bd. 2, 261. Against Dettwiler, *Die Gegenwart des Erhöhten*, 189.

270. Frey, *Die johanneische Eschatologie*, Bd. III, 163.

271. Carson, *The Gospel according to John*, 501; Frey, *Die johanneische Eschatologie*, Bd. III, 150, 161–62, 166; Ridderbos, *Het evangelie naar Johannes*, Dl 2, 153. Against Dettwiler, *Die Gegenwart des Erhöhten*, 180, 189–92. Dettwiler sees the Spirit as 'die neue, zeitlich und räumlich entschränckte Gestalt der Anwesentheit Jesu bei der Gemeinde,' 189. In his position the difference between Christ and the Spirit disappears.

with the Father.[272] Nevertheless, the Spirit plays a necessary mediating role in the communion with Jesus and so with his Father (14:26; cf. 15:26 and 16:13–15).[273]

Given this observation that Jesus departs and that the Spirit comes, how then do we have to understand this return of Jesus (14:3, 18, 28), his self-disclosure to his disciples and not to the world (14:19–21), the love of the Son and the Father for those who keep his commands (14:21, 23), and the coming of Father and Son, making their home with a disciple (14:23)? And how do they relate to the gift of the Spirit—do Father and Son come independently of the coming of the Spirit?

Now we must say something on the return in 14:3. It is almost beyond dispute that this verse refers to the return of Jesus at the *parousia*. Jesus goes to his Father and will return from his Father's realm. This is clearly a motif of future eschatology.[274]

Concerning the threefold divine coming, first the coming of the Spirit is promised (14:16–17). Until now I have argued that this coming of the Spirit cannot be identified with the coming of the Son. These verses affirm this position. The Spirit comes on the prayer of the Son and is sent

272. Frey, *Die johanneische Eschatologie,* Bd. III, 163; Kammler, 'Jesus Christus und der Geistparaklet,' 97, 107.

273. Bornkamm, 'Der Paraklet im Johannes-Evangelium,' 110–13; Van Bruggen, *Het evangelie van Gods Zoon*, 202–3; Crump, 'Re-examining the Johannine Trinity,' 405–8; Van Houwelingen, *Johannes*, 299; Kammler, 'Jesus Christus und der Geistparaklet,' 90–93; Nissen, 'Mission in the Fourth Gospel,' 230–31; Ridderbos, *Het evangelie naar Johannes*, 153; Schnackenburg, *Das Johannesevangelium*, Bd. 3, 85, 94–95; Schnelle, *Neutestamentliche Antropologie*, 161; Scholtissek, *In ihm sein und bleiben*, 270; Stuhlmacher, *Biblische Theologie des Neuen Testaments*, Bd. 2, 261–64.

274. Carson, *The Gospel according to John*, 488; Dettwiler, *Die Gegenwart des Erhöhten*, 148–49; Frey, *Die johanneische Eschatologie,* Bd. III, 147–53; Van Houwelingen, *Johannes*, 291–92; Ridderbos, *Het evangelie naar Johannes*, Dl. 2, 136–38.

Van Hartingsveld differentiates between the last day and the day of 'Heimholung.' 14,3 describes an event on the day of 'Heimholung,' see Van Hartingsveld, *Die Eschatologie des Johannesevangeliums*, 106–10, 129–34, 145. According to Kammler and Schnackenburg, here a traditional future eschatological motive is reinterpreted as present eschatological, see Kammler, 'Jesus Christus und der Geistparaklet,' 103–5; Schnackenburg, *Das Johannesevangelium*, Bd. 3, 70–71. But in this way the future eschatology, also present in John's gospel, is unnecessarily denied. Scholtissek leaves open whether this refers to the *parousia* or to the moment of someone's death, but excludes that it refers to the spiritual coming of Jesus after his resurrection, see Scholtissek, *In ihm sein und bleiben*, 248–49; see also 268.

by the Father. Accordingly, he has to be distinguished from Father and Son and has his own (relative) independence.

The pragmatical intention of the announcement of the threefold divine coming is made explicit again in 14:18a. Jesus will not leave his disciples alone, 'ὀρφανούς,' 'like orphans.' Within this context, this word first refers back to 14:2–3. Jesus is in his Father's house and his disciples are left behind—they might seem fatherless. The motif of the house of the Father and a return of Jesus to bring his disciples in his Father's house is reused here.[275] Secondly, a semantic relation to the death of Christ is present. This must be less prominent, because the death of a brother does not make you an orphan and further the motif of the house of the Father is mentioned already. However, the departure of Jesus to his Father's house consists in his death.[276]

Jesus immediately continues that not only the Spirit comes, but that he will come himself. He repeats his promise that he will return (14,3). After a little while, they will see him (14:19). In the following verse we find the chronological reference of 'ἐν ἐκείνῃ τῇ ἡμέρᾳ' (14:20). The disciples will know that Jesus is in his Father and they in him and he in them. Jesus and his Father will love them if they live in love and Jesus will reveal himself to them (14:21). Even the Father will come to make his home with them (14:23). To which occasion does 14:18–23 refer? When does the Son come to them, in his Easter-appearences or at the *parousia*? Or has this second coming to be understood as a coming in the Spirit after all? Until now we presumed that this cannot be the case, because the second παράκλητος is distinguished from Jesus, he comes to fill the absence of Jesus, and it is not said in John that Jesus comes in the Spirit. However, in 14:19 the opposition world-believers of 14:17 returns: just as the world cannot receive the Spirit, the world will not see the Son.

275. Frey, *Die johanneische Eschatologie,* Bd. III, 166; Van Houwelingen, *Johannes,* 300.

276. See for this relation Carson, *The Gospel according to John*, 501; Dettwiler, *Die Gegenwart des Erhöhten*, 192; Ridderbos, *Het evangelie naar Johannes*, Dl. 2, 153–54.

Frey denies the existence of this relation. However, his argument that 'ὀρφανούς' is very strong if it would refer only to the short time between the death of Jesus and his resurrection, is not convincing. The question is not whether a period can be characterized with the help of this word. Instead, Jesus says that he will *not* leave them as orphans. Against Frey, *Die johanneische Eschatologie,* Bd. III, 165.

Further, the disciples will see Jesus after a little while. Does this suggest yet an identification of the gift of the Spirit and the coming of the Son?[277]

Within the discussion, basically two options exist:

a. a present eschatological interpretation. These verses refer to the time starting with Easter. ἔτι μικρὸν and ἐν ἐκείνῃ τῇ ἡμέρᾳ may be eschatological language, but these expressions are used in a modified form. They indicate the decisive character of cross and resurrection. ἔτι μικρὸν might also just indicate the short time between death and resurrection. Further it is important that only the disciples see Jesus, as was the case in the Easter-appearances. The fact that this is also the case in 14:17 indicates a parallel between the coming of the Spirit and the coming of the Son. This parallel also is an argument for a present interpretation. The Spirit plays a role in the coming of the Son. Although the Spirit is distinguished from Jesus, still the Spirit mediates the inhabitation of Son and Father. That Jesus lives, is not new. He lives always in John's gospel (cf. 11:25). However, in his coming they would see again that death had no power over him as well as over them. Further, seeing the resurrected Jesus, believing that he is in the Father becomes knowing that he is in his Father. Finally, the upward movement of 14:2–3

277. According to Dettwiler, apocalyptic language is used but the traditonal future eschatology (14:2) is modified. 14:16–17 refers to the sending of the Spirit-Paraklete, 14:18–20 to the coming of Jesus at Easter. The coming of the Spirit and the coming of the Jesus are identical, which is indicated by the parallels between 14:16–17 and 14:18–20; see Dettwiler, *Die Gegenwart des Erhöhten*, 191–94.

Kammler does not identify Christ and the Spirit, but still according to him 14:18–20 refer to the coming of the exalted Christ after Easter in the Spirit. It is the Spirit who discloses Christ in his person and work, Kammler, 'Jesus Christus und der Geistparaklet,' 91, 102–8.

Carson, Ridderbos and Schnackenburg read it as referring to the Easter-appearances, see Carson, *The Gospel according to John*, 501–2; Ridderbos, *Het evangelie naar Johannes*, Dl. 2, 154; Schnackenburg, *Das Johannesevangelium*, Bd. 3, 89–90.

Frey distinguishes between the future eschatological passage 14:18, referring to the *parousia* and 14:19–20, which have a present eschatological character. These verses refer to the spiritual vision of Jesus in the time after Easter in the Spirit, see Frey, *Die johanneische Eschatologie*, Bd. III, 164–69.

Van Hartingsveld and Van Houwelingen read 14:18–20 as referring to the day of bringing home (14:2–3). Van Houwelingen identifies this day with the last day, the day of the *parousia*, whereas Van Hartingsveld distinguishes the day of bringing home from the last day, see Van Houwelingen, *Johannes*, 301 and Van Hartingsveld, *Die Eschatologie des Johannesevangeliums*, 114–17, 145.

is changed into a downward movement in 14:23 which indicates a difference between the future eschatology of 14:2–3 and the present eschatology of 14:19–23.[278]

In this option Christ and the Spirit are closely related although they are distinct, and the more stable view of the reciprocal εἶναι distinguished from the more unstable view represented by the μένειν concerns already the present. In the light of the resurrection we already know that Christ is in us and we are in him.

b. a future eschatological interpretation. These verses refer to the time of the return of Jesus to bring his disciples home. ἔτι μικρὸν and ἐν ἐκείνῃ τῇ ἡμέρᾳ are eschatological expressions, indicating a future eschatological understanding of Jesus' return. The fact that only the disciples see Jesus is no problem, for this is also the case in 14:2–3. The parallel with 14:17 is no argument, for the Spirit and the Son are not the same. That Jesus lives, is not new and consequently no argument for a present eschatological interpretation. The change of believing that Father and Son live in each other into knowing that this is the case, and that even Christ is in his disciples and they in him, takes place in the future. The downward movement in 14:23 is a deepening of the upward movement in 14:2–3: as Jesus brings his disciples to where he is, Father and Son come to live with his disciples.[279] In this option Christ and the Spirit remain distinct and the Spirit fills the absence of Jesus. The more stable view of the reciprocal εἶναι remains a matter of the future, in the present we just believe that Father and Son live in each other and we have to remain in Christ and he in us.

Option b. has several advantages. Firstly, it results in a plausible reading of the other passage where the expressions ἔτι μικρὸν and ἐν ἐκείνῃ τῇ ἡμέρᾳ are used (16:16–28). With Van Houwelingen, these expressions can both be read as eschatological expressions, without modification. The first μικρὸν in 16:16 refers to the departure of Jesus in his death and ascension, the second to the *parousia*. The ἐν ἐκείνῃ τῇ ἡμέρᾳ in 16:23

278. See e.g. Frey, *Die johanneische Eschatologie,* Bd. III, 168–71; Kammler, 'Jesus Christus und der Geistparaklet,' 102–8; Ridderbos, *Het evangelie naar Johannes*, Dl. 2, 153–59.

279. See e.g. Van Hartingsveld, *Die Eschatologie des Johannesevangeliums*, 110–17; Van Houwelingen, *Johannes*, 299–303.

refers to the day of the *parousia*. This is the day that all questions will have disappeared (16:23). This is also the day that something changes in the way God deals with a prayer in the name of Jesus. Before the *parousia*, Jesus is the one who reacts to this prayer (14:14), a passage referring to the time after Easter. After the *parousia* however, the prayer in the name of Jesus remains, but now the Father himself reacts to such a prayer, without the intercession of Jesus (16:26f).[280] Secondly, it is no longer necessary to deny that Jesus comes in the Spirit because Jesus and the Spirit are always distinct in John, and still to interpret the coming of Jesus still as a coming in the Spirit.[281] The Spirit comes when Jesus departs and plays a mediating role in our union with Christ and as a result with his Father as we saw (14:25–26; 15:26; 16:12–15). Thirdly, option b. makes clearer how the two views of the relation with Christ, connected to the verbs μένειν and εἶναι are related. As long as Christ has not returned, we are summoned to remain in Christ. At the *parousia*, the relation with Christ receives a more stable character of reciprocal being in each other. The difference between these two views pictures the eschatological tension of the yet and not yet.[282]

This implies a view of the relation between present and future eschatology in John different from what became usual. Present and future are stuck together, but not because John assimilates a future eschatology to his own present eschatology, but the other way round: the future is near and the present is open to the future. This openness of the present to the future can also be seen in John 17:20–23. Here Jesus prays for the realisation of the future, that believers may have perfect unity and may be with him to see his glory. Jesus' departure will realise this future. It will result in a threefold divine coming, of the Spirit immediately after Jesus' departure, and of Son and Father in a near future, resulting in a living together of God and believers. Believers will be taken to the house of the

280. Cf. Van Houwelingen, *Johannes*, 296, 327–28.

According to Frey's interpretation of 16:16–33, verses 16–23a have to be read as future eschatological (including the expressions ἔτι μικρὸν and ἐν ἐκείνῃ τῇ ἡμέρᾳ), whereas he reads 23b–33 as referring to the present situation of the Johannine communion, before the *parousia*. He does not deal with the difference between what is said on prayer in the name of Jesus in 14:14 or 16:23b–24, and 16:26. See Frey, *Die johanneische Eschatologie*, Bd. III, 204–22.

281. As is the case in e.g. the interpretations of Frey, see Frey, *Die johanneische Eschatologie*, Bd. III, 160 and 168–70.

282. Cf. Jerumanis, *Realiser la communion avec Dieu*, 482–83.

Father (14:3). The Son and the Father will even come to the believers to live with them (14:23).

To conclude, the future is near and begins in the present when Jesus departs. He goes back to his Father, dying and ascending, and sends the Spirit to represent himself and to relate his disciples to his words and the life he is in his person. The Spirit fills the emptiness caused by the departure of Jesus. The coming of the Spirit is the beginning of a threefold divine coming, which will be completed at the *parousia* when Son and Father come to live with those who love them. This creates an eschatological tension. This same tension is present in the use of the verbs μένειν and εἶναι. It is necessary to exhort each other as believers to remain in communion with Christ. The necessity to use the verb μένειν will disappear at the *parousia*. From the *parousia* on, the more stable view related to the verb εἶναι will be a reality, as the Son comes and God and man will live together in a perfect communion of reciprocity.

Conclusions

Finally, some conclusions can be drawn now with regard to the interiority-language and to the analogy and differences between the relation, on the one hand, between Father and Son and on the other hand between God or Jesus Christ and the believers.

a. The Father is never subject or object alone within a reciprocal expression with the believer as subject or object, whereas God is never subject or object in a relation with Jesus Christ. Within the gospel expressions of reciprocal being or remaining in are used only with regard to the relation Father—Son or Son—believers.[283] Consequently, the designation 'Father' used alone has a special place within the relation Father—Son[284] and the relation Father—Son has a unique character.

b. The characteristics of the Father—Son relation can analogously be conferred on the relation between the Son and the believers. The Son is for the believers what the Father is for him (cf. 6.2.2).

   First, this implies that the local and communal concepts used to understand the relation between Father and Son can also be

283. Crump, 'Re-examining the Johannine Trinity,' 398–404; Jerumanis, *Realiser la communion avec Dieu*, 405; Scholtissek, *In ihm sein und bleiben*, 332.

284. Malatesta, *Interiority and Covenant*, 34.

used to understand the relation between the Son and the believers: interiority, communion and reciprocal inhabitation. Our relationship of interiority with the Son 'should be understood in the light of the interiority and circumincession of the Divine Persons.'[285] Nevertheless, the use of the verbs μένειν and εἶναι shows that the relation Father—Son has a more stable reciprocal character than the relation God or Jesus Christ—believers, although this second relation has a stable future. The relation between Son and believers is in need of growth toward a perfect reciprocity, which is not the case in the relation Father—Son.[286] The relation between Son and believers has a reciprocal character, but until the *parousia* the exhortation to remain in Christ is necessary.

Second, in the same way as the identity of the Son is not threatened by his communion with his Father, but is founded and determined by it, receiving stability from it, the identity of believers is not threatened and will not disappear as a result of the communion with the Son. Instead, receiving eternal life in the Son, they receive their identity in a renewed and stable form. The symmetry of reciprocal interiority and the asymmetry between the involved persons do not exclude each other. The Father has the primacy and the Son is dependent on his Father and they do not loose their peculiarities. In a comparable way, this is the case in the relation between the Son and the believers.[287] 'Die joh Immanenz-Aussagen reflektieren eine in Gott selbst begründete und diese mitteilende Personalität, die ihre Identität durch eine *Communio* gewinnt, deren dichtester Ausdruck die wechselseitige *Inhabitatio* ist.'[288] Consequently, the relation with the Son must not be understood as a mystical union if this implies an annihilation of identity.

Third, the union between Christ and believers must be transformed more and more into a unity of life, love, knowledge, acts, and privileges, in the same way as Father and Son are one in these

285. Malatesta, *Interiority and Covenant*, 133; cf. Crump, 'Re-examining the Johannine Trinity,' 401–4.

286. Jerumanis, *Realiser la communion avec Dieu*, 482.

287. Jerumanis, *Realiser la communion avec Dieu*, 409–11, 473; Scholtissek, *In ihm sein und bleiben*, 338–39.

288. Scholtissek, *In ihm sein und bleiben*, 372.

respects.[289] At the same time comparable differences exist: the Father commands and sends his Son, and, likewise, so does the Son in respect to the believers.[290]

Fourth, it must be noted that the unity existing between Father and Son is not paralleled with the unity between Son (or God) and believers but the unity between believers among themselves. This unity never results in a unity of Father, Son and believers although this unity of believers is dependent on their being in Son and Father, as we saw when dealing with John 17.[291]

c. Although Father, Son and believers do not constitute a unity together, nevertheless the relation believers—Son—Father is seen as 'I in them and you in me' (17:23), the Father being in the Son, the Son remaining in the believers. As a result of the mediating function of the Son within the relation believers—Son—Father, it can furthermore be said that believers remain 'in God'—as is often the case in the first letter—or 'in us' (John 17:21).

d. A consequence of b. and c. is that the language of being and remaining in has a greater semantic and hermeneutic potential than the concept of unity.[292]

e. The Spirit has a mediating function in the communion with Christ and the Father. The Spirit cannot be identified with the resurrected Christ, but is the One who came to represent Christ after his departure. In the Spirit, believers have communion with Son and Father.[293] This evokes the idea of a Trinity.[294]

f. Jesus makes believers to some extent participate in his position, not only within the communion with his Father, but also in their glory, in the love of the Father for the Son and in his place where his glory can be seen. As the Son participates in the life of the Father, so the believers participate in the life of the Son.

289. Jerumanis, *Realiser la communion avec Dieu*, 407.

290. Jerumanis, *Realiser la communion avec Dieu*, 410–11.

291. See footnote 229; and further Crump, 'Re-examining the Johannine Trinity.'

292. Scholtissek, *In ihm sein und bleiben*, 338.

293. Ridderbos, *Het evangelie naar Johannes*, Dl. 2, 158; Schnackenburg, *Das Johannesevangelium*, Bd. 3, 87.

294. Cf. R.W. Jenson, *Systematic Theology*, Vol. 1, 93. David Crump denies this, see Crump, 'Re-examining the Johannine Trinity.'

g. The dynamism of this relation consists of an intensification of interiority by a movement from the exterior to the interior, in which faith and love play an important role. The Son mediates the love of his Father and by this love his immanence in his disciples is realised (John 17:26). At the same time, believers need faith to receive this love, in this way entering in Jesus Christ and by his mediation in God.[295]

h. Behind this language of being and remaining in lie several ideas as Scholtissek has shown. First, the christological identity of Jesus consists in his being eschatological salvation in person.[296] Jesus is the given salvation because he offers the intimate relation to the resurrected Jesus Christ. Gift and giver become identical.[297] In the gifts that Jesus gives, he gives himself. As a result, structuring moments of the Father-Son relation are conferred on the Son-christian relation.[298] Or as Nissen writes, Jesus provides a place, becomes the entrance to that place or even the place itself; as a result John's Christology has inclusive and exclusive aspects.[299]

i. The Johannine interiority-language itself cannot be understood primarily with the help of the concept of representation. Instead, we need to use here concepts like interiority, communion and reciprocal inhabitation. But because of the identity of giver and gift and because the Son makes us, to a certain extent, participate in his position, the concept of participation is necessary to understand this aspect of the interiority-language.

These conclusions imply that the position of Malatesta is no longer tenable. Because he sees Jesus as the representative of the new covenant, Malatesta differentiates too little between, on the one hand, the Father being in the Son and the Son being in God, and, on the other hand, God being in the believer and the believer being in God. According to him Jesus was the first person realising the new covenant within himself, and as a result a perfect reciprocity between God and man came to exist

295. Jerumanis, *Realiser la communion avec Dieu*, 482.

296. Scholtissek, *In ihm sein und bleiben*, 209.

297. Schnelle, *Neutestamentliche Antropologie*, 170; Scholtissek, *In ihm sein und bleiben*, 312.

298. Scholtissek, *In ihm sein und bleiben*, 372.

299. Nissen, 'Mission in the Fourth Gospel,' 224.

within Jesus' person.[300] The Father-Son relation is a covenant relation, being 'the ground and norm for the relationship between God and all man.'[301] Consequently, believers all have a comparable covenant relation with the Father.[302] Therefore he speaks of 'our relation of mutual remaining with the Father,'[303] where John never does, and of 'our communion with the Father,'[304] reading 'Father' where John writes 'God' several times.[305] More than Malatesta does, we must distinguish between the Father-Son relation and the Son-believers relation, emphasising the exclusiveness of the Son and the special place the designation 'Father' has within the Father-Son relation.

6.3.2 IMAGES FOR UNITY WITH CHRIST IN THE GOSPEL

In this paragraph on soteriology, we started with the Johannine ἐν-language. Now we turn to metaphors for the unity with Christ, used in John. These images we find in chapters we have partly been dealing with already in the previous sub-paragraph, for the metaphors and the ἐν-language occur together: the image of the living bread (John 6) and the image of the wine (John 15). Further I will deal again with John 17, although no images are used there. Moreover, I will deal with the image of the good shepherd we find in John 10. Dealing with these metaphors, I will discuss also the problem of particularity and predestination, for this problem is related with the images of the bread and the living shepherd, and with the theme of unity in John 17.

John 6: The Bread

Already in several sub-paragraphs we have been dealing with this important passage from different perspectives. In 6.2.1 the problem of the sacramental overtones and the reference of 'σάρξ' (6:51) was discussed. In 6.2.2 the central question was the parallel between the Father-Son relation and the Christ-christian relation (6:57). Very briefly the 'I am'-saying received attention in 6.2.3 (6:35, 48, 50, 51). I concluded that this

300. Malatesta, *Interiority and Covenant*, 308.

301. Malatesta, *Interiority and Covenant*, 32, 35, 323.

302. Malatesta, *Interiority and Covenant*, 250–51, 323.

303. Malatesta, *Interiority and Covenant*, 273–74.

304. Malatesta, *Interiority and Covenant*, 304.

305. Malatesta, *Interiority and Covenant*, 126, 273, 322.

metaphor emphasises the difference between Jesus and the believer, and does not evoke an idea of representation. The perspective of the death of Christ for others brought us in 6.2.4 again to a discussion of Jesus' gift of his flesh (6:51). Finally I investigated the ἐν-language in 6.3.1 (6:56). Now I will deal more extensively with the entire section and its central image, the image of the bread as image for the believer's unity with Christ.

The start of the discussion with the Jews determines the bread-discourse. It follows the story of the sign of Jesus feeding the five thousand. The next day Jesus contrasts the food they ate yesterday which perishes, with the food 'that endures to eternal life' (6:27). In response to their ironic question[306] what they must do to do the works of God, he focuses their attention on his own person: it is the work of God if they believe in him, the one God has sent (6:29). As a result, in the following verses the themes of eternal life, the work of God, and the contrast between the Jews' ideal to do the works of God and their factual unbelief, return repeatedly in relation to the central image of the bread.

The crowds associate the feeding of the five thousand with the manna, the bread of heaven in the desert.[307] In his reaction, Jesus contrasts Moses with his Father (6:32), the manna with the true bread (6:32–33), and the death of the forefathers who ate the manna in the desert with the eternal life of all who eat the bread of life (6:49–51, 58).[308] Is seems as if Jesus suggests that for the Jews, Moses has become more important than his Father.[309] Although Jesus is more than the manna, again the Jews start grumbling (6:41) like they did in the desert and do not believe.[310]

306. Cf. Anderson, *The Christology of the Fourth Gospel*, 201.

307. Here a reference sounds to Ps 78:24–25. For a more extensive investigation of the parallels between Ps 78 and John 6, see Anderson, *The Christology of the Fourth Gospel*, 202–4.

According to the analysis of Wierenga, the storyteller uses the strategy of the 'arranged misunderstanding,' using ambiguous signs: the misunderstanding of the crowds gives Jesus the opportunity to expound his teaching; see Wierenga, *Verhalen als bewijzen*, 193–94; 16–22.

308. Cf. Van Houwelingen, *Jezus stelt zich voor*, 17–18; Wierenga, *Verhalen als bewijzen*, 209.

309. According to Anderson, here the adherents of Mosaic piety are accused of idolatry, see Anderson, *The Christology of the Fourth Gospel*, 204. See further Carson, *The Gospel according to John*, 286; Ridderbos, *Het evangelie naar Johannes*, Dl. 1, 264.

310. The verb γογγύζω used to describe the grumbling in reaction to Jesus' words (John 6:41, 43, 61) is the same as the LXX uses to describe the grumbling of Israel in the desert in Exod 17:3; Num 11:1; 14:27, 29; 17:6, 20.

Nevertheless, Jesus aims at their life, not at a death like the death of their forefathers in the desert (6:58).

The image of bread and manna implies a world with different aspects. It is a world of hunger in the desert, where life is in danger. In the desert people live without food, unless food is given from heaven. If food is given, it can spoil. Food that endures to eternal life is a solution to this problem. If it is given, one must come and eat. The food must be taken in and come inside someone. It must be eaten and chewed. And it results in life, the danger of death in the desert is overcome. All these aspects we find in John 6.

The food is given from heaven. Noteworthy is the centrality of the Father from the beginning of this passage (6:27). It is the Father who gives the bread. The crowds mention the works of God and their forefathers, but actually they do not believe in Jesus the Son although they saw him and his sign. With all their self-esteem they are stubborn and blind. Jesus gives life as the living bread and he will not send away anyone who comes to him, but give eternal life according to the will of the Father. Over against this puzzling unbelief, Jesus confronts them with the message that if the Father gives them to come, they will believe (6:37–40). The Father gives Christ as the living bread, and the Father gives persons to Jesus.[311] Consequently, all these persons will come to Jesus and Jesus will keep them in and not throw them out and send them back.[312] For his Father's will is decisive in every respect: the Father gives the living bread and wants all who believe in the Son to have eternal life; the Father gives many people to Jesus, the Son will not lose any of them but raise them up on the last day.[313] Ironically the Jews do not understand that Jesus refers to God as his Father and start talking about his father and mother; Jesus is just

311. Carson, *Divine Sovereignty and Human Responsibility*, 186; Van Houwelingen, *Johannes*, 157; Piper, *The pleasures of God*, 138–39; Stuhlmacher, *Biblische Theologie des Neuen Testaments*, Bd. 2, 252.

Marshall instead denies that these verses suggest that a predestination is at work, see Marshall, *New Testament Theology*, 500–501.

312. Cf. Carson, *Divine Sovereignty and Human Responsibility*, 184, 192; Carson, *The Gospel according to John*, 290; Hofius, 'Erwählung und Bewahrung,' 81–83; Van Houwelingen, *Johannes*, 157.

313. Carson, *The Gospel according to John*, 290–91; Hofius, 'Erwählung und Bewahrung,' 84–86; Van Houwelingen, *Johannes*, 157; Ridderbos, *Het evangelie naar Johannes*, Dl. 1, 269; Schnackenburg, *Das Johannesevangelium*, Bd. 2, 73; Stuhlmacher, *Biblische Theologie des Neuen Testaments*, Bd. 2, 252.

Joseph's son (6:41–42). Now Jesus says it more emphatically: only if the Father draws someone will he believe in Jesus (6:44–45).[314] Particularity of salvation, the gift of faith, perseverance and final resurrection are all centred in the Son who executes his Father's will. The gift of the living bread, the coming, eating and living are all surrounded by the activity and the will of the Father.

It is important to emphasise that Jesus' statements develop in reaction to self-esteem and unbelief. He starts with the gift of bread by the Father, followed by the invitation to come. Reacting to unbelief he adds that all who the Father gives him will come; and everyone who believes in the Son shall have eternal life (6:37, 40); very open and generous formulations. When the Jews start grumbling, Jesus formulates this more sharply: 'No-one can come to me unless the Father . . . draws him (6:44).[315] This drawing consists in a divine teaching, an inner illumination.[316] These statements obviously have a polemic function, directed against the self-satisfaction and unbelief of the Jews. As a consequence, their rhetorical aim is to bring them to critical self-reflection and the embarrassing conclusion that the Jews were not taught by God (6:45), in spite of their forefathers, their self-esteem, and their God-talk. Their primary aim is to bring to conversion, humility and belief, not to exclude, even if they ascribe salvation entirely to God. Further they make clear that rejection by men does not frustrate God's saving purposes.[317] Only as some do not believe, Jesus utters more excluding statements (6:64f).

The metaphor not only implies that Jesus is given by the Father. Apart from the will and activity of the Father, several other aspects are mentioned making Jesus the true, living bread for someone, giving life for ever.[318] Firstly, the metaphor is used in one of the 'I am'-sayings, stressing the exclusive position of Jesus Christ (6:35, 48, 50). Secondly, Jesus mentions the necessity of faith. Apart from explicit references to faith, also several verbs, metaphorical used, refer to faith: to come (ἔρχομαι; 6:35, 36, 44), to look (θεωρέω; 6:40), to eat (εσθίω; 6:51, 53, 56), to drink

314. See Carson, *Divine Sovereignty and Human Responsibility*, 185.

315. Van Houwelingen, *Johannes*, 158.

316. Carson, *The Gospel according to John*, 293.

317. Carson, *Divine Sovereignty and Human Responsibility*, 185; Carson, *The Gospel according to John*, 290; Ridderbos, *Het evangelie naar Johannes*, Dl. 1 268.

318. Note that Jesus gives the bread in that he is the bread of life, cf. Anderson, *The Christology of the Fourth Gospel*, 205.

(πίνω; 6:54, 56), to chew (τρώγω; 6:58).[319] Thirdly, Jesus is the life giving bread because he will raise up all who the Father gave him on the last day (6:39, 40, 44, 54). Hence the gift of everlasting life cannot be separated from future eschatology and the resurrection of the dead on the last day.[320] Fourthly, as we have seen already, Jesus is the living bread because he gave his flesh, dying on the cross for the life of the world (6:51). Fifthly, the metaphor of the bread is related to the ἐν-language and consequently to the idea of reciprocal inhabitation as a present reality (6:56). Sixthly, the sacramental overtones of the passage refer to the Eucharist, where the eating and drinking of the living bread becomes visible. Seventhly, the parallel between the Father-Son relation and the Son-believer relation demonstrates that the life giving relationality of God is opened, taking the believer up into the communion with God in Christ (6:57). Finally, from the comparison with the manna and Israel in the desert believers can be seen as a people and hence as a collective.

To conclude, the metaphor of the bread, given from heaven to let a hungry people live, evokes a view of Christ related with the will and activity of the Father, the exclusiveness of Christ, the cross and the resurrection of the dead on the last day, eternal life, election and perseverance, faith, communion with Christ as reciprocal inhabitation, the Eucharist, and the communion of Father and Son; moreover it has a collective aspect. Further, in this chapter the exhortation to believe in Jesus as the living bread given by God is combined with a stress on the divine activity in election, the gift of faith, illumination, perseverance and resurrection on the last day. Finally, the image does not suggest immediately that the concept of participation is necessary to understand Johannine thinking.

John 10: The Good Shepherd

In a comparable way to John 6, several aspects of John 10 have been discussed already in the preceding part of this chapter. In 6.2.2 we saw that the

319. Anderson sees here a clear parallel to the Pauline idea of justification by faith, see Anderson, *The Christology of the Fourth Gospel*, 201. Van Houwelingen stresses the durative implication of τρώγω, Van Houwelingen, *Johannes*, 106.

See further Burge, *The Anointed Community*, 187; Carson, *Divine Sovereignty and Human Responsibility*, 184; Hofius, 'Erwählung und Bewahrung,' 82–83; Ridderbos, *Het evangelie naar Johannes*, Dl. 1 267, 273, 282–83.

320. Carson, *The Gospel according to John*, 292. Again we find a combination of future eschatology and salvation in the present, cf. Anderson, *The Christology of the Fourth Gospel*, 205–6.

mutual knowing of Father and Son is compared with the mutual knowing of shepherd and sheep (10:14–15). Further, two of the 'I am'-sayings can be found in John 10 as we saw in 6.2.3: I am the door (10:11) and I am the good shepherd (10:14–16). Here I concluded that the discontinuity between shepherd and sheep does not lead to an idea of inclusiveness and hence not to representation. Consequently, this is also the case with regard to participation. And in 6.2.4 discussing the Johannine view of the death of Jesus we found that the Son proves that he is the good shepherd, because he does not run away for the wolf, but lays down his life for the sheep (10:15). He gives his life according to his Father's will, but also takes it up again (10:18). In this section the metaphor of the shepherd as metaphor for the unity with Christ determines the focus.

John 9 relates that Jesus heals a man born blind. When the Pharisees investigate this healing, they throw out the man who had been blind. The end of the story gives it a deeper meaning, for Jesus tells some Pharisees that they are blind themselves. Their behaviour is quite contrary to the behaviour one would expect from a good shepherd. Instead, Jesus has a heart for his sheep.[321] This is elaborated in John 10, the discourse of the good shepherd. In John 10:1–6 a general sketch is given, elaborated in the next verses and grouped around two 'I am'-sayings: 'I am the door' and 'I am the good shepherd.' I concentrate on the second, for the first image is not an image for unity with Christ.

The shepherd is the one who knows his sheep and calls them. The sheep know his voice and follow him. The world of the sheep is a world full of dangers: strangers, thieves and robbers outside the sheep pen coming to kill and destroy, hired hands who forget their flock when a wolf comes, and wolves attacking the flock and scattering it. The good shepherd is different: he cares for his sheep and comes so that his sheep may have life to the full. He is prepared to risk his life for his sheep, and brings different sheep together in one flock with one shepherd.[322]

Important in this metaphor is the reciprocal knowledge of shepherd and his sheep, related to the voice of the shepherd. This shepherd even knows his own sheep individually and calls them by name; his sheep know

321. For the relation between John 9 and 10, see Kowalski, *Die Hirtenrede*, 184–94; and further Van Bruggen, *Het evangelie van Gods Zoon*, 173.

322. See on this image also Van Houwelingen, *Jezus stelt zich voor*, 35–39.

his voice and follow him (10:3–5, 14, 27).[323] This is a polemical aspect of the metaphor, for the sheep did not listen to other 'shepherds,' who were thieves and robbers (10:8). We saw already that Jesus compares this intimate relation of reciprocal knowing each other with the relation he has with his Father. Just as the Father knows him and he knows his Father, shepherd and sheep know each other (10:15). Even sheep living outside 'this' flock, in another flock, have this knowledge of the shepherd's voice.

Another significant aspect is that the shepherd has his eye on the well-being of his flock. In John 10 this well-being is related especially with the image of the door, as the gate to a pasture (10:9–10). Nevertheless, the contrast between the thief as well as the robber and the good shepherd makes it obvious that the good shepherd does not pursue death and destruction.[324] Instead, he is even prepared to give his life if a wolf comes; actually he lays down his life. Therefore, in 10:10 a transition is already prepared from the image of the door to the image of the shepherd. The good shepherd cares for his sheep, in contrast to the hired hand (10:13). In this perspective the death of Jesus is mentioned, as we have seen already. He lays down his life for his sheep (10:11, 15, 17, 18). Within this metaphor, it is not the universal love for the world that is central, but the saving work of the good shepherd as focused on his own sheep.[325] In the second discussion on this theme with the Jews that John relates, this is elaborated as the gift of eternal life and the gift of perseverance. Jesus gives eternal life to his sheep and they shall not perish, even not 'εἰς τὸν αἰῶνα.' No one can snatch them out of his hand. (10:28).[326]

The shepherd has his own flock, but other sheep exist. The suggestion in 10:3 is that more sheep are in the sheep pen, but only his own sheep—τὰ ἴδια πρόβατα—follow the shepherd (10:3–4).[327] Next, in 10:20,

323. Carson, *The Gospel according to John*, 382–83; Kowalski, *Die Hirtenrede*, 199–200; Schnackenburg, *Das Johannesevangelium*, Bd 2, 356, 373–74.

324. See for the contrasting figures Kowalski, *Die Hirtenrede*, 211–16.

325. Carson, *The Gospel according to John*, 387.

326. Carson, *The Gospel according to John*, 393; Carson, *Divine Sovereignty and Human Responsibility*, 194; Van Houwelingen, *Johannes*, 226; Ridderbos, *Het evangelie naar Johannes*, Dl. 1, 429; Schnackenburg, *Das Johannesevangelium*, Bd 2, 385.

327. Bergmeier, *Glaube als Gabe nach Johannes*, 236; Carson, *The Gospel according to John*, 382; Carson, *Divine Sovereignty and Human Responsibility*, 188–89; Van Houwelingen, Johannes, 219; Schnackenburg, *Das Johannesevangelium*, Bd. 2, 352; Wierenga, *Verhalen als bewijzen*, 257. Ridderbos denies that the image implies that more sheep are in the pen, see Ridderbos, *Het evangelie naar Johannes*, Dl. 1, 411.

many Jews made up their minds and uttered their judgment on Jesus: 'He is demon-possessed and raving mad. Why listen to him?' In reaction to this unbelief, Jesus is very clear and sharp also: they who hear his voice and believe in him are his sheep, whereas these Jews are not his sheep and *therefore* do not believe (10:26–27).[328] Now Jesus also talks slightly differently about his death. Whereas he said firstly 'The good shepherd lays down his life for the sheep' (10:11.15), even with an openness to other sheep (10:16), now Jesus formulates exclusively: *My* sheep listen to my voice and I give *them* eternal life (10:27–28).[329] Jesus excludes those who exclude themselves. These statements have a double effect. On the one hand they make clear that whoever does not believe is not a sheep of the good shepherd; an election-statement. On the other hand, the rhetorical effect of these excluding statements in a book aiming at belief in Jesus as the Christ (cf. 20:30) may be that people who regard Jesus as demon-possessed convert and start listening to Jesus.[330] Although these verses have implications for a doctrine of election, their place within the narrative structure (Jesus reacts to the accusation of demon-possession) and their possible rhetorical effect must not be forgotten. To conclude, not all the sheep within this sheep pen are the sheep of Jesus. This means that not all the Jews believe in the Messiah. The Synagogue is no longer a point of reference (cf. John 9:34–35).

But Jesus has more sheep outside this sheep pen, as he says in 10:16. They will also listen to his voice and the result will be one flock with one shepherd. Jesus also has sheep among the gentile peoples. The difference between Israel and the gentiles will disappear, for it will be one flock.[331]

328. Bergmeier, *Glaube als Gabe nach Johannes*, 215; Carson, *The Gospel according to John*, 393; Carson, *Divine Sovereignty and Human Responsibility*, 190; Van Houwelingen, *Johannes*, 224; Piper, *The pleasures of God*, 137; Schnackenburg, *Das Johannesevangelium*, Bd. 2, 384.

Ridderbos opposes strongly against a divine predestination and focuses on birth of the flesh, being from below and of this world. In his justified opposition against determinism, he has less possibility to do justice to the fact that it is said that the Father gives Jesus his sheep, see Ridderbos, *Het evangelie naar Johannes*, Dl. 1, 428.

329. This importance of this difference must not be overstated, for already in 10:3–4 Jesus refers to the sheep as 'τὰ ἴδια πρόβατα.'

330. Cf. Carson, *The Gospel according to John*, 393; Ridderbos, *Het evangelie naar Johannes*, Dl. 1, 428; Schnackenburg, *Das Johannesevangelium*, Bd. 2, 385.

331. Carson, *The Gospel according to John*, 388; Van Houwelingen, *Johannes*, 222–23; Kowalski, *Die Hirtenrede*, 219–20; Ridderbos, *Het evangelie naar Johannes*, Dl. 1, 421; Schnackenburg, *Das Johannesevangelium*, Bd. 2, 376–77; Scholtissek, *In ihm sein und*

As a consequence, the metaphor involves connotations of gentile mission, unity and collectivity.

At first sight the attention paid to the Father is quite unexpected. First the Father is mentioned in 10:15 when the mutual knowledge of shepherd and sheep is compared with the mutual knowledge of Father and Son. Second Jesus says that the Father loves him because he lays down his life according to the command of his Father (10:17). He does all his works in his Father's name (10:25).[332] Third, it is the Father who gives the Son his sheep (10:29).[333] Fourth, the preservation of the sheep by the Son (10:28) is repeated in 10:29 and ascribed now to the Father. In election, salvation, and perseverance, the Father works.[334] The conclusion is logical: the Son and the Father are one. Seeing all these references to the Father, the attention paid to the Father is less strange than it might seem at first. In Ezekiel 34, the prophet Ezekiel protests against the shepherds of Israel who do not take care of their flock. Now the Lord himself will search for his sheep and look after them (Ezek 34,11–16) and provide one shepherd, his servant David (Ezek 34:13). This prophesy is fulfilled in John 10. The care of the Lord for his sheep returns as the care of the Father.

To conclude, the metaphor of the good shepherd has an Old Testament background. This metaphor portrays Jesus as the good shepherd who cares for his sheep. Important aspects are his voice, his knowledge of his sheep and the knowledge his sheep have of him—analogically related with the knowledge of Father and Son—his uniqueness, his protection against dangers resulting in his death for his sheep, his pursuing the well-being of his flock, and his preservation of his sheep until eternity, the difference between his own sheep in the sheep pen and other sheep, the unity of Jewish sheep and gentile sheep that he brings, collectivity, and the place of the Father. Again we find traces of a doctrine of election and perseverance, formulated in reaction to charges of demon-possession. Finally, this metaphor does not hint at a concept of participation.

bleiben, 325 Stuhlmacher, *Biblische Theologie des Neuen Testaments*, Bd. 2, 267.

332. Kowalski, *Die Hirtenrede*, 209–10; Carson, *The Gospel according to John*, 388; Van Houwelingen, *Johannes*, 222; Schnackenburg, *Das Johannesevangelium*, Bd. 2, 378.

333. Van Houwelingen, *Johannes*, 219; John Piper, *The pleasures of God*, 137.

334. Bergmeier, *Glaube als Gabe nach Johannes*, 215–16, 235; Carson, *The Gospel according to John*, 393.

John 15: The Vine

We have discussed John 15 firstly in 6.2.2, concerning remaining in the Son as the Son remained in the Father, by remaining in his love and obeying his commands (15:9–10). Secondly in 6.2.3, where the Old Testament background of the vine-metaphor was discussed and I interpreted the metaphor as meaning that Jesus represents the true Israel. Thirdly, we saw in 6.2.4 that Jesus in 15:13 refers to his death as a death for his friends out of love. Finally in 6.3.1 the ἐν-language was discussed, the coordinates of communion with Christ we find in John 15:3, 7, 9–10, 12, and 16: word, commands, and love, as well as the emphasis of the metaphor on fruit-bearing.

John 15 is a part of the farewell-discourses and different themes we find elsewhere return in this chapter.[335] It refers to the time after the departure of Jesus.[336] Jesus goes to his Father and promises the Holy Spirit. Nevertheless, the time after his departure is not a time of absence and desolation but of communion, as the image of the vine makes clear.

The image of the vine places us in a vineyard. The gardener cuts and prunes, so that the branches of the vine will be more fruitful. Only if vine and branches remain in contact can branches bear fruit, but dead branches are thrown into the fire and burned. However, a fruitful vine is the honour of the gardener.[337]

Jesus is the true vine. Apart from him, his disciples can do nothing (15:5), but remaining in him they will bear much fruit. He is the source of life and only in a communion of reciprocal inhabitation will his disciples find life and be fruitful. One remains in Christ by keeping his words (15:7), praying (15:7), remaining in his love (15:9), obeying his commands (15:10). As a branch of the vine, one is never alone, but always together with the vine and other branches. A branch cannot live of its own, apart

335. Cf. Stibbe, *John*, 163–65.

336. Scholtissek, *In ihm sein und bleiben*, 275.

337. Motifs related to the vine-metaphor return all over 15:1–17. Therefore the entire passage must be read as a creative elaboration of the metaphor. One must not conclude to quickly that the metaphor is left, as Heise does regarding 15:3, see Heise, *Bleiben*, 85. Cf. Dettwiler, *Die Gegenwart des Erhöhten*, 95; Scholtissek, *In ihm sein und bleiben*, 316.

from this communion.[338] The metaphor has not only Christological, but also ecclesiological implications.[339]

Whereas the metaphors of bread and shepherd do not lead to the conclusion that the concepts of representation and participation are necessary to understand Johannine thinking, this is not the case with the vine-metaphor. We have seen already in 6.2.3 that more continuity can be seen between Jesus and the disciples as vine and branches. Further, I concluded that this metaphor implies incorporation and representation. Jesus represents the true Israel. Likewise, in the case of this metaphor the concept of participation is helpful to understand what it is to be in Christ. This implies that the concept of reciprocal inhabitation on the one hand and representation and participation on the other hand do not exclude each other, for all these concepts are helpful to understand the vine-metaphor.

Also in relation to this metaphor the Father is mentioned, and the Father has a prominent place. The Father is mentioned right in the beginning: 'my Father is the gardener' (15:1). Before the union with Christ, the vine, is elaborated (15:3–7), the work of the Father is described: 'He cuts off every branch in me that bears no fruit, while every branch that does bear fruit he prunes so that it will be even more fruitful' (15:2).[340] This metaphor suggests that the care of the Father is very important for the fruit of the vine and the branches. With regard to the disciples, the pruning suggests that the Father may cut into their lives.[341] Further, the elaboration of the union with Christ is finished again with a reference to the Father: 'This is to my Father's glory, that you bear much fruit' (15:8a). It is the gardener's joy if his vine is very fruitful. Moreover, the Father has a central place in 15:9–17. Jesus loves his disciples as his Father has loved him (15:9). The disciples must obey Jesus' commands and remain in his love, just as he has obeyed his Father's commands and remained in his love (15:10). The words of Jesus contain everything he learned from his Father (15:15). And in 15:16 the motif of the Father's care returns: whatever the disciples ask the Father in Jesus' name to be fruitful, he will give

338. Cf. Dettwiler, *Die Gegenwart des Erhöhten*, 90; Stuhlmacher, *Biblische Theologie des Neuen Testaments*, Bd. 2, 267.

339. Scholtissek, *In ihm sein und bleiben*, 280.

340. Heise emphasises that the being of the Son and the being of the believers in the Son both are the work of the Fataher, see Heise, *Bleiben*, 83–84.

341. Schnackenburg, *Das Johannesevangelium*, Bd. 2, 110.

them. It is remarkable that the Father is not related here with themes like election and perseverance as was the case with the metaphors of the bread and the good shepherd, while at the same time the theme of election is mentioned in 15:16, but now related to the Son.[342] In this passage, the Father is the source of love and of Jesus' words, the Father's care guides the believer's life and the Father's glory is the goal of all.[343]

The metaphor makes clear that the life of a believer has to be fruitful. What is the reference of these fruits? According to Van Houwelingen, these fruits must not be understood as the good works of faith, but strictly as the people who will be converted through the preaching of the apostles: 'fruits' has a missionary reference. [344] That this reference is present in the image, becomes clear in 15:16, where Jesus says that he chose his disciples so that they should go, 'ὑπάγω.' Van Houwelingen is right that this exhortation is easier to understand if a missionary reference is presupposed.[345] Nevertheless, it is still the question whether the fruit bearing must be understood as strictly missionary. Or is the missionary fruit a part of the fruit they will bear? Van Houwelingen refers to John 4:36–38 and 12:24, claiming that fruit in these passages also have a missionary reference.[346] However, in 4:36–38 the metaphor is a different one—the harvest of the fields by reapers. Further, I doubt whether in John 12:24 the metaphor of 'fruit' has to be interpreted as strictly missionary. Van Houwelingen moreover claims that the fact that in 15:8 the word 'disciples' is mentioned has a missionary implication.[347] But it is not clear that only missionary fruit proves that they are disciples of Jesus. This can also refer to their communion of love (cf. John 17:23). Further, the Old Testament background of the image of the vine does not suggest a strictly missionary connotation. And finally, until 15:16 an innocent reader would not expect missionary connotations, for the text does not give hints in a missionary direction. Nevertheless, in 15,16 this missionary hints are given. The disciples are

342. Dettwiler, *Die Gegenwart des Erhöhten*, 99; Ridderbos, *Het evangelie naar Johannes*, Dl. 2, 172.

343. Schnackenburg uses the word 'theocentric' with regard to the place of the Father in this passage, see Schnackenburg, *Das Johannesevangelium*, Bd. 2, 110.

344. Van Houwelingen, *Johannes*, 310–15.

345. Van Houwelingen, *Johannes*, 314–15. Cf. also Carson, *The Gospel according to John*, 523.

346. Van Houwelingen, *Johannes*, 312.

347. Van Houwelingen, *Johannes*, 312.

elected and sent to go and bear fruit—preaching the gospel in the world. Therefore, the fruits must be understood in a broader sense, referring to the entire Christian life of which mission is an aspect.[348]

As a consequence, this metaphor has implications for the relation between belief and moral life. Belief in Christ and communion with him are the presupposition of a Christian life. Without Christ, you can do nothing. At the same time, belief in Christ and communion with him must become visible in fruits. A branch without fruit is a dead branch that will be cut off and thrown into the fire. Christology is the foundation of moral life.[349]

Finally I want to mention the intimacy of the metaphor. The communion of a vine and its branches is very close, as is indicated by the language of reciprocal 'remaining in.' This intimacy will lead to a flowering prayer-life (15:7). Further, Jesus stimulates the disciples to do as he did. Moreover, Jesus compares his disciples to friends. Friends, he dies for out of great love (15:13); friends, who are characterized by doing what Jesus commands (15:14);[350] friends, whom he told everything his Father told him and who are not like slaves who do not know their master's business (15:15). It is an image elaborated in the direction of a communion of love (15:9–17)[351] and a communion of joy (15:11). Concerning the death of Christ, this means that his death is not seen as a death for the world, but as a death for his friends, with whom he lives in intimate communion.

To conclude, in the metaphor of the vine different lines and themes come together: the Old Testament background; Jesus as source of life; the communality of the Christian life; the emphasis on the Father; the parallel between the Father-Son relation and the Son-christian relation; a fruitful Christian life with different fruits, including missionary fruits; several coordinates of the communion like word, commands and love, but also prayer; the intimacy of the communion as a communion of

348 Carson, *The Gospel according to John*, 517. Schnackenburg, *Das Johannesevangelium*, Bd. 2 113, 127. Ridderbos concentrates on the broad sense and denies that a missionary accent can be seen in 15,16, see Ridderbos, *Het evangelie naar Johannes*, Dl. 2, 167–68, 172–73. Dettwiler interprets the fruit-bearing as a living in the communion of love, see Dettwiler, *Die Gegenwart des Erhöhten*, 94.

349. Dettwiler, *Die Gegenwart des Erhöhten*, 100; Scholtissek, *In ihm sein und bleiben*, 280, 297.

350. Cf. Carson, *The Gospel according to John*, 522; Ridderbos, *Het evangelie naar Johannes*, Dl. 2, 171; Scholtissek, *In ihm sein und bleiben*, 297.

351. Dettwiler, *Die Gegenwart des Erhöhten*, 101.

loving friends; a joyful communion; and finally the death of Jesus as a death for friends. Unlike in other metaphors, themes such as election and perseverance are not present, although the care of the Father and Jesus' choice of his disciples are mentioned. And also unlike other metaphors, the concept of participation is necessary to understand the meaning of this metaphor.

Conclusions

Having discussed these three images, some conclusions can be drawn with regard to the union with Christ. I will relate these conclusions to John 17 also.

a. As the continuity with the Old Testament indicates, Jesus is the fulfilment of the scriptures.[352] Union with Christ is also a fulfilment of the promises of the Old Testament. As a result, a combination of union with Christ with the motive of the new covenant can be defended quite well.

b. It is impossible to reflect on union with Christ without mentioning the Father. The Father stands at the beginning. He knows and loves the Son, grants him to have life in himself and speaks to him. He sends the Son and gives him as life to the world (cf. 17:4, 6–8, 18). It is the Father who gives persons to the Son and draws them so that they come to the Son (cf. 17:2, 6, 9). The Father cares for them and keeps them in his hand (cf. 17:11). Finally the Father is the goal, for he is glorified in what believers do.

c. The metaphors show that Jesus is unique. All the images are introduced in an 'I am'-saying, emphasising the uniqueness of Jesus. Further Jesus is the unique source of life. All metaphors emphasise that Jesus gives life. Without him no life exists, so that union with Christ is the precondition for life.

d. That Jesus is the source of life and that in union with him life is given, is related to his death, but also with themes of future eschatology. First, his death is a precondition: Jesus gives himself in death for life. This death has a universal and a particular aspect. According to the metaphor of the bread Jesus is given for the world, emphasising the universality of salvation given in him. Nevertheless, in relation

352. Cf. Obermann, *Die christologische Erfüllung der Schrift im Johannesevangelium.*

to this metaphor it is also said that Jesus will raise the persons the Father gave to him, emphasising the relation with particular persons. The other metaphors also emphasise that Jesus dies for particular persons with whom he has a relation: his sheep, his friends (cf. 17:9). Second, the union with Christ as a life giving union is related also to themes of future eschatology: perseverance until eternal life and the gift of eternal life in the resurrection on the last day.

e. The metaphor of the bread and the vine both are associated with ἐν-language. However, it is understandable that this is not the case with the third metaphor, for the metaphor of the shepherd and his flock is difficult to combine with ἐν-language. As a logical consequence, we find further in relation to all metaphors the parallel between the Father-Son relation and the Son-believers relation: a parallel in living by the Father or the Son, in mutual knowing, in being loved and remaining in the other's love, and in keeping commands (cf. 17:20–26).

f. All images indicate the collectivity of the persons united with Christ as a people, a flock or as branches of the same vine (cf. 17:22f).

g. Union with Christ is related to themes traditionally developed in a doctrine of predestination: election, particular redemption and perseverance (cf. 17:2, 6, 9–12, 15, 19). The decision of God precedes human decisions. However, the rhetorical context of statements expressing these themes must not be forgotten. This is not to deny the referential content of these statements, but where the danger of misunderstanding is urgent it is important to see the pragmatic intention of these statements. In the narrative, these statements are a reaction to unbelief. Their intention is not primarily to exclude, for they go together with, or are even preceded by, more open and inviting utterances. We find them in a book written to evoke faith in Jesus as the Christ. But if people who ought to know better refuse to believe in Jesus as the Christ, they are, in their self-esteem confronted with the message that they can not believe, unless the Father gives them faith. The intention of these statements is to encourage the believing reader or to bring the unbeliever to embarrassment and conversion. Human beings are called to believe, but at the same time is made clear that God decides over faith and unbelief, combating human pretensions.[353]

h. With regard to the concepts of representation, substitution, reciprocal inhabitation and participation the following can be concluded. First, because the uniqueness of Jesus is emphasised, the necessity of the concept of substitution is evident. Second, in relation to two of the three metaphors the ἐν-language is utilised, justifying the conclusion that the concept of reciprocal inhabitation is also necessary. Third, the metaphor of the vine shows that these concepts do not exclude the concepts of representation and participation. Although they are less prominent, nevertheless these two concepts also have to be used to understand what it means to be in Christ, seen in a Johannine perspective.

6.3.3 PARTICIPATION: BECOMING LIKE CHRIST

John's Christology has exclusive and inclusive aspects, as we have seen. Jesus provides a place, but is at the same time the entrance to that place and the place itself.[354] If he is given to us as a place, this might imply that we share in his position. Therefore, in this section the central question is, whether and to what extent we participate in the position of Jesus himself. If we share in the position of Christ, the claim that the use of the concept of participation is necessary to reconstruct Johannine thinking is justified.

The first question now is, whether and to what extent believers participate in the position of the Son in his relation to his Father. In 6.2.2 we saw that in the paralleled relations between Father—Son and Christ—Christians, the Son might be representing believers in relation to his Father and the Father in relation to believers. He is unique and several predications used for Jesus can only be applied to believers after

353. For the combating of human pretensions, see Carson, *Divine Sovereignty and Human Responsibility*, 182. Bergmeier notices that John does not give 'eine den Gesetzen der Logik genügende Predestinations*lehre*,' Bergmeier, *Glaube als Gabe nach Johannes*, 231. Further Schnelle remarks: 'Prädestinationsaussagen sind immer theologische Grenzaussagen,' Schnelle, *Neutestamentliche Antropologie*, 151. See further Bergmeier, *Glaube als Gabe nach Johannes*, 231–36; Carson, *Divine Sovereignty and Human Responsibility*, 197–98; Schnelle, *Neutestamentliche Antropologie*, 148–51.

354. Nissen, 'Mission in the Fourth Gospel,' 224.

modification. At the same time, these modifications show that believers to some extent do participate in his position.

Now it is time to deal more extensively with these modifications. They show to what extent believers participate in the position of Christ according to John. In 6.3.1 the use of the designation 'Father' in reciprocal relations appeared to be limited exclusively to the relation with the Son. In the gospel, God is the Father of Jesus; only in John 20:17 Jesus refers to God as 'my Father and your Father,' marking the fact that he has a special relation with his Father as well as the new given possibility for his disciples to call God 'Father.' In the first letter of John, God is called 'Father.'[355] Now, after the departure and glorification of Christ, it is emphasised that God is not just *called* 'Father,' but believers *are* God's children and he is their Father (1 John 3:1).[356] However, it is still the case that Jesus Christ is called 'υἱός,' whereas believers are called 'τέκνα θεοῦ' (1 John 3:1, 2, 10; 5:2), and not 'υἱοὶ' like in Romans.[357] Jesus is μονογενὴς (John 1:18; 3:16; 1 John 4:9), a believer is born from God as 'γεγεννημένος εκ τοῦ θεοῦ' (1 John 3:9; 4:7; 5:1, 4, 18; vgl. 2:29). Jesus came from above, 'ἄνωθεν ἐρχόμενος' (John 3:31) and is from above, 'ἐκ τῶν ἄνω' (John 8:23), believers must be born from above, 'γεννηθῆναι ἄνωθεν' (John 3:3, 7). Jesus is anointed, 'Χριστός,' Christians received a 'χρῖσμα' (1 John 2:20, 27). Many of these examples show, that Rusam is right in stating that the relation between believers and God in the First Letter of John is described with words recalling words used to describe the relation between Jesus and God in the Gospel.[358] The first letter unfolds an ecclesiology that is caused by what is told in the gospel.[359] Whereas in the Gospel the disciples are called friends once (John 15:13–15), in 1 John the believers are called brothers (1 John 2:10f; 3:10, 12, 13, 15, 17; 4:20, 21; 5:16), beloved members of the family of God.[360] Although the Son remains unique and

355. Rusam has shown that in 1 John God is called 'Father' only once in combination with 'children,' in 1 John 3:1. In other instances it is used absolutely or in combination with 'Son.' But he is anxious not to over-interpret these observations. See Rusam, *Die Gemeinschaft der Kinder Gottes*, 110.

356. Rusam, *Die Gemeinschaft der Kinder Gottes*, 125.

357. Rusam, *Die Gemeinschaft der Kinder Gottes*, 124, 147–49; cf. Crump, 'Re-examining the Johannine Trinity,' 411.

358. Rusam, *Die Gemeinschaft der Kinder Gottes*, 153.

359. Rusam, *Die Gemeinschaft der Kinder Gottes*, 127.

360. Rusam, *Die Gemeinschaft der Kinder Gottes*, 109, 126.

stands in a unique relation with his Father, yet the believers participate in the position of the Son. 'Only thanks to the Son the children belong to the great family of God.'[361]

This is confirmed by what we saw in 6.3.1, that Jesus to some extent makes believers participate in his position. He is an example for believers in his dependency on, love for and obedience to his Father. Believers participate in the reciprocal inhabitation that characterizes the relation between Father and Son[362] and the communion with Christ and in Christ with God will have a stable character.[363] However, the unity of Father and Son preserves its unique divine character; believers do not participate in this unity. To conclude, it is the unique divine character of Jesus, that he makes believers participate in his position in his relation to his Father.

We discussed already the inclusive moment of Jesus' death and resurrection in 6.2.5. Passages discussed in this section bring us to a second issue, participation in the death and resurrection of Christ.

John 14:2–4 contains both an exclusive and an inclusive moment. Jesus departs to the Father's house to prepare a place; an activity in which believers do not participate. Nevertheless, Jesus promises the believers that he will come back to bring them to the place where he is—in his Father's house. A participation in his residence in this place is promised here. A similar idea can be found in John 12:26b: 'where I am, my servant also will be.'

John 14,19 indicates that the gift of life the gospel of John promises again and again is a participation in the life of Christ. Here Jesus says that the disciples will see him, for 'ἐγὼ ζῶ καὶ ὑμεῖς ζήσετε.' The difference of present and future tense shows the difference between Jesus and the disciples and their dependency on Jesus: because he lives, they will live.[364] They will participate in his life. Because in the next verse is written that they will know 'that I am in my Father and you in me and I in you' it is reasonable to relate this participation in the life of Christ with reciprocal inhabitation (cf. John 6:57). Participation in the position of Christ in his

361. M. de Jonge, *Jesus: Stranger from Heaven and Son of God*, 152. See further 144, 151.

362. Cf. Scholtissek, *In ihm sein und bleiben*, 262.

363. Cf. Scholtissek, *In ihm sein und bleiben*, 209, 353–54, 365.

364. Dettwiler, *Die Gegenwart des Erhöhten*, 168; Schnackenburg, *Das Johannesevangelium*, Bd. III, 89.

relation with his Father and their communion of reciprocal inhabitation implies also a participation in their fullness of life.[365]

Comparable to John 14:2–4, a combination of the exclusive and the inclusive moment can be found in John 17:19, 24. As we saw, Jesus says in 17:19 that he sanctifies himself so that his disciples too may be sanctified. His disciples do not participate in his sanctifying act, but they do in the resulting situation of being sanctified. And in 17:24, Jesus prays that those whom the Father has given him may be where he is to see his glory. Jesus is unique in his glory, because the Father loved him before the creation of the world, but the disciples participate in his place.

In the first letter of John, an important passage is 1 John 3:2. Here the author writes that on the day of the *parousia*, 'we shall be like him, for we shall see him as he is.' Although it is not totally clear whether 'him' refers to God or to Christ, the last is more probable,[366] but even if it refers to God, it is evident that we will be like Christ because he is like God. We shall participate in the glory he has as the resurrected and glorified Son of God.

To conclude, it is not said that we participate in the death of Christ, but we participate and will participate even more in the result of his death and resurrection. Our life is a participation in his life and we will be like he is and where he is.

As we have seen, Jesus is an example for believers in his dependency, love and obedience. This leads to a third theme, the theme of imitation of Christ. Imitation does not necessarily imply participation, but because participation in Christ does imply following the example of Christ, it is relevant that we find this theme in Johannine thinking. Central in John is the imitation of the love of Christ; we find this motif several times. First in John 13:14–15. After Jesus washed his disciples' feet, he asks his disciples whether they understand what he has done for them. Then he tells them why he did this. He gave them an example to be followed. If he, their lord and teacher has served his disciples, washing their feet, they should also wash one another's feet. Against the background of three other passages

365. See Schnelle, *Neutestamentliche Antropologie*, 168; Scholtissek, *In ihm sein und bleiben*, 192, 209, 314.

366. According to Lalleman and Marshall it refers to Jesus. Smalley thinks it refers to Jesus but leaves open the possibility that it also refers to God. Strecker writes that in the *parousia* we will see God. See Lalleman, 1, 2 *en* 3 *Johannes*, 170; Marshall, *The Epistles of John*, 173; Smalley, 1, 2, 3 *John*, 147; Strecker, *Die Johannesbriefe*, 153–56.

(John 15:12–13, 1 John 2:6 and 3:16), it is very plausible to see in this feet-washing a prefiguration of the death of Jesus as an example.[367] In John 15:12–13 Jesus explicitly identifies his death for his friends as an example to be followed. Elaborating what it is to remain in Christ's love, he gives his disciples a command: 'Love each other as I have loved you. Greater love has no one than this, that he lay down his life for his friends.' This returns in the first letter, in 1 John 3:16: 'We know love by this, that he laid down his life for us. And we ought to lay down our lives for the brothers' (my translation). More generally, the command to follow the example of Christ is given in 1 John 2:6: 'Whoever says to remain in him, must walk in the same manner as he walked' (my translation). Here explicitly remaining in Christ is related to imitation of Christ.[368] And in 1 John 3:3 we find the exhortation to purify oneself, 'just as he is pure.'[369] These five passages make clear that for John imitation of the example of Christ is important for those who belong to Christ and remain in him.[370]

Fourth, in the gospel of John we find the motif of participation in the suffering of Christ, in John 15:18–21. The world hates Jesus because he does not belong to the world. Because the disciples are not of the world, the world will hate them too. Those who persecuted Jesus will persecute his disciples too.[371]

Finally the disciples participate in being sent into the world. Jesus is sent by the Father to make the Father known and to do his work.[372] The Paraclete is sent by Father and Son to enable understanding of Jesus and to equip them for their mission.[373] And the disciples are sent by Jesus to do as he did.[374] This sending of the disciples into the world we find in John 15:16; 17:18 and 20:21.

367. Nissen, 'Community and Ethics in the Gospel of John,' 202.

368. Malatesta, *Interiority and Covenant*, 122.

369. Marshall, *The Epistles of John*, 174; Smalley, *1, 2, 3 John*, 149;

370. See also Hays, *The Moral Vision of the New Testament*, 144–46; Schnelle, *Neutestamentliche Antropologie*, 138.

371. De Jonge, *Jesus*, 154, 157; Marshall, *New Testament Theology*, 507–8.

372. Loader, *The Christology of the Fourth Gospel*, 77–78; Nissen, 'Mission in the Fourth Gospel,' 216.

373. Loader, *The Christology of the Fourth Gospel*, 85–92; Nissen, 'Mission in the Fourth Gospel,' 216.

374. De Jonge, *Jesus*, 152–53, 155; Hays, *The Moral Vision of the New Testament*, 143; Nissen, 'Mission in the Fourth Gospel,' 216; Schnelle, *Neutestamentliche Antropologie*, 146; Stuhlmacher, *Biblische Theologie des Neuen Testaments, Band 2*, 269.

To conclude, in Johannine thinking believers participate in Jesus Christ. This is a participation as far as the inclusive moment of the work of Jesus reaches; the exclusive moment is also strongly emphasised. Believers do not participate totally in Christ. However, they participate in his position in his relation with his Father, although not in their divine unity. God is their Father and they are God's children (not sons). They participate in their relation of reciprocal interiority. Believers do not participate in the death of Jesus, but they do in his resurrection and in his glorification. To live is to participate in the life of Jesus and the believers will be where Jesus is, glorified like he is. Further Jesus is to be imitated in his love. Finally the disciples participate in Jesus' suffering and his mission into the world.

6.3.4 CONCLUSION

How should we understand the Johannine ἐν-language, and is the concept of participation necessary to reconstruct the Johannine view of soteriology?

The relation of Father and Son is a relation of reciprocal interiority, of reciprocal inhabitation and reciprocal remaining in each other. This is indicated by the ἐν-language. This relation has a unique character, and Father and Son live within a unique unity. Nevertheless, in the Son the communion is opened for the believers. The characteristics of this relation can be transferred analogously to the relation of the Son and the believers. Until the *parousia* this relation has a less stable character, so that the exhortation to remain in Christ is necessary. In this relation, identity is given and not annihilated. As a result of this relation with the Son, it can also be said that the believers are in God, for the Son brings them into communion with the Father also. In this communion with Christ, the Spirit has a mediating function, but he cannot be identified with Christ. Presupposed in all of this is the identity of giver and gift: in salvation Jesus gives, he gives himself. As far as this identity of giver and gift is concerned, and the Son makes us participate in his position, the concept of participation is necessary to understand the ἐν-language. Further, we need other concepts: interiority, reciprocal inhabitation and communion.

A comparison of the images used for the unity with Christ—the living bread, the good shepherd and his sheep, and the vine and the branches—made clear the central position of the Father, the uniqueness of Jesus Christ as source of life, and the importance of both his death as well as the final resurrection on the last day. Further we saw that it is related to themes of election and perseverance. Concerning concepts I concluded here that all four concepts are necessary to understand the unity with Christ: substitution as far as the uniqueness of Christ is concerned, less prominently representation indicated especially by the image of the vine, reciprocal inhabitation in relation to the ἐν-language, and finally the concept of participation. I showed that although believers do not participate in Christ in all respects, nevertheless a participation can be seen in (aspects of) his relation with his Father, in his resurrection and glorification, and in his suffering and mission. Further the participation-theme implies imitation of Christ.

6.4 Reality

The third central question concerns the reality of 'being in Christ.' In this section I will deal with several aspects of the reality as Johannine literature sketches it. The character of this reality is first hidden (6.4.1), second determined by a restored relation with God (6.4.2), third complex (6.4.3), fourth eschatological (6.4.4), fifth moral (6.4.5), sixth collective and individual (both 6.4.6).

6.4.1 HIDDEN

At first sight, the reality of 'being in Christ' is a general accessible reality. God loves the world (John 3:16). Everyone can read the gospel of John, and see that it is written 'that you may believe that Jesus is the Christ, the Son of God, and that by believing you may have life in his name' (John 20:31). The invitation to come, to see and to believe is a general one, and the mystagogical gospel intends to bring the reader to its heart: the communion with God in the Son. Looking more closely, it appears that the Word came to his own, but they did not receive him (John 1:11). Especially the Jewish leaders do not believe (John 7:45–52) but suffer from spiritual blindness (John 9:4–41). Confronted with their unbelief, Jesus makes clear that faith must be given by God himself; blindness must be healed. This makes clear that the reality of 'being in Christ' is hidden and only accessible if access is given by God. Its reality can be experienced only in the perspective of faith.

This brings us to the image of a birth, a birth 'ἄνωθεν' or from God.[375] The first time we find this motif in John 1:12–13. It might seem here that this birth from God here is a result of faith, for 'all who received him' and 'believed in his name' (1:12) Christ gave the right to become God's children. But 1:13 makes clear that this concerns those 'which were born not of blood, nor of the will of the flesh, nor of the will of man, but of God' (KJV). This does not entirely exclude the interpretation that a birth from God follows faith. Nevertheless, if faith leads to a birth from God, then still persons born of blood and flesh would believe and John denies exactly this. Further, in more passages we found this order: first a statement inviting faith, second statements making clear that only God can give faith. Consequently, it is more likely that 112–13 must be understood in this way, that those who believe received the right to become God's children from Christ, who gave his life to make them God's children; and that at the same time this faith is caused by a birth of God.[376]

The image of birth returns in John 3. Nicodemus comes in the night, and discloses amicably his disposition towards Jesus, but he is blind to the true identity of Jesus as the Son of God who has to be crucified. Jesus in his reply chooses shock-therapy, destroying the certainty of the Jewish teacher and revealing to the reader Nicodemus' blindness: 'unless someone is born 'ἄνωθεν,' he cannot see the kingdom of God' (3:3; my translation).[377] A birth 'ἄνωθεν' is an ambigious expression, for it can be understood horizontally (temporally) as a new birth or vertically as a birth from above, caused by God.[378] In his response, Nicodemus asks

375. John 1:12–13; 3:1–8; 1 John 3:9; 4:4, 6, 7; 5:1, 4, 18, 19.

376. Bergmeier, *Glaube als Gabe nach Johannes*, 219; Carson, *The Gospel according to John*, 126; Carson, *Divine Sovereignty and Human Responsibility*, 181–82; Van Houwelingen, *Johannes*, 50; Ridderbos, *Het evangelie naar Johannes*, Dl. 1, 60–64; Schnackenburg, *Das Johannesevangelium*, Bd. 1, 237–39.

377. Popp, *Grammatik des Geistes*, 111–13; Wierenga, *Verhalen als bewijzen*, 155; see also 150.

378. The combination of the possibility of Nicodemus' interpretation and Jesus' own explanation makes it necessary to see the expression as ambigious; see Burge, *The Anointed Community*, 167; Carson, *The Gospel according to John*, 189; Frey, *Die johanneische Eschatologie*, Bd. III, 258; Popp, *Grammatik des Geistes*, 116; Wierenga, *Verhalen als bewijzen*, 155.

Hofius chooses 'a new birth,' see Hofius, 'Das Wunder der Wiedergeburt,' 40–43; Van Houwelingen, Ridderbos and Schnackenburg choose a birth from above, see Van Houwelingen, *Johannes*, 91; Ridderbos, *Het evangelie naar Johannes*, Dl. 1, 150 ; Schnackenburg, *Das Johannesevangelium*, Bd. 1, 381.

whether Jesus means another fleshly birth.[379] But Jesus makes clear this is not what he means, but rather a birth of water and Spirit, a birth from above (3:5–8).[380] Such a birth is necessary, because of the hopelessness of human existence.[381] This birth has a hidden character: the effect of this birth is as clear as if the wind blows, but where this birth comes from is hidden—as was the case with the wind in a pre-meteorological age.[382] Because Jesus in his reaction on Nicodemus' question for more explanation (3:9) refers to his death on the cross, the cross must have a foundational meaning for this birth from above.[383] Hence, cross and Spirit together give a person a radical new existence in a new birth from above; a birth with a hidden character. This birth is necessary to see Jesus

379. Carson, Frey, Popp, and Wierenga see the reaction of Nicodemus as proof of his spiritual blindness. According to Wierenga this is a typical Johannine case of 'arranged misunderstanding,' creating the possibility for Jesus to explain his teaching. See Carson, *Divine Sovereignty and Human Responsibility*, 182; Frey, *Die johanneische Eschatologie*, Bd. III, 258; Popp, *Grammatik des Geistes*, 119–20; Wierenga, *Verhalen als bewijzen*, 150–52, 155–56.

According to Van Houwelingen Nicodemus does not show lack of understanding here, but formulates a provoking question to express his objection to the stringent rule Jesus just formulated; Van Houwelingen, *Johannes*, 91. However, Jesus' reaction in 3:10–12 shows that even a teacher as Nicodemus is in need of regeneration. Hence his problem is spiritual blindness.

380. Primarily this must not be understood as a word of Jesus referring to a new birth caused by baptism, although also for Nicodemus in his perspective a reference to the baptism of e.g. John the Baptist would be possible: the emphasis lies on the Spirit. Cf. Burge, *The Anointed Community*, 157–58, 167, 169; Carson, *The Gospel according to John*, 191–95; Ridderbos, *Het evangelie naar Johannes*, Dl. 1, 152. For Christian readers a sacramental reference might be possible, because of the second layer of sacramental overtones of this passage. Cf. Schnackenburg, *Das Johannesevangelium*, Bd. 1, 383. Burge, Carson and Ridderbos do not reckon with this possibility. Popp gives, in his interpretation, too central a place to baptism. See Popp, *Grammatik des Geistes*, 121–23, 125–26. Van Houwelingen gives space for an interpretation that does justice to both layers, see Van Houwelingen, *Johannes*, 92–93. Wierenga reads here also a hint at the Rule of community of Qumran, see Wierenga, *Verhalen als bewijzen*, 156.

381. Carson, *The Gospel according to John*, 196–97; Hofius, 'Das Wunder der Wiedergeburt,' 51, 75–77; Schnackenburg, *Das Johannesevangelium*, Bd. 1, 385.

382. Hofius stresses that the comparison concerns the working of the new birth and not its cause; it concerns 'die Unfaßbarkeit' and 'die Unverfügbarkeit des Geschehens,' see Hofius, 'Das Wunder der Wiedergeburt,' 52. See further Carson, *The Gospel according to John*, 197; Van Houwelingen, *Johannes*, 95.

383. Burge, *The Anointed Community*, 169; Carson, *The Gospel according to John*, 204; Frey, *Die johanneische Eschatologie*, Bd. III, 260; Hofius, 'Das Wunder der Wiedergeburt,' 61–66, 74, 78; Popp, *Grammatik des Geistes*, 143.

as Christ and as Son of God and as a result, this new birth takes place if a person comes to believe in Jesus as the Christ and as Son of God.[384] To conclude, perspective (faith) and reality of a new existence (a new birth from above) belong inseparably together and are totally dependent on the acts of God—Son and Sprit.[385]

This is related with the εἶναι ἐκ-language, we find in the Johannine writings and also in John 1 and 3: of blood, of the flesh, of the will of man, of God (1:13); of water and of the Spirit (3:5); of the flesh, of the Spirit (3:6); of the Spirit (3:8); of the heaven (3:13, 27); of the earth, of the heaven (3:31). This language does not indicate a dualism of a higher and a lower part of reality, but of two realms in reality, one new realm determined by Christ and one old, determined by sin.[386]

In conclusion, both passages make clear that a fleshly person cannot see this reality. Access to this reality must be given, and if access is given the reality itself is given also. This gift has a hidden character, for the Spirit works in a hidden way. In the gift, a person comes to faith. Therefore, the exhortation to believe and the conviction that faith is a gift, implying a new birth from God, do not exclude each other but belong together. Only in the perspective of faith is this reality experienced.

6.4.2 RELATION WITH SPIRIT, SON, AND FATHER

As a result of the preceding investigations, it can be concluded that 'being in Christ' is a reality consisting in a relation with the παράκλητος, the Spirit; a relation with Jesus, the Son; and a relation with the Father. It is the Spirit who relates with Jesus and represents him for us (John 14:26; 16:13–15). If we have the Spririt, we remain in Jesus Christ, the Son (1 John 2:20, 27; 3:24; 4:13). It is Jesus who gives life, for he is our life. Whoever believes in Christ, the resurrection and the life, will live, even though he dies (John 11:25–26). All the 'I am'-sayings confirm this: Jesus is the source of life. Hence a relation with him determines the existence of a believer. If this gift of life and existence is real, this relation with Jesus

384. Popp, Grammatik des Geistes, 145.

385. Cf. Bergmeier, *Glaube als Gabe nach Johannes*, 219; Burge, *The Anointed Community*, 170; Hofius, 'Das Wunder der Wiedergeburt,' 51–52, 75–76, 79–80.

386. Although human decision and faith do play a role within this dualism, this dualism cannot be understood apart from the act of God who gives a new existence. However, this does not imply determinism. See further Bergmeier, *Glaube als Gabe nach Johannes*, 214–16; Keck, 'Derivation as Destiny'; Schnelle, *Neutestamentliche Antropologie*, 151–53.

Christ determines its reality. It is also Jesus who makes the Father known and brings us into communion with Him. To know the Father is eternal life (John 17:3). And it is the Father who gives the disciples to Jesus, so that he will be their life. Hence also the relation with the Father is part of the reality of 'being in Christ.'

The relation with the Son cannot be understood apart from the first creation. We saw that God created the world by the λόγος (6.2.1). Every human being is dependent on the λόγος for life and being. Nevertheless, this relation with the source of life became problematic. The λόγος became flesh to restore this relation. Therefore the restoration of the relation with the λόγος as source of life implies somehow a restoration of creation, or better, a new creation.[387]

Although the gospel and the first letter of John do not explicitly teach a doctrine of the Trinity, nevertheless the existence of a relation between the believer and Father, Son and Spirit is evident and the idea of a Trinity is evoked.[388] The question is now, whether the believer becomes part of the Trinity. This seems to be the case in the interpretation of Malatesta, for in his view the Father-Son relation is a covenant-relation in which the believer participates, participating in Christ. But he tends to forget the exclusivity of the Son. Although an analogy exists between the Father-Son relation and the Son-believer relation, and with Malatesta it can be said that our relation of interiority with Christ can be compared with 'the interiority and circumincession of the divine persons,'[389] nevertheless a difference exists between the Father-Son relation and the Son-believer relation as we have seen (see 6.3.1). The unity of Father and Son is unique, and believers do not come to share in this unity with the Father. Although the believer is surrounded by Father, Son and Spirit, living in communion with the Father by the Spirit and the Son, the Johannine perspective excludes the possibility that a believer would become a part of the Trinity. If deification would imply becoming part of the Trinity, than the idea of deification does not fit within a Johannine perspective.

Further we saw that the relation with Father, Son and Spirit does not lead to a mystical unity if this means dissolution of identity (see 6.3.1).

387. Cf. Bergmeier, *Glaube als Gabe nach Johannes*, 219.

388. Cf. footnote 294.

389. Malatesta, *Interiority and Covenant*, 133.

Instead, the relation with the Son gives identity, just as the identity of the Son is not dissolved by his relation with his Father.

6.4.3 COMPLEX

Being in Christ in a Johannine perspective is a complex reality. Several reasons may clarify why it is a complex reality. Firstly, this reality comes into existence by an event that is referred to with the metaphor of another birth from above. Secondly I discussed several coordinates, as salvation in Christ, the word, love, faith and the acts of a believer which all play their role. This results in complexity. Thirdly, this reality is determined by Christ himself, whose identity as incarnation of the word of God has a complex character. Fourthly, the death of Christ has a constituting function for this unity. Fifthly, Father and Spirit play a role in our unity with Christ as we have seen. But how should we understand what it is to be surrounded by Father, Son and Spirit? This implies as a sixth aspect, that at least four actors, Father, Son, Spirit and the believer, play a role within this reality; three of them are divine and the fourth is a sinful human being, whose relation with God is restored. Seventhly, reciprocal inhabitation appeared to be a central and useful concept to understand this communion with Christ. But how should we imagine two persons living in each other? Spatially conceived it is hard to imagine. If a person is in the other, the second cannot be at the same time in the first also. As a result, it is, eighthly, not surprising that the different metaphors for unity with Christ cannot be combined if they are taken literally: a peace of bread is eaten and taken in, but it is difficult to understand what it is to be in Christ if Christ is compared with bread; a shepherd walks before his sheep but is not united with his sheep, no reciprocal inhabitation is seen normally; and the image of a vine and its branches gives another perspective on this unity. A futher complicating factor is that these images can be understood only within their own rhetorical setting: they are chosen to make a specific point. As a result, it is not surprising that it is not easy to understand the reality of being in Christ and Christ being in us.

6.4.4 ESCHATOLOGICAL

Another complicating factor is the eschatological character of its reality. We have seen that motifs of a future as well as a present eschatology are found within Johannine thinking (6.3.1). What complicates reflection on the reality of being united with Christ and living in reciprocal inhabitation with him is that it is related both to present and to future eschatology. This is clear in the notion of life. First it is a reality given by the crucified and resurrected Christ. The glorified Christ is the present Christ by his Spirit. The believer 'has eternal life and will not be condemned; he has crossed over from death to life' (John 5:24). The last judgment has taken place for whoever believes and Jesus has overcome the world (16:33).[390] Whoever believes in Jesus, has eternal life (6:47). Eternal life begins now and is given in the present.[391] Because Jesus is the resurrection and the life, a believer will live, 'even though he dies; and whoever lives and believes in me will never die' (11:25–26).[392]

This last passage indicates already that a problem still exists. A believer dies, although he lives. Therefore it is not surprising that motifs of future eschatology are used in Johannine thinking in connection with the notion of life. This is very clear in John 6. That Jesus is the true heavenly bread that gives eternal life cannot be separated from the resurrection on the last day

390. Bergmeier writes that both eschatological salvation and judgment are present in John, see Bergmeier, *Glaube als Gabe nach Johannes*, 232. Cf. Frey, who emphasises the eschatological decisiveness of the hour of Jesus, Frey, *Die johanneische Eschatologie,* Bd. II, 291.

391. Frey, *Die johanneische Eschatologie,* Bd. III, 262, 268, 270; Hays, *The Moral Vision of the New Testament*, 149–50; Stuhlmacher, *Biblische Theologie des Neuen Testaments, Band* 2, 259–60.

392. Frey paraphrases John 11:25–26 as follows: 'Wer an Jesus glaubt, wird, auch wenn er [leiblich] stirft, [dann, d.h. zukünftig leiblich auf-]leben [d.h. an der durch Jesus vollzogenen Auferweckung des Lebens teilhaben]. Wer das [ewige] leben hat und [bzw. indem er] an Jesus glaubt, wird niemals [spirituell, definiv, 'in Sünden'] sterben [d.h. er is befreit vom eschatologischen Verdammungsurteil bzw. vom 'ewigen' Tod]. See Frey, *Die johanneische Eschatologie,* Bd. III, 452; cf. Stuhlmacher, *Biblische Theologie des Neuen Testaments, Band* 2, 249.

Van Houwelingen emphasises especially the future eschatological aspect of 11:25–26. He reads it as two statements: a. addressed to Lazarus and those who died with him: I am the resurrection. Whoever believed and died, will be raised by Jesus on the last day; b. addressed to Martha and Maria, together with the living: I am the life. Whoever believes cannot die. However, this implies that eternal life begins now, for already now death is no option any more.

Van Houwelingen modified the interpretation of Van Hartingsveld, who limits the meaning of 11:25–26 to the life of the earthly Jesus: Jesus will raise Lazarus, and Martha and Maria will not die as long as Jesus is on earth. In this way, the relevance of 11:25–26 is limited too strictly to Lazarus and his sisters. See Van Hartingsveld, *Die Eschatologie des Johannesevangeliums*, 55–56; Van Houwelingen, *Johannes*, 240.

(6:39, 40, 44, 54). Until that day perseverance is necessary (10:28). Eternal life includes participation in the resurrection at this day.[393]

That the notion of 'life' has both these dimensions is understandable if is taken into account that 'life' is identified with Jesus.[394] Jesus came in his resurrection and is represented by his Spirit, but at the same time he will come at the *parousia*. And Jesus is understood as ἡ ἀρχὴ και τὸ τέλος (cf. Rev 22:13), embracing the time, and the time of Jesus and the time of the church are united in the Spirit,[395] although they are not identified: Frey uses a model with two focal points.[396] Eschatology has become an inner-aspect of Christology.[397] As a consequence, it is not surprising that apart from the notion of life, the ἐν-language itself contains the eschatological tension, as we have seen (6.3.1). It is necessary to exhort believers to remain in Christ, until our unity with him will be perfect.

Very clearly the eschatological tension is found in 1 John 3:2. We are God's children, but we do not know what it is to be a child of God. But this we know: we will be like God and like his Son, at the *parousia*.[398] This implies that as long as Jesus is not revealed, our true identity is a hidden identity. Believers are children of God, but what it is to be a child of God, has still to be revealed.[399]

Finally we find the eschatological tension in the first letter, in the explicit opposition of 1 John 1:8–10 and 1 John 3:6, 9.[400] Chapter 1 tells of the salvation God gave in the blood of Jesus, his Son. To deny that we are sinners is to deny that we need salvation. Hence it is written, 'if we claim to be without sin, we deceive ourselves,' and 'If we claim we have not sinned, we make him out to be a liar' (1 John 1:8, 10). We have sinned and we have sin. Against the background of atonement, the believer must be

393. Frey, *Die johanneische Eschatologie*, Bd. III, 268, 270; Hays, *The Moral Vision of the New Testament*, 152–53.

394. Frey, *Die johanneische Eschatologie*, Bd. III, 270.

395. Frey, *Die johanneische Eschatologie*, Bd. II, 286–87; Stuhlmacher, *Biblische Theologie des Neuen Testaments, Band* 2, 247.

396. Frey, Die johanneische Eschatologie, Bd. II, 295–97.

397. Stuhlmacher, *Biblische Theologie des Neuen Testaments, Band* 2, 247.

398. Cf. Marshall, *The Epistles of John*, 171–73; Smalley, *1, 2, 3 John*, 144–47; Strecker, *Die Johannesbriefe*, 153–56.

399. Frey, *Die johanneische Eschatologie*, Bd. III, 88–90.

400. To this problem see Wilckens, '"Simul iustus et peccator" im 1. Johannesbrief,' 136–46.

seen as a sinner. Chapter 3 is different. It deals with believers as children of God. Only two kinds of human being exist, children of God and children of the devil. A sinner belongs to the devil, 'because the devil has been sinning from the beginning,' but the Son of God appeared 'to destroy the devil's work' (1 John 3:8). 'Who remains in him, does not sin. Who sins has not seen him and does not know him' (1 John 3:6; my translation). 'Who is born of God does no sin, because God's seed remains in him and he cannot sin, because he is born of God' (1 John 3:9; my translation).[401] Here it is not the blood of Christ that is the central referent, but the new identity given in a birth from God. Although the opposite statements can be understood within their context, nevertheless the opposition is very clear: a believer is a sinner and a believer does not sin. This can be understood if the believer is seen as part of an eschatological reality: a reality (he cannot sin) that has a conditional character (if he remains in Christ).[402] This eschatological reality is partly already reality in the life of the believer, partly not.[403] '*Simul iustus et peccator*.'[404] But it means also that as far as a believer participates in this reality, sin can be overcome. Participation in this eschatological reality is a gift of God that first of all consists of remaining in Christ.[405] Malatesta quotes Augustine: 'In quantum in ipso manet, in tantum non peccat.'[406] 1 John 3 implies no theology of perfectionism and no doctrine of inherent holiness or sinlessness.[407]

To conclude, in relation to the reciprocal inhabitation of Christ and the believer, we find the eschatological tension at different moments: in

401. See on 1 John 3:9 La Rondelle, *Perfection and Perfectionism*, 227–36; and also 6.4.6.

402. Marshall, *The Epistles of John*, 182; Marshall, *New Testament Theology*, 544–45; Lalleman, *1, 2 en 3 Johannes*, 119–21; see also Ulrich Wilckens, "'Simul iustus et peccator" im 1. Johannesbrief,' 137.

403. Marshall, *New Testament Theology*, 545; Schnelle, *Neutestamentliche Antropologie*, 164–65; Smalley, *1, 2, 3 John*, 164.

404. According to Stuhlmacher, who does not find this simul in Paul, the first letter of John is very close to Luther's *simul iustus et peccator*, see Stuhlmacher, *Biblische Theologie des Neuen Testaments, Band* 2, 275. See further Smalley, *1, 2, 3 John*, 164.

405. Malatesta, *Interiority and Covenant*, 246; La Rondelle, *Perfection and Perfectionism*, 232; Smalley, *1, 2, 3 John*, 164; Wilckens, "'Simul iustus et peccator" im 1. Johannesbrief,' 140.

406. Malatesta, *Interiority and Covenant*, 247.

407. Strecker, *Die Johannesbriefe*, 164; Stuhlmacher, *Biblische Theologie des Neuen Testaments, Band* 2, 273; La Rondelle, *Perfection and Perfectionism*, 236.

the notion of 'life,' in the ἐν-language itself, and in 1 John 3, where it is said that it is not revealed what we shall be when Christ is revealed and that the believer does not sin. To understand this tension, it is important to see Christ himself as the gift of life and salvation. Between his resurrection and *parousia*, the believer lives; hence living with an eschatological tension caused by his relation of reciprocal interiority with Christ.

6.4.5 MORAL

Living in communion with Christ as reciprocal inhabitation is a moral reality, because it has moral implications. We have seen already that coordinates of this communion consist in commands, love and the acts of the believer (6.3.1). Participation in Christ includes following his moral example (6.3.3). It is clear that to remain in Christ, it is important to keep his commandments (John 15:10; 1 John 3:24) and his word (1 John 2:3–5), to follow his example (1 John 2:6) and to love each other (1 John 4:12, 14). But this raises the question whether the moral acts of the believer cause his remaining in Christ. This seems to be the case, if we read 'The one who keeps his commands, remains in Him and He in him' (1 John 3:24a; my translation) and 'If we love one another, God remains in us' (1 John 4:12; my translation).

The answer to this question is complicated. It is clear that our moral acts do not have the primacy, for several reasons. First, both passages are followed by the assurance that we know that we remain in him by the Spirit he gave us (3:24b; 4:13). Especially if it might seem that our acts constitute a decisive factor in our remaining in Christ, his Spirit is mentioned—the paraclete. Second, in the first part of 1 John 3, the righteousness of believers is traced back to notions as a child of God (3:2), birth of God (3:9–10) and to Jesus Christ himself (3:5–8). If the acts of the believer result from Jesus Christ and a birth of God, the primacy of God's acts is evident. Third, in the verses preceding 1 John 4:12 it is made clear not that our love is so great, but that everything starts with the love of God. 'This is how God showed his love among us: He sent his one and only Son into the world that we might live through Him' (4:9). And only because God loves us, we have to love one another (4:11). Being loved by God and living through Christ, we are exhorted to love each other. Finally within a broader Johannine framework this is confirmed by the image of the vine and the branches, which makes clear that believers as branches can do nothing without Jesus Christ, the true vine (cf. John 15:4–5). It is possible that a branch does not bear fruit, but this is only the case if a believer does not remain in Christ (15:6). Hence it is the reciprocal inhabitation that results in moral acts. Moral acts show that the reality of which they are an implication is present, but they do not bring this reality to existence. The remaining in Christ is the source of (moral) obedience. Being loved by God, we love one another. Moral works are no precondition for, but an expression of, the unity with Christ.[408]

However, in the case of an absence of these acts, something is wrong. Therefore, believers are summoned to act in accordance with their new being.[409] Further it is possible to say that if we love one another and keep his commands, we remain in Christ. This implies that once the unity with Christ exists, the (moral) obedience becomes at the same time, in a certain sense, a condition of remaining continuously in Christ: the more a believer is disobedient, the less he remains in Christ. In conclusion, both thoughts are present: primarily, the obedient love is an expression of unity with Christ; secondarily, obedience becomes also, to some extent, a condition of remaining continuously in Christ.[410]

6.4.6 COLLECTIVE AND INDIVIDUAL

To conclude this section I want to discuss the question whether 'being in Christ' is a collective or an individual reality.

The collective impliciations of this reality are obvious. We have seen that all the images for unity with Christ have collective implications: the bread and the people in the desert, the shepherd and his flock, and the vine and the branches (6.3.2). How does this collective character relate to the image of regeneration, which suggests a more individual reality?

Within history, the metaphor of another birth from above has been understood individualistically. Popp suggests that although regeneration firstly is an individual occurrence, it must not be understood individualistically. This metaphor also has a collective aspect, because this metaphor has its place within the metaphor of the family of God.[411] This implies

408. Malatesta, *Interiority and Covenant*, 274; Marshall, *The Epistles of John*, 195; Marshall, *New Testament Theology*, 539–40.

409. Stuhlmacher, *Biblische Theologie des Neuen Testaments, Band 2*, 273.

410. Smalley, *1, 2, 3 John*, 211.

411. Popp, *Grammatik des Geistes*, 118.

that collective and individual aspects of 'being in Christ' do not exclude each other. To be in Christ is to be part of the familiy of God, but only individuals can become a part of it by regeneration.

One passage which seems to fit well within a traditional understanding of regeneration is 1 John 3:9. A major difficulty of this passage in this respect however is the reference of 'σπέρμα.' Does it refer to a new life principle, understood as a separate substance (God's nature remains in the believer), as word or Spirit (God's Word or God's Spirit remains in the believer)? Or does it mean 'offspring,' referring to Jesus Christ (God's Son remains in the believer) or to the believer which implies that 'in Him' has to be understood as 'in God' or 'in Christ' (God's offspring, the believers, remain in God/Christ)?[412] The first interpretation would imply a substantial understanding of regeneration, the other interpretations a more relational one. In the last interpretation 'seed' could be understood collectively. It is difficult to make a decision, for the different options are all possible. The interpretation of seed as word could be supported by Jesus' parable of the man sowing good seed (Matt 13 / Mark 4 / Luke 8) and by the Johannine motif of the word which has to remain in the believer; the interpretation of seed as Spirit also fits within a Johannine framework (cf. John 3:5, 8). A further possible interpretation is the translation of 'σπέρμα'as 'offspring,' which is furthermore always the translation in the Johannine literature (John 7:42; 8:33, 37; Rev 12:17). For this systematic-theological investigation it is important that all these interpretations are possible, whereas the first interpretation has no further support in New Testament literature; such a substantial interpretation of 'σπέρμα' would be unique in the New Testament.

To conclude, 'being in Christ' is a reality with both collective and individual aspects.

412. Marshall and Smalley understand 'seed' as referring to the word or the Spirit as the new principle of life, Malatesta prefers a reference to the word, following others without giving further arguments. Lalleman opts for interpretation of 'seed' as God's offspring, the believers. See Malatesta, *Interiority and Covenant*, 247–49; Marshall, *The Epistles of John*, 186; Lalleman, *1, 2 en 3 Johannes*, 175; Smalley, *1, 2, 3 John*, 173; Strecker, *Die Johannesbriefe*, 171–73.

6.5 Conclusion

In this chapter I have investigated the second canonical voice in this conversation on 'being in Christ.' Again three questions have been answered with respect to 'being in Christ': do we need the concept of representation (and maybe substitution) to reconstruct John's Christology? Is it necessary to use the concept of participation (and maybe union) to understand John's soteriology? And how should we reconstruct the character of the reality of 'being in Christ' as the Johannine writings picture it?

Generally it can be said that the framework of Johannine thinking on the issue of 'being in Christ' consists primarily in the idea of reciprocal inhabitation, of Father and Son, and of Jesus Christ and his disciples. With regard to the first question, we saw that the emphasis is on the exclusiveness of Jesus Christ as source of life and hence on the moment of substitution. However, we saw again that substitution and representation do not exclude each other; in the margin also the idea of representation is present. Concerning John's soteriology, we discovered that the relation between Christ and his disciples has characteristics analogous to the relation between Father and Son. Primarily we need concepts like interiority, reciprocal inhabitation and communion, highlighting the moment of union. However, as far as the identity of giver and gift is concerned and the Son making us participate in his position, we also need the concept of participation to understand the ἐν-language. It is further remarkable how theocentric John's vision of 'being in Christ' is. Mediated by the Holy Spirit and by Jesus Christ, we share to some extent in Christ's communion with his Father and are in God. The Father is the source and goal of everything. Finally I dealt with the question concerning the reality of 'being in Christ.' Its reality has a hidden character, accessible only to the perspective of faith. It consists of a relation with Father, Son and Spirit, whose communion envelops the believer. Due to the many actors and aspects involved, it is further a reality with a complex character. 'Being in Christ' carries with it an eschatological tension and has moral implications. Finally it is a reality both collective and individual.

7

CANONICAL SYNTHESIS

7.1 Introduction

IN THE SECOND PART of this study, following our examination of the tradition, we have heard two canonical voices: the apostles Paul and John. In Chapter 5 and 6 we saw how Paul and John use the 'ἐν Χριστῷ' or 'ἐν ἐμοὶ'-language, and how this use fits within a larger framework. Now it is time to formulate some conclusions of this second part. The most important question to be answered in this chapter is whether Paul and John have conflicting, contradicting perspectives, or whether they can be two voices together as one decisive voice. Is it possible to develop a concept of 'being in Christ' and its ontological implications, building both on Paul and John? I will deal with this question in 7.2, comparing Paul and John. In 7.3 I will continue with a short sketch of how Paul and John fit within a canonical whole. This chapter closes with a concluding section (7.4).

7.2 PAUL AND JOHN

Paul and John are different. Paul uses the expression 'ἐν Χριστῷ,' John does not, apart from 1 John 5:20. John wrote a gospel in which it is Jesus himself who speaks of being and remaining 'ἐν ἐμοὶ,' Paul wrote letters. Furthermore, they use different images to refer to the impact of the Christ event in the life of the believer; images for participation in Christ in Pauline literature and images for union with Christ in John. Paul's position can be summarized as 'participation in the story of the representative,' John's position as 'reciprocal inhabitation.' To characterize the framework of Paul we need the concepts representation and participation, whereas in the case of John the emphasis is on substitution and union. Consequently, it might seem impossible to combine these two perspectives in one systematic theological perspective on 'being in Christ.'

On the level of language, the differences are evident. Paul and John use different expressions or use the same language differently. This is not decisive however. On a deeper level there might be more concurrence, for it is possible for two persons to give different descriptions of something, but refer to the same reality, and give descriptions which do not exclude or contradict. The decisive question is, whether the Pauline and Johannine models of 'being in Christ' contradict and exclude each other on an ontological level. Do these models have contradicting ontological implications, or do they have the same or complementary implications, although the models themselves differ?

In this light the harmony we find between Paul and John concerning the character of the reality of 'being in Christ' (5.5 and 6.4) is significant. In both cases it is a reality determined by a relation with Son and Spirit, an eschatological reality characterized by a tension between the already and the not yet, a hidden reality accessible to the perspective of faith, and a reality with collective aspects. Concerning the nature of the reality of 'being in Christ,' the differences are not that big. However, this is not decisive.

To these observations something more important has to be added. Paul can be summarized as 'participation in the story of the representative,' John as 'reciprocal inhabitation.' What happens when we compare the Pauline and the Johannine framework in the light of the four concepts defined in 1.2.6? These are the four concepts: two Christological concepts, a. substitution: the moment of exclusivity of Christ; b. representation: the moment of inclusivity of Christ; and two soteriological concepts, c. union: the moment of contact between Christ and believers; d. participation: the moment of sharing of the believer in Christ.

In Paul the emphasis is on representation and participation. However, representation presupposes substitution, and further Paul uses images for union with Christ, which indicates that we also need a concept of union to reconstruct Paul's framework. John's emphasis is on substitution and union. However, we saw that we also need the concepts of representation and participation to understand parts of John's thinking. Paul's model of 'being in Christ' emphasises the moments of representation and participation, John's model the moments of substitution and union. However, all four moments are present in the theological frameworks of both.

One might still ask whether Paul and John understood these four moments in a similar and at least compatible way. I will deal with all four moments to see whether this is the case.

a. **Substitution**: Paul emphasises different aspects like person substitution (together wit the moment of representation reverse sides of the one coin), the acts of God in Christ, and the exclusivity of moments of the history of Jesus Christ, especially his death. The images Paul uses are juridical and sacrificial, but also images of victory and of a proof of love. John shows that the Father is present in the Son and acts when the Son acts. The I am-sayings stress that Jesus Christ is a divine source of life. Especially with the death of Christ, something unique has happened. The images used to refer to this soteriological significance are juridical and sacrificial, but also other images like victory, a proof of love, exaltation and glorification.

b. **Representation**: Paul refers to Jesus as Christ, *eschatos* Adam, the first one, and head. He has experienced what we will experience. This is expressed with the help of positive semantic relations between the story of Jesus Christ and the biographies of believers. John uses the image of the vine. Further he emphasises that the life of the master and his disciples follow the same pattern: mission, suffering, death, resurrection, glorification.

c. **Union**: Paul uses different images to express our union with Christ, some of which have a more personal character like the image of marriage, whilst others are less personal, like body, body and head, building or temple, and clothing. Furthermore, he sometimes uses reciprocal expressions: we in Christ, but also Christ in us. Finally, the union with Christ is related to the sacraments of baptism (as giving expression to participation in Christ) and Eucharist (in combination with the image of the body). John uses other images than Paul: bread, the good shepherd and vine and branches. He uses reciprocal expressions more than Paul. Finally, he uses the image of bread to relate the moment of union with the sacrament of the Eucharist.

d. **Participation**: According to Paul, we participate in Christ by the Holy Spirit. Participating in Christ, we participate in his story. Further, participation in Christ is expressed with the help of several images, which show that we participate in who Christ is, in his identity and his position. John also refers to the Spirit as the one who makes us share in Christ. We participate in the life of Jesus Christ, as source of life. Finally, to some extent the church participates in the position of Jesus Christ as Son of God, in his suffering, death, resurrection and mission.

To conclude with regard to the way in which Paul and John give expression to these four moments, we find a significant harmony between their two thought-worlds. We have two different models or perspectives, with different accents, words and images, but at a deeper level their models are compatible.

As a result, this second part concentrating on two voices from the canonical scriptures has not lead to an impasse. Paul and John can indeed play a decisive role in this conversation on 'being in Christ.' For the present investigation this implies the following.

Firstly, it is impossible and unnecessary to harmonise the use of the in Christ-language as we find it in Paul and John into one biblical-theological model of 'being in Christ.' Instead, we have reconstructed a Pauline model (or even two Pauline models) and one Johannine model. Systematic theology will have to live with this diversity and utilize the possibilities of each of them in an appropriate context.

Secondly, the hypothesis formulated in 1.2.6 fits Paul well, but not John. After chapters 5 and 6 it should be clear already that the hypothesis was incomplete. We do not only need the concepts of representation and participation, but also the concepts of substitution and union. Theological reflection on the relation between Christ and the church or the believers needs these four concepts to gain access to the nature of this relation. Using these four concepts, it can be made clear that the diversity found in Paul and John does not imply a real opposition, because at a deeper level their thinking harmonises. There is no contradiction at an ontological level.

Thirdly, this convergence between Paul and John on a deeper level can be discovered moreover when the nature of the reality of 'being in Christ' is concerned. I showed this when I started this discussion and compared the results of 5.5 and 6.4.

7.3 'Being in Christ' within the Canon

To make this chapter a real canonical synthesis, something has to be said on the place of 'being in Christ' within the canon. I can only give a rough sketch, drawing faint lines. For reasons of time, I have had to be selective. Something has been said already on fact that the notion of 'Messiah' is a representative one (5.3). Further I could say something on the motif of the servant of the Lord, sometimes referring to the people of Israel, and sometimes to an individual. As individual, the servant represents and serves the community.[1] But I will concentrate on the position of Christ within the history of the covenants, on the relation between 'being in Christ' and synoptic gospels, and on the letters of Peter.

As the fulfilment of the Scriptures, Jesus Christ is 'the climax of the covenants.'[2] Jesus Christ is the seed of Abraham, the fulfilment of the covenant with Abraham (Gen 15; 17). By his obedience to the law and his death, which the apostles understood as a sacrificial death, Jesus Christ is the fulfilment of the Sinai-covenant (Exod 19–24) and its laws. He is more than Moses.[3] As the son of David, Jesus Christ is further the fulfilment of the covenant with David (2 Sam 23:5; Ps 89:3, 28; 1 Kngs

1. Robert Jenson has elaborated the continuity between the servant of the Lord and the concept of totus Christus, 'the risen Christ, *including and included in* his community.' See Jenson, *Systematic Theology. Volume* 1, 80–82; see also Loonstra, *Verkiezing—verzoening—verbond*, 205–7, 225, 297.

2. On the different covenants, see Dumbrell, *Covenant and Creation*; Scobie, *The Ways of our God*, 474–78, 483–84. The term 'climax of the covenants' is a variation on the title of Wright's book *The Climax of the Covenant.*

3. Scobie, *The Ways of our God*, 302–4, 308–9, 315, 318–19, 321–23, 325f; and further Brueggemann, *Theology of the Old Testament*, 662–70.

8:23–24; Jer 33:21).[4] This line of the David-covenant coincides with the Zion-tradition. Jesus Christ is the priestly king in line with Melchizedek.[5] As the one who brings the new covenant, the climax of covenant history, he inaugurates the eschaton as *eschatos* Adam.[6] Jesus Christ is the seed of Abraham, the true Israelite, the king on the throne of David, which all indicates that he is a representative figure, exclusive in his inclusiviness. But he is also the one with an exclusive role, who inaugurates the new covenant with his blood. Against the Old Testament background of the history of the covenants, lines emphasising exclusiveness and inclusiveness come together.[7] If the election of Zion is more fundamental than the covenant with David, we might see already indicated here that the grace of the exclusiveness—the electing presence of God—is more fundamental than the representative figure of the king.[8]

Secondly I will say something on the relation between Jesus Christ and the Kingdom of God. In Jesus' message and acts, the kingdom of God dawns. Attitude towards Jesus is decisive for entrance in the kingdom of God.[9] However, the question is whether Jesus brings the kingdom or whether the kingdom brings Jesus.[10] Van Bruggen defends the first: with Jesus the kingdom of heaven comes, for he is the coming God. Faith in Jesus constitutes the entrance. Jesus himself is the guide, who brings his own by his suffering, death and return into the kingdom.[11] Jüngel's position is more in line with the second option. The kingdom authorises Jesus

4. Brueggemann, *Theology of the Old Testament*, 600–621; De Jong, *Van oud naar nieuw*, 59–74; Loonstra, *Verkiezing—verzoening—verbond*, 202–5, 216–21, 225; Scobie, *The Ways of our God*, 304–8, 315–18, 324–25.

5. Scobie, *The Ways of our God*, 309–10, 318–19, 325–26. See on Zion, Brueggemann, *Theology of the Old Testament*, 654–62; Dekker, *De rotsvaste fundering van Sion*, 207–47; Gese, 'Der Davidsbund und die Zionserwählung,' 113–29; Loonstra, *Verkiezing—verzoening—verbond*, 216–21; Stuhlmacher, *Die Verkündigung des Christus Jesus*, 25–32.

6. Scobie, *The Ways of our God*, 348–54

7. Cf. De Jong, *Van oud naar nieuw*, 74–84

8. Cf. Brueggemann, *Theology of the Old Testament*, 657–58; Dekker, *De rotsvaste fundering van Sion*, 215–20, 233, 255; Gese, 'Der Davidsbund und die Zionserwählung,' 127–28; De Jong, *Van oud naar nieuw*, 20, 28, 32–38.

9. Stuhlmacher, *Biblische Theologie des Neuen Testaments, Band 1*, 71, 74–75, 94–95.

10. According to R. Otto, Jesus does not bring the kingdom, but the kingdom brings Jesus; see Otto, *Reich Gottes und Menschensohn*, 80.

11. Van Bruggen, *Het evangelie van Gods Zoon*, 68–71; Van Bruggen, 'Kingdom of God or Justification of the Sinner?,' 257–60; see also Stuhlmacher, *Die Verkündigung des Christus Jesus*, 28–30.

and makes him the eschatological person, with whom the eschaton identifies. His message of the kingdom promises an existence *extra se*, just like Paul's gospel of God's righteousness.[12] Which option is to be preferred?

In the light of the four concepts necessary to structure our thinking on the relation Christ-believers, one could ask whether a choice has to be made. The first option could be reinterpreted as emphasising the moment of substitution, the second as emphasising the moment of representation. As a consequence, the relation between Jesus and the Kingdom is a double one: he is the king, bringing the kingdom, and he represents the people, providing them with a place in God's reign. Consequently, the existence extra se Jüngel writes about has to be identified with 'being in Christ.' In this light it is significant that Jesus teaches his disciples to say 'our Father' in prayer to God: they are allowed to share in his special relationship with God.[13] This would imply that 'being in Christ' is an important concept for understanding the way in which the kingdom of God comes. The kingdom of God is being realised in our lives as 'being in Christ.'[14]

But the synoptic gospels are not only important for the sake of the kingdom. They further tell the story of the life of Jesus. This story makes the idea of the identification of Christ with sinful people, which we find fairly abstract in Paul, more concrete. Jesus Christ was born as a human being. He was baptised as a penitent, prepared to live our life and to fulfil all righteousness. Being baptised, he was anointed with the Spirit as messiah. He learned to live an obedient life through suffering. He was loyal to his Father, although this brought him into conflict with the religious authorities and would result in his death. In the end he was prepared to drink the cup according to the will of the Father. Although Pilate judged that he was innocent, he was sentenced to death as a blasphemer. In this way he identified with the innocent victims of injustice, forsaken even by God. Hanged on the cross, he died the death of the cursed, becoming a curse. Although he was innocent, he became one with his guilty people and bore their punishment. Finally he died as a criminal and a loser. The

12. Jüngel, *Paulus und Jesus*, 139, 193, 196, 211–12, 266–67, 269–70, 282.

13. Stuhlmacher, *Biblische Theologie des Neuen Testaments, Band 1*, 87.

14. According to Marshall, Jesus is the bringer of the kingdom, which is in line with Van Bruggen. He further writes that in the gospel of the apostles it is realised implicitly that Jesus is the kingdom. This also leads to the conclusion that 'being in Christ' is the way of entering the kingdom; see Marshall, *New Testament Theology*, 471. See also Stuhlmacher, *Die Verkündigung des Christus Jesus*, 35–39.

story shows what it means if Paul writes that he was born from a woman, lived under the law and was made sin. He identified with our lives and with our problems.

Finally, the other apostle who uses the expression 'ἐν Χριστῷ ('Ιησοῦ)' deserves some attention: Peter (1 Pet 3:16; 5:10, 14). I have investigated Paul and John, but what light does Peter's first letter shed on 'being in Christ'? I will deal with these passages and show that we find the four moments present in Paul and John also in Peter.

Firstly, I will say something on the passages where the 'ἐν Χριστῳ-language is used. In 3:16 it is used the first time. Peter exhorts his readers, when suffering for Christ's sake and asked for the reason for their hope, to answer with good behaviour in Christ. Interpreters read the 'in Christ' slightly differently, but it is clear that the relation with Christ is determinative for their way of life. The fact that it can be compared with John as well as with Paul shows the similarity to both.[15] In chapter 5 it is used twice, first in 5:10. According to Peter, God called his readers to eternal glory in Christ. This shows that God acts in Christ as we saw in Paul. But in Christ refers both to the means of God's acts and to the sphere of the Christian existence.[16] We might see here a hint at a communion with the calling of Christ. We are called with Christ to share in his glory. Consequently, we should not limit the significance of the 'in Christ' exclusively to the calling or to the glory.[17] Finally Peter uses it in 5:14, closing his letter with a greeting of peace to all his readers who are in Christ. They are Christians, united with Christ.[18] In conclusion, the expression is used in a way both similar to Paul and John. It sometimes highlights the moment of union, sometimes the moment of participation.

Secondly, we find the moments of substitution, representation, union and participation in Peter's letter. The moment of substitution is important for Peter, as his references to the blood of Christ indicate (1 Pet

15. Selwyn compares it with the Johannine mutual inhabitation: at the one hand Christ lives in their hearts (3:15), at the other hand they walk in Christ. Elliot and Van Houwelingen compare it with Paul, but emphasise the Semitic background of the expression. Michaels finally downplays the expression, interpreting it as 'christian.' See Elliott, *1 Peter*, 632; Van Houwelingen, *1 Petrus*, 126; Michaels, *1 Peter*, 190; Selwyn, *The First Epistle of St. Peter*, 195

16. Cf. Michaels, 1 *Peter*, 302.

17. Elliott, *1 Peter*, 865; Van Houwelingen, 1 *Petrus*, 184–85; Selwyn, *The First Epistle of St. Peter*, 240.

18. Elliott, *1 Peter*, 892; Van Houwelingen, 1 *Petrus*, 192.

1:18f). Christ is presented as the suffering servant of the Lord (2:21–24; 3:18).[19] Further we clearly find the moment of participation, which presupposes someone to participate in, a representative who is exclusive in his inclusiveness. A central motif in his first letter is that believers share in the suffering of Christ, but that they will share in his glory. For the present especially the participation in the suffering of Christ is important. This suffering has an exclusive aspect: Christ suffered for the readers, bore their sins, and died once for all (2:21, 24; 3:18).[20] A comparable exclusive aspect is present in his resurrection, for the readers are saved by Christ's resurrection (3:21). Nevertheless, his suffering also has an inclusive side. It is an example to be followed. Again and again Peter returns to the participation in Christ's suffering (1:6; 2:21–23; 3:17; 4:1, 15f).[21] 'He was put to death in the body and made alive by the Spirit' (3:18) and we will follow him on this path (4:1f, 6, 13).[22] In heaven an imperishable heritage is kept for us (1:4). This hope of the heavenly heritage results in an eschatological tension. Christ still has to be revealed in his return (1:7, 13; 4:13). This revelation will also be the revelation of our participation in this glory (5:1).[23] Nevertheless, the eschatological tension is not only a tension of hope. The believers live already in the last times (ἐπ ἐσχάτων τῶν χρόνων; 1:20) and the judgment of God has begun with them (4:17). Apart from participation (and representation) we also find the moment of union. The readers walk and are in Christ as we saw (3:16; 5:14). They are exhorted to sanctify Christ as Lord in their hearts (3:15).[24] Further Peter uses the image of a building, built with living stones on the stone who is Christ (2:4–8).[25] Apart from these four moments other well known motifs return, like the image of a new birth. In Peter this idea of regeneration is

19. Stuhlmacher, *Biblische Theologie des Neuen Testaments, Band* 2, 75–76.

20. Marshall, *New Testament Theology*, 649–50; Stuhlmacher, *Biblische Theologie des Neuen Testaments, Band* 2, 76–77.

21. Marshall, *New Testament Theology*, 642, 646–47, 649; Stuhlmacher, *Biblische Theologie des Neuen Testaments, Band* 2, 82–83.

22. Marshall, *New Testament Theology*, 647, 652; Stuhlmacher, *Biblische Theologie des Neuen Testaments, Band* 2, 78.

23. Marshall, *New Testament Theology*, 644–45, 651; Stuhlmacher, *Biblische Theologie des Neuen Testaments, Band* 2, 83.

24. Marshall, *New Testament Theology*, 653.

25. Marshall, *New Testament Theology*, 646.

relational, related to resurrection, hope, and the word of God (1:1, 23).[26] Finally we find the motif of sanctification (1:2, 15, 16) and the importance of a life in love (4:8).[27] This short thematic overview of the first letter of Peter shows that apart from the expression 'ἐν Χριστῷ ('Ιησοῦ)' we find the same four moments as reconstructed in the conceptual framework presented above.[28]

What this short sketch has made clear is, firstly, that the representative figure of the Christ has an Old Testament background, as is indicated by titles like seed of Abraham and son of David. 'Being in Christ' as part of reality of the new covenant has to be understood as part of a reality which is the climax of the covenants. Secondly, we have seen that the relation between Jesus Christ and the kingdom of God is a double relation, for Christ represents the king as well as the people. Within this second representation, we find the moment of inclusiveness, related with 'being in Christ.' This implies that one could say that 'being in Christ' is the way in which the kingdom of heaven is becoming a reality. Thirdly, the narrative of the gospels helps to make the idea of Christ's identification with us more concrete. Finally, the first letter of Peter confirms the conclusions concerning 'being in Christ' based on John and Paul, for in this letter we find similar ideas.

7.4 Conclusion

Within the canon we find many different voices. Paul offers two different models of 'being in Christ,' which can both be characterized as 'participation in the story of Jesus Christ.' In John we find another model of 'being in Christ' as part of 'reciprocal inhabitation.' The original hypothesis of this investigation fits Paul well, but not John.

These different models cannot be reduced to one single model. However, it can be shown that they are compatible. Both the Pauline and the Johannine framework contain four moments: substitution, representation, union and participation; moments we also find in Peter's first letter. Because we find these four moments in both canonical voices in this

26. Marshall, *New Testament Theology*, 644.

27. Marshall, *New Testament Theology*, 645–47, 654–56.

28. Stuhlmacher, *Biblische Theologie des Neuen Testaments, Band* 2, 75.

conversation, a systematic-theological concept of 'being in Christ' will have to do justice to these four moments.

Clearly 'being in Christ' is an eschatological theme, related to the last times. Jesus Christ is the climax of the covenants. He is the one who has brought the new covenant as well as the kingdom of God. Within this reality, 'being in Christ' is an important theme, for this is the way in which the coming of the reign of God is being realised.

8

INGOLF U. DALFERTH

ESCHATOLOGICAL REALITY

8.1 Introduction

INGOLF U. DALFERTH (1948) is professor of systematic theology, symbolics and philosophy of religion at the university of Zürich. Educated in Tübingen and Cambridge, he stands in the German hermeneutic tradition of e.g. Eberhard Jüngel,[1] but he also is well acquainted with the Anglo-Saxon analytic tradition. He is praised for his fruitful combination of analytic and hermeneutic method.[2] His many books include a mono-

1. For an introduction to and critical discussion of Bultmann and hermeneutical theology, written by Dalferth himself, see Dalferth, 'God and the Mystery of Words,' 87–100.

2. Van der Kooi, review of I.U. Dalferth, *Der auferweckte Gekreuzigte*, 165; cf. Beck, review of I.U. Dalferth, *Gedeutete Gegenwart*, 351.

According to Rohls, it is Dalferth's merit to have brought Anglo-Saxon philosophy of language into a close relation with German protestant theology. See Rohls, 'Sprachanalyse und Theologie bei I.U. Dalferth,' 200.

graph on Christology, *Der auferweckte Gekreuzigte*, as well as an impressive philosophy of religion, *Die Wirklichkeit des Möglichen*.[3]

In his *Religiöse Rede von Gott*,[4] he extensively studies the analytic tradition of philosophy of language and religion and uses this to develop a theory of religious speech about God. Theologically central to this theory is the analysis of the basic Christian experience of being addressed by God.[5] This experience involves the self-identification of God in Jesus Christ and by the Holy Spirit to a believer.[6] Based on this study, an important motif in his work is the reality of the creating loving presence of God as Father that is identified, defined and universally disclosed in this self-identification.[7] This divine self-identification in the practice of the believer's life is the hermeneutical starting point of his theology, which is an unfolding of the consequences of this divine self-identification. God's self-identification has a soteriological significance and hence necessarily includes a new understanding of self, world and God caused by a change of horizon.[8]

3. Dalferth, *Der auferweckte Gekreuzigte*; Dalferth, *Die Wirklichkeit des Möglichen*.

4. Dalferth, *Religiöse Rede von Gott*. For an analysis of Dalferth's position in *Religiöse Rede von Gott*, see Laube, *Im Bann der Sprache*, Ch. 5.

5. Dalferth, *Religiöse Rede von Gott*, 393–494.

6. Dalferth, *Religiöse Rede von Gott*, 477, 481, 487, 577, 586, 600–606; see further e.g. Dalferth, *Theology and Philosophy*, 159, 188–95, 202; Dalferth, *Gott*, 11–14, 17, 48–50, 240; Dalferth, *Der auferweckte Gekreuzigte*, 27, 85, 86; Dalferth, *Gedeutete Gegenwart*, 206, 266; Dalferth, ‚Inbegriff oder Index?' 100; Dalferth, 'Fremdauslegung als Selbstauslegung,' 170–73; Dalferth, *Die Wirklichkeit des Möglichen*, 445; Dalferth, *Evangelische Theologie als Interpretationspraxis*, 62, 102–3.

7. Dalferth, *Theology and Philosophy*, 193, 220; Dalferth, *Existenz Gottes und christlicher Glaube*, 212–26; Dalferth, *Kombinatorische Theologie*, 134–37; Dalferth, *Gott*, 6, 12, 230–31, 240–41; Dalferth, *Der auferweckte Gekreuzigte*, 25–28, 32–34, 45–47, 57, 62, 74, 93, 96–97, 100, 123, 133–35, 163–67, 174–75, 180–84, 191–92, 205–9, 217–18, 225–28, 230–36, 301–2, 306; Dalferth, *Gedeutete Gegenwart*, 98, 118, 206, 273, 283; Dalferth, 'Volles Grab, leerer Glaube?' 401, 404–5; Dalferth, 'Fremdauslegung als Selbstauslegung,' 172; Dalferth, 'Representing God's Presence,' 254; Dalferth, *Auf dem Weg der Ökumene*, 23, 25, 31; Dalferth, *Die Wirklichkeit des Möglichen*, 125; Dalferth, *Evangelische Theologie als Interpretationspraxis*, 86; Dalferth, 'Gott für uns,' 61–62.

8. Dalferth, *Theology and Philosophy*, 195, 197, 221; Dalferth, *Der auferweckte Gekreuzigte*, 35, 160, 183–84, 237, 284, 310–11; Dalferth, 'Subjektivität und Glaube,' 50–56; Dalferth, *Gedeutete Gegenwart*, 190–92; Dalferth, 'Volles Grab, leerer Glaube?' 401–5; Dalferth, ‚Inbegriff oder Index?' 100, 102–7; Dalferth, *Die Wirklichkeit des Möglichen*, 132–33, 448–52, 475–76; Dalferth, *Evangelische Theologie als Interpretationspraxis*, 33–35, 96, 102; Dalferth, 'Gott für uns,' 62.

The first attempt to unfold its consequences is his 'Habilitation' *Existenz Gottes und christlicher Glaube*. Here he sketches an eschatological ontology that is implied by it.[9] His locative, relational, and subject involving interpretation of existence is important: to say that *a* exists is to localise *a* in relation to me.[10] It is especially this eschatological ontology that will occupy us in this chapter, as we investigate whether it is helpful in understanding the character of the reality of 'being in Christ.'

In *Theology and Philosophy* this eschatological ontology is presented differently with the help of two other important motifs: perspective and orientation. By God's self-identification to a person, a new perspective is introduced. As a result, two perspectives exist simultaneously: the old perspective—*coram mundo*—and the new perspective of faith—*coram deo*. These are perspectives on self, world and God. According to Dalferth, theology must not ignore the *coram mundo* perspective, but reconstruct it within its own *coram deo* perspective.[11] Further Christian theology has to justify its own perspective in the public sphere of the university, of other perspectives and rationalities.[12] Perspectives are always perspectives of participants and open to otherness.[13] Second, the self-identifying revelation of God to someone localizes that person in relation to God and hence localises him absolutely. Based on this absolute localisation, absolute orientation becomes possible for this believer. The concept of orientation builds on *Existenz Gottes*, in which the idea of localisation is a central one.[14]

9. Cf. Dalferth, *Jenseits von Mythos und Logos*, 295–96, 310–12; Dalferth, *Der auferweckte Gekreuzigte*, 214.

10. Dalferth, *Existenz Gottes und christlicher Glaube*, 121.

11. Dalferth, *Theology and Philosophy*, 77–78, 85–87, 158–62; Dalferth, 'Subjektivität und Glaube,' 41; Dalferth, *Gedeutete Gegenwart*, 24, 33, 95, 155–59; Dalferth, 'Creation—Style of the World,' 127; Dalferth, ,Erkundungen des Möglichen,' 55–69; Dalferth, *Die Wirklichkeit des Möglichen*, 119–21, 123–27, 132–33, 196–99, 395; Dalferth, *Evangelische Theologie als Interpretationspraxis*, 61–62, 134–40.

12. Dalferth, *Kombinatorische Theologie*, 50–58, 93; Dalferth, *Gedeutete Gegenwart*, 6, 28, 35–36, 51–55, 79, 81, 187–88; Dalferth, *Evangelische Theologie als Interpretationspraxis*, 124, 126, 128, 135–39. Cf. Dalferth, *Die Wirklichkeit des Möglichen*, 43–44, 46, 60–64, 102–3.

13. Dalferth, *Gedeutete Gegenwart*, 178–88; Dalferth, *Die Wirklichkeit des Möglichen*, 60–63, 92–93.

14. Dalferth, *Theology and Philosophy*, 195, 208–12; Dalferth, *Die Wirklichkeit des Möglichen*, 149–54, 157–59, 164–66.

As the self-identifying act evidences, theology has to be Christological, and therefore Trinitarian and soteriological. God identifies himself definitively as God to us in Jesus Christ. As a result, Christian theology is Christology. However, God is not identified without different acts: the identification of God by Jesus as loving presence, God's identification with Jesus Christ, and his self-identification to someone by the Holy Spirit.[15] That God's identification is an identification to someone necessitates the soteriological character of theology. God's self-identification to me unmasks me as a sinner who does not know God. At the same time, God's active and loving presence is revealed to me. Consequently, God's identification involves me existentially and includes a 'for me-relation.'[16] The saving act of the triune Christ is understood especially as revelation, and Christology has to be constructed as revelation-Christology.[17] Because theology is Christology, it has to be Trinitarian and soteriological theology.

An important drive in Dalferth's theology is to affirm that God is a reality. If God identifies himself to us, then he is a reality, determining his identity himself. If God identifies himself to us, then He gives our entire life a new horizon. If it is really God who is identified as loving presence and if he is present in the perspective of faith, then he is present in all acts of life. If it is true that God identifies himself to us as the Christian faith confirms, then the particular perspective of the Christian faith has

15. Dalferth, *Religiöse Rede von Gott*, 442–43, 485, 600, 604–5, 626; Dalferth, *Theology and Philosophy*, 81, 189–93; Dalferth, *Kombinatorische Theologie*, 83, 132; Dalferth, *Gott*, 7, 11, 13, 18–22, 48–50, 241–43; Dalferth, 'Über Einheit und Vielfalt des christlichen Glaubens,' 135–36; Dalferth, *Jenseits von Mythos und Logos*, 79, 243; Dalferth, *Der auferweckte Gekreuzigte*, 36, 56, 70, 73, 121–22, 159, 163–67, 174, 179, 181–84, 189, 201, 203–7, 212–13, 215–16, 218–19; Dalferth, 'Subjektivität und Glaube,' 51–53; Dalferth, *Gedeutete Gegenwart*, 203, 206–7; Dalferth, 'Volles Grab, leerer Glaube?' 404; Dalferth, 'Inbegriff oder Index?' 100; Dalferth, 'Fremdauslegung als Selbstauslegung,' 171–73; Dalferth, *Die Wirklichkeit des Möglichen*, 124–25; Dalferth, *Evangelische Theologie als Interpretationspraxis*, 102; Dalferth, 'Gott für uns,' 61–62.

16. Dalferth, *Religiöse Rede von Gott*, 394, 399–405, 469–94; Dalferth, *Existenz Gottes und christlicher Glaube*, 117–18, 121, 130, 152–54; Dalferth, *Theology and Philosophy*, 152, 158–60, 188–91, 203, 211–12; Dalferth, *Der auferweckte Gekreuzigte*, 26–27, 31, 35, 42, 83, 123–24, 135–39, 180–86, 213, 236, 239, 251–52, 257, 267, 276–83, 306, 309; Dalferth, 'Inbegriff oder Index?' 106–7; Dalferth, *Die Wirklichkeit des Möglichen*, 451–52; Dalferth, *Evangelische Theologie als Interpretationspraxis*, 100; Dalferth, 'Gott für uns,' 55.

17. Dalferth, 'Gott für uns,' 64.

universal significance.[18] This combination of a sensivity to themes like perspective and particularity and an emphasis on self-determining reality and universality makes Dalferth an interesting dialogue partner reflecting on 'being in Christ' and its ontological implications. Not all human beings have discovered this 'being in Christ' whereas according to the Christian faith it is a reality that concerns everyone.

In this chapter I will give an overview of themes in Dalferth's theology that are relevant for the development of a concept of 'being in Christ.' To order the description of Dalferth's thinking, some difficulties must be overcome. First, Dalferth's theology is hermeneutically structured: it is a comprehensive whole of understanding God, the world and the self that is unfolded from God's self-identification in Jesus Christ. Second, consequently in *Existenz Gottes und christlicher Glaube*, Dalferth's Christology is a part of his eschatological ontology. Third, Dalferth unfolds this new perspective only twice in a larger systematic whole, using different orderings.[19] Therefore, I will structure my chapter in the same way as the other chapters. First I will deal with his Christology (8.2). In a next paragraph his Soteriology will follow (8.3). Then I will continue with his eschatological ontology to describe the character of the reality of 'being in Christ' according to Dalferth (8.4), and I will close this chapter with an evaluation (8.5). As a result, some parts of his eschatological ontology will be described before I have introduced the conceptual apparatus that structures this ontology.[20]

18. Dalferth, *Existenz Gottes und christlicher Glaube*, 16–18; Dalferth, *Gott*, 12; Dalferth, *Gedeutete Gegenwart*, 3, 5–6, 8–9, 24–32, 35, 113–18, 129–32, 187–90, 274–85; Dalferth, 'Inbegriff oder Index?' 104, 106–7, 130; Dalferth, 'Representing God's Presence,' 237, 239–40, 254; Dalferth, *Die Wirklichkeit des Möglichen*, 470–71, 473.

19. In *Existenz Gottes und christlicher Glaube*, Dalferth's order is as follows: experience of God—God—faith—human being—Jesus Christ. In *Der auferweckte Gekreuzigte*, it is different. After having said that a Christology can not start with the incarnation, Dalferth uses this structure: resurrection—the word of the cross—Jesus Christ—Trinity—soteriological significance.

20. Dalferth himself proves that this is possible. The conceptual apparatus of *Existenz Gottes und christlicher Glaube*, is never used again after this book. More specifically, it is noteworthy that some parts of the story of this book are told in other articles but without the entire apparatus. See Dalferth, *Gott*, 23–50; and especially Dalferth, *Gedeutete Gegenwart*, 99–132.

8.2 Christology

To investigate Dalferth's Christology I will first sketch the development of his Christology, while at the same time dealing with some central concepts (8.2.1). In a second section Dalferth's reconstruction of the different moments of the history of Jesus Christ will be described (8.2.2). Finally I will answer the question, what Dalferth's Christology means for the hypothesis for the development of a concept of 'being in Christ' (8.2.3).

8.2.1 CENTRAL MOMENTS OF DALFERTH'S CHRISTOLOGY

For a description of Dalferth's Christology, three books are especially important: *Religiöse Rede von Gott*, *Existenz Gottes und christlicher Glaube* and *Der auferweckte Gekreuzigte*.[21]

In *Religiöse Rede von Gott*, Dalferth uses Christology to explain the experiential foundation of Christian God talk. Is it possible to give a foundation of the truth of Christian God talk and to justify its rationality and legitimacy? Dalferth states this is possible, referring to the Christian experience of Jesus as God's address ('Gottes Anrede').[22] This thesis evokes some problems: is it possible to experience Jesus as God's address and next to identify God based on this experience?[23] This experience presupposes the historical perception of Jesus, the existential or religious interpretation of Jesus as address, and the Christian interpretation of Jesus as God's address.[24] This experience is the experience of Pentecost. This experience is not the experience of God's address *by* Jesus but the experience of Jesus *as* God's address. This presupposes the absence of Jesus, for certain historical events like life or death do not constitute the basic experience, but the experience of this life and death as God's address—an experience that lies outside these historical events. Only after his death was it possible to experience the unity of his words and behaviour, his life, suffering and death as one event that could be experienced as God's address.[25] To

21. Apart from these books, Dalferth wrote two articles about Christology after his *Der auferweckte Gekreuzigte*, one concentrating on the resurrection, 'Volles Grab, leerer Glaube?'; the other on the interpretation of the Christological dogma, 'Gott für uns.'

22. Dalferth, *Religiöse Rede von Gott*, 396–97; Laube, *Im Bann der Sprache*, 232–42.

23. Dalferth, *Religiöse Rede von Gott*, 457, 460–61, 577.

24. Dalferth, *Religiöse Rede von Gott*, 468, 483.

25. Dalferth, *Religiöse Rede von Gott*, 470, 486–88. Cf. Dalferth, *Existenz Gottes und christlicher Glaube*, 185, 330–31.

experience Jesus as God's address is to experience Him as Christ.[26] This experience can be articulated in various different models, building on the Old Testament tradition.[27] Only in this Christological experience is it possible to identify God as the subject of this address. E.g. because Jesus' life, teaching and death is experienced as God's loving action in favour of mankind, God can be articulated as loving Father.[28] Because God Himself makes it possible to experience Jesus as God's address and hence identifies Himself for us as loving Father, the Christological experience necessitates Trinitarian language.[29] This divine self-identification remains central to Dalferth's thinking.[30]

Already in *Religiöse Rede von Gott* it is clear that God's self-identification implies existence presuppositions.[31] In *Existenz Gottes und christlicher Glaube*, Dalferth further develops this in a sketch of an eschatological ontology, which shows that God's self-identification brings with it a new understanding of God, the world and the self.

God's self-identification makes the believer participate in the reality of God. Our spatio-temporal world is a world of sin, in which God cannot be experienced, for he is hidden in his glory. By sin, humanity has blinded himself to God.[32] In Jesus Christ, God makes it possible to experience himself within our spatio-temporal world without becoming spatio-temporal himself. To experience Jesus after Pentecost as God's address and hence as Christ, is to experience God in Jesus Christ.[33] Therefore, God's self-identification opens a new perspective in the world of sin, a perspective on new realities and a new perspective on known

26. Dalferth, *Religiöse Rede von Gott*, 474–75, 487–88.

27. Dalferth, *Religiöse Rede von Gott*, 485, 489.

28. Dalferth, *Religiöse Rede von Gott*, 590, 598.

29. Dalferth, *Religiöse Rede von Gott*, 485, 600–606.

30. See e.g. Dalferth, *Existenz Gottes und christlicher Glaube*, 176, 185, 191–92; Dalferth, *Theology and Philosophy*, 158–58, 189–94; Dalferth, *Kombinatorische Theologie*, 148; Dalferth, *Gott*, 240–41; Dalferth, *Der auferweckte Gekreuzigte*, 85, 164–67, 174, 180–81, 228; Dalferth, *Gedeutete Gegenwart*, 206; Dalferth, 'Fremdauslegung als Selbstauslegung,' 170–73; Dalferth, *Auf dem Weg der Ökumene*, 16–17; Dalferth, *Evangelische Theologie als Interpretationspraxis*, 86, 103, 115.

31. Dalferth, *Religiöse Rede von Gott*, 473–77, 480.

32. Dalferth, *Existenz Gottes und christlicher Glaube*, 172–75, 179–81; cf. Dalferth, *Gott*, 46–47; Dalferth, *Gedeutete Gegenwart*, 118.

33. Dalferth, *Existenz Gottes und christlicher Glaube*, 175–76, 180–92, 305; cf. Dalferth, *Gott*, 48.

realities.[34] In this perspective, Jesus is not known *kata sarka*, but *kata pneuma* as Christ.[35] Thus, Christology presupposes this new perspective on God's reality.

Regarding our understanding of God, within this perspective God is known as the triune God. He addresses us as God the Father, God the Son is God's address to us, and God the Spirit brings us to the experience of Jesus as God's address, of God as subject of this address and of God as creator, reconciler and redeemer.[36] The Son is the one who is originally addressed by the Father in the Spirit and who entirely corresponds and conforms ('entsprechen') to the Father. Because he corresponds and conforms to the Father, he wants to live in communion like the Father who opens himself up for communion. Hence the incarnation of the Son is originally given with his being addressed to divine conformity.[37] God is an eternal self constituting event of address and answer. God does not limit the dynamics of his life to himself, but relates himself to others and lets them participate in his original life by inclusion in his eternal relation to himself.[38] God is a perichoretic event of address and answer that opens himself up to communion. God is love, giving others to exist within his horizon. God lives for others and towards others. To state God's Trinitarian existence is to state his pro-existence.[39]

God is essentially love, always directed towards others and intending to let others share within his own life.[40] In the case of Father, Son, as well as Spirit, Dalferth speaks of pro-existence, an existence for others. In the story of Jesus Christ it is definitively confirmed that God Father, Son and Spirit, exists as love.[41] It seemed at the cross of Jesus Christ that pro-existence would lead to non-existence. Only two alternatives seem possible: existing for others resulting in not existing, or possessing the own existence and not living for others. The existence of the relata seems to be the presupposition of the relation. On the cross God has shown that this

34. After *Existenz Gottes und christlicher Glaube*, Dalferth refers to this perspective as coram deo perspective. See footnote 11.

35. Dalferth, *Existenz Gottes und christlicher Glaube*, 305–12.

36. Dalferth, *Existenz Gottes und christlicher Glaube*, 189, 194–95.

37. Dalferth, *Existenz Gottes und christlicher Glaube*, 196–97.

38. Dalferth, *Existenz Gottes und christlicher Glaube*, 206–7.

39. Dalferth, *Existenz Gottes und christlicher Glaube*, 210–11.

40. Dalferth, *Existenz Gottes und christlicher Glaube*, 212.

41. Dalferth, *Existenz Gottes und christlicher Glaube*, 217–18.

is not true of his love, for God's love is creative. God's love transcended the dilemma. God's love lets himself be pulled into the death communion with human beings by jeopardizing his divinity. But he pulled Jesus Christ, and with him everything else, into communion with himself. Therefore his love proved to be stronger than death. With this, God remained true to his essence also in the face of death.[42] This was possible because of the human existence of Jesus Christ, which was divine pro-existence. Jesus Christ existed for others, as God corresponding ('entsprechend') human being. As such, he is the human beings addressing ('ansprechende') God.[43] Is he both God and man, then is his death a death for others, because God let himself be pulled so totally in the communion of death with Jesus Christ that this Jesus as Christ was incorporated in God's communion of life. His death and eternal life in communion with God are because of his pro-existence not just his personal affair, but they have soteriological significance: every human being is included in the history of Jesus Christ and thus integrated in the communion of life with God.[44] Because of the pro-existence of Jesus Christ, he is at the same time the address of God to us and our answer to God. In him God opens his communion of life for us and pulls us into this communion, and in him we turn ourselves toward God because he lives in God's communion.[45] This all shows that love as pro-existence is a central concept for Dalferth.[46]

Apart from the Trinity and God's love or pro-existence, God's glory is important for Dalferth.[47] God exists in glory, the horizon within which

42. Dalferth, *Existenz Gottes und christlicher Glaube*, 218–19, 221.

43. Dalferth, *Existenz Gottes und christlicher Glaube*, 232, 310, 313, 315.

44. Dalferth, *Existenz Gottes und christlicher Glaube*, 310.

45. Dalferth, *Existenz Gottes und christlicher Glaube*, 313, 317.

46. This love is further specified as original, creative, fatherly, redemptive, forgiving, and merciful. Cf. Dalferth, *Theology and Philosophy*, 158–59, 193, 200, 202–3, 219–23; Dalferth, *Kombinatorische Theologie*, 130, 134, 136–37, 148; Dalferth, *Gott*, 6, 12, 187, 210, 230–31, 240–41; Dalferth, 'Über Einheit und Vielfalt des christlichen Glaubens,' 119, 130–31; Dalferth, *Der auferweckte Gekreuzigte*; Dalferth, *Gedeutete Gegenwart*, 96, 98, 118, 131, 206, 266, 273, 282–83; Dalferth, 'Volles Grab, leerer Glaube?' 401, 404–9; Dalferth, 'Fremdauslegung als Selbstauslegung,' 172; Dalferth, 'Representing God's Presence,' 254; Dalferth, *Auf dem Weg der Ökumene*, 23–25, 31; Dalferth, *Evangelische Theologie als Interpretationspraxis*, 86; Dalferth, 'Gott für uns,' 61, 73–74.

47. In terms of the conceptual apparatus that will be introduced in 8.4.1, Dalferth writes that it is the 'Gegenstand' God Father, Son and Spirit that exist; that it is his 'Gegenstandsart' to exist as love, and His 'Gegenständlichkeit' to exist in glory. Cf. footnote 20.

he realises his love. At the cross, God glorified himself by bearing the contrast of life and death and incorporating Jesus in his glory, thus realising his love. As a result, the contrast of life and death was unmasked as a false alternative: in God's glory, the glorified Jesus received life despite his death—resurrection (including ascension) is glorification.[48] As a result, Jesus cannot be located in our spatio-temporality any more, but within the horizon of God's glory he exists as Christ and hence as the realisation of God's love. (Nevertheless, the one who exists within God's glory as Christ, the Son of God, is the same as the earthly Jesus.[49]) At the cross, the reality of God's glory proved to be a greater and more encompassing reality than our spatio-temporal reality of sin.[50] The glorified existence Jesus received is existence freed from sin and in eternal communion with the Creator.[51] As the glorified one, Jesus Christ's existence remains pro-existence, intending to incorporate others in this communion of life with God.[52]

Because Jesus as Christ is God's address to us, he opens for us God's reality and presence. Jesus existed and exists enhypostatically based on God's relation to Him and for others. Therefore he confronts us with God. He realised his existence anhypostatically, which means that his communion with God, which is non spatio-temporally structured but still determines his existence, is yet realised and manifested within our spatio-temporality. Only in his being is God brought to us as Father and are we brought to God as his children. As a result, he makes it possible for us to live within God's eschatological reality. In him we are with God and God is with us. In him God's presence is made accessible within space and time, whereas God remains non spatio-temporal.[53]

In *Der auferweckte Gekreuzigte*, Dalferth gives another triple: God's identity (Who is God?): Father, Son and Spirit; God's being (How is God?): Trinitarian act; God's essence (What is God?): inexhaustible originating love ('unerschöpfliche schöpferische Liebe'), see Dalferth, *Der auferweckte Gekreuzigte*, 33.

48. Dalferth, *Existenz Gottes und christlicher Glaube*, 228–30.

49. Dalferth, *Existenz Gottes und christlicher Glaube*, 306–9, 312, 314–15.

50. Dalferth, *Existenz Gottes und christlicher Glaube*, 230–31, 309.

51. Dalferth, *Existenz Gottes und christlicher Glaube*, 235.

52. Dalferth, *Existenz Gottes und christlicher Glaube*, 232–33, 310.

53. Dalferth, *Existenz Gottes und christlicher Glaube*, 314–320; Dalferth, *Gott*, 48, 240.

In *Der auferweckte Gekreuzigte* Dalferth further unfolds the hermeneutical logic of Christian theology, building on earlier work but using more biblical material.[54]

First he makes clear that the resurrection is the hermeneutical starting point of theology. The referent of Christological confessions is not Jesus of Nazareth, but the crucified One who is raised from death ('der auferweckte Gekreuzigte'), who is alive and present.[55] Theology starts with the resurrection of Jesus Christ. This resurrection must be understood in view of the crucifixion, which leads to Christology. The cross must be understood in view of God, and God in view of the light of Jesus' message and God's acts in Jesus' cross and resurrection, what leads to the doctrine of God and the Trinity. God's acts in cross and resurrection must be understood in view of us and our world, leading to pneumatology.[56] Concentrating on Christology, this implies that Jesus' life and message of the kingdom of God and God's nearness as loving Father are understood in the light of his resurrection, cross and resurrection in the light of his message, and God and his kingdom in the light of the story of Jesus Christ.[57] Or stated differently, we need historical (concerning the historical identity of Jesus of Nazareth and his message), eschatological (concerning God's eschatological acting in cross and resurrection), soteriological (concerning God's acting towards us for our salvation) and Trinitarian theological questions (concerning the divine identity of Jesus Christ).[58]

A central concept in Dalferth's Christology is the concept of identification. Dalferth sees different identifications. First, Jesus identified God as loving Father. Second, in cross and resurrection God identified himself with Jesus, in this way confirming the identification Jesus gave of God. Third, in this way God identified himself in Jesus Christ with humanity. This has to be elaborated.[59]

54. See on this book Kühn, *Christologie*, 62–63; Wenz, 'Christologische Paralipomena II,' 414–17.

55. Dalferth, *Der auferweckte Gekreuzigte*, 21–24.

56. Dalferth, *Der auferweckte Gekreuzigte*, 27, 31–36. Cf. how Dalferth in *Religiöse Rede von Gott* the experience of address by God takes as starting point, that can be unfolded in different perspectives and models, see 443, 463–66, 472, 489–93, 606, 672.

57. See esp. Dalferth, *Der auferweckte Gekreuzigte*, 78 note 81, 87–139, 161.

58. Dalferth, *Der auferweckte Gekreuzigte*, 86.

59. These identifications at the same time imply differentiations. Identifying God as Father, Jesus differentiates himself as Son from God. In relation to Jesus, God differentiates himself as Father from the Son. In relation to us, God differentiates himself in the

The first concerns the Jesus of history. According to Jesus' message, God's kingdom is coming, and God is near as a loving Father. Jesus also addresses God as Father. The Father-image is the summary of Jesus' understanding of God.[60]

The second is more complex. The resurrection of Jesus Christ shows that God maintains the life communion with Jesus, in which Jesus lived all his life, even in death. This makes him what he is: the Son of God. God identifies himself as Son with Jesus and makes this man by his Spirit participate in his own divine identity. In this way, He identifies himself as Father of the Son, thus confirming Jesus' identification of God as loving Father. But if God is as he has proven himself in Jesus, then he can never be anything else, and must be near his children as a loving Father, who remains loyal through death. This is confirmed when he makes Jesus the place of his nearness and presence.[61]

Thirdly, Christ identified himself with humanity. Explicitly this is said only once by Dalferth.[62] More explicitly Dalferth describes how when Jesus died, speaking in a Trinitarian way, the Son of God died, making himself like us sinners. We sinners wanted to be like God, but acting like this we made ourselves incapable of action, as death ultimately shows. The cross shows that we are made like God, because God makes himself like us: sentenced, rejected, desolate, excluded, and alone. In this way God discloses his divinity to us: not self sufficiency, but selfless love. Death, sin and our distance from God are not decisive, rather God's creative love is. In Christ, we are with God and God is with us.[63]

The central soteriological images 'Lord,' 'Christ' and 'Son of God' used in reference to Jesus, manifest this soteriological significance. According to Dalferth, they all show that the history of Jesus effectuates God's kingdom as all changing nearness of the loving Father, a love which is present

difference of Father and Son from his creatures as creative Spirit. See e.g. Dalferth, *Der auferweckte Gekreuzigte*, 59, 77–78, 114, 279; Dalferth, 'Gott für uns,' 59–61.

60. Dalferth, *Der auferweckte Gekreuzigte*, 27, 78 note 81, 111, 114, 120, 123, 133–33, 164–65, 279.

61. Dalferth, *Der auferweckte Gekreuzigte*, 27, 133–34, 136–39, 279–81; and further 77, 78 note 81, 85–86, 93, 128–29, 160–65, 174, 205, 207, 213, 217, 229, 303. See further Dalferth, 'Volles Grab, leerer Glaube?' 404–5.

62. Dalferth, *Der auferweckte Gekreuzigte*, 276–77. See on inclusivity 8.2.3.

63. Dalferth, *Der auferweckte Gekreuzigte*, 27, 40–45, 277. Cf. Dalferth, *Existenz Gottes und christlicher Glaube*, 344; Dalferth, *Gedeutete Gegenwart*, 60–65.

by the Holy Spirit. As Lord, Jesus is the one who is glorified with God, who reigns over life and death, and whose reign is a reign of love and loyalty. As Christ, he is the one in whom God's reign has been realised, exclusively in him but as a result of his inclusiveness with a universal openness. As the Son of God He is the Son of David, representing his people and living with God as a loving Father whose love He discloses universally.[64]

Dalferth in this book further makes his eschatology-concept more precise. Until *Der auferweckte Gekreuzigte*, 'eschatology' seemed a concept that referred generally to everything concerning God, although eschatological ('eschatologisch') was contrasted with 'eschatic' ('eschatisch').[65] 'Eschatologisch' concerns present eschatology, 'eschatisch' the ultimate goal of future eschatology.[66] In this book, Dalferth shows a development in 19th and 20th century theology. Eschatology concerned successively (a) the eschata, (b) the eschaton, and (c) the *Eschatos*, Jesus Christ. Accordingly, Dalferth relates Christology and eschatology, resulting in a more specified eschatology-concept.[67] Nevertheless, this specification implies a change, for the emphasis on the incompleteness of 'eschatological' in the light of what is still 'eschatisch' has disappeared in *Der auferweckte Gekreuzigte*, where he does not use the word 'eschatisch.'[68] He now describes God's eschatological action as final, universally valid, and renewing.[69] As a result, God's eschatological action can not just be a historical action, for it concerns the whole of history, making this world of histori-

64. Dalferth, *Der auferweckte Gekreuzigte*, 127–34.

65. See e.g. Dalferth, *Existenz Gottes und christlicher Glaube*, 268–70. Here it is important that the identification system of God's reality (God's 'Gegenständlichkeit') as a whole can be characterized as eschatological. That Dalferth's eschatology-concept refers to the entire reality of God and his acts does not imply that in *Existenz Gottes und christlicher Glaube* this concept is dark and ambigious, as Browarzik writes; see Browarzik, 'Onto-Theo-Logie,' 372.

66. Dalferth distinguishes e.g. between an 'eschatologisch' and an 'eschatisch' eschaton, Dalferth, *Existenz Gottes und christlicher Glaube*, 272. See further for his use of 'eschatisch' *Existenz Gottes und christlicher Glaube*, 234, 237, 264–66, 272, 287, 299, 319, 336, 343; Dalferth, *Kombinatorische Theologie*, 148, 157.

67. Dalferth, *Der auferweckte Gekreuzigte*, 197–200.

68. In this light it is remarkable, that Dalferth in *Jenseits von Mythos und Logos* does not oppose to the idea that the resurrection of the death and the last judgment are mythical. See Dalferth, *Jenseits von Mythos und Logos*, 158. Cf. Dalferth, 'Volles Grab, leerer Glaube?' 396–97, where Dalferth equates the resurrection of Christ with the situation of a deceased believer in stead of with the resurrection of the flesh at the last day.

69. Dalferth, *Der auferweckte Gekreuzigte*, 80.

cal events the old world by putting it in the light of the new world and a new life. This leads to a fundamental change in frame of reference: a new perspective and a new life are opened up.[70]

Summarizing, Dalferth's Christology is unfolded from the self-identification of God in Jesus Christ, that is Jesus raised from death by God and experienced as the place of God's identifying or loving presence by the Holy Spirit.

In *Existenz Gottes und christlicher Glaube* the implications of this identification for reality are elaborated. God is the Trinitarian God, an event of address and answer. In Jesus Christ we participate in this event. God is love, he wanted to open his life toward others. The existence of this loving God is pro-existence, as was the existence of Jesus, who lived for others. By his death and resurrection in the glory of God, he was incorporated in God's glory, hence opening God's glorified existence also for us. As Christ, Jesus makes God's reality accessible for us and makes it possible to participate within this reality.

In *Der auferweckte Gekreuzigte* Dalferth further elaborates this position, exploring the hermeneutical logic of Christology and referring more extensively to the New Testament. He shows the development from the identification of God as loving Father by Jesus to the gospel of Jesus Christ as the one in whom God's reign is realised and God's loving presence is disclosed universally. God's eschatological action in the resurrection of Jesus Christ made this possible. The confessions that Jesus is Christ, Lord, and Son of God all make clear that he is the place of the disclosure of God's loving presence.

8.2.2 THE STORY OF JESUS CHRIST

Having sketched some moments of Dalferth's Christology, I will now investigate in greater detail the soteriological relevance of the history of Jesus Christ according to his theology. I will structure my treatment of the different moments of this history following the hermeneutical logic Dalferth describes.

70. Dalferth, *Der auferweckte Gekreuzigte*, 32, 58–59, 74, 76, 79–83, 99, 161, 202, 208–9, 217–18. Cf. Dalferth, *Auf dem Weg der Ökumene*, 22–23. Here Dalferth describes the resurrection as not an act of God in history, but as the beginning of the eschatological end of history. 'Eschatological' concerns here the end of history; cf also Dalferth, 'Volles Grab, leerer Glaube?'404.

It is evident that the whole of the history of Jesus Christ is important to Dalferth. Only as a whole and after Pentecost can Jesus' history be experienced as God's address, as we have seen his emphasis in *Religiöse Rede von Gott*.[71] In this history God's character and loving nearness are disclosed.[72] His history is central to the proclamation of the gospel.[73] But more important is that the history of Jesus Christ is the paradigm of all our histories. All human biographies are integrated in his story, which is '*Vor*geschichte, *Grund*geschichte und *Nach*geschichte' of all other human histories.[74] In the history of Jesus Christ God judges our lives.[75] This significance of the history of Jesus Christ makes it worth a closer look.

As has been said in the preceding section, the hermeneutical starting point of telling the story of Jesus Christ is the resurrection and not the incarnation. It was the combination of two opposed experiences that constituted a cognitive dissonance and lead to the belief that Jesus was raised from death by God: the death of Jesus and the experience of Jesus as living Lord.[76] Historical facts like an empty tomb did not lead to this incredible faith, but only the experiences of Jesus as the living Christ worked by the Holy Spirit.[77] As a consequence, Dalferth does not differentiate between Easter, (Ascension,) and Pentecost. This experience is repeated in every human life where faith in Jesus Christ comes into being;[78] telling the story of Jesus Christ without Ascension it is impossible to differentiate between the experience of the first disciples and our experience. However, he does distinguish between the resurrection and the experience of Jesus as

71. See footnote 25.

72. Dalferth, *Gott*, 20, 45; Dalferth, *Der auferweckte Gekreuzigte*, 186, 213, 218.

73. Dalferth, *Existenz Gottes und christlicher Glaube*, 325, 330; I. U. Dalferth, 'Über Einheit und Vielfalt des christlichen Glaubens,' 132.

74. Dalferth, *Der auferweckte Gekreuzigte*, 305; and further Dalferth, *Existenz Gottes und christlicher Glaube*, 310; Dalferth, *Theology and Philosophy*, 222; Dalferth, *Gott*, 45; Dalferth, *Der auferweckte Gekreuzigte*, 186, 213, 218, 238, 253, 302, 304–5; Dalferth, *Gedeutete Gegenwart*, 91; Dalferth, 'Der Mensch in seiner Zeit,' 175–77; Dalferth, *Evangelische Theologie als Interpretationspraxis*, 102.

75. Dalferth, *Auf dem Weg der Ökumene*, 31.

76. Dalferth, *Der auferweckte Gekreuzigte*, 64, 67, 70; Dalferth, 'Volles Grab, leerer Glaube?' 389–90.

77. Dalferth, *Der auferweckte Gekreuzigte*, 62–67; Dalferth, 'Volles Grab, leerer Glaube?' 385–88, 394–96, 404.

78. Dalferth, *Religiöse Rede von Gott*, 470; Dalferth, 'Volles Grab, leerer Glaube?' 403–4; Dalferth, *Auf dem Weg der Ökumene*, 23.

risen. Jesus is not raised because He is experienced as such, but, because God raised Jesus from death, Jesus is experienced as the living Christ.[79] Resurrection is incorporation in God's glory, when God gives the crucified Jesus access to his glory. As the resurrected one, Jesus Christ participates in God's reality and lives in his eternal communion of life. This reality transcends our historical reality.[80] Because this act of God, raising Jesus from death is an eschatological act of God, not *in* history ('in der Welt') but *on* history ('an der Welt') determining history as a whole and beginning the end of history, it cannot be discerned within history if the Holy Spirit does not make an experience of Jesus as the resurrected Christ possible.[81] The resurrection of Jesus Christ is not an historical fact that once happened, but neither is it a myth, for it is an eschatological act of God that determines everything.[82] The resurrection does not even necessarily lead to historical facts like an empty tomb; according to Dalferth, these do not matter theologically. He can say this because he equates the resurrection of Christ with the situation of a deceased person, lying in the grave with a decaying body, but nevertheless living in, by and with God; and not with the resurrection of the flesh on the last day. As a result, the soteriological significance of the resurrection is that also in our death, we live in God's reality.[83] God's eschatological acts transcend and comprise our historical reality.

79. Dalferth, *Kombinatorische Theologie*, 91; Dalferth, *Der auferweckte Gekreuzigte*, 55–56; Dalferth, 'Volles Grab, leerer Glaube?' 403–4.

80. Dalferth, *Existenz Gottes und christlicher Glaube*, 219, 230, 310; Dalferth, *Der auferweckte Gekreuzigte*, 57, 76–77; Dalferth, 'Volles Grab, leerer Glaube?' 402; Dalferth, *Auf dem Weg der Ökumene*, 22.

81. Dalferth, *Der auferweckte Gekreuzigte*, 69–70, 80; Dalferth, 'Volles Grab, leerer Glaube?' 387–88.

82. Dalferth, *Jenseits von Mythos und Logos*, 107, 112, 115, 123, 132, 141–43, 154–59, 162–64; Dalferth, *Der auferweckte Gekreuzigte*, 78–80; Dalferth, 'Volles Grab, leerer Glaube?' 385, 402, 404.

83. Dalferth, *Der auferweckte Gekreuzigte*, 65–66; Dalferth, 'Volles Grab, leerer Glaube?' 396–97. esp 47, 399.

I agree with Dalferth that the relevance of the empty tomb must not be misunderstood as *ground* of faith. However, the empty tomb is soteriologically relevant because it determines the content of our faith. Consequently, I see a problem where Dalferth does not differentiate between, on the one hand, the period between someone's death and the resurrection on the last day when human bodies in their graves suffer from decay, and, on the other hand, the period after the resurrection of the flesh, when our graves will be empty and we receive a new glorified body. Now Dalferth equates the resurrection of Jesus Christ with our post mortem presence with God. As a result, the soteriological

The hermeneutical process that leads to the belief 'Jesus is risen from death' and the hermeneutical consequences of Jesus' resurrection for our understanding of God, world and self, Dalferth describes as the application of Jesus' preaching to himself and the resulting universalising of his message. His message becomes the horizon of the understanding of his life and death and at the same time the horizon of understanding of the whole of humanity. He is the place of God's definitive self determination as loving Father, and we are God's children and heirs. This implies that we exist in an eschatological, fundamental new existence.[84] This new life is a life in the body of Christ as we will see in 8.3.1.

From the resurrection, we look back to the cross. However, Dalferth emphasises that this must not result in rendering the cross harmless ('verharmlosung'). Seen in our perspective, the cross is soteriologically mute and makes mute. Striving to be like God, we die as failures and drop-outs. God makes himself like us, mortal and without answer to the last why question. This muteness does not disappear by progression to a next stage of glory in the resurrection, although the church often acted as if it did. The cross only speaks when it is placed in the middle of God's life and with this context within our lives. This renders the cross not harmless, but says in the word of the cross more than could have ever been seen or expected within our horizon. This cross brings God so near that he is with us even in death and we therefore are with him also in our death. It tells us that by making himself like us, God determines and discloses his divinity as selfless love. It changed God and changed our lives, making us free to love like God.[85]

In this way, Dalferth closely relates cross and resurrection, emphasising the crucial importance of God's eschatological action in cross and

---

significance of the resurrection of Jesus Christ is understood as disclosure of our eternal existence in God's loving presence. In this way, the empty tomb is not soteriologically necessary. Equated with the resurrection of the flesh, the empty tomb *is* soteriologically relevant: it shows that our graves will be empty one day, when we will receive a new glorified body. The hope of our resurrection is *not dependent on* the empty tomb, but the *content* of this hope does change if the grave was not empty.

84. Dalferth, *Der auferweckte Gekreuzigte*, 57–58, 76–83, 207; Dalferth, 'Volles Grab, leerer Glaube?' 401–3, 405.

85. Dalferth, *Der auferweckte Gekreuzigte*, 43–46; Dalferth, *Gedeutete Gegenwart*, 60–65; Dalferth, 'Volles Grab, leerer Glaube?' 385, 404; Dalferth, *Auf dem Weg der Ökumene*, 22–25, 32. Concerning the 'verharmlosungen' of the cross, see Dalferth, *Der auferweckte Gekreuzigte*, 48–51; Dalferth, *Gedeutete Gegenwart*, 75–78.

resurrection. In the death of Christ his loving Father stays with him, and incorporates him in his life. God's presence with his Son implies that the Son lives even if he dies. In God's reality he lives for ever beyond the alternatives of life and death. God's love is stronger than death and creates life; it is a love that is not limited by death. Determining himself in this way according to Jesus' identification of God as Father, God determines his identity also for us. Incorporating the Son in his glory, he opens his communion of life also to us. In the light of the resurrection, the cross is the realisation of the reign of Gods love.[86]

This soteriological significance of the cross is referred to when the image of sacrifice is used.[87] Understanding Jesus' death as a sacrifice leads to a Christological modification of the sacrifice image, in which the category of sacrifice is spiritualised.[88] Following Hartmut Gese, Dalferth sees three moments in the Old Testament sacrifices: a. the act of consecration by laying hands on the head of the animal, leading to a transfer of subject; b. killing of the animal; c. symbolic incorporation in the sacred: by the blood of the sacrifice the life consecration of the person who sacrifices is accomplished symbolically.[89] Not only does something negative take

86. Dalferth, *Existenz Gottes und christlicher Glaube*, 176, 218–21, 229–30, 232, 309–10; Dalferth, *Der auferweckte Gekreuzigte*, 44–45, 57, 77–79, 205–6, 208, 252–53, 276–81; Dalferth, 'Volles Grab, leerer Glaube?' 398, 400, 402, 404, 406; Dalferth, *Auf dem Weg der Ökumene*, 31.

87. Dalferth warns against the idea that interpretation of the cross is just a subjective activity. Interpretations of Jesus' death must be understood pneumatologically and within a Trinitarian hermeneutic. These interpretations refer to God's eschatological action that Christians understand as God's self-interpretation; Dalferth, *Der auferweckte Gekreuzigte*, 246 note 42. Cf. concerning the resurrection Dalferth, *Kombinatorische Theologie*, 91.

88. Dalferth, *Jenseits von Mythos und Logos*, 193; Dalferth, *Der auferweckte Gekreuzigte*, 253–54, 270, 297–300. That the sacrifice-metaphor is used, does not imply that Jesus' death *is* a sacrifice. Speaking of the soteriological significance of Jesus' death is speaking of this death in such a way, that is said what the New Testament tries to say if this death is characterized as a sacrifice. According to Dalferth, the image of sacrifice is used to indicate that this death is the end of all sacrifices; that sacrifices are not necessary any more; and even that Jesus' death shows that all sacrifices are ineffectual and needless. Jesus' death is interpreted as sacrifice to indicate that his death has transcended all sacrifices and even was no sacrifice itself. See Dalferth, *Der auferweckte Gekreuzigte*, 293–96.

Jüngel criticised Dalferth, for according to Jüngel it is not possible to understand Jesus' death without the sacrifice-metaphor. Jesus' death was a sacrifice, but this metaphor must be understood christologically. See Jüngel, *Das Evangelium von der Rechtfertigung*, 141.

89. Dalferth, *Jenseits von Mythos und Logos*, 194; Dalferth, *Der auferweckte Gekreuzigte*, 275.

place (death), but also something positive: the relation of the person who sacrifices with the sacred is restored. A sacrifice incorporates in the sacred. The interpretation of Jesus' death—as legal execution—as a cultic sacrifice shows that something comparable takes place: eschatological incorporation in the communion with God. This moment of incorporation is the soteriologically relevant moment of the death of Jesus, not an isolated idea of work-substitution; an incorporation that is worked by God alone.[90] Something comparable takes place in the death of Jesus for us, but in a different order. In our perspective the order a. consecration—b. killing—c. incorporation becomes c. Christ: incorporation—b. cross: killing—a. faith: transfer of identity. We do not transfer our identity onto Christ, but we submit to his identification with us. The resurrection discloses the incorporation that has taken place proleptically. This incorporation in God is identical with 'being in Christ.'[91] In God's perspective the cross is at the same time an act of consecration and incorporation.[92] In the perspective of Jesus it becomes a. cross: consecration—b. killing—c. resurrection: incorporation. This does not mean that Jesus identifies with something, but in his life, culminating on the cross Jesus receives an identity that makes him what he is: Christ, Son of God. God makes Jesus the created place of his nearness and presence. Consecration and incorporation do not take place symbolically, but really.[93]

In this interpretation of 'sacrifice' all emphasis is on what God does. It is not what Jesus does that is soteriologically significant (Jesus gives himself in his death to the life and salvation creating nearness of his Father to disclose this also to others). It is not his work, but his person, that is important, for soteriologically it matters only that God acts eschatologically, making Jesus Christ the place of his presence. It is the resurrection that gives the cross its saving character. As a result, Jesus Christ, in his person, is our salvation. He *is* the new covenant, although he did not create this covenant by his blood. His death is the execution of God's

90. According to Dalferth, something goes wrong if the image of sacrifice is isolated or privileged. Only together with other images, the sacrifice-metaphor is understood correctly. See Dalferth, *Der auferweckte Gekreuzigte*, 253, 257, 260–62, 270, 272–74, 286–93, 295–96, 299–300, 305.

91. Dalferth, *Jenseits von Mythos und Logos*, 194; Dalferth, *Der auferweckte Gekreuzigte*, 276–79.

92. Dalferth, *Der auferweckte Gekreuzigte*, 276, 278–79, 281.

93. Dalferth, *Der auferweckte Gekreuzigte*, 279–80.

covenant loyalty, insofar as God unified himself with Jesus in his death to realise his union with us. We do not come to God through the death judgment, but God comes to us, performing the atonement. Humanity gives nothing, God gives everything.[94]

Less emphasised but still present is the idea of the divine judgment in cross and resurrection. In Jesus Christ, God takes over our sin and gives us a new existence in God's presence. Here the stress is on the quality of the new existence that is given, not on the condemnation of the old existence.[95]

From cross and resurrection looking back on the life of Jesus, we see Jesus' message of the Kingdom, his identification of God as Father, and the divine ground of his existence. Jesus' message of the nearness of the kingdom and the identification of God as Father, evoke the question of who he is, as does the resurrection. If the resurrected Jesus Christ is the same as Jesus of Nazareth, and if God remains loyal to Jesus and continues his existence, giving him access to his glory, what can be said about Jesus' identity and his relation with the Father?[96]

Jesus' message shows a special relation of Jesus with God, whom he identified as Father. In a special way, Jesus lived totally from his relation with God and for others.[97] He distinguished himself from God the Father, to serve this Father and his compassionate love.[98] This was possible because of the work of God's Spirit in Jesus' life.[99] How special this relation with God was, is indicated by the resurrection: God stays near his Son in death and even identifies himself with Jesus, confirming Jesus'

94. Dalferth, *Der auferweckte Gekreuzigte*, 251–53, 277–78, 281–82; Dalferth, 'Gott für uns,' 64–65, 70.

According to David Ford, the problem of this account of sacrifice is that Dalferth does not do justice to the physicality of a sacrifice and 'the bodily particularity of the dead Jesus and the continuing importance of this, represented in his face,' see Ford, *Self and salvation*, 209.

95. Dalferth, *Existenz Gottes und christlicher Glaube*, 318–19; Dalferth, *Der auferweckte Gekreuzigte*, 79; Dalferth, *Auf dem Weg der Ökumene*, 30–32.

96. Dalferth, *Der auferweckte Gekreuzigte*, 85.

97. Dalferth, *Existenz Gottes und christlicher Glaube*, 232, 315; Dalferth, *Der auferweckte Gekreuzigte*, 23 note 65, 93.

98. Dalferth, *Der auferweckte Gekreuzigte*, 109 note 54, 166.

99. Dalferth, *Der auferweckte Gekreuzigte*, 110, 118, 123; Dalferth, *Evangelische Theologie als Interpretationspraxis*, 107.

identification of God as Father as a self-identification.[100] That Jesus could live his life in this way totally *coram deo*, according to Dalferth, was only possible based on the special relation God had with Jesus; even his human existence is confessed as an act of God.[101] The cross and resurrection show the identity of Jesus as Christ, an identity that determined the way He lived his life on earth in God's presence.[102] This identity and this special relation of God with Jesus are the presupposition of God's relation with us via Jesus.[103]

The disclosure of this divine ground of Jesus' being Dalferth describes as a hermeneutical process. During his life, Jesus identified God as Father. As a result, after the resurrection Jesus receives the title 'Son.' Originally, this title has a background in hereditary right, a background it retains primarily. Because Jesus discloses God's nearness, he is called 'firstborn son' in a second stage. In a third stage, the son-metaphor becomes independent of the Hebrew background. The combination with the Hellenistic *Logos*- and *Sophia*-concepts stimulates this. Further, if the Son is Son, there can be no time that Father and Son were not together. This third stage of the development Dalferth finds again in the New Testament in the use of titles like 'Lord,' 'Christ,' 'Son of God,' but also in narratives with a secondary character in respect to the narrative of cross and resurrection, about pre-existence, sending, descent, conception by the Holy Spirit, virgin birth, incarnation, ascension, and ascent.[104] This divine ground of Jesus' being is important for soteriological reasons: God

100. Dalferth, *Der auferweckte Gekreuzigte*, 27, 133–37, 160–61, 165–66, 279–80.

101. Dalferth, *Existenz Gottes und christlicher Glaube*, 185, 308, 310–12, 314–15; Dalferth, *Der auferweckte Gekreuzigte*, 110, 135–36.

Dalferth distinguishes his position from the position of Pannenberg. Where Pannenberg works with the human relation with God as a general characteristic of being human and a concept of humanity that is creation theological, Dalferth starts with the special humanity of Jesus Christ, his special relation with God and therefore a Christological-soteriological starting point. The universality of salvation has to be understood as the universality of God's presence, and not in the light of a general essence of human nature. See Dalferth, *Der auferweckte Gekreuzigte*, 23 note 65 and 148 note 126; Dalferth, 'Gott für uns,' 72–74. Cf. Dalferth, Jüngel, 'Person und Gottebenbildlichkeit,' 60.

102. Dalferth, *Existenz Gottes und christlicher Glaube*, 230, 310–11, 314–15.

103. Dalferth, *Existenz Gottes und christlicher Glaube*, 315–16.

104. Dalferth, *Der auferweckte Gekreuzigte*, 30, 111–19, 132–33; cf. Dalferth, *Existenz Gottes und christlicher Glaube*, 134, 316.

takes the initiative to determine himself as love and to disclose himself to us as loving presence.[105]

Theologically this divine ground must be articulated further. According to Dalferth, this cannot be done in reference to a dual ontology of human-divine state of affairs, using temporal or ontological categories of metaphysics.[106] The classical doctrine of the two natures is a problematic elaboration of this divine ground, because it interprets Christological images and texts uncritically in a realist way within the framework of a substance ontology.[107] Instead, it must be articulated as the saving act of the triune God, who is the referent of Christological statements. This saving act is the self communication of God, in which all our communication with and about God is founded.[108] This divine self communication is unfolded in the doctrine of the Trinity. The doctrine of the Trinity shows that the concept of person has to be understood relationally. The person of Jesus Christ was constituted entirely by God, by God's communication with himself.[109] In his life, culminating at the cross, he receives an identity that makes him what he is: Christ, the Son of God.[110]

Summarizing, the emphasis in Dalferth's Christology is on the saving and eschatological action of the triune God. This culminates in the resurrection, which gives Jesus Christ his soteriological significance. God incorporates Jesus in his glory and determines and discloses himself to us as loving nearness, communicating himself to us in Christ and the Spirit. That the resurrection gives soteriological significance to the cross is not to render the cross harmless. Here we see who we are: humans striving to be like God, but ending in the blind alley of death. However,

105. Dalferth, *Existenz Gottes und christlicher Glaube*, 316–17; Dalferth, *Der auferweckte Gekreuzigte*, 135, 139.

106. Dalferth, *Der auferweckte Gekreuzigte*, 152, 159. Although Dalferth declines a dual ontology, in *Existenz Gottes* he uses a new duality as we will see in 8.4, of two 'Gegenständlichkeiten.'

107. Dalferth, *Der auferweckte Gekreuzigte*, 146.

108. Dalferth, *Der auferweckte Gekreuzigte*, 152–53.
How important this self communication of God is to Dalferth can be seen in his evaluation of the patristic doctrine of the Trinity. He values that the Cappadocians broke the Greek metaphysics with their concepts of *ousia* and *hypostasis*, but regrets that epistemologically the impossibility of knowing the transcendent God is maintained, see Dalferth, *Jenseits von Mythos und Logos*, 91.

109. Dalferth, *Der auferweckte Gekreuzigte*, 156.

110. Dalferth, *Der auferweckte Gekreuzigte*, 279.

as the image of sacrifice indicates, the cross is a death for us. In cross and resurrection, God incorporates Jesus Christ in his life and makes him the created place of his nearness, the place where his kingdom is realised. The emphasis is on the quality of the new existence in God's loving presence, not on the condemnation of the world of sin. God confirms that Jesus lived a true message: God is, as loving Father, a near God. That Jesus could live this life can be only understood if this life is seen as a life with a divine ground, as a work of the triune God communicating with himself to communicate with us.

8.2.3 INCLUSIVITY AND EXCLUSIVITY

Having described aspects of Dalferth's Christology, it is now the moment for analysing his work in regard to the hypothesis of this investigation. Does his work contain a moment of representation? Can a concept of 'being in Christ' be developed using the concept of representation and in continuity with Dalferth's Christology? And what about the moment of substitution and its relation to the moment of representation?

An inclusive moment is present in his Christology, although Dalferth does not use the concept of representation itself. It can be traced in different aspects. First, it can be seen in the idea that Jesus is the true human being ('wahrer Mensch'). He accomplishes himself the life in correspondence ('Entsprechung') to God, which humanity had refused. In Jesus Christ is realised the possibility of true human being. In him we humans come to God. He is the first true human being, by the Spirit this possibility is realised also in our lives, making us true human beings too. As a result, the true human being of Jesus Christ has an inclusive and prospective character.[111] Second, it is presupposed in the idea that Jesus is not only God's address to us, but also our answer to God. In him God turns to us and him alone God accepts as our answering return to him.[112] Here we participate by the Spirit in the Trinitarian perichoretic relation of address and answer between Father and Son, and also the essence of being human is realised: living with God as communicating persons.[113] Third,

111. Dalferth, *Existenz Gottes und christlicher Glaube*, 185, 223, 225, 274, 313, 316, 344; Dalferth, *Der auferweckte Gekreuzigte*, 73, 253; cf. Dalferth, 'Gott für uns,' 59–60.

112. Dalferth, *Existenz Gottes und christlicher Glaube*, 313, 317–18, 320.

113. Dalferth, *Existenz Gottes und christlicher Glaube*, 196–98, 204, 283, 316; Dalferth, *Der auferweckte Gekreuzigte*, 231, 235–36.

Jesus' history can only be the frame of reference for all our histories if his history includes ours. Jesus' history is our fore- and after-history ('Vor- und Nachgeschichte'), the eschatological paradigm of all our histories. What it is to be human can only be understood if the human being is seen integrated in the history of Jesus Christ. His history is open and inclusive.[114] Fourth, Dalferth explicitly emphasises the inclusiveness of Jesus as Christ, collective person and corporate personality within the horizon of God's action; for Christ is soteriologically inclusive as a result of God's action as Dalferth emphasises several times.[115] This all shows that the moment of inclusiveness is present in Dalferth's Christology. However, this inclusiveness plays no direct role in Dalferth's understanding of 'being in Christ,' which is identified with 'being incorporated in God' or with 'glorified being.'[116] Based on the preceding chapters, 'being in Christ' could also be understood as a precondition for being incorporated in God or glorified being.

A moment of inclusivity is present in Dalferth's Christology, but this moment is coloured by the emphasis on God's eschatological action that creates this inclusiveness (it is not Jesus who is inclusive, but God's eschatological action)[117] and by the metaphor of place (Christ is the place of God's loving creative presence).[118] Dalferth does not understand the history of Jesus Christ as a representative act, but instead warns against jesuologies (or Christologies) which concentrate too much on Jesus.[119]

What can be said concerning the moment of substitution? Concerning this moment, I have distinguished between work-substitution and person-substitution (see 1.2.6).

114. Dalferth, *Existenz Gottes und christlicher Glaube*, 325, 330; Dalferth, *Gott*, 20; Dalferth, *Der auferweckte Gekreuzigte*, 56–57, 186, 213, 218, 238, 253, 302, 304–5; Dalferth, ‚Subjektivität und Glaube,' 56; Dalferth, *Gedeutete Gegenwart*, 91

115. Dalferth, *Der auferweckte Gekreuzigte*, 54, 127, 131, 135, 214, 301, 304. Cf. Dalferth, 'Der Mensch in seiner Zeit,' 176–77; Dalferth, 'Gott für uns,' 64–65, 66.

116. Dalferth, *Existenz Gottes und christlicher Glaube*, 234; Dalferth, *Jenseits von Mythos und Logos*, 194; Dalferth, *Der auferweckte Gekreuzigte*, 278.

117. Dalferth, 'Gott für uns,' 72–74.

118. For the idea of Christ as place, see Dalferth, *Existenz Gottes und christlicher Glaube*, 229; Dalferth, *Der auferweckte Gekreuzigte*, 306; Dalferth, 'Volles Grab, leerer Glaube?' 405; Dalferth, *Evangelische Theologie als Interpretationspraxis*, 102; Dalferth, 'Gott für uns,' 60–66. It is closely related to the notions of localisation and orientation.

119. Dalferth, 'Gott für uns,' 62–68.

The moment of person-substitution can be traced obviously in his Christology. The uniqueness of Jesus Christ is emphasised by Dalferth for soteriological reasons. His relation with the Father is not a soteriological outcome, but the Christological presupposition of such a soteriological outcome in the life of others.[120] This uniqueness can be articulated in different ways. First, Christ is God's address to us based on God's relation to him. In this sense, we cannot be like Christ for his position in our relation with God is unique. He lives in conformity with God because he is the Son of God who conforms to his Father—a Trinitarian relation—and as such he lives a human life in conformity with God. We are enabled to live in conformity with God because of the relation we have with God in Christ.[121] Second, he is the first, enabling others to be like him: the firstborn Son, the first one raised from death;[122] the first true human being as we have seen. Third, Christ is the place where God and man are together again. He is, in his person, the new covenant.[123] Fourth, he is the sacramentum of salvation.[124] Fifth, he is, in his person, the realisation of his message of the coming Kingdom of God; the Kingdom brings Jesus as representative, with whom and in whose life his message is realised.[125] Sixth, his becoming a person is decisive for our becoming persons. Jesus is a person based on God's relation to him, just as is the case with us. However, Jesus Christ as a person is not distinguished from God, but is the second person of the Trinity and part of God's communication with himself. We are, as persons, distinguished from God and our constitution as a person is part of God's communication with others than God; already in our constitution as person, Christ and the Spirit play a decisive role.[126] Seventh, he is unique because his history includes ours and constitutes the truth of our histories.[127] All emphasis is on the person

120. Dalferth, *Existenz Gottes und christlicher Glaube*, 316–17; Dalferth, 'Gott für uns,' 61.

121. Dalferth, *Existenz Gottes und christlicher Glaube*, 314–19; Dalferth, *Der auferweckte Gekreuzigte*, 280 note 110.

122. Dalferth, *Der auferweckte Gekreuzigte*, 29, 123, 132–33.

123. Dalferth, *Der auferweckte Gekreuzigte*, 251.

124. Dalferth, *Der auferweckte Gekreuzigte*, 21, 253, 306.

125. Dalferth, *Der auferweckte Gekreuzigte*, 95, 101, 106, 110.

126. Dalferth, *Der auferweckte Gekreuzigte*, 156f. Cf. Dalferth, Jüngel, 'Person und Gottebenbildlichkeit,' 67–97; Dalferth, *Die Wirklichkeit des Möglichen*, 201–6.

127. Dalferth, *Der auferweckte Gekreuzigte*, 305.

of Christ, and clearly the moment of person-substitution is central to Dalferth. Christ's person as place of God's presence plays a decisive role in our relation with God.

At the same time, he explicitly denies that we need something like a moment of work-substitution. Jesus did not accomplish a certain work, by his acting and suffering, that has an influence that is understood quasi-causally. Not the acts of Jesus Christ, but the eschatological act of God realises our salvation.[128] It is in line with this rejection of work-substitution, that according to Dalferth the uniqueness of (the person of) Christ can only be maintained if his uniqueness is understood as a saving act of God.[129] All emphasis is on the work of God and the acts of Jesus Christ himself play no role in the constitution of salvation.[130] Further, his person is important only because of God's acts. Dalferth denies that a Christology should concentrate on the person of Christ, creating a distance between Jesus Christ, the God-man and other human beings.[131] Regarding 'being in Christ,' this leads to an identification of 'being in Christ' with being incorporated in God or glorified being.[132] The history and person of Jesus Christ receive insufficient separate attention.[133]

The moments of inclusivity and person-substitution are interwoven. The moment of person-substitution and the inclusiveness of the person of Jesus Christ are reverse sides of the one coin. Further, it can be traced in the idea that Jesus Christ is the true human being and therefore the true God. God realises true humanity in Christ, opening for us the possibility of living in relation to Jesus Christ a human life in communion with God.

128. Dalferth, *Der auferweckte Gekreuzigte*, 205–6, 251–52, 274, 286–92, 299, 305–6.

129. Dalferth, *Der auferweckte Gekreuzigte*, 26–27, 31–33, 57–59, 62, 79, 139, 143 n. 112, 152, 159, 239, 252, 301, 303, 306.

130. According to Dalferth, both the active as well as the passive dimensions of the history of Jesus Christ are important (Dalferth, *Der auferweckte Gekreuzigte*, 186). What the active dimension consists in, does not become very clear apart from Jesus' identification of God. Maybe the example Jesus gives in his death as a self sacrifice is another part of this active dimension, see *Der auferweckte Gekreuzigte*, 253.

131. Dalferth, 'Gott für uns,' 62–64, 70.

132. See footnote 116.

133. It might even be asked, whether this leads to less emphasis in recent work on the uniqueness of Christ In *Evangelische Theologie als Interpretationspraxis*, Dalferth writes that Jesus Christ does not add something to faith in God, but that in Christianity, faith in God is articulated in a special way (81). Faith is a gift from the Spirit and can be given apart from Jesus Christ, if only God's presence is disclosed in the way this presence is disclosed in and by Jesus Christ (86).

The Son, becoming the true human being becomes the true God. Or: as true man he is true God; as true God he is true man.[134]

Summarizing, the moments of inclusivity and exclusivity (as person-substitution) are both present in Dalferth's Christology. They are intertwined, for the first is the reverse side of the second. Both are the result of God's eschatological saving act. Christ is our representative, in so far as we are included in what God does to Jesus Christ. However, because all emphasis is on God's eschatological act, the role of Jesus Christ is not understood as a representative acting on behalf of the people he represents, be it in his inclusivity (going where they will go, acting like they will do)—although he does say that Christ is the true human being who lives in conformity with God—or in his exclusivity (going where they do not have to go, acting where they could not act). Of course, any idea of work-substitution is declined in this line. Christ is the *place* where God acts on our behalf, not the second *person* of God who himself acts on our behalf.

8.3 Soteriology

In this paragraph I will concentrate on the anthropological side of 'being in Christ.' I will investigate Dalferth's theology to see whether it is helpful to develop a concept of 'being in Christ' with regard to this other side, after having investigated his Christology. First I will give a more general analysis of Dalferth's soteriology (8.3.1). In a next section I will focus especially on the moments of union and participation, to see whether these moments are necessary to develop a concept of 'being in Christ' and to test the hypothesis of this investigation (8.3.2).

8.3.1 LIVING IN A NEW PERSPECTIVE

The resurrection of Christ cannot be isolated from the gift of the Holy Spirit. God is the triune God who reveals himself in Christ and in the Spirit. Jesus is not Christ, God's address unless human beings are addressed in him. God is not identified if he does not identify himself to someone. Christ's resurrection and cross have no saving relevance if sinners are not saved. This saving significance of the death of Christ is

134. Dalferth, *Existenz Gottes und christlicher Glaube*, 185, 223, 225, 274, 316–18, 344.

interpreted in the New Testament with the image of sacrifice, understood by Dalferth as incorporation in God as we have seen.[135]

A fundamental idea to Dalferth as we have seen is that if God addresses someone and identifies himself to that person, a new perspective is opened and as a result a change of perspectives takes place. If God identifies himself to us, he exists. If Jesus lives in God's reality, although he died and lives no more in our spatio-temporal reality, God has his own reality which is greater than our reality. If God addresses us, we also live in God's reality, a life *coram deo*. If God shows his presence, we find ourselves in Gods loving presence, incorporated in God and being localised absolutely *coram deo*. As a result, we begin to see our own reality and our world in a new perspective. We are sinners, but justified by God. Our world is fallen, but God's creation. Becoming Christian is a changing of perspective, thanks to God's eschatological act in Christ and the Spirit. This change is a change from sin and unbelief to faith and love.[136]

This change of perspective implies a change from an old to a new life. The resurrected Christ has disclosed to us a new life in communion with the Father. In him we know God as the One who is creating and loving nearness. Whoever believes is included in God's saving act and lives in Christ. In what follows, I will give some characteristics of this new life according to Dalferth.

This new life is a life that is transformed by God's eschatological act. The eschatological act must be understood as a Trinitarian act, in which God raises Jesus from death as Christ, and the Spirit works faith in the believer and opens a new perspective.[137] God's eschatological act qualifies our world eschatologically and creates a difference between the

135. Consequently, Dalferth discusses the image of sacrifice in *Der auferweckte Gekreuzigte* in pneumatology.

136. See on these two perspectives, the *coram mundo* and the *coram deo* perspective and the change from the perspective of sin to the perspective of faith here esp. Dalferth, *Existenz Gottes und christlicher Glaube*, 176, 180, 185–89; Dalferth, *Der auferweckte Gekreuzigte*, 47, 78–79, 80–83, 208–10; Dalferth, 'Volles Grab, leerer Glaube?' 404; Dalferth, *Die Wirklichkeit des Möglichen*, 125–27, 450–51; Dalferth, *Evangelische Theologie als Interpretationspraxis*, 82–83, 102–3; Dalferth, *Auf dem Weg der Ökumene*, 29–30, 33, 35; and further footnote 11, 14, and 70.

See further Van der Kooi, *De ziel van het christelijk geloof*, 47, 82.

137. Dalferth, *Der auferweckte Gekreuzigte*, 201, 204–5, 208–10; Dalferth, 'Volles Grab, leerer Glaube?' 404; Dalferth, *Evangelische Theologie als Interpretationspraxis*, 62, 80, 86, 102.

old world of death and life and the new world in which the death reigns no more. The continuity between both worlds lies in God's creating act. God annihilates what is old and preserves what is good.[138] Hence, within our reality we can distinguish that which is ambivalent, which obscures and covers the saving presence of God (old) from that which makes unmistakably clear God's creating act as a saving act (new). We live within an eschatological process aiming at a world in which all ambivalence is gone and God's presence is evident everywhere.[139] Because it is a process, Dalferth distinguishes between eschatological ('eschatologisch'—related to the *Eschatos*) and 'eschatic' ('eschatisch'—related to the eschata) as we have seen, a distinction that indicates the eschatological tension of the 'yet' and 'not yet.'[140]

The change is a change from unbelief to a life in faith. Faith is a relation, worked by the triune God. The human being is passive in the constitution of this relation, because the constitution of the relation creates the believer. Faith lives entirely from God's saving presence as disclosed in Jesus Christ, and is a gift of the Holy Spirit. Christian faith is eschatological, worked by God, and constitutes a new creation. As such it is justifying faith.[141] Summarizing, the faith-relation has three characteristics: the relation to Jesus Christ (resurrection-faith), to God (*fiducia promissionis*) and to ourselves (*fides justificans*).[142] Therefore, faith cannot be understood as a kind of epistemic belief. It has to be distinguished from believing that something is the case, believing someone, or believing in someone, and is not the result of a (psychological) process of transformation.[143] Further, faith also has to be distinguished from beliefs about the faith-relation,

138. Dalferth, *Der auferweckte Gekreuzigte*, 7879; cf. Dalferth, 'Volles Grab, leerer Glaube?' 399. And further Dalferth, *Kombinatorische Theologie*, 46; Dalferth, *Leiden und Böses*, 204–6.

139. Dalferth, *Gedeutete Gegenwart*, 227–31.

140. See footnote 66. Further Dalferth, *Theology and Philosophy*, 220.

141. Dalferth, *Existenz Gottes und christlicher Glaube*, 239–48, 252–55; Dalferth, 'Über Einheit und Vielfalt des christlichen Glaubens,' 100, 107, 136; Dalferth, *Der auferweckte Gekreuzigte*, 36, 62–64, 70, 202–10, 233; Dalferth, *Evangelische Theologie als Interpretationspraxis*, 77, 86, 103.

142. Dalferth, 'Über Einheit und Vielfalt des christlichen Glaubens,' 107; Dalferth, 'Glaube,' 193; Dalferth, 'Faith,' 265.

143. Dalferth, *Existenz Gottes und christlicher Glaube*, 245; Dalferth, 'Über Einheit und Vielfalt des christlichen Glaubens,' 108–12.

or from ways of confessing and articulating it.[144] In his work, a shift of emphasis can be seen, from faith as faith in Jesus Christ in *Existenz Gottes* to faith in God in his later work. In *Existenz Gottes,* faith is the pneumatological reverse of God's address in Christ. Here it is faith in Jesus Christ.[145] In *Der auferweckte Gekreuzigte* faith is the completion of God's self-identification when the Spirit opens someone's eyes for God's love as Jesus Christ identified it and God confirmed this identification in the resurrection. From the article 'Faith' in *Encyclopedia of Christianity* on, faith according to Dalferth has to be understood as faith in God, and faith in Jesus Christ is only a concrete version of faith in God.[146] The question is: what does this imply for the relation to Jesus Christ?

In this new life the isolating solitude of sin is broken. This is the case when someone believes. To live in faith is living in glorified being or living in faith. As we have seen, glorified being and being in Christ are identical. But Dalferth also equates living in Christ with living in faith, or in the Spirit. Being in Christ is glorified being in communion with God.[147] Spatio-temporally this is lived in the church, but it is a life that transcends the spatio-temporal world. Although the believer still exists spatio-temporally, he also exists eschatologically, incorporated in Christ as member of the body of Christ. There is no more death, damnation or separation from the love of God. It is a life in communion with God that is realised in Christ, for in Christ we are incorporated in God.[148] In accordance with the being of Jesus Christ, it is being in God's reign, being with God and

144. Dalferth, *Existenz Gottes und christlicher Glaube*, 288–89; Dalferth, 'Über Einheit und Vielfalt des christlichen Glaubens,' 111; Dalferth, *Der auferweckte Gekreuzigte*, 31 (cf. 225, 259, 266); Dalferth, *Evangelische Theologie als Interpretationspraxis*, 79–80.

145. Dalferth, *Existenz Gottes und christlicher Glaube*, 239, 242, 245, 248, 252–55, 259; Dalferth, 'Glaube,' 194.

146. Dalferth, 'Faith,' 265; Dalferth, *Evangelische Theologie als Interpretationspraxis*, 80–81; Dalferth, 'Gott für uns,' 60.

The article 'Faith' is the English translation of the article 'Glaube' in the *Evangelische Kirchenlexicon,* where faith is still described as faith in Christ. The English translation marks the shift of emphasis. Cf. Dalferth, 'Glaube,' 194.

147. Dalferth, *Existenz Gottes und christlicher Glaube*, 233–34, 280; Dalferth, 'Über Einheit und Vielfalt des christlichen Glaubens,' 119; Dalferth, *Der auferweckte Gekreuzigte*, 309.

148. Dalferth, *Existenz Gottes und christlicher Glaube*, 234–35, 280; Dalferth, *Der auferweckte Gekreuzigte*, 277–78.

for others, being together in the horizon of God's glory. Living a new life, the believer lives in communion.[149]

Being in Christ, the believer is distinguished from himself as sinner. In this new life we receive a new identity and are constituted as persons. Faith '*ponit nos extra nos*.' This can be experienced only as a fundamental experience of difference, between how we experience ourselves and how God experiences us in Christ. We can first experience who we are in truth, when God makes this known to us in Christ by the Holy Spirit in faith. This difference is explicated as *simul creatura et peccator* or *simul iustus et peccator*. Our life as life in Christ is integrated in the life of Jesus Christ.[150] Because Christ identified himself with us at the cross, we receive a new identity together with Christ, who is incorporated in God.[151] God's self-disclosure also discloses who we are in truth as the history of Jesus Christ shows it. Our identity is an identity *extra se*, for it lies outside our relation to ourselves, to the world and to God but in the pneumatological relatedness to Jesus Christ, in justification by faith.[152] It is an identity in becoming, for it is constituted by the eschatological act of God, and lies in its eschatological final form. Fundamental for our identity therefore is the eschatological difference between old and new as well as the related category of justification.[153] This leads to a permanent identity crisis, experienced as contestation. We live as differentiated beings, for we are justified sinners. Only God guarantees the unity of our person and its identity.[154]

Here the difference between becoming a person ('Werden zur Person') and becoming as a person ('Werden als Person') is central. We live in two histories, the history of God's action—the history of Jesus Christ—and our own history. In the first we become a person, in the second we become as persons. Becoming a person, human beings become human as a person opposite God. In the history of Jesus Christ, God

149. Dalferth, *Existenz Gottes und christlicher Glaube*, 236; Dalferth, *Auf dem Weg der Ökumene*, 14f, 19–21.

150. Dalferth, *Existenz Gottes und christlicher Glaube*, 300, 343–44; Dalferth, *Gedeutete Gegenwart*, 91–92.

151. Dalferth, *Der auferweckte Gekreuzigte*, 276–78.

152. Dalferth, *Existenz Gottes und christlicher Glaube*, 283–84; Dalferth, ‚Subjektivität und Glaube,' 57; Dalferth, *Die Wirklichkeit des Möglichen*, 198.

153. Dalferth, *Existenz Gottes und christlicher Glaube*, 283–84; Dalferth, ‚Subjektivität und Glaube,' 53–54, 57.

154. Dalferth, *Existenz Gottes und christlicher Glaube*, 285, 301; Dalferth, ‚Subjektivität und Glaube,' 53–54; Dalferth, 'Volles Grab, leerer Glaube?' 398.

constitutes our person in its eschatological truth by his judgment, and he goes on doing so, discharging from offences and making us true. The *rectitudo* of our person is not a result of our life, but is grounded in God's justifying judgment.[155]

Becoming as a person concerns the way in which we give form to the person we are in the history of our lives. Here we face the central problem of a Christian anthropology: how can I be who I am in truth eschatologically?[156] First, this concerns the appropriation of God's judgment in the process of our lives that invites us to interpret our lives in the light of God's judgment. At the same time, this is an appropriation *by* God's judgment, for God makes us what he declares us, and declares us what he makes us.[157] It includes a fundamental new orientation, characterized as penitence and conversion. In the light of the fundamental eschatological difference of old and new, our understanding of self, God and world has to be reshaped. Faith learns to pierce the multiplicity of meanings of experience and to live within this multiplicity yet with God's unambiguous judgment and in God's loving presence.[158] For, second, it concerns the attempt to live according to our eschatological truth. As long as we do not do so, we exist in self-contradiction.[159] Once we discover the self-centredness of our old lives and the eschatological truth of the new life, it has to come to a God-centred new life in accordance with this eschatological truth. We are called to live in our entire life in gracious dedication to God, enforcing tendencies of love so that more and more God's love receives a non-ambivalent and recognisable form.[160] This radical new orientation in our view of life and in our acts justifies the use of images like new creation, regeneration or new life.[161]

155. See footnote 126, and further Dalferth, *Existenz Gottes und christlicher Glaube*, 255.

156. Dalferth, *Existenz Gottes und christlicher Glaube*, 284.

157. Dalferth, *Gedeutete Gegenwart*, 93, 97; Dalferth, *Auf dem Weg der Ökumene*, 31–32.

158. Dalferth, *Der auferweckte Gekreuzigte*, 83, 185–86, 201–2, 208–9; Dalferth, *Gedeutete Gegenwart*, 91; Dalferth, *Leiden und Böses*, 206–11.

159. Dalferth, Jüngel, 'Person und Gottebenbildlichkeit,' 66; Dalferth, *Existenz Gottes und christlicher Glaube*, 224, 282, 284–85, 338.

160. Dalferth, *Existenz Gottes und christlicher Glaube*, 262, 285–86; Dalferth, *Theology and Philosophy*, 220; Dalferth, *Der auferweckte Gekreuzigte*, 208, 306–15; cf Dalferth, *Gedeutete Gegenwart*, 228–30.

161. Dalferth, *Der auferweckte Gekreuzigte*, 208.

This new life is a life that is conformed to Christ. We do not know what we shall be if God acts to save us apart from Christ. Key to the knowledge of what we are and what we will be, is the *conformitas Christi*. This *conformitas* is realised where the history of Jesus Christ becomes effective in the individual life history of someone by the work of God. Baptism shows that this *conformitas* cannot be understood as just glorification, for it includes a burial in the death of Christ. We are conformed to the cross of Christ.[162] This idea of *conformitas Christi* again shows the importance of the history of Jesus Christ for the history of the believer.[163]

The importance of the history of Jesus Christ makes it also important to tell this history, to baptise and to celebrate the Lord's Supper, as the church does in her liturgy. Jesus has to be presented as Christ, to make co-presence with Christ possible. This co-presence is *communicative* co-presence.[164] In *Existenz Gottes*, the idea of co-presence has its place within an explanation of the question of how Jesus can be experienced as God's address. Here co-presence is the co-presence with Jesus Christ. Jesus Christ becomes co-present when he is preached as Christ and God uses this preaching to make Jesus God's address. By the Holy Spirit, Jesus becomes not only verbally (or sacramentally), but really present in faith.[165] In later work, the idea of co-presence is maintained and again interpreted in a pneumatological way. We are co-present with God by the Holy Spirit.[166] Nevertheless, the telling of the history of Jesus Christ and its representation in the sacraments in the liturgy of the church remain important, for here God disclosed his presence to us.

Finally, this new life is a life in the body of Christ. In *Existenz Gottes*, Dalferth writes that the new life in Christ is lived eschatologically in time and space in the church, but hoped 'eschatically.'[167] But this life in the body of Christ is described most extensively in *Volles Grab, leerer*

162. Dalferth, *Existenz Gottes und christlicher Glaube*, 233; Dalferth, *Theology and Philosophy*, 223; Dalferth, ‚Subjektivität und Glaube,' 56.

163. See footnote 68.

164. Dalferth, *Religiöse Rede von Gott*, 362–63; Dalferth, *Theology and Philosophy*, 220, 222–23; Dalferth, *Kombinatorische Theologie*, 156; Dalferth, *Jenseits von Mythos und Logos*, 194.

165. Dalferth, *Existenz Gottes und christlicher Glaube*, 321–31; cf. Dalferth, *Gott*, 50.

166. Dalferth, 'Representing God's Presence,' 254; cf. Dalferth, 'Fremdauslegung als Selbstauslegung,' 170–71; Dalferth, *Der auferweckte Gekreuzigte*, 171, 182, 213, 216.

167. Dalferth, *Existenz Gottes und christlicher Glaube*, 234, and further 328; Dalferth, *Der auferweckte Gekreuzigte*, 213.

Glaube? The resurrected Christ has a body, but this must not merely be understood as his spiritual body that replaces his earthly body. A body is our mediated relatedness with others and ourselves. In faith, our bodily existence receives a new eschatological determination. Now it is the mediated relatedness only via God with others and ourselves in the mode of love. Eschatological corporeality is being interwoven in God's life which is working love. It is life in God as existence in Christ, which is lived in the church as body of Christ under the precondition of the difference of faith and unbelief. Eschatological corporeality is being with others and for others in the mode of love, as is God's life.[168]

In summary, the resurrection of Christ leads, by the Holy Spirit, to a new life where the difference of old and new is made actual in someone's life. It is a life created by God, in faith and leading to a new perspective, a new understanding of the self, the world and God. This eschatological life is lived in faith, in Christ, in the Spirit and it is hoped 'eschatically'; a tension of yet and not yet characterizes it. It is a life in communion and in love, as the church—the body of Christ—has to show. The new life is possible because we exist in two histories, the history of God in which we become person and our own history in which we become as persons. As such, we exist *extra nos* in Christ and receive our identity in him in justification. Although we are simul iustus et peccator, the identity in Christ has to lead to a new understanding and a new way of life in growing conformity with Christ. To live in Christ, it is necessary that the church tells the story of Jesus Christ and re-enacts it in baptism and eucharist. Life in Christ is a life in love, in the body of Christ in which we are mediated via God related with others, sharing in God's life of love.

8.3.2 UNION AND PARTICIPATION?

For a further evaluation of my hypothesis in conversation with Dalferth, we must investigate whether the moments of union and participation are present in his theology.

The idea of participation is the reverse of the inclusiveness of Christ as representative (see 8.2.3). I will give a short recapitulation of what we have seen in this section. If Jesus is the true human being, we participate in him when we become true human beings. If he is our answer to God, we participate in him when we live in conformity to God. As we have

168. Dalferth, 'Volles Grab, leerer Glaube?' 406–8.

seen, in this way we participate in the Trinitarian relation of address and answer. Where his history is the paradigm of all our histories, we participate in his history.

The history of Christ has to be understood from the beginning as a history in which we are included.[169] By participation in the history of Jesus Christ, we participate in his eschatological life and live in communion with God.[170] Jesus Christ is our resurrection and our life.[171] If we want to know how God experiences us and who we really are, we need to know how God experiences Jesus Christ.[172] And we may know God as Jesus Christ identified God: as loving Father, as we have seen repeatedly. The manifestation of God's love in the history of Jesus Christ promises and confirms that this love will be the ultimate reality in our lives.[173] Further we participate in the person of Christ. Christ is a collective person, the corporate Christ. We need to participate in Christ to participate in the new covenant. Everything which is soteriologically relevant is present in the person of Christ and we are constituted as persons together with him.[174] As a result of the participation in the person of Christ, we participate in the eschatological nearness of God, which creates life. He is, in his person, the *extra nos* of our salvation.[175] In this participation, baptism and Eucharist play an important role. In baptism, we are buried together with Christ in his death, and included in relation to Jesus Christ in God's life communion.[176] In the Eucharist, God makes it possible to participate in the life in communion with God, retracing ('nachvollziehen') cross and resurrection.[177] This participation is the work of God, especially of the Holy Spirit. Pneumatologically, we are conformed to Jesus Christ and live as true human beings in conformity to God. Only pneumatologically is

169. Dalferth, *Der auferweckte Gekreuzigte*, 302.

170. Dalferth, *Existenz Gottes und christlicher Glaube*, 280 note 110, 310, 344; Dalferth, *Theology and Philosophy*, 220; Dalferth, 'Über Einheit und Vielfalt des christlichen Glaubens,' 131. Cf. Dalferth, *Auf dem Weg der Ökumene*, 19.

171. Dalferth, *Existenz Gottes und christlicher Glaube*, 234 note 2.

172. Dalferth, *Gott*, 91.

173. Dalferth, *Der auferweckte Gekreuzigte*, 218, 302; Dalferth, *Auf dem Weg der Ökumene*, 23; Dalferth, 'Gott für uns,' 73.

174. Dalferth, *Der auferweckte Gekreuzigte*, 156f, 251–52, 282, 301.

175. Dalferth, *Der auferweckte Gekreuzigte*, 277–78.

176. Dalferth, *Existenz Gottes und christlicher Glaube*, 233, 261.

177. Dalferth, *Existenz Gottes und christlicher Glaube*, 329.

the history of Jesus Christ continued biographically in our own histories.[178] Finally, of course, faith plays its important role: we participate in Christ by faith also.[179] It may be evident, that the moment of participation is a central moment in Dalferth's theology.

At the same time, it must be noted that the emphasis is on the participation in the end of the history of Jesus Christ. Although Dalferth writes that participation in the history of Christ includes participation in his death and burial, nevertheless he writes more often (mostly) about participation in the new eschatological life of Christ. Participation must not be understood in the light of the universal humanity of Jesus Christ, but in the light of the universality of God's presence, revealed in the history of Jesus Christ.[180] Again we may ask how important the human life of Jesus is to Dalferth.

The critical question regarding my hypothesis is whether we also need a moment of union. In *Existenz Gottes*, this clearly is the case. By faith, we live in communion with Christ. The church is united with Jesus Christ in faith. We live with him, in co-presence. The Lord's Supper is a moment of real co-presence and communion with Jesus Christ.[181] Again, the Holy Spirit plays a central role: we are related with Jesus Christ pneumatologically.[182] According to Dalferth, this union cannot be understood as a mystical union.[183] Hence, if a moment of union is necessary, this union with Christ is a non mystical union in faith and in the Spirit.

In his later work however, the moment of union seems to become less important. This is not to say that the moment of union is entirely absent, for in relation to, e.g., the new covenant Dalferth writes that union with Christ is essential; and further he writes that by God's word, believers are united in faith with Christ and each other.[184] Different factors contribute to the fact that the union with Christ seems to become less important. Already in *Existenz Gottes*, the emphasis is on communion with God,

178. Dalferth, *Existenz Gottes und christlicher Glaube*, 243, 255, 280 note 110, 284, 329; Dalferth, *Gedeutete Gegenwart*, 20.

179. Dalferth, *Der auferweckte Gekreuzigte*, 280 note 110, 282.

180. Dalferth, 'Gott für uns,' 72–74.

181. Dalferth, *Existenz Gottes und christlicher Glaube*, 232–33, 281, 328.

182. Dalferth, *Existenz Gottes und christlicher Glaube*, 243, 284.

183. Dalferth, 'Fremdauslegung als Selbstauslegung,' 169.

184. Dalferth, *Der auferweckte Gekreuzigte*, 252; Dalferth, *Auf dem Weg der Ökumene*, 48.

although this communion is mediated christologically.[185] Second, according to Dalferth, we participate in communion with God based on the action of God rather than on the acts of Jesus Christ. The history of Jesus Christ is especially important because of what God does in this history, and not because of acts of Jesus himself apart from his understanding of God as Father, as we have seen already (see 8.2.3). Instead, Dalferth claims that Christology should not focus on Jesus Christ, and absolutely not on the human being Jesus of Nazareth.[186] Further the fact that the resurrection of Jesus Christ is not necessarily a bodily resurrection makes it impossible to use e.g. the idea of an organic union between the head of the new creation and its body. Moreover the conceptuality of localisation and Christ as the place of God's action make an idea of union superfluous. Finally, the theme of the inhabitation of the Holy Spirit is absent in Dalferth's theology.[187]

To conclude, for the development of a concept of 'being in Christ,' the participation in the person and history of Christ are both important, if it is developed building on Dalferth's work. This participation in Christ is participation by the Spirit and by faith. We participate in his human being and in his relation to the Father; in his eschatological life in the nearness of God's love. Apart from this moment, also a moment of union with Christ is important. However, the importance of a moment of union diminishes, because Dalferth focuses on the eschatological act of God, and not on the acts of Jesus Christ. Further, this union should no be a mystical union according to Dalferth.

8.4 Eschatological Ontology

What especially concerns us in this investigation are the ontological implications of 'being in Christ.' Therefore we now turn to Dalferth's eschatological ontology, to see how he reconstructs these ontological implications. In 8.4.1 first a description will be given of his concept of ontology and of some central concepts in his eschatological ontology. Second, I will

185. Dalferth, *Existenz Gottes und christlicher Glaube*, 197, 232–34, 283, 317; cf. Dalferth, 'Fremdauslegung als Selbstauslegung,' 169.

186. Dalferth, 'Gott für uns,' 62–68.

187. Rikhof regrets that Dalferth's pneumatology in *Der auferweckte Gekreuzigte* is constructed as doctrine of reconciliation and does not give a treatise of the theme of inhabitation; Rikhof, review of review of Dalferth, *Der auferweckte Gekreuzigte*, 259.

describe how these concepts are used in his reconstruction of a Christian, eschatological, understanding of reality (8.4.2).

8.4.1 ONTOLOGICAL REFLECTION

Before further investigating Dalferth's eschatological ontology, I will first say something on his view of ontological reflection.

He takes his starting point in the work of Willard van Orman Quine.[188] With him he asks for the ontological implications of a language or theory. A given proposition can be analysed to determine the ontological commitments of a person if he states that this proposition is true. Which entities have to exist if that proposition is true? As a result, ontological reflection is relative to a given language, discourse or theory. An ontological theory is always relative to the theory or language that has been chosen as frame of reference.[189]

In his eschatological ontology, Dalferth seeks to elaborate the ontological implications of the Christian story. Given the Christian faith it can be asked under which ontological presuppositions it actually makes its truth claim. What are the ontological implications of the faith in Jesus Christ?[190] Ontology bound in this way to the perspective of the Christian faith is ontology '*sub specie fidei*.'[191]

Ontological reflection is more than analysing the ontological implications of separate propositions. The different reconstructed entities do not exist independently. In a second, step a system of functionalities and relations has to be reconstructed in which the different entities have their place.[192] In a third step, different ontological reconstructions have to be integrated in a more complex ontological reconstruction that encompasses as much as possible theories. This is to overcome the plurality of isolated experiences, theories and ontologies.[193] This does not mean that ontology is a metaphysical super-science. Instead, its aim is to do justice to the difference between reality and models of reality in respect to

188. On Dalferth and Quine, see Brandt, 'Quines Tranchiermesser und Dalferths Wetzstein'; cf. Mühling-Schlapkohl, *Gott ist Liebe*, 16 note 25.

189. Dalferth, *Existenz Gottes und christlicher Glaube*, 16, 31–32, 56–57, 63–67, 88.

190. Dalferth, *Existenz Gottes und christlicher Glaube*, 16, 31, 66, 75–77.

191. Dalferth, *Existenz Gottes und christlicher Glaube*, 76.

192. Dalferth, *Existenz Gottes und christlicher Glaube*, 57–60.

193. Dalferth, *Existenz Gottes und christlicher Glaube*, 60–62, 67–68.

all different kinds of claims of knowledge.[194] Further this does not imply choosing an already existing ontological system. The aim is first of all to reconstruct the ontology of the Christian faith itself. A possible choice for a given ontology (Platonist, constructivist, nominalist etc.) is determined by the question of which ontology is most able to reconstruct the ontology of the Christian faith and to integrate other ontologies.[195] The truth claim of the Christian faith is universalised in an eschatological ontology, to provoke contradiction and to make the ontological framework itself object of the fight for truth.[196] In his later work, Dalferth is more explicit than in his *Existenz Gottes und christlicher Glaube* about the perspectivity of all orientation. He emphasises differences that cannot be overcome and denies that it is necessary to see reality as a unity.[197] Still he maintains that although a religious perspective is fragmentary, it remains a universal perspective that orientates the whole of life.[198]

To come to an eschatological ontology, ontological reflection has two tasks: a hermeneutical and a critical task. Given are the texts and the discourse of the Christian faith. Its grammar has to be described to see how different images are used. This makes it possible to ask for the ontological implications of the Christian *use* of images, not of the images themselves, for, that a name is used does not necessarily imply that it stands for an entity.[199] To do this, an ontology criterion is needed, that discloses the presupposed entities in the Christian faith.[200] In recent work, Dalferth embeds claims of truth and knowledge more in an entire religious practice, stressing the importance of hermeneutical sensivity. Religious discourse is part of a religious way of life and communicates no

194. Dalferth, *Existenz Gottes und christlicher Glaube*, 36.

195. Dalferth, *Existenz Gottes und christlicher Glaube*, 66–67.

196. Dalferth, *Existenz Gottes und christlicher Glaube*, 76–77.

197. Dalferth, *Gedeutete Gegenwart*, 206–8; Dalferth, 'Creation—Style of the World,' 136–37; Dalferth, *Die Wirklichkeit des Möglichen*, 137–39, 158.

198. Dalferth, *Die Wirklichkeit des Möglichen*, 106.

199. This makes Dalferth's eschatological ontology post-metaphysical but not post-modern: he rejects a metaphysical identification of image and entity, but still is interested in ontological implications and in truth. See Dalferth, *Existenz Gottes und christlicher Glaube*, 56; Dalferth, *Jenseits von Mythos und Logos*, 310–12; Dalferth, *Evangelische Theologie als Interpretationspraxis*, 60.

200. Dalferth uses Quine's criterion that is formulated as 'to be is to be the value of a bound variable' or as '(Ex)(x=a).' See Dalferth, *Existenz Gottes und christlicher Glaube*, 55–56, 64; Mühling-Schlapkohl, *Gott ist Liebe*, 11–12.

direct truth claims, but in religious discourse we find communicated how people see, understand and interpret themselves and their world. Not just the truth of something that is said, but the truth of an entire way of life is up for debate.[201]

The first task, executed by hermeneutically operating textual studies is followed by the second task, carried out by a language-critical dogmatical theory.[202] The hermeneutical reconstruction of ontological implications does not suffice, for the first hermeneutical step leaves open the question whether an entity exists really or not and is just a semiotic construction. In Quine's theory, this second step is missing.[203] Building on Quine, Dalferth formulates his existence principle as follows: 'to be is to be related to our story.'[204] Properly speaking only that exists which stands in a *real* relation to us, whether we are intentionally related to it or not.[205] In strict sense only in the case of a *real* relation is an ontological implication given.[206]

This necessitates differentiation between the representation of an entity in our language and the entity, represented in our language.[207] Signs are used to represent something as something for someone.[208] Ontological reflection has to reflect critically on the question whether an entity really exists, i.e. whether the semiotic construction that the entity is, really represents something that exists independently from its being intended.[209] At the same time, reality is more than what is semiotically disclosed and symbolically reconstructed.[210] Ontological reflection has to guard the ontological difference between our concept of reality and reality itself, to

201. Dalferth, 'Erkundungen des Möglichen,' 50–51; Dalferth, *Die Wirklichkeit des Möglichen*, 39–40, 113–14, 184–85.

202. Dalferth, *Existenz Gottes und christlicher Glaube*, 77.

203. Dalferth, *Existenz Gottes und christlicher Glaube*, 32, 36, 55, 63.

204. Dalferth, *Existenz Gottes und christlicher Glaube*, 73; Dalferth, *Gott*, 43.

205. Dalferth, *Existenz Gottes und christlicher Glaube*, 73.

206. Dalferth, *Existenz Gottes und christlicher Glaube*, 32.

207. Dalferth, *Existenz Gottes und christlicher Glaube*, 32–34.

208. Dalferth, *Gedeutete Gegenwart*, 122, 125–27; Dalferth, 'Fremdauslegung als Selbstauslegung,' 157; Dalferth, *Die Wirklichkeit des Möglichen*, 6–7, 22. In his recent work, Dalferth states with C.S. Peirce that a sign is a triadic relation, see Dalferth, *Die Wirklichkeit des Möglichen*, 6f; Dalferth, *Evangelische Theologie als Interpretationspraxis*, 60.

209. Dalferth, *Existenz Gottes und christlicher Glaube*, 33–36; Dalferth, *Gedeutete Gegenwart*, 127–29, 188.

210. Dalferth, *Existenz Gottes und christlicher Glaube*, 35.

strive at a concept of reality that is as true as possible.[211] However, still the question is open as to what it means to be really related to our story.

This question must be solved to avoid a relativist ontology according to which everything referred to must exist somewhere. That someone refers to some entity as *x* does not necessarily imply that the semiotic construction *x* actually is a reconstruction of something that exists. Dalferth tries to solve this question on the basis of the existence of God.[212] However, Dalferth wants to avoid a position in which existence is equated with existence within time and space, for according to Dalferth God exists, but not spatio-temporally.[213]

Dalferth's starting point is a given proposition, in which an entity is identified as something and something is predicated of that entity. The first of these two acts—identifying and predicating—is crucial: without being identified as *x* something cannot appear in language as *x*.[214] We identify something by referring to it with a name, a characterisation, or by deixis—pointing at something or showing it. As a result, entities are always relative in respect to this act of identification and exist as entities only within a system of signs. They are products of a semiotic process in which something as entity is demarcated from other semantic objects.[215] That does not imply that something exists merely if it is identified and referred to in language. But that something exists, can only be a subject of discussion if it has been identified as something. How it becomes a subject of discussion, depends on the manner of conceptualisation.[216]

To be identified as an entity for someone presupposes a system of identification, a 'Gegenständlichkeit,' within which something by a speech-act can be identified as an entity, so that it can be discussed in language. Common existence so that I know that the other exists is possible only within the same 'Gegenständlichkeit,' for otherwise I cannot

211. In guarding this difference, we are again bound to language, but we experience this reality in concrete life and acts and meet other perspectives on this reality. See Dalferth, *Existenz Gottes und christlicher Glaube*, 33–35; cf. Dalferth, *Gedeutete Gegenwart*, 127–29, 176, 180, 186–88.

212. Dalferth, *Existenz Gottes und christlicher Glaube*, 83–84.

213. Dalferth, *Existenz Gottes und christlicher Glaube*, 32–33, 110–12; Dalferth, *Gott*, 37.

214. See on identification and predication Dalferth, *Religiöse Rede von Gott*, 242–61; Laube, *Im Bann der Sprache*, 270–80.

215. Dalferth, *Existenz Gottes und christlicher Glaube*, 32–34, 39.

216. Dalferth, *Gedeutete Gegenwart*, 122–27.

identify the other as something and refer to it or discuss it. This concept of 'Gegenständlichkeit' plays a crucial role in Dalferth's ontology.[217]

If something is identified for someone as *x*, that person can say '*x* exists.' Preceding discussions of existence show different aspects: its locative character, the impossibility of determining it semantically, and its relational function that involves the subject.[218] Dalferth now interprets this singular existence sentence as a pragmatic act of localisation. By stating '*x* exists,' a person localises himself in relation to *x*, within the same context that we call 'reality.' He does not say something about *x* by ascribing the predicate 'existence' to *x*, but he says something about himself: he stands in a certain relation to a given *x*.[219] This concept of relational localisation is also crucial in Dalferth's thinking.

If an entity really exists and is not just a semiotic construction but a real entity, that entity stands in an ontological relation to us. An ontological relation is a real relation that states the existence of the related relata. A singular existence sentence states that between the speaker and the entity an ontological relation exists.[220] This ontological relation has to be distinguished from an epistemic relation, or an intentional relation, or an ontic, spatio-temporal relation. Existence is independent of being intended or being known, and is not necessarily only spatio-temporal. An epistemic relation of possible experience also presupposes an ontological relation, but not everything that exists can be known.[221] An intentional relation presupposes an ontological relation if a real entity is concerned instead of an ideal entity.[222] In the case of a real entity, being intended and existence are not identical, as in the case of an ideal entity.[223] It is possible to isolate a real entity within a given state of affairs.[224] A spatio-temporal relation presupposes an ontological relation, but the reverse is not the case. In this way, distinguishing between ontic and ontological relation, Dalferth

217. Dalferth, *Existenz Gottes und christlicher Glaube*, 44–48.

218. Dalferth, *Existenz Gottes und christlicher Glaube*, 113–20; Dalferth, *Gott*, 40–41.

219. Dalferth, *Existenz Gottes und christlicher Glaube*, 121–22, 126–27, 183; Dalferth, *Gott*, 41–42.

220. Dalferth, *Existenz Gottes und christlicher Glaube*, 126, 128–29, 147, 150, 152; Dalferth, *Gott*, 44.

221. Dalferth, *Existenz Gottes und christlicher Glaube*, 122–24.

222. Dalferth, *Existenz Gottes und christlicher Glaube*, 125–26; Dalferth, *Gott*, 43.

223. Dalferth, *Existenz Gottes und christlicher Glaube*, 32–33.

224. Dalferth, *Existenz Gottes und christlicher Glaube*, 39.

distinguishes between spatio-temporality and existence.[225] Existence is the ontological 'Urfaktum.'[226]

8.4.2 EXISTENCE WITHIN TWO 'GEGENSTÄNDLICHKEITEN'

Why Dalferth distinguishes between ontic and ontological relations, between spatio-temporality and existence, and why he uses the concept of 'Gegenständlichkeit' becomes clear at the moment he introduces the Christian experience of address by God, in which God identifies himself to us.

Because God identifies himself as God to us at the moment when Jesus is experienced as God's address and therefore as Christ, several things appear to be the case. It appears that God exists, without being spatio-temporal.[227] Before God we discover that we are sinners who have made absolute our spatio-temporality, pretending it to be the one and only reality and ignoring the creator and our creatureliness. Within our spatio-temporal, ontic 'Gegenständlichkeit,' God cannot be identified any more, for it is perverted because of our sin.[228] But because God identifies himself to us in our spatio-temporality, it appears that another 'Gegenständlichkeit' exists: God's eschatological 'Gegenständlichkeit,' an identification system within entities can also be identified that we cannot identify spatio-temporally. God's 'Gegenständlichkeit' is not spatio-temporal, but it must make it possible that God as entity of this 'Gegenständlichkeit' can make himself experienced within space and time, without becoming spatio-temporal himself. The ontic 'Gegenständlichkeit' and the eschatological 'Gegenständlichkeit' are not total alternatives, excluding each other. Ontic entities can be localised within God's identification system, but entities in God's identification system are not necessarily spatio-temporal. God's 'Gegenständlichkeit' has the priority.[229]

Identifying himself to someone, God localises someone within his identification system. From now on, he can be identified in the ontic identification system, but also in God's 'Gegenständlichkeit.' God's address and the resulting self-identification in Christ have a pneumatologi-

225. Dalferth, *Existenz Gottes und christlicher Glaube*, 130–46.

226. Dalferth, *Existenz Gottes und christlicher Glaube*, 155–56.

227. Dalferth, *Existenz Gottes und christlicher Glaube*, 176, 185–86.

228. Dalferth, *Existenz Gottes und christlicher Glaube*, 179–81.

229. Dalferth, *Existenz Gottes und christlicher Glaube*, 182–84; Dalferth, *Gott*, 48.

cal reverse: faith, a real relation worked by God. By faith as a non ontic but eschatological relation, the believer is identifiable localised within the horizon of God's non ontic but eschatological identification system. Now a communal 'Gegenständlichkeit' is given within which communal existence of God and man is possible. An ontic difference and an ontological relation coincide.[230]

As a result of the idea of God's eschatological 'Gegenständlichkeit,' Dalferth writes about 'eschatological states of affairs' and an 'eschatological indicative.' Eschatological states of affairs cannot be identified or verified ontically, although they can be propagated as possibility. These states of affairs are constituted by God alone and cannot be identified, described or understood without mentioning God explicitly. Without giving attention to the constitutive relation with God, the true character of these eschatological states of affairs remains unknown. They cannot be produced or reproduced ontically. Only afterwards and after articulation in language, can they be recognised by subjects who also experienced eschatological states of affairs. Their existence can be confessed based on faith given by the Holy Spirit. Examples of eschatological states of affairs are the existence of God, of God's 'Gegenständlichkeit,' of Christ and of believers.[231] Although eschatological state of affairs cannot be identified ontically, they can be propagated as a possibility in language.[232] This is what theology does, speaking in the 'eschatological indicative.' The eschatological indicative tries to express reality together with all its possibilities in the light of her eschatological, final truth *coram deo*.[233] Therefore it is localising, not descriptive language.[234] It sounds like a conjunctive or an irrealis; it might seem fiction. The difference with fiction is its truth claim (which cannot be decided in time and space).[235]

230. Dalferth, *Existenz Gottes und christlicher Glaube*, 174, 181–82, 186–85, 242–43, 253–54; Dalferth, *Gott*, 50.

231. Dalferth, *Existenz Gottes und christlicher Glaube*, 184, 268–71, 275, 289, 304, 333.

232. Dalferth, *Existenz Gottes und christlicher Glaube*, 184, 271, 273.

233. Dalferth, 'Creation—Style of the World,' 127; Dalferth, 'Erkundungen des Möglichen,' 58; Dalferth, *Die Wirklichkeit des Möglichen*, 122; cf. Dalferth, *Leiden und Böses*, 204–7.

234. Dalferth, *Der auferweckte Gekreuzigte*, 74, 296; Dalferth, *Die Wirklichkeit des Möglichen*, 132–33.

235. Dalferth, *Existenz Gottes und christlicher Glaube*, 272, 305, 331–32. Cf. Dalferth, *Gott*, 50.

It should be clear that the self-identification of God also introduces God's 'Gegenständlichkeit' within the ontic 'Gegenständlichkeit.' Now more has to be said on the nature of God's 'Gegenstandlichkeit.' God's 'Gegenständlichkeit' is God's glory. Every ontic entity, which can be identified in the ontic identification system, can also be identified and localised within Gods identification system. But not every entity that can be identified in the eschatological 'Gegenständlichkeit' can be identified ontically. Therefore, within the horizon of God's 'Gegenständlichkeit; more entities can be identified than in the ontic one. These are the entities that the faith presupposes, which can be understood and identified only in the light of their relation with God that constitutes them. Because God's 'Gegenständlichkeit' is ordered christologically and all relations with God run through Jesus Christ, none of these entities can be understood without paying attention to its relation to Jesus Christ.[236]

Entities that can be identified in both identification systems, can only be understood fully within the horizon of God's eschatological 'Gegenständlichkeit,' because here they can be seen as God sees them. Within the horizon of God's 'Gegenständlichkeit,' a richer perspective on reality is possible than within the ontic 'Gegenständlichkeit' within which God's dimension has come to lack.[237]

The nature of God's 'Gegenständlichkeit' can be explained further in reference to the resurrection of Jesus Christ. Here God's 'Gegenständlichkeit' showed itself to be stronger and more encompassing than the ontic 'Gegenständlichkeit.' Also, in his death, the crucified Jesus remained localised within God's 'Gegenständlichkeit.' He died, but received life in God's glory despite his death. God's 'Gegenständlichkeit' is more powerful ontologically, for it encompasses more entities. Ontologically, Jesus always was localised in God's 'Gegenständlichkeit,' but cross and resurrection make it possible to experience Jesus as such (epistemologically). Because Jesus exists also within the horizon of God's 'Gegenständlichkeit' and can be experienced in this quality, God's glory becomes accessible as the horizon of perfect, true and eternal life in God's communion. Death is not the last horizon of life. The cross is the place where God glorified himself, showing his glory, that is, his 'Gegenständlichkeit,'

236. Dalferth, *Existenz Gottes und christlicher Glaube*, 225–27.

237. Dalferth, *Existenz Gottes und christlicher Glaube*, 226, 232.

under the conditions of space and time.[238] Within this framework of two 'Gegenständlichkeiten,' the idea of a bodily resurrection is not necessary. He exists no more ontically with a fleshly body ('Körper'), but he exists eschatologically and is represented ontically in preaching.[239]

The resurrection not only makes known that God and Jesus exist within the horizon of this 'Gegenständlichkeit,' but also opens a new way of being. By faith we are also localised within God's 'Gegenständlichkeit,' participating in Christ's glory and receiving eternal life. We exist in Christ and God's love for us is also stronger than death.[240]

The resurrection of Jesus Christ for us shows that he as well as we exist within two identification systems. Ontically, Jesus can be identified only as the earthly Jesus. But Jesus must not be known only according to the flesh, but also according to the Spirit. Jesus also is localised within God's eschatological 'Gegenständlichkeit' as Jesus Christ, God's address. Jesus realised his identity as spatio-temporal human being completely within the horizon of God's 'Gegenständlichkeit'; it can be said even more strongly: Jesus Christ lives in his ontic life the identity he has in Gods eschatological 'Gegenständlichkeit' as Son of God[241] Jesus Christ is a relational being ('Verhältniswesen'), a relation between the eschatological 'Gegenständlichkeit' within which he is God's address, and the ontic 'Gegenständlichkeit' in which he realised this identity uniquely as Jesus. As God's address he broke open our closed ontic 'Gegenständlichkeit,' opening our eyes for God's 'Gegenständlichkeit.'[242]

Now we can understand why we have seen on several occasions that the human life of Jesus has received insufficient attention. The significance of Jesus Christ lies in the identity he has in God's 'Gegenständlichkeit,' an identity that he lives ontically. All emphasis is on the eschatological 'Gegenständlichkeit.' The human, ontic life of Jesus does not contribute something to salvation apart from revealing God, his loving presence, and his 'Gegenständlichkeit,' hence making it possible for us also to live in God's eschatological 'Gegenständlichkeit.' As a result, bodily resurrection and work-substitution are not important, and all emphasis is on the

238. Dalferth, *Existenz Gottes und christlicher Glaube*, 229–31.

239. Dalferth, *Existenz Gottes und christlicher Glaube*, 322–27; cf. 161–63.

240. Dalferth, *Existenz Gottes und christlicher Glaube*, 231–37.

241. Dalferth, *Existenz Gottes und christlicher Glaube*, 306–10, 314–19.

242. Dalferth, *Existenz Gottes und christlicher Glaube*, 310–12, 319–21.

eschatological action of God. The fact that Jesus is the true human being does not change this.

Human beings also exist within two identification systems and are relational beings, although in a way different from Christ. We have seen already that a human being exists in two histories; Dalferth thus can also say that someone exists in two 'Gegenständlichkeiten.' A human being is a relation between eschatological being in the horizon of God's eschatological 'Gegenständlichkeit' and ontic being in the horizon of the 'Gegenständlichkeit' of time and space.[243] The believer knows this and lives in two 'Gegenständlichkeiten' as justified *sinner, simul iustus et peccator*, whereas other people do not realise this and live as sinners, *simul creatura et peccator*. The difference is not an ontic process, but the eschatological action of God, identifying himself and localising the sinner in his own glory; the change from unbelief to faith, that constitutes the believer. In this way God liberates the sinner to be really human, not as if a human being possesses himself living in contradiction with God's address as old man, but by God's justifying address living *extra se*. As old man, the sinner lives in denial of God who constitutes and guarantees his unity as person—a unity between what constitutes him as person in God's 'Gegenständlichkeit' and his ontic life in the ontic 'Gegenständlichkeit.' As new man, the justified sinner lives in accordance with God's address that constitutes and guarantees his person.[244] The believer lives in God's 'Gegenständlichkeit' in a new way and he knows this: he is a new creation in Christ.

The conceptuality of two 'Gegenständlichkeiten' is fundamental to Dalferth's interpretation of the reality of 'being in Christ.' Different aspects of his theology that we have been dealing with above can be understood against this background. The new being, glorified being, being in Christ is being in two 'Gegenständlichkeiten' in a new way: constituted as a new creation by the faith-relation we have with God in Christ and in the Spirit. Something new is created: eschatological being in Christ. Whoever does not believe, falls short of the glory of God; whoever believes however lives in God's glory, not only under the conditions of time and space, but freed

243. A human being is a relational being because of this relation between eschatological and ontic being, and not just because he stands in a self relation, a world relation and a God relation, see Dalferth, Jüngel, 'Person und Gottebenbildlichkeit,' 60, 95–96; Dalferth, *Existenz Gottes und christlicher Glaube*, 299–300.

244. Dalferth, Jüngel, 'Person und Gottebenbildlichkeit'; Dalferth, *Existenz Gottes und christlicher Glaube*, 300–302.

from sin (the closed ontic 'Gegenständlichkeit') to live in eternal communion with God, the loving Father. We do this in Christ. The relation we have with Christ is not only intentional, but real; otherwise it would be fiction. Jesus Christ is represented ontically in word and sacrament, but we are related to Christ when this ontic representation receives eschatological quality by the action of the Spirit. If this happens we are really co-present with Christ. By this relation with Christ in the Spirit we are localised in God's 'Gegenständlichkeit,' *coram deo*. Because this localisation creates something new and a sinner can not from his own possibilities identify God in his ontic 'Gegenständlichkeit,' this reality is only accessible to those who have received access to this 'Gegenständlichkeit' from God himself. As such it is bound to a participant's perspective.

Living in two 'Gegenständlichkeiten,' the believer is freed to live a true human life, no more in contradiction with God and his destiny as God corresponding ('entsprechender') human being. Now he lives free from the illusion of self possession and may live in correspondence ('Entsprechung') with God, who constitutes his person by his address. However as we have seen, existence in two 'Gegenständlichkeiten' not only implies peace and rest, but also temptation and an ongoing identity crisis. The believer needs the justifying judgment of God and has to try to live ontically in accordance with his eschatological identity. As we have seen, we do not only become persons, we also become as persons. This becoming as persons is the attempt to live in the ontic 'Gegenständlichkeit' in accordance with how God localises us in his eschatological 'Gegenständlichkeit.'[245]

It seems to me that Dalferth understands the eschata in this light: the more we live ontically in accordance with our eschatological identity in Christ, the more the ontic realm is transformed to openness for God's loving presence. It is a hermeneutical process, in which all ambivalence disappears and God's loving nearness becomes evident.[246] The question is whether this is enough. Because Dalferth identifies 'being in Christ' with glorified being, and does not pay enough attention to the ontical, bodily

245. Dalferth, Jüngel, 'Person und Gottebenbildlichkeit,' 67–97; Dalferth, *Existenz Gottes und christlicher Glaube*, 224–25, 260, 262, 282, 284–86, 297, 338–42; Dalferth, *Der auferweckte Gekreuzigte*, 156–57; Dalferth, *Leiden und Böses*, 206–11.

246. Dalferth, *Gedeutete Gegenwart*, 228–30.

existence of Jesus Christ, and sees the bodily resurrection as unnecessary, it remains unclear what salvation means 'eschatically' ('eschatisch').[247]

Summarizing, in the self-identification of God, he addresses us and opens our sinful ontic 'Gegenständlichkeit' to his eschatological 'Gegenständlichkeit,' by localising us again in this 'Gegenständlichkeit' as new creatures in Christ. Christ, the believer and sinners all exist in both 'Gegenständlichkeiten,' but differently. Jesus Christ has always had his identity in God's 'Gegenständlichkeit' as Son of God, in his Trinitarian relation with his Father. Believers have received a new identity in this 'Gegenständlichkeit' when they were constituted anew by faith as justified sinners, *simul iustus et peccator*. Sinners finally live in both 'Gegenständlichkeiten' as God's creatures who deny God's loving presence, living in contradiction to God and their own destiny *simul creatura et peccator*. 'Being in Christ' must be understood within this framework. It is the new eschatological existence in God's 'Gegenständlichkeit' that the believer receives in Christ. Because all emphasis is on the eschatological 'Gegenständlichkeit,' the impact of salvation on the ontic reality of *bodily* existence seems neglected.

8.5 Evaluation

Ingolf U. Dalferth's theology as described above is an important contribution to the conversation on 'being in Christ' of this book, concerning the hermeneutical as well as the ontological implications of 'being in Christ.'

Hermeneutically, in line with his theology 'being in Christ' can be understood as a new localisation that offers a new orientation and an understanding of self, world and God. In Christ, a believer is localised *coram*

247. Glorified being is lived eschatologically and hoped eschatically. All creatures will share in the Christological communion with the Creator, when God's reign is realised and created liberated. Eschatical being in Christ is realised, if all creatures live in the glory of God's reign and if God is all in all. Dalferth writes about an 'eschatic' consummation of the world, so that this world has a *telos* that transcends all historic destinations and an origin that transcends all intrahistorical origins. He further differentiates between the eschatological and 'eschatical' experience of God's nearness. Jesus Christ confronts us eschatologically with God's 'Gegenständlichkeit' and not 'eschatically,' so that the ontic is not ignored but broken through, Dalferth, *Existenz Gottes und christlicher Glaube*, 234, 237, 265, 272, 319, 336. What in this light is meant with resurrection of the dead and what it is to exist freed from the bounds of sin and dead, is not described.

Orally, Dalferth explained to me that the difference eschatological-eschatic has to be made in reference to the world, not in reference to my life.

deo and *extra se*. A new perspective is opened, a participant's perspective that is given by God himself. Believers may learn to understand their lives in the light of God's justifying judgment and of the history of Jesus Christ. This implies a fundamental change of understanding. The world of sin, ignoring God, is broken open and a new life in the loving presence of God is made possible. This shows very well the epistemic impact of sin as well as of salvation: knowing according to the flesh or according to the Spirit makes a difference.

Ontologically, he offers an ontology *sub specie fidei*; a sketch of a new understanding of reality in the light of what God does in Christ and in the Spirit. His eschatological ontology is an important contribution to the understanding of the reality of 'being in Christ.' 'Being in Christ' can be understood as an eschatological state of affairs, a state of affairs related to God, that can only be identified in faith; which existence cannot be verified ontically and can be denied; that is related to the universal and definitive eschatological action of God, which concerns the end of history. Theological descriptions of 'being in Christ' can be understood as an eschatological indicative. Further, the difference between eschatological and 'eschatic' is important. If the Christian faith is true, its particular perspective concerns reality and not fiction. The least that can be done is to show what the implications of the Christian faith are, including its ontological implications, if it is true indeed. However, as we will see below, I have some critical questions concerning his eschatological ontology.

But also theologically he reminds us of important aspects. 'Being in Christ' has to be understood as the work of the triune God. By the Holy Spirit we participate in the communicative relation of Father and Son and live in the loving nearness of the Father, as the Son does. Jesus Christ is a collective person, a corporate person, by whom we are included in God's reality. Another valuable idea is the relation between eschatological and the *Eschatos*. In this light, an eschatological state of affairs might be understood as a state of affairs constituted by its relation to the *Eschatos*.

My questions all concern the impact of the new existence in God's eschatological 'Gegenständlichkeit' on our created bodily (ontical) existence.

If we start, with Dalferth, with the resurrection of Jesus Christ, he is right in stating that to be convinced of the resurrection of Jesus Christ, faith is necessary. The empty tomb is not enough; faith worked by the Spirit is required. Historical evidence would not suffice to create faith in the resurrection of Jesus Christ. But although this is true, it is not impossible that the tomb was empty. In any case, if the grave was empty as the New Testament says, this influences our understanding of the resurrection and of salvation. As a result, it is unsurprising that Dalferth's thesis that it is not necessary that the grave was empty is related to other moments of his theology.

During his bodily existence in the ontic 'Gegenständlichkeit,' Jesus lived ontically in accordance with his eschatological identity, and identified God as loving Father. Apart from this, the life of Jesus in the ontic has no soteriological relevance. We do not conform ('entsprechen') to the existence of Jesus Christ, but to our relation with God in Jesus Christ. Furthermore, Dalferth emphasises the person of Christ, and denies the importance of his work and any idea of work-substitution.

What is not necessarily healed is not necessarily assumed. This variation of Gregory of Nazianzus' 'what is not assumed, is not healed' shows the relation between resurrection and incarnation in Dalferth's theology. If the grave was not necessarily empty, it is not necessary that the incarnation-stories say more than that Jesus' existence had a divine ground. That a divine identity assumes a human body to heal the human bodily existence is an idea from another conceptual framework. Further, it is unsurprising that in his Christology Dalferth has no place for the divine and human Christ of classic Christology, with whom we need to be united to live. Jesus Christ is the place of God's eschatological act, but the God-man himself does not add anything substantial to salvation.

Concerning the work of the Spirit, Dalferth emphasises the importance of the Spirit with regard to faith and our new understanding of self, world and God. The bodily life in the ontical, however, is more than faith, knowing, understanding and interpreting. The believer's life is an attempt to live in the ontic in accordance with the eschatological identity in Christ. This is true, but the work of the Spirit in this attempt is not mentioned. The biblical image of 'fruits of the Spirit' suggests that more must be said on the work of the Spirit in the renewal of our existence.

Finally, corresponding to the resurrection of Christ, it is not clear what the eschatological tension between the yet and not yet consists in according to Dalferth. The identification of 'being in Christ' and 'glorified being' shows that here lies a problem. The difference of 'eschatological' and 'eschatic' might very well be used here to give expression to this tension. However, although according to Dalferth this world becomes more and more transparent to God's loving presence, does this difference also imply the end of dying and the resurrection of persons who have died already?

What does salvation consist of? Is it possible to think within the framework of Dalferth's eschatological ontology of two 'Gegenständlichkeiten' that we are not saved from the ontic, but that the ontic, God's fallen creation itself is saved? What does the salvation of the body mean? Is it possible to think this without a resurrection that is more than a new localisation, but also the recreation of our bodily existence and hence the creation of a new kind of body, resulting in historical facts: empty graves? Is a healing of creation possible without resurrection of the body of Christ and without the growth of the body of Jesus by the power of the Holy Spirit in the virgin Mary? Dalferth's understanding of salvation is more than hermeneutical, because what is revealed is the effective presence of God's love. However, it is not clear how salvation could include furthermore the resurrection of the dead and the end of dying. According to my view, Dalferth structurally forgets the *bodily* reality of our human, created existence.[248]

If the grave was empty and if something more must be said on the spiritual resurrection body than Dalferth does, then his eschatological ontology has to be modified. This modification could be carried out using his own conceptuality. First, we have to see that it is possible to be localised in God's eschatological 'Gegenständlichkeit' in two ways, *simul creatura et peccator* or *simul iustus et peccator*. Second, whereas the difference between the two is God's eschatological act, nevertheless God's 'Gegenständlichkeit' is called 'eschatological' by Dalferth. Protology and eschatology, creation and recreation are not distinguished. If the new being is the result of God's eschatological action in Jesus Christ, the *Eschatos*, it is better not to call God's 'Gegenständlichkeit' eschatological, but to differentiate within God's 'Gegenständlichkeit' between created and recreated being (eschatological and eschatic, both related to the *Eschatos*). If the difference between the first body of Jesus and the spiritual resurrection of Jesus Christ has to be defended, another reason for this modification is given. Third, the new eschatological existence cannot be understood

248. For comparable criticisms although from a different angle, see Kühn, *Christologie*, 63; Wenz, 'Christologische Paralipomena II,' 416. Kühn blames Dalferth for leaving open the question concerning the historical access to the reality of Jesus of Nazareth as archetype or example of the human relatedness with God. Wenz doubts whether the conceptuality of God's acts suffices for understanding the person of Jesus Christ.

solely as a new localised existence in a new relation to God (in Christ, in the Spirit, in faith). The identification of 'being in Christ' and 'glorified being' cannot be maintained. In Dalferth's terms, this identification has to be replaced by a difference between the two, as difference between a new eschatological localisation in Christ (being in Christ) and a new 'eschatic' spiritual bodily existence after the resurrection of the dead (glorified being). This modification requires more attention to concepts like substance. The focus of his ontology on epistemic questions (identification) and on relations is a factor that contributes to what I see as a loss of the substance of salvation in his theology.

Something still has to be said about the hypothesis formulated in chapter 1. We have seen that Jesus Christ has an inclusive character. Resulting from the eschatological action of God, he is collective or corporate person. However, corresponding to the criticism just formulated, the history of Jesus Christ could be soteriologically relevant in more aspects than Dalferth suggests. More could be said on his life as an act of a representative. In any case, both the moments of representation and person-substitution can be found in his theology and are necessary to understand 'being in Christ.'

Dalferth concentrates on the end of the history of Jesus Christ—the resurrection or glorification—and denies that a moment of work-substitution is necessary. I can understand his resistance to an isolated idea of work-substitution. However, this leaves unsolved how the powers of guilt, evil, satan, and death are broken. The motif of restoration of justice is neglected. The New Testament imagery suggests to me that in this way the gospel becomes too harmless. Images like victory of the powers and paying of a ransom deserve more attention as a precondition of the new creation in Christ.

Concerning union and participation, Dalferth shows that union with Christ in faith is necessary and that we participate in the history of Christ. Nevertheless, because Dalferth resists a focus on Jesus, the union with Christ only is important for the sake of our relation with the Father. It has no further value. Moreover, the participation in the history of Christ is a motif in Dalferth's theology that has to be 'unpacked' to make it more than an idea.

To conclude, Dalferth's thinking offers a lot of valuable insights. Hermeneutically, it shows that 'being in Christ' is a localising reality that offers a new interpretation of self, world and God. The history of Jesus

Christ and God's judgment in Christ constitute a new God-given perspective that has to be appropriated in a life process. Ontologically, his eschatological ontology elaborates this new perspective concerning its ontological implications. Theologically, he emphasises the eschatological action of the triune God.

My questions concern the bodily (ontical) reality and salvation's impact on it. At different moments of his theology, Dalferth seems to have a blind spot here. As a result, his eschatological ontology has to be modified on several points. Important to this modification is the difference of 'being in Christ' and 'glorified being' which Dalferth wrongly identifies.

Dalferth confirms the hypothesis, that to develop a concept of 'being in Christ' we need the concepts of representation (the inclusive moment) and participation. Further we have seen again that representation and person-substitution are reverse sides of the one coin. Dalferth denies that a moment of work-substitution is necessary.

9

OLIVER O'DONOVAN

MORAL REALITY

9.1 Introduction

OLIVER O'DONOVAN (1945) IS Professor of Christian Ethics and Practical Theology at the University of Edinburgh. He has his theological roots in research on Augustine.[1] After his Augustine-study, O'Donovan wrote two works, that both attracted much attention, *Resurrection and Moral Order*[2] and *The Desire of the Nations*.[3] These two works are especially relevant with regard to the present investigation, to-

1. See his dissertation, O'Donovan, *The Problem of Self-Love in St. Augustine*; and further O'Donovan, '*Usus* and *fruitio* in Augustine, *De Doctriana Christiana 1*.' See further De Bruijne, *Levend in Leviatan*, 82–84, 155–56.

2. O'Donovan, *Resurrection and Moral Order.*

3. O'Donovan, *The Desire of the Nations*. See for the discussion this book has caused *Studies in Christian Ethics*, 11 (1998) 2; Schweiker, 'Freedom and Authority in Political Theology'; Wolterstorff, 'A discussion of Oliver O'Donovan's *The Desire of the Nations*'; Bartholomew (Ed.), *A Royal Priesthood?*; De Bruijne, *Levend in Leviatan*.

gether with a third book, *On the Thirty Nine Articles*, in which O'Donovan presents his theological position in conversation with the 39 articles of the Anglican Church.[4] Oliver O'Donovan is especially regarded as an authority in the field of political theology, a status he confirmed publishing *From Irenaeus to Grotius*[5] and *Bonds of Imperfection*,[6] both together with his wife Joan Lockwood O'Donovan, and recently the sequel to *The Desire of the Nations*: *The Ways of Judgment*.[7]

In *Resurrection and Moral Order*, O'Donovan is active in the area of what he calls 'Christian moral concepts,'[8] sketching an outline for evangelical ethics. A central notion in this book is the Augustinian concept of order, but he gives it a place within a more Pauline framework than Augustine was able to, due to his Neo-Platonism.[9] He uses the concept of moral order to correct the modern voluntarist climate, but also his own tradition that worked only with a simple divine command theory. Influenced by his teacher Paul Ramsey and by Karl Barth, his theological framework is strongly determined by Christology, pneumatology and eschatology.[10] In the resurrection of Christ, the order of creation is vindicated and transformed eschatologically. In this way he tries to bridge the gap between a 'creation ethics' and an 'ethics of the kingdom.' Central is the history of Jesus Christ, our representative, in which we participate through the Holy Spirit. This indicates the importance of two concepts, representation and participation; two concepts that also play a central role in the present investigation.

Much of his later work is determined by the rediscovery of what he calls 'a Great Tradition of political theology, almost unknown to today's

4. O'Donovan, *On the Thirty Nine Articles*.

5. O'Donovan & Lockwood O'Donovan (Eds.), *From Irenaeus to Grotius*.

6. O'Donovan & Lockwood O'Donovan, *Bonds of Imperfection*.

7. O'Donovan, *The Ways of Judgment*.

8. O'Donovan, *Resurrection and Moral Order*, vii.

9. Cf. O'Donovan, *The Problem of Self-Love in St. Augustine*, 139. Although he highly values Augustine, O'Donovan criticises Augustine and the Augustinian tradition for abstracting from salvation-history. He values in the Reformers that they reintroduced 'the forgotten middle-term of the relation of God and the soul, the effective agent of God and the representative of man, Jesus Christ, whose work of salvation is complete and decisive.' See O'Donovan, *On the Thirty Nine Articles*, 77–78.

10. See on O'Donovan's eschatology Carroll, 'The Power of the Future in the Present,' 120–28; De Bruijne, *Levend in Leviatan*, 64–69; and 87–91, 152–55 for the influence of Barth and Ramsay.

theologians.'[11] *The Desire of the Nations* is the first book resulting from this discovery, praised by Wolterstorff as 'the most important contribution to political theology in our century.'[12] In *The Desire of the Nations* the theological framework sketched in *Resurrection and Moral Order* is used in political theology. In the fullness of the time, the kingdom of God triumphed by the representative act of Jesus Christ. In the church, participating in Christ by the Holy Spirit, this is recapitulated. Again, Christology, pneumatology and eschatology determine the theological lines O'Donovan draws. It becomes obvious now, that representation (and participation) is a concept with political connotations.[13]

The centrality of Christology, pneumatology and eschatology determines O'Donovan's non-foundationalism and the way he relates particularity and universality. O'Donovan writes in the preface of *Resurrection and Moral Order* about his discovery of the force of anti-foundationalism.[14] In accordance with this discovery he regards epistemology as 'a reflexive, not an absolute, intellectual operation.'[15] A neutral starting point is not available, but we actually have knowledge of God, that need not be justified on a priori grounds.[16] Knowing implies loving.[17] Christians simply believe the truth constituted by what God has done for his world and for mankind in Jesus Christ, centred in his resurrection.[18] As a result, particular events

11. O'Donovan, *The Desire of the Nations*, xi.

12. Wolterstorff, 'A discussion of Oliver O'Donovan's *The Desire of the Nations*,' 100. For an analysis of O'Donovan's political theology, see De Bruijne, *Levend in Leviatan*.

13. Very clearly the political background of the concept of representation can be seen in two later works, O'Donovan, *Common Objects of Love*, 5, 28–37, 44, 48, 53–54, 56, 59, 64–67, 69, 71; O'Donovan, *The Just War Revisited*, Cambridge 2003, 3, 22, 27, 29–31, 36, 50; O'Donovan, *The Ways of Judgment*, 149–63. But already in *Resurrection and Moral Order* these political connotations are present, see O'Donovan, *Resurrection and Moral Order*, 15.
On O'Donovan's eschatological Christology, see De Bruijne, *Levend in Leviatan*, 64–69.

14. O'Donovan, *Resurrection and Moral Order*, vii.

15. O'Donovan, *Resurrection and Moral Order*, 76.

16. O'Donovan, *Resurrection and Moral Order*, 76–77.

17. O'Donovan, *Common Objects of Love*, 11.

18. About the resurrection as starting point see O'Donovan, *Resurrection and Moral Order*, 13–15; O'Donovan, *The Desire of the Nations*, 19–20. In the preface to the second edition of *Resurrection and Moral Order*, O'Donovan characterizes his position with three principles: the realist principle, the evangelical principle and the Easter principle, see O'Donovan, *Resurrection and Moral Order*, ix–xviii.

and particular traditions have a universal impact. The particularity of the history of Jesus Christ and of revelation have to be maintained, but in this particularity a universal reality is disclosed, if Jesus Christ really represents mankind, if he is really raised from the dead, if in his resurrection the moral order of creation is restored and transformed eschatologically, and God's kingdom has triumphed.[19]

Consequently, O'Donovan moves in his theology from particularity to universality. Theology implies description and theory. To describe and to develop theories good concepts are needed. These are necessary because concepts 'disclose the elementary structure of reality in relation to which we can begin to identify questions for theoretical development.'[20] Good theological concepts can be found by careful exegesis, reading the scriptures of the canonical history. This history must be read as a whole and theology has to do justice to this whole of salvation history, without abstracting from it. The reading of the particular biblical narrative precedes theoretical reflection in relation to contemporary questions. Good concepts mediate between the narrative and theoretical reflection.[21] With regard to 'being in Christ,' two concepts are important to O'Donovan as we have seen: representation and participation. In *On the Thirty Nine Articles*, these concepts are elaborated in general and soteriologically, whereas both are elaborated in a more specific direction in *Resurrection and Moral Order* (in relation to the moral order) and in *The Desire of the Nations* (in relation to the kingdom of God).[22]

In this chapter I will now give a description of O'Donovan's theology as far as it is relevant for our conversation aiming at the develop-

19. O'Donovan, *Resurrection and Moral Order*, 13–15, 17, 31, 53–55, 65, 76–91, 143–44, 147–50, 156–62, 228, 242; O'Donovan, *On the Thirty Nine Articles*, 29; O'Donovan, 'Evangelicalism and the Foundations of Ethics,' 96–97; O'Donovan, *The Desire of the Nations*, 141–44; O. O'Donovan & Lockwood O'Donovan, *Bonds of Imperfection*, 318.

20. O'Donovan, *The Desire of the Nations*, 15.

21. O'Donovan, *The Desire of the Nations*, 12–29; O'Donovan, 'Response to Respondents,' 92–99; De Bruijne, *Levend in Leviatan*, 33–34.

For a criticism of O'Donovan's method, see Furnish, 'How Firm a Foundation?'; Hauerwas, Fodor, 'Remaining in Babylon,' 34–49; Schweiker, 'Freedom and Authority in Political Theology,' 115, 117–19, 123. See for O'Donovan's reaction O'Donovan, 'Deliberation, History and Reading,' 128–30, 140–44; O'Donovan, 'Response to Respondents,' 92–98.

22. O'Donovan, *Resurrection and Moral Order*, e.g. 15, 22, 33, 66, 74, 101–2, 109, 121, 140, 150, 163, 246; O'Donovan, *On the Thirty Nine Articles*, esp. 27–49, 77–82; O'Donovan, *The Desire of the Nations*, esp. 120–92.

ment of a concept of 'being in Christ.' First in 9.2 I will concentrate on his Christology, analysing the concept of representation within its theological context. Second in 9.3 I turn to his soteriology as this is centred around the concept of participation. In 9.4 more theoretical questions will be dealt with, concerning the reality of 'being in Christ.' Finally I will present a short evaluation of O'Donovan's contribution to the conversation in 9.5.

9.2 Christology

In this paragraph I will first deal generally with the concept of representation (9.2.1). In a second section the different moments of the representative act which O'Donovan distinguishes will be investigated (9.2.2). Finally I will describe the relation between representation and substitution as O'Donovan sees it, to come to a first evaluation of the hypothesis of this investigation in conversation with O'Donovan (9.2.3).

9.2.1 REPRESENTATION

Representation is a concept with political connotations as we have seen.[23] More generally, representation as a social phenomenon is a special kind of signification, 'which extracts from the universe of objects some that will assume a representative meaning and will stand concretely for the sphere of communication itself.'[24] As a result of this act of signification, an object, idea or person represents a community. Hence members of a community conceive of their community as such. Political representation is a special case of social representations. It can even be said that political representation is only possible based on a system of social representation. Social representation is necessary for a community to discern its own community as such. Political representation makes it possible that the representative acts on behalf of the represented community.[25]

As a case of symbolisation, representation presupposes moral imagination. It is necessary that we see ourselves in the representative, as someone who '"stands for" our consciousness of our common asso-

23. See footnote 13.

24. O'Donovan, *Common Objects of Love*, 28–29.

25. O'Donovan, *Common Objects of Love*, 28–31; De Bruijne, *Levend in Leviatan*, 96–97.

ciation.'[26] Consequently, one has to know the representative in relation to oneself, which implies an affective dimension.[27] Recognition is essential to true representation, implying an affective relation and existential involvement.

Jesus Christ is representative in a double sense: he represents God and he represents the community.[28] Already in the Old Testament the king was God's 'son,' which was a role of double representation: the king presented God's rule to Israel and Israel to God.[29] In Christ the two roles meet. The first is the role of the Davidide monarch, who mediates God's rule. The second is the role of the representative individual who lonely like Jeremiah carries in his own destiny the fate and promise of the people.[30] The necessity of the meeting of these two roles can be found in the figure of the Servant of YHWH in Deutero-Isaiah, having royal characteristics and at the same time bearing the suffering caused by the sin of his people. Jesus Christ represents 'at once the divine rule and faithful response to it.'[31] But, according to O'Donovan, firstly Jesus must be Israel's representative before he represents their God. Before appearing as the answer to their prayers of penitence and of longing for salvation, he has to bring these prayers before God, as the representative of Israel.[32] Because he represents his people he can also be the representative of their God: Israel's saviour.

It is an interesting question whether this double representation amounts to ontological assertions like the two natures doctrine. O'Donovan warns against a formal use of the two natures doctrine. Christology must conform to the event of God's revelation and to the narrative form of the gospels that tell about this event. A strict use of the Nicene and Chalcedonian framework allows no room for important biblical categories. O'Donovan especially emphasises the eschatological character of

26. O. O. Donovan, *The Ways of Judgment*, 159, 175.

27. O. O. Donovan, *The Ways of Judgment*, 161, 163, 180; De Bruijne, *Levend in Leviatan*, 100.

28. O'Donovan, *The Desire of the Nations*, 123–24, 134–35; O'Donovan, *Common Objects of Love*, 44.

29. O'Donovan, *The Desire of the Nations*, 61.

30. O'Donovan, *The Desire of the Nations*, 123. Remarkably the duplicity of the representation is on 61 already present in the monarchy itself, as is the case in *The Ways of Judgment*, 4 and 158. On 123 of *Desire* however it seems as if the king only represents God while the representation of the people is introduced by the representative individual.

31. O'Donovan, *The Desire of the Nations*, 123–24.

32. O'Donovan, *The Desire of the Nations*, 134.

Christology that is lost in a formal two natures doctrine. As examples he mentions the apocalyptic eschatological significance of the title 'Son of man' and the emphasis on the presence of God's eschatological Kingdom.[33] He wants to reemphasise this eschatological colour: Christ is the eschatological and therefore '*decisive* presence of God and the *decisive* presence of God's people.'[34] Christology concerns events which can be dated.[35] He emphasises that Christ appeared in the last days, and God spoke in him 'once for all.'[36] In this way temporal and narrative factors are reintroduced into Christology. However, this does not justify the conclusion that purely functional categories would suffice in Christology. O'Donovan suggests that if that conclusion is drawn, the import of the *eschatological* claims is missed. Only with regard to Jesus is it claimed 'that the very presence of the ruling God is present to the true people of God once and for all the time' in his person;[37] which is an eschatological statement. Time and eschatology do not necessarily exclude a two nature doctrine, but they could rather reinforce each other.[38] As a consequence O'Donovan speaks

33. O'Donovan, *On the Thirty Nine Articles*, 23–24, 33–34; O'Donovan, *The Desire of the Nations*, 124, 134.

34. O'Donovan, *The Desire of the Nations*, 124; cf. O. Donovan, *The Ways of Judgment*, 185.

35. O'Donovan, *The Desire of the Nations*, 136.

36. O'Donovan, *On the Thirty Nine Articles*, 33–34.

37. O'Donovan, *The Desire of the Nations*, 124.

38. O'Donovan does not see an opposition between history and eschatology in the way Dalferth does. According to O'Donovan, the eschatological event is an event *in* history. God, his rule and his word, is in his incarnate Son present within the created reality.

Nevertheless, more must be said because in Jesus' resurrection the moral order is transformed eschatologically. History and change are possible, based on the framework of the moral order. Creation and moral order are the presupposition of history. For this reason O'Donovan emphatically distinguishes natural (ends generically anchored in the moral order) and historical teleology (the end of the process of time). The history of Jesus Christ—his incarnation, death, resurrection and glorification—concerns historical events. However, in the resurrection of Christ the moral order not only has been vindicated, but also transformed toward its eschatological *telos*. In Christ, the representative, the meaning of the whole has been focussed. He is a concrete universal. His eschatological transformation includes the eschatological transformation of what he represents, humanity and the moral order. This eschatological fulfilment of history is not generated immanently from within history. If Christ brings history and world-order to its fulfilment, he receives an eschatological quality that transcends history. Although the eschatological event takes place *within* history, it is an event that *transcends* history. History and eschatology cannot be identified: the eschatological act in history transforms history towards its eschatological end. See O'Donovan, *Resurrection and Moral Order*, 15, 53, 55–66, 143–44, 150.

of two natures, although he recognises the problem that the formulae have lost their historical context. As a consequence, few theologians are really able to understand the process of thought which resulted in these formulae. However, he wants to maintain the classical doctrine, while at the same time emphasising the narrative-historical and eschatological aspect of Christology.[39]

Although the representation of God by Jesus Christ is interesting also, I will further concentrate on the representation of the people, for this representation is most relevant in the present investigation.

In *Resurrection and Moral Order* and in *On the Thirty Nine Articles* O'Donovan characterizes Christ as the representative of humanity. He is head, the first-born from the dead, the pre-eminent one, the *archè*. He is the head of creation, in whose fate the whole created order is taken up and in whom all and everything are represented. O'Donovan emphasises the universality and cosmic dimension of Christ's representation. Due to the position of humanity in creation, the fate of the entire creation 'is taken up in the fate of this particular representative man.'[40] Christ is a figure like Adam, but as the last Adam he is an eschatological figure. His resurrection is the affirmation of life, in a way that goes beyond and transcends the initial gift of life. In him creation is restored and transformed to its eschatological *telos*. The last Adam is not just a living soul, but a life giving spirit.[41] Because he has this representative significance, one is not

39. O'Donovan, *On the Thirty Nine Articles*, 22–23; Cf. O'Donovan, *The Desire of the Nations*, 134–35; and further his remarks on the doctrine of the two natures: O'Donovan, *Resurrection and Moral Order*, 143, 147; O'Donovan, *The Desire of the Nations*, 82.

It is interesting to see how ethical interests colour O'Donovan's Christology. I will give two examples. The first concerns his choice for a diphysite rather than a monophysite Christology. Christ represents the created order in his human nature. According to O'Donovan, this order is a *created* order and not a divine expression of God's character. To preserve the creatureliness of this moral order, O'Donovan proposes a diphysite Christology, for in a monophysite solution this creatureliness is less safe. See O'Donovan, *Resurrection and Moral Order*, 147.

The second example concerns his idea of God's transcendence. Instead of emphasising the transcendence of God in a Barthian way as the humility of his incarnate presence within creation, O'Donovan wants to preserve in his political theology the supreme authority of God. As a consequence, he can write: 'A self-sufficient divine sovereignty, self-justified and complete, has come to be a rule in which all human nature finds itself represented.' See O'Donovan, *The Desire of the Nations*, 135.

40. O'Donovan, *Resurrection and Moral Order*, 15.

41. O'Donovan, *Resurrection and Moral Order*, 14–15, 33, 54, 57, 255; O'Donovan, *On the Thirty Nine Articles*, 29, 34, 77–79, 126; O'Donovan, 'Evangelicalism and the

justified in saying that only *one* man has been raised and exalted, and that the redeeming work is hardly begun. God's decision in the resurrection of Christ is a final one: if the righteous representative is raised, what remains to be done? Salvation is accomplished in the representative, it is finished and complete. What the Spirit does is communicate the definitive triumph, 'realising the implications of what has already been accomplished.'[42] God does not offer Christ to us as a representative leaving it open to us to decide whether Christ shall be in fact the last Adam or not. Therefore the question is not 'shall all mankind be saved in Christ?' but 'shall we ourselves be saved with all mankind in Christ?'[43]

Like Adam, Christ as representative of mankind and creation has universal significance. As a result, universality is a property of createdness, not of the incarnation. For a better understanding of the double representation I want to say something on the relation between representation and universality/particularity. O'Donovan criticises the conceptual scheme of most modern idealism that understood the universal as the divine and the concrete as the human. As a consequence incarnation has been understood as the focussing of the meaning of the whole in the representative one. According to O'Donovan this scheme has to be reversed. 'Universality is a property of worldliness' and incarnation is 'the coming within universal order of that which belongs outside it.'[44] Christ's particularity belongs to his divine nature, his universality to his human nature. 'As the one whom God has sent he is irreplaceable; as the new man he is the pattern to which we may conform ourselves.'[45] As human being—as 'concrete universal'—he is the one in whom the restored creation is summed up.[46] The *saving* significance of Jesus Christ as representative of mankind still depends on the incarnation. But that Jesus represents mankind cannot be concluded from incarnation. His universality lies in the fact that he represents his people, not in the fact that he represents God.

Foundations of Ethics,' 97; O'Donovan, *The Ways of Judgment*, 185, 232.

42. O'Donovan, *On the Thirty Nine Articles*, 79; and further 124, 126; cf. O'Donovan, *Resurrection and Moral Order*, 255; O'Donovan, *The Desire of the Nations*, 143.

43. O'Donovan, *On the Thirty Nine Articles*, 124–25.

44. O'Donovan, *Resurrection and Moral Order*, 144.

45. O'Donovan, *Resurrection and Moral Order*, 143. See further 146–50.

46. O'Donovan, *Resurrection and Moral Order*, 150.

However, O'Donovan also compares Christ with a national leader.[47] This evokes the question whether Christ represents Israel or mankind as a whole. In *The Desire of the Nations* O'Donovan answers this question: the representative of Israel becomes the representative of all humanity.

How is this possible? Jesus' teaching, announcing the coming of God's kingdom, is a disclosure of the reign of God.[48] His works of power show God's saving rule. He proclaimed the coming judgment of Israel. And he made God's law accessible to God's people.[49] Implicitly, Jesus claimed to be the great Davidic heir. To refer to his own role he used the title of 'the Son of man,' taken from Daniel 7. This title 'places the Son of man in a representative role and gives priority to the Kingdom itself.'[50] The conflict between Jesus and the Jewish authorities however leads to a climax in the history of God with his rebellious people: Jesus' death. The resurrection of Jesus is God's triumph over Israel.[51] Nevertheless, God's self-vindication and his judgment against Israel is at the same time the vindication of Israel itself. From an Easter-perspective can be said that the vindication of God implies the vindication of Israel over against Israel's corruption. Israel struggled against God and against itself; God struggled against Israel for Israel. Representing God, Jesus Christ suffers the resistance of Israel on God's behalf; representing Israel, he suffers God's resistance on Israel's behalf. In him, the causes of God and of Israel have been made one. The death of Jesus is at the same time Israel's rebellion against God and God's condemnation of Israel.[52] His resurrection however, freed Israel from the forces that had taken possession of Israel. The victory over these demonic powers and over sin, affirming the new identity of Israel in its representative, appears as the conquest of death. This makes possible the restoration of mankind as a whole, for sin and death are conquered. As a result, Paul compares Jesus Christ not with Abraham, 'the national patriarch,' but with Adam, 'the founder of the human race.'[53] Christ is 'the

47. O'Donovan, *Resurrection and Moral Order*, 15.

48. O'Donovan, *The Desire of the Nations*, 88–89.

49. O'Donovan, *The Desire of the Nations*, 93, 96, 100.

50. O'Donovan, *The Desire of the Nations*, 116–17.

51. O'Donovan, *The Desire of the Nations*, 129.

52. O'Donovan, *The Desire of the Nations*, 130.

53. O'Donovan, *The Desire of the Nations*, 141; Oliver O'Donovan, 'Gerechtigkeit und Urteil,' 2.

true Israelite and the true representative of the human race.'[54] The eschatological act of Christ is an act of grace that exceeds the protological act of transgression.[55] The decisive moment that ensures that Christ can be seen as representing mankind and not just Israel is that in the restoration of Israel he conquers death, sin, and demonic forces of bestiality.

On a conceptual level, O'Donovan characterizes representation with two statements: '(a) The representative *alone* constitutes the presence of the represented; (b) The represented are *really present* in what the representative does and experiences on their behalf.'[56] If the second is forgotten, representation becomes a kind of fiction; if the first is forgotten representation becomes a heuristic tool to discover a pattern, for the representative does nothing more than the people represented do. Then the pattern of actions receives attention, but it is forgotten that this constitutes the represented. An important interest for O'Donovan is the integration of objective and subjective aspects of salvation. What is realised in our subjectivity, is realised first in the subjectivity of Jesus Christ—which is from our point of view objectively.[57] Another interest is the decisive character of the representative act.[58]

By his new and irreplaceable role, the representative constitutes a new reality that was not already there. He is new and innovative, transcending the represented. O'Donovan compares him with a mould or template, for he provides a *hupogrammos* and he is the *prototokos*. As representative, he is irreplaceable and unique.[59]

To be unique in this way, he had to be not just a 'supremely *average* figure.' His atypicality was understood in the theological tradition as his sinlessness. Because Christ is unique in his sinlessness, he is unique in his capacity to represent true humanity. To represent a guilty people, he had to be innocent, 'because only the innocent can confer upon the guilty the public standing they lack.' Jesus Christ was made like his brothers, but he was not simply like them. Christ was in the likeness of the sinful flesh 'by

54. O'Donovan, *The Desire of the Nations*, 148.

55. O'Donovan, *The Desire of the Nations*, 128.

56. O'Donovan, *The Desire of the Nations*, 125.

57. O'Donovan, *Resurrection and Moral Order*, 23–24.

58. O'Donovan, *The Desire of the Nations*, 128–29; cf. O'Donovan, *On the Thirty Nine Articles*, 42–43, 78–80.

59. O'Donovan, *The Desire of the Nations*, 125–26.

an act of identification that went beyond simply conformity to type.'[60] His sinlessness was required to be the decisive representative of mankind.

The represented are not absent while the representative stands in, as statement (b) says. Further the constitution of the represented by the representative alone (statement (a)) is not temporary, but demands permanence. Hence representation must not be understood as replacement, as Dorothee Sölle thought. Furthermore, representation is not temporary as she proposed. Political representation is not replacement, but co-presence. It is a creative innovation, that 'multiplies freedom and authority, leaving everyone with more.' Here O'Donovan follows Hannah Arendt, but remarks that this idea of political representation can be seen as conferring freedom only if we have learned to think in terms of a salvific rule. The perception of political representation as conferring freedom rather than taking it away depends on the eschatological transformation of politics by the Christ-event. There we see that freedom is perfected in his act of representation. Christ 'is at one and the same time alone and accompanied, always representing, always together with those he represents.'[61]

To sum up, representation is a social phenomenon with political implications. As a case of symbolisation, representation presupposes moral imagination and an affective aspect. Jesus Christ is representative in a double sense, representing God's rule and representing his people. He is the eschatological representative, the last Adam; head, firstborn from the dead, and life giving spirit. As last Adam he has universal significance. That he, as representative of the people of Israel, is at the same time the eschatological Adam, representing humanity as a whole, is brought about by his resurrection, which shows that he conquered the powers of sin, death and bestiality. This victory has universal significance. Two statements characterize the concept of representation: (a) The representative *alone* constitutes the presence of the represented; (b) The represented are *really present* in what the representative does and experiences on their behalf. Therefore he is a unique figure, who represents his people not just temporarily, but always. Political representation does not take away freedom, but confers it.

60. O'Donovan, *The Desire of the Nations*, 125–26; see further O'Donovan, *On the Thirty Nine Articles*, 78.

61. O'Donovan, *The Desire of the Nations*, 126–27.

9.2.2 THE MOMENTS OF THE REPRESENTATIVE ACT

In the history of theology, according to O'Donovan, the focus of the theological exploration of the representation of Christ has been laid especially on his death, the incarnation being its precondition, establishing Christological conditions for atonement.[62] The emphasis on death and incarnation led to a neglect of the kingdom of God and the resurrection, especially in the western Anselmic tradition.[63] Further, without the resurrection the death of Christ is a last and hopeless word. Hence the cross of Christ cannot be understood without the resurrection, for cross and resurrection are related teleologically.[64] But not only does the western (Reformed) tradition isolate one moment of the history of Jesus Christ from the others, other theologies also privilege one moment above others.[65] O'Donovan wants to proceed differently, doing justice to the entire narrative of the representative act. Jesus' person in two natures is not the only precondition of his work, rather his whole life is important. Good theology should treat all the different moments separately and in their interaction, showing them to be one act of God. Christian thought has to be concerned with all the moments of the Christ-event, although the resurrection provides the starting point for telling the story.[66] Jesus Christ is representative of his people in his entire life and his representative act comprises the whole of his history. 'If Christ alone upon the cross bore the judgment upon sin, that is because he alone was acknowledged as God's Son by the Jordan, he alone rose from the dead, he alone took his seat on the right hand of majesty on high when 'a cloud hid him'.'[67]

The re-telling of the narrative, aptly concentrates on several central moments of the representative act. O'Donovan identifies four moments: Advent, Passion, Restoration and Exaltation. He emphasises that this is

62. O'Donovan, *On the Thirty Nine Articles*, 33–34; O'Donovan, *The Desire of the Nations*, 127.

63. O'Donovan, *Resurrection and Moral Order*, xv; O'Donovan, *On the Thirty Nine Articles*, 30; O'Donovan, *The Desire of the Nations*, 128, 134; O'Donovan, 'Gerechtigkeit und Urteil,' 12.

64. O'Donovan, *Resurrection and Moral Order*, 95; O'Donovan, *On the Thirty Nine Articles*, 32.

65. O'Donovan, *On the Thirty Nine Articles*, 27.

66. O'Donovan, *Resurrection and Moral Order*, ix, xv, xvii, 13–14; O'Donovan, *On the Thirty Nine Articles*, 27–32; O'Donovan, *The Desire of the Nations*, 127–29.

67. O'Donovan, *The Desire of the Nations*, 127.

only an exegetical schema without any theoretical function; but still an exegetical summary that claims to represent the essential structure of the story.[68] In what follows in this section I will investigate these different moments in their respective significance and interrelation.

The first moment is the advent of Jesus Christ. Although the gospels differ in their approach to the advent of Jesus Christ, telling of the baptism of Christ or also of his incarnation and birth, O'Donovan still sees continuity between them. Birth and baptism constitute together one movement of coming, which can be summarized in the idea of condescension.[69]

O'Donovan regrets the non-eschatological character of the traditional doctrine of the incarnation, reducing in his view the incarnation to the preface of the story. Instead, the incarnation is itself a part of it.[70] As we have seen already, incarnation concerns the particularity and uniqueness of Jesus Christ. He is God's unique presence in creation; the saviour is a particular person: this specific, incarnate logos with his particular history. That which belongs outside this world, the transcendent God, becomes part of this world, bridging the gap of his transcendence and assuming universal significance. The incarnation makes it possible to take up the fate of creation in the fate of the representative. The representative guarantees that the universe does not explode, but holds together as an ordered cosmos. The identification of the Son of God with creation means that the visible presence of God, who is the end of creation, is also, as a creature, the first one. On this level of creation also, there is a teleological ordering εἰς αὐτὸν. Because God is located beyond his creation (he transcends our time-space field in a metaphysical sense) the story of incarnation has some mythopoetic traces. However, incarnation is not a true myth, for something that can be dated in history really happened. As the incarnate logos, Christ is the unique and saving presence of God within creation. Christology rests in being, not simply in event.[71]

68. O'Donovan, *Resurrection and Moral Order*, xviif; O'Donovan, *The Desire of the Nations*, 133. See further De Bruijne, *Levend in Leviatan*, 40, 66–67.

In *On the Thirty Nine Articles* O'Donovan identifies five moments, related to the text of the Thirty Nine Articles: Incarnation, Cross, Descent into hell, Resurrection and Ascension. However, dealing with the sacraments he suggests a number of four sacraments, related with four moments; see O'Donovan, *On the Thirty Nine Articles*, 27, 127–28.

69. O'Donovan, *The Desire of the Nations*, 133–35.

70. O'Donovan, *On the Thirty Nine Articles*, 33–34.

71. O'Donovan, *Resurrection and Moral Order*, 15, 33, 85, 143–44, 146; O'Donovan,

The incarnation is followed by the baptism of Jesus by John the Baptist, which marks the coming of Christ. His baptism is a divine act of authorisation, but before this authorisation Jesus takes upon himself the role of Israel. Jesus is identified as the Son of God, an identification that leads to the beginning of the movement of disciples away from John the Baptist to Jesus. This movement 'signals the gathering of Israel to the Kingdom of God.'[72] Advent is the coming of Jesus, his appearance and the beginning of his ministry to fulfil the hopes of Israel.[73]

If the Advent-moment is forgotten, a political theology is left only with two contrasting spheres of old and new being. This leads to the idea that a positive use of power for political interests is impossible, as O'Donovan criticises Karl Barth. Seen from the Advent-moment, earthly politics is part of the unfulfilled salvation history. The gospels do not start by telling of cross and resurrection, but of Jesus' coming. This gives place to a time of waiting before the time of fulfilment, a time for politics.[74]

The second moment is the suffering and cross of Jesus Christ. The cross introduces God's judgment over this world. At first sight, it seems logical to see the judgment of God in the resurrection as divine intervention. However, a deeper analysis in the light of the resurrection shows the activity of God's judgment already in the cross of Jesus. The cross was more than the work of wicked men, something which happened according to God's plan and foreknowledge. In the cross we see the mystery of representative judgment. Analysing O'Donovan's writings, the following reconstruction of this representative judgment can be given.[75]

a. Judgment is understood as bringing the distinction between good and evil into public observation, separating guilt and innocence, and saying 'yes' to the good—the life in the Spirit—and 'no' to the evil—

On the Thirty Nine Articles, 23, 35–36; O'Donovan, *The Desire of the Nations*, 135; and De Bruijne, *Levend in Leviatan*, 64.

72. O'Donovan, *The Desire of the Nations*, 133–34.

73. O'Donovan, *Resurrection and Moral Order*, xvii.

74. O'Donovan & Lockwood O'Donovan, *Bonds of Imperfection*, 247, 256, 260–63. Cf. O'Donovan, *Resurrection and Moral Order*, xvii–xviii; De Bruijne, *Levend in Leviatan*, 66.

75. O'Donovan, *Resurrection and Moral Order*, 95; O'Donovan, *On the Thirty Nine Articles*, 28; O'Donovan, *The Desire of the Nations*, 136, 256.

the life in the flesh. Public ambiguity comes to an end and by God's judgment—a performative judgment—a new reality is created.[76]

b. In the conflict around Jesus, rebellion against God becomes manifest. The old is confronted and challenged. The darkness refuses the light and the false destroys the true. The true nature of darkness and falsehood is shown. It is the work of the Spirit to show that the rejection of Jesus is not just a Jewish problem, but that unbelief in Jesus Christ, the judgment of the world, becomes our sin and our repudiation of him.[77]

c. The innocent one suffers most from this conflict. Israel judges Jesus, condemning him to death. This repudiation of the innocent Jesus makes him not just the representative of the innocent, but also of the guilty. He identifies himself with guilty humanity in his death, with the guilty Israel, becoming a slave.[78]

d. Because of this identification, in the judgment of Jesus by Israel and Pilate, God judges the guilty, the old age, and Israel. Jesus Christ bore the curse of the law. In this way, God condemned sin in the flesh. The old authority of the law with its oppressions of flesh and condemnation is not only confronted and challenged, but also destroyed.[79]

e. In this way, the cross is not only an act of judgment, but also an act of reconciliation. Already in the cross, not only rejection but also acceptance can be found. The 'no' is the presupposition of the 'yes' that is pronounced more clearly in the resurrection. Further the identification with the guilty creates space for the guilty to share

76. O'Donovan, *Resurrection and Moral Order*, 14; O'Donovan, *On the Thirty Nine Articles*, 31–32; O'Donovan, *The Desire of the Nations*, 38, 136, 256; O'Donovan, 'Gerechtigkeit und Urteil,' 3–5, 11; O'Donovan, *The Ways of Judgment*, 7–12, 16.

In his criticism of O'Donovan, Carroll focuses too much on the negative side of judgment, not seeming to see that the performative character of God's judgment creates something new. See Carroll., 'The Power of the Future in the Present.'

77. O'Donovan, *Resurrection and Moral Order*, 94–95, 105; O'Donovan, *The Desire of the Nations*, 128, 136; O'Donovan, 'Gerechtigkeit und Urteil,' 12; O'Donovan & Lockwood O'Donovan, *Bonds of Imperfection*, 2.

78. O'Donovan, *Resurrection and Moral Order*, 74, 105; O'Donovan, *On the Thirty-Nine Articles*, 32; O'Donovan, *The Desire of the Nations*, 130, 135–36.

79. O'Donovan, *Resurrection and Moral Order*, 14, 74; O'Donovan, *On the Thirty-Nine Articles*, 29, 31–33; O'Donovan, *The Desire of the Nations*, 128, 130.

in the vindication of the innocent. Moreover, the obedience that led to Christ's death is already God's reversal of Adam's choice. And finally, the prayer of Jesus Christ for forgiveness is not a prayer against divine justice, but a demonstration of a divine justice that is 'more complete and more satisfying' than all other justice.[80]

Understanding the cross in this way as an act of judgment (and as a result of this judgment as an act of reconciliation) means that it can also be understood as a perfect sacrifice and a propitiation for the sins of mankind. It is necessary to speak of divine punishment. However, the obedient suffering of Christ was not simply a reversal of man's plight, but a participation in and identification with it.[81] It can only be understood as such within the history of salvation, and hence within the framework of an eschatological conception of Christ's work. His death is the end of an age. Only the coming of the Kingdom of God and the last Adam could bring reconciliation.[82]

The third moment of the representative act is the resurrection of Jesus Christ. In the resurrection, God's judgment continues.

However, before dealing further with God's judgment it is important to see that the resurrection has two aspects, an aspect of restoration and an aspect of eschatological transformation or empowerment. That these two aspects belong inseparably together shows how resurrection and ascension, the fourth moment, are closely related. Below I will further discuss the relation between resurrection and ascension. For now it suffices that they are closely related but can be treated separately. Doing so, O'Donovan relates the third moment especially with restoration and the fourth moment with glorification.[83]

80. O'Donovan, *Resurrection and Moral Order*, 75; and further 14, 74; O'Donovan, *On the Thirty Nine Articles*, 31–32; O'Donovan, *The Desire of the Nations*, 136; O'Donovan, 'Gerechtigkeit und Urteil,' 12.

81. O'Donovan, *On the Thirty Nine Articles*, 31–32; O'Donovan, *The Desire of the Nations*, 137; O'Donovan, *The Ways of Judgment*, 107–8. For O'Donovan's concept of punishment, see *The Ways of Judgment*, 101–24; De Bruijne, *Levend in Leviatan*, 132–34.

82. O'Donovan, *On the Thirty Nine Articles*, 33–34.

83. O'Donovan, *Resurrection and Moral Order*, 56; O'Donovan, *On the Thirty Nine Articles*, 34; O'Donovan, *The Desire of the Nations*, 142–43; O'Donovan, *The Ways of Judgment*, 85–86.

Returning to the judgment of God, it is important to note that the resurrection is not the positive word in contrast to which crucifixion and death is the negative word of God's judgment. The positive aspect is already present in the cross, as the Reformation's emphasis on the cross rightly claims. However, the resurrection does add something to the cross as we will see.[84]

In a way comparable to the cross, the resurrection as part of God's judgment has several layers:

a. First of all the resurrection of Jesus Christ is God's judgment on Jesus. In the cross God reverses the judgment of Israel on Jesus and vindicates him. God and his reign triumph over the Jewish authorities and God's people.[85]

b. Because Jesus was sentenced to death yet he was innocent, he dies as representative of the innocent victims of injustice. Like Abel's blood, their blood cries out from the ground. In the vindication of Jesus Christ, he reconciles the innocent to God and gives them vindication. In this way 'the cry of outraged innocence which Cain's civilisation could never silence,' is put to rest. Nature's claim on behalf of the innocent is satisfied. This vindication 'puts an end to the unfinished business of nature's justice.'[86]

c. Because Jesus was condemned and made to be sin, he also became representative of his guilty people. Because Jesus Christ identified himself with them, he made it possible that they also would participate in his vindication. The resurrection is not only God's judgment against Israel but also for Israel. Israel's sin is conquered and a new identity is given in the representative. Jesus Christ 'becomes a new focus of identity for those who inherit Abraham's faith.'[87]

84. O'Donovan, 'Gerechtigkeit und Urteil,' 12–13.

85. O'Donovan, *Resurrection and Moral Order*, 105; O'Donovan, *The Desire of the Nations*, 129.

86. O'Donovan, *Resurrection and Moral Order*, 74–75; O'Donovan, *The Ways of Judgment*, 26–27.

O'Donovan denies that in the punishment of the offender satisfaction has to be given to the victim. This would be no more than personal vengeance. The victim's grievance is simply God's concern. 'It is a measure of the deep de-Christianisation of our times that it is once again possible to speak in public of the victim's interest in punishment . . .' see *The Ways of Judgment*, 115–16.

87. O'Donovan, *The Desire of the Nations*, 141.

d. '(T)he form the rejection and vindication of Jesus takes is the conquest of death.'[88] As we have seen already, this makes Christ comparable to the representative of mankind, Adam. His resurrection is 'God's reversal of Adam's choice of sin and death.'[89] God's decision that Adam should live is affirmed anew. In the resurrection of the representative, it is promised that all shall be made alive. Because his vindication (and transformation) is on behalf of all man, it is the climax of his identification with humanity. In his resurrection, he represents humanity. Therefore the physical reality of the restored body is important. Taking his body again, Christ's resurrection concerns material reality. His body represents the perfection of human nature as first fruit of a renewed humanity. The resurrection gives humanity a new form, showing that God's judgment is no mathematical point but is unfolded in the life of the second Adam. In conclusion, the resurrection of Jesus Christ is the restoration of humanity.[90]

e. The resurrection is not only the restoration of mankind, but also of the created order and of the entire creation. Concerning the restoration of the moral order more will be said in relation to the fourth moment. With the confirmation of humanity and moral order, creation is also affirmed again and will be restored together with the representative. The resurrection is a sign of the end to that futility that characterizes the entire created nature in its bondage to decay.[91]

This is not all that can be said on God's judgment, below I will continue (see 9.3.1). The result of God's judgment in cross and resurrection is objective justice.[92] Something has been said already concerning justice under c. In the vindication of Jesus Christ, vindicating both the innocent and the guilty, a divine justice is demonstrated 'that was more complete

88. O'Donovan, *The Desire of the Nations*, 141.

89. O'Donovan, *Resurrection and Moral Order*, 13.

90. O'Donovan, *Resurrection and Moral Order*, 13–15, 31, 57; O'Donovan, *On the Thirty Nine Articles*, 29, 34; O'Donovan, 'Evangelicalism and the Foundations of Ethics,' 97; O'Donovan, *The Desire of the Nations*, 142; O'Donovan, 'Gerechtigkeit und Urteil,' 13; O'Donovan, *The Ways of Judgment*, 86.

91. O'Donovan, *Resurrection and Moral Order*, 15, 22, 56; O'Donovan, *On the Thirty Nine Articles*, 34; O'Donovan, 'Evangelicalism and the Foundations of Ethics,' 97; O'Donovan, *The Desire of the Nations*, 143.

92. O'Donovan, *The Desire of the Nations*, 38.

and more satisfying than any eye had yet seen or ear heard of.'[93] God's performative judgment makes objective justice possible and creates a new reality.

Finally the character of Jesus' body has to be explained, for it is a spiritual body. According to O'Donovan, the spiritual nature of Jesus' body does not exclude the physical and material, but points to the transformation of the material. In the resurrection, Christ receives a spiritual body that does not conform to the laws and normative patterns of material existence. The material is transformed in ways 'that require a different phenomenology and a different pattern of perception.' It is important that a human person is brought back from death in a human body, to prevent 'a gnostic preference for the spiritual.' Resurrection concerns the vindication of creation.[94]

Jesus Christ is more than Adam. He is not just a living soul, but a life-giving spirit, leading humanity to its 'supernatural' destiny. The vindication of humanity in the resurrection of Christ includes both its redemption and its transformation.[95] This is especially evident in the fourth moment, the ascension of Christ, unfolding 'the implications of what is present already in the resurrection.' Ascension is not just a sign of the resurrection, for the elevation of Christ to the Father marks the eschatological transformation, one of the two sides of the resurrection. Unfortunately, contemporary theology has shown a tendency to ignore the ascension of Christ. O'Donovan sees cosmological questions contributing to this tendency.[96] Below I will describe O'Donovan's solution to these problems. I will first concentrate on the soteriological significance of the ascension.

Like the resurrection, the ascension is the vindication of Jesus Christ. However, the ascension has a more clearly public and political character: 'it was the fulfilment of the political promise which Jesus had come to bring, and his own authorisation as the representative of the Kingdom of God.'[97] Therefore the ascension-story is not to be demythologised, for this implies immediately its depoliticising, because exactly the political affir-

93. O'Donovan, *Resurrection and Moral Order*, 75.

94. O'Donovan, *On the Thirty Nine Articles*, 29.

95. O'Donovan, *Resurrection and Moral Order*, 14, 56–57, 142.

96. O'Donovan, *On the Thirty Nine Articles*, 35; O'Donovan, *Resurrection and Moral Order*, 57.

97. O'Donovan, *The Desire of the Nations*, 145.

mations are lost in this process. The language of coronation is essential to the story of ascension and its political significance. Because the Father confers his authority to his Son, to speak of divine authority after ascension is to speak of the authority of Christ. In this way, it is the climactic conclusion of the story of Jesus Christ. The final moment expresses the accomplishment of the representative act, confirming what the whole story was about, as the anticipations of the glorification show.[98]

Ascension is not only significant for Jesus Christ himself and God's kingdom, for it is the foundation which determines all future time and all public existence, although it is a secret foundation. It shows the eschatological transformation of humanity to its 'supernatural' destiny as I have written already. In its representative humanity is glorified, for Jesus Christ is glorified at God's right hand. In this eschatological transformation the *telos* of humanity is reached in the last Adam. Unanswered questions of creation are answered and all those possible ends to which God did not destine creation are ruled out. Creation is freed from corruption and disintegration. The possibility of disruption is vanished.[99]

The exaltation of Christ to God's right hand is at the same time the restoration and transformation of the moral order of creation. The privileged place of humanity within the created order is the position of dominion, set over all the works of God's hands and 'lacking a very little of God' as Psalm 8 says. In Christ this created order is vindicated and perfectly realised. 'In his conquest over death and in his glorification at the Father's right hand we see man as he was made to be, . . . able for the first time to take his place in the cosmos as its lord.'[100] Hence the glorification of Christ is the restoration of moral order. Because Jesus Christ represents humanity, his triumph prepares the way for the future triumph of humanity as a whole. This triumph does not imply a new innovative order, but is the vindication and fulfilment of the primal order in a way that was always implied but not realised due to the fallen state of mankind. That it is a fulfilment shows that the glorification of Christ results not only in a restoration, but also in a transformation of the moral order. The seat at God's right hand which belongs to the Son, the position to that which humanity

98. O'Donovan, *Resurrection and Moral Order*, 141; O'Donovan, *The Desire of the Nations*, 145.

99. O'Donovan, *Resurrection and Moral Order*, 55–56; O'Donovan, *The Desire of the Nations*, 145–46.

100. O'Donovan, *Resurrection and Moral Order*, 54.

is elevated in Christ, is a position humanity never has enjoyed before. In Christ humanity is elevated to share in the glory of God.[101]

That the exaltation of the Son implies the restoration and eschatological transformation of the moral order also, can only be understood with the help of the concepts of representation and judgment. That Jesus Christ is the one in whom that order has come to be, is possible because he is the representative of mankind. God has willed that the restored creation should take form in and in relation to him. He is the concrete and irreplaceable embodiment of the renewed moral order. God chose and 'elected a small segment of reality' (the reality of Jesus Christ) to shape all the reality that we encounter.[102] In this choice of God we again meet the judgment of God. Raising Jesus Christ from the dead, God conferred authority upon Jesus, quite apart from us. The resurrection (restoration and glorification) is God's final and decisive word on creation.[103] Because of this decisiveness, God's judgment in Christ and the last judgment are closely connected. The resurrection is the revelation of God's final judgment. In him the final judgment had arrived. All the material for judgment is present in Jesus Christ. 'It is enough that he has spoken his word upon creation in the person of its head, in whom all and everything are represented.'[104] God has rejected all that rejects him, speaking his condemning 'No' on all which denies and detracts from humanity and creation. His final 'Yes' is spoken to Christ and in him to mankind and the created universe. After the resurrection and exaltation of the righteous representative to God's right hand, nothing remains to be done except from the realization of the implications of what has been accomplished already. Although resurrection and last judgment have to be distinguished, the content of the last judgment is known: what is in Christ, is accepted and justified; what is not in Christ is condemned.[105]

Finally we have to deal with the cosmological questions related to ascension, which often lead to a demythologisation or a neglect of ascension in 20th century theology. According to O'Donovan, the reality of

101. O'Donovan, *Resurrection and Moral Order*, 38, 53–54, 57, 81; O'Donovan, 'Evangelicalism and the Foundations of Ethics,' 97.

102. O'Donovan, *Resurrection and Moral Order*, 121; and further 150.

103. O'Donovan, *Resurrection and Moral Order*, 13, 105, 140.

104. O'Donovan, *Resurrection and Moral Order*, 255.

105. O'Donovan, *Resurrection and Moral Order*, 14, 255–56; O'Donovan, *On the Thirty Nine Articles*, 38, 79; O'Donovan, *The Desire of the Nations*, 177.

ascension is very important because of its moral and political implications. However, this event is an indescribable and unspeakable event that can only be expressed with images. It can be described as an event in so far as the ascension has one foot in our space and time, for it is the end of the resurrection appearances of Jesus. But the ascension is more, although this more is veiled by the cloud that hid Jesus on the mountain top. And that this more has occurred is soteriologically significant. The material body of Jesus has been transferred from our spatio-temporal order into an order that is greater than the physical and spatio-temporal, into an existence in the presence of God which lies beyond the conditions of our physical existence. The verb 'ascend,' used to tell about this transfer to an existence that transcends time and space, can refer to no form of known spatial movement. We are not able to localise the right hand of God. Further, we can not describe the form of a human body outside space and time as we know it. The result of the eschatological transformation of humanity remains invisible. We do not know what it is to be a new creation or to participate perfectly in the restored order of creation. The only model for a description of the new creation is hidden for our eyes by a cloud. But we know that the path has been taken and that we are to take it too, and we wait for the public manifestation of this reality.[106]

For O'Donovan, not only are the different moments important, but also the relations between these moments. I will list the different observations O'Donovan makes concerning these relations.

First, the perspective on the representative act is determined by the resurrection.[107] Without the resurrection the cross is the last word, and a hopeless word. The resurrection shows that the cross is more. It is not only the result of obedience, leading to exclusion and death. Already in the cross God is at work, judging the world. Further, the resurrection is the ground for the conviction that this world is an ordered cosmos. Without resurrection, no reasons for the idea that this world is an ordered one could be given.[108]

106. O'Donovan, *Resurrection and Moral Order*, 14, 247, 249; O'Donovan, *On the Thirty Nine Articles*, 35–38; O'Donovan, *The Desire of the Nations*, 144–45; O'Donovan, *The Ways of Judgment*, 86.

107. O'Donovan, *Resurrection and Moral Order*, 14; O'Donovan, *The Desire of the Nations*, 131, 256.

108. O'Donovan, *Resurrection and Moral Order*, 14–15; 19, 95.

Second, cross and resurrection together form the centre of the narrative of the representative act.[109]

Third, cross and resurrection belong together. They cannot be isolated from each other, but must also not be played off against each other.[110] Without the resurrection, the cross is hopeless. It leads to a gnostic otherworldliness or a depoliticising of the gospel. The elements of abnegation and criticism present in the cross become destructive without the resurrection. This does not imply that the cross can be forgotten in the light of the resurrection, for it says that obedient participation in the moral order will lead to exclusion.[111] Cross and resurrection are related narratively and teleologically.[112] Therefore, the resurrection is more than the annulment of the cross. The cross is the negative side of the judgment of God, but even the positive side of God's judgment is already at work in the cross. The resurrection affirms this 'pro nobis' of the cross and gives the positive judgment of God its form. In this last aspect becomes clear that the resurrection really adds something to the cross. The resurrection does more than presenting the significance of the cross, for the life of the second Adam in which we participate is more than a mathematical point.[113]

Fourth, the resurrection is the vindication of creation in a double sense, redeeming and transforming. As a result, it can be seen together with ascension and it can be distinguished from ascension. On the one hand, it is possible to look forward. In this perspective, as we find it in Matthew and Mark, resurrection and ascension are identified. On the other hand, one can look backwards. Now the recovery of the lost is distinguished from the transformation and elevation of humanity. The emphasis is on the physical reality of the restored body. This is the pre-

109. O'Donovan, *On the Thirty Nine Articles*, 27.

110. O'Donovan, *The Desire of the Nations*, 128–30.

111. O'Donovan, *Resurrection and Moral Order*, 14–15, 95; O'Donovan, *On the Thirty Nine Articles*, 28; O'Donovan, *The Desire of the Nations*, 128.

112. The descent to the dead shows the teleological link between death and resurrection. The proclamation of the gospel to the dead shows that Christ's identification with mankind in death is at the same time a proclamation of God's favour. The conquest of death is already preached. Jesus makes himself one with us in the darkness of God's wrath, and as a result he brings us out from darkness into the light of God's favour. See O'Donovan, *On the Thirty Nine Articles*, 32.

113. O'Donovan, *On the Thirty Nine Articles*, 28–30, 32; O'Donovan, *The Desire of the Nations*, 130, 256; O'Donovan, 'Gerechtigkeit und Urteil,' 12–13.

sentation we find in Luke and John. Because the resurrection has both senses, both perspectives are possible.[114]

Fifth, just like the cross the ascension needs the resurrection. Just as the cross becomes destructive without the resurrection, the aspects of transcendence and revolution become negative without the affirmation of creation in the resurrection. Again the danger of gnostic other-worldliness has to be prevented.[115] Together with the resurrection, cross and ascension can qualify creation without denying it.

In summary, the representative act is itself a history consisting of four different related moments: advent, cross, resurrection and ascension. These moments need and qualify each other.

Advent is the beginning of the story and of the identification of God with humanity in Jesus Christ. The other three moments all contain aspects of the judgment of God. The conflict between Jesus Christ and the Jewish authorities that leads to his cross, introduces the judgment of God, not only in its negative side but also already in its positive side. In his suffering, Jesus identified himself with the innocent but also with the guilty. He suffered as a result of and for our sins. In the resurrection, Jesus is vindicated. Because of his identification with humanity and the resulting representative character of his life, humanity and creation participate in this vindication. In Jesus Christ humanity is not only redeemed, but also glorified and brought to its eschatological *telos*, sharing in the glory of God. This eschatological *telos* is hidden until it is manifested publicly.

9.2.3 REPRESENTATION AND SUBSTITUTION

Having described the relevant aspects of the Christology of Oliver O'Donovan, the time has come for a first evaluation of the hypothesis of this inquiry in the light of his theology. Does he support a theological concept of 'being in Christ' with the help of a concept of 'representation' in so far as its Christological side is concerned?

Although O'Donovan does not explicitly reflect on the concept of 'being in Christ,' it is evident that the concept of 'representation' is very central to his Christology, if not *the* central concept. The matter of 'being in Christ' is also present, although he does not often use the words 'being-

114. O'Donovan, *Resurrection and Moral Order*, 56–57; O'Donovan, *On the Thirty Nine Articles*, 34–35.

115. O'Donovan, *Resurrection and Moral Order*, 14–15.

in-Christ.'[116] It is evidently in line with his theology to develop a concept of 'being in Christ' using the concept of representation.

Much has been said already on his concept of representation, especially in its use in reference to Christ as representative of his people and of humanity. That a moment of inclusiveness is present may be evident. What has not yet been said is that the concept of representation is a central concept in O'Donovan's description of the objective reality.[117] O'Donovan follows Karl Barth in differentiating between the work of Christ and the Spirit using the words 'objective' and 'subjective.' The reality of the representative is the objective reality that determines the subjective reality of believers. In Christ, what it is to be human is determined, participating in the vindicated and transformed moral order, living under the reign of God's kingdom. From our point of view, Jesus Christ as representative (including his subjectivity) is the objective reality.[118]

Apart from this, something still has to be said on the exclusive moment to test the hypothesis formulated in 1.2.6. In relation to this exclusive moment, three concepts are important: the concept of representation in so far as it is used for Jesus Christ as representing God, the concept of substitution, and the concept of judgment.

First, the concept of representation is used in a double sense as we have seen already. Jesus Christ also represents God to his people. Again this is a political representation. When concentrating on the representation of God's rule, it is worth noting that O'Donovan sometimes writes about a double representation, and sometimes reserves the concept of representation for the representative individual that represents his people, distinguishing this representative role from the mediating role of the king. Sometimes the king represents both God and his people, sometimes the king does not represent but only mediates God's rule.[119] In any case, it may be clear that Jesus Christ represents or mediates God's rule. The triumph of Jesus Christ is also the triumph of the kingdom of God. The principali-

116. He does so e.g. in O'Donovan, *Resurrection and Moral Order*, 24.

117. The first part of his *Resurrection and Moral Order* is titled 'The objective reality.'

118. O'Donovan, *Resurrection and Moral Order*, 24, 101–2, 109.

119. For the idea of the double representation, see O'Donovan, *The Desire of the Nations*, 61, 134; O'Donovan, *Common Objects of Love*, 44, 56; for the distinction between the king as mediator of God's rule and the representative individual representing the people, see O'Donovan, *The Desire of the Nations*, 123. Cf. also footnote 30.

ties and powers have been disarmed in the victory of Jesus Christ.[120] In *Common Objects of Love*, O'Donovan shows the liberating effect of this representation. Only a real image of God can liberate human societies from idolatry to other political representations, hence making a universal society possible. 'We must become actual members of a real community constituted by the real and present image of God as unique lord, and the real and present image of mankind as subject uniquely to God.'[121] The representation of humanity does not suffice. We need a representation of God also to liberate mankind of its idols. In Christ both representations are realised.[122] This double concept of representation shows that both the inclusive and the exclusive moment are present in O'Donovan. Both even need each other.

Second, O'Donovan's use of the concept of substitution shows his ambivalence regarding this concept. O'Donovan clearly rejects the idea of substitution if this amounts to the isolation of one moment of the representative act. Used in isolation, the concept of substitution is misleading. He criticises the Anselmic tradition for being unable to do justice to the resurrection. Further the cross cannot be understood as a 'voluntary act of heroism,' for this gives the cross 'the appearance of a new, pioneering achievement.' Instead, the cross was the suffering of an age-old fate, and not an action in reversal of man's plight but in identification with it.[123] Together with Dorothee Sölle, he rejects a concept of substitution understood as replacement. Positively, he describes substitution as a concept identifying 'one of the two necessary poles of the representative role, the point of initiative and innovation.'[124] In this way, substitution is understood as the exclusive moment of the representative act. This concept of substitution, interpreted as innovation and initiative, includes both person- and work-substitution. Christ suffered as a propitiation for the sins of mankind, as we have seen. In his death, Christ suffered 'the judgment

120. O'Donovan, *The Desire of the Nations*, 146–47.

121. O'Donovan, *Common Objects of Love*, 44.

122. O'Donovan, *Common Objects of Love*, 44, 54–57; O'Donovan, *The Ways of Judgment*, 159, 184; De Bruijne, *Levend in Leviatan*, 98–100.

123. O'Donovan, *On the Thirty Nine Articles*, 30–32.

124. O'Donovan, *The Desire of the Nations*, 127; and further 126.

invoked by others' guilt';[125] God condemned sin in the flesh.[126] This condemnation of sin leads to the third concept.

For thirdly, in the death and resurrection of Jesus Christ, God acts, condemning sin and creating a new reality by his performative judgment, a new reality even implying objective justice as we have seen. In a juridical and even ontological sense, a new state of affairs has come into being. After this judgment only one thing has to be done, the realisation of the implications of this judgment. This again emphasises the exclusiveness of Jesus Christ and his representative act.

Summarizing, an inclusive and an exclusive moment are present. They cannot be separated but belong together, as two poles of one concept. The exclusive moment is identified in three concepts: the representation or mediation of God's rule, substitution and the judgment of God.

9.3 Soteriology

After having investigated the Christological, objective side of O'Donovan's contribution to the development of a concept of 'being in Christ,' it is now time to continue with the pneumatological, subjective side. In this subjective side the concept of participation is a central one. In the first section of this paragraph I will deal generally with the concept of participation (9.3.1). Secondly I will elaborate how according to O'Donovan the church participates in the different moments of the representative act (9.3.2). Finally three soteriological images will be discussed, justification, election and adoption (9.3.3).

9.3.1 PARTICIPATION

In Christ, Israel, humanity and creation are restored and transformed eschatologically. God's kingdom has triumphed. The Christian life must respond to this reality. It is not self-evident that this response does not amount to a superhuman effort, and that the message of Jesus Christ is a good message indeed. It is also not logical that this restoration, which has taken place independently of us, is relevant to our subjective existence. That the apostolic message is definitely evangelical is the work of the Holy

125. O'Donovan, *The Desire of the Nations*, 136.

126. O'Donovan, *Resurrection and Moral Order*, 14, 23, 74; O'Donovan, *The Desire of the Nations*, 136; O'Donovan, *The Ways of Judgment*, 107–8.

Spirit. It is the Spirit who makes participation possible, being its ground, and not the church or the sacraments.[127]

With regard to this concept of participation, it is noteworthy that in O'Donovan's use of the concept we participate in different things. Believers will participate in the moral order,[128] in Christ's authority within the created order,[129] in the redeemed or restored creation,[130] 'in the life of the one who reveals himself as love,'[131] in the cross of Christ,[132] in the righteousness of Christ,[133] in the eternal purpose which the Father has for the Son,[134] in the representative act,[135] in the Christ-event,[136] and in the coming of the Kingdom.[137] It might seem now that the concept of participation is a very broad one. However, it has a focus in Jesus Christ. To participate in the new creation is for ever participation in Christ.[138] All other things in which we participate are included in this participation in Christ, the representative.

This participation concerns subjective reality. However, the characterisation as subjective does not intend to make object and subject lose their relational sense. Instead, subjective reality is not a different reality from objective reality. Participation only concerns the realisation of the implications of the representative act. The Spirit does not add something to what is accomplished in Christ, but takes from what is his. He speaks what he hears and glorifies Jesus. The redeemed creation is 'apart from us (in Christ and once for all),' 'but includes us and enables us to participate in it,' immediately engaging us 'through the Spirit here (and now).'[139]

127. O'Donovan, *Resurrection and Moral Order*, 101; O'Donovan, *On the Thirty Nine Articles*, 42–44, 125; O'Donovan, *The Desire of the Nations*, 129.

128. O'Donovan, *Resurrection and Moral Order*, 22, 25, 76, 87, 94, 95, 247, 248.

129. O'Donovan, *Resurrection and Moral Order*, 24.

130. O'Donovan, *Resurrection and Moral Order*, 101, 249.

131. O'Donovan, *Resurrection and Moral Order*, 246.

132. O'Donovan, 'Evangelicalism and the Foundations of Ethics,' 103.

133. O'Donovan, *On the Thirty Nine Articles*, 77.

134. O'Donovan, *On the Thirty Nine Articles*, 77.

135. O'Donovan, *The Desire of the Nations*, 129.

136. O'Donovan, *The Desire of the Nations*, 174.

137. O'Donovan, *The Desire of the Nations*, 146, 161.

138. O'Donovan, *Resurrection and Moral Order*, 150.

139. O'Donovan, *Resurrection and Moral Order*, 101 and 109, and further 102, 140–41; O'Donovan, *On the Thirty Nine Articles*, 42–44, 79, 123–25.

The distinction objective-subjective might arouse questions concerning the position of the church in participation. O'Donovan has been wrestling with a post-liberal emphasis on the church, but maintains a Protestant position. The work of God in Christ must precede the church and the individual.[140] Further he unmistakably distinguishes the Holy Spirit from the church. [141] With regard to the relationship individual—church, his position has seen development. In *Resurrection and Moral Order* (1986), he chose the order individual—church, which he regards later as unsatisfactory, as he writes in the preface to its second edition (1994).[142] It seems that O'Donovan gradually became more aware of the importance of the church. In *On the Thirty Nine Articles* (1986) already a tendency toward a more ecclesiological accent can be discovered, in his exposition of election, church and the sacraments.[143] In *The Desire of the Nations* (1996) the church has the primacy, for this book concerns the political character of the community of the church. But the primacy of the community in this book not only serves his political interest, for the primacy of the community over the individual has a more general character.[144] However, he remains critical of a post-liberal communitarism, as becomes clear in the final chapter of *The Ways of Judgment*. Church and subject are in need of each other. He writes, 'the subject is realised in the church, the church completed in the subject.'[145] One might conclude that the soteriological framework surrounding the concepts representation and participation is Christ—Spirit—Church/Individual.

O'Donovan distinguishes various aspect of this enabling to participate through the Spirit. In elaborating this work of the Spirit, O'Donovan builds on the centrality of the concept of judgment as we have discovered it in relation to his concept of representation. The following aspects can be distinguished:

a. God the Father has given authority to Jesus, raising him from the dead. In this judgment of the Father lies the origin of the authority

140. O'Donovan, *Resurrection and Moral Order*, xviii–xx, 164.

141. O'Donovan, *Resurrection and Moral Order*, 106–7; O'Donovan, *On the Thirty Nine Articles*, 42.

142. O'Donovan, *Resurrection and Moral Order*, xix.

143. O'Donovan, *On the Thirty Nine Articles*, 86, 91–93, 128.

144. O'Donovan, *The Desire of the Nations*, 73; cf. De Bruijne, *Levend in Leviatan*, 74.

145. O'Donovan, *The Ways of Judgment*, 314; and further 312–15.

of Christ. The exaltation of the Son of man, in which the Father confers authority upon Jesus, is what we call also the Kingdom of God. In the exaltation of Christ, God has authorised a public event: it is located in the public realm, and has a meaning which is open to speech and thought. Consequently, the authority of God in Christ is not incommunicable.[146]

b. The Holy Spirit makes this reality present to us. The cross and resurrection of Jesus Christ are events in the past and Jesus himself is absent from us. The universal manifestation of their saving significance belongs to the future. It is the Holy Spirit who makes the reality of Jesus Christ present to us and us to it. 'The work of the Holy Spirit defines an age—the age in which all times are immediately present to that time, the time of Christ.' O'Donovan refers to Kierkegaard's idea of the 'absolute contemporaneousness with Christ.'[147]

c. The Spirit makes this reality of redemption, the reality of Jesus Christ, authoritative to us, so that it comes to claim us. He will convict the world concerning sin, righteousness and judgment. This reality is present in the mode of authority. Redemption in Christ is God's final, eschatological act, and in the eschaton history is given its meaning. As such the different redemptive moments 'stand equidistant from all moments of time and determine what the reality of each moment is.' Hence this reality exercises its authority over the already existing reality; it has the power to determine the present reality of our world.[148]

d. The Spirit evokes our free response to this reality. Asking after this free response is asking about the 'fruits of the Spirit.' We are included in the reality of salvation and enabled to participate in it. This means that 'the renewal of the universe touches me at the point where I am a moral agent.' The external reality of salvation is internalised. '(P)sychological barriers which prevent us from responding to God's deeds' are removed and we are liberated 'from

146. O'Donovan, *Resurrection and Moral Order*, 140–42.

147. O'Donovan, *Resurrection and Moral Order*, 103; and further 102, 140, 163; O'Donovan, *On the Thirty Nine Articles*, 43, 126; O'Donovan, *The Ways of Judgment*, 87; De Bruijne, *Levend in Leviatan*, 40, 43, 65; and 163–68 more general on the relation O'Donovan-Kierkegaard.

148. O'Donovan, *Resurrection and Moral Order*, 103; and further 104–5, 109, 121.

the incapacity to obey.'[149] We are made free to act again in accordance with reality. The dividedness of will and reason is recreated, the will is detached from its self-chosen orientation, and reason is, by repentance, brought to the commitment of faith. '(R)eason and will together are turned from arbitrariness to reality.'[150] This must not be understood causally or deterministically, for belief is not inauthentic but a decision of man in one sense. But O'Donovan warns us not to overestimate the human capacity of decision. God has to evoke the existential act of belief through the Holy Spirit. However, this liberation of the will would be misunderstood if only the work of the Spirit were mentioned. The gift of subjective freedom is 'an aspect of our being-in-Christ.' The freedom which the Spirit gives us is the freedom of Christ.[151]

e. The Holy Spirit not only gives us the possibility to act freely, but also makes us participate in the authority of Christ. The church is united with the authorisation of Jesus Christ in his exaltation. In the Spirit the church participates in the representative act. In this way the Spirit gives 'social form to the triumph of Christ.'[152] This implies that we are no longer slaves, but sons. We are no longer under the law, but are free to do what we were not permitted to do before, sharing in the position of Christ within the moral order, the position of dominion as lord over creation. The Spirit gives legitimacy to the existence of the church, effect to its mission and right to its various relations. As a result of this authorisation, the church has its own authority and is a political society which is 'not answerable to any other authority.'[153]

It may be clear that in this reconstruction, concepts like authority and authorisation play a central role. That this is the case especially in *Resurrection and Moral Order* and in *The Desire of the Nations* can be un-

149. O'Donovan, *Resurrection and Moral Order*, 23; 101, 182.

150. O'Donovan, *Resurrection and Moral Order*, 113, 111–12.

151. O'Donovan, *Resurrection and Moral Order*, 24; 101–2, 109, 140; O'Donovan, *On the Thirty Nine Articles*, 44, 73–74.

152. O'Donovan, *The Desire of the Nations*, 161.

153. O'Donovan, *The Desire of the Nations*, 159; and further O'Donovan, *Resurrection and Moral Order*, 24–25; O'Donovan, *On the Thirty Nine Articles*, 97–98, 111–12; O'Donovan, *The Desire of the Nations*, 159, 161, 169, 174.

derstood if O'Donovan's interests are made explicit. In *Resurrection and Moral Order*, he sketches an outline for evangelical ethics. In this context he wants to make clear that objective reality is an authoritative reality and that a Christian participates in the position of Christ within the moral order. In *The Desire of the Nations*, O'Donovan argues for the political character of the church. To have such a political character, the church has to be authorised. These specific moral and political interests focus the participation-concept. Further, authorisation is especially important concerning participation in Christ's resurrection and glorification, but less concerning the participation in his suffering. In *On the Thirty Nine Articles*, the idea of the authorisation of the church is present also, but this book has a more general character. As a result, the question concerning participation also has a more general character and the concept of authority and authorisation do not play that central role. Here e.g. the concept of communication is used.[154]

The gift of the Spirit has the character of a first and incomplete anticipation on our complete eschatological participation in Christ, the final enjoyment of salvation. O'Donovan uses the concept of anticipation in a pneumatological context, not in a Christological one; Christ is the *eschatos* and not an anticipation of the end. The present is dependent on the future and universal manifestation of Christ's glory. In hope, 'that future is present . . . by anticipation; it encourages us and sustains us by promising to our present experience' a final completion. In faith however, we 'conceive that future as something apart from our present, wholly independent of it.'[155] We have our existence in the middle of the end, between the last things and the last things. We live in an eschatological frame, with the resurrection of Jesus Christ behind us and ahead the full appearance of salvation. We do not know what we shall be, for the only model for a description of this new life is concealed from our sight by a cloud at ascension. The Christian life is a life *in Christ*, with a hidden and waiting character. The existence of the church has a secret foundation and its essential nature is hidden also. An apophatic element in what we say about the future is inescapable. Despite its hidden character and its secret foundation, the gift of the Spirit as earnest of our inheritance already points us forward to the end. The eschatological reality already has a transforming,

154. Cf. O'Donovan, *On the Thirty Nine Articles*, 43, 77, 79. On communication, see De Bruijne, *Levend in Leviatan*, 101–4.

155. O'Donovan, *Resurrection and Moral Order*, 247.

formative effect. The hidden reality of salvation receives a public form in the sacraments. And the status of believers as God's children is not merely a name, but a present eschatological reality, despite our waiting for its final disclosure. The eschatological gift was given once and for all in Christ. The present existence of the children of God is 'a mode of existence which is already ours, yet not fully clear to us, and which is, before it can be our mode of existence, Christ's mode of existence.'[156] Only the moment of universal manifestation of salvation will bring complete participation in Christ; until then the Spirit is the first gift of the end.[157]

Summarizing, by the Holy Spirit believers participate in Christ and in the reality of salvation he constitutes. In this participation, that does not add something to the representative act, the implications of the Christ event are realised. Just as in the concept of representation, in participation also the concepts of judgment and authority are important. God the Father makes the reality of Jesus Christ authoritative; the Holy Spirit makes this reality present and authoritative for us. He evokes our free response to this reality, by letting us participate in the freedom of Christ. This freedom of Christ also implies the authorisation of the church to participate in the authority of Jesus Christ. Because the Spirit is given as anticipation of full participation in Christ, we wait for the full manifestation of the reality of salvation.

9.3.2 RECAPITULATION OF THE REPRESENTATIVE ACT

Our relation with Christ is not a formless relation. Instead, the relation of the church to the Christ event, to which the Spirit admits, is formed as a recapitulation of the Christ-event. It is not the biographical shape of the life of believers that determines the form of the relation, as was the case in Roman Catholic theology of justification and sacraments, but the form of the Christ event itself. It is not an external narrative that gives coherence, but its coherence is the inner logic of the Christ-narrative. O'Donovan

156. O'Donovan, *Resurrection and Moral Order*, 260.

157. O'Donovan, *Resurrection and Moral Order*, 22, 247, 249, 258–59; O'Donovan, *On the Thirty Nine Articles*, 38, 42; O'Donovan, *The Desire of the Nations*, 146, 166, 182; O'Donovan, 'Response to Daniel Carroll R.,' 145; O'Donovan, *The Ways of Judgment*, 86.

According to Carroll, O'Donovan's eschatology lacks a sustained exposition of the 'not yet.' In the light of what has been said on the Spirit as merely anticipation of the full enjoyment of salvation, this criticism has to be modified. Against Carroll, 'The Power of the Future in the Present,' 123.

does not intend to exclude a concept of Christian progress and make individual biography irrelevant, but our biographies do not determine the shape of the relation with Christ. We participate in the new creation by conformity to Jesus Christ and by *imitatio Christi*. In this recapitulation the community participates in the acts and experiences which the representative first undertook. In describing the narrative shape of the relation, O'Donovan uses the same four moments as heuristic guide as he has used in his description of the representative act: Advent, Passion, Restoration and Exaltation. The church participates in these four moments at the same time as they are internally (Christologically) related. However, the shape of the relationship with Christ is not merely narrative, but also sacramental. The sacraments give the church its institutional form and order. They are effective signs of the mystery of redemption in Christ, which make this mystery palpable in the participating church. The hidden mystery of salvation receives a public form in the sacraments. In this way, we are assured publically in our ambiguous existence that the redemptive grace of God is active in our world. Each of the moments is related to a sacrament as we will see. Hence the sacraments receive their place within a Christological and ecclesiological framework.[158]

Before dealing with the different moments again, the question arises as to how these moments relate to Pentecost. O'Donovan distinguishes Pentecost emphatically from the four moments of the narrative of the Christ-event, as if Pentecost would be a fifth moment. As a result, Pentecost does not have the 'once for all' character that the Christ-event has. The descent of the Spirit is not accomplished forever in the first filling of the apostles. Ascension is the sign of the accomplished and finished work of Christ, not a penultimate or antepenultimate occurrence to which something has to be added. The representative act in which the church is represented, is complete; Pentecost makes it possible to participate in this act in the Holy Spirit. Pentecost is not a supplement to the ascension, but a fruit of it. Christ shares his triumph with humanity and gives his Spirit as a consequence of his coronation. Because the ascension is already the

158. O'Donovan, *Resurrection and Moral Order*, xviii, 95, 249, 259; O'Donovan, *On the Thirty Nine Articles*, 80–81, 126–29; O'Donovan, *The Desire of the Nations*, 171–72, 191. See further De Bruijne, *Levend in Leviatan*, 52–54.

In *On the Thirty Nine Articles* (127–28) O'Donovan announces the program developed in *The Desire of the Nations*, relating four sacraments with the four moments of the representative act.

triumph of the Kingdom of God, Pentecost is an anticipation of the coming Kingdom, a downpayment of our inheritance. Christian faith and experience are in this way coextensive with the Holy Spirit. An important aspect of Pentecost is the authorisation of the church to participate in the authority of Christ as we have seen. However, although Pentecost is related immediately to Ascension, the recapitulation in the Spirit concerns not only this fourth moment, but the whole saving event with its four different moments. Pentecost is not an isolated moment, 'but sums up the whole Christ-event.'[159]

Participating in Christ, the church participates in the four moments. I will now describe how O'Donovan elaborates this recapitulation of the four moments of the representative act. Remarkably, O'Donovan not only shows that the church participates in this recapitulation. The witness of the church in society gives society the opportunity to be reshaped, becoming affected by the narrative structure of the Christ-event. Furthermore, modernity as a child of Christianity is interpreted by O'Donovan in its last phase as a parodic and corrupt development of Christian social order. Hence O'Donovan gives in *The Desire of the Nations* three sketches of the influence of the Christ-event, once in its recapitulation in the church, once in a description of liberal society, and once in a critique of modernity.[160] I will concentrate on the first, for this is the relevant one in relation to 'being in Christ.'

Participating in the first moment of Advent, the church is a gathering community. This gathering started immediately after the baptism of Jesus as the disciples of the Baptist started to follow Jesus. The church can only exist as a community that is always gathering, continually adding to its membership from all people, leaping over all existing communal boundaries. The mission of the church is the implication of this aspect of the being of the church. This gathering continues until the coming of the Kingdom is complete. The centre of this movement is Jesus and the confession that he is the Christ, the son of the living God. As a result, the act of faith corresponds to the advent moment.[161] Each believer has to

159. O'Donovan, *The Desire of the Nations*, 161; see further O'Donovan, *Resurrection and Moral Order*, xvii–xviii; O'Donovan, *On the Thirty Nine Articles*, 42–46; O'Donovan, *The Desire of the Nations*, 162, 171.

160. O'Donovan, *The Desire of the Nations*, 249–52, 271–75.

161. O'Donovan, *Resurrection and Moral Order*, xvii; O'Donovan, *The Desire of the Nations*, 134, 175–76;

make this confession, for it is the criterion of the church's membership. The church has the authority 'to recognise those who gather and to claim them for the community.'[162] The unity of the church lies in this confession, that is an acknowledgment and acceptance that in Christ final judgment has arrived. What remains to the church is to discern the implications of this judgment, 'demonstrating transforming righteousness and discriminating between the works done in Christ and those done in defiance of him.'[163] The sign that marks the gathering community is baptism. In accepting baptism, a believer 'accepts Jesus as his or her representative, and accepts Jesus' people as his or her people.'[164]

The second moment of Passion corresponds to the suffering of the church. The church is engaged in the same conflict with the principalities and powers as Christ was, overcoming them. 'The church stands at the heart of the contradiction of the end-time,' between 'the new order restored in Christ' and 'the old array of rebellion, chaos and death.'[165] Living as a Christian involves obedient suffering in the pattern of the suffering of Christ himself. '(J)oyful and obedient participation in the moral order must conflict with disobedience,' the false excluding the true.[166] Conformity to Christ includes even conformity to his death. This suffering has two different aspects, the exclusion from life on earth, culminating in martyrdom, and the mortification of those aspects of our own nature 'which are inclined to compromise "upon the earth."'[167]

The first aspect concerns the exclusion from life on earth and from created good. This exclusion may be caused by our own fallen humanity or by others. The church stands in a conflict: a controversy against humanity, in which the church struggles for humanity. Standing in this struggle, the church is authorised to 'to confront and overcome resistance to God's saving will by enduring suffering. . . .' O'Donovan mentions different kinds of this suffering, like 'pressure that an unbelieving society puts on the church,' 'worries over the welfare of the church and the frus-

162. O'Donovan, *The Desire of the Nations*, 176.

163. O'Donovan, *The Desire of the Nations*, 177.

164. O'Donovan, *The Desire of the Nations*, 178; O'Donovan, *On the Thirty Nine Articles*, 127.

165. O'Donovan, 'Evangelicalism and the Foundations of Ethics,' 105.

166. O'Donovan, *Resurrection and Moral Order*, 94.

167. O'Donovan, *Resurrection and Moral Order*, 95–96; xvii, 249; O'Donovan, *The Ways of Judgment*, 294.

trations of physical weakness and mortality.' This suffering is vicarious, for it is undertaken for the benefits of others. This is the case very obviously in suffering following directly out of the Christian mission. O'Donovan writes of a chain of suffering, which originates in Christ and in which each 'suffers for the welfare of others' and 'each benefits from others' suffering.' Suffering, the church imitates the suffering of Christ in its double representation: the suffering of the church represents the innocence of God whom the world judges and the guilt of mankind, whom God judges. As such, the church witnesses to the righteous God and to the sin of the world. This witness-character resulted in the rise of the word 'martyr.' What we now call martyrdom is the final consequence of this conflict, when nothing else is left over, as a testimony to God's faithfulness.[168]

The second aspect concerns the mortification of the flesh. This is the work of the Spirit who makes us participate in the death of Christ, leading believers whom he inhabits 'in ways that accomplish the "death" of the "flesh."'[169] We have to abandon the 'I' that had hitherto been our project to realise. Our 'I' 'becomes to us the "old man" who . . . is crucified with Christ,' something which involves 'a moment of self-annihilation.'[170]

The Eucharist is the sign marking the suffering community. This sacrament is effective in the formation of the community of the church, determining its identity in relation to the passion of Christ. The church is the community of believers who have died with Christ. The Eucharist is not, according to O'Donovan, an individualistic feeding on the living Christ, seated in heaven on the right hand of God, but a participation in the cross and death of Christ. Another aspect colours the relation to his cross: its opening to the eschatological Kingdom. A 're-enacting of Christ's death' could not be 'without its affirmation of divine victory.'[171]

Participation in the resurrection concerns two aspects, a present aspect of joy and a future aspect of hope. I will concentrate first on the present aspect. The church is a glad community in response to Christ's resurrection. This gladness is essential to keep the church from pathology

168. Quotations are all taken from O'Donovan, *The Desire of the Nations*, 179. See further 178–80, 256; O'Donovan, *Resurrection and Moral Order*, 94–96; O'Donovan, 'Evangelicalism and the Foundations of Ethics,' 106; O'Donovan, *The Just War Revisited*, 10.

169. O'Donovan, *The Desire of the Nations*, 129.

170. O'Donovan, *Resurrection and Moral Order*, 112; and further 94–96, 112, 249.

171. O'Donovan, *The Desire of the Nations*, 181; and further 180; O'Donovan, *On the Thirty Nine Articles*, 127.

if it suffers injustice. We may note here that this shows that the church participates in the four moments at the same time. The church 'has to live in the gladness of the resurrection, while it still suffers the hostility of the cross.'[172] At the same time it shares in the death and resurrection of Jesus Christ. That the shape of the relation with Christ is not biographical but Christological as we saw, has this consequence that the recapitulation of the four moments takes place at the same time.

The risk of pathology is evident, for a community finding its identity in unjust treatment by others comes to depend on this injustice. The joy, found in her participation in the resurrection, together with the forgiving of its enemies, guards against this pathology. On the one hand O'Donovan writes that by forgiving enemies, the church is able 'to sustain its Easter joy in conflict.'[173] On the other hand he writes later that joy provides the church with a position of strength in which 'it has no need of the oppressors' oppression, and so can offer reconciliation.'[174] Whether joy or forgiveness has the primacy, it is clear that both in their relation are necessary to keep the church from a dependency on injustice. In this way the enemy is liberated from his power, in the resurrection faith that all rebellion against God has been defeated.[175]

The resurrection of Jesus Christ is a source of joy, for it concerns the restoration of creation. But gladness does not just belong to created life as such, more has to be said. This gladness is related to the moral order. Not only is creation restored but necessarily also its order, for according to O'Donovan creation is ordered. 'Gladness belongs essentially to the creature,' in the case of human beings even to our place within the moral order. Joy is a 'moral attitude,' 'appropriate to the recognition of God's creative goodness,' without which the order of creation cannot be restored.[176] This means that in Christ humanity is restored in the recovery of original joy and that the gladness of the church is the gladness of Jesus Christ himself for in him the renewed order of creation is present. Hence not the cross, but the resurrection and the gladness belonging to it constitute the point

172. O'Donovan, 'Evangelicalism and the Foundations of Ethics,' 106; O'Donovan, *The Desire of the Nations*, 181.

173. O'Donovan, 'Evangelicalism and the Foundations of Ethics,' 106.

174. O'Donovan, *The Desire of the Nations*, 181. Cf. O'Donovan, 'Gerechtigkeit und Urteil,' 14; O'Donovan, *The Just War Revisited*, 5.

175. O'Donovan, *The Desire of the Nations*, 181.

176. O'Donovan, *The Desire of the Nations*, 181.

of departure for the Christian life and ethics. Discipleship is primarily participation in the resurrection although it involves also participation in the cross of Christ. Christian morality is the morality of a new creation in Christ. Living with the fulfilment of the law, the law written on our hearts, we may now, in Christ, live and act acceptably to God. However, it remains open whether believers participate in this delightful life. 'It remains an open question for these members of the church whether their lives will be shaped by that exalted delight which is participation in the new creation of God, or whether they will be shaped by the old and habitual dispositions of the affections.'[177]

The second aspect of participation in the resurrection of Christ concerns the future. In Christ's resurrection we see the resurrection of the whole human race. The first born from the dead is raised with the promise that all shall be made alive. The general resurrection of the dead is a future event, part of the public manifestation of the salvation we wait for.[178]

Finally, the sign of the resurrection gladness is the keeping of the Lord's Day. Just as the Sabbath celebrated the comprehensive completeness of creation, the Lord's Day marks the acceptance of Christ's work and the completion and re-creation of creation order. At the same time, this day marks the identity of the community; the church receives its identity in participating in the fulfilment.[179]

Finally the church participates in the fourth moment. As in the resurrection-moment, we here discover again and even more explicitly the tension between the yet and not-yet.

Regarding the present, Christians participate in the position of Christ within the moral order, the position of humanity within creation. This position is the place of 'dominion.' This includes a participation in the authority of Christ, by virtue of which we are no longer slaves but sons. Now humanity is no longer in a subservient position under the law, for this puts him in a different relation to the natural order, 'humbly and proudly

177. O'Donovan, *The Desire of the Nations*, 182; and further O'Donovan, *Resurrection and Moral Order*, xviii, 14–15; O'Donovan, 'Evangelicalism and the Foundations of Ethics,' 96–97, 103–5; O'Donovan, *The Desire of the Nations*, 181–83; O'Donovan, 'Gerechtigkeit und Urteil,' 13.

178. O'Donovan, *Resurrection and Moral Order*, 15, 33, 249; O'Donovan, *On the Thirty Nine Articles*, 39–40; O'Donovan, 'Evangelicalism and the Foundations of Ethics,' 97; O'Donovan, *The Desire of the Nations*, 127.

179. O'Donovan, *On the Thirty Nine Articles*, 127; O'Donovan, *The Desire of the Nations*, 186.

in command.' Man is allowed 'to make moral responses creatively.'[180] This position is also the position needed for adequate knowledge. Christian knowledge is 'knowledge from man's position in the universe,' grounded in Christ's human being.[181] At the same time O'Donovan emphasises that dominion easily becomes domination. True knowledge is challenged constantly by false forms of reality. Therefore we need the Spirit who forms and brings to expression the appropriate pattern of free response to objective reality. Further, our present participation within this position is only an anticipation of our complete participation, but this concerns the future aspect with which I will deal below.[182]

Moreover, the church is authorised to speak the words of God. This includes prophecy, 'the speech that God addresses to mankind' and prayer, 'the speech that he invites mankind to address to him.' The church participates in the glory of Christ, his heavenly position at the right hand of the Father and is authorised to 'deploy the powers of the Kingdom of God.'[183] These powers are displayed through speech, for God's Kingdom becomes a reality by his word. Prophecy is according to O'Donovan 'to speak a word from God to the church as it is placed here and now; to declare that the present situation is this and not that.'[184] Prophecy is impossible without a careful reading of the scriptures, for it shows the light that the scriptures shed on the present. In this way however, something new is discovered. In prayer, the church asks God to let his power work in itself and in the world surrounding it. Prayers 'seek only one thing, the final manifestation of God's rule on earth.'[185]

Regarding the future, participation in the fourth moment evidently shows the incompleteness of our participation in Christ. Our life in Christ, the new creation is hidden and indescribable as we have seen already.[186]

The sign of the empowerment of the church is the laying-on of hands. Doing this, the church asks her heavenly Lord for the manifestation of his gifts in its individual members. It shows that the church is

180. O'Donovan, *Resurrection and Moral Order*, 24; and further 22, 25.

181. O'Donovan, *Resurrection and Moral Order*, 81; and further 25, 76.

182. O'Donovan, *Resurrection and Moral Order*, 22, 87, 94, 140, 146.

183. O'Donovan, *The Desire of the Nations*, 186–87. Cf. O'Donovan, *Resurrection and Moral Order*, xvii.

184. O'Donovan, *The Desire of the Nations*, 188.

185. O'Donovan, *The Desire of the Nations*, 189.

186. See footnote 156 and 157.

authorised to invoke 'the powers of the age to come' and ask for the gift of the Holy Spirit. In different situations (new membership, threat of illness and death, particular tasks of great difficulty) it supplicates God to make his power effective. Because it singles out a particular member, this sign protects against collectivism.[187]

Summarizing, the gift of the Holy Spirit at Pentecost is a consequence of the representative act, culminating in the glorification of Christ. Pentecost has to be distinguished from the representative act, for it does not complete this act but is its consequence. Pentecost does not have the 'once for all' character that this act has. The shape of the participation in Christ through the Spirit is a narrative-sacramental one, formed by the narrative of the Christ-event itself. The representative act of Christ is recapitulated in the church by her participation in Christ. All four moments of the Christ-narrative return in the Christian existence. The moment of Advent returns in the gathering of the church in faith around the sign of baptism. Participating in the moment of the cross, the church is a suffering community, in martyrdom—a suffering with a vicarious character—as well as in mortification of the flesh. The sign of this participation is the sacrament of the Eucharist. In the last two moments the tension between the yet and not yet becomes explicit. Sharing in the resurrection of Christ, the church lives a new joyful life, but waits also for the resurrection of the flesh. In communion with the exaltation of Christ, Christians share in the position of Christ, authorised to live in freedom as sons and to speak the word of God. At the same time we wait for the complete manifestation of the new creation, which is now hidden in God. O'Donovan relates the third moment with the keeping of the Lord's Day, the fourth with the laying-on of hands.

9.3.3 JUSTIFICATION, ELECTION AND ADOPTION

Having examined our participation in Christ as a participation in the history of Jesus Christ, I now turn to O'Donovan's use of three soteriological images, justification, election and adoption, to see whether he relates them with the concept of participation.

187. O'Donovan, *On the Thirty Nine Articles*, 127; O'Donovan, *The Desire of the Nations*, 190.

The doctrine of justification concerns the question 'how we participate in the righteousness of Christ,' O'Donovan writes.[188] We participate in the representative act of Jesus' death and resurrection. Justification is participation in God's acceptance of Christ. As a result, we find that justification is not only *sola fide*, but rather that *solus Christus* has to be especially emphasised. The God-man relation exists thank to its 'middle-term,' Jesus Christ, 'the effective agent of God and the representative of man.' We are justified in 'moral union' with him.[189] Only in him, not apart from him are we acceptable and accepted. The transaction of the representative from death to life was 'a final and decisive act of history.'[190] Therefore, God has revealed his final judgment in the cross and resurrection of Jesus Christ. Even the material for this final judgment is present in Christ. God has spoken his word upon creation in the person of its head, in whom all and everything are represented. This word is 'God's final decision on mankind,' 'decisively creative for all ages before and after.' In accepting Jesus Christ, God has accepted the whole of humanity.[191] God has spoken his 'Yes' to humanity in Christ and 'No' to all which refuses and denies him, to all which detracts from him. Justification is finished and accomplished in world-history with the death and resurrection of Jesus Christ. All is finished and complete; what still has to be done is the realisation of the implications of what has been accomplished. God's decision in the resurrection of Christ, the representative, is a final decision.[192]

Because God's judgment in Christ and the future judgment of God are closely related, justification has at the same time a past and a future character. The divine judgment in man's favour is complete in Christ. At the same time, the present is ambiguous and incomplete and we wait for the hope of righteousness. The eschatological judgment of God in Christ is an 'invasive reality'[193] which touches and shapes human lives. The present time is a time for the realisation of the implications of God's judgment, until this judgement is finally manifest.[194]

188. O'Donovan, *On the Thirty Nine Articles*, 77.

189. O'Donovan, *On the Thirty Nine Articles*, 78–79.

190. O'Donovan, *The Desire of the Nations*, 129; O'Donovan, *On the Thirty Nine Articles*, 79–80.

191. O'Donovan, *Resurrection and Moral Order*, 255.

192. O'Donovan, *Resurrection and Moral Order*, 255–56.

193. O'Donovan, *Resurrection and Moral Order*, 258.

194. O'Donovan, *Resurrection and Moral Order*, 253–54.

The idea of God's judgment as an invasive reality has several implications. First, we contribute nothing to our justification. We are justified by faith and apart from works, which means that justification 'is the foundation of possible works of love and presupposes none of them.'[195] Neither me nor the Spirit, add anything to what has been accomplished in Christ. Therefore the Reformers said that we are *accounted* righteous, not made righteous.[196]

Second, the meaning of the lives of believers, however ambiguous they may be, is determined exclusively by God's justifying judgment. This is not the case for biographical reasons, but because we encounter in Jesus Christ the decisive reality which must shape our life whenever we meet it. There is no 'before justification' in the life of a believer, for justification is the death and resurrection of Jesus Christ. A biographical concept of justification fails to grasp the eschatological dimension of justification in Christ. The choice for or against God's new creation in Christ is decisive. 'The final question is whether this life, this act, this character, belong to the renewed and transformed world which God is bringing into being, and that question can be answered only in terms of the relation to Christ in whom the transformed world is already present to us.'[197] This implies that we have no 'ongoing encounter with transgression.'[198] We must understand our lives as totally renewed, free of the reign of sin. We cannot live at the same time in the realm of condemnation and in the realm of justification. The judgment of God, his 'Yes' determines our identity. The eschatological gift of our existence in Christ is crucial here.[199]

Third, O'Donovan regrets the separation of sanctification from justification in Protestantism. The Reformation started with the discovery that Paul uses the same noun (δικαιοσύνη) for the active noun corresponding to the verb δικαίοω and the moral status of righteousness. Therefore, the term justification was chosen to display the connection between moral righteousness and God's favourable verdict. However, the Reformation came to use two words, justification and sanctification, obscuring this

195. O'Donovan, *Resurrection and Moral Order*, 254.

196. O'Donovan, *Resurrection and Moral Order*, 253–55; O'Donovan, *On the Thirty Nine Articles*, 79.

197. O'Donovan, *Resurrection and Moral Order*, 259–60.

198. O'Donovan, *The Desire of the Nations*, 128.

199. O'Donovan, *Resurrection and Moral Order*, 254–57, 259–61; O'Donovan, *On the Thirty Nine Articles*, 81–82; O'Donovan, *The Desire of the Nations*, 128–29.

connection again. This led to 'a justification which had nothing to do with righteousness' and 'a righteousness which had nothing to do with justification.' O´Donovan tries to restore the relation between our acts and God's judgment. The concept of righteousness relates eschatology and ethics, for the eschatological decision has to influence all historical decisions. Everything that we accomplish in our acts or character depends for its form, meaning and value upon the justifying 'Yes' of God. '(A)ny rightness which may belong to a human act or character derives from God's final judgment.' Our good works are an effect of our being united with Christ in faith.[200]

Understood in this context, sanctification is a reality. Although everything is given in Christ, moral learning is possible, which is more than repeated repentance, yet also not accumulative. The new reality in Christ receives historical embodiment in present human actions and decisions. It is possible to ask for the fruits of the Spirit. But this is a communication of what has been achieved already in Christ. Sanctification also is no afterword.[201] God's justification of humanity in Christ is decisive and apart from works, but this justification has to become visible in works of righteousness and love.

The doctrine of predestination, according to O'Donovan, concerns the question of 'how we participate in the eternal purpose which the Father has for his Son.'[202] Election concerns our participation in the position of the Son and in his relation with his Father. From eternity he is his Father's beloved Son.[203]

The Reformation tried to rediscover the connection with Christology, as it did in the case of justification. In the Augustinian tradition a Christological foundation for the doctrine is lacking. It speaks of God's eternal purposes independently of God's revelation in Jesus, and is therefore purely theistic. Renaissance libertarian thought's criticism of the Augustinian doctrine brought the Reformers to a defence of it, which made it more difficult to rework the doctrine on a Christological foundation. Classically, the decree is said to foreordain the destiny of the individual.

200. O'Donovan, *Resurrection and Moral Order*, 253–54; and further 257–58, 262; O'Donovan, *On the Thirty Nine Articles*, 79.

201. O'Donovan, *Resurrection and Moral Order*, 92, 104, 182; O'Donovan, *On the Thirty Nine Articles*, 79; O'Donovan, *The Desire of the Nations*, 182.

202. O'Donovan, *On the Thirty Nine Articles*, 77.

203. O'Donovan, *On the Thirty Nine Articles*, 83.

Christ and his community serve the elaboration of the decree in history. According to O'Donovan, this order has to be reversed. Predestination concerns Christ and his community, whereas the individual and his destiny are a matter of history, following out of the decree. God has chosen in Christ, which means that Christ the representative is chosen together with the community of the redeemed. In this way, the doctrine of predestination and the doctrine of the Trinity are closely related. Predestination shows that the relations within the Trinitarian Godhead constitute the foundation of the salvation of humanity. It is not that we are chosen whereas Christ was the means to realise our choosing, but 'we are chosen in him, because *he* is the chosen one.'[204] All emphasis is on the election of the representative, in whom we participate.[205]

Concerning history this implies several things. First, that individuals refuse to hear the gospel and do not believe cannot be understood as a consequence of the divine decrees. According to O'Donovan it is impossible to believe in a double decree, for this belief does not pass a crucial test for theological utterances: 'Do they show us the same God that is revealed to us in Christ?'[206] Second, that the dialectic of belief and unbelief and even the refusal to believe is used to reveal the greatness of God's might and mercy. Finally, election is intended to serve mankind. The elect are chosen to reach other people through them, and they are chosen to reach others again. Jesus Christ 'was chosen that we might be chosen in him. We are chosen in him that others may be chosen in him through us.'[207] A chosen people receives God's blessing to pass it on to others, letting them also share in this blessing. In this way O'Donovan tries to do justice to salvation history.

The image of adoption is used by O'Donovan in his discussion of the concept of conscience. He understands the Christian concept of conscience in the light of the internal dialogue of the human spirit with the

204. O'Donovan, *On the Thirty Nine Articles*, 83.

205. O'Donovan, *On the Thirty Nine Articles*, 82–87.

It is noteworthy that O'Donovan refers to a Bible passage that is often used in the Reformed tradition to argue for a limited atonement: 'All that the Father gives me will come to me,' John 6:37. According to O'Donovan this means that a company of redeemed will be gathered around the Representative, whereas who they will be is not specified before the foundations of the earth. See O'Donovan, *On the Thirty Nine Articles*, 86.

206. O'Donovan, *On the Thirty Nine Articles*, 85.

207. O'Donovan, *On the Thirty Nine Articles*, 87.

Spirit of God. This dialogue of the Spirit of God with our spirit 'adopts us into the family-relations of the godhead in the economy of salvation.' In the Spirit we discover our identity as sons of God. O'Donovan specifies this in different directions: together with Jesus Christ we call on God as Father, we share the glory of God's presence, and our own lives are conformed to his cross and glorification.[208] Again O'Donovan shows that believers participate in the representative, Jesus Christ through the Holy Spirit. The explicitly Trinitarian framework of his elaboration of the adoption-image is remarkable.

To conclude, in the elaboration of these three soteriological images, the concepts of representation and participation play a central role. Christ, the representative, is chosen and accepted. We participate in his election and are accepted with him, being justified. We share in his identity as son of God the Father. This again shows the importance of these two concepts in O'Donovan's theology.

9.3.4 PARTICIPATION AND UNION

In the last section of this paragraph we come to the final question, whether in a concept of 'being in Christ,' developed in conversation with O'Donovan, the moments of participation and union need to be present.

It may be obvious that according to O'Donovan a concept of participation is essential (see 9.3.1). This participation in the representative returns as participation in the history of the representative and as participation explicated with the help of soteriological images. This participation is not possible without God's judgment to make the reality of the representative authoritative for us. Interestingly, justification is not separated from participation, but understood as a participation in the acceptance of Jesus Christ. Further, the Holy Spirit plays an important role, making this authoritative reality present to us and evoking a free reaction of faith. Within this juridical and pneumatological context, the concept of participation has its place.

It is less evident that we need a moment of union according to O'Donovan. Images for union with Christ, like body, head and body, building and cornerstone, vine and branches, the living bread eaten by believers do not play a role in his theology. At two moments he denies that a moment of union plays a role. Firstly, election is not election in

208. O'Donovan, *The Ways of Judgment*, 316.

union with individuals. The representative is predestined together with a collective that is not specified further regarding individuals.[209] Secondly, O'Donovan denies that the Eucharist can be understood as a feeding on the living ascended Christ. This interpretation is suggested by John 6, but O'Donovan nowhere deals with this passage. Nevertheless, when dealing with justification he explicitly refers to a moment of union. In faith we are united with Christ. 'The Reformers' doctrine of justification, then, is a doctrine of the believer's moral union with Christ.'[210] Here he qualifies the concept of union as a union 'in faith' and as 'moral.' Further it is important that O'Donovan is here in discussion with Cranmer and the Reformers. In his own language the moment of union does not play an important role. Combined with other denials or noted silences this leads to the conclusion that a moment of union is not necessary within O'Donovan's conceptuality. Representation, participation together with the concepts of judgment, authority and faith suffice to explain the salvation of humanity.

9.4 Moral Reality

Concerning the reality of 'being in Christ' a lot has been said above. Central is the eschatological representative, in whom humanity is decisively present. In him salvation is finished and complete. Jesus Christ, the representative, constitutes the people he represents. (9.2.1). The reality of 'being in Christ' is an eschatological reality.

Incarnation makes it possible that the fate of the entire creation is taken up into the fate of the one Representative. In the cross and resurrection the old is condemned and a new creation is established in Jesus Christ, raised from the dead in a new spiritual body. He is glorified at the right hand of God and receives again the position of dominion, the position humanity ought to have within creation. In this way, creation is vindicated and transformed eschatologically. By God's judgment, Jesus Christ is the concrete and irreplaceable embodiment of the renewed moral order. God chose and elected the reality of Jesus Christ to shape all the reality that we encounter, although it is a small segment of reality. God's performative judgment creates a new reality. However, elevated in

209. O'Donovan, *On the Thirty Nine Articles*, 83–87.

210. O'Donovan, *On the Thirty Nine Articles*, 79.

heaven, this reality is hidden and not manifest to us, although it does determine even public existence. (9.2.2). 'Being in Christ' is a moral reality (related to the moral order of the universe) and a hidden reality.

Further it is a reality that presupposes objective justice. No restoration of the moral order is possible unless the demands of justice are satisfied. This satisfaction is given in the cross and the resurrection of Jesus Christ (9.2.3). This concerns again the moral character of the reality of 'being in Christ.' Further, it reminds us of the relation O'Donovan sees between Christology and objectivity. Christology concerns objective reality. Consequently, 'being in Christ' is a reality with an objective character.

The eschatological reality of Christ has an absolute character, making possible the believer's absolute contemporaneousness with Christ. By the Holy Spirit this authoritative reality comes to influence our lives, laying its claim on us. The reality of 'being in Christ' is an invasive reality, open for participation and influencing even our subjective existence. In this influence, Christ has the primacy over the Spirit. Because it has a hidden character until its final public manifestation, also our participation in it has an incomplete character. The gift of the Spirit is a first anticipation of our complete participation in it. Our existence has its place in the middle of the end, in an eschatological frame (9.3.1). This confirms the eschatological and hidden character of the reality of 'being in Christ.' Further, it is a reality with a collective aspect.

In faith, believers accept Jesus Christ as their representative and become active participants. This participation involves pain and joy. Participating in the representative act implies authorisation. At the same time, we hope for a full participation in the resurrection and glorification of Jesus Christ. In any case, it is an invasive reality that influences the life of the believer (9.3.2 and 9.3.3). This again reminds us of the eschatological character of this reality.

Speaking from this reality as 'eschatological' demands further clarification, for it concerns several related aspects. First, it is a reality that constitutes the end of history. An eschatological reality is a definitive reality, giving meaning to history. Jesus Christ is the *eschatos* Adam in that he determines the end of history and the definitive form of mankind, transformed to its *telos*.[211] Second, the end comes in the representative but we

211. The message of the gospel concerns the end of history, see O'Donovan, *The Just War Revisited*, 5. See on Christology and history in O'Donovan further De Bruijne, *Levend in Leviatan*, 65, 68–69.

live in the middle of the coming of the end. The end is an open space between resurrection and *parousia*, in which we live. Living within the end, we live in the middle of the communication of what has been achieved already in Christ. Third, therefore this reality is characterized by a tension between the already and the not yet. In the Spirit it is anticipated, but it retains a hidden character. To this hidden character we turn now.

'Being in Christ' is a hidden reality. As a result, our existence has a hidden and waiting character. But we also do not know what we shall be. The manifestation of Christ at the *parousia* will not only imply that we see ourselves fully participating in Christ, but also the redemption of non-human creation. However, it is impossible to speculate on what 'redemption' will mean here. As we have seen, our knowledge of salvation retains an apophatic element.[212]

As a result of this hidden character, it is difficult to recognise this reality. This is especially the case for an outside perspective. From the outside, the church is a religious organisation. From an inside perspective of faith however, the church is discerned e.g. as a political community of obedience and freedom, governed by its Lord in heaven. Until the appearance of Christ, this tension between perspectives will not be resolved.[213] However, also in the life of others it is difficult to discern someone's identity in Christ. Normally, acts reveal someone's character. This is complicated by conversion, 'since it introduces an inner contradiction, a conflict of flesh and Spirit . . . into the hidden reality of the character itself.'[214] Although the encounter with God's love shapes a life, outward ambiguity is still a possibility. Even our judgments about ourselves are provisional, because this ambiguity also attaches to us due to the hiddenness of the formative moment of the reality of Christ. Only the word of God and the sacraments transcend this ambiguity. Even our own perspective on our own life asks for the *parousia* which will bring an end to this ambiguity.[215] Nevertheless we need an inside perspective to know this reality.

That even our own perspective remains ambiguous raises questions concerning our biography and 'being in Christ.' As we have seen, O'Donovan criticises the Roman-Catholic doctrines of justification and

212. O'Donovan, *Resurrection and Moral Order*, 55, 247, 260; O'Donovan, 'Response to Daniel Carroll R.,' 145.

213. O'Donovan, *The Desire of the Nations*, 166.

214. O'Donovan, *Resurrection and Moral Order*, 257.

215. O'Donovan, *Resurrection and Moral Order*, 257–59.

of the sacraments for their biographical character. In both cases, these doctrines have to be reframed in a Christological-eschatological framework. Salvation is not achieved within a biographical process of justification, or within a range of sacraments that lead the believer during his lifetime. In the death and resurrection of Jesus Christ everything has been achieved. However, he leaves space for the reflection of this once-and-for-all redemption in our individual biographies.[216] If this were not the case, our relation with Christ would be a formless relation. O'Donovan instead affirms that this relation is a shaped relation as we have seen. This shape is not the shape of our biographies, but of the narrative of the Christ-event. This implies that even our biographies have to be shaped by the narrative of the Christ-event. 'Being in Christ' is no biographical concept, but our lives need to be shaped by our 'being in Christ.'

About the formative effect of 'being in Christ' on our lives much has been written already. The representative act is recapitulated in the life of the church, in faith, suffering, rejoicing, and speaking. The sacraments further give this reality a public form within an ambiguous world (9.3.2). Moreover, in 9.3.1 we have seen the influence on the self. Our old self is crucified with Christ. Psychological barriers are taken away and we are made free. The dividedness of will and reason is recreated. When the Spirit makes us participate in Christ, a conflict of flesh and Spirit is introduced in the self. The flesh is the merely human that 'becomes dangerous when it is conceived as an alternative source of strength to the Spirit.'[217] However, it is not the condemning 'No' that is determinative for our self-interpretation. Because we as persons are saved by God's 'Yes' there is no more need for us 'to save the faces of our old selves.' Faith is 'able to relax the compulsive grip of self-justification.' Openness to repentance is given. We only need to fear that we try to defend the old man of our past against the divine 'No,' hence ceasing to live in the light of the divine 'Yes.'[218] Further we receive a place within the universe, the human position within the moral order, for 'being in Christ' is participation in the position of Christ. This place is the position of 'dominion' (9.2.2, 9.3.1 and 2). The concept of moral order is an important one within O'Donovan's ontology. It has moral implications, but also affective, because joy is the appropri-

216. O'Donovan, *On the Thirty Nine Articles*, 80.

217. O'Donovan, *Resurrection and Moral Order*, 12; and further 112, 257.

218. O'Donovan, *Resurrection and Moral Order*, 256.

ate moral attitude towards God's creative goodness. However ambiguous our lives may be, they are influenced by the invasive, formative reality of Christ our representative.

Finally I want to mention that according to O'Donovan redemption as restoration *and* transformation includes divinisation, a 'dangerous but exciting term' according to O'Donovan.[219] In salvation, humanity receives more than the life in communion with God that was possible in the first creation. However, this supernatural end is not the denial of humanity (neither 'dehominisation') or creation (nor 'uncreation'),[220] but an elevation to a higher destiny: participation in the divine life. In our responsive love to the divine love, 'the divine mode of being becomes our own.'[221]

To conclude, the reality of 'being in Christ' can be characterized as follows. It is an eschatological reality, which means first that Christ, the *eschatos* and the end of history, determines it, and second that it is marked by the eschatological tension between the already and not yet of a first anticipating participation through the Holy Spirit while we live within the end. It is a moral reality, for it concerns the position of humanity within the moral order, the position of 'dominion.' Because Jesus Christ is hidden in heaven after his ascension, it is a hidden reality, although it is formative and shapes our lives. As a result, our lives maintain an ambiguous character. The objective reality of Jesus Christ determines our lives, but we still wait for the complete public manifestation of salvation at the *parousia*. This is not to deny that it influences the community of the church and the self of the believer, creating space for a honest self knowledge and repentance. The manifestation of salvation will include our divinisation.

9.5 Evaluation

Oliver O'Donovan is the last conversation partner in this investigation in search for a concept of 'being in Christ.' Before presenting my conclusions in the next chapter, I will give a short evaluation of the position of O'Donovan as described in this chapter.

219. O'Donovan, *Resurrection and Moral Order*, 65.

220. O'Donovan, *Resurrection and Moral Order*, 56.

221. O'Donovan, *Resurrection and Moral Order*, 248; O'Donovan, *On the Thirty Nine Articles*, 34.

Important in his contribution to the conversation is the double concept of representation and participation as he presents it. The representative act comprises the story of the life of Jesus Christ as the gospels tell it. His scheme of four different moments makes it possible to distinguish different aspects of this story. In the representative act, salvation has been achieved. At the same time, this does not lead to a static idea of a salvation that leaves open the question of how it influences our lives, as was the case in the idea of a corporate personality. The difference between the 'in Christ' and the 'in the Spirit' is warranted, without doing injustice to the achievement in Christ. He emphasises that representation presupposes moral imagination as well as existential and affective involvement. Sanctification is necessary, but it is not the realisation of something lacking in Christ. Furthermore it is interesting to see how the double concept is combined with the concept of judgment. O'Donovan does not separate the juridical from the mystic or the organic in an artificial way, suggesting two separate compartments.

Concerning participation, several things are important. First, the distinction he makes between the representative act and Pentecost is intriguing. Pentecost does not add something to the identity and position of the representative, but concerns our participation in Christ. However, the story of Jesus Christ continues after Ascension, for he is active in his intercession and in the gift of his Spirit to make his people share in his position. Does the continuation of his story imply a continuation of the representative act, although it does not add something to the eschatologically transformed position of Jesus Christ? Second, O'Donovan is able to do justice to a broad spectrum of our participation in the history of Jesus Christ, including a participation in his suffering, a neglected theme. Third, he re-establishes the relation between justification and moral righteousness, without doing injustice to the justification 'apart from works.'

I regard his reflection on the hidden reality of Christ that nevertheless influences our lives to be just as significant. Our relation with Christ has hidden aspects, but it is a relation formed by the different moments of the recapitulated representative act and by the sacraments. Our lives remain ambiguous and our biography does not have the primacy, but our lives are formed by the eschatological reality of Jesus Christ and our biographies can be reframed within the story of the Christ-event.

In this way he makes clear the eschatological nature of 'being in Christ.' He shows that the *eschatos* and the *eschata* are related inseparably.

Nevertheless, this does not lead to a disappearance or emptying of the *eschata*. Jesus Christ is risen, taking again his body. The resurrection concerns material reality. Therefore, the *eschata* and our full participation in Christ's resurrection will also concern our material reality. The gift of the Holy Spirit is only a first incomplete anticipation of our complete participation in the reality of Jesus Christ.

Because it has not yet been made known what we will be, it is difficult, even impossible to determine the relation between the already and the not yet. However, sometimes I wonder whether O'Donovan gives too positive an impression of our participation in Christ in the present. Knowing in Christ, we participate in his knowledge, but it must not be forgotten that we now see but a poor reflection as in a mirror. And does O'Donovan suggest that the restoration of the subject, the reintegration of reason and will in faith is complete? O'Donovan seems to have an optimistic view here.

O'Donovan would confirm our hypothesis that the concepts of representation and participation give a good opportunity for the development of a concept of 'being in Christ.' Further, he shows that we also need a concept of substitution. This concept safeguards that everything is accomplished in Christ, but also that participation in Christ is impossible without objective justice and a real confrontation with guilt and evil. At the same time, O'Donovan rightly resists the isolation of the substitution-moment. However, his position raises an important question concerning this hypothesis and his own theology. We have seen that a moment of union is not present in his theology. However, it might be asked whether the New Testament does not contradict O'Donovan's statements on predestination (predestination is concerned with Christ and the church, not with individuals) and on the Eucharist (Eucharist is not feeding on the living Christ). But to answer these questions we turn now to the last chapter.

10

A SYSTEMATIC-THEOLOGICAL CONCEPT OF 'BEING IN CHRIST'

10.1 Introduction

WITH THIS TENTH CHAPTER we come at the end of this conversation on 'being in Christ.' In this chapter I will present my conclusions, consisting of a proposal for a systematic-theological concept of 'being in Christ' with a special emphasis on its ontological implications. It is based on the preceding investigation of John Owen, Herman Bavinck, Paul and John, Ingolf U. Dalferth and Oliver O'Donovan. Consequently, the emphasis is on the clarification of the gospel of Jesus Christ and the implied Christian understanding of reality. Furthermore, this proposal is developed in answer to the theological climate and cultural-philosophical context as signalled in 1.1.1 and 1.1.2. Finally, I hope to show the integrative power of the theme of 'being in Christ': it embraces Christology, pneumatology, spirituality, biography and ethics.

I will start with the discourse of the Christian community and some of its grammatical structures (10.2). Based on these structures, I will develop a systematic-theological framework (10.3). The chapter closes with an elaboration of the ontological implications of 'being in Christ' (10.4). Here I will return to the discussions I referred to in 1.1.3 concerning a theological ontology.

10.2 Grammatical Structures

Systematic theology is critical reflection on the practice of the church. Its aim is the saying of the gospel in preaching and doxology, and a church growing in a life in communion with the triune God and each other to the glory of God (cf. 1.2). The church is a community gathering in worship and prayer, reading the Scriptures, preaching and hearing the gospel, and celebrating the sacraments of baptism and the Lord's Supper. These liturgical activities constitute the centre of the life of the Christian community, a life with moral, spiritual and many other aspects. Linguistic activities are central in the practice of the church (cf. 1.2.4). Consequently, systematic theology has to do justice to this Christian discourse and reflect on the saying of the gospel in the church. Before structuring this discourse in a theological grammar and unfolding a systematic-theological framework, we have to form a notion of the discourse itself.

Within this discourse, several elements can be distinguished, which are relevant for a concept of 'being in Christ.' First, the language of 'being in Christ.' As we have seen in chapter 5 and 6, two different usages of the expression 'in Christ' can be found in the New Testament. 'Being in Christ' in Pauline perspective is a phase in between, an incomplete participation in the story of Jesus Christ. In a Johannine fashion, 'being in Christ' is one side of the reciprocal inhabitation of Christ and his disciples. Strictly speaking, it is impossible to develop *one* concept of 'being in Christ,' because based on the New Testament two different models of 'being in Christ' can be reconstructed.

Second, this in Christ-language has its place within a larger context. To mention some elements of it: a. the story of Jesus Christ as told in the gospels; b. images referring to Jesus Christ (Adam, head; the first one, the firstborn, the Son, the bread of life, the door, the shepherd, the true vine); c. soteriological images, showing the significance of Jesus' cross and resurrection (sacrificial and juridical images, images of victory, reconciliation, and liberation, Jesus' death as a death for others and as a moral example);[1] d. semantic relations between the story of Jesus Christ and the biography of believers;[2] e. images for union with Christ (body, body and head, marriage, clothing, building with cornerstone, bread, vine and branches, inhabitation); f. parallels drawn between the Father-Son relation and the Son-disciples relation; g. images for salvation as participation in the position of Jesus Christ (justification, adoption, election, sanctification, glorification).

This discourse is structured by a theological 'grammar.' Concerning 'being in Christ,' at least two grammatical structures have to be distinguished: the doctrine of the Trinity (10.2.1) and the four moments of the relation between Christ and the church (see ch. 7; 10.2.2).

10.2.1 TRINITARIAN GRAMMAR

We have seen that both John Owen and Herman Bavinck were Trinitarian thinkers. According to both the love of the Father has the primacy. Christ is head and representative, and it is the Spirit who unites us with Christ and makes us participate in the benefits acquired by Christ. But the reverse is also true: Christ is formed as head in the Spirit as we saw in Owen's pneumatology, and Christ unites us with him and his benefits by his Spirit. Hence, the Trinity is not only relevant for understanding their theology as a whole, but also for their contribution to this conversation on 'being in Christ.'

Paul and John both are not explicitly Trinitarian. However, according to a Pauline understanding it is God who acts in Christ and in the Holy Spirit. 'Being in Christ' has a Christological side and a pneumatological reverse. John at first sight is binitarian with his emphasis on Father and Son. Nevertheless, it is the Spirit who lets us participate in the Son as source of life and in his relation with his Father. Therefore it is necessary to mention the work of the Spirit. Consequently, 'a fully trinitarian logic' determines both Paul and John.[3]

1. See further Boersma, *Violence, Hospitality and the Cross*, 99–201; Gunton, *The Actuality of Atonement*, 53–141; McIntyre, *The Shape of* Soteriology, 29–52.

2. McIntyre uses here the concepts of universalisers, relaters and contemporanisers, see McIntyre, *The Shape of Soteriology*, 88–108.

3. Jenson, *Systematic Theology. Volume 1*, 92; and more general 90–94. Crump denies

According to Dalferth, theology is Christology and therefore Trinitarian. Theological reflection on the self-identification of God, resulting in a glorified 'being in Christ,' needs a Trinitarian grammar. Further, looking back from the resurrection, the life of Jesus already demands a Trinitarian grammar. He lived his life thanks to the work of the Spirit and to his special relation with his Father. O'Donovan is less explicitly Trinitarian, apart from his elaboration of the adoption-image. However, his Christology and pneumatology demand a Trinitarian framework.

To conclude, a concept of 'being in Christ' has to be Trinitarian. Firstly, no 'being in Christ' is possible without Christ, who provides sinners with a new position and a new identity and makes them participate in his position and identity as the church. Secondly, 'being in Christ' is impossible without the Holy Spirit who lived in Christ and makes the church share in Christ, in his place and his identity. In this way, united with Christ, the church participates to some extent in the relation that Father and Son have together in the Holy Spirit. Thirdly, as a consequence 'being in Christ' is impossible without the Father who acts in his Son and his Spirit to bring us into his house, into his family. The Father, his love and his glory, constitutes the origin and the goal of the divine action of which 'being in Christ' is an important element. Christology and pneumatology together constitute two sides of 'being in Christ.' Son and Spirit are the hands of God (as Irenaeus said), or the arms of the Father embracing us in love.[4]

10.2.2 FOUR MOMENTS

The second grammatical structure is evoked by four moments we have discovered in the relation of Christ with the church. We did not find all four moments in all our conversation-partners. However, the fact that we find these four moments both in Paul and John makes it necessary to use four concepts. I have concluded already that the hypothesis with which I started this investigation, has proved insufficient (see ch. 7). To develop a concept of 'being in Christ' we not only need the concepts of 'representation' and 'participation,' but also 'substitution' and 'union.' Four concepts

this as far as John is concerned. However, later on in his article the Trinity emerges again, see Crump, 'Re-examining the Johannine Trinity.'

4. Cf. Gunton, *The One, the Three and the Many*, 120, 159; Volf, *Exclusion & Embrace*, 128.

have to structure the discourse on the relation with Christ. Further, emphases differ as we saw. Consequently, these four concepts are useful tools in the investigation of (reflection on) the relation with Christ, stimulating a debate on how these four moments have to be understood.

Two Christological Moments:

a. **Substitution**: the moment of exclusivity of Christ.

b. **Representation**: the moment of inclusivity of Christ.[5]

Within the Reformed tradition these moments are evidently present. The Son is God and man, guarantee, mediator and high priest. These concepts are related with the exclusiveness of his office and work, which I called work-substitution. He makes satisfaction for our sins, acquiring the benefits of our salvation, and prays as our intercessor in heaven. He is our salvation in person. As such he is also inclusive. As inclusive person, he is exclusive in his inclusiveness. Christ is head, public person, representative, second Adam, mystical person. Consequently, the exclusive and the inclusive moments are intertwined and belong together as far as person-substitution is concerned.

In the work of O'Donovan and Dalferth we discovered a comparable pattern. Person-substitution and representation are reverse sides of the one coin. According to O'Donovan, Christ is representative of both God and God's people. Hence he is the last Adam, representative of humanity. Two of his conceptual statements are important: '(a) The representative *alone* constitutes the presence of the represented; (b) The represented are *really present* in what the representative does and experiences on their behalf.'[6] Representation requires some form of moral imagination, to see oneself represented in the representative. Moreover, O'Donovan speaks of a 'representative act' with different moments. I will return to this theme of imagination in 10.4.2. Dalferth stresses that Jesus Christ is the place of God's eschatological act on our behalf. Regarding work-substitution we find some hesitation in both. Dalferth denies that Christ did *something* to 'produce' salvation; all emphasis is on personal categories and on the eschatological act of God, who identified himself with Jesus. O'Donovan wants to prevent an isolation of the moment of substitution as present in

5. See on the history of the concepts of *substitutio* and *repraesentatio*, Schaede, *Stellvertretung*, 92–115, 171–238.

6. O'Donovan, *The Desire of the Nations*, 125.

the Anselmic tradition. However, seen as the reverse side of representation, substitution includes work-substitution. This indicates that some problems are attached to the concept of substitution.[7]

In Paul and John we also found the inclusive and the exclusive moments as intertwined aspects of the history of Jesus. Paul refers to Jesus as Christ, last Adam, firstfruits, firstborn, and head. His history is decisive because of its inclusiveness. This implies at the same time substitution, even work-substitution. John stresses the exclusiveness of Christ, but we found also the moment of inclusiveness. Concerning work-substitution, the first letter of John is more explicit than the gospel of John. However, the moment of work-substitution is present.

What does this survey of the results of this investigation imply for the concept of work-substitution? The distinction person-work has a problematic side, if it implies a static person-concept. A given person is primary, the works this person does, follow. A comparison with the distinction identity-acts suggests a more dynamic concept of person. The identity of a person is expressed in his acts, but his acts also influence his identity. With regard to Christology, this implies the following. First, the identity of Christ developed during his history. He is our salvation, in his person, because he realised salvation objectively in his life, death and glorification. Second, the separation of person and work may result in an isolation of his work, of the juridical aspect, from his representative person, as threatens to be the case in the substantialist language of benefits in the Reformed tradition.[8] Third, the difference person-work, if it has to be made, is not a difference within the moment of substitution alone. This difference is also present in the other moments: Christ is inclusive in his person and work, we are united with his person and work, and we participate in his person and work. However, in the case of human sin the difference person-work makes some sense. First, the person has to be good before his works can be good (Matt 7:16–20; Luke 6:43–44). This

7. Stephan Schaede differentiates between satisfaction and 'Stellvertretung.' The concept of satisfaction he describes as a businesslike concept, which generates a quantifying interpretation of the work of Christ. It cannot do justice to the recreating impact of the history of Jesus Christ, and did not really facilitate the genesis of the concept of 'Stellvertretung,' a more personal and relational concept. According to Schaede, we need the concept of 'Stellvertretung,' but not the satisfaction-concept. His analysis affirms the problems attached to the concept of substitution. See Schaede, *Stellvertretung*, 273, 308–9, 453–54, 474–75, 478–85, 543–44, 627–29, 635–37.

8. See also Boersma, *Violence, Hospitality and the Cross*, 163–70, 173–79.

applies also to Jesus: if he has to save us from sin, his person has to be of a quality that he is able to do so. Accordingly, his identity at the beginning of his story is important.[9] Second, Colin Gunton reminds us of an important issue concerning the atonement: 'whether the real evil of the real world is faced and healed *ontologically* in the life, death and resurrection of Christ.'[10] The metaphors of ransom, sacrifice, liberation, and victory all suggest that Christ has done something once and for all. The distinction of person and work is an important reminder in this respect: a part of the answer to the Christological question has to be: 'He is the one who did this *something* for us.' Christ paved the way for us to God the Father, removing all obstacles. This 'something' has to be understood as a part of the larger representative act. How this 'something' has to be conceptualised, is a question which lies beyond the scope of this investigation.[11]

Another aspect which deserves separate attention is the fact that according to O'Donovan Jesus Christ represents God as well as his people. This double representation is important for two reasons. First, one of the characteristics of sin is its blindness towards God, as Dalferth emphasises: God is not the problem, but the sinner is. To enable a saved believer to

9. Cf. Berkouwer, *De persoon van Christus*, 80–85.

10. Gunton, *The Actuality of Atonement*, 165.

11. Cf. Boersma, *Violence, Hospitality and the Cross*, 158–63; Van de Beek, *Jezus Kurios*, 150–56; Gestrich, *Christentum und Stellvertretung*, 354–92.

A comparable combination of exclusivity and inclusivity is present in the work of many other theologians, although differences exist in the way of conceptualising the exclusive aspect of the work of Christ, referring to *something* Christ has done. See e.g. Boersma, *Violence, Hospitality and the Cross*, 177–79; Douma, *Grondslagen christelijke ethiek*, 158–59; Gunton, *The Actuality of Atonement*, 160–67; Loonstra, *God schrijft geschiedenis.*, 193. Even in Berkhof, Jüngel and Schaede the exclusive aspect of the work of Christ can be found more implicitly; see Berkhof, *Christelijk geloof*, 282, 300–304; Jüngel, *Das Evangelium von der Rechtfertigung des Gottlosen als Zentrum des christlichen Glaubens*, 71–74, 128–43; Schaede, *Stellvertretung*, 627–29, 631.

Robert Jenson does not use these concepts, but his concepts of the *totus Christus* and identification lead to a analogous model. Nevertheless he is critical of substitutionary satisfaction; see Jenson, *Systematic Theology. Volume 1*, 76, 80–82, 85, 89, 138, 170, 186, 191–92.

A. van de Beek works with the same combination of exclusivity and inclusivity, emphasising also the exclusive aspect of the work of Christ. However, his concept of a Christ who is *anhypostaton* but not *enhypostaton* leads to a limited inclusivity. It is important to Van de Beek that God bore our existence in Christ, not that God renewed our existence. See Van de Beek, *Jezus Kurios*, 29–30, 42–43, 52, 56–57, 81–82, 144–56, 201–2, 216–19, 226–32; Van de Beek, *De kring om de Messias*, 39–40, 92–93, 109, 119, 172–77, 190–91, 227–29, 233–34, 260–65.

live in a restored relation with God, God has to identify himself for us. Consequently, Jesus Christ has to be God's representative, who makes us to some extent participate in his relation with his Father.[12] Secondly, O'Donovan shows that a restoration of the human community is impossible if humanity is not saved from its idols and false representations of God. Jesus Christ can not be the last Adam and the head of humanity if he is not at the same time God's true representative.

Whether this double representation implies that Jesus Christ has to be God and man is another question. Nevertheless, we saw with John that he maintains a distinction between the unique (divine) Father-Son relation and our participation in the Father-child relation.[13] For another reason also, it is essential for 'being in Christ' that Jesus Christ is God. To be the source of life as the Johannine language shows him, he has to be God. This aspect is neglected in the theologies of Dalferth and O'Donovan. Both emphasise the eschatological act of God in Christ (God's judgment) and reject (Dalferth) or maintain some distance from (O'Donovan) the ontology of substance of the classical doctrine of the two natures.

To conclude, both moments are important for a concept of 'being in Christ,' but in a different way. The inclusive moment denotes the 'side' of the story of Jesus Christ in which we will participate, the exclusive moment the other 'side' of the story, which is the soteriological precondition of this participation. Although we participate in Christ, we do not *become* Christ.[14] Jesus Christ needs to be God to save us, he needs to be the first

12. Schaede criticises Anselm in this respect for his *remoto Christo* method. This makes it impossible to see that in Christ our knowledge of God is renewed. Comparably he criticises Calvin, who also does not conceptualise the reality that God and man mutually rediscover each other in Christ. The sinner is renewed in the cross and resurrection of Christ, the knowledge of God is not; Schaede, *Stellvertretung*, 309, 392–93; and further more generally on double representation 226–27, 630.

13. Berkhof does use the concepts of exclusivity and inclusivity and sees Jesus Christ as representative of God and of his people. However, interpreting the God-Jesus relation as a covenant-relation in a way comparable with Edward Malatesta, he does not do justice to the difference between the Father-Son relation Jesus has with God and our Father-child relation with God, and loses the divinity of God as divine source of life. See Berkhof, *Christelijk geloof*, 280–91, 294, 326–33. For Malatesta, see in 6.2.2 the excursus on the new covenant and the conclusions of 6.3.1.

14. Garcia, 'Imputation and the Christology of Union with Christ,' 219, 223, 246, 248. Because we are not to be like Christ in his exclusiveness, Gestrich is right writing that not all Christian life can be in conformity with Christ, see Gestrich, *Christentum und Stellvertretung*, 421–22.

one, and he needs to be the one who breaks open a way by his victory and atonement. Both moments need each other and are reverse sides of the one coin.

Two Soteriological Moments

c. **Union**: the moment of contact between Christ and the believers.

This moment was evidently present in the two representatives of the Reformed tradition, especially in the concept of mystical union. This concept implies a narrative: its origin lies in the *pactum salutis*, Christ is mystical person during whose life this mystical union is realised objectively, the Spirit incorporates us in Christ and unites us with him and lives within us, Christ communicates his fullness, the believers have communion with Christ and the mystical union is enjoyed in the Lord's Supper. With regard to Owen, it has to he said that his reflection on personal communion with Christ partly exceeds the subject of 'being in Christ.'[15] This mystical union with the person of Christ is the presupposition of our participation in Christ. According to Owen, unification with Christ is related to the creation of a new habit.

The moment of union is central in Johannine thinking, although it is also present in Paul. For John the mutual indwelling of Christ and the disciples, analogous to the mutual indwelling of Father and Son, is vital. Apart from the language of being and remaining in each other, it is indicated by images like bread and vine with branches. The same is the case in Paul, where we find images like body, body and head, building and temple, marriage and clothing.

Dalferth and O'Donovan complicate this consensus. According to Dalferth we are united with Christ in faith and in the Spirit, but this union cannot be understood as a mystical union. Furthermore, the presence of God in Christ and the Spirit has a revelatory character and is not understood as divine indwelling. In O'Donovan's conceptuality, this moment of union also does not play an important role.[16]

15. He highlights an important aspect of the relation with Christ, a face to face relation with him, but this aspect cannot be understood as 'being in Christ.' The idea of the face of Christ is also a central concept in the book of Ford, *Self and Salvation*.

16. Dalferth and O'Donovan share this neglect of the moment of union with many others. To mention two of them: Berkhof uses the concepts of exclusiviness, inclusiveness (representation) and participation, see *Christelijk geloof* 282, 313, 316–26. Gestrich in his *Stellvertretung* distinguishes between exclusive, inclusive and prospective 'Stellvertretung,' see 222–23, 388–90.

The position of Dalferth and O'Donovan has to be understood as a position after Albrecht Ritschl. His criticism of the mystical union marks a watershed in the history of theology and leads to a neglect of this theme in protestant theology. Ritschl identified the concept of mystical union with neo-Platonist metaphysics. Further, he criticised it as Pietism, an individualistic spirituality presupposing a substantialist understanding of God's inhabitation. According to Lehmkühler, Ritschl did not see the difference between neo-Platonism with its emphasis on the dissolution of the individual in the highest being, and the orthodox concept of a mystical union. Further, Ritschl is not interested in a philosophical discussion concerning a definition of a relation with God.[17] Consequently, Lehmkühler makes a plea for a rehabilitation of the inhabitation of God in the believers. Nevertheless, Ritschl's criticism marks out two important features for a concept of mystical union: a concept of mystical union should not suggest dissolution of identity,[18] and it should not be thought in substantialist terms but in a more relational fashion.[19]

The gospel of John, in particular, offers material for such a concept of mystical union. The union between Christ and the church has to be distinguished from the Trinity as a union. We have seen that an analogy exists between the intertrinitarian *perichoresis* and the union between Christ and the believers, but it is only an analogy.[20] The Trinity is not

17. Lehmkühler, *Inhabitatio*, 199–216.

18. Loonstra, *God schrijft geschiedenis*, 222

19. In this respect the Reformed tradition is more vulnerable to Ritschl's criticism than Lutheran orthodoxy; cf. Ch. 2 on Owen with Lehmkühler, *Inhabitatio*, 164–65, 171.

20. To emphasise that this is just an analogy I would be very cautious about using the term 'perichoresis' to characterize the relation between Christ and the church as has become usual in debates on Trinitarian ontology. A perichoretic paradigm emphasises: God in us, we in God, and we in another. But all these relations are not perichoretic, only the first two are analogous to a perichoretic relation. I would never use this concept to characterize generally relations between God and the cosmos or within human society or cosmos. Colin Gunton e.g. uses the concept too generally, although he is aware of the fact that only an analogy exists between the Trinitarian perichorese and other relations. See Gunton, *The Promise of Trinitarian Theology*, xviii, 140, 151, 198; Gunton, *The One, the Three and the Many*, 163–73; Speidell, 'A Trinitarian Ontology of Persons in Society,' 283–88.

McCormack goes too far however, writing that the concept of *perichoresis* describes 'that which is *dissimilar* in the analogy between intra-trinitarian relations among the divine "persons" on the one hand and human to human relations on the other.' As a result, a quasi-perichoretic indwelling of the historical humanity of Christ is ontologically impossible. In his 'ontology of correspondence,' the inhabitation of Jesus Christ by his Spirit

open, although it envelops us, being 'roomy.'[21] The reciprocal inhabitation does not lead to dissolution or loss of identity, but instead is a source of identity. Further this idea of mutual indwelling is obviously relational, and the many coordinates restrain a substantialist fixation of this union. This union remains a mystery.[22] However, it is a reality which results in a new presence of God which differs from his omnipresence.[23]

The narrative structure of the concept of mystical union in the Reformed tradition highlights an important aspect of the moment of union. Both in Owen and Bavinck, the union is a story with different episodes, in God's council, in the history of Jesus Christ, and in our own biography. This signals a problem related to the mysterious character of this union: its beginning has a fluid character, at least for our understanding. In this light it is significant that it is not clear in Luther's theology whether the exchange of place between Christ and the believer takes place in or after the cross. Luther localises the exchange in the cross as well as in the present. The exchange does not take place in an isolated incarnation, cross or conversion, for these occurrences have an inner connection. Preaching, Luther even formulates in the present: Christ takes my sin and dies on the cross.[24] The word of faith 'synchronises' the believers with the cross. Although this concerns the exchange and not the mystical union, the problem of its fluid character is the same. This fluid character of the beginning of the union should not be lost in the name of theological clarity. Theology has to do justice to the participant's perspective and not to distort this with a theoretical solution. The relational nature of the union should not be lost in a separation of the objective and the subjective.[25]

---

also seems impossible. Consequently, union with Christ has to be understood as a union of wills; see McCormack, 'What's at Stake in the Current Debates over Justification?' 110–11, 115.

21. According to Jürgen Moltmann, the Trinity is open, see Moltmann, *Trinität und Reich Gottes*, 110–11, 166–67, 193–94. The idea that the Trinity envelops us and is roomy I owe to Robert Jenson, see Jenson, *Systematic Theology. Volume 1*, 122, 226.

22. See for a proposal of the doctrine of God's inhabitation in man Lehmkühler, *Inhabitatio*, 287–336.

23. Lehmkühler emphasises that in the inhabitation, God is present 'novo modo,' see Lehmkühler, *Inhabitatio*, 74–75, 114, 155, 171, 310, 315; see also 316–26.

24. Schaede, *Stellvertretung*, 327–29, 342, 347.

25. Sometimes it is necessary to differentiate between Christology and soteriology, between objective and subjective. I did this myself, as did Bavinck and O'Donovan. However, it is necessary to be very cautious that the relational nature of Christology and

The relation we find in Luther between the exchange and the preaching of the gospel of Jesus Christ is significant: the union has to be understood in the light of the Christus *pro nobis*, who identified with us, who is preached in the gospel and with whom we identify. Because the gospel has the character of *promissio*, the union also has to be understood in the light of the *promissio*.

To conclude, we need a moment of union, concerning the ongoing union with Christ, as the one who became who he is by his entire history. This moment has different aspects, related to the beginning of this union (incorporation, unification, faith) and its ongoing continuation (inhabitation, communion, communication).[26] Its nature is analogous to the intertrinitarian *perichoresis*. Due to Ritschl's theology it has been neglected, but this moment deserves rehabilitation in contemporary theology. Because this union itself is a story, a movement of identification of Christ with us and our identification with Christ, the beginning of this union has a fluid character. This fluid character should not be forgotten in the name of theoretical clarity.

d. **Participation**: the moment of the believers' sharing in Christ.

Within the Reformed tradition, this moment created the most problems. In particular John Owen differentiates strictly between an anti-Roman Catholic line of actual obedience and an anti-Remonstrant line of habitual being. Participation in the obedience of Christ is unthinkable. Comparably, a juridical line of forensic imputation and a mystical line of organic participation can be found in Bavinck. Further complication follows with the concept of benefits, acquired by Christ, in which we participate. Although the concept of participation is used here, it is reinterpretated as participation in quasi-substantialist benefits. However,

---

soteriology is not lost. More than the Lutheran tradition, the Calvinist tradition risks a separation by the creation of a theoretical solution too clear, due to the presence of the difference between Christ *extra nos* and *in nobis*, which we find in Calvin. See on this distinction in Calvin Van 't Spijker, ' 'Extra nos' en 'in nobis' bij Calvijn in pneumatologisch licht.'

26. Frigato presupposes that every human being has in his anthropological structure an innate, ontological relation with Christ. Consequently, humanity is able to answer the new situation determined by the call in Christ. He does not reflect on pneumatology, regeneration, the change from old to new, from flesh to spirit. Life in Christ seems to be an anthropological possibility. See Frigato, *Leven in Christus en moreel handelen*, 155–56, and more generally 138–58.

Owen teaches a participation in the position of Christ as son and heir, as well as in his suffering and death. In Bavinck's theology participation is present concerning election, the position and identity of Christ, and the supernatural life of Jesus Christ. Further it is the background of a process of growing conformity to Christ. I concluded that using the concept of participation will be an apposition but also an improvement of the Reformed tradition.

That it is an improvement indeed is confirmed by the importance of the concept in Pauline thinking. 'Being in Christ' is a moment in a process of growing participation in Christ and in his history. Further, different soteriological images imply a moment of participation. The investigation of John confirmed the necessity of a concept of participation. To some extent we participate in the Son's relation with his Father and in his position. We do not participate in his death, but even more in the result of his death and resurrection. Other aspects of participation concern the imitation of Christ's example, his suffering and his mission into the world.

Both Dalferth and O'Donovan emphasise the inclusive nature of the history of Jesus Christ. According to Dalferth, the history of Jesus has to be continued biographically in our lives by the Spirit. However, the emphasis is on participation in the new eschatological life of Jesus Christ and less on his death and burial. In O'Donovan's soteriology participation is the central concept. The church participates in the different moments of the story of Christ—his advent, suffering, resurrection and glorification—but also the images of justification and election contain a moment of participation.

For a concept of 'being in Christ' the moment of participation is important to do justice to, especially, the Pauline model as well as to the eschatological nature of 'being in Christ,' characterized by the tension between already and not yet. 'Being in Christ' in Pauline understanding is not the ultimate end, but a phase in between. Furthermore it opens a hermeneutical potential for the interpretation of a believer's biography. Finally it gives the life of the believers an orientation towards a full participation in Christ, his identity and his destination: a christomorphic life.[27]

For the Reformation the concept of participation proved to be problematic, as a result of the Roman-Catholic doctrine of justification. Participation implied self-justification and uncertainty of salvation.

27. Van der Kooi, *De ziel van het christelijk geloof*, 106, 119, 133.

Consequently, all emphasis was laid on the cross of Christ and his 'It is finished.' However, the Reformed solution created new problems as we saw in the chapters on Owen and Bavinck and did not succeed in doing justice to all aspects of the New Testament, which contains a moment of participation. Therefore, the concept of participation has to be rehabilitated, while avoiding the faults of late medieval Roman-Catholic theology.

That this rehabilitation is necessary, is proved in the negative by the attempt of Christoph Gestrich to make the concept of 'Stellvertretung' the central concept for understanding the relation between Christ and the church, as well as by the evaluation of this concept by Stephan Schaede. Gestrich distinguishes three modalities of 'Stellvertretung,' related to three questions: what does someone *do* as 'Stellvertreter,' who *is* someone as 'Stellvertreter,' and where does someone *stand* as 'Stellvertreter'? In relation to Jesus Christ, the answers to these three questions refer to exclusive, inclusive and prospective 'Stellvertretung' respectively.[28] However, this solution raises several problems. First, not only the person (who Christ is), but also the work (what Christ does), and the place of Christ (where Christ stands) have an exclusive and an inclusive aspect.[29] We participate in his acts, his identity and his position, but only to a certain extent. The difference between exclusiveness and inclusiveness indicates to what extent we participate in Christ's identity (person) and acts (work). Second, it is suggested that the present is inclusive, whereas the future is not. But prospectivity also implies the inclusive nature of the future. The past (death and burial), the present (being in Christ, suffering) and the future (glorification) all have an inclusive aspect. In conclusion, the three questions concerning acts, identity and position cannot be answered referring to the exclusive, inclusive and prospective modality of 'Stellvertretung.'

Stephan Schaede described the history of the concept of 'Stellvertretung.' Several of his observations and conclusions are interesting. He signals that Lutheran orthodoxy limits the concepts of *surrogatio* and *substitutio* to the context of suffering. That sinners might also become the righteousness of God in Christ is not mentioned. All emphasis is on the person of Christ and not on the change with regard to the person of

28. Gestrich, *Christentum und Stellvertretung*, 222–23, 388–90.

29. Consequently, it is misleading to relate the Son to our identity and the Spirit to our place. The Son determines our identity as well as our place. It is the work of the Spirit to make us participate in the identity and place of the Son. Contra Gestrich, *Christentum und Stellvertretung*, 245, 248–49.

the sinner. The renewing effect of the person of Christ receives no attention. He deals with the problem of the law, but the fulfilment of the law in the gospel seems forgotten.[30] Consequently, he concludes that the concept of 'Stellvertretung' does not do justice to the renewing potential of Jesus Christ. 'Stellvertretung' contains a moment of exclusion, but its soteriological aim is that this exclusion is overcome. In Christ we are a new creation.[31] The direction of Schaede's argument is the same as Morna Hooker's proposal to replace the concept of exchange by the concept of interchange (see 5.3.6). The concept of participation makes it possible to say something on participation in the righteousness of Christ, in his vindication and resurrection.

Using the concept of participation in Jesus Christ, it is clear that this participation includes different aspects of Jesus Christ: his identity, his acts and his position, as well as his past, his present and his future. The concept contains possibilities which solve problems signalled in reference to Gestrich and Schaede.[32] This concept of participation does not imply a Platonic metaphysics of being. We do not participate in the substance of the human nature of Jesus Christ, but in his history, his identity and position.[33]

Rehabilitation for the concept of participation should not lead to self-justification and uncertainty of salvation. To prevent this, the Reformation emphasised the *extra nos* of salvation in Christ. The distinction of forensic imputation and organic participation was used to maintain the justification of the sinner as a justification apart from works. These two interests are worth remembering. Accordingly, a twofoldness has to be maintained, although it is maintained differently: not by distinguishing the juridical

30. Schaede, *Stellvertretung*, 524, 545.

31. Schaede, *Stellvertretung*, 635.

32. The concept of participation is central in the theology of Robert Jenson, see Jenson, *Systematic Theology. Volume 1*, 138, 191, 204–5, 227–30. In the theology of A. van de Beek the motive of participation also is important, but here it is limited to participation in his suffering regarding our present reality and participation in his resurrection with regard to our salvation from this present reality, see Van de Beek, *Jezus Kurios*, 43; Van de Beek, *De kring om de Messias*, 23, 39, 176–77, 261.

33. Cf. for a comparable concept of participation McCormack, 'Participation in God, Yes, Deification, No.' What is missing in his understanding of participation is the inhabitation of the Spirit of God, which McCormack unfortunately identifies with metaphysics, see 349. As a consequence, he cannot appreciate Calvin's understanding of the Lord's Supper; see McCormack, 'What's at Stake in the Current Debates over Justification?' 104–6. Cf. footnote 20.

from the organic-mystical, but by the distinction between substitution and representation, between the exclusive and the inclusive moment. As a result, the moment of participation evokes the question to what extend we participate in Christ. The difference between the exclusive and the inclusive moment indicate the answer. We participate in Christ in so far as his inclusiveness is concerned. Another important aspect is related to the concept of judgment as O'Donovan has elaborated it. Christ is given to us by a judgment of God and made authoritative and present to us by the Holy Spirit, evoking our free response and making us participate in Christ. Participation is not to be distinguished from the forensic aspect, but our participation in Christ has itself a forensic aspect. That this is enough to do justice to the central interests of the Reformation will be shown in 10.3.[34]

Excursus: Emphasis on Substitution in the Reformed Churches ('Liberated')

In the Reformed churches ('liberated') the emphasis has been laid on the moment of substitution. This has several causes. First, to loosen the relation between election and covenant, it was denied that Christ is head of the covenant (see 4.3). In the covenant he is the mediator. Second, in reaction to Kuyperian theology an anxiety over subjectivism and mysticism developed. As a result, the mystical union was not the object of a lot of reflection.[35] Third, the concept of corporate personality was criticised for the following reasons: this concept implied collectivism, it was introduced in theology despite the fact that in sociology the concept was already outdated, it downplays individual responsibility, it cannot be found in the Old Testament, it does not differentiate between 'in Christ' and 'in the Spirit' and hence is too static,[36] whereas the exclusive nature of the work of Christ as a guarantee is neglected (cf. 5.5.2).[37] However, the concept was criticised but not replaced by another concept to express yet

34. I agree with Garcia that the *extra nos* of salvation and the exclusiveness of Christ are important theological interests. However, my solution with the distinction exclusiveness-inclusiveness differs from his solution, using Calvin's Christological doctrine of the two natures and the concept of justification as imputation; see Garcia, 'Imputation and the Christology of Union with Christ.'

35. Maybe here also the influence can be seen from Ritschl's objections to the mystical union as result of his understanding of this concept in the light of neo-Platonism.

36. Cf. Kamphuis, *Een eeuwig verbond*, 93–97.

37. Kamphuis, 'De kerk—een corporatieve persoonlijkheid?' 146–64.

the inclusiveness of Christ. Fourth, in reaction to criticisms of satisfaction by liberal theologians this concept was defended. As a result of these causes, much emphasis was on the exclusiveness of Christ as mediator and on the objectivity of the promise. Christ reconciled us with God by his *intercessio* and not by *processio*.[38] This emphasis on one moment carries the risk of forgetting the other moments, as seems to be the case in the present situation on the level of spirituality (see 1.1.1).[39]

Furthermore the relation between both grammatical structures has to be clarified. One might at first sight expect that the concepts of substitution and representation are Christological concepts, whereas union and participation are pneumatological concepts. However, this is not the case. Especially in Owen's pneumatology, but also in Dalferth's Christology it becomes very clear that the Spirit is active in Christology as well as in soteriology.[40] The Reformed emphasis on the continuation of the activity of Christ after his glorification in his intercession shows that the Son as well is active in Christology and soteriology.[41]

To conclude, the discourse of the New Testament contains several elements, based on which two models of 'being in Christ' can be reconstructed. Consequently it is impossible to develop *one* concept of 'being in Christ' in a strict sense. These two models of 'being in Christ' each highlight different aspect of the relation between Christ and the church.

The Christian discourse is structured. With regard to 'being in Christ,' two grammatical structures are important: firstly the doctrine of the Trinity, and secondly the four concepts substitution (the exclusive moment of Jesus Christ), representation (the inclusive moment of Jesus Christ), union (the moment of contact between Christ and the church) and participation (the moment of sharing in Christ). Substitution is the precondition of 'being in Christ,' according to the Pauline model 'being

38. Kamphuis, *Een eeuwig verbond*, 87.

39. The other three moments are present evidently in Douma's *Grondslagen*, see 155–59, 175–79. Further, K. Schilder opposes the idea of a simple exchange and defends an integration of the substitution-moment in a more complex concept of 'plaatsbekleding'; see Veenhof, 'Jezus Christus de plaatsbekleder.'

40. Cf. on Jesus as bearer of the Spirit Jenson, *Systematic Theology. Volume 1*, 88–89.

41. Robert Jenson emphasises the activity of the *Trinity* in one united agency. Father, Son and Spirit are acting together in a mutually single act; see Jenson, *Systematic Theology. Volume 1*, 36–37, 110–13.

in Christ' is constituted by representation and participation, whereas the Johannine model emphasises the union.

10.3 Systematic-Theological Framework

Based on these two grammatical structures a systematic-theological framework can be developed further. I will deal firstly with Christology (10.3.1) and secondly with soteriology (10.3.2). Two aspects of soteriology deserve separate attention, the different metaphors of salvation traditionally used in an order of salvation (10.3.3) and finally the question: who are the represented (10.3.4)?

10.3.1 CHRISTOLOGY

Central in Christology is the history of Jesus Christ. We only have history as story. Consequently, it is important to reflect on the narrative structure of this story. Dalferth retells the story from a hermeneutical perspective. Because our perspective of Jesus as the Christ is determined by the resurrection, his Christology is a reconstruction of the genesis of this perspective. Consequently, his story starts with the resurrection and not with the incarnation. Although Dalferth is right that the resurrection is determinative for our perspective on Jesus Christ, I will not follow his hermeneutical reconstruction of the *story* as resurrection, cross, life, and birth. The perspective of the storyteller as well as the genesis of the story have to be distinguished from the story itself. The resurrection determines the perspective of the storyteller, but the story starts with the birth of Jesus. Therefore, I chose a combination of a perspective determined by the resurrection and a 'heilsgeschichtliche' ordering of the narrative, following the narrative structure of the gospels, of birth, life, cross, death and resurrection. The narrative of the history of salvation should be foundational for systematic theology (see 1.2.4).

Regarding 'being in Christ' this has several implications. Christology starts with the birth of Jesus. However, the narrative of Christology is the end of another story, the story of Israel, as is emphasised by O'Donovan.[42] This has two further consequences.

42. See also Van de Beek, *De kring om de Messias*.

First, the story of Jesus Christ does not start with the council of God. In the Reformed tradition, God's eternal council seems to be the beginning of the story. The choice for another perspective, a divine eternal perspective, results in another beginning of the story, God's eternal council. In the canonical scriptures however the story is told differently. Concentrating on the theme of election in Paul and John, we see a different rhetorical strategy. The beginning of the story is open and inviting. Election is a matter of doxology and praise in the end of the story (Paul), or it is used to encourage or to bring the unbeliever to embarrassment and conversion, whereas the inviting statements have the primacy (John). Theology from a human point of view should not start telling the story with election, but end the story with it to the praise of God. As an alternative, the theme of election should return at different moments within the story with the pragmatic functions we find in John.

Second, Christology has to be told as the end of Israel's history and consequently as eschatology.[43] This eschatological emphasis is underdeveloped in the Reformed tradition, but we found it clearly in Paul, John, Dalferth and O'Donovan. Jesus Christ inaugurated the new covenant, which is the climax of a long history of covenants. He is the *eschatos* Adam. Where Adam failed, he succeeded, conquering the devil, sin and death, and restoring the image of God in humanity. Irenaeus used the concept of recapitulation here. Christ recapitulated by his obedience and annulled the disobedience of Adamic humanity.[44] Notwithstanding the modification of Jewish eschatology, wherein an entire period opens up between the resurrection of the promised Messiah and his public reappearance in glory as eschatological judge, the very eschatological nature of Christology

43. A. van de Beek stresses the eschatological nature of Christology, writing beautiful passages using much biblical-theological material. However, his eschatology has no implications for cosmology. Eschatology is salvation from this cosmos, not of the cosmos itself which will disappear in a big crunch. See Van de Beek, *Schepping*, 209–10, 214, 223; Van de Beek, *Jezus Kurios*, 173–79; Van de Beek, *De kring om de Messias*, 20–23, 38–46, 172–77, 192, 211, 298.

Further K. Schilder, although he used 'eschatology' in its traditional meaning, nevertheless shows the relation between Christology and eschatology, see Doekes, 'Van de alpha tot de omega,' 130–34.

See further Gaffin, 'The Vitality of Reformed Dogmatics,' 30; Van der Kooi, *De ziel van het christelijk geloof*, 24, 30, 157.

44. Van de Beek, *Jezus Kurios*, 29–30; Van de Beek, *De kring om de Messias*, 176; Boersma, *Violence, Hospitality and the Cross*, 119–26, 187–89.

remains incontestable.[45] Instead, this means that pneumatology, soteriology and ecclesiology share in the same eschatological character.[46] Obviously the rediscovery of the eschatological nature of Christology leads to a confusing situation where, in the name of the eschaton, the reality of the eschata can be denied. However, this confusing situation is caused by the complexity of the story of the *eschatos* Adam itself.[47] Within the end itself a hole opened and the end appeared as a period of time. Consequently, I will follow Dalferth in his difference between 'eschatological' (related to the *eschatos* Adam) and 'eschatic' (related to the eschata) hence maintaining the eschatological nature of Christology.[48]

This eschatological nature of Christology has implications for the relation between our stories and the story of Jesus Christ. His story is not a story which precedes our story and which our stories follow. Instead, it is a history in which our lives are comprised. The history of Jesus Christ has not come to an end yet, for he still has to reappear in glory. The end of our story and the end of his history coincide.

Having said this on the narrative structure of the story of Jesus Christ and its eschatological nature, I will deal further with the story itself. First I will sum up some of the results of 10.2 with regard to this story. In Trinitarian perspective, this history has a Christological and a pneumatological side. The Holy Spirit is active in the incarnation, life, death and resurrection of Jesus Christ. Further this history has an exclusive and an inclusive side. Exclusivity and inclusivity must be kept together, to prevent an isolation of the substitution-moment. Our relation with Christ is not determined by a simple exchange, but by a representative act consisting in different moments and by a more complex movement of identifications: Christ identifies with us more and more, becoming our representative. And we are identified with Christ and identify with him, participating in his history.

45. Cf. Robert Jenson in his *Systematic Theology. Volume 1*: 'By Jesus' resurrection occurring "first," a sort of *hole* opens *in* the event of the End, a space for something like what used to be history, for the church and its mission' (85). He shows that Jesus' resurrection "first" was unexpected, but resolves the antinomies present in Jewish eschatology until then. See 84–86.

46. See on the eschatological nature of pneumatology Gaffin, 'The Vitality of Reformed Dogmatics,' 33; Van der Kooi, *De ziel van het christelijk geloof*, 157; Loonstra, *God schrijft geschiedenis*, 212–18.

47. Cf. Hjelde, *Das Eschaton und die Eschata*, 487–99.

48. See on this difference also Eberhard Jüngel in his *Paulus und Jesus*, 285–89.

This identification of Christ with us was a process with different steps. It started with the birth of the Son of God as incarnation of the divine word. He was born of a woman, born under law. He was baptised as a penitent to fulfil all righteousness. He was chosen as God's beloved Son and received the Holy Spirit. He lived a life in the Spirit. He shared our existence, being tempted by the devil. He was obedient to his Father until the end, even when this became dangerous. He was prepared to die. He identified with the innocent victims of injustice, being sentenced to death although he was innocent. He shared our suffering and our experience of the absence of God. In this identification however, he also identified with the guilty, he was made to be sin for us and died as a blasphemer. He bore the curse of sin, abandoned by God. He identified with losers, becoming a loser hanging on a cross. He identified with mortal human beings, dying on that same cross. Identifying with us, Christ became what we are and took our place. He became our representative during this process of identification. He was God with us, even unto his death.

That this identification was a process and his identity developed during his history is not to deny that he could do this because he was the *eschatos* Adam. We saw that Christ did not become the *eschatos* Adam during his life, but that he could live his life the way he did because he was the *eschatos* Adam (see 5.3.2).

Jesus Christ did not take our place to become what we are and to stay in his tomb. His history continues with his resurrection, glorification and ascension to be seated at the right hand of God. Here he reigns and is our high priest, interceding for us, giving his Spirit to the church and making the church participate in his story. The representative act comprises more than his identification with us.

According to the Pauline model of 'being in Christ' it is a phase 'in between' which waits for a more complete participation in the story of Jesus Christ. Consequently, the end of his story has to be understood in such a way that it is possible for us to share in this end. In this light it is important to reflect on the nature of the resurrection. This question became pressing in the context of modern cosmology. According to Dalferth, the resurrection is God's eschatological act, not in but on history, and determining the end of history as a whole. Within history it can only be discerned if the Holy Spirit makes possible an experience of Jesus Christ. The empty tomb is not a necessary consequence of the resurrection, Dalferth writes.

Christ remains accessible through his body, the church.[49] I concluded that more has to be said on the bodily resurrection (8.5). This is important because of the clarification of our participation in the resurrection of Christ. O'Donovan maintains the physical and material nature of the body of Christ, and points to the transformation of the material. A human person is brought back from death in a human body. Resurrection and ascension raise cosmological questions, which O'Donovan solves claiming that Jesus Christ has been transferred into an existence in the presence of God, beyond the conditions of our physical existence. We are not able to describe this transfer or the form of a human body outside time and space as known to us nor to localise the right hand of God.

The eschatological character of the resurrection is important in Dalferth's position. The resurrection as God's eschatological act confirms his identity. Further Jesus did not rise to die again, but into a new reality where death is no longer a possibility. His resurrection brings in a new age. In O'Donovan's position it makes sense to say that we will participate in his resurrection and receive a body like his. His position can be understood in the light of the proposal of Van den Brom that ascension is the transfer of the body of Jesus Christ from our three-dimensional system to the higher dimensional system of heaven.[50] Further clarification of the nature of the resurrection body is impossible. Nevertheless, to guarantee our participation in the resurrection of Christ, this resurrection should at least have the following historical consequences: the disappearance of his dead body, the resurrection appearances to the disciples, the new life of

49. The positions of A. van de Beek and Robert Jenson are comparable to the position of Dalferth. Van de Beek values many aspects of Bultmann's position and criticises Pannenberg comparably to Dalferth, and he writes that the resurrection is not an event in history but an eschatological act determining the whole and the end of history. However, different from Dalferth, he emphasises the importance of the empty tomb and of the bodily resurrection. See Van de Beek, *Jezus Kurios*, 163–73, 232–44; Van de Beek, *De kring om de Messias*, 20, 39–40, 42–45, 94, 98, 367–68.

According to Jenson, Jesus Christ is risen into the future of God. Like Dalferth, he clarifies the resurrection not by analogy to our resurrection of the flesh, but by analogy to a dead body lying in a tomb. Jesus is risen into his body, the church. Different from Dalferth he insists that the tomb had to be empty , but only because Jesus is now available to us by church and sacraments and not by relics. See Jenson, *Systematic Theology. Volume 1*, 194–206, 229.

50. Van den Brom, *God alomtegenwoordig*, 230–31.

the church, and the future public appearance on the last day together with the public visible appearance of our risen bodies.[51]

In conclusion: narrating the story of Christ I will follow the story of the history of salvation. In this light, Christology is eschatology. Jesus Christ is not significant for the sake of one moment of his life, but because of his entire history as the gospels tell it. His life is a representative act, consisting in different moments. During his life, he identified with us during a process of growing conformity to our existence until he died on the cross. He became what we are, to make us participate in what he is now. Hence it is especially important that the nature of his resurrection is conceptualised in a way that allows us to understand that we participate in his destiny.

10.3.2 SOTERIOLOGY

The eschatological story of Jesus Christ continues in our lives. In this subsection I first want to develop two images for union with Christ which have great integrative power, a Pauline image which is forgotten but deserves rehabilitation, the image of clothing, and a Johannine image, the image of the vine and branches.

The Pauline image of clothing is an image for union with Christ, but in this image we can find all four moments. Christ is our clothing. He is the new man and in him salvation is complete. We do not add something to salvation but simply put on something which is already there. He is the first, exclusive in his inclusivity. The image shows further that we cannot be united with Christ without participating in him. In the light of this image, 'being in Christ' implies literally being *in* him, or being covered with him. With regard to the modern subject, it is noteworthy that this image does not focus on interiority, but has exocentric implications. Christ is *extra nos*, but still he is near. United with Christ, we also participate in him. Man and woman participate in him alike, both receiving a position as full-fledged heir. Before elaborating aspects of this participation, I want to say something more general on sin and salvation. Sin and its consequences are understood as filth or nakedness, both causing shame. Salvation is a gift implying acceptance, for a new garment is given and the shameful nakedness covered. However, it is not just acceptance, for the filthy clothing is removed. Moreover, the image implies forgiveness

51. See on the resurrection further Berkhof, *Christelijk geloof*, 305–16.

because a new innocent identity is given. This new identity is the first aspect of participation in Christ. Being clothed with Christ, we participate in his innocence and his position as full citizen of the kingdom of God and heir of the Father (adoption). The second aspect of participation concerns our acts. We cannot be clothed with Christ if we do not put off our old garment, referring to the sinful way of life. At the same time, clothing oneself with Christ means doing the good works prepared in Christ, acting in conformity with Christ and following his example. Consequently, possibilities for growth are given. A third aspect of participation is eschatic: we will be clothed with our heavenly dwelling. And finally, the new clothing can be interpreted as the wedding-dress for the wedding of the lamb.

The Johannine image is the image of the vine and the branches. It has been shown already that in this image all four elements are also present. Christ is the true Israel, inclusive and exclusive (see 6.2.5). The image shows that we cannot participate in Christ without union with him. This image shows 'being in Christ' as being grafted upon him and grown together with him. Exocentricity and interiority are kept together, for we remain in him and he remains in us. With regard to sin, this image highlights the aspect of loss of contact with the source of life. Sin leads to death, salvation restores the relation with the source of life and makes possible a new flowering in a fruitful life. Clearly the fruits do not give life to the tree, but the tree gives life to bear fruits. Consequently, the acts of the believers do not restore the relation with God, but the reconciled relation with God in Christ results in acts of a renewed life. Furthermore, union with the vine results in joy. The image has ecclesiological implications as most of the other images for union with Christ have. The one vine has many branches. Further it has missionary implications. To bear fruit is secondary in John 15 to bring people to Jesus Christ to make them branches of him as his disciples.

What neither image shows is the relation to the Holy Spirit, to the sacraments, to the story of Jesus Christ and to the judgment of God. On these four elements I will say something now.

First I start with the work of the Holy Spirit. The role of the work of the Spirit in soteriology is evident in the Reformed tradition, in the New Testament as well as in the work of Dalferth and O'Donovan. However, this is not to be understood as if soteriology is especially the area of pneumatology, as Dalfeth and O'Donovan say. Christology also has a pneumatological aspect, and soteriology has a Christological aspect. This last is important in the Reformed tradition: it is Jesus Christ who unites us with himself and makes us participate in his story. This reality can at the same time be formulated pneumatologically: the Spirit unites us with Christ and makes us participate in his story. The inhabitation of Christ in us in the present is the inhabitation of his Spirit (see 6.3.1). The Holy Spirit is given as a deposit or downpayment of the future heritage. Consequently, the Spirit is essential in our relation with Christ. Moreover, Christ's Spirit, living in us, is a source of moral and spiritual renewal.[52]

Second, in relation to union and participation the sacraments have to be mentioned. The chapter on John Owen is exceptional because the sacraments play almost no role in it. This is different in the other chapters. According to Bavinck, baptism is the sacrament of incorporation in Christ, Eucharist the sacrament of the ongoing mystical union with Christ. For Paul, baptism is baptism into Christ by which the beginning of our participation in Christ is marked. We die and are buried with him, and are clothed with Christ in baptism. Further the image of the body is related to the Lord's Supper. In Johannine thinking the image of the living bread has sacramental overtones. In Dalferth's understanding, baptism and Eucharist play an important role in our participation in the story of Jesus Christ. O'Donovan writes that the—four—sacraments together with the story of Jesus Christ determine the shape of our relation with him. The hidden reality of salvation becomes publicly manifest in baptism, Eucharist, the keeping of the Lord's day, and the laying-on of hands. O'Donovan is reluctant to let the shape of the relation with Christ be determined by our biography as is the case in the Roman-Catholic tradition, because its shape is Christological. Further his understanding of the Lord's Supper does not include an individual feeding on the living Christ. When the Eucharist, with the Reformed tradition and the gospel of John, is understood as a public manifestation of our mystical union with Christ, an opening is created for a closer relation with our biographies: the sacrament of baptism marks the beginning of our 'being in Christ,' the Eucharist the ongoing reality of 'being in Christ.'

52. Alston, 'The Indwelling of the Holy Spirit'; Van den Brink, 'De geestelijke groei van de nieuwe mens,' 95–105; Douma, *Grondslagen Christelijke Ethiek*, 173–79; Van der Kooi, *De ziel van het christelijk geloof*, 82, 84, 106–13; Lovelace, *Dynamics of spiritual life*, 119–33.

A. van de Beek cannot do justice to this aspect of the work of the Holy Spirit, cf. Van de Beek, *Jezus Kurios*, 216–19, 224–32, 247–54.

Third, I need to say something on the story of Jesus Christ.[53] It has been said in 10.2.2.2 that we participate in this story but only to a certain extent. This 'to a certain extent' has to be elaborated, which I will do now. I will not limit myself to the four moments of O'Donovan in order to do justice to other aspects we have discovered in Paul and John.

a. The beginning of the story: Jesus began his life as representative. The church begins her life in Christ by accepting the representative in faith. Just as Jesus was chosen and anointed with the Spirit, the church is chosen in Christ and receives the Spirit. Hereby the church never herself becomes a representative, but she exists as a body constituted by the representative.

b. The Father-Son relation: Jesus Christ lived as the Son of God. In this way he represents the people of God, called the son of God in the Old Testament, or the righteous people which were called God's children.[54] Still this Old Testament background is not sufficient to understand his Father-Son relation. The gospel of John shows that in the case of Jesus Christ this Father-Son relation has a special character. Their unity, mutually being in each other, is unique and not open to participation. He is the one and only Son of God. Consequently, the Christian tradition came to speak of an eternal generation. Although this relation is unique, the Son does enable believers to become God's children. Paul makes the difference between Jesus the Son and the believers still smaller. In Christ, the believers become full grown sons and consequently heirs of God. It is the Spirit of the Son who makes us call God 'Father.' We share in the loving nearness of God in which Jesus lived. In communion with Christ we pray 'our Father' as we find it in the Lord's Prayer. John emphasises the difference, Paul the similarity because of the hereditary connotations. The Son is unique, the children, however, share in his position and his relation with the Father.[55]

c. Life in the world: the life of Jesus was a life in obedience to his Father, a life of serving love, a life for others: pro-existence as Dalferth calls

53. It is important that systematic theologies do not disturb the narrative relation between Jesus Christ and the believers. Cf. Milbank's criticism of Anselm's *Cur Deus Homo*, Milbank, *Theology and social theory*, 396.

54. Van Bruggen, *Het evangelie van Gods Zoon*, 126.

55. Van der Kooi, *De ziel van het christelijk geloof*, 79,

it. Our obedience will not result in our justification or in the justification of others. Rather this was the case in Jesus' life: his obedience makes many righteous. Here we have the difference between Jesus Christ and the church. At the same time, Jesus Christ is presented as example to be followed, especially with regard to the loving attitude shown in his death for others. He is even more than an example: our good works are prepared in Christ. We clothe ourselves with his righteousness to live a life for others in love and obedience.[56]

d. Mission: Christ has been sent into the world by his Father. His mission has been accomplished. Nevertheless, he sends his disciples into the world to do as he did, in the power of the Holy Spirit. Jesus is sent to make known the Father and his work, the church is sent to make known Jesus Christ and his work.[57]

e. Cross: The cross of Christ has many aspects. First, Christ suffered the presence of sin and its consequences in the world. He identified with our existence, its illness and failure. It brought him to tears and stirred his anger. He suffered the hiddenness of God in this world. The second aspect concerns the activity of evil. Christ lived an obedient life in conformity with God's law. This resulted in his exclusion from life, although he was innocent. Third, he suffered for the benefit of others. He was willing to suffer for others, to show them God's love and reconcile them with God. Fourth, he suffered the judgment of God. He drank the cup, was made to sin and became a curse for us.

We participate in all aspects. Our suffering the presence of sin and its consequences, the first aspect, is not in itself a participation in the suffering of Christ. But because of Christ's identification with our existence and our union with Christ in faith, our suffering receives a new significance as participation in Christ's suffering, if we endure it in imitation of him. Moreover, just as God was hidden in Jesus Christ, he will often be hidden in the life of the believers. However, the hiddenness of God that Christ experienced during the three hours darkness on the cross will never be our experience.

56. Cf. Boersma, *Violence, Hospitality and the Cross*, 205–34; Gestrich, *Christentum und Stellvertretung*, 66, 425–26, 443–46; Ford, *Self and Salvation*, 79, 91, 97, 166, 172, 219, 233, 240.

57. Cf. Gestrich, *Christentum und Stellvertretung*, 398–400.

Second, living in conformity with Christ, the church may be excluded from life as was the case with Jesus. Martyrdom is its climax. Third, the church may also suffer for the benefit of others, enduring hardship to reach others with the love of God. This suffering may contribute to reconciliation, even with God, but not to the atonement of sin. Because making atonement is part of the exclusive moment, the suffering of the church for others never has the atoning quality present in the suffering of Christ.[58] Fourth, the church will agree with God's judgment on sin, taking up the cross and mortifying sin. This fourth aspect clearly indicates at the same time the exclusivity of the cross of Christ in which the church does not participate.[59] The church will not drink the cup Christ had to drink, or be made a curse as he was. He gave himself for our justification.[60]

f. Death and burial: The death and burial of Christ are the climax of his suffering. He died for our sins to make us live. This immediately indicates the exclusive aspect of his death. But his death also has two inclusive aspects: by his death our existence in sin came to an end, and we have to put our sinful existence to death together with Christ. Consequently, we are freed from ourselves.[61]

g. Resurrection: Christ died as a blasphemer, but he was innocent. Consequently, he was vindicated and brought to life again. He is risen from death. The exclusive aspect of his resurrection concerns the fact that he is the firstborn from the dead. The inclusive side of his resurrection again has three aspects. First, the church partici-

58. See on suffering and reconciliation Volf, *Exclusion & Embrace*, 125–27.
John Milbank emphasises the suffering of the church in a praxis of reconciliation, but looses the exclusive side of the story in this respect; see Milbank, *The Word Made Strange*, 151–52, 158–62.

59. Note that the sacrifice-image is not exclusive, see Rom 12:1.

60. Harmannij was right in calling attention to the inclusive aspect of the suffering of Christ, reacting against an overemphasis on the exclusive aspect. Christ identified with our suffering, making e.g. Psalm 22 his own prayer. His position is comparable to Hooker's, opposing the idea of exchange and offering interchange as an alternative. However, Harmannij's formulations fail to do complete justice to the exclusive aspect of Christ's suffering. Therefore, he took back his book. See K. Harmannij, *Jezus leed wat wij nu lijden*, 17, 20–28, 32–35, 37, 40–47, 53–54, 69–80.
See further on participation in the suffering of Christ Calvin, *Institutes of the Christian Religion*, Book III, 8; Douma, *Grondslagen christelijke ethiek*, 191–93.

61. Van der Kooi, *De ziel van het christelijk geloof*, 83.

pates in his vindication and justification. This offers hope for victims of injustice and justification by faith for sinners. Participation in his vindication corresponds to joy and peace. Second, the church will be raised from death in the resurrection of the flesh in the last day. Injustice will be set right, and the salvation of sinners will be completed. Third, the church is alive in her representative and lives a new life already.

h. Glorification and inheritance: After his resurrection Christ received the highest name and a position as king and highpriest. He inherited the glory of God. He is the head of the church as well as of the cosmos. Further he is the first of humanity living according to God's intention and taking his place within the moral order as O'Donovan pointed out. As such, Christ is unique for several reasons. He is the first, he is head, highpriest and king of kings. However, he is also the last Adam living as a glorified human being, in which the church participates. The present participation of the church concerns authorisation. Again I will follow O'Donovan here, who writes that this authorisation concerns participation in Christ's position of dominion, allowing creative moral responses, as well as authorisation to speak the words of God, displaying the powers of the kingdom of God.[62] The future participation will bring visible glorification and public appearance in glory, as well as inheriting together with Christ.[63]

i. Intercession: In heaven at the right hand of God, Christ prays for his church and the salvation of the world. This intercession is especially emphasised by the Reformed tradition. The activity of Christ as saviour continues after his resurrection and glorification. What the Reformed tradition did not say, probably for anti-Roman Catholic reasons, is that the church participates in this intercession. Christ is unique in making intercession on the grounds of his own sacrifice, as blameless and exalted high priest. The church never pleads on the grounds of her own works, but only in the name of Jesus Christ.

62. The authorisation of the church is important for the discussion concerning the gifts of the Spirit (like wisdom, knowledge, healing, miracles, prophecy, distinguishing spirits, teaching, exhorting, leadership). Cf. on authority in spiritual conflict Lovelace, *Dynamics of spiritual life*, 133–44.

63. See for a further elaboration of e-h in relation to the work of the Spirit and his gifts, Burger, 'Theologia crucis, theologia gloriae, of geen van beide?.'

This does not change the fact that the church together with Christ prays for the church and for the world.[64]

j. Giving the Holy Spirit: Christ promised that he would pray to his Father to give the Holy Spirit. At Pentecost, the Holy Spirit was given as downpayment of the eschatological inheritance. According to O'Donovan, Pentecost does not have the 'once for all character' of the Christ-event. With the ascension, the representative act is complete, and Pentecost makes participation in this act possible. What O'Donovan does not seem to see, is that the saving activity of Jesus Christ after his ascension continues in his intercession. Further, the participation of the church in Christ can be described as a result of the act of the Spirit, but at the same time of an act of Jesus Christ himself, as we have seen. Consequently, Pentecost is a moment in the story of Jesus Christ. I do not want to suggest that something has to be added to cross, resurrection and glorification, but Christ is yet active in distributing the fruits of his achievement. Another question is, whether Pentecost has the character of a 'once for all' event. Ferguson distinguishes two dimensions of Pentecost: the redemptive-historical which is unrepeatable and the personal-existential which is an aspect of the continuing work of the Spirit. What the apostles experienced is unique, but Christ's activity, experienced as a new filling of the Spirit, baptism with the Spirit, revival and renewal continues.[65] With regard to substitution and representation, one might expect that giving the Spirit is exclusively an activity of Jesus Christ. However, John 7:38f says about a believer that streams of living water will flow from within him, suggesting that the church plays a role in giving the Spirit. The laying on of hands and the gift of the Spirit are related.

k. Appearance in glory: after his death Christ, in his glory, appeared to the select few rather than to all. Consequently his vindication has to be completed in his *parousia*. This moment will be at the same time the moment of the salvation of the bodies of the members of

64. Gestrich, *Christentum und Stellvertretung*, 444–49; Van der Kooi, *De ziel van het christelijk geloof*, 76–85, 115–17, 133, 157.

65. See Ferguson, *The Holy Spirit*, 79–92, 235–37. To maintain a careful balance between the redemptive-historical and the personal-existential is important for the discussion concerning the gifts of the Spirit between continuation and cessation.

the church. In the resurrection of the flesh the believers will receive a spiritual body and be glorified to live with Christ.

In 10.2.2.2 we faced the problem of whether I could do justice to the central interests of the Reformation in rehabilitating the concept of participation. I have shown now that using the difference of exclusivity and inclusivity the *extra nos* of salvation is guaranteed, although we participate in the entire story of Jesus Christ.

After elaborating the extent to which the story of Jesus Christ has an inclusive character, fourth something has to be said on the judgment of God. I will do this in 10.3.3 in relation to the image of justification.

It is especially in the field of soteriology that the contextual relevance of 'being in Christ' for the present cultural context can be shown.[66] Therefore I will use Charles Taylor's four terms to formulate conclusions of this conversion with regard to the self: notions of the good, our understanding of self, the kinds of narrative in which we make sense of our lives, and conceptions of society (see 1.1.2). In this way I will show that in Christ the subject is saved and the contact with God, self and world is restored.

a. Notions of the Good: Jesus Christ is determinative for our notion of the good. No one is good except God alone, but God acts in Christ, identifying himself to us in Christ and in the Spirit and reconciling us to him. 'Being in Christ' is the place where the triune God meets us. We even discover ourselves in God. Being in Christ we are united to the source of life again. We confess that Jesus Christ is the good life and the way to the good life. As a result, the shape of the story of his life has to determine our ideas of a good life.[67] A life in communion with Christ is a life in which we reflect his face more and more. As far as his inclusiveness is concerned, we are changed to conformity with Christ. 'Being in Christ' is the place where our relations with our moral sources are restored: God, the moral order of creation, a new humanity, and God's history with this world.

66. For a comparable Christian response on nihilism from the viewpoint of salvation as conformity to Christ, see Hoogland, 'Christelijk geloof: oplossing of verlossing,' 107–19.

67. Milbank, *Theology and social theory*, 398. On the relation between atonement and the good life, see Van den Brink, 'Narrative, Atonement and the Christian Conception of the Good Life.'

b. Our understanding of the self: by being in Christ, the subject is relocated. It is no longer localised in the world, in the flesh, in the old world, but in Christ and in the Spirit. As a result, the subject is liberated from incurvation in itself, decentered and recentered. It becomes a self without idols, worshipping the true God alone. The subject no longer possesses himself and no longer needs to secure himself in self-justification, but lives excentrically, with its life *extra se* in Christ.[68] This implies a loss of identity (the old self dies), but at the same time the gift of a new identity (a new self). As a result, the identity and the position of the subject are no longer threatened, but Christ and the Spirit determine his identity and position, securing it against decay and mortality and offering hope of a future with Christ in a renewed world.[69] Living in Christ and in the Spirit, the self lives in God's love. It enjoys the hospitality of God, who wants to communicate his abundance.[70] As a result, the self receives joy, rest and peace. Worship, singing and gladness are appropriate responses to God's attitude towards us. God's love and goodness are to be enjoyed, praised and celebrated.[71] In Christ, the subject is enabled to live a new life in love. Clothing ourselves with Christ, we are not just confronted with his perfect example but also covered with his perfect life. In this way it becomes possible to be honest about guilt and failure, about the difference between high moral standards and our power to live in accordance with these standards. This difference has lost its destructive character, because the justice of Christ covers us. Being in Christ is the place where the subject is saved and restored. It is liberated for a new identity and receives a place to live from God's abundance, facing the loving eyes of God in Jesus Christ and rejoicing in him.[72]

68. Cf. Gestrich, *Christentum und Stellvertretung*, 390, 410–14, 420–22; Jüngel, *Gott als Geheimniss der Welt*, 228–29, 235, 246–47, 529, 7536–43; Jüngel, *Das Evangelium von der Rechtfertigung des Gottlosen als Zentrum des christlichen Glaubens*, 176–77, 181–83, 191–92, 205–7; Volf, *Exclusion & Embrace*, 69–71, 92; Ford, *Self and Salvation*, 45–106.

69. Gestrich, *Christentum und Stellvertretung*, 245, 248–50, 252, 397, 410–15; Ford, *Self and Salvation*, 117, 127–28.

70. See on God's abundance Ford, *Self and Salvation*, 98, 101–3, 107–36, 144–45; on God's hospitality Boersma, *Violence, Hospitality and the Cross*.

71. Ford, *Self and Salvation*, 75, 80–81, 99, 107–36, 167. See further Brümmer, 'Ultimate Happiness and the Love of God.'

72. See on 'being in Christ' and our relation with ourselves also Burger, 'Mens in

c. The kinds of narrative in which we make sense of our lives: Participation in Christ includes participation in his story. This means that we experience what Christ experienced, in accordance with the Pauline model of 'being in Christ.' Enough has been said on this theme already. But the story of Jesus Christ is a part of a larger history, the history of Israel. It is the story of the coming of the promised kingdom of God. Both stories in which we have come to participate, the smaller story of the life of Jesus Christ and the larger story of God and his people, have not come to an end yet, although we know the outcome. Consequently, 'being in Christ' is an existence of hope and desire for the coming of the kingdom of God.

d. Conceptions of society: It is remarkable that the images the New Testament uses for union with Jesus Christ are all collective. United with Christ, we live in communion; not just with Jesus Christ but with all other people who have found their life in him. It is impossible to be in Christ solitarily.[73] In Christ, the last Adam, a new humanity is created. This has universal significance, which is made especially clear in Paul's letters to the Ephesians and the Colossians. The community which came into existence with Christ is a world community, in which ethnic lines no longer bring division. Only the salvation of humanity from its idols by God's self-identification makes a world community possible, reuniting humanity. The other we meet in Christ is also someone in Christ: Jesus Christ mediates all relationships with other people. He stands between me and the other.[74] This community exists in Christ only, marked by baptism and Eucharist. It is a community where new life is lived already, worshipping God, practicing forgiveness, living for others in love with hospitality and generosity; a community of reconciliation and hope. The message of atonement has to result in practices and new social mechanisms that seek peace and reconciliation.[75] This community is the necessary context for our lives in Christ to have a public shape, to offer an exemplary practice which we can imitate, to learn the idiom of 'being in Christ,' to understand our identity and world as being

---

Christus,' 118–20.

73. Van der Kooi, *De ziel van het christelijk geloof*, 76, 89–91.

74. Ford, *Self and Salvation*, 251f.

75. Boersma, *Violence, Hospitality and the Cross*, 205–34; Milbank, *Theology and Social Theory*, 397.

in Christ and to practice it as a skill.[76] 'Being in Christ' therefore introduces a new community into this world of competing groups, testifying of the coming Christ and the coming kingdom of God.

Summarizing, we are clothed with Christ and live as branches of the true vine. This is possible because of the Holy Spirit. Sacraments give our union with and participation in Christ a public manifestation. Participation in Christ has to be understood further as participation in the story of Jesus Christ, many moments of which story have an inclusive aspect. 'Being in Christ,' finally is a concept offering hope for the postmodern subject, restoring its relation with the good, relocating the subject, giving it a place in the story of Jesus Christ and in his community, the church.

10.3.3 METAPHORS FOR SALVATION

Different images are used to express the importance of the story of Jesus Christ in the biography of the believers.

The first image which has to be elaborated is the forensic image of justification. This is an important image because in the elaboration of this forensic image the relation between God's judgment and participation in Christ can be unfolded. We have seen that in the Reformed tradition participation-language is avoided with regard to justification. However, I concluded that in the Pauline framework justification and participation cannot be separated. The imputation-language made it possible to separate justification and participation, but we found that Paul uses the verb λογίζομαι in relation to justification only if Christ cannot be mentioned and the continuity in God's dealing with Abraham and the New Testament believers is discussed. Because I am especially interested in 'being in Christ' and hence in the relation with Jesus Christ, I will avoid the language of imputation. We do not need it (see 5.4.4).[77] How then should we relate justification and participation without losing the central

76. Gestrich, *Christentum und Stellvertretung*, 136; Milbank, *Theology and social theory*, 396, 398.

77. Here I differ from McCormack and Garcia. McCormack sees in the positive imputation of the righteousness of Christ the heart of the Reformation understanding of justification; see McCormack, 'What's at Stake in the Current Debates over Justification?' 83–84, 109; McCormack, 'Protestant Identity as a Theological Problem.' Garcia uses the doctrine of imputation as a tool to maintain the exclusivity of Christ, see Garcia, 'Imputation and the Christology of Union with Christ,' 246–48.

interests of the Reformation which are also Pauline interests: the justification of the wicked and the *extra nos* of salvation?[78] I have shown in 10.3.2 that the distinction between exclusiveness and inclusiveness is necessary here. Both moments play a role in justification: Christ died for our sins, and he was raised for our justification (see 5.4.4). In the removal of sin, the exclusive moment is especially important. In acceptance, forgiveness and the gift of innocence and a new identity the identification of Christ with us and our participation in him is essential. Now I will say more on the concept of judgment to show how this concept safeguards the interests of the Reformation.

Discussing Owen and Bavinck, we saw how they emphasised the forensic aspect of salvation. God's judgment justifies the ungodly. O'Donovan's analysis of God's judgment is especially important here. He shows how in the cross and resurrection God successively condemns sin, accepts the sinner, vindicates Jesus Christ and with him all innocent victims of injustice, restores humanity from death, and makes the representative authoritative and present to us in the Spirit, who evokes our free response in faith and makes our participation possible. God's performative judgment separates good from evil, condemning it, and creates a new reality which includes us. Consequently, God's judgment comprises the justification of Jesus Christ as well as the justification of the wicked, making them participate in God's judgment on Jesus Christ who died for sin and is raised for our justification. This means that the justification of Jesus Christ and the justification of the sinner, consisting of the gift of Jesus Christ to the believer, should not be identified. Nevertheless, the justification of the sinner consists in the gift of participation in the justification of Jesus Christ. God's performative judgment, the gift of Jesus Christ, is, further, an effective judgment which results in our good works.[79] We are not justified by works, but still God's judgment creates our good works. The gift of Christ is like the gift of new clothing: a new identity leading to a new way of life. To conclude, the concept of God's perfective judgment makes it possible to understand how justification is a justification apart from works by faith, a justification of the wicked, whereas it is at the same

78. Cf. Garcia, 'Imputation and the Christology of Union with Christ.'

79. Where the language of imputation is maintained, it becomes difficult to see how we receive a participation in the justification of Jesus Christ and how God's justifying judgment is effective. Contra Garcia, 'Imputation and the Christology of Union with Christ.'

time the gift of participation in Christ, i.e. in God's judgment on him and in his obedient life.[80]

This effective understanding of justification implies that the eschatological tension is present within the image of justification. Whoever believes, is justified. Consequently, the judgment is a reality. Furthermore, the judgment effects a process of change in the life of the believer, resulting more and more in righteous acts. Finally, eschatically we shall be saved from the wrath of God as Paul writes. In the end, God's judgment on all human beings will be public, leading to salvation or to wrath. Further, if justification is effective, it has to result in visible righteousness and innocence, for others as well as for ourselves. Reconciliation is not really possible as long as the consequences of our injustice are not healed and restored. Justification without resurrection and re-creation is incomplete. Consequently, justification has to be completed in a cosmic event: the resurrection of the flesh and the re-creation of the entire cosmos, when all consequences of sin will be healed.[81]

A second important image is the image of adoption. The interest of this image lies in the fact that it highlights the identity and position which is given in Christ. The image is similar to the image of justification because it is a forensic image—adoption is a forensic act—and because the image of justification also concerns our identity. However, the image of adoption says more about our identity. This image implies our participation in the position of Christ as son and heir in a Pauline understanding, or as child in a Johannine understanding. To be adopted means that we will

80. See on justification as an effective judgment of God further Jüngel, *Das Evangelium von der Rechtfertigung des Gottlosen als Zentrum des christlichen Glaubens*, 174–83, 205–6; McCormack, 'What's at Stake in the Current Debates over Justification?' 107–10.

Robert Jenson tries, in his doctrine of justification, to combine the Augustinian, transformative doctrine with the hermeneutical doctrine of justification of the Reformation, using the Finnish Luther research (the 'Mannermaa school'). Augustine's doctrine appears under pneumatology as the achieving of righteousness. The Christological doctrine of the Reformation is a metalinguistic doctrine instructing teachers about characters of the language preachers are to use. God's gifts are 'bespoken to us' and therefore the speaking of the gospel has to be promising. Luther's theology provides a bridge between both, because 'according to Luther, the soul becomes what it hearkens to.' Jenson shows that the promise of God effects something in the believer. His concept of promise functions as the concept of judgment in the proposals of O'Donovan and Jüngel. See Jenson, *Systematic Theology. Volume 1*, 13–14; Jenson, *Systematic Theology. Volume 2: The Works of God*, Oxford 2001, 291–98.

81. Volf, *Exclusion & Embrace*, 137–40.

be glorified. Further it gives us the right to call God 'Father.' As children of God we participate to some extent in the Father-Son relation between God the Father and Jesus Christ.

However, the grammar of this image is not just binitarian but Trinitarian. We receive the Spirit of sonship by which we cry 'Abba, Father.' The adoption-image shows that the identity and position we receive is possible only because we are enveloped in the Trinity: as children we participate in the triune community, although we do not participate in the unity that Father, Son and Spirit have together (see 6.3.1). Maybe we should even say that the same love who fills us is the Holy Spirit who unites Father and Son in love.[82] This evokes the question whether adoption includes deification. What it does not imply is participation in the Trinitarian unity of Father, Son an Spirit, or the end of humanity. Being saved, humans become really human again. At the same time we will receive a spiritual body (although I do not know what a spiritual body is). Adoption does imply participation in the divine nature and in the divine glory. Whether we should call this deification or not is just a matter of words.[83]

Finally, like the image of justification this image contains an eschatological tension also. We are now children of God, but that we are children is not yet visible. The children still have to be revealed, which will happen when the Son is revealed in his glory at the *parousia*.

A third image I will deal with is the image of election. We have seen that according to Bavinck, Paul and O'Donovan election is participation in the election of Christ. Consequently, the image has similarities with the image of adoption, indicating that we participate in the Father-Son relation. The church shares in the love of the Father for the Son. Further, it is important to see with O'Donovan the missionary intention of election. The chosen representative has to include others. Likewise, those included in the representative invite others to participate together in the representative. Election is like a magnet, attracting others to the love of God.[84] According to O'Donovan election does not concern the predestination

82. As Jenson does, together with Augustine, Jonathan Edwards and Martin Luther; see Jenson, *Systematic Theology. Volume 1*, 148–49. See further Van der Kooi, *De ziel van het christelijk geloof*, 79.

83. Boersma and Jenson both use the term deification, McCormack does not; see Boersma, *Violence, Hospitality and the Cross*, 257–61; Jenson, *Systematic Theology. Volume 1*, 71, 83, 226–27; McCormack, 'Participation in God, Yes, Deification, No.'

84. For a comparable position see Gestrich, *Christentum und Stellvertretung*, 262–69.

of individual members of Christ. The gospel of John shows something different: the Father gives individuals to the Son, whereas it is impossible to believe in the Son unless the Father draws someone to the Son. Faith, perseverance and resurrection all are gifts of God. This implies some kind of doctrine of election which concerns individual salvation.

Finally, I want to say something on the image of regeneration. Within the New Testament, the theological concept of regeneration as it was developed in the history of theology appears to include three different words: παλιγγενεσία (Matt 19:28; Titus 3:5), ἀναγεννάω (1 Pet 1:2, 23), and a birth ἄνωθεν (John 3:3, 7). The first, παλιγγενεσία, is an image which refers to a cosmic event of re-creation (Matt. 19:28), or which is used in a context of justification, washing and renewal (Titus 3:5). In Peter the new birth is related to Christ's resurrection, hope and the word of God. In a Johannine understanding it is related to water and Spirit. The different words refer to an inward spiritual renewal today and a cosmic renewal in the future. Both are related to Jesus Christ and his resurrection.[85] The first is related further with word, water and Spirit. This suffices for a plea for a relational understanding of regeneration in the light of participation in Christ's resurrection.

The process of salvation is traditionally analysed in the order of salvation. Different images refer to different moments of this order. What this survey of several images makes clear is that the process of salvation is present within several images. Justification, adoption, election and regeneration should not be understood as different moments in the process of salvation. Instead, each image highlights different aspects of the entire process.[86]

To conclude, the image of justification shows the relation between God's judgment and our participation in Christ. We participate in Christ by God's judgment, participating in God's judgment on Jesus Christ. God's judgment is effective, consequently implying an eschatological tension. Until the eschatic re-creation of the cosmos, the process caused by God's judgment will continue. The image of adoption shows the identity and position the believers receive in Christ, an identity still invisible. This identity is determined by a Trinitarian grammar: we share in the position of the Son by the Spirit as glorified children of the Father. Election

85. Toon, *Born Again*, 185–86.

86. Hoekema, *Saved by Grace*, 11–17.

concerns the participation of the church in the love of the Father for his Son, and has a missionary focus. Regeneration finally refers to the new life given together with Christ. In all these images we find aspects of the process of salvation as well as the eschatological tension related to this process.

10.3.4 WHO ARE REPRESENTED?

Until now I left undefined to whom I refer with the 'we' who are represented by Christ and participate in him. With regard to justification, I did not deal with the opposition between Owen and Bavinck, and O'Donovan. In the Reformed tradition the atoning death of Christ on the cross presupposes the imputation of guilt unto Christ based on God's decree of predestination. This results in an understanding of mystical union, representation and particular atonement limited to the elect. According to O'Donovan, in a process of identification Christ becomes the representative of Israel and because of his resurrection and the function of Israel in redemptive history the representative of humanity. Humanity is represented and saved in Christ, and now it is only the question of whether we shall be saved with humanity. Christ represents humanity, by faith we participate in humanity saved in Christ. The Reformed tradition especially affirms the line of particularity; O'Donovan (as well as Dalferth) affirms the line of universality. Which line is to be preferred?

We find both lines in Paul as well as in John. Both use particular, affirming or excluding as well as universal, open and inviting statements. Consequently the question of when a particular statement is used and when a universal one will be decisive. It is especially here the narrative and rhetorical structure of a systematic-theological text has to be reflected on to do justice to the pragmatic intentions of the different statements. We saw that both in Paul and John election-statements come in the end, in doxology or because of unbelief. Further, if we reconstruct the story of Jesus Christ, following the narrative structure of the bible, the structure of this reconstruction will be redemptive-historical and not begin with God's eternal decree. Finally, I concluded in 4.4 that theology should not give a theoretical reconstruction which undermines the practice of the preaching of the gospel and does no justice to its communicative character. Consequently, one simple answer on the question 'who are the represented' cannot be given. Instead, rules have to be formulated as to when the different answers have to be given.

Two different ranges of answers can be given to this question. The first is determined by the process of identification. Primarily, Christ represents the innocent victims of injustice. Secondarily, sentenced as if he were guilty, Christ becomes representative of the guilty. In this way he represents all Israel, the people of God. But Israel has a position within God's redemptive purposes. In Israel, God wants to save the world. Consequently, Christ's death and resurrection removes 'the dividing wall of hostility' between Jew and gentile. His resurrection proves that he is the last Adam, representing humanity. In him, humanity is saved.

The second range is determined by different contexts. The following answers have to be distinguished:

a. An inviting answer. Christ represents all humanity. He represents you. No one has to exclude himself from Christ and doubt whether he is represented by him. This is the first answer which should be given where the gospel is preached

b. A descriptive answer: Christ represents the church. We see that not all Jews believed in the Jewish Messiah. Not all humanity confesses Christ as Lord. This answer should be given to make clear that not all participate in Christ, but only those who believe in Christ and are incorporated in his body.

c. An encouraging answer: Christ represents all who are given him by the Father and no one can snatch them out of his hand. This answer should be given to those who are afraid of losing their faith.

d. A confronting answer: Christ represents only those who are drawn by the Father. Whoever does not belong to Jesus' sheep, does not believe. This answer should be given to those who trust their own capacities before God and do not want to believe in Jesus Christ.

e. A doxological answer: Christ represents God's elect, those who have received faith by God's grace. This answer should be given to praise the triune God.

f. An eschatic-descriptive answer: Christ represents all who we see as glorified beings, to live with him forever. This answer should be given in the end.

It is impossible for human beings, who do not see the heart, to give the eschatic answer. It is the limited character of human knowledge which leads to the fluid character of the beginning of the union with Christ (see 10.2.2.2). 'Being in Christ' implies that someone can be in Christ as well as outside Christ. However, theological reflection should not focus on the border between inside and outside as if the eschatic answer could be given already. This can be done in relation to union with Christ, regeneration, conversion, the moment of justification, or the sacrament of baptism. We should not focus on the border between outside and inside, but on Christ and on a process of growing conformity with him. Moreover, reflection on the border between inside and outside Christ is not fruitful, because of the complexity of this border. Many different actors are involved in the crossing of the line between unbelief and faith (cf. 5.5.5 and 6.3.1), a line which shares in the complexity of the eschaton:

a. God the Father: coming with light, loving, pulling, inviting;
b. Jesus Christ, the Son: having lived, suffered and risen in Christ life and salvation can be found, being preached, making the church participate in his person and story;
c. Holy Spirit: illuminating, living in the church, making her participate in Christ;
d. Church: representing Christ in word, sacraments and community, baptising;
e. Subject: conversion and faith, discovering their being in Christ, remaining in Christ.

The Reformed tradition emphasised the work of God, the Roman-Catholic tradition the activity of the church in baptism, modern evangelism the acts of the subject, the Charismatic movement the work of the Spirit.[87] Consequently, reflection on 'border disputes' is a cause of many confessional differences. Instead of specialising as a Christian sub-tradition in one of the actors, we should see the complexity of the border and do justice to them all.

To conclude, the border between unbelief and faith, between being outside Christ and in Christ is a complex phenomenon. Many actors are involved, historical but eschatological acts play a role, our human knowl-

87. Cf. Toon, *Born Again*.

edge is limited and ignorant of the end of history. Consequently, the beginning of the union with Christ has a fluid character. Furthermore, different answers have to be given to the question 'who are those represented,' answers each with their own pragmatic intention and suited for different contexts.

10.4 Eschatological Reality

In 1.1.3 I argued for some form of theological realism, in the end, for soteriological reasons: that *God* saves us, that God *saves* us, and that God saves *us* has to be a reality. Because Christians believe 'being in Christ' is a reality, it has all kinds of implications: spiritual, affective, psychological, moral, or social. In this investigation, I focus especially on the ontological implications of 'being in Christ.' Before I deal with the ontological implications themselves (10.4.2), I will first start with some methodological considerations (10.4.1)

10.4.1 METHOD

In 1.2.4 I started this investigation with a 'complex pragmatic realism,' an extended version of Lindbeck's cultural-linguistic approach. In this position theological concepts are bound up with the praxis pietatis, without neglecting truth claims of the Christian faith. Theology reflects on the speech acts of the church, including the narratives of redemptive history.

Although O'Donovan does reflect on the reality of 'being in Christ' and develops a moral ontology, his work does not offer much concerning a method for ontological reflection. This is evidently not the case with Dalferth. His position is compatible with the position sketched in 1.2.4. Ontological reflection starts with a given language, discourse or theory. The pragmatic dimension of language understood as speech acts has to be investigated with hermeneutical sensitivity, before the question concerning ontological implications can be answered. Consequently, ontological reflection is not an absolute activity, but an ontological theory is always relative to the chosen language or theory. To be is to be related to our story. This means that it is possible to ask for the ontological implications of the in Christ-language.[88] Its aim is not to replace the in Christ-language and

88. Cf. Mühling-Schlapkohl, *Gott ist Liebe*, 11–15.

the related images by a more adequate conceptual language or by reconstructing a more real reality behind this language, but to clarify the meaning of the language of faith. Before reconstructing ontological implications we have to investigate the use of the in Christ-language, as I did especially in ch. 5 and 6. The grammar of its use has been described in 10.2.

Secondarily, the question has to be answered whether entities to which we refer in our story, do really exist.[89] This means, according to Dalferth: does someone stand in an ontological relation with the entity he refers to? With regard to 'being in Christ,' an important question is whether we stand in an ontological relation with Father, Son and Spirit. According to Dalferth, the ontological commitment of Christian believers is that this is the case.[90] We have this ontological commitment because we believe that we stand also in an epistemic relation with God because of his self-identification. By God's self-identification, God is identified as loving Father. This self-identification opens an identification system—a 'Gegenständlichkeit,' in which God identifies himself to us. Dalferth is especially interested in the identification of God, but, further, he makes clear that in God's 'Gegenständlichkeit' other entities and states of affairs can be identified. This makes it possible to understand the distinction between knowing according to the flesh and the Spirit: if God's identification-system is opened to us because God has identified himself to us, we can identify differently. Here Dalferth uses the concept of 'eschatological states of affairs.'

How do we identify eschatological states of affairs, of which 'being in Christ' is an instance? We identify something by referring to it using a system of signs. A sign represents something as something to someone. God is identified by the words of Jesus, the affirmation of the identification of God by Jesus in the resurrection of Jesus Christ, and by the assurance of the Holy Spirit. In the case of the identification of eschatological states of affairs, something similar has to be the case:

a. the teaching of Jesus provides a first reference;
b. his teaching is confirmed by the resurrection;
c. his apostles elaborate Jesus' teaching and resurrection in their gospel of Jesus Christ under the guidance of the Holy Spirit;

89. Cf. Mühling-Schlapkohl, *Gott ist Liebe*, 15–17.

90. See on 'ontological commitments' also Mühling-Schlapkohl, *Gott ist Liebe*, 15.

d. common existence is provided in God's 'Gegenständlichkeit' where word, sacraments and the life of the church give the eschatological states of affairs a public manifestation;

e. believers are assured of their identification and existence by the Holy Spirit.[91]

Consequently, the identification of eschatological states of affairs is secondary to the resurrection of Jesus Christ and the self-identification of God in Christ. Further, identification of these states of affairs presupposes the perspective of faith, the 'Gegenständlichkeit' of God and the work of the Holy Spirit. It presupposes a life in faith, a participant's perspective. Therefore their identification remains contested until Christ returns. We are not able to solve the resulting conflict of interpretations, a conflict with a spiritual nature because it is the conflict of the old and the new reality.[92]

This implies that the identification of 'being in Christ' is complex for at least two reasons. First, 'being in Christ' as eschatological state of affairs is a reality of which the identification is bound to the perspective of faith. Second, the reality itself is complex. It is a divine mystery which we can more easily refer to with images than we can describe it conceptually. We need these images which demand a new way of thinking about our relation with Jesus Christ.[93] To identify 'being in Christ,' we have to learn to use the 'in Christ' language and the images related to this language, and to live its reality in the church with word and sacraments and in a Christian life. A moment of imagination is necessary, as O'Donovan says. Verification apart from this perspective is impossible as long as Christ has not appeared in glory publicly.

Because 'ontic' verification is impossible, Dalferth defines the language referring to eschatological states of affairs as 'eschatological indicative': localising language, suggesting a possibility in the light of a final eschatological truth, but not descriptive. Understood in this way, the Christian faith concerns a different interpretation of reality. What then is

91. Cf. on the identification of the eschaton and Jesus as Christ Jenson, *Systematic Theology. Volume 1*, 170, 174–75; on identification in general Mühling-Schlapkohl, 18–20.

92. See on the conflict of interpretations e.g. Schürger, *Wirklichkeit Gottes und Wirklichkeit der Welt.*

93. Cf. Colin Gunton on the necessity of classic metaphors of atonement, see Gunton, *The Actuality of Atonement*, 48–52.

the reality of the 'eschatological states of affairs'? Here questions concerning method change into questions concerning content.

To summarize: the Christian faith has ontological implications, and even includes ontological commitments. Fundamental for the reconstruction of the ontological implications of the Christian faith is the resurrection of Jesus Christ. In the resurrection of Jesus Christ, God definitively identifies himself to us. Following God's self-identification other entities and 'eschatological states of affairs' also have to be identified. Their identification is bound to the perspective of faith in which we live in the identification-system of God.

10.4.2 REALITY IN CHRIST

It is evident from the foregoing that 'being in Christ' has hermeneutical implications. A new perspective is opened, showing that the world of sin is not all there is. Christian believers know in Christ, as O'Donovan emphasises, and according to the Spirit. But this new perspective belongs to a new reality, in which the believer participates.[94] Both Dalferth and O'Donovan show that hermeneutical implications have ontological implications.[95] Now it is finally the moment to formulate some of the ontological implications of 'being in Christ.'

Bavinck tried to reconstruct the reality of 'being in Christ' using the concept of organism. In his organic thinking, organic images from the New Testament referring to union with Christ were used as a cosmological concept. (Only in is Colossians the body-image used as an image with cosmological implications.) Its result is a kind of Christocentric, holistic process-thought, although it is not pan(en)theistic. As such his concept of organism is a 19th century concept. Still it has deeper roots in the Christian tradition. The metaphor of organism is an evocative image, which is developed as a powerful model incorporating different aspects of the reality of 'being in Christ.' For a real contemporary evaluation of his organic thinking however, a more extensive dialogue with modern cosmologies is necessary. Consequently, I will limit myself to a more moderate reconstruction of the ontological implications of 'being in Christ.'

These ontological implications have to be reconstructed in an eschatological ontology as Dalferth has constructed it. Christology is eschatol-

94. For the hermeneutical implications, see J. M. Burger, 'Hermeneutiek en bekering.'

95. Cf. Schaede, *Stellvertretung*, 230.

ogy because Jesus Christ is the *eschatos* Adam, as we have seen (10.3.1). 'Being in Christ' is an eschatological reality because it concerns our union with the *eschatos* (Johannine) or our incomplete participation in Jesus Christ (Pauline) and is hence characterized by a tension between what is already realised in our lives and what will be realised when Jesus Christ appears in glory. We live within the end. Consequently I concluded that we have to distinguish with Dalferth between 'eschatological' (related to the *eschatos* Adam) and 'eschatic' (related to the eschata).

In 8.5 I concluded nevertheless that Dalferth's eschatological ontology has its shortcomings and has to be improved. This firstly concerns his concept of eschatological 'Gegenständlichkeit.' It is true that God identifies himself definitively to us by the resurrection of Jesus Christ. However, the people of Israel already knew God, for he was identified by the exodus from Egypt.[96] God's revelation did not start with Jesus Christ. Consequently, God's identification-system was already to some extent open to participation before Jesus Christ. Further, re-creation is more than the opening of a new identification-system. Re-creation concerns the salvation of creation, including our bodies, from the bondage of decay. God's 'Gegenständlichkeit' has to be distinguished from the eschatological reality which exists in Christ.

Second, we have to redefine 'eschatological states of affairs.' According to Dalferth, they are constituted by their relation to God and God's eschatological act, which is universally valid, definitive and recreating. With O'Donovan, greater emphasis should be placed on the fact that they are constituted by their relation to the eschatological representative, Jesus Christ. The representative has an identity, a glorified body and a position in which he makes us participate. This relation with the eschatological representative is established by God's eschatological judgment and by the Holy Spirit, the down-payment of the eschatological inheritance. Our relation with the representative is real and not fictive, although we have the reality of these eschatological states of affairs in faith and in hope. They remain invisible, or their visibility is disputed and contested. Consequently, empirical verification is impossible until the *parousia*. Eschatological states of affairs receive a public and visible character when Jesus Christ appears in his glory and these states of affairs will participate definitively in his glory.

96. According to Robert Jenson, God is identified by the exodus as well as by the resurrection, see Jenson, *Systematic Theology. Volume 1*, 42–60.

Third, this necessitates a reconsidering of the nature of the eschatological indicative. This language is locative and suggests a possibility in the light of the eschatological truth. Because of the hidden character of eschatological states of affairs, language referring to these realities necessarily has an evocative moment, stimulating imagination. But is this all that can be said? The glorified body of Christ is a human reality in the glorified presence of God. The inhabitation of the Holy Spirit is a reality in the life of the believer. Our knowledge of these eschatological states of affairs is very limited. Verification apart from the language of the Christian discourse is impossible. But if I say that Christ is raised in a glorified body, or that the Holy Spirit lives in the church, this speech act has (at least) a descriptive-constative function, however limited my description. I refer to a reality which exists at least according to my Christian faith. To conclude, the concept of 'eschatological indicative' is helpful as long as its (limited but still) descriptive character is not denied.

Fundamental to an eschatological ontology is the act of re-creation in the cross and the resurrection of Jesus Christ. This act is more than just revelatory. A small segment of reality, Jesus Christ, risen as a spiritual body and glorified at the right hand of God, is made authoritative as the destination of humanity, as O'Donovan writes. His resurrection creates a difference between old and new creation. New creation exists in Christ. We do not know what it is to exist as a risen human person in a spiritual, glorified body. Still it is soteriologically important to maintain the existence of this new glorified but created being, for Christ's present bodily existence is our future bodily existence. Jesus Christ also provides the continuity between old and new creation as we saw in Bavinck, Paul and John. The one in whom God recreates is the incarnation of the word by whom God created. This new eschatological being is communicative being, for he exists as our representative who makes all believers participate in his eschatological being.

The death, resurrection and exaltation of Jesus Christ constitute the borderline between old and new creation. But we saw that within the end, a line separating old from new, a gap opened up in which the church lives. The church lives within the end, on the border between old and new. She still lives in the old reality, waits and hopes for the new reality, and already receives a first downpayment of the new reality in the Spirit. In the Spirit she has a first participation in the representative, his identity and position. This incomplete participation in the new eschatological reality makes the development of an eschatological ontology so complicated. Christ and the Spirit determine the reality of the church, but in which sense?

It is important that the identity and position of the church is determined by a Trinitarian framework: in the representative, the Son Jesus Christ and in the Spirit who makes the church participate in the Son, the church is the family of the beloved children of God the Father.

Further, as I wrote already, the new being is communicative being which encounters our lives in the Spirit, in the gospel of Jesus Christ and in the sacraments. Hence new realities are opened, faith is evoked and we are enabled to participate in this new reality.

In this way the church is determined by a reality which exists *extra se*. Primarily, church and believers exist in Christ. Determinative for the identity, position and acts of church and believers is not what we see, think or feel; where we are and in which position, or what we do. Neither the subject with his self-reflection, nor his morality, his feelings, his bodily and psychological health, nor even his religion constitutes the believer. Church and believers live exocentrically. Christ's existence is pro-existence: he lives for the church, for the believers.

The reality *extra nos* touches and influences our existence. This influence presupposes a real, ontological relation between Jesus Christ, the first new human being and the believers, as Dalferth writes. This relation is constitutive for the existence of the believer.[97] From this new constitution a new life follows, leading to a complete future participation in the identity, acts and position of Jesus Christ. At least two models are used to understand this constitution.

The first model is a relational model, with Lutheran and existential influences. This model we find in Dalferth. The emphasis is on relations, like the relation of the self with God, and the self as relation. The model shows that the self is always excentrical, oriented on a judgment, an image, a future identity. A sinner is characterized as *homo incurvatus in seipsum*. A sinner is oriented towards idols, the judgments of other human beings, or has his own self-project, and self-justifying attempts to stabilise himself. Because the believer lives in Christ *extra se* and because God addresses the sinner in his liberating judgment, the self is liberated from the need of incurvation and self-justification. Christ is in God's judgment given as an image into which we will be changed. By the love of God in

97. See on constitutive relations Mühling-Schlapkohl, *Gott ist Liebe*, 47–48.

Christ we are freed from bondage to love again. Living *extra se* in Christ our person is constituted anew. The identity of the self is a future identity, given excentrically in Christ.[98] This model is apt to show religious, psychological, affective and moral implications of the relation with Jesus Christ. What this model neglects is the moment of union.[99]

The second model is a substantialist model. We found this model in the Reformed tradition. United with Christ by the Holy Spirit, a new habitus is created in the sinner. This model emphasises the ontological change in the believer: a new being is given. The relation with Jesus Christ really touches the existence of the sinner and changes this existence by giving a new principle of life. From this change a new Christian life springs. The weakness of this model is that it threatens to isolate the new being from the constitutive relation with Jesus Christ, as we saw in Owen. Moreover, the change from unbelief to faith is duplicated as we found in Bavinck: first an ability of faith is given, second the change from unbelief to faith is made.

Consequently, both models have disadvantages, but where the first model is not sufficient when used alone, the second model itself is problematic. Lehmkühler stresses that we need more than the first model to remind us of the presence of God in the believer. In line with the first model we could think that God is present in the believer by his effects, as the warmth of the sun is present whereas the sun itself remains distant. The New Testament and the theological tradition up to Ritschl suggest that more has to be said: God himself is present in believers. To express this presence, distinct from God's omnipresence, relational concepts are insufficient. (This emphasis is no less Lutheran than the first model, as the new Finnish Luther-research has shown.)[100] Consequently, the second model has to be reconstructed in a more relational way focussing not on the new nature created in the sinner, but on the new presence of God in the believer by his Spirit, a presence ontologically different from God's

98. See e.g. Gestrich, *Christentum und Stellvertretung*, 341, 367–71, 377, 390, 396–97, 410 , 412–15, 419, 422, 434–35; Jüngel, *Das Evangelium von der Rechtfertigung des Gottlosen als Zentrum des christlichen Glaubens*, 110, 120–24, 170–73, 181–83, 191–92, 202–13; Lehmkühler, *Inhabitatio*, 299–310; McCormack, 'What's at Stake in the Current Debates over Justification?' 106–17.

99. According to Lehmkühler this model neglects the inhabitation of the Holy Spirit, see Lehmkühler, *Inhabitatio*, 309–10.

100. Lehmkühler, *Inhabitatio*, 199–216 (on Ritschl's influence), 238–86 (on the Finnish Luther-research), 287–336 (on God's inhabitation).

omnipresence. The images of clothing and the Johannine model of mutual indwelling with its images of living bread as well as vine and branches all highlight aspects of this presence. Further, the Spirit as Spirit of communion makes an individualistic interpretation impossible. Understood in this way the second model is also a relational model. The first model focuses on the judgment of God in his word, the second on the presence of God in his Spirit.[101]

Because both models explain the constitution of the existence of the believer, they focus on the individual. The truth of this emphasis is that without an existential involvement of the believer the reality of Christ makes no difference. This existential involvement is emphasised in different respects by all theologians in this conversation. Consequently, its reality has spiritual, affective, and psychological implications. Furthermore it is important to see that we need imagination to participate in this reality. Dalferth relates this with the eschatological indicative, O'Donovan with the concept of representation.

However, we should not forget that the subject must not be isolated. A Christian always is a Christian in communion. Firstly, no Christian existence is possible without communion with the triune God, who established himself his relation with us in Christ and in the Spirit. Secondly, nobody becomes or remains a believer without the church. Almost all images for union with Christ are collective images. Christian existence is existence in Christ and therefore existence in the church.[102] Church and subject are in need of each other, as O'Donovan writes: 'the subject is realised in the church, the church completed in the subject.'[103]

Until now I have focussed on the new being in Christ and its influence on our existence. But finally something has to be said on the presence of the old reality. According to Dalferth, we have to distinguish here between the 'Gegenständlichkeit' of sin and the eschatological 'Gegenständlichkeit'

101. These two models seem very similar to the two lines we found in John Owen: actual obedience and habitual being, but still differences exist. The acts of Jesus Christ have relevance to both models. Both models have to be understood as providing participation in Christ. We need both models to understand the image of justification. This is not the case in Owen's theology.

102. In this light it is remarkable that the New Testament never refers to the Spirit in *my heart* (sg.). Always a plural is used. Where the concept of heart could stimulate a focus on the individual, the plural 'hearts' or 'your heart' draws the attention back to the communion of Christian believers.

103. O'Donovan, *The Ways of Judgment*, 314.

of the Triune God. I concluded however, that the difference between old and new being has to be made within the 'Gegenständlichkeit' of God. Hermeneutically, we have to differentiate between knowing according to the flesh (Dalferth's 'Gegenständlichkeit' of sin) and knowing according to the Spirit (the 'Gegenständlichkeit' of God). Ontologically, a difference has to be made between the old creation, fallen in sin, and the new creation, existing in Christ who is raised from death.

We live on the border of these two realities. Our fleshly bodies relate us with the old reality, the Holy Spirit relates us with the new reality. We still wait for the redemption of our bodies. Living on the border, the appearance of the Spirit in our lives introduces a struggle between flesh and Spirit. This implies an inner conflict and an ongoing identity crisis. Outward ambiguity characterizes our existence as both O'Donovan and Dalferth write. The identification of eschatological states of being remains contested. Faith and hope are necessary for the believer to see himself in the light of the judgment of God and the gift of a new life *extra se* in Christ.

Both realities influence us. It is impossible to say where the old reality ends and the new reality starts. We can refer to the influence of the new in the old and experience it, although description and identification of the new are contested and influenced by the active presence of the old. Our knowledge, our interpretations and judgments are renewed by the Spirit, but still our understanding is incomplete. Our affections are renewed, but still they can demonstrate lack of love for God. Morally we learn to live in accordance with the Spirit, but the new life remains imperfect. The power of evil and sin may be broken, but yet we experience its strength. As a sign of the coming kingdom, diseases may be healed, but at the same time Christians suffer and die. At the same time, we participate in the suffering and the cross of Jesus Christ as well as in his resurrection and glorification.[104] Consequently, a believer needs a practical competence of understanding to distinguish the old from the new, and to see the old in the light of the new. Until the resurrection our bodies participate in the old creation and our lives remain imperfect. Hence the new eschatological being remains invisible to public discernment, although word and sacraments make it publicly manifest. The old reality and the resulting

104. This is important with regard to discussions concerning healing: Christians may be healed through prayer, but the Spirit may also let a believer participate in the suffering of Christ.

struggle remains until Christ appears in glory and creation is brought into glorious freedom.

We live in union with Christ, but our participation in his story remains incomplete. Until the resurrection of the flesh to everlasting life with Christ, our being is *being in Christ.*

SUMMARY IN DUTCH

Zijn in Christus. Een bijbels en systematisch onderzoek in een gereformeerd perspectief.

1. Introductie

1.1 Er zijn allerlei redenen te geven om opnieuw na te gaan denken over 'zijn in Christus.' Het zou een centraal thema in de christelijke theologie en spiritualiteit moeten zijn, maar is dat vaak toch niet. In het huidige theologische klimaat krijgen veel thema's de aandacht, maar staat de christologie vaak niet bovenaan de agenda. Onderzoek naar 'zijn in Christus' zou kunnen laten zien dat dit thema bij tal van vragen behulpzaam is en een grote integrerende kracht heeft. Dat 'zijn in Christus' een verwaarloosd thema is, is juist binnen de gereformeerde traditie merkwaardig. In de gereformeerde theologie heeft de mystieke eenheid met Christus een centrale rol gespeeld. Ook in het huidige cultureel-filosofische klimaat kunnen redenen gevonden worden om over dit thema na te denken. Veel vragen in onze cultuur cirkelen rond het menselijk subject. Wellicht is het voor het subject van groot belang dat het 'in Christus' een plaats ontvangt waar het zichzelf kan hervinden. Tenslotte sluit het vragen naar 'zijn in Christus' aan op de zoektocht naar een theologische ontologie in de huidige theologie.

1.2 Theologie is reflectie op de praxis van de kerk met als doel bij te dragen aan de communicatie van het evangelie van Jezus Christus, zodat de leden van de kerk in Christus en door de Geest leven in gemeenschap tot eer van God. Theologie kan vervolgens verstaan worden als een complexe hermeneutische beweging, die in dit onderzoek gedeeltelijk gemaakt zal worden: evaluatie van de eigen traditie, herlezing van de canonieke geschriften in de Bijbel en vervolgens het systematisch doordenken van vragen binnen de eigen context. In deze paragraaf wordt dit verder uitgewerkt en de methodologie verantwoord.

De hypothese van dit onderzoek is dat er twee concepten nodig zijn om over 'zijn in Christus' na te denken: representatie (de inclusiviteit van Christus als onze vertegenwoordiger) en participatie (ons delen in Christus). Om deze hypothese te testen zal gekeken worden in hoeverre daarnaast twee andere begrippen noodzakelijk zijn: substitutie (de exclusiviteit van Christus) en eenheid (het contact tussen Christus en de gelovige). Binnen substitutie wordt in dit onderzoek onderscheiden tussen werksubstitutie (de exclusiviteit van wat Christus doet) en persoonsubstitutie (de exclusiviteit van wie Christus is).

1.3 In deze studie wordt een concept van 'zijn in Christus' ontwikkeld met speciale aandacht voor de ontologische implicaties ervan. Dit zal gebeuren in gesprek met twee vertegenwoordigers van de gereformeerde traditie (John Owen en Herman Bavinck), met twee apostelen (Paulus en Johannes) en met twee contemporaine theologen (Ingolf U. Dalferth en Oliver O'Donovan).

2. John Owen – liefde voor de priesterlijke bruidegom

2.1 John Owen was een Engelse puritein en scholasticus, die leefde na de synode van Dordrecht en in die context een trinitarische en christocentrische theologie ontwikkelde. Het christocentrische aspect is sterk gekleurd door twee motieven: Christus als hogepriester en als bruidegom.

2.2 Owen onderscheidt drie verbonden: het werkverbond, het verbond van de middelaar en het genadeverbond. In alle drie verbonden speelt een representatieve figuur een grote rol: Adam in het werkverbond, Jezus Christus in beide andere verbonden. De relatie tussen de verbonden en de theologische belangen die hier spelen worden geanalyseerd.

De mystieke eenheid met Christus begint volgens Owen al in de raad van God, in verkiezing en het verbond van de middelaar. Hier krijgt de Zoon zijn positie als representant.

2.3 Het verhaal van de mystieke eenheid met Christus krijgt zijn tweede episode in de geschiedenis van Jezus Christus. In verschillende stappen wordt de christologie van Owen onderzocht. Als eerste worden verschillende relevante christologische concepten beschreven, zoals representatie, mystieke persoon, hoofd en eenheid.

Vervolgens wordt onderzocht welke momenten uit de geschiedenis van Jezus Christus benut worden om hun betekenis voor de verlossing te laten zien. Niet alleen de incarnatie en het offer maar ook andere momenten spelen een rol. Hier wordt steeds meer duidelijk dat Owen twee conceptuele velden hanteert die naast elkaar staan als gescheiden compartimenten: de eerste, juridische wordt gestuurd vanuit het *actus*-begrip, de tweede, zijnsmatige door het *habitus*-begrip. Beide dienen verschillende theologische belangen.

Tenslotte worden de exclusiviteit en de inclusiviteit van Jezus Christus onderzocht: beide zijn aanwezig en houden elkaar in balans. Werksubstitutie vormt bij Owen duidelijk een onderdeel van de exclusiviteit van Christus.

2.4 De derde stap die de mystieke unie compleet maakt vindt plaats in het leven van de gelovigen. Owens soteriologie wordt geanalyseerd door eerst verder in kaart te brengen hoe de beide conceptuele velden uitgewerkt worden. Dit gebeurt aan de hand van de vraag naar de plaats van de rechtvaardiging in Owens theologie en het gebruik van verschillende beelden voor heil: rechtvaardiging, wedergeboorte en heiliging.

Daarna komen Owens gedachten over de mystieke eenheid met Christus aan bod. Hier blijkt dat het concept van de nieuwe *habitus* een belangrijke rol speelt, naast andere concepten als eenheid, communicatie en participatie.

Na onderzoek van Owens heilsorde wordt de analyse van zijn soteriologie afgesloten met de vraag naar de vier centrale concepten. Representatie en participatie, maar ook eenheid en substitutie blijken van belang om in het spoor van Owen na te denken over 'zijn in Christus.'

2.5 De werkelijkheid van het zijn in Christus is alleen toegankelijk via het perspectief van het geloof. Om de aard van deze werkelijkheid te begrijpen speelt bij Owen het concept van de nieuwe *habitus* een belangrijke rol.

3. Herman Bavinck – mystieke eenheid met het hoofd van het organisme

3.1 Herman Bavinck is een van de twee grote theologen van het Neo-Calvinisme. Op de drempel van de 20e eeuw schreef hij zijn Gereformeerde Dogmatiek, een trinitarische en christocentrische dogmatiek. De *unio mystica cum Christo* vormt één van de rode draden in dit werk.

3.2 De centrale rol van Jezus Christus gaat terug op Bavincks gods- en scheppingsleer. Jezus Christus is de geïncarneerde *logos asarkos*, de middelaar van de schepping. De schepping is teleologisch gericht op de geïncarneerde Zoon van God, die tegelijk middelaar van de herschepping is. Niet alleen de schepping, ook de mensheid is gericht op Jezus Christus. Hij is het hoofd van de nieuwe mensheid die Adam, het hoofd van de gevallen mensheid overtreft.

3.3 Om Bavincks christologie in beeld te krijgen, wordt eerst zijn concept van 'hoofd' geanalyseerd. Als hoofd van het organisme van de nieuwe mensheid heeft Christus steeds de centrale plaats: in de verkiezing, in het *pactum salutis* en in het genadeverbond. Het hoofd-zijn van Christus is bij Bavinck zowel verbonden met representatie als met werksubstitutie.

Daarna wordt nagegaan hoe Bavinck in zijn christologie spreekt over de *unio mystica*. Het is een narratief concept dat zelf een verhaal omvat: Gods raad, de objectieve realisering in de geschiedenis van Jezus Christus en de subjectieve toepassing in het leven van de gelovige. De mystieke eenheid is enerzijds voorwaarde voor de toerekening en zo onderdeel van de rechtvaardigingsleer, anderzijds onderscheidt Bavinck het juridische aspect van het heil nadrukkelijk van het mystieke om het exclusieve van Christus veilig te stellen.

Bavinck benadrukt verder dat Christus in eigen persoon ons heil is. Al zijn weldaden zijn in zijn persoon omvat, zodat werk en persoon niet gescheiden kunnen worden. Bavinck doet recht aan meerdere momenten uit het verhaal van Christus en laat hun soteriologische betekenis uitkomen.

Afsluitend wordt uiteengezet hoe exclusiviteit en inclusiviteit van Christus bij Bavinck terugkomen. Beide houden elkaar in balans. Persoon- en werksubstitutie worden teveel van elkaar onderscheiden, wat tot problemen leidt in Bavincks concept van de mystieke unie en van de mystieke weldaden.

3.4 Aansluitend bij zijn christologie benadrukt Bavinck in zijn soteriologie dat er alleen verlossing is door eenheid met de persoon van Christus. Daarom begint deze paragraaf over zijn soteriologie met een verdere analyse van het *unio mystica*-concept: enerzijds de voorwaarde om in Christus te delen, anderzijds een mystieke weldaad die later in de heilsorde zijn plek heeft.

In de analyse van Bavincks heilsorde blijkt de centrale rol van de wedergeboorte, de gave van een kiem van nieuw leven. Naast dit organische beeld staat de forensische rechtvaardiging.

Om Bavincks soteriologie goed te begrijpen, moet in elk geval de eenheid met Christus aandacht krijgen. Participatie speelt geen hoofdrol in zijn denken. Daar staat tegenover dat geconstateerde problemen in zijn soteriologie juist opgelost kunnen worden door aan participatie een grotere plaats te geven.

3.5 Tot slot wordt Bavincks concept van organisme onderzocht om te ontdekken hoe Bavinck de werkelijkheid van het 'zijn in Christus' ziet, een concept met wortels in de gereformeerde traditie en in de 19[e] eeuwse filosofie.

4. Kritische evaluatie van de gereformeerde traditie

4.1 Na de eerste stap in de hermeneutische beweging van dit onderzoek, het gesprek met de eigen gereformeerde traditie is het tijd voor een balans: een kritische evaluatie.

4.2 Belangrijk om vast te houden is de nadruk op Gods liefde en het daarmee verbonden trinitarische framework. Deze liefde heeft zijn oorsprong in God zelf en komt uit in verkiezing, verzoening en de gave van de eenheid met Christus.

4.3 Waardevol is verder de centrale rol van de mystieke eenheid met Christus. Dit concept van de *unio mystica* wordt gekarakteriseerd als een narratief concept, omdat het een verhaal omvat. Dit narratieve karakter maakt dat het concept gebruikt kan worden om recht te doen aan allerlei theologische belangen.

4.4 De gereformeerde traditie loopt het risico om vooral een theoretische reconstructie te geven van het handelen van God bij het nadenken over de mystieke eenheid. Deze theoretische reconstructie heeft de verkondiging van het evangelie ondergraven. In plaats daarvan zou een concept van 'zijn in Christus' de verkondiging van het evangelie juist moeten stimuleren.

4.5 De beelden die het Nieuwe Testament gebruikt om het heil aan te duiden, zijn in de theologie op verschillende manieren gebruikt. In meer of mindere mate zijn ze gebruikt als theologische concepten om met deze concepten in theologische discussies een positie in te nemen. Om hiervan los te komen is het belangrijk deze beelden opnieuw te onderzoeken op het punt van hun relatie tot 'zijn in Christus.' Ditzelfde geldt voor de narratieve relaties die het Nieuwe Testament legt tussen de geschiedenis van Jezus Christus en het leven van de gelovigen.

4.6 Het onderzoek van twee gereformeerde theologen levert voor de onderzoekshypothese een aantal voorlopige conclusies op. Een concept van 'zijn in Christus' moet recht doen aan de inclusiviteit van Christus, die direct verbonden is aan de exclusiviteit van zijn persoon. De exclusiviteit van zijn werk geldt als voorwaarde voor het 'zijn in Christus,' niet zelf als onderdeel ervan. De onderzoekshypothese moet gecorrigeerd worden door de eenheid met Christus te verstaan als onderdeel van 'zijn in Christus.' Uit het vervolg moet duidelijk worden of explicietere aandacht voor participatie in Christus leidt tot oplossing van een aantal gesignaleerde problemen bij de onderzochte theologen.

4.7 Met betrekking tot de werkelijkheid van 'zijn in Christus' is het nodig om het relationele karakter ervan opnieuw te doordenken, los van het meer substantiële concept van wedergeboorte dat in de gereformeerde traditie centraal is komen te staan.

5. Paulus – participatie in het verhaal van Christus

5.1 De intentie van dit onderzoek is om aan de canonieke stemmen een doorslaggevende betekenis te geven. Daarom worden zes brieven van de apostel Paulus onderzocht op het punt van 'zijn in Christus': vier vroegere brieven (1 en 2 Korintiërs, Galaten, Romeinen) en twee latere (Kolossenzen, Efeziërs).

5.2 Eerst wordt de rol onderzocht die Christus toegekend wordt in verkiezing en schepping in een viertal passages. Representatie, persoonsubstitutie en participatie komen hier naar voren.

5.3 Deze paragraaf gaat over de christologie van Paulus vanuit de vraag of het representatiebegrip hier nodig is. Een aantal aspecten passeren de revue.

Nagegaan wordt hoe Paulus in de geschiedenis van Jezus Christus een proces ziet waarin de Zoon van God zich identificeert met de gevallen mensheid; een proces dat erop uitloopt dat hij tot zonde gemaakt wordt en een vloek wordt voor ons.

Daarna wordt bekeken welke rol de figuur van Adam, door Paulus getekend als een representatieve figuur, speelt in Paulus' christologie.

Vervolgens wordt Paulus' gebruik van een aantal christologische metaforen geanalyseerd: eersteling, eerstgeborene en hoofd. Dit levert allemaal materiaal op voor een antwoord op de vraag naar de noodzaak van de vier concepten: representatie, substitutie, eenheid en participatie.

Expliciet wordt de vraag gesteld of de begrippen representatie en substitutie zelf nodig zijn om Paulus te begrijpen. De inclusiviteit is op allerlei plaatsen terug te vinden, waar Paulus positieve semantische relaties legt tussen wat Jezus meegemaakt heeft en wat de gelovigen mee zullen maken. Jezus heeft dingen gedaan of meegemaakt die beslissend zijn voor wat wij doen of mee zullen maken (bijv. Christus sterft - wij sterven; Christus leeft - wij leven). Hier is het representatieconcept nodig om te begrijpen dat volgens Paulus het verhaal van Christus beslissend is voor ons levensverhaal. Tegelijk legt Paulus - soms in dezelfde passages - negatieve semantische relaties tussen de geschiedenis van Christus en onze eigen geschiedenis (bijv. Christus stierf - wij sterven niet maar leven). Hier is het concept van werksubstitutie nodig om een aspect van de betekenis van de dood van Christus te begrijpen. Niet als een geïsoleerde plaatsvervanging, maar als onderdeel van een complexe beweging, waarin exclusiviteit en inclusiviteit met elkaar verweven zijn. Deze beweging kan aangeduid worden als 'interchange.' Substitutie staat niet op zichzelf, maar is onderdeel van een groter geheel.

5.4 In de volgende paragraaf wordt de soteriologie van Paulus onder de loep genomen, waarbij de aandacht zich concentreert op het moment van participatie. Als eerste wordt in kaart gebracht hoe Paulus de uitdrukking 'in Christus' gebruikt, voor zover dat voor dit onderzoek van belang is. Het gebruik is verbonden met de notie van een representatieve Messias, in wie wij zijn. 'In Christus' kan een instrumentele en een lokaliserende betekenis hebben. Dit lokaliserende blijkt ook uit andere uitdrukkingen: er is een nieuwe sfeer of *aeon* die bestaat in Christus. In

Christus is de redding werkelijkheid. Juist hier blijkt ook dat de uitdrukking 'in Christus' verbonden kan zijn met een eschatologische spanning van incomplete participatie in de representant. Dit wordt bevestigd in de analyse van Paulus' gebruik van de uitdrukking 'met Christus.' Hierbij ligt de nadruk op een intensievere participatie, gedeeltelijk met betrekking tot het verleden (met Christus gestorven en begraven), gedeeltelijk met betrekking tot de toekomst (met Christus leven of erven), maar ook tot het heden (met Christus lijden).

Op zoek naar een moment dat aangeduid moet worden met het concept eenheid is de volgende stap een beschrijving van Paulus gebruik van vier beelden: lichaam, gebouw / tempel, huwelijk en kleding. Hierin is steeds een concept van eenheid nodig om Paulus' christologie en soteriologie te begrijpen.

Afsluitend worden vier andere metaforen onderzocht: rechtvaardiging, adoptie, heiliging en verlossing. Deze beelden benutten elk verschillende semantische velden en hebben eigen mogelijkheden, maar toch komt de verlossing steeds naar voren als een vorm van participatie in Christus. De conclusie is dat zowel het concept van eenheid als van participatie nodig zijn om Paulus te begrijpen in zijn soteriologie.

5.5 Het hoofdstuk sluit af met een reconstructie van de aard van de werkelijkheid van het 'zijn in Christus' volgens Paulus. Een aantal aspecten komt naar voren aan de hand van verschillende interpretaties die gegeven zijn. Het is een werkelijkheid die bepaald wordt door de aanwezigheid van Christus en van de Heilige Geest. Wie in Christus is, leeft in de invloedssfeer van Christus' koninkrijk door de Heilige Geest. Het is een corporatieve werkelijkheid, al is het begrip van 'corporatieve persoonlijkheid' zelf niet bruikbaar. Het is een eschatologische werkelijkheid. Christus en de Geest realiseren beide het *eschaton*. Tot de dag van de *parousia* leven christenen in een eschatologische spanning, zolang we nog buiten ons zelf in Christus leven, of ver van Christus in het sterfelijke vlees. Het is een werkelijkheid waar we toegang toe krijgen door geloof. Als actieve subjecten worden we er bij betrokken, in geloof, in de kerk en in een nieuw leven. Gesproken zou kunnen worden van mystieke ervaringen.

6. Johannes - wederzijdse inwoning

6.1 De tweede canonieke stem in dit onderzoek is de stem van Johannes. Ook in het Johannes-evangelie en de eerste Johannes-brief komt het in Christus-zijn regelmatig naar voren. Daarom gaat hoofdstuk 6 over deze beide geschriften.

6.2 Ook hier wordt begonnen met de christologie, vanuit de vraag naar representatie (en substitutie). Een eerste aspect van Johannes' christologie is het mens-zijn van Jezus. De *logos* is vlees geworden en wordt aangeduid als 'zoon van de mens.' Beide blijken in het Johannes-evangelie geen representatieve connotaties te hebben. De titel 'zoon van de mens' benadrukt eerder de exclusiviteit van Jezus Christus.

Belangrijk is verder de relatie tussen de Vader en Jezus als de Zoon. Deze relatie staat model voor de relatie tussen Jezus en de leerlingen. De verschillende manieren waarop beide relaties met elkaar vergeleken worden, worden in deze paragraaf onderzocht. Steeds komt naar voren: wat de Vader is voor de Zoon, dat is de Zoon voor zijn leerlingen. Primair komt hier de exclusiviteit van de Zoon naar voren, in zijn eenheid met de Vader. Tegelijk is er ook enige ruimte om de Zoon in zijn relatie met de Vader als representant van zijn volk te zien.

Ook de 'ik ben'-woorden benadrukken vooral de exclusiviteit van Jezus Christus, al laat de wijnstok-metafoor ruimte voor inclusiviteit. Ook met betrekking tot de dood van Jezus valt de nadruk op de exclusiviteit van deze gebeurtenis. Hoewel dit de noodzaak van een concept van (werk)substitutie laat zien, is wel belangrijk dat er allerlei verschillende beelden worden gebruikt om de betekenis van de dood van Jezus aan te duiden en niet alleen beelden ontleend aan de wereld van het offer. Toch zit er volgens Johannes ook aan de dood van Jezus een moment van inclusiviteit. Exclusiviteit staat dus op de voorgrond, al is er voor inclusiviteit wel ruimte.

6.3 In de soteriologie krijgt de eenheid met Christus veel ruimte door zijn nadruk op wederzijdse inwoning.

Eerst wordt het gebruik van uitdrukkingen als 'in mij,' 'in hem,' zijn en blijven onderzocht. De Vader-Zoon relatie heeft een uniek karakter, maar bij wijze van analogie worden de karakteristieken van deze relatie wel overgedragen op de relatie tussen Jezus en zijn leerlingen. Hier wordt duidelijk dat het concept van eenheid van groot belang is om Johannes hier te begrijpen: interioriteit, gemeenschap en wederzijdse inwoning spelen een grote rol. Het spreken van zijn en blijven laat de dynamiek van de relatie tussen Jezus en zijn leerlingen zien. Vader en Zoon zijn in elkaar, Jezus roept zijn leerlingen op om ook in hem te blijven. Wanneer we blijven in de Zoon, delen we ook steeds meer in zijn positie tegenover de Vader. Gave en gever zijn identiek. Zo is er niet alleen ruimte voor eenheid (en exclusiviteit), maar ook voor een zekere mate van participatie (en inclusiviteit).

Verbonden met het in hem zijn en blijven zijn beelden voor eenheid met Christus, die vervolgens voorwerp van onderzoek zijn (samen met Johannes 17): levensbrood, goede herder, ware wijnstok. Deze beelden laten een aantal dingen zien: de oudtestamentische achtergrond van de eenheid met Christus: hij vervult een oudtestamentisch beeld in een nieuw verbond; de centrale rol van God de Vader; de uniciteit van Jezus als levensbron; het belang van Jezus' dood maar ook van de *eschata*; de collectiviteit van degenen die met Jezus verbonden zijn (de kerk); en het belang van thema's die thuishoren in de verkiezingsleer. Ook hier blijkt weer de nadruk op substitutie en wederzijdse inwoning, waarnaast er ook ruimte is voor representatie en participatie.

Dat laatste blijkt waar er in Johannes aandacht is voor het worden als Jezus. Leerlingen delen tot op zekere hoogte in zijn relatie met de Vader, in zijn opstanding en verheerlijking, zijn lijden en zijn zending. Tot slot wordt Jezus ook als voorbeeld aan de lezers voorgehouden.

6.4 Over de aard van 'zijn in Christus' zijn op grond van Johannes een aantal dingen te zeggen. Het is een verborgen werkelijkheid, die alleen toegankelijk is door de gave van geloof en in het perspectief van dit geloof. Het is een werkelijkheid die bestaat in een relatie met Vader, Zoon en Geest. Om deze en om andere redenen is het ook een complexe werkelijkheid. Het is een werkelijkheid die gekenmerkt wordt door een eschatologische spanning. Het is een werkelijkheid met morele implicaties en tot slot met zowel een collectief als een individueel aspect.

7. Canonieke synthese

7.1 Als afsluiting van het Bijbelstheologische middendeel wordt in dit hoofdstuk de balans opgemaakt.

7.2 In deze paragraaf worden Paulus en Johannes naast elkaar neer gezet. Op het niveau van woord- en beeldgebruik zijn de verschillen groot.

Het Paulinische model van 'zijn in Christus' (participatie in het verhaal van de representant) verschilt van het Johanneïsche (wederzijdse inwoning). Paulus legt de nadruk op representatie en participatie, Johannes op substitutie en eenheid. De systematische theologie moet deze diversiteit laten staan en de mogelijkheden van beide modellen zo goed mogelijk benutten. Toch zijn er ook grote overeenkomsten, in de manier waarop beide de werkelijkheid van het 'zijn in Christus' zien, maar ook als het gaat om substitutie, representatie, eenheid en participatie. Wat die laatste vier begrippen betreft wordt nu heel duidelijk dat deze vier begrippen nodig zijn en de onderzoekshypothese onvolledig was.

7.3 Om echt canoniek te werk te gaan, worden in deze paragraaf enkele lijnen getrokken vanuit de rest van de canon: vanuit het Oude Testament, vanuit het koninkrijk van God en vanuit Petrus, die ook de uitdrukking 'in Christus' gebruikt. In deze laatste brief blijkt opnieuw dat de hierboven genoemde begrippen alle vier nodig zijn. Tot slot maakt de canonieke rondgang te meer duidelijk dat 'zijn in Christus' een eschatologisch thema is: Jezus Christus is de climax van de verbonden, die het nieuwe verbond en het koninkrijk van God tot een werkelijkheid maakt.

8. Ingolf U. Dalferth – eschatologische werkelijkheid

8.1 Ingolf Dalferth is thuis in zowel de Duitse hermeneutische traditie als de angelsaksische analytische traditie. Kort wordt een schets gegeven van zijn ontwikkeling en van enkele belangrijke motieven in zijn theologie. Van belang voor dit onderzoek is o.a. zijn eschatologische ontologie.

8.2 Uitgangspunt in Dalferths christologie is Gods zelfidentificatie voor ons in Jezus Christus: door God opgewekt uit de dood en door ons ervaren als de plaats van Gods presentie door de Heilige Geest. De drieenige God is een gebeuren van aanspraak en antwoord, hij is liefde en daarom open voor anderen. Door Jezus Christus worden wij opgenomen in dit verheerlijkte zijn van God, omdat hij door zijn sterven en opstanding Gods werkelijkheid voor ons toegankelijk maakt. Belangrijk is verder hoe Dalferth de hermeneutische genese van de christologie reconstrueert vanuit de opstanding.

Nadat eerst Dalferths christologie getypeerd is, wordt vervolgens meer gedetailleerd ingegaan op wat Dalferth ziet als de soteriologische relevantie van de geschiedenis van Jezus Christus. Het verhaal begint volgens Dalferth bij de opstanding. Centraal in de opstanding is het eschatologische handelen van God, niet zozeer *in* maar vooral *aan* de wereld en de daarmee samenhangende ervaring van Jezus Christus als levende Heer. Door Gods reddende handelen wordt Jezus opgenomen in zijn glorie en ontsluit God zich voor ons als liefdevolle nabijheid. Vanuit de opstanding wordt teruggekeken naar het kruis. Het kruis laat als eerste zien wie wij zijn: zondige mensen die willen zijn als God, maar die daarin vastlopen. Tegelijk laat het gebruik van het offerbeeld in het Nieuwe Testament zien dat de dood van Jezus een dood voor ons was. In kruis en opstanding incorporeert God Jezus Christus in zijn leven. Daarbij ligt dus alle nadruk op wat God doet: hij maakt Jezus Christus tot de plaats van zijn liefdevolle nabijheid voor ons. Zo is Jezus Christus in eigen persoon ons heil, een nieuwe existentie voor Gods aangezicht. De opstanding bevestigt zo ook de boodschap van Jezus tijdens zijn leven. Dit leven kan terugkijkend alleen begrepen worden als een leven met een goddelijke grond, een reddende activiteit van de drie-enige God.

Op deze wijze krijgen zowel de exclusiviteit als de inclusiviteit van Jezus Christus hun plek. De nadruk ligt op Gods reddende, eschatologische handelen waarin wij opgenomen worden door Jezus Christus, onze representant. Dit betekent dat de rol van Jezus Christus niet zelf verstaan wordt als een representatieve handeling voor de mensen die hij vertegenwoordigt. Voor werksubstitutie heeft Dalferth dan ook geen ruimte.

8.3 Centraal in de soteriologie van Dalferth staat dat we mogen leven in een nieuw perspectief. De opstanding van Jezus Christus leidt door de Heilige Geest tot een nieuw leven, waar de differentie tussen oud en nieuw leven in iemands leven werkelijkheid wordt. Het nieuwe leven is geschapen door God, in geloof. Als nieuw perspectief brengt het een nieuw verstaan van het zelf, de wereld en God met zich mee. Het wordt gekenmerkt door een eschatologische spanning: het wordt geleefd in geloof en in Christus, en 'eschatisch' gehoopt. In de kerk moet dit nieuwe leven zichtbaar worden, een leven in liefde en in gemeenschap. Nieuw leven is mogelijk doordat we leven in twee geschiedenissen: de geschiedenis van God waarin we *tot* persoon worden en onze eigen geschiedenis waarin we worden *als* persoon. Op deze wijze bestaan we buiten onszelf in Christus. We ontvangen onze identiteit in Christus in de rechtvaardiging. *Simul iustus et peccator*, moet de identiteit in Christus leiden tot een nieuw verstaan en tot een nieuwe levenswijze in groeiende gelijkvormigheid aan

Christus. De kerk moet het verhaal van Jezus Christus blijven vertellen en zichtbaar laten worden in doop en avondmaal.

In deze soteriologie krijgt participatie duidelijk een plaats: participatie in de persoon en in de geschiedenis van Jezus Christus, door de Heilige Geest en door geloof. We delen in zijn mens-zijn, in zijn relatie tot de Vader en in zijn eschatologisch leven in Gods nabijheid. Daarnaast is ook bij Dalferth een moment van eenheid aanwezig, die overigens volgens Dalferth niet gezien mag worden als een mystieke eenheid. Omdat Dalferth focust op de eschatologische act van God en niet op de handelingen van Jezus Christus, komt deze eenheid wel meer op de achtergrond te staan.

8.4 In deze paragraaf wordt een beschrijving gegeven van Dalferths eschatologische ontologie. Eerst wordt ingegaan hoe Dalferth aankijkt tegen ontologische reflectie. In zijn eschatologische ontologie vraagt Dalferth naar de ontologische implicaties van het christelijke verhaal. Een paar belangrijke begrippen uit zijn ontologie: Dalferth hanteert een existentie-principe: 'bestaan is verbonden zijn met ons verhaal.' 'Bestaan' kan niet beperkt worden tot wat bestaat binnen tijd en ruimte, omdat God niet tijdruimtelijk bestaat. Om te weten dat iets bestaat, moet dat iets eerst als entiteit worden geïdentificeerd. Identificatie is alleen mogelijk wanneer er een gemeenschappelijke 'Gegenständlichkeit' is die de identificerende persoon en de te identificeren entiteit omvat. Wie iets identificeert als iets verricht daarmee een pragmatische act van lokalisering.

Theologisch werkt Dalferth dit vervolgens uit. Door Gods zelfidentificatie opent God voor ons zijn eschatologische 'Gegenständlichkeit.' Onze zondige tijdruimtelijke 'Gegenständlichkeit' wordt op deze wijze opengebroken. We worden hierdoor opnieuw gelokaliseerd binnen Gods 'Gegenständlichkeit' en krijgen daar een nieuwe, eschatologische identiteit. Voortaan bestaan we in twee 'Gegenständlichkeiten.' De impact van de verlossing op ons lichamelijke bestaan lijkt verwaarloosd te worden, waar Dalferth alle aandacht richt op de eschatologische 'Gegenständlichkeit.'

8.5 Dalferths denken biedt een aantal waardevolle inzichten. Hermeneutisch laat hij zien dat 'zijn in Christus' een lokaliserende werkelijkheid is, die een nieuw verstaan biedt van God, zelf en wereld. De geschiedenis van Jezus Christus en Gods oordeel in Christus constitueren een nieuw perspectief dat in het levensproces eigen gemaakt moet worden. Ontologisch werkt hij dit nieuwe perspectief uit door de ontologische implicaties ervan na te gaan in een eschatologische ontologie. Theologisch legt hij de nadruk op Gods eschatologische handelen.

Mijn vragen betreffen de lichamelijke werkelijkheid en de impact van de verlossing daarop. Het lijkt dat Dalferth hier te weinig oog voor heeft. Daarom zou zijn eschatologische ontologie op een aantal punten bijgesteld moeten worden. Belangrijke verbetering zou kunnen zijn dat onderscheid gemaakt wordt tussen 'zijn in Christus' en 'verheerlijkt zijn,' die Dalferth ten onrechte met elkaar identificeert.

9. Oliver O'Donovan – morele werkelijkheid

9.1 Oliver O'Donovan heeft zijn theologische wortels in zijn Augustinus-onderzoek. In eerste instantie is hij bekend geworden door zijn pleidooi voor een eerherstel van de 'morele orde.' Daarna heeft hij zich vooral gericht op politieke theologie en ethiek.

9.2 Het representatiebegrip heeft een centrale rol in de christologie van O'Donovan. Deze paragraaf begint met een analyse van dit begrip zoals O'Donovan het hanteert. Representatie is een sociaal en politiek begrip, een vorm van symbolisering die vraagt om morele verbeelding en affectieve betrokkenheid. Jezus Christus is volgens O'Donovan representant in dubbele zin: representant van God en van zijn volk. Als representant van zijn volk is hij tegelijk als laatste Adam ook representant van de mensheid.

Volgens O'Donovan moet de geschiedenis van Jezus Christus begrepen worden als een representatieve act met meerdere momenten. Die momenten en de relaties daartussen worden vervolgens op een rij gezet. O'Donovan onderscheidt vier momenten: advent, kruis, opstanding en hemelvaart. Door deze momenten heen speelt een ander belangrijk concept uit O'Donovans christologie: het oordeel van God.

Representatie speelt dus een belangrijke rol bij O'Donovan. Tegelijk vraagt hij aandacht voor de exclusiviteit van Christus. Representatie en substitutie hebben elkaar nodig. De exclusiviteit van Christus is terug te vinden in zijn bemiddeling van Gods koningschap, in het oordeel van God en in het eigenlijke concept substitutie.

9.3 In O'Donovans soteriologie staat het begrip participatie centraal. Deze paragraaf begint met O'Donovans participatiebegrip. Door de Heilige Geest delen gelovigen in Christus en in zijn verlossing. Ze delen in de representatieve act van Christus, die compleet is. Er wordt dus niets aan de representant toegevoegd, maar de implicaties van wat bereikt is worden in de gelovigen gerealiseerd. Ook hier speelt het oordeelsbegrip een belangrijke rol. Participatie wordt mogelijk door het oordeel van God. Op deze wijze wordt de kerk bovendien geautoriseerd om te delen in het gezag van Christus. De gave van de Geest is een eerste anticipatie op de volledige participatie in het heil.

Omdat de representatieve act in vier momenten uiteengelegd is, valt ook de participatie in vier momenten uiteen. Deze vier momenten van de recapitulatie van de representatieve act worden vervolgens geanalyseerd. Pinksteren hoort hier overigens niet bij, omdat Pinksteren de consequentie is van de representatieve act, welke vervolgens tot participatie in Christus leidt in vier momenten. Deze vier momenten hebben elk een narratieve, sacramentele vorm. Ook hier gaat het dan om advent (doop), kruis (avondmaal), opstanding (zondag) en hemelvaart (handoplegging).

Een volgend element van O'Donovans soteriologie betreft zijn gebruik van soteriologische beelden, waarvan er drie beschreven worden: rechtvaardiging, verkiezing en adoptie. In de uitwerking hiervan blijkt dat de concepten representatie en participatie een belangrijke rol spelen. Participatie is in O'Donovans soteriologie duidelijk een belangrijk begrip, voor eenheid geldt dit echter niet.

9.4 In deze laatste paragraaf wordt de aard van de werkelijkheid van het 'zijn in Christus' onderzocht, aan de hand van de verschillende aspecten die O'Donovan hieraan onderscheidt: een eschatologische werkelijkheid, een morele werkelijkheid en een nu nog verborgen werkelijkheid.

9.5 Tot slot wordt O'Donovans bijdrage aan dit onderzoek geëvalueerd. Belangrijk is zijn dubbel-concept van representatie en participatie. Op een aantal punten wordt dit nader uitgewerkt. Speciaal van belang is verder zijn reflectie op het verborgen karakter van de werkelijkheid ervan, terwijl Christus tegelijkertijd als representant het bestaan van de gelovigen wel degelijk beïnvloedt. De relatie tussen de *eschata* en de *eschatos* komt zo goed voor het voetlicht. Een kritische vraag waar het hoofdstuk mee eindigt is die naar het concept eenheid.

10. Een systematisch-theologisch concept van 'zijn in Christus'

10.1 In dit laatste hoofdstuk wordt een voorstel geboden voor een systematisch-theologisch concept van 'zijn in Christus,' gebaseerd op het voorgaande onderzoek en met speciale aandacht voor de ontologische implicaties ervan.

10.2 Deze paragraaf begint met de grammaticale structuren van het christelijk spreken waarin ook het 'zijn in Christus' ter sprake komt. Op grond van dit spreken zijn twee modellen te reconstrueren, die niet tot elkaar te reduceren zijn: een Paulinisch en een Johanneïsch model. Met betrekking tot 'zijn in Christus' zijn twee structuren van belang, die beide aandacht krijgen: de leer van de triniteit en de vier momenten (substitutie, representatie, eenheid en participatie).

10.3 Op basis hiervan kan vervolgens een systematisch-theologisch framework ontwikkeld worden. Christologisch wordt als uitgangspunt genomen het verhaal van de heilsgeschiedenis. Dat wil zeggen: Christologie is eschatologie, het hele verhaal dat de evangeliën vertellen is soteriologisch van belang. In zijn leven, een representatieve act vond een steeds verdergaande identificatie plaats met ons bestaan tot Jezus Christus stierf aan het kruis. Hij werd wat wij waren, om ons te laten delen in wat hij nu is. Daarom is het belangrijk dat de opstanding zo begrepen wordt, dat wij ook werkelijk kunnen delen in zijn bestemming.

Voor de soteriologie wordt begonnen met het uitwerken van twee beelden voor eenheid met Christus, die een grote integrerende kracht hebben. Wij worden bekleed met Christus en leven als takken van de ware wijnstok. Niet helder in deze beelden maar wel essentieel is dat het door de Heilige Geest is dat wij een zijn met Christus. De sacramenten geven de eenheid met en participatie in Christus een publieke manifestatie. Delen in Christus is ook delen in zijn verhaal. We delen in de aspecten van het verhaal die elk een inclusief aspect hebben. Meerdere aspecten worden nagegaan, waarbij steeds het inclusieve en het exclusieve onderscheiden worden. Afsluitend wordt de contextuele relevantie van 'zijn in Christus' verwoord. Het biedt hoop voor het postmoderne subject, herstelt de relatie met het goede en geeft het subject een plaats terug.

Centraal in de gereformeerde soteriologie is traditioneel de heilsorde. De beelden voor heil worden in de heilsorde als concepten gebruikt en verwijzen in die heilsorde naar verschillende momenten in het proces van verlossing. In plaats daarvan wordt in dit onderzoek verdedigd dat de verschillende beelden – rechtvaardiging, adoptie, verkiezing en wedergeboorte – elk op hun manier aspecten van dit hele proces laten oplichten. Dit wordt aangetoond aan de hand van de vier genoemde beelden.

Ook wordt ingegaan op de vraag wie de gerepresenteerden zijn en waar de grens tussen in Christus en buiten Christus ligt. In de gereformeerde traditie wordt vooral de particulariteit benadrukt van de *unio mystica*, O'Donovan en Dalferth benadrukken de universaliteit van het heil in Christus. Zowel de particulariteit als de universaliteit zijn terug te vinden in Paulus en Johannes. Daarom is er geen eenvoudig antwoord te geven op de vraag: Wie zijn de gerepresenteerden? Belangrijker is om te zien welke verschillende antwoorden gegeven worden, in welke context en met welke pragmatische intentie. Omdat wij het hart van mensen niet kennen kunnen wij de grens tussen buiten en binnen nu nog niet exact aangeven. Van belang is bovendien dat de grens tussen binnen en buiten een complex fenomeen is, omdat bij het overschrijven van deze grens meerdere actoren betrokken zijn.

10.4 In deze paragraaf wordt de balans opgemaakt met betrekking tot de ontologische implicaties van 'zijn in Christus.' Het christelijk geloof heeft ontologische implicaties en omvat ontologische commitments. Fundamenteel voor de reconstructie van deze implicaties is de opstanding van Jezus Christus. Hier identificeert God zichzelf definitief voor ons. In het vervolg van Gods zelfidentificatie kunnen ook andere entiteiten en 'eschatologische standen van zaken' geïdentificeerd worden. Zo opent zich een nieuwe perspectief dat bij een nieuwe werkelijkheid hoort, waarin de gelovige deelt.

Wat zijn die ontologische implicaties van 'zijn in Christus'? Daarmee sluit deze paragraaf af. Er wordt geen omvattende reconstructie gegeven, zoals Bavinck dat deed. Dit zou vragen om een dialoog met moderne kosmologieën. Er moet onderscheiden worden tussen Gods 'Gegenständlichkeit' die al vóór Jezus Christus tot op zekere hoogte toegankelijk was en de eschatologische werkelijkheid die sinds Pasen bestaat. Verder moeten eschatologische standen van zaken begrepen worden vanuit hun relatie tot Jezus Christus, de *eschatos*. Ook wordt ingegaan op de eschatologische indicatief, waaraan het descriptieve karakter niet ontzegd mag worden. Complicerend is echter, dat de kerk leeft de op grens van oud en nieuw zijn. Hoe moet het delen van de kerk in dit nieuwe zijn begrepen worden? Er worden twee modellen besproken die dit proberen te verhelderen: een relationeel model en een substantieel model. Afsluitend wordt ingegaan op de voorlopig nog blijvende presentie van het oude zijn. We leven in eenheid met Christus, maar voorlopig is onze participatie in Christus nog incompleet: 'zijn in Christus.'

BIBLIOGRAPHY

Primary Sources

Acta of Handelingen der Nationale Synode, in den naam onzes Heeres Jezus Christus, gehouden door autoriteit der Hoogmogende Heeren Staten-Generaal der Vereenigde Nederlanden te Dordrecht, ten jare 1618 en 1619: hier komen ook bij de volledige beoordeelingen van de Vijf Artikelen en de Post-acta of Nahandelingen/in de tegenwoordige spelling naar de oorspronkelijke Nederduitsche uitgave onder toezicht van J.H. Donner en S.A. van den Hoorn. Leiden: D. Donner 1883–1886.

Bavinck, Herman. *De wetenschap der H. Godgeleerdheid. Rede ter aanvaarding van het leeraarsambt aan de Theologisch School te Kampen, uitgesproken den 10 Jan. 1883*, Kampen G. Ph. Zalsman 1883.

———. *De theologie van prof. dr. Daniel Chantepie de la Saussaye. Bijdrage tot de kennis der ethische theologie.* 2d ed. Leiden: D. Donner, 1903.

———. *Kennis en leven. Opstellen en artikelen uit vroegere jaren.* Kampen: Kok.

———. *De katholiciteit van christendom en kerk. Rede bij de overdracht van het rectoraat aan de Theol. School te Kampen op 18 dec. 1888.* Kampen: G. Ph. Zalsman 1888.

———. 'De theologie van Albrecht Ritschl.' *Theologische Studiën* 6 (1888) 369–403.

———. *De algemene genade. Rede bij de overdracht van het rectoraat aan de theologische school te Kampen op 6 december 1894.* Kampen: G. Ph. Zalsman, 1894.

———. *De offerande des lofs. Overdenkingen vóór en na de toelating tot het heilige avondmaal.* 's Gravenhage: Fred. H. Verschoor, [1901].

———. *De zekerheid des geloofs.* Kampen: Kok 1918.

———. *Godsdienst en godgeleerdheid. Rede gehouden bij de aanvaarding van het Hoogleeraarsambt in de Theologie aan de Vrije Universiteit te Amsterdam op Woensdag 17 december 1902.* Wageningen: Naamloze Vennootschap Drukkerij 'Vada,' 1902.

———. *Gereformeerde Dogmatiek.* 4th ed. Kampen: Kok, 1928.

———. *Roeping en wedergeboorte.* Kampen: Ph. Zalsman, 1903.

———. *Christelijke wereldbeschouwing.* 2d ed. Kampen: Kok, 1913.

———. *Wijsbegeerte der openbaring. Stone-lezingen voor het jaar 1908*, gehouden te Princeton N.J. Kampen: Kok, 1908.

———. *Magnalia Dei. Onderwijzing in de Christelijke religie naar Gereformeerde belijdenis.* Kampen: Kok, 1909.

———. *Modernisme en orthodoxie. Rede gehouden bij de overdracht van het rectoraat aan de Vrije Universiteit op 20 october 1911.* Kampen: Kok, 1911.

———.*Bijbelsche en religieuze psychologie.* Kampen: Kok, 1920.

———. *Verzamelde opstellen op het gebied van godsdienst en wetenschap.* Kampen: Kok, 1921.

Calvin, John. *Institutes of the Christian Religion.* The Library of Christian Classics Vol. XX and XXI. Translated by Ford L. Battles. Philadelphia: The Westminster Press, 1960.

Dalferth, Ingolf U. *Religiöse Rede von Gott.* Beiträge zur evangelischen Theologie 87. München: Kaiser, 1981.

———, and Eberhard Jüngel. 'Person und Gottebenbildlichkeit.' In *Christlicher Glaube in moderner Gesellschaft.* Enzyclopedische Bibliothek 24. Freiburg, Basel, Wien: Herder, 1981, 60–99.

———. *Existenz Gottes und christlicher Glaube. Skizzen zu einer eschatologischen Ontologie.* Beitrage zur evangelischen Theologie 93. München: Kaiser, 1984 .

———. 'Glaube. Systematisch-theologisch.' In *Evangelisches Kirchenlexikon. Internationale theologische Enzyklopädie*, 3th ed.. Göttingen: Vandenhoeck & Ruprecht, 1989, 193–202.

———. *Theology and Philosophy.* Oxford: Basil Blackwell, 1988. Reprinted: Eugene, OR: Wipf & Stock, 2001.

———. *Kombinatorische Theologie. Probleme Theologischer Rationalität.* Quaestiones Dis-putae 130. Freiburg, Basel, Wien: Herder, 1991.

———. *Gott. Philosophisch-theologische Denkversuche.* Tübingen: Mohr Siebeck, 1992.

———. 'Über Einheit und Vielfalt des christlichen Glaubens. Eine Problemskizze.' In *Marburger Jahrbuch Theologie IV*, edited by Wilfried Härle, and Reiner Preul, 99–137. Marburg: N.G. Erwert, 1992.

———. 'God and the Mystery of Words.' *Journal of the American Academy of Religion*, 60 (1992) 1, 79–104.

———. *Jenseits von Mythos und Logos. Die christologische Transformation der Theologie.* Quaestiones Disputae 142. Freiburg, Basel, Wien: Herder, 1993.

———. *Der auferweckte Gekreuzigte. Zur Grammatik der Christologie.* Tübingen: Mohr Siebeck, 1994.

———. 'Subjektivität und Glaube. Zur Problematik der theologischen Verwendung einer philsophischen Kategorie.' *Neue Zeitschrift für Theologie und Religionsphilosophie* 36 (1994) 18–58.

———. *Gedeutete Gegenwart. Zur Wahrnehmung Gottes in der Erfahrungen der Zeit.* Tübingen: Mohr Siebeck, 1997.

———. 'Volles Grab, leerer Glaube? Zum Streit um die Auferweckung des Gekreuzigten.' *Zeitschrift für Theologie und Kirche* 95 (1998) 379–409.

———. 'Creation—Style of the World.' *International Journal of Systematic Theology* 1 (1999) 2, 119–37.

———. 'Inbegriff oder Index? Zur philosophischen Hermeneutik von "Gott."' *Gott der Philosophen—Gott der Theologen. Zum Gesprächsstand nach der analytischen Wende*, edited by Chr. Gestrich, 89–140. Beiheft 199 zur Berliner Theologischen Zeitschrift 16 (1999).

———. 'Erkundungen des Möglichen. Perspektiven hermeneutischer Religionsphilosophie.' In *Perspectives in contemporary Philosophy of Religion*. Schriften der Luther-Agricola-Gesellschaft 46. Edited by Tommi Lehtonen und Timo Koistinen, 31–87. Helsinki: Luther-Agricola-Society, 2000.

———. 'Fremdauslegung als Selbstauslegung. Vorüberlegungen zu einer trinitarischen Hermeneutik der Abwesendheit Gottes.' In *Fremdheit und Vertrautheit. Hermeneutik im europäischen Kontext*, edited by H.J. Adriaanse and R. Enskat, 145–73. Leuven: Peeters, 2000.

———. 'Der Mensch in seiner Zeit.' *Zeitschrift für Dialektische Theologie* 16 (2000) 2, 152–80.

———. 'Faith. Systematic Theology.' In *Encyclopedia of Christianity*. Grand Rapids: Eerdmans/Leiden: Brill, 2001, 265–74.

———. 'Representing God's Presence.' *International Journal of Systematic Theology* 3 (2001) 3, 237–56.

———. *Auf dem Weg der Ökumene. Die Gemeinschaft evangelischer und anglikanischer Kirchen nach der Meissener Erklärung*. Leipzig: Evangelische Verlagsanstalt, 2002.

———. *Die Wirklichkeit des Möglichen. Hermeneutische Religionsphilosophie*. Tübingen: Mohr Siebeck, 2003.

———. *Evangelische Theologie als Interpretationspraxis. Eine systematische Orientierung*. Forum theologische Literaturzeitung 11/12 (2004). Leipzig: Evangelische Verlagsanstalt, 2004

———. 'Gott für uns. Die Bedeutung des christologischen Dogmas für die christliche Theologie' In *Denkwürdiges Geheimnis. Beiträge zur Gotteslehre. Festschrift für Eberhard Jüngel zum 70. Geburtstag*, edited by Ingolf U. Dalferth et al., 51–75. Tübingen: Mohr Siebeck, 2004.

———. *Leiden und Böses. Vom schwierigen Umgang mit Widersinnigem*. Leipzig: Evangelische Verlagsanstalt, 2006.

Luther, Martin. *Tractatus de libertate Christiana*. In *Martin Luthers Werke* 7, 49–73 Weimar: Hermann Böhlhaus Nachfolger 1897.

O'Donovan, Oliver. *The Problem of Self-Love in St. Augustine*. New Haven and London: Yale University Press, 1980.

———. 'Usus and fruitio in Augustine, De Doctriana Christiana 1.' *The Journal of Theological Studies* 33 (1982) 361–97.

———. *Resurrection and Moral Order: An Outline for Evangelical Ethics*. 2d ed. Leicester England: Apollos / Grand Rapids, MI: Eerdmans, 1994.

———. *On the Thirty Nine Articles: A Conversation with Tudor Christianity*. Oxford: The Paternoster Press Exeter for Latimer House, 1986.

———. 'Evangelicalism and the Foundations of Ethics.' In *Evangelical Anglicans: Their Role and Influence in the Church Today*, R.T. France, A.E. McGrath, 96–107. London: SPCK, 1993.

———. *The Desire of the Nations: Rediscovering the Roots of Political Theology*. Cambridge: Cambridge University Press, 1998 (1996).

———. 'Gerechtigkeit und Urteil.' *Neue Zeitschrift für Systematische Theologie und Religionsphilosophie* 40 (1998) 1–16.

———. 'Response to Respondents: Behold, the Lamb.' *Studies in Christian Ethics*, 11 (1998) 2, 91–110.

———, and Joan Lockwood O'Donovan. *From Irenaeus to Grotius: A Sourcebook in Christian Political Thought 100–1625*. Grand Rapids, MI / Cambridge, UK: Eerdmans, 1999.

———. 'Deliberation, History and Reading: A Response to Schweiker and Wolterstorff.' *Scottish Journal of Theology* 54 (2001) 1, 127–44.

———. *Common Objects of Love. Moral Reflection and the Shaping of Community* The 2001 Stob Lectures. Grand Rapids, MI / Cambridge UK: Eerdmans, 2002.

———. 'Response to Daniel Carroll R.' *A Royal Priesthood? The Use of the Bible Ethically and Politically: A Dialogue with Oliver O'Donovan*, edited by Craig Bartholomew, 144–46. Grand Rapids, MI: Paternoster Press Carlisle / Zondervan, 2002.

———. *The Just War Revisited, Current Issues in Theology*. Cambridge: Cambridge University Press 2003.

———, and Joan Lockwood O'Donovan, *Bonds of Imperfection: Christian Politics, Past and Present*. Grand Rapids, MI / Cambridge UK: Eerdmans, 2004.

———. *The Ways of Judgment: The Bampton Lectures 2003*. Grand Rapids, MI / Cambrigde, UK: Eerdmans, 2005.

Owen, John. ΘΕΟΜΑΧΙΑ ΑΥΤΕΞΟΥΣΙΑΣΤΙΚΗ, *or A Display of Arminianism*. (1643) In *The Works of John Owen*, edited by William H. Goold, Vol. X, 2–137. Edinburgh: T. & T. Clark, 1862.

———. *Two Short Catechisms, Wherein the Principles of the Doctrine of Christ Are Unfolded and Explained*. (1645). In *The Works of John Owen*, edited by William H. Goold, Vol. I, 464–94. Edinburgh: T. & T. Clark, 1862.

———. *Salus Electorum, Sanguis Jesu; or the Death of Death in the Death of Christ* (1647). In *The Works of John Owen*, edited by William H. Goold, Vol. X, 140–428. Edinburgh: T. & T. Clark, 1862.

———. *Of the Death of Christ, the Price He Paid and the Purchase He Made* (1650). In *The Works of John Owen*, edited by William H. Goold, Vol. X, 429–79. Edinburgh: T. & T. Clark, 1862.

———. *Of Communion with God the Father, Son and Holy Ghost* (1657). In *The Works of John Owen*, edited by William H. Goold, Vol. II, 2–274. Edinburgh: T. & T. Clark, 1862.

———. *A Vindication of Some Passages in a Discourse Concerning Communion with God* (1674). In *The Works of John Owen*, edited by William H. Goold, Vol. II, 276–364. Edinburgh: T. & T. Clark, 1862.

———. ΠΝΕΥΜΑΤΟΛΟΓΙΑ, *or A Discourse Concerning the Holy Spirit* (1674). In *The Works of John Owen*. edited by William H. Goold, Vol. III, 2–651; Vol. IV, 1–520. Edinburgh: T. & T. Clark, 1862.

———. *The Reason of Faith* (1677). In *The Works of John Owen*, edited by William H. Goold, Vol. IV, 2–115. Edinburgh: T. & T. Clark, 1862.

———. *The Doctrine of Justification by Faith, through the Imputation of the Righteousness of Christ* (1677). In *The Works of John Owen*, edited by William H. Goold, Vol. V, 1–400. Edinburgh: T. & T. Clark, 1862.

———. ΣΥΝΕΣΙΣ ΠΝΕΥΜΑΤΙΚΗ, *or Causes, Ways, and Means of Understanding the Mind of God as Revealed in His Word, with Assurance Therein* (1678). In *The Works of John Owen*, edited by William H. Goold, Vol. IV, 118–234. Edinburgh: T. & T. Clark, 1862.

———. ΧΡΙΣΤΟΛΟΓΙΑ: *Or, A Declaration of the Glorious Mystery of the Person of Christ* (1678). In *The Works of John Owen*, edited by William H. Goold, Vol. I, 2–272. Edinburgh: T. & T. Clark, 1862.

———. *A Discourse of the Work of the Holy Spirit in Prayer* (1682). In *The Works of John Owen*, edited by William H. Goold, Vol. IV, 236–350. Edinburgh: T. & T. Clark, 1862.

———. *Meditations and Discourses on the Glory of Christ* (1684). In *The Works of John Owen*, edited by William H. Goold, Vol. I, 274–415. Edinburgh: T. & T. Clark, 1862.

———. *Meditations and Discourses Concerning the Glory of Christ, Applied unto Unconverted Sinners and Saints under Spiritual Decays* (1691). In *The Works of John Owen*, edited by William H. Goold, Vol. I, 418–61. Edinburgh: T. & T. Clark, 1862.

———. *Two Discourses Concerning the Holy Spirit and His Work: The One, of the Spirit as a Comforter; the Other, as He Is the Author of Spiritual Gifts* (1693). In *The Works of John Owen*, edited by William H. Goold, Vol. IV, 352–520. Edinburgh: T. & T. Clark, 1862.

Secondary Sources

Alston, Wallace M. Jr., and Michael Welker, et al. *Reformed Theology: Identity and Ecumenicity.* Grand Rapids, MI / Cambrigde: Eerdmans, 2003.

Alston, William P. 'The Indwelling of the Holy Spirit.' In *Divine Nature and Human Language: Essays in Philosophical Theology*, 223–52. Ithaca / London: Cornell University Press, 1989.

Anderson, Paul N. *The Christology of the Fourth Gospel: Its Unity and Disunity in the Light of John 6.* Wissenschaftliche Untersuchungen zum Neuen Testament 2. Reihe 78. Tübingen: Mohr Siebeck, 1996.

Angenendt, Arnold. *Geschichte der Religiosität im Mittelalter.* Darmstadt: Wissenschaftliche Buchgesellschaft, 1997.

Asselt, Willem J. van. 'Puritanism Revisited: een poging tot evaluatie.' *Theologia Reformata* 44 (2001) 3, 221–32.

Baarlink, H. *Romeinen 1. Een praktische bijbelverklaring.* Tekst en toelichting. Kampen: Kok, 1987

Baars, Arie *Om Gods verhevenheid en zijn nabijheid. De Drie-eenheid bij Calvijn.* Theologie en Geschiedenis. Kampen: Kok , 2004.

Balla, Peter. *Challenges to New Testament Theology. An Attempt to Justify the Enterprise.* Wissenschaftliche Untersuchungen zum Neuen Testament 2. Reihe 95. Tübingen: Mohr Siebeck, 1997.

Ballauf, Scherer, et al. 'Organismus.' In *Historisches Wörterbuch der Philosophie* Bd. 6. Darmstadt: Wissenschaftliche Buchgesellschaft.

Barcley, William B. *"Christ in You": A Study in Paul's Theology and Ethics*, Lanham, New York, Oxford: University Press of America, 1999.

Ulrich Barth. *Religion in der Moderne.* Tübingen: Mohr Siebeck 2003.

———. *Aufgeklärter Protestantismus.* Tübingen: Mohr Siebeck, 2004.

Bartholomew, Craig, editor. *A Royal Priesthood? The Use of the Bible Ethically and Politically: A Dialogue with Oliver O'Donovan.* The Scripture and Hermeneutic Series Vol. 3. Carlisle: Paternoster Press / Grand Rapids, MI: Zondervan 2002.

Bassler, Jouette M., editor. *Pauline Theology Vol. 1: Thessalonians, Philippians, Galatians, Philemon.* Minneapolis: Fortress Press, 1991.

Bibliography

Batey, Richard. 'The MIA SARX Union of Christ and the Church.' In *New Testament Studies* 13 (1966/1967), 270–81.

Bayer, Oswald. *Promissio. Geschichte der reformatorische Wende in Luthers Theologie.* Darmstadt: Wissenschaftliche Buchgesellschaft, 1989.

———. *Theologie.* Handbuch Systematischer Theologie, Bd. 1. Gütersloh: Gütersloh Verlagshaus, 1994.

———. 'Wer ist Theologe?' In *Rechtfertigung und Erfahrung: für Gerhard Sauter zum 60. Geburtstag* edited by Michael Beintker, 208–13. Gütersloh: Kaiser, Gütersloher Verlagshaus 1995.

———. *Martin Luthers Theologie. Eine Vergegenwärtigung.* Tübingen: Mohr Siebeck 2004.

Bauckham, Richard. *The Gospels for All Christians.* Grand Rapids, MI / Cambridge U.K: Eerdmans, 1998.

———. 'For Whom Were Gospels Written?' In *The Gospels for All Christians*, 9–49. Grand Rapids, MI / Cambridge UK: Eerdmans, 1998.

Baum, Armin D. *Pseudepigraphie und literarische Falschung im frühen Christentum* Wissenschaftliche Untersuchungen zum Neuen Testament 2. Reihe 138. Tübingen: Mohr Siebeck, 2001.

Beck, Andreas. Review of *Gedeutete Gegenwart*, by Ingolf U. Dalferth. *Nederlands Theologisch Tijdschrift* 55 (2001) 4, 351–52.

Becker, Jürgen. *Paulus. Der Apostel der Völker.* Tübingen: Mohr Siebeck, 1989.

Beek, A. van de. *Schepping. De wereld als voorspel voor de eeuwigheid.* Baarn: Callenbach, 1996.

———. *Jezus Kurios. De Christologie als hart van de theologie.* Spreken over God 1,1. Kampen: Kok, 1998.

———. *De kring om de Messias. Israël als volk van de lijdende Heer.* Spreken over God 1,2. Zoetermeer: Meinema, 2002.

———. 'Een aantrekkelijke kerk—maar voor wie?' *Wapenveld* 54 (2004) 4:17–27.

Beeke, Joel R. *Assurance of Faith. Calvin, English Puritans and the Dutch Second Reformation.* New York: Peter Lang, 1991.

Beker, J. Christiaan. *The Triumph of God. The Essence of Paul's Thought.* Minneapolis: Fortress Press, 1990.

Belt, Henk van den. 'De autonomie van de mens of de autopistie van de Schrift.' In *Ontmoetingen met Bavinck.* AD Chartasreeks 9, edited by Harinck, George et al., 287–306. Barneveld: De Vuurbaak 2006.

Benthem, Hans van, and Klaas de Vries, 'Meer dan genoeg. Het verlangen naar meer: een balans.' In *Meer dan genoeg. Het verlangen naar meer van de Geest,* edited by H. ten Brinke et al., 144–68 Barneveld: De Vuurbaak Barneveld 2004.

Bergmeier, Roland. *Glaube als Gabe nach Johannes. Religions- und theologiegeschichtliche Studien zum prädestinatianischen Dualismus in dem vierten Evangelium.* Beiträge zur Wissenschaft vom Alten und Neuen Testament Bd 112. Stuttgart Berlin Köln Mainz: W. Kohlhammer, 1980.

Berkhof, Hendrikus. *Christelijk geloof. Een inleiding tot de geloofsleer.* Nijkerk: Callenbach, 1990.

Berkouwer, G.C. *Geloof en rechtvaardiging.* Dogmatische Studiën. Kampen: Kok, 1949.

———. *Geloof en heiliging* Dogmatische Studiën. Kampen: Kok, 1949.

———. *De persoon van Christus* Dogmatische Studiën. Kampen: Kok, 1952.

———. *De verkiezing Gods.* Dogmatische Studiën. Kampen: Kok, 1955.

Bibliography

Best, Ernest. *A Critical and Exegetical Commentary on Ephesians.* Edinburgh: T. & T. Clark, 1998.

Betz, Hans-Dieter. *Galatians: A Commentary on Paul's Letter to the Churches in Galatia* (Hermeneia). Philadelphia: Fortress Press, 1979.

Biezeveld, de Boer, et al. *In iets geloven: Ietsisme en het christelijk geloof.* Kampen: Kok 2006.

Boersma, Hans. *A Hot Peppercorn: Richard Baxter's Doctrine of Justification in Its Seventeenth-Century Context of Controversy.* Zoetermeer: Boekencentrum, 1993.

———. *Violence, Hospitality and the Cross: Reappropriating the Atonement Tradition.* Grand Rapids, MI: Baker Academics, 2004.

Bolt, John. 'The Imitation of Christ Theme in the cultural-ethical Ideal of Herman Bavinck.' Ph.D. diss., University of St. Michael's College (Toronto School of Theology), 1982.

———. 'Christ and the law in the ethics of Herman Bavinck.' *Calvin Theological Journal* 28 (1993) 45–73.

Bornkamm, Günther. 'Der Paraklet im Johannes-Evangelium.' In *Studien zum Neuen Testament,* 96–117. München: Kaiser, 1985.

Bouttier, Michel. *En Christ. Étude d'éxégèse et de thëologie Pauliennes.* Paris: Presses Universitaires de France, 1962.

Brandt, Reinhard. 'Quines Tranchiermesser und Dalferths Wetzstein—zu einigen ontologischen Voraussetzungen der Theologie.' *Zeitschrift für Theologie und Kirche,* 91 (1994) 2, 210–29.

Bremmer, Rolf H. *Herman Bavinck als dogmaticus.* Kampen: Kok , 1961.

———. *Herman Bavinck en zijn tijdgenoten.* Kampen: Kok Kampen, 1966.

Brink, Gijsbert van den. *Almighty God: A Study in the Doctrine of Divine Omnipotence.* Studies in Philosophical Theology 7. Kampen: Kok Pharos, 1993

———. 'De geestelijke groei van de nieuwe mens (Op het snijvlak van theologie en psychologie).' In *Onrustig is ons hart. Mens-zijn in christelijk perspectief,* edited by Henri Veldhuis, 88–109. Zoetermeer: Boekencentrum, 1994.

———. *Een publieke zaak. Theologie tussen geloof en wetenschap.* Boekencentrum Essay. Zoetermeer: Boekencentrum, 2004.

———. 'Narrative, Atonement, and the Christian Conception of the Good Life.' In *Religion and the Good Life.* Studies in Theology and Religion 10, edited by Marcel Sarot and Wessel Stoker, 113–29. Assen: Royal van Gorcum, 2004.

Brinkman, Martien E. 'De toekomst van de Gereformeerde theologie.' *Gereformeerd Theologisch Tijdschrift,* 41 (1998) 3, 138–56.

Brom, Luco J. van den. *God alomtegenwoordig.* Dissertationes Neerlandicae Series Theologica 7. Kampen: Kok, 1982.

Browarzik, Ulrich. 'Onto-Theo-Logie.' *Evangelische Theologie* 45 (1985) 4, 367–73.

Browning, Don S. *A Fundamental Practical Theology: Descriptive and Strategic Proposals.* Mineapolis: Fortress Press, 1991.

———. *Creatieve twijfel. Een studie in de wijsgerige theologie.* Kampen: Kok, 1990.

Bruce, F.F. *The Epistle of Paul to the Galatians: A Commentary on the Greek Text* (NIGTC). Exeter: The Paternoster Press, 1982.

Brueggemann, Walter, *Theology of the Old Testament: Testimony, Dispute, Advocacy.* Minneapolis: Fortress Press, 1997.

Bruggen, Jakob van. *Christus op aarde. Zijn levensbeschrijving door leerlingen en tijdgenoten.* Commentaar op het Nieuwe Testament derde serie. Kampen: Kok, 1987.

———. 'The Authority of Scripture as a Presupposition in Reformed Theology.' In *The Vitality of Reformed Theology: Proceedings of the International Theological Congress June 20–24th 1994 Noordwijkerhout the Netherlands*, edited by J.M. Batteau et al., 63–83. Kampen: Kok, 1994.

———. *Het evangelie van Gods Zoon. Persoon en leer van Jezus volgens de vier evangeliën.* Commentaar op het Nieuwe Testament derde serie. Kampen: Kok, 1996.

———. *Paulus. Pionier voor de Messias van Israël.* Commentaar op het Nieuwe Testament derde serie. Kampen: Kok, 2001.

———. "Kingdom of God or Justification of the Sinner? Paul between Jesus and Luther.' *In die Skriflig* 35 (2001) 2, 253–67.

———. *Het kompas van het Christendom. Ontstaan en betekenis van een omstreden bijbel.* Kampen: Kok, 2002.

———. *Galaten. Het goed recht van gelovige Kelten.* Commentaar op het Nieuwe Testament derde serie. Kampen: Kok, 2004.

———. *Romeinen. Christenen tussen stad en synagoge.* Commentaar op het Nieuwe Testament derde serie. Kampen: Kok, 2006.

Bruijne, A.L. Th. de. 'Romeinen: pionierswerk nodig?' *De Reformatie* 72 (1996) 5, 91–94.

———. 'Christelijke ethiek tussen wet, schepping en gemeenschap. Een positionering naar aanleiding van Romeinen 12,1 en 2.' *Radix* 27 (2001) 2/3, 116–48.

———. 'Navolging en verbeeldingskracht' In *Woord op schrift. Theologische reflecties over het gezag van de bijbel*, edited by C. Trimp, 195–237. Kampen: Kok 2002.

———. 'Gereformeerde theologie vandaag.' In *Gereformeerde theologie vandaag: oriëntatie en verantwoording.* TU-Bezinningsreeks 4, edited by A.L. Th. de Bruijne, 11–29. Barneveld: De Vuurbaak, 2004.

———. *Levend in Leviatan. Een onderzoek naar de theorie over 'christendom' in de politieke theologie van Oliver O'Donovan.* Kampen: Kok, 2006.

Brümmer, Vincent. *Theology and Philosophical Inquiry: An Introduction.* London: The MacMillan Press Ltd, 1981.

Brümmer, Vincent. *The Model of Love: A Study in Philosophical Theology.* Cambridge: Cambridge University Press, 1993.

———. 'Ultimate Happiness and the Love of God.' In *Religion and the Good Life.* Studies in Theology and Religion 10, edited by Marcel Sarot and Wessel Stoker, 241–65. Assen: Royal van Gorcum, 2004.

Buchegger, Jürg. *Erneuerung des Menschen. Exegetische Studien zu Paulus.* Texte und Arbeiten zum neutestamentlichen Zeitalter 40. Tübingen: Francke, 2003.

———. Burge, Gary M. *The Anointed Community: The Holy Spirit in the Johannine Tradition.* Grand Rapids, MI: Eerdmans, 1987.

Burger, J.M. 'Mens in Christus: lichaam, ziel en geest.' *Radix* 30 (2004) 3, 109–22.

———. 'Theologia crucis, theologia gloriae, of geen van beide?' In *Levend water. Gereformeerd debat over charismatische vernieuwing.* TU-bezinningsreeks 5, edited by E.A. de Boer, 135–50. Barneveld: De Vuurbaak, 2006.

———. 'Hermeneutiek en bekering.' In: *Charis. Theologische opstellen, aangeboden aan prof. dr. J. W. Maris*, edited by A. Baars et al., 57–66.Heerenveen: Groen 2008.

Burkett, Delbert. *The Son of Man Debate. A History and Evaluation.* Society for New Testament Studies Monograph Series 107. Cambridge: Cambridge University Press, 1999.

Carroll R., M. Daniel. 'The Power of the Future in the Present: Eschatology and Ethics in O'Donovan and Beyond.' In *A Royal Priesthood? The Use of the Bible Ethically and Politically: A Dialogue with Oliver O'Donovan*. Edited by Craig Bartholomew, 116–43. Grand Rapids, MI: Paternoster Press Carlisle / Zondervan, 2002.

Carson, D.A. 'Unity and Diversity in the New Testament: the Possibility of Systematic Theology.' In *Scripture and Truth*, edited by D.A. Carson and John Woodbridge, 65–95. Grand Rapids, MI: Zondervan, 1983.

———. *The Gospel according to John*. Leicester England: InterVarsity Press / Grand Rapids, MI: Eerdmans, 1991.

———. *Divine Sovereignty and Human Responsibility: Biblical Perspectives in Tension*. Grand Rapids, MI: Marshall Pickering / Baker Books, 1994.

Childs, Brevard S. *Biblical Theology of the Old and New Testaments: Theological Reflections on the Christian Bible*. London: SCM Press Ltd, 1992.

Clifford, Alan C. *Atonement and Justification: English Evangelical Theology 1640–1790, An Evaluation*. Oxford: Clarendon Press, 1990.

Collins, Raymond F. *First Corinthians*. Sacra Pagina Series Vol. 7. Collegeville Minnesota: The Literugical Press, 1999.

Crump, David. 'Re-examining the Johannine Trinity: perichoresis or deification?' *Scottish Journal of Theology* 59 (2006) 4, 395–412.

Dawes, Gregory W. *The Body in Question: Metaphor and Meaning in the Interpretation of Ephesians 5:21–32*. Biblical Interpretation Series 30. Leiden Boston Köln: Brill, 1998.

Deissmann, Adolf. *Die neutestamentliche Formel "in Christo Jesu."* Marburg: N.G. Elwert'sche Verlagsbuchhandlung, 1892.

———. *Paulus. Eine kultur- und religionsgeschichtliche Skizze*. Tübingen: Mohr Siebeck, 1911.

Dekker, Eef. *Rijker dan Midas. Vrijheid, genade en predestinatie in de theologie van Jacobus Arminius (1559–1609)*. Zoetermeer: Boekencentrum, 1993.

Dekker, Jacob. *De rotsvaste fundering van Sion. Een exegetisch onderzoek naar het Sionswoord van Jesaja 28,16*. Zoetermeer: Boekencentrum, 2004.

Dettwiler, Andreas. *Die Gegenwart des Erhöhten. Eine exegetische Studie zu den johanneischen Abschiedsreden (Joh 13,31–16,33) unter besonderer Berücksigtigung ihres Relecture-Charakters*. Forschungen zur Religion und Literatur des Alten und Neuen Testaments 169. Göttingen: Vandenhoeck und Ruprecht, 1995.

Dietzfelbinger, Christian. 'Sühnetod im Johannesevangelium?' In *Evangelium Schriftauslegung Kirche. Festschrift für Peter Stuhlmacher zum 65. Geburtstag*, edited by Jostein Ådna et al., 65–76. Göttingen: Vandenhoeck & Ruprecht, 1997.

Dingemans, G.D.J. *De stem van de Roepende. Pneumatheologie*, Kampen: Kok 2000.

Doekes, L. 'Van de alpha tot de omega.' In *K. Schilder. Aspecten van zijn werk*, edited by J. Douma et al., 119–46. Barneveld: De Vuurbaak, 1999.

Douma, Jochem. *Algemene genade. Uiteenzetting en beoordeling van de opvattingen van A. Kuyper, K. Schilder en Joh. Calvijn over 'algemene genade.'* 3d ed. Goes: Oosterbaan & Le Cointre B.V., 1976.

———. *Grondslagen christelijke ethiek*. Christelijke ethiek 1. Kampen: Kok, 1999.

Douma, Jos R. 'Christocentrische prediking.' *De Reformatie* 77 (2002) 34, 723–25.

———. 'Spirituele christologie.' *De Reformatie* 77 (2002) 35, 741–43.

———. 'De preek: stem van Christus.' *De Reformatie* 77 (2002) 36, 761–63.

———. 'Preken: roepen tot gemeenschap met Christus.' *De Reformatie* 77 (2002) 37, 775–78.

———. 'De prediker: passie voor Christus.' *De Reformatie* 77 (2002) 38, 797–800.

Douty, Norman F. *Did Christ Die Only for the Elect? A Treatise of the Extent of Christ's Atonement*. Eugene, OR: Wipf and Stock Publishers, 1998.

Dumbrell, W.J. *Covenant and Creation, A Theology of the Old Testament Covenants*. Carlisle: Paternoster Press, 2000.

Dunn, James G.D. *Unity and Diversity in the New Testament: An Inquiry into the Character of Earliest Christianity*. London: SCM Press, 1977.

———. *Romans 1–8*. Word Biblical Commentary. Dallas Texas: Word Books, 1988.

———. *Romans 9–16*. Word Biblical Commentary. Dallas Texas: Word Books, 1988.

———. "The Body of Christ' in Paul.' In *Worship, Theology and Ministry: Essays in Honor of Ralph P. Martin*. Journal for the Study of the New Testament Supplement Series 87, edited by Michael J. Wilkins and Terence Paige, 146–62. Sheffield: Sheffield Academic Press, 1992.

———. 'The "Body" in Colossians.' In *To Tell the Mystery: Essays on New Testament Eschatology in Honor of Robert H. Gundry*. Journal for the Study of the New Testament Supplement Series 100, edited by Thomas E. Schmidt and Moisés Silva, 163–81. Sheffield: Sheffield Academic Press, 1994.

———. *The Epistles to the Colossians and to Philemon*. The New International Commentary on the New Testament. Grand Rapids, MI: Eerdmans / Carlisle: The Paternoster Press, 1996.

———. 'Once more, ΠΙΣΤΙΣ ΧΡΙΣΤΟΥ.' In *Pauline Theology Vol. IV Looking Back, Pressing On*, edited by E. Elisabeth Johnson and David M. Hay, 61–81. Georgia: Scholars Press Atlanta, 1997.

———. *The Theology of Paul the Apostle*. Edinburgh: T. & T. Clark, 1998.

Ebeling, Gerhard. 'Was heißt "Biblische Theologie"?' In: *Wort und Glaube* [I], 69–89. Tübingen:, Mohr Siebeck, 1960.

Elliott, John H. *1 Peter: A New Translation with Introduction and Commentary*. The Anchor Bible. New York etc.: Doubleday, 2000.

Endo, Masanobu. *Creation and Christology: A Study on the Johannine Prologue in the Light of Early Jewish Creation Accounts*. Wissenschaftliche Untersuchungen zum Neuen Testament 2. Reihe 149. Tübingen: Mohr Siebeck, 2002.

Faber, Jelle. *American Secession Theologians on Covenant and Baptism*. Pella, Iowa: Inheritance Publications, 1996.

Fatehi, Mehrdad. *The Spirit's Relation to the Risen Lord in Paul*. Wissenschaftliche Untersuchungen zum Neuen Testament 2. Reihe 128. Tübingen: Mohr Siebeck, 2000.

Fee, Gordon J. *The First Epistle to the Corinthians*. The New International Commentary on the New Testament. Grand Rapids, MI: Eerdmans, 1987.

Ferguson, Sinclair B. *John Owen on the Christian Life*. Edinburgh/Carlisle Pennsylvania: The Banner of Truth Trust, 1987.

———. 'John Owen on the Spirit in the Life of Christ.' *Banner of Truth Magazine* 293 (1988), 10–15 and 294 (1988), 10–14.

———. *The Holy Spirit*. Contours of Christian Theology. Leicester: InterVarsity Press, 1996.

———. 'John Owen and the doctrine of the person of Christ.' In *John Owen—the Man and His Theology: Papers Read at the Conference of the John Owen Centre for Theological Study September 2002*, edited by Robert W. Oliver, 69–100. New Jersey: P&R, Phillipsburg / Darlington: Evangelical Press, 2002.

———. 'John Owen and the doctrine of the Holy Spirit.' In *John Owen—the Man and His Theology: Papers Read at the Conference of the John Owen Centre for Theological Study*

September 2002, edited by Robert W. Oliver, 101–30. New Jersey: P&R, Phillipsburg / Darlington: Evangelical Press, 2002.

Ford, David F. *Self and Salvation: Being Transformed*. Cambridge Studies in Christian Doctrine. Cambridge: Cambridge University Press, 1999.

Frey, Jörg. *Die johanneische Eschatologie. Bd. II Das johanneische Zeitverständnis*. Wissenschaftliche Untersuchungen zum Neuen Testament 110. Tübingen: Mohr Siebeck, 1998.

———. *Die johanneische Eschatologie. Bd. III Die eschatologische Verkündigung in den johanneischen Texten*. Wissenschaftliche Untersuchungen zum Neuen Testament 117. Tübingen: Mohr Siebeck, 2000.

———. 'Die "*theologia crucifixi*" des Johannesevangeliums.' In *Kreuzestheologie im Neuen Testament*. Wissenschaftliche Untersuchungen zum Neuen Testament 151, edited by Andreas Dettwiler et al., 169–238. Tübingen: Mohr Siebeck, 2002.

Frigato, Sabino, *Leven in Christus en moreel handelen. Inleiding in de fundamentele moraaltheologie*. Translated by C. Verdonk. Budel: Damon, 2002.

Furnish, Victor P. 'How Firm a Foundation? Some Questions about Scripture in *The Desire of the Nations*.' *Studies in Christian Ethics*, 11 (1998) 2, 18–29.

Gadamer, Hans-Georg, *Hermeneutik I. Wahrheit und Methode. Grundzüge einer philosophischen Hermeneutik*. Tübingen: Mohr Siebeck, 1990.

Gaffin, Richard B. 'Resurrection and Redemption. A Study in Pauline Soteriology.' Th.D. diss., Philadelphia: Westminster Theological Seminary, 1969.

———. 'The Vitality of Reformed Dogmatics' In *The Vitality of Reformed Theology. Proceedings of the International Theological Congress June 20–24th 1994 Noordwijkerhout The Netherlands*, edited by J.M. Batteau et al., 16–50. Kampen: Kok, 1994.

Garcia, Mark A. 'Imputation and the Christology of Union with Christ: Calvin, Osiander, and the Contemporary Quest for a Reformed Model.' *Westminster Theological Journal* 68 (2006), 219–51.

Genderen, J. van, and W.H. Velema, *Beknopte Gereformeerde Dogmatiek*, Kampen: Kok, 1992.

———. *Covenant and Election*. Neerlandia Alberta Canada / Pella Iowa U.S.A: Inheritance Publications, 1995.

Gese, Hartmut. 'Erwägungen zur Einheit der biblischen Theologie.' In *Vom Sinai zum Zion. Alttestamentliche Beiträge zur biblischen Theologie*, 11–30. München: Kaiser, 1974.

———. 'Der Davidsbund und die Zionserwählung.' In *Vom Sinai zum Zion. Alttestamentliche Beiträge zur biblischen Theologie*, 113–29. München: Kaiser, 1974.

———. 'Die Sühne' In *Zur biblischen Theologie. Alttestamentische Vorträge*, 85–106. München: Kaiser, 1977.

Gestrich, Christof. *Christentum und Stellvertretung. Religionsphilosophische Untersuchungen zum Heilsverständnis und zur Grundlegung der Theologie*. Tübingen: Mohr Siebeck, 2001.

Glas, Gerrit. 'Geloofszekerheid. Over psychologische en antropologische voorwaarden om te geloven.' In *Geloven in zekerheid? Gereformeerd geloven in een postmoderne tijd*. TU-Bezinningsreeks 1, edited by Koert van Bekkum and Rien Rouw, 19–34. Barneveld: De Vuurbaak, 2000.

Gleason, Randall C. *John Calvin and John Owen on Mortification: A Comparative Study in Reformed Spirituality*. Studies in Church History. New York [etc.]: Peter Lang, 1995.

Bibliography

Gleason, Ronald N. 'The Centrality of the *Unio Mystica* in the Theology of Herman Bavinck.' Th.D. thesis, Philadelphia: Westminster Theological Seminary, 2001.

Gnilka, Joachim. *Paulus von Tarsus. Apostel und Zeuge.* Herders theologischer Kommentar zum Neuen Testament. Freiburg, Basel, Wien: Herder, 1996.

Goldingay, John. 'Biblical Narrative and Systematic Theology.' In *Between Two Horizons. Spanning New Testament Studies and Systematic Theology,* edited by Max Turner and Joel B. Green, 123–42. Grand Rapids, MI / Cambridge UK: Eerdmans Company, 2000.

Gorman, Michael J. *Cruciformity. Paul's Narrative Spirituality of the Cross.* Grand Rapids, MI / Cambridge: Eerdmans, 2001.

Graafland, Cornelis. *Van Calvijn tot Barth. Oorsprong en ontwikkeling van de leer der verkiezing in het Gereformeerd Protestantisme.* 's-Gravenhage: Boekencentrum, 1987.

———. *Gereformeerden op zoek naar God. Godsverduistering in het licht van de gereformeerde spiritualiteit.* Kampen: De Groot-Goudriaan, 1990.

Green, Joel B. 'Scripture and Theology: Uniting the Two So Long Divided.' In *Between Two Horizons: Spanning New Testament Studies and Systematic Theology,* edited by Max Turner and Joel B. Green, 23–43. Grand Rapids, MI / Cambridge UK: Eerdmans, 2000.

Grenz, Stanley J., and Olson, Roger E. *20th Century Theology: God and the World in a Tran-sitional Age.* Downers Grove, IL: InterVarsity Press, 1992.

Grondin, Jean. *Einführung in die philosophische Hermeneutik.* Die Philosophie. Darmstadt: Wissenschaftliche Buchgesellschaft, 1991.

Gundry, Robert H. *Sōma in Biblical Literature. With Emphasis in Pauline Antropology.* Society for New Testament Studies—Monograph Series 29. Cambridge etc.: Cambridge University Press, 1976.

Gunton, Colin E. *The Actuality of Atonement: A Study of Metaphor, Rationality and the Christian Tradition.* Edinburgh: T. & T. Clark, 1994.

———. *The Promise of Trinitarian Theology.* Edinburgh: T. & T. Clark, 1997.

———. *The One, the Three and the Many: God, Creation and the Culture of Modernity.* The 1992 Bampton Lectures. Cambridge: Cambridge University Press, 1998.

———. *Theology through the Theologians. Selected Essays 1972–1995.* Edinburgh: T. & T. Clark, 1996.

———. 'Election and Ecclesiology in the Post-Constantinian Church.' *Scottish Journal of Theology* 53 (2000) 2, 212–27.

Guthry, Donald. *New Testament Introduction.* Leicester, England Apollos / Downers Grove, IL: InterVarsity Press, 1990.

Hafemann, Scott J. *Suffering and the Spirit. An Exegetical Study of II Cor. 2:14—3:3 within the Context of the Corinthian Correspondence.* Wissenschaftliche Untersuchungen zum Neuen Testament 19. Tübingen: Mohr Siebeck, 1986.

Hägerland, Tobias. 'John's Gospel: A Two-Level Drama?' *Journal for the Study of the New Testament* 25 (2003) 3, 309–22.

Han, Cheon-Seol. *Raised for our Justification. An Investigation on the Significance of the Resurrection of Christ within the Theological Structure of Paul's Message.* Kampen: Kok, 1995.

Harinck, George, and Gerrit W. Neven, editors. *Ontmoetingen met Bavinck.* AD Chartasreeks 9. Barneveld: De Vuurbaak, 2006.

Harmannij, *Kornelis . Jezus leed wat wij nu lijden.* Kampen: Kok Voorhoeve, 1997.

Hartingsveld, Lodewijk van. *Die Eschatologie des Johannesevangeliums. Eine Auseinandersetzung mit Rudolf Bultmann.* Van Gorcum's Theologische Bibliotheek 36. Assen: Van Gorcum, 1962.

Hart, Trevor. 'Humankind in Christ and Christ in Humankind: Salvation as Participation in our Substitute in the Theology of John Calvin.' *Scottish Journal of Theology* 42 (1989), 67–84.

Hartvelt, G.P. *Verum Corpus. Een studie over een central hoofdstuk uit de avondmaalsleer van Calvijn.* Delft: W.D. Meinema N.V., 1960.

Hauerwas, Stanley, and James Fodor. 'Remaining in Babylon: Oliver O'Donovan's Defense of Christendom.' *Studies in Christian Ethics*, 11 (1998) 2, 30–55.

Hay, David M., editor. *Pauline Theology Vol. II: 1 & 2 Corinthians.* Minneapolis: Fortress Press, 1993.

———, and E. Elisabeth Johnson, editors. *Pauline Theology Vol. III: Romans.* Minneapolis: Fortress Press, 1995.

Hays, Richard B. 'Crucified with Christ: A Synthesis of the Theology of 1 and 2 Thessalonians, Philemon, Philippians and Galatians.' In *Pauline Theology Vol. 1: Thessalonians, Philippians, Galatians, Philemon*, edited by Jouette M. Bassler, 227–46. Minneapolis: Fortress Press, 1991.

———. *The Moral Vision of the New Testament. Community, Cross, New Creation: A Contemporary Introduction to New Testament Ethics.* Edinburgh: T. & T. Clark, 1996.

———. "ΠΙΣΤΙΣ and Pauline Christology: What is at Stake?' In *Pauline Theology Vol. IV Looking back, pressing on*, edited by E. Elisabeth Johnson and David M. Hay, 35–60. Atlanta Georgia: Scholars Press, 1997.

———. *The Faith of Jesus Christ. The Narrative Substructure of Galatians 3:1—4:11.* Grand Rapids, MI: Eerdmans, 2002.

Heim, S. Mark. *Salvations. Truth and Difference in Religion.* Maryknoll, New York: Orbis Books, 994.

Heise, Jürgen. *Bleiben. Menein in den Johanneischen Schriften.* Hermeneutische Untersuchungen zur Theologie 8. Tübingen, Mohr Siebeck, 1967.

Hensley, Jeffrey. 'Are Postliberals Necessarily Antirealist? Re-examining the Metaphysics of Lindbeck's Postliberal Theology.' In *The Nature of Confession: Evangelicals and Postliberals in Conversation*, edited by Timothy R. Phillips and Dennis L. Okholm, 69–80. Downers Grove, IL: InterVarsity Press, 1996.

Herms, Eilert. 'Was haben wir an der Bibel? Verschuch einer Theologie des christlichen Kanons.' In *Jahrbuch für biblische Theologie 12 Biblische Hermeneutik*, 99–152. Neukirchen-Vluyn: Neukirchener Verlag, 1998.

Hettema, Theo L. *Reading for Good: Narrative Theology and Ethics in the Joseph Story from the Perspective of Ricoeur's Hermeneutic.* Kampen: Kok Pharos, 1996.

Hielema, Syd. 'Herman Bavinck's Eschatological Understanding of Redemption.' Ph.D. diss., Wycliffe College, Toronto School of Theology, 1998.

Hill, Charles E. *The Johannine Corpus in the Early Church.* Oxford / New York: Oxford University Press, 2004.

Hjelde, Sigurd *Das Eschaton und die Eschata. Eine Studie über Sprachgebrauch und Sprachverwirrung in protestantischer Theologie von der Orthodoxie bis zur Gegenwart.* Beiträge zur evangelischen Theologie 102. München: Kaiser, 1987.

Hodgson, Peter C. *Winds of the Sprit. A Constructive Christian Theology.* London: SCM Press Ltd. 1994.

Hoekema, Anthony A. 'Herman Bavinck's Doctrine of the Covenant.' Ph.D. diss., Princeton Theological Seminary, 1953.

———. *Saved by Grace*. Grand Rapids, MI: Eerdmans / Exeter, UK: The Paternoster Press Ltd, 1989.

Hofius, Otfried. 'Das vierte Gottesknechtlied in den Briefen des Neuen Testaments.' In *Der leidende Gottesknecht. Jesaja 53 und seine Wirkungsgeschichte*, edited by Bernd Janowski, Peter Stuhlmacher, 107–27. Tübingen, Mohr Siebeck 1996.

———. 'Struktur und Gedankengang des Logos-Hymnus in Joh 1,1–18.' In *Johannesstudien. Untersuchungen zur Theologie des vierten Evangeliums*. Wissenschaftliche Untersuchungen zum Neuen Testament 88, edited by Otfried Hofius and Hans-Christian Kammler, 1–23. Tübingen: Mohr Siebeck, 1996.

———. 'Das Wunder der Wiedergeburt. Jesu Gespräch mit Nikodemus Joh 3,1–21.' In *Johannesstudien. Untersuchungen zur Theologie des vierten Evangeliums*. Wissenschaftliche Untersuchungen zum Neuen Testament 88, edited by Otfried Hofius and Hans-Christian Kammler, 33–80. Tübingen: Mohr Siebeck, 1996.

———. 'Erwählung und Bewahrung. Zur Auslegung von Joh 6,37.' In *Johannesstudien. Untersuchungen zur Theologie des vierten Evangeliums*. Wissenschaftliche Untersuchungen zum Neuen Testament 88, edited by Otfried Hofius and Hans-Christian Kammler, 81–86. Tübingen: Mohr Siebeck, 1996.

Hollander, H.W. *1 Korintiërs I. Een praktische bijbelverklaring*. Tekst en Toelichting. Kampen: Kok, 1996.

Holleman, Joost. *Resurrection and Parousia. A Traditio-Historical Study of Paul's Eschatology in 1 Corinthians 15*. Supplements to Novum Testamentum 84. Leiden, New York, Köln: E.J. Brill, 1996.

Holwerda, B. 'De Heilshistorie in de prediking.' In . . . *Begonnen hebbende van Mozes*, 79–118. Terneuzen: Littooij, 1953.

Hoogland, Jan. 'Christelijk geloof: oplossing of verlossing.' In *Om de verstaanbaarheid. Over bijbel, geloof en kerk in een postmoderne samenleving*, edited by W. Dekker and P.J. Visser, 102–19. Zoetermeer: Boekencentrum 2002.

Hooker, Morna D. *From Adam to Christ. Essays on Paul*. Cambridge etc.: Cambridge University Press, 1990.

House, Paul R., 'Biblical Theology and the Wholeness of Scripture: Steps toward a Program for the Future.' In *Biblical Theology: Retrospect and Prospect*, edited by Scott J. Hafemann, 267–79. Downers Grove, IL: InterVarsity Press / Leicester England: Apollos, 2002.

Houwelingen, P.H.R. van. *1 Petrus. Rondzendbrief uit Babylon*. Commentaar op het Nieuwe Testament derde serie. Kampen: Kok, 1991.

———. *Het evangelie van het Woord*. Commentaar op het Nieuwe Testament derde serie. Kampen: Kok, 1997.

———. *Jezus stelt zich voor*, Kampen: Kok, 1998.

Howard, George. 'The Head / Body Metaphors of Ephesians.' *New Testament Studies* 20 (1974), 350–56.

Janowski, Bernd. *Sühne als Heilsgeschehen: Studien zur Sühnetheologie der Priesterschrift und zur Wurzel KPR im Alten Orient und im Alten Testament*. Wissenschaftliche Monographien zum Alten und Neuen Testament 55. Neukirchen: Neukirchener Verlag, 1982.

Bibliography

Jansen, Henry. *Relationality and the Concept of God*. Currents of Encounter: Studies on the Contact between Christianity and Other Religions, Beliefs and Cultures 10. Amsterdam–Atlanta: Rodopi, 1995.

Jenson, Robert W. *Systematic Theology. Volume 1: The Triune God*. Oxford: Oxford University Press, 2001.

———. *Systematic Theology. Volume 2: The Works of God*. Oxford: Oxford University Press, 2001.

Jerumanis, Pascal-Marie *Realiser la communion avec Dieu. Croire, vivre et demeurer dan l'évangile selon S. Jean*. Etudes Bibliques Nouvelle série. 32. Paris: Librairie Lecoffre J. Gabalda et Cie, Éditeurs, 1996.

Johnson, E. Elisabeth, and David M. Hay, editors. *Pauline Theology Vol. IV: Looking Back, Pressing On*. Atlanta, Georgia: Scolars Press, 1997.

Johnson, Luke T. 'Fragments of an Untidy Conversation: Theology and the Literary Diversity of the New Testament.' In *Biblical Theology: Problems and* Perspectives, edited by Steven J. Kraftchick et al., 276–89. Nashville: Abingdon Press, 1995.

Jones, R. Tudur. 'Union with Christ: the Existential Nerve of Puritan Piety.' *Tyndale Bulletin* 41 (1990), 186–208.

Jong, Hendrik de. *Van oud naar nieuw. De ontwikkelingsgang van het Oude naar het Nieuwe Testament*. Kampen: Kok, 2002.

Jonge, M. de. *Jesus: Stranger from Heaven and Son of God. Jesus Christ and the Christians in Johannine perspective*. Edited and translated by John E. Steely. Sources for Biblical Study 11. Missoula, MT: Scholars Press for the Society of Biblical Literature.

Jüngel, Eberhard. *Paulus und Jesus. Eine Untersuchung zur Präzisierung der Frage nach dem Ursprung der Christologie*. Tübingen: Mohr Siebeck, 1986.

———. *Gott als Geheimniss der Welt. Zur Begründung der Theologie des Gekreuzigten im Streit zwischen Theismus und Atheismus*. Tübingen: Mohr Siebeck, 1986.

———. *Das Evangelium von der Rechtfertigung des Gottlosen als Zentrum des christlichen Glaubens. Eine theologische Studie in ökumenischen Absicht*. Tübingen: Mohr Siebeck, 1999.

Kammler, Hans-Christian 'Jesus Christus und der Geistparaklet. Eine Studium zur johanneischen Verhältnissbestimmung von Pneumatologie und Christologie.' In *Johannesstudien. Untersuchungen zur Theologie des vierten Evangeliums*. Wissenschaftliche Untersuchungen zum Neuen Testament 88, edited by Otfried Hofius and Hans-Christian Kammler, 87–190. Tübingen: Mohr Siebeck, 1996.

Kamsteeg, A., et al. 'Antwoord op vragen.' *De Reformatie* 72 (1996) 4, 72–74.

Kamphuis, Barend. 'Systematische theologie.' In *Gereformeerde theologie vandaag: oriëntatie en verantwoording*. TU-Bezinningsreeks 4, edited by A. L. Th. de Bruijne, 59–71. Barneveld: De Vuurbaak, 2004.

Kamphuis, J. 'De kerk–een corporatieve persoonlijkheid?'In *Altijd met goed accoord. Opstellen uit de jaren* 1959–196, 138–67. Amsterdam: Ton Bolland, 1973.

Kamphuis, J. *In dienst van de vrede. De kerkelijke consensus als dogmatische factor*. Kamper Bijdragen XXIII. Groningen: De Vuurbaak, 1980.

———. *Een eeuwig verbond*. Haarlem: Vijlbrief, 1984.

Käsemann, Ernst. 'Begründet der Neutestamentliche Kanon die Einheit der Kirche?' In *Exegetische Versuche und Besinnungen*. Bd. 1, 214–23. Göttingen, Vandenhoeck & Ruprecht 1960.

———. 'Zum Verständniss von Römer 3,24–26.' In *Exegetische Versuche und Besinnungen*, Bd.1, 96–100. Göttingen: Vandenhoeck & Ruprecht, 1970.

Keck, Leander E. 'Derivation as Destiny: "Of-ness" in Johannine Christology, Anthropology, and Soteriology.' In *Exploring the Gospel of John. In Honor of D. Moody Smith*, edited by R. Alan Culpepper and C. Clifton Black, 274–88. Louisville Kentucky: Westminster John Knox Press, 1996.

Kelsey, David H. *Proving Doctrine. The Uses of Scripture in Modern Theology.* Harrisburg: Trinity Press International, 1999.

Kennedy, Kevin D. *Union with Christ and the Extend of the Atonement in Calvin.* Studies in Biblical Literature 48. New York etc: Peter Lang, 2002.

Kim, Jung H. *The Significance of Clothing Imagery in the Pauline Corpus.* Journal for the Study of the New Testament Supplement Series 268. London / New York: T. & T. Clark International, 2004.

Kim, Seyoon. *Paul and the New Perspective. Second Thoughts on the Origin of Paul's Gospel.* Tübingen: Mohr Siebeck / Grand Rapids: Eerdmans, 2002.

King, David M. 'The Affective Spirituality of John Owen.' *Evangelical Quarterly* 68 (1996), 223–33.

Kiuchi, N. *The Purification Offering in the Priestly Literature: Its Meaning and Function.* Journal for the Study of the Old Testament Supplement Series 56. Sheffield: JSOT Press, 1987.

Klapwijk, Jacob. 'Honderd jaar filosofie aan de Vrije Universiteit.' In *Wetenschap en rekenschap* 1880–1980. *Een eeuw wetenschapsbeoefening aan de Vrije Universiteit*, edited by M. van Os and J. Wieringa, 528–93. Kampen: Kok, 1980.

Klooster, Fred H. 'The Uniqueness of Reformed Theology: A Preliminary Attempt at Description.' *Calvin Theological Journal* 14 (1979) 1, 32–54.

Knöppler, Thomas. *Die theologia crucis des Johannesevangeliums. Das Verständnis des Todes Jesu im Rahmen der johanneischen Inkarnations- und Erhöhungschristologie.* Wissenschaftliche Monographien zum Alten und Neuen Testament 69. Neukirchen-Vluyn: Neukirchener Verlag, 1994.

———. *Sühne im Neuen Testament. Studien zum urchristlichen Verständnis der Heilsbedeu-tung des Todes Jesu.* Wissenschaftliche Monographien zum Alten und Neuen Testament 88. Neukirchen-Vluyn: Neukirchener Verlag, 2001.

Koeyer, R.W. de. "Pneumatologia': enkele aspecten van de leer van de Heilige Geest bij de puritein John Owen (1616–1683).' *Theologia Reformata* 34 (1991), 226–46.

Kolfhaus, Wilhelm. *Christusgemeinschaft bei Calvin.* Beiträge zur Geschichte und Lehre der Reformierten Kirche 3. Neukirchen: Buchhandlung des Erziehungsvereins Neukirchen Kr. Moers, 1939.

Kontekstueel 20 (2005) 1.

Kooi, Akke van der. *De ziel van het christelijk geloof. Theologische invallen bij de praktijk van geloven.* Kampen: Kok , 2006.

Kooi, Kees van der. Review of *Der auferweckte Gekreuzigte*, by Ingolf U. Dalferth. *Nederlands Theologisch Tijdschrift*, 51 (1997) 2, 165–66.

———. 'Enkele perspectieven en uitdagingen voor de dogmatiek.' In *Heroriëntatie in de Theologie*, edited by Wessel Stoker and Henk C. van der Sar, 6–15. Kampen: Kok, 2003.

———. 'Het beroep op het innerlijk getuigenis van de Geest, in het bijzonder bij Herman Bavinck.' In *Ontmoetingen met Bavinck*, edited by George Harinck and Gerrit W. Neven. AD Chartasreeks 9, 253–64. Barneveld: De Vuurbaak, 2006.

Kooten, Geurt H. van. *The Pauline Debate on the Cosmos. Graeco-Roman Cosmology and Jewish Eschatology in Paul and the Pseudo-Pauline Letters to the Colossians and the Ephesians*, Ph.D. diss., Leiden University, 2001.

Köstenberger, Andreas J. 'Diversity and Unity in the New Testament.' In *Biblical Theology: Retrospect and Prospect*, edited by Scott J. Hafemann, 144–58. Downers Grove, IL: InterVarsity Press / Leicester, England: Apollos, 2002.

Kowalski, Beate. *Die Hirtenrede (Joh 10,1–18) im Kontext des Johannesevangeliums*. Stuttgarter Biblische Beiträge 31. Stuttgart: Katholisches Bibelwerk GmbH, 1995.

Kreuzer, Thomas. *Kontexte des Selbst. Eine theologische Rekonstruktion der hermeneutischen Anthropologie Charles Taylors*. Öffentliche Theologie 12. Gütersloh: Kaiser Gütersloh Verlagshaus, 1999.

Kuijpers, G. *Abraham Kuyper over de mens*. Dordrecht: Kuijpers, 1998.

Kuitert, H.M. *Zeker weten. Voor wie geen grond meer onder de voeten voelt*. Baarn: Ten Have, 1994.

———. *Jezus. Nalatenschap van het christendom. Schets voor een christologie*. Baarn: Ten Have, 1998.

Kühn, Ulrich. *Christologie*. Göttingen Vandenhoeck & Ruprecht, 2003.

Kuyper, Abraham. *Het werk van den Heiligen Geest*. 2d ed., Kampen: Kok. 1927.

Lalleman, Pieter J. *The Acts of John: A Two-Stage Initiation into Johannine Gnosticism*. Leuven: Peeters, 1998.

———. *1, 2 en 3 Johannes. Brieven van een kroongetuige*. Commentaar op het Nieuwe Testament derde serie. Kampen: Kok, 2005.

Lambrecht S.J., Jan. *Second Corinthians*. Sacra Pagina Series Vol. 8. A Michael Glazier Book. Collegeville, Minnesota: The Literugical Press, 1999.

Lange, Frits de. 'Semper Reformanda. Het protestantisme in de 21e eeuw.' *Theologisch Debat* 1 (2004) 4, 44–48.

Laube, Martin *Im Bann der Sprache. Die analytische Religionsphilosophie im 20. Jahrhundert*. Theologische Bibliothek Töpelmann 85. Berlin, New York: Walter de Gruyter, 1999.

Lehmkühler, Karsten. *Inhabitatio. Die Einwohnung Gottes im Menschen*. Forschungen zur systematischen und ökumenischen Theologie 104. Göttingen: Vandenhoeck & Ruprecht, 2004.

Leijgraaf, Monique. *Brood en wijn binnen de spanning van Gods verkiezing. Een bijbelstheologische interpretatie van het brood des levens (Johannes 6), de wijn van de bruiloft te Kana (Johannes 2,1–12) en de betrouwbare wijnstok (Johannes 15,1–8)*. Baarn: Ten Have, 2001.

Lichtenberger, Hermann. *Das Ich Adams und das Ich der Menschheit*. Wissenschaftliche Untersuchungen zum Neuen Testament 164. Tübingen: Mohr Siebeck, 2004.

Lindbeck, George. *The Nature of Doctrine: Religion and Theology in a Postliberal Age*. Philadelphia: The Westminster Press, 1984.

Link, Hans-Georg. 'Der Kanon in ökumenischer Sicht. Für Ellen Flesseman van Leer.' In *Jahrbuch für biblische Theologie 3 Zum Problem des biblischen Kanons*, 82–96. Neukirchen-Vluyn: Neukirchener Verlag, 1998.

Loader, William. *The Christology of the Fourth Gospel*. Beiträge zur biblischen Exegese und Theologie 23. Frankfurt am Main, Bern, New York, Paris: Peter Lang, 1989.

Loonstra, Bert. *Verkiezing—verzoening—verbond. Beschrijving en beoordeling van het* pactum salutis *in de gereformeerde theologie*. Zoetermeer: Boekencentrum, 1990.

———. *God schrijft geschiedenis. Disputaties over de eeuwige.* Zoetermeer: Boekencentrum, 2003.

Lovelace, Richard F. *Dynamics of Spiritual Life: An Evangelical Theology of Renewal.* Downers Grove, IL: InterVarsity Press / Exeter: The Paternoster Press, 1979.

Mak, Geert. *Nagekomen flessenpost.* Amsterdam / Antwerpen: Atlas, 2005.

Malatesta, Edward S.J. *Interiority and Covenant. A Study of εἶναι ἐν and μένειν ἐν in the First Letter of Saint John.* Analecta Biblica 69. Rome: Biblical Institute Press, 1978.

Marquard, Odo. 'Frage nach der Frage, auf die die Hermeneutik die Antwort ist.' In *Abschied vom Prinzipiellen. Philosophische Studien,* 117–46. Stuttgart: Reclam, 1982.

Marshall, I. Howard. *The Epistles of John.* The New International Commentary on the New Testament. Grand Rapids, MI: Eerdmans, 1978.

———, *New Testament Theology, Many Witnesses, One Gospel.* Downers Grove, IL: InterVarsity Press 2004.

Martin, Ralph P. *2 Corinthians.* Word Biblical Commentary. Waco, Texas: Word Books, 1986.

Martyn, J. Louis. *Galatians. A New Translation with Introduction and Commentary.* The Anchor Bible. New York etc: Doubleday, 1997.

McCormack, Bruce L. 'What's at Stake in the Current Debates over Justification? The Crisis of Protestantism in the West.' In *Justification: What's at Stake in the Current Debates*, edited by Mark Husbandsand and Daniel J. Treier, 81–117. Downers Grove, IL: InterVarsity Press / Leicester: Apollos 2004,

———. 'Participation in God, Yes, Deification, No: Two Modern Protestant Responses to an Ancient Question.' In *Denkwürdiges Geheimnis. Beiträge zur Gotteslehre. Festschrift für Eberhard Jüngel zum 70. Geburtstag,* edited by Ingolf U. Dalferth et al., 347–74. Tübingen: Mohr Siebeck, 2004.

———. 'Protestant Identity as a Theological Problem.' Lecture given in Kampen, Holland at a conference celebrating the 150th anniversary of the founding of that Theological University of Kampen, September 3, 2004. The theme of the conference is 'Reshaping Protestantism in a Global Context.'

McGrath, Alister E. *The Genesis of Doctrine. A Study in the Foundations of Doctrinal Criticism.* The 1990 Bampton Lectures. Oxford: Basil Blackwell, 1990.

———. 'An Evangelical Evaluation of Postliberalism.' In *The Nature of Confession. Evangelicals and Postliberals in Conversation*, edited by Timothy R. Phillips and Dennis L. Okholm, 23–44. Downers Grove, IL: InterVarsity Press, 1996.

———. *Christian Theology: An Introduction.* Oxford: Blackwell Publishers, 1997.

McIntyre, John. *The Shape of Soteriology. Studies in the Doctrine of the Death of Christ.* Edinburgh: T. & T. Clark, 1992.

Meijer, Remmelt J. 'De preek: op (zoek) naar echte spiritualiteit.' *De Gereformeerde kerkbode van Groningen, Friesland en Drenthe. Waarin opgenomen de officiele mededelingen van de kerken in deze provincies*, 59 (2003), 12, 163–66.

———. 'Christus preken: niet meer en niet minder!' *De Gereformeerde kerkbode van Groningen, Friesland en Drenthe. Waarin opgenomen de officiele mededelingen van de kerken in deze provincies*, 59 (2003), 13, 179–82.

Meijers, S. *Objectiviteit en existentialiteit. Een onderzoek naar hun verhouding in de theologie van Herman Bavinck en in door hem beïnvloede concepties.* Kampen: Kok, 1979.

Michaels, J. Ramsey. *1 Peter.* Word Biblical Commentary. Waco, Texas: Word Books, 1988.

Milbank, John. *Theology and Social Theory: Beyond Secular Reason*. Signposts in Theology. Oxford: Basil Blackwell, 1990.

———. *The Word Made Strange. Theology, Language, Culture*. Oxford: Blackwell Publishers, 1997.

Mildenberger, Friedrich. 'Biblische Theologie als kirchliche Schriftauslegung.' In *Jahrbuch für biblische Theologie 1 Einheit und Vielfalt biblischer Theologie*, 151–62. Neukirchen-Vluyn: Neukirchener Verlag, 1988.

Moltmann, Jürgen. *Trinität und Reich Gottes. Zur Gotteslehre*. München: Kaiser, 1980.

Moo, Douglas J. *The Epistle to the Romans*. The New International Commentary on the New Testament. Grand Rapids, MI / Cambridge, UK: Eerdmans, 1996.

Moxter, Michael. *Güterbegriff und Handlungstheorie. Eine Studie zur Ethik F. Schleiermachers*. Morality and the Meaning of Life, 1. Kampen: Kok Pharos, 1992.

Mühling-Schlapkohl, Markus. *Gott ist Liebe. Studien zum Verständnis der Liebe als Modell das trinitarischen Redens von Gott*. Marburger Theologische Studien 58. Marburg: N.G. Elwert, 2000.

Muller, Earl C. *Trinity and Marriage in Paul: The Establishment of a Communitarian Analogy of the Trinity Grounded in the Theological Shape of Pauline Thought*. American University Studies Series VII 60. New York , Bern, Frankfurt am Main, Paris: Peter Lang, 1990.

Muller, Richard. *Scholasticism and Orthodoxy in the Reformed Tradition: An Attempt at Definition*. Grand Rapids: Calvin Theological Seminary, 1995.

Neugebauer, Fritz. *In Christus. En cristw. Eine Untersuchung zum Paulinischen Glaubensverständnis*. Göttingen: Vandenhoeck & Ruprecht, 1961.

Nielsen, Helge K. 'Johannine Research.' In *New Readings in John. Literary and Theological Perspectives. Essays from the Scandinavian Conference on the Fourth Gospel Århus 1997*. Journal for the Study of the New Testament Supplement Series 182, edited by Johannes Nissen and Sigfred Pedersen, 11–30. Sheffield: Sheffield Academic, Press 1999.

———. 'John's Understanding of the Death of Jesus.' In *New Readings in John. Literary and Theological Perspectives. Essays from the Scandinavian Conference on the Fourth Gospel Århus 1997*. Journal for the Study of the New Testament Supplement Series 182, edited by Johannes Nissen and Sigfred Pedersen, 232–54. Sheffield: Sheffield Academic Press, 1999.

Nissen, Johannes. 'Community and Ethics in the Gospel of John.' In *New Readings in John. Literary and Theological Perspectives. Essays from the Scandinavian Conference on the Fourth Gospel Århus 1997*. Journal for the Study of the New Testament Supplement Series 182, edited by Johannes Nissen and Sigfred Pedersen, 194–212. Sheffield: Sheffield Academic Press, 1999.

———. 'Mission in the Fourth Gospel: Historical and Hermeneutical Perspectives.' In *New Readings in John. Literary and Theological Perspectives. Essays from the Scandinavian Conference on the Fourth Gospel Århus 1997*. Journal for the Study of the New Testament Supplement Series 182, edited by Johannes Nissen and Sigfred Pedersen, 213–31. Sheffield: Sheffield Academic Press, 1999.

Noordegraaf, A. 'Paulus' spreken over rechtvaardiging. Tendensen in het nieuwere onderzoek.' *Theologia Reformata* 45 (2002) 1, 4–26.

Nüssel, Friederike. '"Ich lebe, doch nun nicht ich, sondern Christus lebt in mir" (Gal. 2,20a). Dogmatische Überlegungen zur Rede vom "Sein in Christus."' *Zeitschrift für Theologie und Kirche* 99 (2002) 480–502.

Obermann, Andreas. *Die christologische Erfüllung der Schrift im Johannesevangelium.* Wissenschaftliche Untersuchungen zum Neuen Testament 2. Reihe 83. Tübingen: Mohr Siebeck, 1996.

Oberman, Heiko A. *Spätscholastik und Reformation. Bd. 1 Der Herbst der mittelalterlichen Theologie.* Translated by Martin Rumscheid and Henning Kampen. Zürich: EVZ-verlag 1965.

O'Brien, Peter T. *Colossians, Philemon.* Word Biblical Commentary. Waco, Texas: Word Books, 1982.

———. *The Letter to the Ephesians.* The Pillar New Testament Commentary. Grand Rapids, MI: Eerdmans / Leicester: Apollos, 1999.

Oliver, Robert W., editor. *John Owen—the Man and His Theology. Papers Read at the Conference of the John Owen Centre for Theological Study September 2002.* Phillipsburg, New Jersey: P&R / Darlington: Evangelical Press 2002.

———. 'John Owen—His Life and Times.' In *John Owen—the Man and His Theology. Papers Read at the Conference of the John Owen Centre for Theological Study September 2002*, edited by Robert W. Oliver, 9–40. Phillipsburg, New Jersey: P&R / Darlington: Evangelical Press 2002.

Otto, Rudolf. *Reich Gottes und Menschensohn. Ein religionsgeschichtlicher Versuch.* München: C.H. Beck, 1934.

Packer, James I. 'What did the Cross achieve? The Logic of Penal Substitution.' In *Celebrating the Saving Work of God. Collected Shorter Writings of J. I. Packer* Vol. 1, 85–123. Carlisle: Paternoster, 1998.

———. *A Quest for Godliness. The Puritan Vision of the Christian Life.* Wheaton, IL: Crossway Books, 1990.

Park, Heon-Wook. *Die Kirche als "Leib Christi" bei Paulus.* Giessen / Basel: Brunnen, 1992.

Patterson, Sue. *Realist Christian Theology in a Postmodern Age.* Cambridge Studies in Christian Doctrine. Cambridge: Cambridge University Press, 1999.

Payne, Jon D. *John Owen on the Lord's Supper.* Edinburgh: The Banner of Truth Trust, 2004.

Pelikan, Jaroslav. *The Christian Tradition: A History of the Development of Doctrine* Vol. 1–5. Chicago / London: The University of Chicago Press, 1971–1989.

Peters, Albrecht. *Rechtfertigung.* Handbuch Systematischer Theologie Bd. 12 Gütersloh: Gütersloh Verlagshaus, 1984.

Piper, John 'The Demonstration of the Righteousness of God in Romans 3:25–26.' *Journal for the Study of the New Testament* 7 (1980), 2–32.

———. *The Justification of God. An Exegetical and Theological Study of Romans 9:1–23*, Grand Rapids, MI: Baker Book House, 1983.

———. *The Pleasures of God: Meditations on God's Delight in Being God.* Portland, Oregon: Multinomah 1991.

Popp, Thomas. *Grammatik des Geistes. Literarische Kunst und theologische Konzeption in Johannes 3 und 6.* Arbeiten zur Bibel und ihrer Geschichte 3. Leipzig: Evangelische Verlagsanstalt, 2001.

Post, J.S. 'De Unio Mystica.' *Gereformeerd Theologisch Tijdschrijft*, 31 (1930) 1, 1–26

Powers, Daniel Glenn. *Salvation through Participation: An Examination of the Notion of the Believers' Corporate Unity with Christ in Early Christian Soteriology*, Ph.D. diss., Leiden University, 2001.

Räisänen, Heikki. *Neutestamentliche Theologie? Eine religionswissenschaftliche Alternative.* Stuttgarter Bibelstudien 186. Stutttgart: Katholisches Bibelwerk, 2000.

Rehnman, Sebastian. 'John Owen: A Reformed Scholastic at Oxford.' In *Reformation and Scholasticism: An Ecumenical Enterprise.* Texts and Studies in Reformation and Post-Reformation Thought, edited by Willem J. van Asselt and Eef Dekker, 181–203. Grand Rapids, MI: Baker Academic, 2001.

———. *Divine Discourse. The Theological Methodology of John Owen.* Texts and Studies in Reformation and Post-Reformation Thought. Grand Rapids, MI: Baker Academic, 2002.

Reid, J.K.S. *Our Life in Christ.* The Library of History and Doctrine. London SCM Press, 1963.

Reitsma, *B.J.G. Geest en schepping. Een bijbels-theologische bijdrage aan de systematische doordenking van de verhouding van de Geest van God en de geschapen werkelijkheid.* Zoetermeer: Boekencentrum, 1997.

Ricoeur, Paul. 'Explanation and Understanding.' In *Interpretation Theory: Discourse and the Surplus of Meaning*, 71–88. Forth Worth: Texas Christian University Press 1976.

———. 'The Hermeneutical Function of Distanciation.' In *From Text to Action: Essays in Hermeneutics, II*, translated by Kathleen Blamey and John Thompson, 75–88. London: The Atholone Press, 1991.

———. 'What Is a Text? Explanation and Understanding.' In *From Text to Action: Essays in Hermeneutics, II*, translated by Kathleen Blamey and John Thompson, 105–24. London: The Atholone Press, 1991.

Ridderbos, Herman. *Paulus. Ontwerp van zijn theologie.* Kampen: Kok 1966.

———. 'De theologie van het Nieuwe Testament.' In *Inleiding tot de studie van het Nieuwe Testament*, edited by Karel A. Deurloo et al., 173–90. Kampen: Kok, 1982.

———. *Zijn wij op de verkeerde weg? Een bijbelse studie over de verzoening.* Theologie en Gemeente 5. Kampen: Kok, 1972.

———. *Het evangelie naar Johannes. Proeve van een theologische exegese* (2 dl.). Kampen: Kok, 1987.

Rikhof, Herwi. Review of *Der auferweckte Gekreuzigte*, by Ingolf. U. Dalferth. *Kerk en theologie*, 49 (1998) 3, 258–59.

Rohls, Jan. 'Sprachanalyse und Theologie bei I. U. Dalferth.' *Theologische Rundschau*, 55 (1990), 200–217.

Rondelle, H.K. la. *Perfection and Perfectionism. A Dogmatic-Ethical Study of Biblical Perfection and Phenomenal Perfectionism.* Kampen: Kok, 1971.

Ru, Gerrit de. *Heeft het lijden van Christus aanvulling nodig? Onderzoek naar de interpretatie van Col. 1:24.* Amsterdam: Ton Bolland, 1981.

Ruiter, A. de. *De hartkwaal van de kerken. Hoe kunnen bleke kerken weer kleur krijgen.* Kampen: Kok Voorhoeve, 1997.

Ruler, A.A. van. *De vervulling van de wet. Een dogmatische studie over de verhouding van openbaring en existentie.* Nijkerk: C.F. Callenbach, 1947.

Rusam, Dietrich. *Die Gemeinschaft der Kinder Gottes. Das Motiv der Gotteskindschaft und die Gemeinde der johanneischen Briefe.* Beiträge zur Wissenschaft vom Alten und Neuen Testament Bd 133. Stuttgart, Berlin, Köln: W. Kohlhammer, 1993.

Ruyter, B.W.J. de. *De gemeente van de evangelist Johannes: haar polemiek en haar geschiedenis.* Delft: Eburon, 1998.

Sanders, E.P. *Paul and Palestinian Judaism: A Comparision of Patterns of Religion.* London: SCM Press Ltd, 1977.

Sasse, Markus. *Der Menschensohn im Evangelium nach Johannes*. Texte und Arbeiten zum neutestamentlichen Zeitalter 35. Tübingen / Basel: Francke, 2000.

Scalise, Charles J. 'Canonical hermeneutics: Childs and Barth.' *Scottish Journal of Theology* 47 (1994), 61–88.

Schaede, Stephan. *Stellvertretung. Begriffsgeschichtliche Studien zur Soteriologie*. Beiträge zur historischen Theologie 126. Tübingen: Mohr Siebeck, 2004.

Schnackenburg, Rudolf. *Das Johannesevangelium* (Drei Bände). Herders Theologischer Kommentar zum Neuen Testament. Freiburg, Basel, Wien: Herder, 1965–1975.

Schnackenburg, Rudolf *Der Brief an die Epheser*. Evangelisch-Katholischer Kommentar zum Neuen Testament. Zürich, Einsiedeln, Köln: Benziger Verlag / Neukirchen-Vluyn: Neukirchner Verlag, 1982.

Schnackenburg, Rudolf. 'Neutestamentliche Theologie im Rahmen einer gesamtbiblischen Theologie. In *Jahrbuch für Biblische Theologie 1 Einheit und Vielfalt Biblischer Theologie*, 31–47. Neukirchen-Vluyn: Neukirchener Verlag, 1988.

Schnelle, Udo. *Antidoketische Christologie im Johannesevangelium. Eine Untersuchung des vierten Evangeliums in der johanneischen Schule*. Göttingen: Vandenhoeck & Ruprecht, 1987.

———. *Neutestamentliche Antropologie. Jesus—Paulus—Johannes*. Biblisch-Theologische Studien 18. Neukirchen-Vluyn: Neukirchener Verlag, 1991.

———. 'Transformation und Partizipation als Grundgedanke paulinischer Theologie.' *New Testament Studies* 47 (2001) 58–75.

Scholtissek, Klaus. *In ihm sein und bleiben. Die Sprache der Immanenz in den johanneischen Schriften*. Herders Biblische Studien 21. Freiburg etc.: Herder, 2000.

———. 'Johannine Studies: A Survey of Recent Research with Special Regard to German Contributions.' *Currents in Research* 6 (1998), 227–59.

Schrage, Wolfgang. *Der erste Brief an die Korinther*. Evangelisch-Katholischer Kommentar zum Neuen Testament (4 Bände). Braunschweig: Benziger Verlag / Neukirchen-Vluyn: Neukirchner Verlag 1991–2001.

Schuit, J.J. van der. *Het verbond der verlossing. Antwoord op de vraag: Twee of drie verbonden?* Apeldoornse Studies 18. 2d ed. Kampen: Kok, 1982.

Schürger, Wolfgang. *Wirklichkeit Gottes und Wirklichkeit der Welt. Theologie im Konflikt der Interpretationen*. Forum Systematik 12. Stuttgart: W. Kohlhammer, 2002.

Schweiker, William. 'Freedom and Authority in Political Theology: A Response to Oliver O'Donovan's *The Desire of the Nations*.' *Scottish Journal of Theology* 54 (2001) 1, 110–26.

Scobie, Charles H.H. *The Ways of our God: An Approach to Biblical Theology*. Grand Rapids, MI / Cambridge, UK: Eerdmans, 2003.

Seifrid, Mark A. *Justification by Faith: The Origin and Development of a Central Pauline Thema*. Supplements to Novum Testamentum 68. Leiden, New York, Köln: E.J. Brill, 1992.

———. 'In Christ.' In *Dictionary of Paul and his Letters*, edited by Gerald F. Hawthorne et al., 433–36. Downers Grove / Leicester: InterVarsity Press, 1993.

Selwyn, Edward G. *The First Epistle of St. Peter: The Greek Text with Introduction, Notes, and Essays*. London Macmillan & Co., 1947.

Siber, Peter *Mit Christus leben. Eine Studie zur paulinischen Auferstehungshoffnung*. Abhandlungen zur Theologie des Alten und Neuen Testamentes 61. Zürich: Theologischer Verlag Zürich, 1971.

Smalley, Stephen S. *1, 2, 3 John*. Word Biblical Commentary. Waco, TX: Word Books.

Smedes, Lewis B. *Union with Christ: A Biblical View of the New Life in Jesus Christ*, Grand Rapids, MI: Eerdmans, 1983.

Söding, Thomas, editor. *Johannesevangelium—Mitte oder Rand des Kanons? Neue Standortbestimmungen.* Quaestiones Disputatae 203. Freiburg, Basel, Wien: Herder, 2003.

Son, Sang-Won (Aaron). *Corporate Elements in Pauline Anthropology. A Study of Selected Terms, Idioms, and Concepts in the Light of Paul's Usage and Backgrounds.* Analecta Biblica 148. Roma Editrice Pontificio Instituta Biblico: 2001.

Spanje, T.E. van. *Inconsistency in Paul? A Critique of the Work of Heikki Räisänen.* Wissenschaftliche Untersuchungen zum Neuen Testament, 2. Reihe 110. Tübingen: Mohr Siebeck, 1999.

Speidell, Todd H. 'A Trinitarian Ontology of Persons in Society.' *Scottish Journal of Theology* 47 (1998), 283–300.

Spence, Alan. 'Christ's Humanity and Ours: John Owen.' In *Persons, Divine and Human. King's College Essays in Theological Anthropology*, edited by Christoph Schwöbel and Colin E. Gunton, 74–94. Edinburgh: T. & T. Clark, 1991.

———. 'John Owen and Trinitarian Agency.' *Scottish Journal of Theology*, 43 (1994), 157–73.

Spijker, Willem van 't. *Gemeenschap met Christus. Centraal gegeven van de gereformeerde theologie.* Apeldoornse Studies 32. Kampen: Kok, 1995.

———. "Extra nos' en 'in nobis' bij Calvijn in pneumatologisch licht.' In *Geest, woord en kerk. Opstellen over de geschiedenis van het gereformeerd protestantisme*, 114–32. Kampen: Kok. 1991.

———, et al. *Het puritanisme. Geschiedenis, theologie en invloed.* Zoetermeer: Boekencentrum, 2001.

———. 'Puriteinen op de agenda.' *Theologia Reformata* 44 (2001) 3, 233–45.

Stibbe, Mark W.G. *John.* Readings: A New Bible Commentary. Sheffield: JSOT Press, 1993.

———. *John as Storyteller: Narrative Criticism and the Fourth Gospel.* Society for New Testament Studies, Monograph Series 73. Cambridge, New York, Melbourne: Cambridge University Press, 1994.

Strack, Wolfram. *Kultische Terminologie in ekklesiologischen Kontexten in den Briefen des Paulus.* Bonner Biblische Beiträge 92. Weinheim: Beltz Athanäum, 1994.

Strecker, Georg. *Die Johannesbriefe.* Kritisch-exegetischer Kommentar über das Neue Testament. Göttingen: Vandenhoeck & Ruprecht, 1989.

Stuhlmacher, Peter. 'Zur neueren Exegese von Röm 3,24–26.' In *Versöhnung, Gesetz und Gerechtigkeit. Aufsätze zur biblischen Theologie.* Göttingen: Vandenhoeck & Ruprecht, 1981.

———. *Wie treibt man Biblische Theologie?* Biblisch-Theologische Studien 24. Neukirchen-Vluyn Neukirchener, 1995.

———. *Biblische Theologie des Neuen Testaments, Band 1 Grundlegung Von Jezus zu Paulus.* 2d ed. Göttingen: Vandenhoeck & Ruprecht, 1997.

———. *Biblische Theologie des Neuen Testaments, Band 2 Von der Paulusschule bis zur Johannesoffenbarung. Der Kanon und seine Auslegung*, Göttingen: Vandenhoeck & Ruprecht, 1999.

———. 'My Experience with Biblical Theology.' In *Biblical Theology: Retrospect and Prospect*, edited by Scott J. Hafemann, 174–91. Downers Grove, IL: InterVarsity Press / Leicester England: Apollos, 2002.

———. *Die Verkündigung des Christus Jesus. Neutestamentliche Beobachtungen.* Wuppertal: R. Brockhaus, 2003.

Tamburello, Dennis E. *Union with Christ: John Calvin and the Mysticism of St. Bernard.* Columbia Series in Reformed Theology. Louisville Kentucky: Westminster John Knox Press, 1994.

Tannehill, Robert C. *Dying and Rising with Christ: A Study in Pauline Theology.* Berlin: Alfred Töpelmann, 1967.

Taylor, Charles. *Sources of the Self: The making of Modern Identity.* Cambridge: Cambridge University Press 1989

Theobald, Michael. 'Eucharistie in Joh 6. Vom pneumatologischen zum inkarnationstheologischen Verstehensmodell.' In *Johannesevangelium—Mitte oder Rand des Kanons? Neue Standortbestimmungen.* Quaestiones Disputatae 203, edited by Thomas Söding, 178–257. Freiburg, Basel, Wien: Herder. 2003.

Thiselton, Anthony C. *The Two Horizons: New Testament Hermeneutics and Philosophical Description with Special Reference to Heidegger, Bultmann, Gadamer, and Wittgenstein.* Exeter: The Paternoster Press, 1980.

———. *New Horizons in Hermeneutics: The Theory and Practice of Transforming Biblical Reading.* London: Harper Collins Pulbishers, 1992.

———. *Interpreting God and the Postmodern Self: On Meaning, Manipulation and Promise.* Scottish Journal of Theology. Current Issues in Theology. Edinburgh: T. & T. Clark, 1995.

Thomas, G. Michael. *The Extent of the Atonement. A Dilemma for Reformed Theology from Calvin to the Consensus.* Paternoster Biblical and Theological Monographs. Carlisle: Paternoster, 1997.

Thompson, Marianne M. *The Humanity of Jesus in the Fourth Gospel.* Philadelphia: Fortress Press, 1988.

Thompson Michael. *Clothed with Christ: The Example and Teaching of Jesus in Romans 12:1—15:13.* Journal for the Study of the New Testament Supplement Series 59. Sheffield: Sheffield Academic Press, 1991.

Thrall, Margaret E. *A Critical and Exegetical Commentary on the Second Epistle to the Corinthians* Vol. 1. Edinburgh: T. & T. Clark, 1994.

Toon, Peter. *God's Statesman. The Life and Work of John Owen.* Exeter: Paternoster Press, 1971.

———. *Born Again. A Biblical and Theological Study of Regeneration.* Grand Rapids, MI: Baker Book House, 1987.

Tovey, Derek. *Narrative Art and Act in the Fourth Gospel.* Journal for the Study of the New Testament Supplement Series 151. Sheffield: Sheffield Acedemic Press, 1997.

Trimp, Cornelis. *Tot een levendige troost zijns volks. Goes:* Oosterbaan & Le Cointre N.V., 1954.

———. *Klank en weerklank. Door prediking tot geloofservaring.* Barneveld: De Vuurbaak, 1989.

Troxel, A. Craig. '"Cleansed Once for All": John Owen on the Glory of the Gospel Worship in 'Hebrews.'' In *Calvin Theological Journal* 32 (1997), 468–79

Trueman, Carl R. *The Claims of Truth: John Owen's Trinitarian Theology.* Carlisle, Cumbria: Paternoster, 1998.

———. 'John Owen's *Dissertation on Divine Justice*: An Exercise in Christocentric Scholasticism.' *Calvin Theological Journal* 33 (1998), 87–103.

———. 'A Small Step towards Rationalism: The Impact of the Metaphysics of Tommaso Campanella on the Theology of Richard Baxter.' In *Protestant Scholasticism: Essays in Reassessment,* edited by Carl R. Trueman and R. Scott Clark, 181–95. Carlisle: Paternoster Press, 1999.

———. 'John Owen as a Theologian.' In *John Owen—the Man and His Theology. Papers Read at the Conference of the John Owen Centre for Theological Study September 2002,* edited by Robert W. Oliver, 43–68. Phillipsburg New Jersey: P&R, / Darlington: Evangelical Press, 2002.

Veenhof, Cornelis. *Prediking en uitverkiezing. Kort overzicht van de strijd, gevoerd in de Christelijk Afgescheidene Gereformeerde kerk tussen 1850 en 1870, over de plaats van de leer van de uitverkiezing in de prediking.* Kampen: Kok 1959.

Veenhof, Jan. *Revelatie en inspiratie. De openbarings- en schriftbeschouwing van Herman Bavinck in vergelijking met die der ethische theologie.* Amsterdam: Buijten en Schipperheijn N.V., 1968.

———. 'Jezus Christus de plaatsbekleder.' In *Ontmoetingen met K. Schilder. Prof. dr. K. Schilder 1890 - 19 december - 1990,* edited by G. Puchinger, 76–83. Kampen: Kok, 1990.

———. *The relationship between nature and grace according to H. Bavinck.* Wetenskaplike Bydraes van die PU vir CHO, Reeks F no. 332. Potchefstroom: Institute for Reformational Studies, 1994.

———. 'De God van de filosofen en de God van de bijbel. Herman Bavinck en de wijsbegeerte.' In *Ontmoetingen met Bavinck.* AD Chartasreeks 9, edited by George Harinck and Gerrit W. Neven, 219–33. Barneveld: De Vuurbaak, 2006.

Veluw, A.H. van. *De straf die ons de vrede aanbrengt. Over God, kruis, straf en de slachtoffers van deze wereld in de christelijke verzoeningsleer.* Zoetermeer: Boekencentrum, 2002.

Verbrugge, Ad. *Tijd van onbehagen. Filosofische essays over een cultuur op drift.* Filosofische diagnosen. Amsterdam: Sun, 2004.

Versteeg, J.P. *Christus en de Geest. Een exegetisch onderzoek naar de verhouding van de opgestane Christus en de Geest van God volgens de brieven van Paulus.* Kampen: Kok, 1971.

Volf, Miroslav, *Exclusion & Embrace: A theological Exploration of Identity, Otherness, and Reconciliation.* Nashville: Abingdon Press, 1996.

Vree, Jasper. 'Organisme en instituut. De ontwikkeling van Kuypers spreken over kerkzijn (1867–1896).' In *Abraham Kuyper: vast en veranderlijk,* Cornelis Augustijn, Jasper Vree, 86–108. Zoetermeer: Meinema, 1998.

———. 'Tegen de evolutie de palingenesie. Abraham Kuypers rede over de Verflauwing der grenzen.' In *Abraham Kuyper: vast en veranderlijk,* Cornelis Augustijn, Jasper Vree, 149–64. Zoetermeer: Meinema, 1998.

Vries, Pieter de. *"Die mij heeft liefgehad." De betekenis van de gemeenschap met Christus in de theologie van John Owen (1616–1683).* Heerenveen: Groen, 1999.

Wagner, Falk. 'Religion der Moderne—Moderne der Religion.' In *Religion als Thema der Theologie. Geschichte, Standpunkte und Perspektiven theologischer Religionskritik und Religionsbegründung,* edited by Wilhelm Gräb, 12–44. Gütersloh: Kaiser, 1999.

———. *Metamorphosen des modernen Protestantismus.* Tübingen: Mohr Siebeck, 1999.

Wall, Robert W. 'Reading the Bible from within Our Traditions: The 'Rule of Faith' in Theological Hermeneutics.' In *Between Two Horizons. Spanning New Testament*

Studies and Systematic Theology, edited by Max Turner and Joel B. Green, 88–107. Grand Rapids, MI / Cambridge UK: Eerdmans, 2000.

———. 'Canonical Context and Canonical Conversation.' In *Between Two Horizons. Spanning New Testament Studies and Systematic Theology*, edited by Max Turner and Joel B. Green, 165–82. Grand Rapids, MI / Cambridge UK: Eerdmans, 2000.

Wallace, Ronald S. *Calvin's Doctrine of the Christian Life*. Edinburgh and Londen: Oliver and Boyd Ltd., 1959.

Walt M.A., B.D., S.P. van der. *Die Wijsbegeerte van Dr. Herman Bavinck*. Potchefstroom: Pro Rege-Pers Beperk, 1953.

Walter, Matthias. *Gemeinde als Leib Christi. Untersuchungen zum Corpus Paulinum und zu den "Apostolischen Vätern."* NTOA 49. Freiburg Schweiz: Universitätsverlag / Göttingen: Vandenhoeck und Ruprecht, 2001.

Wedderburn, A.J.M. 'The Body of Christ and related concepts in 1 Corinthians.' *Scottish Journal of Theology* 24 (1971) 1, 74–96.

———. 'Some Observations on Paul's use of the Phrases "in Christ" and "with Christ."' *Journal for the Study of the New Testament* 25 (1985), 83–97.

———. *Baptism and Resurrection. Studies in Pauline Theology against Its Graeco-Roman Background*. Tübingen: J.C.B. Mohr (Paul Siebeck) 1987.

Welker, Michael. 'Biblische Theologie. II. Fundamentaltheologisch.' In *Religion in Geschichte und Gegenwart*. Vierte Auflage, 1549–1552. Tübingen: Mohr Siebeck, 1998.

Wenham, David. 'Appendix: Unity and Diversity in the New Testament.' In *A Theology of the New Testament*, George Eldon Ladd, 684–719. Grand Rapids, MI: Eerdmans, 1997.

Wenz, Gunter. 'Christologische Paralipomena II.' *Theologische Rundschau* 64 (1999), 396–420.

Westerholm, Stephen. *Perspectives Old and New on Paul. The "Lutheran" Paul and His Critics*. Grand Rapids, MI / Cambridge, UK: Eerdmans / 2004.

Wierenga, Lambert. *Verhalen als bewijzen. Strategieën van narratieve retoriek in Johannes. Verslag van een cursorische lectuur van het Johannes-evangelie*. Kampen: Kok, 2001.

Wikenhauser, Alfred. *Die Christusmystik des hl. Paulus*. Biblische Zeitfragen Folge 12, Heft 8–10. Münster i. W.: Verlag der Ulchendorffschen Verlagsbuchhandlung, 1928.

Wilckens, Ulrich. '"Simul iustus et peccator" im 1. Johannesbrief.' In *Der Sohn Gottes und seine Gemeinde. Studien zur Theologie der Johanneischen Schriften*. Forschungen zur Religion und Literatur des Alten und Neuen Testaments 200, 136–46. Göttingen: Vandenhoeck & Ruprecht, 2003.

Williams, David J. *Paul's Metaphors. Their Context and Character*. Massachusetts: Hendrickson Publishers Peabody, 1999.

Witkamp, L. Th. *Kolossenzen. Een praktische bijbelverklaring*. Tekst en toelichting. Kampen: Kok, 1994.

Wright, N.T. *The Climax of the Covenant. Christ and the Law in Pauline Theology*. Edinburgh: T. & T. Clark, 1991.

———. 'Romans and the Theology of Paul.' In *Pauline Theology Vol. III: Romans*, edited by David M. Hay, E. Elisabeth Johnson, 30–68. Minneapolis: Fortress Press, 1995.

———. *What Saint Paul Really Said: Was Paul of Tarsus the Real Founder of Christianity?* Oxford: Lion, 1997.

Wolterstorff, Nicholas, *Divine Discourse: Philosophical Reflections on the Claim That God Speaks*. Cambridge: Cambridge University Press, 1995.

———. 'A Discussion of Oliver O'Donovan's *The Desire of the Nations*.' *Scottish Journal of Theology* 54 (2001) 1, 87–109.

Won, Jonathan J.-C. '*Communion with Christ: an Exposition and comparison of the Doctrine of Union with Christ in Calvin and the English Puritans*.' Ph.D. Thesis, Westminster Theological Seminary, 1989.

Yee, Gale A. *Jewish Feasts and The Gospel of John*. Zacchaeus Studies: New Testament. Wilmington, Delaware: Michael Glazier, 1989.

Yoo, Hae M. *Raad en daad. Infra- en supralapsarisme in de nederlandse gereformeerde theologie van de 19e en 20e eeuw*. Kampen: Dissertatie-uitgeverij Mondiss, 1990.

Zumstein, Jean. *Kreative Erinnerung. Relecture und Auslegung im Johannesevangelium*. Zürich: Pano, 1999.

SCRIPTURE INDEX

Scripture Index

NAME INDEX

Name Index

CPSIA information can be obtained
at www.ICGtesting.com
Printed in the USA
BVHW06*1119201018
530457BV00008B/600/P

9 781498 252072